P9-DBI-541

THE BRUMBACK LIBRARY

IN MEMORY OF:

Mrs. Eloise Wilson

PRESENTED BY:

Mrs. Dolores Balyeat

Southern Living

2009 ANNUAL RECIPES

641.5975
S04

Oxmoor
House®

Best Recipes of 2009

Creole Shrimp and Grits ▶
(page 29) A great dish to serve at a casual dinner party, the rich sauce for this regional favorite starts with a roux.

Oven-Roasted Tomatoes
(page 31) Try these slow-roasted canned tomatoes in your favorite chili recipe, or use them as a topping for pizza.

◀ **Red Wine Beef Stew** *(page 30)*
Pull out your Dutch oven to enjoy the comfort of vegetables cooked in a delicious broth.

Triple Chocolate-Cookie Trifle Pie *(page 44)* Store-bought cookies make handy ingredients on this spin of a splurge-worthy Southern dessert.

Pot Likker Soup *(page 28)* A mess of greens mixed with ham hocks that have simmered for hours make up this scrumptious winter favorite.

Cinnamon-Orange Coffee *(page 47)* and **Biscuit Beignets** *(page 50)* A made-from-scratch mix is the secret ingredient to this divine beverage that pairs nicely with these New Orleans-style treats.

▲ **Nutter Butter®-Banana Pudding Trifle**
(page 44) Layers of bananas and crunchy peanut butter cookies make this homemade pudding absolutely irresistible.

Croissant French Toast With Pecans *(page 248)*
A honey-pecan butter sauce tops this melt-in-your-mouth breakfast specialty.

Peanut Butter-Banana Sandwich Bread Puddings With Dark Caramel Sauce *(page 244)*
Serve this scrumptious dessert straight from the oven to guests.

Pecan-Honey Butter *(page 246)* Just three ingredients mix together to make this incredible spread that can be made ahead and frozen.

Barbecue Sundae *(page 53)* Set up a station at your next gathering for guests to create these individual treats filled with Baked Pork Butt Roast, coleslaw, and chopped fresh cilantro.

Pressed Cuban Sandwiches, Italian-Style Sandwiches, and Barbecue Sandwiches *(pages 52-53)* Put together an assortment of melt-in-your-mouth sandwiches that begin with a pork loin roast or a Boston butt.

Ultimate Vanilla Layer Cake *(pages 62–63)* This moist cake boasts a rich and creamy frosting that makes for an unbelievable dessert.

▲ Lemon Curd-Filled Angel Food Cupcakes *(page 79)*
Lemon curd and a cream cheese frosting add to the flavor of these little cakes.

Vanilla-Champagne Soaked Fruit *(page 61)*
This fuss-free dish combines the delicious flavors of fresh fruit, vanilla bean, mint, and Champagne.

Strawberry-Fruit Toss With Cornmeal Shortcakes *(page 85)* Pillow-soft shortcakes topped with fruit make a tasty and colorful springtime concoction.

Strawberries Romanoff Pancakes With Brown Sugar-Sour Cream Sauce *(page 86)* Savor this dessert that boasts fluffy pancakes and sweet strawberries.

▲ **Grilled Potato Salad** *(page 114)* A homemade dry rub and dressing help make this recipe an enormous hit.

Hominy Grill's Shrimp and Grits *(page 95)* The shrimp and mushrooms in this specialty that hails from Charleston sauté in hot bacon drippings.

Chocolate Sugar Cookies *(page 106)* Fun to bake, this quick-to-mix dough makes treats that are even more fun to decorate.

Toasted Coconut-Cashew Brownies *(page 145)* Add coconut, cashews, and ginger to one of our best-ever brownie recipes for a rich chocolaty treat.

Fried Green Tomatoes With Bread-and-Butter Pickle Rémoulade *(page 116)* Creole seasoning and a delicious sauce made with bread-and-butter pickles give this Southern specialty a one-of-a-kind taste.

Shrimp-and-Pasta Salad *(page 138)*
Fresh fruit, shrimp, pasta, and arugula
mixed with a tarragon-mint dressing
come together in just 20 minutes.

◀**Heirloom Tomato Salad With Fresh Lady Peas** *(page 139)* Perfectly ripe summer tomatoes team up with Lady pcas for a cool and refreshing dish.

Caramel-Pecan Bars *(page 251)* Taste autumn in every bite of this pecan-and-honey favorite.

Brandy Alexander Cheesecake *(page 256)* Chocolate bear-shaped crackers help create the crust of this luscious and creamy sweet ending.

▼ **Grilled Fingerling Potato Salad** *(page 138)* It takes just a little chopping and dicing to whip up this no-fuss recipe.

Cornbread Focaccia *(page 153)* Feta cheese, olives, tomatoes, and rosemary add a delightful flavor to this quick bread.

Cornbread Crostini *(page 152)*
Miniature cornbreads baked in small muffin tins replace baguettes as the base in this Southern-style appetizer.

Meet the *Southern Living* Food Staff

For over 40 years, the *Southern Living* Food Staff has been the trusted source of Southern cuisine. On these pages, we invite you to match the names and faces of the people who plan, kitchen-test, and write about our favorites.

▲ (seated) Scott Jones, *Executive Editor;* Shannon Sliter Satterwhite, *Food Editor;* (standing) Lyda Jones Burnette, *Test Kitchen Director;* Pat York, *Editorial Assistant*

▲ (seated) Kristi Michele Crowe *and* Angela Sellers, *Test Kitchen Professionals;* Rebecca Kracke Gordon, *Assistant Test Kitchen Director;* (standing) Marian Cooper Cairns, *Test Kitchen Specialist/Styling;* Pam Lolley, *and* Norman King, *Test Kitchen Professionals;* Vanessa McNeil Rocchio, *Test Kitchen Specialist/Styling*

(seated) Ashley Arthur, *Assistant Recipe Editor;* ▶ Ashley Leath, *Senior Recipe Editor;* Donna Florio, *Senior Writer;* Natalie Kelly Brown, *Assistant Food Editor;* (standing) Shirley Harrington *and* Mary Allen Perry, *Senior Food Editors;* Marion McGahey, *Assistant Food Editor*

Our Year at Southern Living®

Dear Food Friends,

I know there are long-time readers out there who have all 30 previous volumes of *Southern Living* Annual Recipes. I'm also certain some of you are picking this up for the very first time. Whatever the case, let me assure you this 2009 edition—our 31st volume—is one of our best ever. It's packed with delicious recipes, gorgeous photography, and our expert cooking advice.

It was with the *Southern Living* readers in mind that we decided to transition to a new time format with our October 2009 issue. This new format utilizes a hands-on, total time approach, which allows us to provide readers with a more accurate portrayal of how long a recipe will take, start to finish, with just one glance. Now, instead of readers adding up a long list of times and calculating for themselves how long it will take before dinner gets to the table, we've done the work for you.

"Food in the South is about so much more than sustenance—it's about connecting with family and friends ..."

You continue to make us part of your extended family, and we definitely think of each and every reader as part of ours. (Check out Cook's Chat beginning on page 24, a perfect example of this relationship and a way for readers to share comments and their own kitchen know-how about some of their favorite recipes.)

Don't miss bonus features such as the Test Kitchen Notebook, where, regardless of whether you're a new cook or comfortable in the kitchen, you'll uncover our top secrets for success and learn everything you need to know about preparing these irresistible recipes. I'm also particularly fond of this year's "5-Ingredient Comfort Food" section starting on page 327. Food in the South is about so much more than sustenance—it's about connecting with family and friends around the supper table. The recipes in this section absolutely speak to this tradition.

This coming year, please allow us to set the *Southern Living* table with you in mind.
- How is the economy affecting the way you cook for your family or entertain for friends? What are your favorite money-saving tips? Share them with us.
- Have you reinvented a favorite dish (i.e. something from mom) or made it better for you? Tell us about it.
- Have a kitchen question or want to know how to make a classic Southern recipe? Ask us.
- Do you know someone who makes the "best something" you've ever tasted? Introduce us to them.

We remain committed to reflecting today's Southern kitchen and giving you more of what you want in practical and affordable ways that fit your lifestyle. Thanks for inviting us into your homes, and I look forward to hearing from you and seeing more of your recipes soon.

Sincerely,

Scott Jones
Executive Editor
sl_foodedit@timeinc.com

©2009 by Oxmoor House, Inc.
Book Division of Southern Progress Corporation
P.O. Box 2262, Birmingham, Alabama 35201-2262

Southern Living, *Healthy Living*, and *Holiday Dinners* are federally registered trademarks of Southern Living, Inc.

All rights reserved. No part of this book may be reproduced in any form or by any means without the prior written permission of the publisher, excepting brief quotations in connection with reviews written specifically for inclusion in magazines or newspapers, or limited exerpts strictly for personal use.

ISBN-13: 978-0-8487-3285-1
ISBN-10: 0-8487-3285-5
ISSN: 0272-2003

Printed in the United States of America
First printing 2009

To order additional publications, call 1-800-765-6400.

For more books to enrich your life, visit **oxmoorhouse.com**

To search, savor, and share thousands of recipes, visit **myrecipes.com**

Cover: Chocolate-Citrus Cake With Candied Oranges, page 298

Page 1: Pumpkin Pie Spectacular, page 249

Southern Living ®

Executive Editor: Scott Jones
Food Editor: Shannon Sliter Satterwhite
Senior Writer: Donna Florio
Senior Food Editors: Shirley Harrington, Mary Allen Perry
Assistant Food Editors: Natalie Kelly Brown, Marion McGahey
Senior Recipe Editor: Ashley Leath
Assistant Recipe Editor: Ashley Arthur
Test Kitchens Director: Lyda Jones Burnette
Assistant Test Kitchens Director: Rebecca Kracke Gordon
Test Kitchens Specialist/Food Styling: Marian Cooper Cairns,
    Vanessa McNeil Rocchio
Test Kitchens Professionals: Norman King, Pam Lolley, Angela Sellers
Editorial Assistant: Pat York
Production Manager: Jamie Barnhart
Copy Chief: Paula Hunt Hughes
Assistant Copy Chief: Katie Bowlby
Copy Editors: Stephanie Gibson, JoAnn Weatherly
Assistant Copy Editors: Marilyn R. Smith, Ryan Wallace
Senior Food Photographer: Jennifer Davick
Photographers: Ralph Anderson, Beth Dreiling Hontzas
Senior Photo Stylist: Buffy Hargett
Production Coordinators: Christy Coleman, Paula Dennis, Ryan Kelly

Oxmoor House, Inc.

VP, Publishing Director: Jim Childs
Editorial Director: Susan Payne Dobbs
Brand Manager: Daniel Fagan
Managing Editor: L. Amanda Owens

Southern Living ® *2009 Annual Recipes*

Editor: Susan Hernandez Ray
Photography Director: Jim Bathie
Senior Production Manager: Greg A. Amason

Contributors

Designer: Nancy Johnson
Copy Editor: Donna Baldone
Editorial Consultant: Jean Liles
Proofreader: Julie Gillis
Indexer: Mary Ann Laurens
Index Copy Editor: Jasmine Hodges
Editorial Interns: Georgia Dodge, Allison Sperando, Christine Taylor

Contents

Favorite Columns

Each month, we focus on topics that are important to our readers—
from delicious menus to healthy options to handy tips for almost anything.

What's for Supper?

■ Rice and chicken make perfect partners. Discover three
of our favorite versions of this down-home comfort food:
Simple Chicken and Rice, Baked Chicken and Rice With
Black Beans, and Salsa Verde Chicken Casserole (page 51).

■ Try our Speedy Pork Chops supper that centers around
good food that's easy to prepare and has few ingredients.
We've even included a timeline that makes it a snap to prepare dinner in just 40 minutes (page 64).

■ Busy cooks will appreciate this dinner that features a
main dish with fast prep and cook time, few ingredients,
and enticing enough to satisfy hungry appetites. Add to it
a quick tossed salad or green vegetable and a dessert that
bakes while your family enjoys the main meal (page 105).

■ Surprise your family with the comforting combination of
sausage, fluffy mashed potatoes, and crunchy onions that
make a a fuss-free casserole (page 121).

■ A deli-roasted chicken makes it easy to make a classic
Mexican dish for a weeknight fiesta night (page 147).

■ Pair one of these quick and easy main dishes with a simple
side for a weeknight meal that your family is sure to love
(page 295).

Healthy Living

♥ Yogurt might just be the perfect food. Discover some great tips
when choosing the best product to buy, as well as some scrumptious recipes that you can make with this tasty treat (page 36).

♥ Kids are more willing to try any food if they've helped to
prepare it. A Dunwoody, Georgia, family shares some recipes
that they like to make together. And, keep hunger at bay with
an energizing, nutrient-packed snack mix (page 55).

♥ Choose ingredients wisely for a colorful salad that can't be
beat. What you decide to put in your salad has a great impact
on the good-for-you impact (page 72).

♥ Fire up the grill to create this lightened meal that begins
with a perfectly seasoned flank steak that requires only
5 minutes to prep and ends with melt-in-your-mouth Grilled
Banana Splits. And, stir up some recipes that take advantage
of nature's sugar substitute (page 82).

♥ Gather a group of friends for a lightened menu of small
delicious bites that will leave everyone satisfied, not stuffed.
Best of all, the recipes are mostly make-ahead (page 102).

♥ The owner of Austin's Taco Xpress shares her unforgettable recipes that boast Texas-size flavor without any of the
guilt (page 118).

♥ The cofounder of Slow Food Oklahoma City takes a
fresh approach to food and shares her tips for healthy eating
(page 131).

♥ Celebrate summer by indulging in everybody's favorite cool treat. We have the scoop on some great-tasting recipes and some of our favorite brands (page 148).

♥ If you love tailgating, but don't want the fuss or the extra calories, then try these four simple, healthful recipes that make for a great outdoor gathering (page 158).

♥ A Houston chef and busy mom shows you that eating well is easier than you think and shares some of her best recipes for eating healthy on-the-go (page 236).

♥ Make smart food choices during the holiday season with some better-for-you sides (page 252).

♥ Reap all the high fiber and protein benefits of oats by using them in some great-tasting recipes. Plus, give the gift of wellness this holiday season (page 264).

♥ Discover some healthy Southern comfort food recipes that help you to incorporate beans into your daily diet. Beans are truly superfoods because they fill you up and help fight against diseases (page 301).

From Our Kitchen

■ Test Kitchen Professionals Marian Cooper Cairns and Angela Sellers share their secrets to cooking chicken that can be used in all types of recipes. (page 42).

■ Find some of our chocolate tips and tricks. We'll share with you our best information on cocoa powder, how to cut chocolate, and all about bittersweet chocolate (page 58).

■ Create beautiful layer cakes using one of our favorite tools and our foolproof frosting tips. Also check out a clever little idea for serving petits fours and pick up a few tips on cake flour (page 74).

■ When you're looking for a quick dinner, give fish a try. Discover all sorts of luring tips, from selecting just the right fish to some great ways to cook it (page 90).

■ Summer ushers in a delicious variety of vegetables from local farmers markets and roadside stands. Take advantage of this bountiful produce with our insider shopping tips and terrific frittata recipe (page 108).

■ If you're looking for the perfect appetizer, cheese trays are fast, easy, and always a hit. Get some advice on arranging cheese in style and some of our favorite quick and impressive recipes (page 122).

■ Fresh herbs add a refreshing flavor to marinades, salad dressings, and more. (page 136).

■ Fall is a great month to clean out your spice pantry. Test Kitchen Specialist/Food Stylist Marian Cooper Cairns shares her list of favorite spices for fall cooking (page 200).

Cook's Chat

Our readers chat online about what they think of our recipes and how they use them. Here, they brag about some of their favorites.

Appetizers and Beverages

Layered Lima Bean Dip, page 37—"I love this layered dip. It's great for pot-lucks. I just get the green, red, yellow, and orange bell peppers, cut them into a dipping size slice, and put them around the edge of the serving bowl. Everyone loves it--even people who do not like lima beans like it! I served it for a Christmas dinner and it was a hit. I will make it again !"

Spicy Boiled Shrimp With Creamy Buttermilk-Avocado Sauce, page 60—"I used Old Bay seasoning for the shrimp boil along with some bottled lemon juice. The buttermilk-avocado sauce was a hit as well. I will definitely keep recipe and make it again. I served this to accompany cold cuts sandwiches for a surprise birthday party."

Shrimp-and-Blue Cheese Spread, page 76—"I loved this! Surprisingly, it was better on the veggies than the crackers. I made it for a party and the combination was wonderful. I wasn't sure how blue cheese and shrimp would be together but loved it. I cut the recipe in half because it makes a lot."

Fresh Herb-Tomato Crostini, page 103—"Delicious! You must try this for the summer—it's refreshing and satisfying! I actually served it as a side dish with a tenderloin. Don't deny yourself this one! "

Entrées

Chicken Tetrazzini With Prosciutto and Peas, page 32—"Awesome! I really enjoyed this. I did make it a little healthier with healthy soups and alfredo. I used a bottle of wine that has been open forever and chicken tastes perfect! Will def. make again!"

Pecan-Crusted Tilapia, page 34—"This was a very easy and outstanding dinner. I substituted mahi mahi for the tilapia and served it with rice and green beans. It was fast and looked like a meal you would order in a restaurant. There is a lot of butter in this recipe, and I would be interested in trying to omit some of it to make this a little healthier. We will definitely make this again!"

Pan-Fried Chicken-and-Ham Parmesan, page 49—"I work for a large fire department in Texas. I've recently been transferred to a new station and it was my turn to cook. We were so busy all day, but I still managed to put this on the table in an hour (along with all my sides). I also served a mixture of zucchini/yellow squash with a can of Rotel added—oh, and a side of corn. Literally, as soon as they took one bite we had another call to go on. One of the guys thought it ws so good that he took it and ate in the back of the fire engine! They all loved it and it helped me with being accepted in. Now they know I can cook. I will cook this again for sure!"

Cajun Omelet, page 50—"This is a very nice dish for brunch or supper. It makes large portions so plan accordingly; you can probably get by on 8 or 10 eggs. I made it with the addition of shrimp and, with a salad, it was an excellent meal that I would gladly serve to guests. We're making it again tomorrow."

Baked Chicken and Rice With Black Beans, page 51—"This casserole was easy and delicious on a cold winter's day! Tastes similar to King Ranch chicken but healthier with the addition of black beans and omission of cream soups. I simply baked some chicken breasts earlier for the meat. Perfect with a green salad and crusty bread. Everyone loved it and I'll definitely make it again."

Thai Pesto Shrimp, page 55—"This is an excellent recipe. I increased the honey and the pepper flakes to give it a nice sweet spicy kick! I double the recipe for other uses; great over fish or a grilled flank steak. It's a keeper."

Jerk Chicken, page 98—"This was delicious with just the right amount of heat. Just as delicious (and maybe a little spicier) when reheated."

Herb-Marinated Flank Steak, page 124—"Great recipe. The fresh herbs really make this dish. Love that you don't have to marinate overnight."

Lime Tortilla-Crusted Chicken Tenders, page 130—"Very easy, and quick prep and cook time make it a great weeknight meal. I served it with a microwaveable packet of Mexican-style rice because I was short on time but, the chicken would go well with a variety of sides. I will definitely make this again."

Natalie's Cajun-Seasoned Pan-Fried Tilapia, page 156—"Wonderful! It had great taste and easy enough to make on a weeknight. I used more oil/butter than the recipe had noted. I will make it again."

Soups and Sandwiches

Southwestern Soup, page 29—"My family already calls this soup one of their favorites! I did add a quarter cup of chopped celery to my hamburger meat as it was browning and an additional four cups of beef broth to this recipe so there was more liquid in the soup. With a pan of homemade cornbread, this soup was a wonderful dinner on a cold evening. Yum-yum!"

Pressed Cuban Sandwiches, page 52—"I roasted the pork roast and used a picnic ham from the grocery store, and this turned out great. I couldn't find soft Cuban bread and used hoagie rolls but they were a bit too crusty. Might try a softer roll next time. I made eight sandwiches on a cookie sheet and placed a cookie sheet over them and smushed it down. I wrapped each sandwich in foil and served them poolside. They stayed warm for a long time. Guests loved the change. Load on the mustard and always use the pickles. It was de-lish with kettle chips and lemonade."

Strawberry-Turkey-Brie Panini, page 86—"This was even better than I expected. The only thing I changed is I didn't use the melted butter and I cooked it in a panini skillet. The sweet, spicy, fresh flavors are wonderful. I'm usually not a fan of the flavor of Brie but the pepper jelly balanced it nicely."

Shrimp Burgers With Sweet 'n' Spicy Tartar Sauce, page 92—"This recipe is absolutely fabulous! Everyone is still talking about it a week later. I served the burgers with coleslaw and sweet potato fries. I highly recommend this recipe."

Salads

Corn-and-Lima Bean Salad, page 61—"This dish is very tasty and easy to prepare. It's low in fat, not a lot of 'dressing' taste. I prepared this for a large family dinner and everyone enjoyed it. It can be made ahead so there is no last-minute salad prep."

Spinach-Grape Chopped Salad, page 72— "This was an outstanding salad. All of the flavors blended beautifully. Wanting a little more protein (as well as substance for a main-dish meal), I added chilled shrimp that had been drizzled in just a little bit of lemon juice. Fabulous! I also added chopped endive because to me there is nothing fresher than endive in a spinach salad. Many requests from guests to make it "again and again." Presents beautifully and is impressive enough to serve to company."

Grilled Potato Salad, page 114—"One word: Wow! I followed the recipe exactly, except for the grilling method. I kept everything in my iron skillet and covered it with aluminum foil, set the grill to medium-low, and stirred every 6-7 minutes. My husband took one bite and declared it "dinner-party worthy." You have to try this one!

Herbed Potato Salad, page 132—"Very easy and quick prep and cook time make it a great weeknight meal. I served it with a microwavable packet of mexican-style rice because I was short on time but it would go well with a variety of sides. I will definitely make this again."

Green Bean, Grape, and Pasta Toss, page 143—"This was very good and different. I might cut down on the amount of dressing used on the salad, but overall a nice summer side dish. I would definitely make it again."

Sides

Baked Onions, page 41—"Tried this tonight and we all loved it. We had some friends over and they wanted the recipe. I served them with a stuffed tenderloin and mushroom sauce. This would be a good side dish for special occasions or just for a treat on a weeknight. I did cook them about 15 minutes longer than directed."

Roasted Cauliflower With Pine Nuts and Raisins, page 57—"This is a terrific, healthful recipe, bursting with flavor, and will perk up any dinner party menu. The pine nuts and raisins complement the garlicky sauce perfectly. I didn't change a thing in the recipe. Served it with seared cod and my guests practically licked their plates clean. Two forks up!"

Sides *(continued)*

Basmati Rice and Peas, page 64—"This had a surprising amount of flavor from so few simple ingredients. It was fast and easy to make. As part of a menu, it was a true favorite. We'll return to this one again and again."

Baked Grits and Greens, page 68—"I thought I hated grits until I tried this. Absolutely fabulous!! A great new side dish for anytime of the day, not just breakfast. This is something I have recommended to many."

Grilled Fresh Artichokes, page 70—"Super yummy and super easy. The only change I made was to brush the artichokes with olive oil and balsamic vinegar before grilling. (I think the balsamic helped them get those yummy grill marks that, to me, adds to the taste and presentation of this beautiful vegetable.) This recipe will be made again and again."

Asparagus-New Potato Hash, page 77—"This recipe is easy, delicious, and good for you. It's a great way to have a carb and green vegetable in the same dish. I found that it kept surprisingly well on very low heat for several minutes between cooking it and serving it. I doubled the recipe and sautéed it in a Dutch oven, which worked very well for the larger amount."

Peppery Grilled Okra With Lemon-Basil Dipping Sauce, page 126—"If you like okra you will love this because it is so easy to make. At first I didn't think this would work but I was wrong. Covering the okra with foil helps it to cook faster, and it is wonderful. I did not use the sauce."

Breads

Cornbread Focaccia, page 54—"This is a good solid recipe. It's easy, tasty, and not demanding. I served it as a side with broiled salmon and sliced strawberries to make an easy weeknight dinner."

Beer-Cheese Cornbread, page 153—"This tasty bread was definitely a hit. I used Heineken as the beer, which gave a nice tang to the cornbread. It pairs great with both chili and barbecue."

Desserts

Hot Fudge Brownie Cake, page 40—"This was so good and so easy! What a fast, deliciously gooey and chocolatey recipe! Wow, this will be my new spur-of-the moment dessert. I have everything in the pantry—chocolate cake for either last-minute guests or a chocolate attack! The fudgy pudding is to die for when warm, along with the spongy chocolate cake. You must serve it with whipped cream or ice cream—it's delicious. It's also good for breakfast, snack, lunch, dinner, and bedtime."

Nutter Butter®-Banana Pudding Trile, page 44—"Wow! This is so easy to make and beautiful too! A footed trifle bowl makes the dessert more showy. I made this one several times and got raves each time. Also, I once substituted the Nutter Butters with Vienna finger sandwich cookies. Delicious! The longer you can let it chill, the better! When traveling to family get-togethers, we take a cooler with ice and put the trifle dish covered with plastic wrap down in the ice. The folks you are visiting like this because they don't have to rearrange their fridge for your food."

Basic Vanilla Cake Batter, page 62—"I fixed the basic vanilla cake with the Key lime icing for my daughters birthday and it drew raves. Really good and easy. Be sure to use cake flour—what a difference that makes. YUM! I would definitely make it again."

Free-form Strawberry Cheesecake, page 87—"This was creamy, delicious, and so easy. The perfect summer dessert! I used chocolate chip cookie pieces, which added a nice flavor. Also, I'll never use granulated sugar to sweeten strawberries again—-the powdered sugar dissolved so well!"

So Good Brownies, page 144—"Best brownie recipe ever! Made them (in mini cupcake size) for a large engagement party and they were the biggest hit of all the goodies on the dessert table! Making them again ASAP! So easy!"

January

Soothing Suppers

Winter is the right time to make big steaming pots of food—the kind that nourishes the spirit as well as the body.

There's nothing quite so cozy as a pot of soup or stew bubbling away on the stove. So celebrate cold weather—pull out your Dutch oven, and try one of these bountiful batches.

Simmer the ham hocks for hours to make the base for Pot Likker Soup. You'll get the nutritional goodness of a mess of greens bathed in lots of rich, smoky ham broth. Creole Shrimp and Grits, our twist on two regional favorites, would be great to serve at a casual dinner party. Red Wine Beef Stew offers the warmth of vegetables cooked in a delicious broth.

Best of all, these offer enough for leftovers. Prepare an extra batch or two to freeze, and life will be less stressful when you're too busy or tired to cook.

Pot Likker Soup

MAKES 6 TO 8 SERVINGS; **PREP:** 20 MIN.;
COOK: 4 HR., 3 MIN.; **COOL:** 30 MIN.;
CHILL: 8 HR.

This would be wonderful alongside a bowl of hoppin' John. Cooking the ham hocks the day before and chilling the broth overnight allows you to skim the fat easily. (Pictured on page 3)

2 (1-lb.) smoked ham hocks
1 medium onion, chopped
1 medium carrot, diced
1 Tbsp. vegetable oil
1 garlic clove, chopped
½ cup dry white wine
½ tsp. salt
¼ tsp. dried crushed red pepper
1 (14.5-oz.) can vegetable broth
½ (16-oz.) package fresh collard greens, washed and trimmed
Cornbread Croutons

1. Bring ham hocks and 8 cups water to a boil in a Dutch oven over medium-high heat. Boil 5 minutes; drain. Reserve hocks; wipe Dutch oven clean.
2. Sauté onion and carrot in hot oil in Dutch oven over medium heat 4 to 5 minutes or until tender; add garlic, and cook 1 minute. Add wine; cook, stirring occasionally, 2 minutes or until wine is reduced by half.
3. Add hocks, 8 cups water, salt, and crushed red pepper to onion mixture, and bring to a boil. Cover, reduce heat to low, and simmer 3 hours or until ham hocks are tender.
4. Remove hocks, and let cool 30 minutes. Remove meat from bones; discard bones. Transfer meat to an airtight container; cover and chill. Cover Dutch oven with lid, and chill soup 8 hours.
5. Skim and discard fat from soup in Dutch oven. Stir in meat and vegetable broth.
6. Bring mixture to a boil. Gradually stir in collards. Reduce heat, and simmer, stirring occasionally, 45 to 50 minutes or until collards are tender. Serve with Cornbread Croutons.

Kitchen Express Pot Likker Soup: Omit ham hocks and salt. Prepare recipe as directed in Step 2, sautéing ½ lb. smoked boneless pork loin, chopped, with onion and carrot. Stir in 2 Tbsp. jarred ham soup base, broth, 8 cups water, and red pepper. Bring to a boil. Gradually stir in collards; reduce heat, and simmer 45 minutes or until collards are tender. Prep: 20 min., Cook: 53 min.

Spanish Kale-and-White Bean Soup: Omit ham hocks, broth, salt, and red pepper. Sauté ½ lb. smoked chorizo, chopped, in Dutch oven over medium-high heat 6 to 8 minutes or until browned. Remove with a slotted spoon; wipe Dutch oven clean. Proceed with recipe as directed in Step 2, sautéing 1 medium potato, cubed, with onion and carrot. Stir in 1 (48-oz.) container chicken broth. Proceed with recipe as directed in Step 6, substituting ½ (16-oz.) package fresh kale, washed and trimmed, for collards, and stirring in chorizo with kale. Stir in 1 (15.5-oz.) can white beans, rinsed and drained, and, if desired, 1 (14-oz.) can chicken broth during last 5 minutes of cooking. Omit Cornbread Croutons. This hearty soup makes a great meal by itself, or serve it with crusty bread and cheese (we like Manchego). Prep: 20 min.; Cook: 1 hr., 6 min.

Cornbread Croutons:
make ahead
MAKES 6 TO 8 SERVINGS; **PREP:** 10 MIN.,
BAKE: 45 MIN., **COOL:** 1 HR.

2 Tbsp. bacon drippings or vegetable oil
1 cup self-rising white cornmeal mix
1 cup buttermilk
1 large egg
½ tsp. salt, divided
½ tsp. pepper, divided

1. Preheat oven to 450°. Coat bottom and sides of an 8-inch square pan with bacon drippings; heat in oven 5 minutes.
2. Whisk together 1 cup cornmeal mix, buttermilk, egg, ¼ tsp. salt, and ¼ tsp. pepper; pour batter into hot pan.
3. Bake at 450° for 15 to 17 minutes or until lightly browned. Turn out onto a wire rack; cool completely (about 30 minutes). Reduce oven temperature to 325°.
4. Cut cornbread into 1½-inch squares. Place on a baking sheet; sprinkle with remaining salt and pepper.
5. Bake at 325° for 30 to 35 minutes or until crisp and lightly browned. Remove to a wire rack; cool completely (about 30 minutes). Store in airtight container up to 1 day.

Southwestern Soup

freezeable

MAKES 6 SERVINGS; **PREP:** 15 MIN.,
COOK: 45 MIN.

(Pictured on page 161)

1 lb. ground beef
1 cup coarsely chopped onion
2 garlic cloves, minced
2 (16-oz.) cans light red kidney beans,
    rinsed and drained
1 (15-oz.) can black beans, rinsed and
    drained
1 (14.5-oz.) can petite diced tomatoes and
    jalapeños, undrained
1 (14.5-oz.) can diced tomatoes and mild
    green chiles, undrained
1 (14-oz.) can beef broth
2 cups frozen yellow and white whole kernel
    corn
1 (1-oz.) envelope taco seasoning mix
¼ tsp. salt
¼ tsp. pepper
2 Tbsp. chopped fresh cilantro
Toppings: sour cream and chopped fresh
    cilantro

1. Brown ground beef, chopped onion,
and garlic in a large Dutch oven over
medium-high heat, stirring often, 10 to
12 minutes or until meat crumbles and
is no longer pink and onion is softened;
drain.
2. Stir in kidney beans, next 8 ingredients, and 4 cups water. Bring to a boil over
medium-high heat. Cover, reduce heat
to low, and simmer 30 minutes or until
thoroughly heated. Stir in cilantro just
before serving. Serve soup with desired
toppings.

Why We Love Dutch Ovens

Dutch ovens—large heavy pots with tight-fitting lids—may be the perfect
big cookware. These muscular, two-handled cooking vessels perform equally
well when boiling water for pasta, making the sauce, frying hushpuppies, or
roasting a pork butt. Enameled cast-iron versions are favorites for their ability
to surround food with heat, allowing them to cook low and slow as well as sear-
ingly fast. This makes cast-iron Dutch ovens an excellent choice for browning
meat such as a pot roast and then cooking it over very low heat on the cooktop or in the oven. Best of all, they come in a rainbow of colors, so they are as
enjoyable to look at as they are to use.

Slightly lighter models—stainless steel or anodized aluminum, for
example—also work very well for any of these tasks. You likely have one if you
purchased a set of cookware or received one as a wedding present. But most
Dutch ovens can be purchased individually, and it can be useful to have two of
them for those times when you're cooking pasta sauce in one and want to cook
the spaghetti to go along with it at the same time. Just be sure to choose one
with a good, heavy bottom for even heat distribution.

Creole Shrimp and Grits

MAKES 6 TO 8 SERVINGS; **PREP:** 30 MIN.;
COOK: 1 HR., 32 MIN.

*The sauce starts with a roux, which is
browning flour in oil. Be sure to get into
the corners of the pan when you stir so
the flour there doesn't scorch. (Pictured
on page 2)*

2 lb. unpeeled, medium-size raw shrimp
    (26/30 count)
¼ cup vegetable oil
⅓ cup all-purpose flour
1 medium onion, finely chopped
2 celery ribs, chopped
1 medium-size green bell pepper, chopped
2 garlic cloves, chopped
1 (6-oz.) can tomato paste
1 bay leaf
1½ tsp. Creole seasoning
1 tsp. lemon juice
½ tsp. Worcestershire sauce
2½ cups milk
1 tsp. salt
1½ cups uncooked quick-cooking grits

1. Peel shrimp, reserving shells; devein
shrimp, if desired. Bring shells and
4 cups water to a boil in a medium
saucepan over medium-high heat;
reduce heat to low, and cook 20 minutes. Pour shrimp broth through
a colander over a large bowl,
pressing shells with back of a spoon;
discard shells.
2. Heat oil in a Dutch oven over medium heat; stir in flour, and cook, stirring
constantly, until flour is caramel colored (about 8 to 10 minutes). Add onion
and next 3 ingredients, and cook, stirring often, 5 to 7 minutes or until tender. Stir in 2 cups shrimp broth, tomato
paste, and next 4 ingredients. Reduce
heat to low, and cook mixture, stirring
occasionally, 45 minutes. Add shrimp,
and cook 10 minutes, stirring in ¼ to
½ cup remaining shrimp broth to reach
desired consistency.
3. Meanwhile, bring milk, 2½ cups
water, and salt to a boil in a saucepan
over high heat. Gradually stir in grits.
Reduce heat to low, and simmer, stirring occasionally, 10 to 12 minutes or
until thickened. Serve Creole Shrimp
over grits.

—ANGELA JEFFERS,
MONCKS CORNER, SOUTH CAROLINA

Red Wine Beef Stew

MAKES 6 TO 8 SERVINGS; **PREP:** 20 MIN.;
COOK: 3 HR., 6 MIN.

This recipe is pure comfort but it takes a while to prepare, so make it on a day when you have some time to spare. Serve it with crusty bread or over rice to capture every drop of the rich gravy. (Pictured on page 2)

1 (4-lb.) boneless chuck roast, trimmed
4 Tbsp. flour, divided
1¾ tsp. salt, divided
1 tsp. paprika
½ tsp. pepper
2 Tbsp. vegetable oil
1 cup dry red wine*
2 (14½-oz.) cans low-sodium beef broth
½ tsp. dried thyme
1 bay leaf
1 small turnip
1 (8-oz.) package fresh mushrooms
1 (16-oz.) package baby carrots

1. Cut beef into 2- to 2½-inch pieces; pat with paper towels to absorb excess moisture. Combine 3 Tbsp. flour, 1 tsp. salt, paprika, and pepper in a bowl; toss beef with flour mixture.
2. Cook beef, in batches, in hot oil in a Dutch oven over medium-high heat, stirring often, 4 to 6 minutes or until brown. Remove beef from Dutch oven. Add red wine, stirring to loosen particles from bottom of Dutch oven. Return beef to Dutch oven; add broth, thyme, bay leaf, and ½ tsp. salt. Bring to a boil. Cover, reduce heat to low, and cook, stirring occasionally, 1 hour.
3. Meanwhile, peel turnip, and cut into 1-inch cubes. Halve mushrooms. Add turnip, mushrooms, and carrots to stew. Cover and cook, stirring occasionally, 1 to 1½ hours or until meat is fork-tender.
4. Whisk together remaining 1 Tbsp. flour and ¼ tsp. salt until blended; whisk ½ cup hot broth into flour mixture until smooth. Whisk flour mixture into stew until smooth. Cook, stirring often, 20 minutes or until thickened.
*Beef broth may be substituted.

Big Flavor From the Pantry

These great-tasting dishes start with one simple gadget—a can opener.

We value the creativity that comes from our readers' kitchens. Such is the case with Cappy Hall Rearick of St. Simons Island, Georgia, who turned us on to the power of canned tomatoes. After trying her recipes for Hearty Tomato Blend and Quick Salsa, we tinkered with the idea of slow-roasting canned tomatoes. The result: Oven-Roasted Tomatoes—one of the tastiest recipes we've produced in a long time.

Test Kitchens Notebook

Canned tomatoes can be stored in the pantry for up to six months. It's best that they are stored in a cool, dry place. Once the can has been opened, the tomatoes can be stored in a covered glass container in the refrigerator for a week.

—**CHARLA DRAPER,** ASSOCIATE FOOD EDITOR

Hearty Tomato Blend

freezeable • make ahead
MAKES 12 CUPS; **PREP:** 20 MIN.

Use this mixture in gazpacho, as a base for Bloody Marys, or as an addition to your favorite spaghetti sauce. Portion out one-to-two cup servings to keep on-hand in the freezer for up to three months.

3 (28-oz.) cans diced tomatoes, drained
4 (8-oz.) cans tomato sauce
2 medium-size sweet onions, diced (about 2 cups)
1 large green bell pepper, diced (about 1½ cups)
1 large red bell pepper, diced (about 1½ cups)
1 tsp. black pepper
½ tsp. ground red pepper
½ tsp. dried crushed red pepper

1. Stir together all ingredients in a large bowl. Use immediately, or store in an airtight container in refrigerator up to 7 days.

— **CAPPY HALL REARICK,**
ST. SIMONS ISLAND, GEORGIA

To freeze: Place 2 cups of tomato mixture in a 1-qt. zip-top freezer bag; seal bag. Repeat procedure with remaining tomato mixture. Place bags flat on a baking sheet, and freeze up to 3 months. Thaw in refrigerator 24 hours.

Quick Salsa

fast fixin's • make ahead

MAKES 3 CUPS; **PREP:** 10 MIN., **CHILL:** 1 HR.

1. Stir together 3 cups Hearty Tomato Blend, 1½ Tbsp. chopped fresh cilantro, and 1 Tbsp. fresh lime juice. Cover and chill 1 hour before serving. Serve with tortilla chips.

—CAPPY HALL REARICK,

ST. SIMONS ISLAND, GEORGIA

Italian-Seasoned Chicken Breasts

MAKES 4 SERVINGS; **PREP:** 30 MIN., **COOK:** 14 MIN.

1 cup uncooked extra long-grain rice
⅓ cup chopped celery
4 skinned and boned chicken breast cutlets
    (about ¾ lb.)
½ tsp. salt, divided
⅛ tsp. pepper
½ cup Italian-seasoned breadcrumbs
1 large egg, beaten
1 Tbsp. vegetable oil
2 cups Hearty Tomato Blend
2 Tbsp. chopped fresh parsley
Garnish: shredded Parmesan cheese

1. Prepare rice according to package directions, adding celery with rice.
2. Meanwhile, sprinkle chicken with ¼ tsp. salt and ⅛ tsp. pepper.
3. Combine breadcrumbs and remaining ¼ tsp. salt in a shallow dish. Dip chicken in egg; dredge in breadcrumb mixture.
4. Cook chicken in hot oil in a 10-inch nonstick skillet over medium-high heat 3 to 4 minutes on each side or until lightly browned and done. Remove from skillet, and drain well on paper towels. Keep warm.
5. Heat 2 cups Hearty Tomato Blend in a small saucepan over medium heat 5 to 6 minutes or until thoroughly heated.
6. Toss hot cooked rice with parsley, and place on a serving plate. Top with chicken. Spoon Hearty Tomato Blend over chicken and rice. Garnish, if desired.

Oven-Roasted Tomatoes

freezeable • make ahead

MAKES ABOUT 2 CUPS; **PREP:** 20 MIN., **BAKE:** 3 HR., **COOL:** 20 MIN.

Try stirring these into your favorite chili recipe, or use them as a topping on pizza.

3 (28-oz.) cans whole tomatoes, drained and
    halved
¾ cup coarsely chopped sweet onion
½ cup loosely packed fresh basil leaves,
    chopped
⅓ cup olive oil
5 large garlic cloves, halved
1½ tsp. dried oregano
½ tsp. freshly ground pepper

1. Preheat oven to 300°. Place tomato halves in a colander, and press gently to remove excess liquid.
2. Stir together tomatoes, onion, and remaining ingredients in a large bowl. Place tomato mixture in a single layer in an aluminum foil-lined 15- x 10-inch jelly-roll pan.
3. Bake at 300° for 2½ to 3 hours or until tomato mixture is deep red and lightly browned, stirring every 45 minutes. Cool in pan on a wire rack 15 to 20 minutes or until completely cool. Store in an airtight container in refrigerator up to 3 days.

To freeze: Place tomato mixture in an airtight container, and freeze up to 3 months. Thaw in refrigerator 24 hours.

Super Snack

Let us help you resolve to eat healthful, even if your schedule remains maxed to the limit. This energy-rich, homemade treat guarantees to please at work, school, or play.

Peanut Butter Granola

MAKES 6 CUPS; **PREP:** 15 MIN., **COOK:** 3 MIN., **BAKE:** 20 MIN., **COOL:** 20 MIN.

1. Preheat oven to 350°. Toss together 3 cups uncooked regular oats, ½ cup dry-roasted peanuts, ½ cup sweetened flaked coconut, and 3 Tbsp. sesame seeds in a large bowl. Cook ½ cup creamy peanut butter, ½ cup firmly packed brown sugar, ¼ cup butter, 1 Tbsp. light corn syrup, and ¼ tsp. salt in a small saucepan over medium heat 3 minutes or until smooth. Stir peanut butter mixture into oat mixture until blended.
2. Spread mixture in a single layer on a lightly greased, aluminum foil-lined 17- x 12-inch jelly-roll pan. Bake 20 minutes or until lightly golden, stirring after 10 minutes. Transfer to wax paper, and cool completely (about 20 minutes). Serve with vanilla yogurt and sliced bananas.

Shortcut Chicken Favorites

Put together a great-tasting meal in minutes with a few cups of rotisserie chicken. This grocery store staple is a terrific time-saver that we use often. But it's also super-easy to simply cook a whole chicken—and much less expensive. We share our two favorite methods in "From Our Kitchen" on page 42. Both deliver delicious results every time.

Chicken Tetrazzini

MAKES 6 SERVINGS; **PREP:** 10 MIN.,
BAKE: 35 MIN.

Served from a silver chafing dish on a sideboard or passed around the kitchen table for a casual supper, Chicken Tetrazzini reigns as the hallmark of Southern casseroles. This quick-and-easy version, originally published in 2001, is a five-star favorite with our readers. It's every bit as good prepared with reduced-fat cream of mushroom soup and light Alfredo sauce and freezes beautifully. Be sure to try our new variations—and then create your own special twists.

1 (7-oz.) package vermicelli
3 cups chopped cooked chicken
1 cup (4 oz.) shredded Parmesan cheese, divided
1 (10¾-oz.) can cream of mushroom soup
1 (10-oz.) container refrigerated Alfredo sauce
1 (4-oz.) can sliced mushrooms, drained
½ cup chicken broth
¼ cup dry sherry
¼ tsp. freshly ground pepper
½ cup slivered almonds

1. Preheat oven to 350°. Prepare pasta according to package directions.
2. Meanwhile, stir together chicken, ½ cup Parmesan cheese, and next 6 ingredients; stir in pasta. Spoon mixture into 6 lightly greased 8-oz. ramekins or a lightly greased 11- x 7-inch baking dish.

Sprinkle with almonds and remaining ½ cup Parmesan cheese.
3. Bake at 350° for 35 minutes or until bubbly.

Chicken Tetrazzini With Marsala and Fresh Mushrooms:
Substitute Marsala for sherry and 1 (8-oz.) package sliced fresh mushrooms for canned mushrooms. Melt 2 Tbsp. butter in a large skillet over medium-high heat; add mushrooms, and sauté 4 to 5 minutes or until tender. Proceed with recipe as directed, adding mushrooms with chicken. Prep: 10 min., Cook: 5 min., Bake: 35 min.

Chicken Tetrazzini With Prosciutto and Peas: *(Pictured on page 172)*
Substitute dry white wine for sherry. Sauté 3 oz. finely chopped prosciutto in 2 tsp. hot vegetable oil in a small skillet over medium-high heat 2 to 3 minutes or until crisp. Proceed with recipe as directed, stirring in prosciutto and 1 cup frozen baby English peas, thawed, with pasta. Prep: 10 min., Cook: 3 min., Bake: 35 min.

Chicken Tetrazzini With White Cheddar and Green Chiles:
Substitute shredded white Cheddar cheese for Parmesan cheese; 2 (4.5-oz.) cans chopped green chiles, undrained, for canned mushrooms; and dry white wine for sherry. Proceed with recipe as directed.

Chicken Tetrazzini With Caramelized Onions:
Melt 2 Tbsp. butter in a large skillet over medium heat; add 1 large sweet onion, diced, and sauté 20 minutes or until caramel colored. Stir in 1 Tbsp. balsamic vinegar, ¼ tsp. salt, and ⅛ tsp. pepper. Proceed with recipe as directed, stirring caramelized onion in with pasta. Prep: 10 min., Cook: 20 min., Bake: 35 min.

Chicken-Chile Cobbler With Smoked Sausage and Black-eyed Peas

MAKES 8 TO 10 SERVINGS; **PREP:** 15 MIN.,
COOK: 40 MIN., **BAKE:** 35 MIN.

We love the fresh taste and texture of frozen black-eyed peas, but they do need to cook before being added to the filling. For a speedier option, substitute 3 cups canned peas (about two 15-oz. cans), or double up on a side dish earlier in the week, and save the leftovers. To ensure even baking, spread the Wild Rice Crust Batter over a hot filling.

1 (16-oz.) package frozen black-eyed peas
2 Tbsp. butter
1 lb. smoked sausage, cut into ¼-inch-thick slices
1 large sweet onion, diced
1 large poblano pepper, seeded and diced
¼ cup all-purpose flour
1 (1.25-oz.) envelope white chicken chili seasoning mix
3 cups chicken broth
3 cups chopped cooked chicken
Wild Rice Crust Batter

1. Cook peas according to package directions; drain.
2. Preheat oven to 425°. Melt butter in a Dutch oven over medium-high heat; add sausage, and sauté 3 minutes or until lightly browned. Add onion and poblano pepper, and sauté 3 minutes. Add flour and seasoning mix; cook, stirring constantly, 1 minute.
3. Gradually add chicken broth, stirring to loosen particles from bottom of Dutch

Make the Most of Your Chicken

Depending on the size, one chicken will yield 3 to 4 cups of chopped, cooked meat. Remove the meat from the bones when it's still warm, and freeze up to one month in a zip-top plastic freezer bag. If you have extra pan juices, drizzle them over the meat for additional moistness. To preserve the fresh flavor and texture, allow 24 hours for the chicken to thaw in the refrigerator before using.

oven. Cook, stirring constantly, 3 minutes or until broth begins to thicken. Stir in black-eyed peas and chicken, and bring to a boil.

4. Meanwhile, prepare Wild Rice Crust Batter as directed. Spoon hot chicken mixture into a lightly greased 13- x 9-inch baking dish. Spoon Wild Rice Crust Batter immediately over hot chicken mixture.

5. Bake at 425° for 35 to 40 minutes or until crust is golden brown and cooked through.

Wild Rice Crust Batter:

MAKES 1 (13- X 9-INCH) CRUST;
PREP: 5 MIN.

1 (8.8-oz.) pouch ready-to-serve long-grain and wild rice mix
1 cup all-purpose baking mix
¾ cup milk
1 large egg, lightly beaten

1. Stir together rice and baking mix in a large bowl. Make a well in center of mixture, and stir in milk and egg just until moistened. Use immediately.
Note: For testing purposes only, we used Uncle Ben's Long Grain & Wild Ready Rice.

Chicken-and-Potato Pancakes

MAKES 6 TO 8 SERVINGS (ABOUT 18 CAKES);
PREP: 15 MIN., **COOK:** 9 MIN. PER BATCH

The secret to tender pancakes? Mix the batter just long enough to incorporate the ingredients, and flip them only once.

2 cups instant pancake mix
2 cups milk
2 cups shredded cooked chicken
1½ cups (6 oz.) shredded colby-Jack cheese blend
1 cup refrigerated shredded hash browns
4 green onions, finely chopped
2 Tbsp. butter, melted
½ tsp. salt
¼ tsp. pepper
Quick Cream Gravy (optional)

1. Whisk together pancake mix and milk in a large bowl, whisking just until dry ingredients are moistened. Stir in chicken and next 6 ingredients, stirring just until blended.
2. Pour about ¼ cup batter for each cake onto a hot (350°), lightly greased griddle or large nonstick skillet. Cook pancakes 3 minutes or until tops are covered with bubbles and edges look dry and cooked; turn and cook other side 5 to 6 minutes or until done. Serve with Quick Cream Gravy, if desired.

—**MARY KAY**, NEW LLANO, LOUISIANA

Note: For testing purposes only, we used Aunt Jemima Complete Pancake & Waffle Mix and Simply Potatoes Shredded Hash Browns.

Chicken-and-Rice Cakes: Substitute shredded Italian six-cheese blend for colby-Jack cheese blend and 1 cup cooked rice for hash browns. Proceed with recipe as directed.

Quick Cream Gravy: Bring ¼ cup dry white wine to a boil over medium heat in a small saucepan. Reduce heat to medium-low, and cook 1 minute. Add 1 cup water; whisk in 1 (1.2-oz.) package roasted chicken gravy mix and ¼ tsp. pepper. Increase heat to medium, and return to a boil. Reduce heat to low, and simmer 3 minutes or until thickened. Whisk in 2 Tbsp. heavy cream. Makes 1¼ cups; Prep: 5 min., Cook: 5 min.
Note: For testing purposes only, we used Knorr Roasted Chicken Gravy Mix.

Apricot-Pecan Chicken Salad

fast fixin's • make ahead
MAKES 6 SERVINGS; **PREP:** 15 MIN.,
COOK: 5 MIN.

Serve over salad greens with sliced avocado, or grill between slices of whole grain bread with Muenster cheese and fresh arugula.

1 cup coarsely chopped pecans
3 cups chopped cooked chicken
1 cup chopped dried apricots
¼ cup mayonnaise
¼ cup sour cream
2 Tbsp. country-style Dijon mustard
2 Tbsp. honey
Salt and pepper to taste

1. Heat nuts in a nonstick skillet over medium-low heat, stirring often, 4 to 5 minutes or until toasted and fragrant.
2. Stir together chicken and next 5 ingredients in a large bowl. Season with salt and pepper to taste; stir in pecans. Serve immediately, or cover and chill until ready to serve. Store in an airtight container in refrigerator up to 3 days.

—**LESLEY PEW**, LYNN, MASSACHUSETTS

Any-Occasion Menu

Serve these simple and delicious dishes at your next get-together. The secret to having a hassle-free gathering is all in the planning. After you prepare the fish, keep it warm in a 200° oven for up to 20 minutes. This gives you time to finish the rest.

Simple Supper

SERVES 4

Pecan-Crusted Tilapia

Herb Mashed Potatoes

Balsamic Green Beans

Quick Apple Bundles

Pecan-Crusted Tilapia

fast fixin's

MAKES 4 SERVINGS;
PREP: 10 MIN., **COOK:** 8 MIN.

Try this tasty tilapia with a simple squeeze of lemon or, if you a have a little more time, delicious Golden Rum-Butter Sauce. If you don't have a skillet large enough to hold all the fillets easily, we recommend cooking them in batches and keeping them warm in a 200° oven. You can substitute catfish, flounder, or orange roughy for tilapia.

½ cup pecan halves
4 (6-oz.) fresh tilapia fillets
1 tsp. salt
½ tsp. garlic powder
¼ tsp. pepper
3 Tbsp. butter
Golden Rum-Butter Sauce
Garnishes: lemon wedge, fresh parsley sprig

1. Process pecans in a food processor until finely chopped. Sprinkle fish fillets with salt, garlic powder, and pepper. Dredge fish in finely chopped pecans.
2. Melt butter in a large nonstick skillet over medium-high heat; add fish, and cook 3 to 4 minutes on each side or until well browned and fish flakes with a fork. Serve with Golden Rum-Butter Sauce. Garnish, if desired.

Golden Rum-Butter Sauce:

MAKES ⅓ CUP; **PREP:** 10 MIN.,
COOK: 6 MIN.

This sauce also tastes great on shrimp or scallops.

3 Tbsp. butter
1 shallot, minced
1 garlic clove, minced
2 Tbsp. rum*
2 Tbsp. fresh lemon juice
2 Tbsp. fresh orange juice
1 tsp. honey
½ tsp. salt

1. Melt 1 Tbsp. butter in a small skillet over medium-high heat; add shallot and garlic, and cook, stirring occasionally, 5 minutes or until shallot is tender. Reduce heat to low, and slowly whisk in rum, next 4 ingredients, and remaining 2 Tbsp. butter. Cook, stirring occasionally, 1 minute; serve warm.

—INSPIRED BY KIM BANDSTRA,
FAIRFIELD, CALIFORNIA

*Fresh lemon juice may be substituted.

Herb Mashed Potatoes

fast fixin's

MAKES 4 SERVINGS; **PREP:** 25 MIN.

We recommend using the in-bag method described on the package for cooking the frozen potatoes.

3 Tbsp. butter
2 garlic cloves, chopped
1 (24-oz.) package steam-and-mash frozen garlic-seasoned potatoes
2 Tbsp. chopped fresh parsley
2 Tbsp. chopped fresh chives
½ tsp. salt
½ tsp. pepper

1. Microwave butter and garlic in a 3-qt. glass bowl at HIGH 2 minutes or until golden brown and bubbly.
2. Prepare potatoes according to package directions. Stir in butter mixture and remaining ingredients. Serve immediately.
Note: For testing purposes only, we used Ore-Ida Steam n' Mash Garlic Seasoned Potatoes.

Balsamic Green Beans

fast fixin's

MAKES 4 SERVINGS; **PREP:** 10 MIN.,
COOK: 7 MIN.

1 lb. tiny green beans (haricots verts), trimmed
2 Tbsp. balsamic vinegar
1 Tbsp. light brown sugar
1 tsp. Dijon mustard
2 shallots, minced
2 Tbsp. olive oil
1 tsp. salt
½ tsp. pepper

1. Cook green beans in boiling salted water to cover 5 to 6 minutes or until crisp-tender; drain. Plunge green beans into ice water to stop the cooking process, and drain.
2. Stir together vinegar, brown sugar, and mustard until smooth.

3. Cook shallots in hot oil in skillet over medium heat, stirring often, 1 minute or until tender. Stir in vinegar mixture, salt, and pepper. Add green beans; toss to coat. Serve immediately.

Quick Apple Bundles

test kitchen favorite

MAKES 4 SERVINGS; **PREP:** 10 MIN.,
BAKE: 20 MIN.

½ (15-oz.) package refrigerated piecrusts
1 (12-oz.) package frozen spiced apples, thawed
1 egg white, lightly beaten
Sugar
1 (12-oz.) jar butterscotch topping, warmed

1. Preheat oven to 425°. Unfold piecrust according to package directions. Cut into fourths. Place apples evenly in center of each fourth. Pull corners over apples, pinching to seal. Place on a baking sheet; brush evenly with egg white, and sprinkle with sugar.
2. Bake at 425° for 18 to 20 minutes or until golden. Serve warm with butterscotch topping.
Note: For testing purposes only, we used Stouffer's Harvest Apples.

Cookin' With Tyler Florence

This popular chef has elevated finger food to its finest.

We asked South Carolina native Tyler Florence to share a few of his favorite appetizers from his cookbook *Tyler's Ultimate* (Clarkson Potter, 2006). His easygoing style comes through in the recipes we've adapted.

Herbed Goat Cheese Bites

chef recipe

MAKES 12 APPETIZER SERVINGS;
PREP: 25 MIN., **CHILL:** 2 HR., **BAKE:** 7 MIN.,
COOL: 5 MIN.

1 Tbsp. fresh thyme leaves
1 Tbsp. fresh flat-leaf parsley leaves
1 Tbsp. fresh tarragon leaves
1 Tbsp. fresh mint leaves
1 (8-oz.) goat cheese log
1 (8-oz.) French bread baguette, cut into ¼-inch-thick slices
2 Tbsp. extra virgin olive oil
½ cup sun-dried tomatoes in oil, drained and chopped
½ cup loosely packed fresh basil leaves

1. Combine and finely chop first 4 ingredients. Roll cheese log evenly in herb mixture; wrap in plastic wrap. Chill at least 2 hours or up to 24 hours.
2. Preheat oven to 350°. Drizzle baguette slices with olive oil. Gently press slices into 24 muffin cups in muffin pans.
3. Bake at 350° for 7 to 9 minutes or until crisp and lightly browned. Remove from oven; let cool in pans 5 minutes.
4. Spread goat cheese into baguette cups; top with sun-dried tomatoes and basil leaves.

The Ultimate Chicken Wings With Curry-Lime Butter

chef recipe

MAKES 6 TO 8 APPETIZER SERVINGS;
PREP: 25 MIN., **BAKE:** 40 MIN.

4 lb. chicken wings*
2 Tbsp. olive oil
2 tsp. salt
1 tsp. freshly ground pepper
½ cup unsalted butter, softened
1 Tbsp. grated lime rind
2 Tbsp. fresh lime juice
1 Tbsp. honey
2 tsp. red curry paste
¼ tsp. soy sauce
2 Tbsp. chopped fresh cilantro

1. Preheat oven to 425°. Cut off wing tips, and discard; cut chicken wings in half at joint, if desired. Place wings in a large bowl, and drizzle with olive oil. Season with salt and pepper, tossing to coat. Arrange wings in a single layer on a lightly greased aluminum foil-lined 15- x 10-inch jelly-roll pan.
2. Bake at 425° for 40 to 45 minutes or until browned and skin is crisp, turning after 20 minutes.
3. Stir together butter and next 5 ingredients in a large bowl; add wings, and toss until evenly coated. Transfer to a platter; drizzle with any remaining butter mixture. Sprinkle with cilantro.
*1 (4-lb.) package frozen party-style chicken wings, thawed, may be substituted.
Note: For testing purposes only, we used Thai Kitchen Red Curry Paste.

Healthy Living®

Discover a few of our tips and recipes to get your
year off to a nutritious start.

The Dish on Yogurt

Find out what we learned about this simple snack. Even if
you're not a fan, you'll love these recipes.

Yogurt is quite possibly the perfect food. Not only is it a great source of calcium, but it also has many health benefits and happens to be a perfect snack. Still, we get dizzy just looking at the dairy case. There are an overwhelming number of products— plain, flavored, creamy, fruity, fruit on the bottom, granola-topped, whole, low-fat, fat-free, light, reduced-calorie, sugar-free, drinkable, organic, and something called "probiotic." How can you make a smart choice? We did some research, and this is what we learned.

What Are Probiotics?

The term is making headlines, but it's actually nothing new. It simply refers to live bacteria that are beneficial to health. Probiotic bacteria naturally live in our digestive tracts to fight off pathogens, but they need to be replenished, particularly if you smoke, drink alcohol, eat poorly, or take antibiotics.

In order for yogurt to be called "yogurt," two probiotic starter cultures must be added—*Streptococcus thermophilus* and *Lactobacillus bulgaricus,* which are known to have a positive effect on digestion. No matter what you hear in TV ads, all yogurts contain some beneficial bacteria. Some brands, such as Horizon Organic and Stonyfield Farm, add three to four more cultures, which may help strengthen the natural defenses of our bodies. Dannon Activia, on the other hand, adds a culture that targets intestinal transit, potentially regulating the digestive system. Although some probiotics can be beneficial for certain health functions, results may vary among individuals.

Cooking destroys live bacteria, but even when heated, yogurt still serves as a low-fat alternative for dips, spreads, and sauces.

Orange-Berry Swirl
MAKES 5 CUPS; **PREP:** 5 MIN.

2 (10-oz.) packages frozen strawberries in
   light syrup
1 (6-oz.) container plain low-fat yogurt
1 cup fresh orange juice
1 cup fat-free milk

1. Process all ingredients in a blender until smooth, stopping to scrape down sides. Serve immediately.

—**LAURA MORRIS**, BUNNELL, FLORIDA

Per 1-cup serving: Calories 121; Fat 0.6g (sat 0.4g, mono 0.2g, poly 0g); Protein 4.3g; Carb 24.7g; Fiber 1g; Chol 2.6mg; Iron 0.3mg; Sodium 51mg; Calc 116mg

Sweet Onion Yogurt Dip
make ahead
MAKES 2 CUPS; **PREP:** 10 MIN.,
COOK: 21 MIN., **COOL:** 5 MIN.,
CHILL: 30 MIN.

1 medium-size sweet onion, thinly sliced
½ tsp. sugar
1 tsp. canola oil
1 garlic clove, pressed
1 cup plain low-fat yogurt
½ cup light sour cream
¼ cup crumbled feta cheese
1 Tbsp. chopped fresh parsley
¼ tsp. salt
¼ tsp. pepper

1. Cook onion and sugar in hot oil in a large nonstick skillet over medium-low heat, stirring often, 15 to 20 minutes or until onions are caramel colored. Stir in garlic, and cook 1 more minute. Let cool 5 minutes; chop onions.
2. Stir together caramelized onion mixture, yogurt, and remaining ingredients in a medium bowl. Cover and chill 30 minutes or until ready to serve.

—**INSPIRED BY GWEN MOSSER**, PLAINFIELD, INDIANA

Per ⅓ cup: Calories 96; Fat 4.5g (sat 2.7g, mono 0.9g, poly 0.3g); Protein 4.9g; Carb 9.2g; Fiber 0.6g; Chol 8mg; Iron 0.3mg; Sodium 217mg; Calc 119mg

Healthy Living

Don't Be Lured by Labels

Health and weight-loss claims are popping up everywhere on product labels, and yogurt is no exception. Consider these facts on your next grocery run.

- Fat-free doesn't always mean lower in calories. In fact, sometimes sugar and other ingredients are added to fat-free products to enhance texture and flavor. Compare the calories of various fat-free and low-fat yogurts. Some fat-free products may have 10 to 20 more calories per serving.
- Watch out for high fructose corn syrup. It's the leading sweetener added to many commercial foods. Recent TV ads have recommended high fructose corn syrup in moderation, but it's hard to know what that means. Here's the skinny: Fructose contributes to more than 10% of America's daily calories. One study suggests that the average consumption of high fructose corn syrup among Americans tops 315 calories a day.
- Ingredients are listed in descending order on product labels, so it's easy to figure out what the main ones are. The first few usually contribute the most to calorie content.
- "Light," "reduced-calorie," and "sugar-free" typically mean that the sugar calories have been replaced with no-calorie sweeteners, such as NutraSweet or Splenda.
- Organic yogurt contains no artificial sweeteners, flavorings, or preservatives, and it should come from cows that haven't been treated with artificial growth hormone.

Layered Lima Bean Dip

MAKES 4 CUPS; **PREP:** 25 MIN.,
CHILL: 2 HR., **BAKE:** 10 MIN.

2 cups plain low-fat yogurt
½ (10-oz.) whole-wheat French bread
   baguette
Olive oil cooking spray
½ tsp. freshly ground pepper
1 small cucumber, seeded and diced
¼ tsp. salt
Lima Bean Mash
¼ cup (1 oz.) freshly grated 1.5% reduced-
   fat sharp Cheddar cheese
1 medium tomato, seeded and diced
   (about ½ cup)
3 cooked bacon slices, crumbled
Assorted vegetable slices

1. Preheat oven to 350°. Line a fine wire-mesh strainer with 1 coffee filter. Place strainer over a bowl; spoon yogurt into strainer. Cover yogurt with plastic wrap, and chill 2 hours.
2. Meanwhile, cut baguette into ¼-inch slices, and place on a baking sheet. Lightly coat 1 side of bread with cooking spray, and sprinkle with pepper.
3. Bake at 350° for 8 to 10 minutes or until toasted.
4. Spoon yogurt into a bowl, discarding strained liquid. (Yogurt will be thick.) Stir in cucumber and salt.
5. Spread Lima Bean Mash on bottom of a 9-inch deep-dish pie plate. Spread yogurt mixture over Lima Bean Mash. Top with cheese, tomato, and bacon. Serve with toasted bread slices and assorted vegetable slices.

Per ½ cup: Calories 172; Fat 5.6g (sat 1.7g, mono 1.9g, poly 0.5g); Protein 10.9g; Carb 20.6g; Fiber 5g; Chol 9mg; Iron 1.6mg; Sodium 362mg; Calc 184mg

Lima Bean Mash:

make ahead
MAKES 1½ CUPS; **PREP:** 10 MIN.,
COOK: 15 MIN., **COOL:** 15 MIN.,
CHILL: 30 MIN.

2 cups frozen baby lima beans
2 garlic cloves, chopped
¼ tsp. kosher salt
1 Tbsp. olive oil
½ tsp. lemon zest
2 tsp. fresh lemon juice

1. Combine lima beans, garlic, kosher salt, and 1 cup water in a medium saucepan. Bring to a boil over medium heat. Cover, reduce heat to low, and cook 15 minutes. Remove from heat, and let cool 15 minutes. Drain, reserving ¼ cup liquid.
2. Process lima bean mixture, reserved liquid, olive oil, and remaining ingredients in a food processor 30 seconds or until smooth. Cover and chill 30 minutes to 1 hour. Store in an airtight container up to 3 days.

Per 3 Tbsp.: Calories 64; Fat 1.9g (sat 0.3g, mono 1.3g, poly 0.3g); Protein 3.1g; Carb 9.1g; Fiber 2.7g; Chol 0mg; Iron 0.9mg; Sodium 73mg; Calc 14mg

Sip-able Sweets

All you need is a Southerner's craving for chocolate and a chilly day; we have the recipes to match. For adults, there's a decadent, honey-sweetened, Italian-style Rich 'n' Thick Hot Chocolate. In Everyday Hot Chocolate, we upped the chocolate factor by stirring hot fudge topping into the milk along with chocolate syrup. Add a special topping or stir-in if you like, and enjoy.

Rich 'n' Thick Hot Chocolate

MAKES ABOUT 4 CUPS (8 [½-CUP] SERVINGS); **PREP:** 10 MIN., **COOK:** 8 MIN.

This is a luxurious, unexpected offering for dessert. Take it over the top with a dollop of Marshmallow Whipped Cream. Find the chocolate bars on the candy aisle at the grocery store. Traditional hot chocolate recipes usually call for arrowroot as a thickener, but we used the more common cornstarch. It's hard to wait, but give this drink a chance to cool off after pouring. You'll love how the whipped cream in Marshmallow Whipped Cream melts into the chocolate before the mini marshmallows.

2 tsp. cornstarch
4 cups milk, divided
2 (3.5-oz.) dark chocolate bars (at least 70% cacao), chopped
⅓ cup honey
1 tsp. vanilla extract
Pinch of salt
Marshmallow Whipped Cream (optional)

1. Whisk together cornstarch and ½ cup milk until smooth.
2. Cook remaining 3½ cups milk in a large, nonaluminum saucepan over medium heat until bubbles appear around edge of saucepan (about 4 minutes; do not boil). Whisk in chocolate, honey, vanilla extract, and salt until blended and smooth. Whisk in cornstarch mixture.
3. Bring milk mixture to a light boil, whisking frequently (about 4 minutes). Remove from heat. Let cool slightly. (Mixture will thicken as it cools.) Serve immediately with Marshmallow Whipped Cream, if desired.
Note: For testing purposes only, we used Ghirardelli Intense Dark Twilight Delight 72% Cacao dark chocolate bar.

Mexican Rich 'n' Thick Hot Chocolate: Prepare recipe as directed through Step 2, whisking in 1¼ tsp. ground cinnamon and 1 tsp. ancho chili powder with chocolate. Proceed with recipe as directed.

Orange-Almond Rich 'n' Thick Hot Chocolate: Prepare recipe as directed through Step 2, whisking in 3 Tbsp. orange juice and 2 Tbsp. almond liqueur with chocolate. Proceed with recipe as directed.
Note: For testing purposes only, we used Amaretto for almond liqueur.

Grown-up Rich 'n' Thick Hot Chocolate: Prepare recipe as directed through Step 2, whisking in ½ cup Southern Comfort with chocolate. Proceed with recipe as directed.

Marshmallow Whipped Cream:
fast fixin's • make ahead
MAKES ABOUT 1½ CUPS; **PREP:** 10 MIN.

Maximum make-ahead time is two hours. After that, the marshmallows start to dissolve.

½ cup whipping cream
1 Tbsp. powdered sugar
½ cup miniature marshmallows

1. Beat whipping cream at medium-high speed with an electric mixer until foamy; gradually add powdered sugar, beating until soft peaks form. Fold in marshmallows. Serve immediately, or cover and chill up to 2 hours.

◆ **TIPS** ◆

- Our drink is thick enough to lightly coat a spoon. If you don't serve it all at one time, remove pan from heat. When you go back for seconds, it will have thickened. Reheat over low heat and thin by stirring in additional milk (¼ cup at a time).
- Secret ingredient: Salt. It enhances the rich, smooth taste of chocolate while toning down the naturally occurring bitterness.

Party Spoons

If you love chocolate-covered spoons, we think you'll like Whipped Topping Dollops on Spoons. You can prep them and store in the freezer up to two days. Take the spoons out of the freezer before you pour Everyday Hot Chocolate. They'll thaw quickly and won't cool off the beverage. This clever idea adds something special to an already delicious drink.

Everyday Hot Chocolate

fast fixin's

MAKES ABOUT 4½ CUPS; **PREP:** 10 MIN., **COOK:** 8 MIN.

The younger crowd will love adding stir-ins to their mugs, while the adults may want to go fancier. Offer Whipped Topping Dollops on Spoons to add to theirs.

4 cups milk
⅔ cup chocolate syrup
3 Tbsp. hot fudge topping
Pinch of salt
Stir-ins: crushed hard peppermint candies, chopped thin crème de menthe chocolate mints, miniature marshmallows, milk chocolate kisses, cherry cordial crème chocolate kisses
Whipped Topping Dollops on Spoons (optional)

1. Cook milk in a large nonaluminum saucepan over medium heat, stirring frequently, 6 to 8 minutes or until thoroughly heated (do not boil). Whisk in chocolate syrup, fudge topping, and salt, whisking vigorously until chocolate is well blended and mixture is frothy. Serve immediately with desired stir-ins or, if desired, Whipped Topping Dollops on Spoons.

Note: For testing purposes only, we used Hershey's Chocolate Syrup, Smucker's Hot Fudge Topping, Andes Crème de Menthe Thins, and Hershey's Kisses Limited Edition Cherry Cordial Crème.

Lightened Everyday Hot Chocolate: Substitute 2% reduced-fat milk for regular milk. Proceed with recipe as directed.

Whipped Topping Dollops On Spoons

freezeable • make ahead

MAKES 8 DOLLOPS; **PREP:** 10 MIN.; **FREEZE:** 1 HR., 5 MIN.

To pipe, gather the top of a zip-top plastic bag just above the level of the whipped topping, and twist. Snip the corner of the bag as directed, and then use the heel of your hand to squeeze topping onto spoons.

Parchment paper
1 cup thawed frozen whipped topping
¼ cup desired topping (chopped toffee bars, shaved white chocolate, shaved dark chocolate, ground cinnamon and nutmeg, finely chopped crystallized ginger, chopped chocolate-covered coffee beans)

1. Line a jelly-roll pan with parchment paper. Place 8 spoons on pan, and freeze 15 minutes.

2. Spoon whipped topping into a 1-qt. zip-top plastic freezer bag. (Do not seal.) Snip 1 corner of bag to make a ½-inch hole. Pipe dollops onto spoons. Freeze 5 minutes.

3. Sprinkle each dollop with about 1½ tsp. desired topping. Freeze dollops 45 minutes. Serve immediately on a tray. Or, transfer to a 13- x 9-inch baking pan; cover tightly, and freeze up to 2 days.

Two-in-One Treats

Pudding meets cake in these easy-to-make sweets.

This Southern dessert begins with a thick cake batter. Once the batter is in the pan or oven-safe dish, gently spoon boiling water over the top. The water and batter blend while baking to form the pudding layer. Try Hot Fudge Brownie Cake capped with a fluff of whipped cream or Apple Pudding Cake flavored with apple juice, freshly chopped apples, and cinnamon. Serve warm, and enjoy.

Hot Fudge Brownie Cake

MAKES 8 SERVINGS; **PREP**: 15 MIN.,
BAKE: 45 MIN., **COOL**: 25 MIN.

1 cup all-purpose flour
2 Tbsp. unsweetened cocoa
2 tsp. baking powder
¼ tsp. salt
1¼ cups granulated sugar, divided
½ cup milk, at room temperature
3 Tbsp. vegetable oil
1 tsp. vanilla extract
½ cup firmly packed light brown sugar
¼ cup unsweetened cocoa
1½ cups boiling water
Whipped cream or ice cream

1. Preheat oven to 350°. Stir together flour, next 3 ingredients, and ¾ cup granulated sugar in a large bowl; stir in milk, oil, and vanilla. Spread batter in a lightly greased 8-inch square pan.
2. Combine brown sugar, cocoa, and remaining ½ cup granulated sugar in a small bowl; sprinkle over batter in pan. Using a spoon, gently drizzle 1½ cups boiling water over batter, being careful not to disturb layers. (Do not stir.)
3. Bake at 350° for 45 minutes or until a cake layer forms on top and layer springs back when touched. Let cool on a wire rack 25 minutes. Serve warm with whipped cream or ice cream.

Chocolate-Cherry Pudding Cake: Thaw 1 (12-oz.) package frozen dark, sweet, pitted cherries; drain. Pat cherries dry with paper towels. Prepare recipe as directed through Step 2, gently sprinkling cherries over batter in pan. Proceed with recipe as directed.

Mocha Pudding Cake: Substitute hot freshly brewed coffee for boiling water. Proceed with recipe as directed.

Gently spoon boiling water over the batter. It's the water that creates the pudding layer while the cake bakes.

Spoon out Hot Fudge Brownie Cake and plenty of the creamy pudding. If there are leftovers, warm cake in a microwave-safe bowl at HIGH 30 seconds. Continue to microwave at 30-second intervals until warm.

Apple Pudding Cake

MAKES 8 SERVINGS; **PREP**: 20 MIN.,
BAKE: 30 MIN., **COOL**: 25 MIN.

1 medium-size Granny Smith apple, peeled,
    cored, and finely chopped
1 Tbsp. lemon juice
¼ cup firmly packed light brown sugar
1½ cups just-add-water pancake-and-
    waffle mix
½ cup granulated sugar
¾ tsp. ground cinnamon
½ cup milk
3 Tbsp. butter, melted
1 tsp. vanilla extract
2 cups apple juice
Ice cream (optional)

1. Preheat oven to 350°. Toss chopped apples with lemon juice in a medium bowl. Add brown sugar, stirring well to coat.
2. Whisk together pancake-and-waffle mix, granulated sugar, and cinnamon in a medium bowl; stir in milk, butter, and vanilla. Fold apple mixture and any accumulated juices into batter. Spread into a lightly greased 8-inch square pan.
3. Microwave apple juice in a 2-cup glass measuring cup at HIGH 2 to 3 minutes or until boiling. Using a spoon, gently drizzle hot apple juice over batter in pan. (Some batter may float once juice is added.)
4. Bake at 350° for 30 to 35 minutes or until a cake layer forms on top and layer springs back when touched. Let cool on a wire rack 25 minutes. Serve warm with ice cream, if desired.
Note: For testing purposes only, we used Aunt Jemima's Original Complete Pancake and Waffle Mix.

Fresh Sides for Winter Meals

Let us show you why summer is not the only time to enjoy fresh vegetables. Take advantage of the season's bounty with these sensational recipes.

Red Cabbage and Apples

MAKES 6 SERVINGS; **PREP:** 15 MIN., **COOK:** 1 HR.

Apples lend sweetness to the cabbage in this traditional combination.

1 medium head red cabbage, chopped
1 medium onion, chopped
2 Tbsp. vegetable oil
2 Granny Smith apples
1 Tbsp. lemon juice
1 Tbsp. sugar
¾ tsp. salt
½ tsp. pepper

1. Cook cabbage and onion in hot oil in a large nonstick skillet or Dutch oven over medium-low heat, stirring occasionally, 30 minutes.
2. Meanwhile, peel and chop apples; toss with lemon juice. Stir apple mixture, sugar, salt, and pepper into cabbage mixture. Cook, stirring occasionally, 30 minutes.
—**PEGGY NANCE LYLE**, RALEIGH, NORTH CAROLINA

Red Cabbage and Pears: Prepare recipe as directed, substituting Bartlett pears for apples.

Baked Onions

MAKES 4 TO 6 SERVINGS; **PREP:** 25 MIN.,
COOK: 3 MIN., **STAND:** 5 MIN.,
BAKE: 50 MIN.

3 (10-oz.) bags pearl onions
¼ cup butter
⅓ cup dry white wine
5 tsp. light brown sugar
3 garlic cloves, chopped
¾ tsp. salt
½ tsp. pepper

1. Preheat oven to 425°. Cook onions in boiling water to cover 3 minutes; drain. Rinse thoroughly under cold running water. Let stand 5 minutes.
2. Cut off root end of 1 onion. Using a towel, gently squeeze pointed end of onion toward root end, slipping outer peel off onion. Discard outer peel. Repeat procedure with remaining onions.
3. Melt butter in a 12-inch ovenproof skillet in a 425° oven 5 minutes. Stir in onions.
4. Bake onions at 425° for 15 minutes. Stir together wine and next 4 ingredients. Stir wine mixture into onions, and bake 35 to 40 minutes or until caramelized. Stir onions to coat and loosen particles from bottom of skillet.
—**ELLEN MILLER CROW**, TEXARKANA, TEXAS

Cauliflower With Cheese Sauce

MAKES 6 SERVINGS; **PREP:** 15 MIN.,
BAKE: 55 MIN., **COOK:** 6 MIN.

After the cauliflower has baked almost 40 minutes, start the cheese sauce.

1 head cauliflower (about 2 lb.)
3 Tbsp. butter
3 Tbsp. all-purpose flour
1 (12-oz.) can evaporated milk
1 cup grated sharp Cheddar cheese
½ tsp. salt
¼ tsp. ground white pepper
Pinch of paprika

1. Preheat oven to 400°. Trim bottom leaves from cauliflower. Remove core, leaving head intact. Place cauliflower on a large piece of heavy-duty aluminum foil. Loosely fold sides of foil up and over cauliflower; crimp sides of foil together to seal, leaving top of foil open. Sprinkle 2 Tbsp. water over cauliflower. Crimp top of foil together to seal. (Foil should be loose, allowing cauliflower to steam). Place foil-covered cauliflower in a roasting pan.
2. Bake at 400° for 45 minutes.
3. Meanwhile, melt butter in a medium saucepan over medium heat; gradually whisk in flour until a paste forms, and cook, whisking constantly, 1 minute. Whisk in evaporated milk, and cook, whisking constantly, 5 minutes or until thickened and smooth. Whisk in cheese until melted. Whisk in salt and pepper.
4. Remove cauliflower from oven, and fold foil halfway down sides of cauliflower. Top cauliflower with cheese sauce, and sprinkle with paprika.
5. Bake at 400° for 10 minutes. Serve immediately.
—**INSPIRED BY LINDA LAMPRECHT**,
CORPUS CHRISTI, TEXAS

Cauliflower With Southwest Cheese Sauce: Prepare recipe as directed, substituting Monterey Jack cheese with peppers for sharp Cheddar cheese and adding 1 (10-oz.) can diced tomatoes and green chiles, drained, to cheese sauce with salt and pepper. Sprinkle with salt to taste.

Good and Easy Chicken

Tips, tricks, and recipe secrets.

Chicken on the Double
Planning ahead for leftovers is one of the smartest ways we know to save time and money. You're actually creating your own home-cooked convenience products. Here, Test Kitchens Professional Marian Cooper Cairns shares her hands-off recipe for roasting two chickens at once. (See page 33 for freezing instructions.) She sometimes places lemon slices and fresh herbs under the skin and inside the cavity for additional flavor, but the taste is just as wonderful without. Feel free to substitute your favorite seasoning blend for the salt and pepper.

Marian's Easy Roast Chicken

MAKES 8 SERVINGS; **PREP:** 10 MIN.;
BAKE: 1 HR., 30 MIN.; **STAND:** 10 MIN.

4 tsp. kosher salt
2 tsp. freshly ground pepper
2 (4- to 5-lb.) whole chickens
1 Tbsp. olive oil

1. Preheat oven to 375°. Stir together salt and pepper.
2. If applicable, remove necks and giblets from chickens, and reserve for another use. Pat chickens dry. Sprinkle ½ tsp. salt mixture inside cavity of each chicken. Rub 1½ tsp. olive oil into skin of each chicken. Sprinkle with remaining salt mixture; rub into skin. Place chickens, breast sides up, facing in opposite directions (for even browning), on a lightly greased wire rack in a lightly greased 17- x 12-inch jelly-roll pan.
3. Bake at 375° for 1½ hours or until a meat thermometer inserted in thigh registers 180°. Let stand 10 minutes before slicing.

Roasting Notes

- To ensure even cooking, remove chicken from the refrigerator 30 minutes before baking.
- Large (4- to 5-lb.) chickens labeled as roasters have a higher fat content than smaller broiler-fryers, so the meat remains moist without basting.
- There's no need to truss. While trussing does create a beautifully shaped roast chicken, it can increase the bake time for the dark meat and prevent areas of the skin from browning.
- Try replacing the wire roasting rack with an aromatic layer of carrots and celery ribs or sliced onions. The vegetables and pan juices make a delicious start for soups or stews, and because you have no rack to wash, cleanup is a breeze.

Pot Luck
Test Kitchens Professional Angela Sellers prefers to cook her chicken on the stovetop. Seared to a golden brown, then simmered with a small amount of liquid in a Dutch oven, the meat is extra juicy and fork-tender, making it perfect for chicken salad, pot pies, and dumplings—plus you get the added bonus of a delicious broth for soup.

Angela's Stovetop Chicken

MAKES 4 SERVINGS; **PREP:** 10 MIN.;
COOK: 1 HR., 5 MIN.

1 (4- to 5-lb.) whole chicken
1½ tsp. salt
¼ tsp. garlic powder
¼ tsp. pepper
2 Tbsp. butter
2 Tbsp. olive oil
¼ cup dry white wine

1. If applicable, remove neck and giblets from chicken, and reserve for another use. Sprinkle chicken with salt, garlic powder, and pepper.
2. Melt butter with oil in a Dutch oven over medium-high heat; add chicken, and cook, breast side down, 5 minutes or until golden brown. Turn chicken, breast side up, and reduce heat to medium-low. Add ¼ cup water and ¼ cup wine to Dutch oven. Cover and cook 1 hour or until a meat thermometer inserted in thigh registers 180°.

February

Dreamy, Creamy Cookie Desserts

Give in to the temptation of our luscious, layered spin-offs of a favorite Southern sweet.

Store-bought cookies make some of the handiest dessert ingredients around. They'd be perfect, Associate Food Editor Shirley Harrington thought, for a few recipe spins on the beloved trifle. All she'd have to do is swap crispy cookies for the softer cake layer usually found in this Southern dessert. Enter Marian Cooper Cairns, Test Kitchen Professional. With pen, paper, and a few favorite cookies to munch on, she and Shirley imagined the creamy filling, fresh fruit, and whipped cream combos to best play up the shape, style, and flavor personality of our chosen cookies. The results? Splurge-worthy cookie trifles.

Triple Chocolate-Cookie Trifle Pie

editor's pick • make ahead
MAKES 10 TO 12 SERVINGS; **PREP:** 25 MIN., **COOL:** 20 MIN., **CHILL:** 8 HR.

It's unusual, but we call for the cream to stand at room temperature before whipping. If it's too cold when folded into the melted chocolate mixtures, the chocolate may harden into tiny pieces.

3¼ cups heavy cream, divided
1½ (4-oz.) bittersweet chocolate baking bars, chopped
1 (4-oz.) white chocolate baking bar, chopped
1 tsp. vanilla extract
1 (12.5-oz.) package assorted cookies
2 Tbsp. mocha liqueur (optional)
2 (6-oz.) containers fresh raspberries
Raspberry Glaze

1. Microwave ½ cup cream at HIGH 30 seconds to 1 minute or until hot (do not boil). Place bittersweet chocolate in a large bowl. Pour hot cream over chocolate, and stir until smooth. Repeat procedure with ¼ cup cream and white chocolate. (If chocolate does not melt completely after stirring, microwave at HIGH for 10-second intervals just until chocolate is melted and mixture is smooth.) Stir ½ tsp. vanilla into each chocolate mixture until well blended. Cool 20 minutes.
2. Meanwhile, let 2½ cups cream stand at room temperature 20 minutes.
3. Beat 1½ cups cream at medium-high speed with an electric mixer until medium peaks form. Gently fold one-fourth of whipped cream into cool bittersweet chocolate mixture. Repeat procedure with remaining whipped cream.
4. Beat remaining 1 cup cream at medium-high speed until medium peaks form. Gently fold one-fourth of whipped cream into cool white chocolate mixture. Repeat procedure with remaining whipped cream.
5. Crush 6 to 7 cookies to equal ½ cup crumbs. Sprinkle on bottom of a lightly greased 9-inch springform pan. Spread half of bittersweet chocolate mixture over crushed cookies in pan. Arrange cookies around sides of pan (about 19 cookies). Spread white chocolate mixture over bittersweet chocolate mixture.
6. Crush remaining cookies, and sprinkle over white chocolate mixture in springform pan. Drizzle with liqueur, if desired. Spread remaining bittersweet chocolate mixture over crushed cookies. Cover and chill 8 to 24 hours.
7. Remove sides from pan. Mound raspberries in center of trifle, and brush with Raspberry Glaze. Serve trifle immediately.
Note: For testing purposes only, we used Ghirardelli 60% Cacao Bittersweet Baking Bars, Ghirardelli White Chocolate Baking Bar, Pepperidge Farm Distinctive Entertaining Cookie Collection, and Godiva Mocha Liqueur.

Raspberry Glaze: Combine 3 Tbsp. seedless raspberry jam and 2 tsp. water in a small glass bowl. Microwave at HIGH 10 to 15 seconds or until smooth.

Nutter Butter®-Banana Pudding Trifle

MAKES 8 TO 10 SERVINGS; **PREP:** 35 MIN., **COOK:** 20 MIN., **STAND:** 30 MIN., **CHILL:** 2 HR.

This homemade pudding is divine, economical, and uses on-hand ingredients. The pudding has thickened enough when a distinct trail is left in the mixture when you stir with a spoon. The cookies will soften the longer the dessert chills. (Pictured on page 5)

3 cups milk
3 large eggs
¾ cup sugar
⅓ cup all-purpose flour
2 Tbsp. butter
2 tsp. vanilla extract
5 medium-size ripe bananas
1 (1-lb.) package peanut butter sandwich cookies
2 cups sweetened whipped cream
Garnishes: peanut butter sandwich cookies, dried banana chips, fresh mint sprigs

1. Whisk together first 4 ingredients in a large saucepan over medium-low heat. Cook, whisking constantly, 15 to 20 minutes or until thickened. Remove from heat; stir in butter and vanilla until butter is melted.
2. Fill a large bowl with ice. Place saucepan in ice, and let stand, stirring occasionally, 30 minutes or until mixture is thoroughly chilled.

3. Meanwhile, cut bananas into ¼-inch slices. Break cookies into thirds.

4. Spoon half of pudding mixture into a 3-qt. bowl or pitcher. Top with bananas and cookies. Spoon remaining pudding mixture over bananas and cookies. Top with sweetened whipped cream. Cover and chill 2 to 24 hours. Garnish, if desired.

Note: For testing purposes only, we used Nabisco Nutter Butter® Sandwich Cookies. For photography, we divided mixture between 2 (1½- to 2-qt.) wide-mouthed pitchers.

Shortcut Nutter Butter®-Banana Pudding Trifle: Omit eggs, sugar, flour, and butter. Substitute thawed extra creamy whipped topping for sweetened whipped cream. Reduce vanilla to 1 tsp. Place 3 cups milk and vanilla in large bowl; add 2 (3.4-oz.) packages vanilla instant pudding mix. Beat with an electric mixer at medium speed 2 minutes or until thickened; let stand 5 minutes. Stir in 1 (8-oz.) container sour cream. Proceed with recipe as directed in Steps 2 through 4.

Note: For testing purposes only, we used Jell-O Vanilla Instant Pudding and Pie Filling and Cool Whip Extra Creamy.

• T I P S •

- **Our Nutter Butter®-Banana Pudding Trifle, Clementine-Gingersnap Trifles, and Triple Chocolate-Cookie Trifle Pie** call for chill time. Written as a range, such as 2 to 24 hours, the numbers indicate the minimum and maximum amount of chill time for the dessert to be at peak flavor and texture.
- **Homemade Whipped Cream to top Nutter Butter®-Banana Pudding Trifle:** Make 2 cups sweetened whipped cream by beating 1 cup whipping cream and 2 Tbsp. sugar at medium speed with an electric mixer until soft peaks form.
- **The Triple Chocolate-Cookie Trifle Pie** was originally tested in a bowl. Our Food staff noted it held its shape and decided to throw out the wild idea of assembling it in a springform pan. Next day, this trifle pie invention was sliced instead of scooped and received our top rating.

Clementine-Gingersnap Trifles

MAKES 6; **PREP:** 30 MIN., **CHILL:** 2 HR.

Clementines, a variety of Mandarin orange, are plentiful in winter. In a pinch substitute 2 (29-oz.) cans mandarin oranges in light syrup, drained. Garnish with leftover cookies.

1 (8-oz.) package cream cheese, softened
¼ cup sugar
1 tsp. lemon zest
1 tsp. vanilla extract, divided
¾ cup heavy cream, whipped
10 to 12 clementines
¼ cup orange marmalade
1½ tsp. poppy seeds
1 (5.25-oz.) package thin ginger cookies
Garnishes: sliced kiwi, thin ginger cookies

1. Beat cream cheese, sugar, zest, and ½ tsp. vanilla at medium-high speed with a heavy-duty electric stand mixer 30 seconds or until smooth and sugar is dissolved. Fold in whipped cream, and spoon into a 1-gal. zip-top plastic bag. Seal bag, and chill 2 to 24 hours.

2. Peel clementines, and separate into segments. (Yield should be 4 cups.)

3. Microwave marmalade in a medium bowl at HIGH 20 seconds or until melted. Stir in clementine segments, poppy seeds, and remaining ½ tsp. vanilla. Remove and reserve 6 segments. Divide half of clementine mixture among 6 (10- to 13-oz.) glasses. Top each with 2 cookies. Repeat layers once.

4. Snip 1 corner of bag with cream cheese mixture with scissors to make a 1-inch hole. Pipe mixture onto cookies in glasses. Serve immediately, or cover and chill 2 hours. Top with reserved segments just before serving, and garnish, if desired.

Note: For testing purposes only, we used Anna's Ginger Thins. A 2½- to 3-qt. trifle dish may be substituted for 6 (10- to 13-oz.) glasses.

Lightened Clementine-Gingersnap Trifles: Substitute reduced-fat cream cheese for regular cream cheese and 1 (8-oz.) container reduced-fat whipped topping, thawed, for whipped heavy cream. Decrease sugar to 1 Tbsp. Proceed with recipe as directed.

Budget Matchup

Lowest cost: Nutter Butter®-Banana Pudding Trifle. On-hand ingredients are used in the pudding, cookies usually cost less than $3.50, and bananas are a bargain at less than $1 per pound.

Moderate spending: Clementine-Gingersnap Trifles. Clementines are sometimes sold individually but are most often available in mesh bags or small wooden crates for $4 to $7. Gingersnaps cost just more than $2. Don't skip the poppy seeds (about $4 a bottle). You'll like them in this recipe as much as in lemon-poppy seed bread.

Splurge sensation: Triple Chocolate-Cookie Trifle Pie. It would cost double to buy this style of dessert at a bakery. Allow $15 for chocolate and cookies, $4 for whipping cream, and probably $7 for raspberry garnish. To save money on the garnish, buy one container of raspberries instead of two. Use 10 to 12 arranged near outside edge of pie to garnish each piece. Skip the Raspberry Glaze. Serve remaining berries for guests to add to their servings.

Luscious Coffee Liqueur

This rich elixir is the perfect addition to a hot cup of coffee. Or use it as an ingredient in our recipes.

A few months ago, our coffee-loving Food staff wondered if we could develop made-from-scratch coffee liqueur. Test Kitchen Professional Kristi Michele Crowe, PhD, not only delivered, but she also created an easy recipe (only five ingredients) that received our highest rating.

Here's the catch: While it takes just 20 minutes to prepare, it needs to stand for one month to allow the hint of vanilla and bold coffee undertone flavors to fully develop. It complements the creamy, buttery interior of Coffee-Pecan Brie and lends subtle sweetness to Coffee Liqueur Barbecue Sauce. Our best advice is to make two batches, so you'll have plenty to share with friends.

For the perfect treat, pair these beverages with the Biscuit Beignets on page 50.

Homemade Coffee Liqueur
make ahead
MAKES 6 CUPS; PREP: 10 MIN., COOL: 10 MIN., STAND: 1 MONTH

4 cups sugar
¼ cup instant espresso
2 cups vodka
2 Tbsp. chocolate liqueur (optional)
1 (8-inch) vanilla bean, split lengthwise

1. Bring 2 cups water to a boil in a large saucepan over medium-high heat. Remove from heat, and whisk in sugar and instant espresso, whisking until completely dissolved. Let mixture cool 10 minutes.
2. Stir in vodka and, if desired, chocolate liqueur until well blended. Pour mixture into a 2-qt. glass bottle. Add vanilla bean. Cover tightly with lid, and shake thoroughly. Let stand in a cool, dark place 1 month, shaking at least once weekly.
Note: For testing purposes only, we used Godiva Original Chocolate Liqueur.

Coffee-Pecan Brie
MAKES 10 SERVINGS; PREP: 15 MIN., BAKE: 28 MIN., STAND: 10 MIN.

This recipe is perfect for entertaining and will easily double. We do recommend baking one recipe at a time so the Brie will stay nice and soft.

¾ cup pecans, chopped
2 (8.5-oz.) Brie rounds
¼ cup Homemade Coffee Liqueur*
3 Tbsp. brown sugar
Crackers or chocolate wafers

1. Preheat oven to 350°. Bake pecans in a single layer in a shallow pan 8 to 10 minutes or until toasted and fragrant.
2. Meanwhile, trim and discard rind from top of each Brie round, leaving a ¼-inch border. Place each Brie round in a shallow ovenproof serving dish.
3. Stir together Homemade Coffee Liqueur and brown sugar in small bowl until blended. Pour mixture over Brie rounds.
4. Bake at 350° for 18 to 20 minutes or until cheese bubbles on top. Sprinkle with pecans. Let stand 10 minutes. Serve with crackers or chocolate wafers.
—JULIE BECKER, MURFREESBORO, TENNESSEE
*Store-bought coffee liqueur may be substituted.

Coffee Liqueur Crème
make ahead
MAKES 2 CUPS; PREP: 5 MIN., CHILL: 2 HR.

A dollop of this silky goodness elevates a slice of chocolate pie to something truly heavenly. We also love it atop pecan pie.

1 cup heavy cream
¼ to ⅓ cup Homemade Coffee Liqueur

1. Beat heavy cream at medium-high speed with a heavy-duty electric stand mixer until soft peaks form. Add ¼ to ⅓ cup Homemade Coffee Liqueur, and beat 30 seconds. Gently stir until well blended. Cover and chill up to 2 hours.

Cinnamon-Orange Coffee Mix
fast fixin's • make ahead
MAKES ⅔ CUP; PREP: 10 MIN.

Combine the dry ingredients in small containers to give as gifts.

½ cup coarsely ground coffee
2 Tbsp. dark brown sugar
1½ tsp. ground cinnamon
1 tsp. dried orange peel*

1. Stir together all ingredients. Store in an airtight container up to 1 month. Do not freeze.
*1 tsp. orange zest may be substituted.

Cinnamon-Orange Coffee

MAKES 8 SERVINGS; **PREP:** 5 MIN.
(Pictured on page 4)

Cinnamon-Orange Coffee Mix
8 Tbsp. Homemade Coffee
    Liqueur (optional)*
Coffee Liqueur Crème (optional)

1. Brew Cinnamon-Orange Coffee Mix according to coffeemaker manufacturer's instructions for 8 (6-oz.) cups of coffee. If desired, stir 1 Tbsp. Homemade Coffee Liqueur into each serving, and dollop with Coffee Liqueur Crème. Serve immediately.
*Store-bought coffee liqueur may be substituted.

Coffee Liqueur Barbecue Sauce

make ahead

MAKES 1 CUP; **PREP:** 10 MIN.,
COOK: 6 MIN., **COOL:** 30 MIN.

The sweet-and-tangy flavor cozies up nicely to everything from baby back ribs to brisket. We like the addition of dried crushed red pepper to make it extra tasty.

1 (8-oz.) can tomato sauce
⅓ cup Homemade Coffee Liqueur*
¼ cup finely chopped yellow onion
2 Tbsp. Worcestershire sauce
1 Tbsp. fresh lemon juice
2 tsp. all-purpose flour
½ tsp. salt
¼ tsp. chili powder
¼ tsp. dried crushed red pepper (optional)

1. Whisk together first 8 ingredients and, if desired, crushed red pepper in a medium saucepan. Bring to a boil over medium heat; reduce heat to low, and simmer, whisking occasionally, 5 to 6 minutes or until slightly thickened. Cool completely before serving (about 30 minutes). Store in an airtight container in refrigerator up to 7 days.
*Store-bought coffee liqueur may be substituted.

Pretty Mini Desserts

We hope you'll try one or more of our cookie desserts starting on page 44. (We've included even more tips here.) Those recipes call for a chill time and serve four or more. But in a time crunch, you can assemble a pair of these single-serving trifles for you and a loved one. First, choose a cookie. Then, layer Creamy Filling and cookies. To finish up, drizzle with a Fruity Topping, sprinkle with chopped candies, and garnish with fresh mint sprigs. Serve immediately. Try these fun combinations, or design your own and let your inner creativity come out.

Fruity Topping: Place ½ cup frozen cherries, raspberries, or blackberries in a small glass bowl. Microwave at HIGH 30 seconds or until thawed; drain. Stir in 1 Tbsp. orange liqueur or orange juice and 2 tsp. powdered sugar. Makes about ½ cup (enough for 2 mini trifles); Prep: 5 min.
Note: For testing purposes only, we used Grand Marnier for orange liqueur.

Combinations To Inspire You

- Pecan shortbread cookies + Creamy Filling + Cherry Fruity Topping
- Pure butter shortbread rounds + Creamy Filling + finely chopped peanut brittle
- Sugar cookies + Creamy Filling + Blackberry Fruity Topping
- Double chocolate-filled vanilla wafer sandwich cookies + Creamy Filling + Raspberry Fruity Topping
- Soft-baked chocolate chip cookies + Creamy Filling + your favorite chopped candy bar
- Homemade snickerdoodle cookies + Creamy Filling + crumbled chocolate-covered crispy peanut-buttery candy bar
- Brownies + Creamy Filling + chopped turtle candies
- Fudge-mint graham cracker cookies + Creamy Filling + chopped thin crème de menthe chocolate mints

Creamy Filling: Stir together 1 (3.5-oz.) container refrigerated prepared vanilla pudding and 3 Tbsp. sour cream. Makes about ½ cup (enough for 2 mini trifles); Prep: 5 min.

Switch the Look

Assemble your choice of our Mini Trifle ideas in margarita glasses for a casual gathering or in old-fashioned Champagne saucer-type glasses for a ladies' get-together. Serve with forks if plated, spoons if in glasses. *Pecan Shortbread Cookie Trifle (right) and Peanut Brittle Cookie Trifle (far right)*

Superfast Suppers

Ready in 30 minutes or less, each of these menus features a quick skillet entrée paired with simple-to-fix sides. The inspiration is Italian, but the taste is pure Southern comfort. They're every bit as good as the special dishes we enjoy at our favorite restaurants, yet are a fraction of the cost.

Steak and Potatoes Supper

SERVES 4

Steak Balsamico With Mushrooms

Warm Roasted Potato Salad

Steak Balsamico With Mushrooms

family favorite • fast fixin's

MAKES 4 SERVINGS; **PREP:** 10 MIN.,
COOK: 19 MIN.

We used flat-iron steaks for this recipe, but boneless chuck-eye steak, a distant cousin of the rib-eye, is an equally tender and inexpensive choice. Both cuts are best cooked medium to medium rare.

4 (6-oz.) flat-iron steaks (about 1¼ inches thick)
1¼ tsp. salt, divided
¾ tsp. freshly ground pepper, divided
2 Tbsp. olive oil
2 garlic cloves, minced
1 (8-oz.) package sliced fresh mushrooms
½ cup balsamic vinegar

1. Rub steaks with 1 tsp. salt and ½ tsp. pepper. Cook steaks in hot oil in a large skillet over medium-high heat 4 to 5 minutes on each side or to desired degree of doneness. Transfer steaks to a serving platter, and keep warm.
2. Add garlic to skillet; sauté 30 seconds, stirring constantly. Add mushrooms and remaining ¼ tsp. salt and ¼ tsp. pepper to skillet; sauté 3 minutes. Stir in vinegar; cook, stirring frequently, 3 to 5 minutes or until mushrooms are tender. Spoon mushroom mixture over steaks, and serve immediately.

Pork Balsamico With Mushrooms: Substitute 2 lb. pork tenderloin, cut in ½-inch-thick slices, for steaks. Proceed with recipe as directed.

Time-saver:

Mushrooms and balsamic vinegar cook in the same skillet as the steaks, deglazing the flavorful bits from the bottom of the pan, while preseasoned frozen potato wedges roast in the oven.

Warm Roasted Red Potato Salad

family favorite • fast fixin's

MAKES 4 SERVINGS; **PREP:** 5 MIN.,
BAKE: 20 MIN.

1 (22-oz.) package frozen olive oil, Parmesan, and roasted garlic red potatoes
1 (5-oz.) package salad greens, thoroughly washed
½ cup refrigerated blue cheese vinaigrette

1. Prepare potatoes according to package directions. Toss salad greens with warm potatoes and vinaigrette just before serving.
Note: For testing purposes only, we used Alexia Olive Oil, Parmesan, and Roasted Garlic Oven Reds, and Marie's Blue Cheese Vinaigrette.

Southern Comfort Food

SERVES 4

Turkey Scaloppine

Roasted Zucchini

Cream Grits With Sweet Corn

Turkey Scaloppine

family favorite • fast fixin's

MAKES 4 SERVINGS; **PREP:** 5 MIN.,
COOK: 6 MIN.

½ cup all-purpose flour
1¼ tsp. Cajun seasoning, divided
1½ lb. turkey cutlets
2 Tbsp. olive oil
1 cup dry white wine

1. Combine flour and 1 tsp. Cajun seasoning in a shallow dish; dredge turkey cutlets in flour mixture, shaking off excess.
2. Cook turkey in hot oil in a large skillet over medium-high heat 1 to 2 minutes on each side or until done. Transfer turkey to a serving platter, and keep warm.
3. Add wine and remaining ¼ tsp. Cajun seasoning to skillet; cook 1 to 2 minutes or until liquid is reduced by half, stirring to loosen particles from bottom of skillet. Drizzle sauce over turkey. Serve immediately.

▪TIP▪

The secret to moist-and-tender Turkey Scaloppine is to have both the skillet and oil hot enough to brown the cutlets the minute they hit the pan. Roasted Zucchini and Creamy Grits With Sweet Corn round out the menu.

Roasted Zucchini

family favorite • fast fixin's
MAKES 4 SERVINGS; PREP: 10 MIN.,
BAKE: 15 MIN.

1 lb. small zucchini
2 Tbsp. olive oil
1 tsp. jarred minced garlic
1 tsp. dried Italian seasoning
½ tsp. dried crushed red pepper
½ tsp. salt

1. Preheat oven to 450°. Cut zucchini lengthwise into quarters; cut each piece in half crosswise. Toss zucchini with oil and remaining 4 ingredients; arrange zucchini in a single layer on a baking sheet. Bake 15 minutes or until golden brown and tender, turning once after 7 minutes.

Creamy Grits With Sweet Corn

family favorite • fast fixin's
MAKES 4 SERVINGS; PREP: 5 MIN.,
COOK: 10 MIN.

1 tsp. salt
¾ cup uncooked quick-cooking grits
1 cup frozen whole kernel corn, thawed
1 (4-oz.) container light garlic-and-herb
    spreadable cheese
½ tsp. freshly ground pepper

1. Bring 3 cups water and 1 tsp. salt to a boil in a large saucepan over medium-high heat; gradually stir in grits. Reduce heat to medium-low, and cook, stirring often, 5 minutes or until thickened. Stir in corn, cheese, and pepper; cook, stirring constantly, 1 minute or until cheese is melted.
Note: For testing purposes only, we used Alouette Light Garlic & Herbs Spreadable Cheese.

Broccoli-Cheese Grits: Substitute 2 cups frozen broccoli florets and 1 cup (4 oz.) shredded sharp Cheddar cheese for corn and garlic-and-herb spreadable cheese. Proceed with recipe as directed.

Spicy Cheese Grits: Substitute 1 (6.5-oz.) container pepper-Jack-and-jalapeño pepper spreadable cheese for garlic-and-herb spreadable cheese. Proceed with recipe as directed.
Note: For testing purposes only, we used J. L. Kraft Specialty Gourmet Pepperjack and Jalapeño Spreadable Cheese.

Italian Inspired

SERVES 4

Pan-Fried Chicken-and-
Ham Parmesan

Garlic-Herb Pasta

Sautéed Grape Tomatoes

Pan-Fried Chicken-and-Ham Parmesan

fast fixin's
MAKES 4 SERVINGS; PREP: 10 MIN.,
COOK: 8 MIN., BAKE: 8 MIN.

4 (6-oz.) skinned and boned chicken breasts
1 tsp. salt
½ tsp. pepper
1 large egg
¼ cup all-purpose flour
⅔ cup Italian-seasoned breadcrumbs
2 Tbsp. olive oil
8 thinly sliced smoked deli ham slices
    (about ¼ lb.)
4 (1-oz.) fresh mozzarella cheese slices
Garlic-Herb Pasta
Sautéed Grape Tomatoes

1. Preheat oven to 350°. Sprinkle chicken with salt and pepper. Whisk together egg and 2 Tbsp. water. Dredge chicken in flour; dip in egg mixture, and dredge in breadcrumbs, shaking off excess.
2. Cook chicken in hot oil in a large ovenproof skillet over medium-high heat 3 to 4 minutes on each side or until golden. Top chicken with ham and cheese.

3. Bake chicken in skillet at 350° for 8 minutes or until cheese is melted. Serve over Garlic-Herb Pasta; top with Sautéed Grape Tomatoes.

Time-saver:

Boneless chicken breasts brown on the stovetop, and then get a hands-off finish in the oven during the short time it takes to prepare the rest of the meal.

Garlic-Herb Pasta: Cook 8 oz. vermicelli according to package directions; drain. Toss with ¼ cup Garlic-Herb Butter. Season with salt to taste. MAKES 4 SERVINGS.

Garlic-Herb Butter: Stir together ½ cup softened butter; 1 large garlic clove, pressed; ⅔ cup chopped fresh basil; ¼ cup chopped fresh parsley; and ¼ tsp. salt until well blended. Use immediately, or cover and chill up to 3 days. For longer storage, form into a log or press into ice cube trays, and wrap tightly with plastic wrap; freeze up to 1 month. Makes ½ cup; Prep: 15 min.

Sautéed Grape Tomatoes

family favorite • fast fixin's
MAKES 4 SERVINGS; PREP: 10 MIN.,
COOK: 3 MIN.

Grape tomatoes deliver a sweet taste of summer and cook in minutes.

1 pt. grape tomatoes, halved
1 Tbsp. light brown sugar
3 Tbsp. balsamic vinegar
¼ tsp. salt
1 tsp. olive oil
2 Tbsp. thinly sliced fresh basil

1. Sauté tomatoes and next 3 ingredients in hot oil in a small skillet over medium-high heat 2 to 3 minutes or until thoroughly heated. Remove from heat, and stir in basil.

Omelets Make a Meal

They're not just for breakfast anymore.

Eggs are Assistant Food Editor Marion McGahey's great go-to ingredient when she's short on time or cooking on a budget. Test Kitchen Professional Norman King bulked up the average breakfast omelet with sliced andouille sausage, bell pepper, onion, and Monterey Jack cheese to create a delicious Cajun-inspired dish that can be enjoyed any time of the day. Be sure to try our delicious shrimp variation too. Keep in mind, the first omelet takes a little longer (45 seconds to 1 minute) to cook than the last due to the heat of the pan.

New Orleans Supper

SERVES 4

Cajun Omelet

Green salad

French bread

Cajun Omelet

MAKES 4 SERVINGS; PREP: 20 MIN., COOK: 22 MIN.

5 tsp. butter, divided
1¼ cups sliced andouille sausage
2 small plum tomatoes, seeded and chopped
½ medium onion, chopped
½ medium-size red bell pepper, chopped
1 celery rib, chopped
1 tsp. minced garlic
1 tsp. Creole seasoning, divided
12 large eggs
1 Tbsp. chopped fresh parsley
Vegetable cooking spray
1½ cups (6 oz.) shredded Monterey Jack cheese
Hot sauce

1. Melt 1 tsp. butter in a 10-inch non-stick heavy skillet over medium-high heat; add sausage, and cook, stirring occasionally, 6 to 7 minutes or until sausage is well browned. Add tomatoes, next 4 ingredients, and ½ tsp. Creole seasoning. Cook 5 to 7 minutes or until vegetables are tender and most of liquid has evaporated. Remove from skillet.
2. Whisk together eggs, parsley, and remaining ½ tsp. Creole seasoning.
3. Melt 1 tsp. butter in skillet coated with cooking spray over medium heat, rotating pan to evenly coat bottom. Pour one-fourth of egg mixture into skillet. As egg mixture starts to cook, gently lift edges of omelet with a spatula, and tilt pan so uncooked portion flows underneath. Cook until almost set (about 1 minute). Cover skillet, and cook 1 minute.
4. Sprinkle 1 side of omelet with one-fourth each sausage mixture and cheese. Fold omelet in half over filling. Slide omelet onto a serving plate; cover with aluminum foil to keep warm. Repeat procedure 3 times with remaining butter, egg mixture, sausage mixture, and cheese. Serve with hot sauce.

Cajun Omelet With Shrimp:

Prepare recipe as directed in Step 1. Stir 1 cup chopped large, peeled and deveined raw shrimp (21/30 count) into sausage mixture. Cook 1 minute or just until shrimp turn pink. Remove from skillet. Proceed with recipe as directed. Prep: 25 min., Cook: 23 min.

SO SOUTHERN

Biscuit Beignets

MAKES 4 TO 6 SERVINGS; PREP: 5 MIN., COOK: 3 MIN. PER BATCH

Tip your hat to the Crescent City, and honor Mardi Gras month by preparing these New Orleans-style treats. (Pictured on page 4)

1. Separate 1 (12-oz.) can refrigerated buttermilk biscuits into individual rounds, and cut into quarters. Pour oil to a depth of 2 inches into a Dutch oven, heat over medium heat to 350°. Fry biscuit quarters, in batches, 1 to 1½ minutes on each side or until golden. Drain on paper towels, and dust generously with powdered sugar. Serve immediately. **Note:** For testing purposes only, we used Pillsbury Golden Layers Buttermilk Biscuits.

Easy Chicken and Rice

These dishes provide variety, value, and family-pleasing flavor.

Rice is welcome on most tables, especially when it's paired with chicken. These ingredients are such perfect partners that nearly every family has a favorite recipe for this down-home dish. Its plain, sturdy comfort makes it appealing to children, especially basic versions, such as Simple Chicken and Rice. Adults may prefer the Tex-Mex flair of Salsa Verde Chicken Casserole or Baked Chicken and Rice With Black Beans. All are mildly seasoned, so if you like a little more spice, stir in some chopped pickled jalapeños or serve with hot sauce on the side. With or without the heat, these are great choices to warm up a winter night.

Simple Chicken and Rice

family favorite

MAKES 6 SERVINGS; **PREP:** 15 MIN.;
BAKE: 1 HR., 30 MIN.

2 cups uncooked jasmine rice
1 (14-oz.) can chicken broth
¾ cup buttermilk
½ cup dry white wine*
1 (8-oz.) package sliced fresh
    mushrooms
2 tsp. salt, divided
1 (3½ lb.) cut-up whole chicken
½ tsp. pepper
3 Tbsp. chopped fresh parsley

1. Preheat oven to 350°. Stir together rice, chicken broth, buttermilk, wine, mushrooms, and ½ tsp. salt. Spoon rice mixture into a lightly greased 13- x 9-inch baking dish. Sprinkle chicken with pepper and remaining 1½ tsp. salt. Place chicken on top of rice mixture.

2. Bake, covered, at 350° for 1½ hours or until chicken is done. Sprinkle with parsley just before serving.
*½ cup chicken broth may be substituted.

Baked Chicken and Rice With Black Beans

MAKES 6 TO 8 SERVINGS; **PREP:** 25 MIN.,
COOK: 10 MIN., **BAKE:** 40 MIN.

Yellow rice, chicken, black beans, and cheese make this dish robust and delicious.

1 (10-oz.) package yellow rice mix
1 cup chopped onion
½ cup chopped green bell pepper
½ cup chopped carrot
1 Tbsp. olive oil
2 cups cubed cooked chicken
1 (15-oz.) can black beans, drained
1 (10-oz.) can diced tomatoes and green
    chiles, undrained
2 cups (8 oz.) grated Monterey Jack cheese

1. Preheat oven to 350°. Prepare rice according to package directions.
2. Meanwhile, sauté onion, bell pepper, and carrot in hot oil in a medium skillet over medium heat 10 minutes or until tender.
3. Combine hot cooked rice, onion mixture, chicken, beans, diced tomatoes and chiles, and 1½ cups cheese in a large bowl. Spoon into a lightly greased 3-qt. or 13- x 9-inch baking dish; sprinkle with remaining ½ cup cheese.
4. Bake, covered, at 350° for 30 minutes; uncover and bake 10 minutes or until cheese is melted.

—**MEREDITH BALDWIN**, LAWRENCEVILLE, ILLINOIS

Salsa Verde Chicken Casserole

family favorite

MAKES 8 SERVINGS; **PREP:** 25 MIN.,
COOK: 15 MIN., **BAKE:** 30 MIN.

2 (3.5-oz.) bags boil-in-bag rice
2 ripe avocados
¾ cup salsa verde
1 (4-oz.) can chopped green chiles
1 Tbsp. fresh lime juice
2 cups chopped cooked chicken breast
1 (10¾-oz.) can reduced-fat cream of
    chicken soup
1 cup light sour cream
1 cup (4 oz.) grated Monterey Jack cheese
2 Tbsp. chopped fresh cilantro
Topping: chopped tomatoes

1. Preheat oven to 350°. Prepare rice according to package directions.
2. Meanwhile, cut avocados in half. Scoop avocado pulp into a medium bowl, and mash with salsa verde, chopped green chiles, and lime juice. Stir in hot cooked rice.
3. Stir together chicken, soup, and sour cream in a small saucepan over low heat; cook, stirring occasionally, 5 minutes or until blended and slightly heated.
4. Spoon rice mixture into a lightly greased 13- x 9-inch baking dish; spoon chicken mixture over rice. Sprinkle with Monterey Jack cheese.
5. Bake at 350° for 30 minutes or until cheese is melted and casserole is bubbly. Sprinkle with chopped cilantro. Top with chopped tomatoes.

—**GINNY RASKA**, BRAZORIA, TEXAS

One Great Pork Roast, Four Delicious Ideas

Any way you serve it, you'll rake in the compliments. Start with a pork loin roast or Boston butt, and offer an assortment of melt-in-your-mouth sandwiches. Alternate them between white or natural parchment paper on a tray for an enticing display. We guarantee they'll be gone almost as soon as you serve them. Read on for another creative serving suggestion for any occasion.

Slow-Cooker Pork Butt Roast

make ahead

MAKES 8 TO 10 SERVINGS; PREP: 20 MIN.; COOK: 8 HRS., 8 MIN.

1. Trim 1 (4- to 5-lb.) boneless pork shoulder roast (Boston butt). Rinse roast, and pat dry. Rub roast with 1 Tbsp. olive oil. Sprinkle with 2 tsp. salt and 2 tsp. pepper; cut roast in half.
2. Cook roast halves in 3 Tbsp. hot oil in a large skillet 2 minutes on each side or until lightly browned. Place roast halves in a lightly greased 6-qt. slow cooker, fat sides up.
3. Cover and cook on HIGH 1 hour. Reduce heat to LOW, and cook 6 to 7 hours or until meat is tender and slices easily. Remove pork, reserving liquid; slice meat. Add 1 cup reserved liquid to pork to moisten.

Baked Pork Loin Roast

MAKES 8 TO 10 SERVINGS; PREP: 10 MIN.; BAKE: 1 HR., 30 MIN.; STAND: 15 MIN.

1 (3- to 4-lb.) boneless pork loin
1 Tbsp. olive oil
2 tsp. salt
2 tsp. pepper

1. Preheat oven to 350°. Trim boneless pork loin roast. Rinse and pat dry. Rub roast with olive oil. Sprinkle with salt and pepper; place in an aluminum foil-lined 13- x 9-inch pan.
2. Bake at 350° for 1½ to 2 hours or until a meat thermometer inserted into thickest portion registers 150°. Let stand 15 minutes before slicing.

—TERRI MATHEWS, LEEDS, ALABAMA

Baked Pork Butt Roast:

Substitute 1 (4- to 5-lb.) boneless pork shoulder roast (Boston butt) for boneless pork loin roast. Prepare recipe as directed in Step 1. Bake at 350° for 4 to 4½ hours or until a meat thermometer inserted into thickest portion registers 180°. Let stand 15 minutes before slicing. Makes 8 to 10 servings. Prep: 10 min., Bake: 4 hr.

Pressed Cuban Sandwiches

fast fixin's

MAKES 4 SERVINGS; PREP: 10 MIN., COOK: 12 MIN.

We made these sandwiches in a skillet, but feel free to use a hot panini press instead. You'll still get the same tasty results. (Pictured on page 7)

1 (12-oz.) Cuban bread loaf, cut in half crosswise
6 to 8 Tbsp. yellow mustard
⅓ lb. thinly sliced Baked Pork Loin Roast (about 8 to 10 slices)*
⅓ lb. thinly sliced baked ham
⅓ lb. thinly sliced provolone cheese
¼ to ⅓ cup dill pickle chips
2 Tbsp. butter, softened

1. Cut bread halves lengthwise, cutting to but not through opposite side. Spread mustard on cut sides of bread. Layer with Baked Pork Loin Roast and next 3 ingredients. Close sandwiches, and spread outsides with butter.
2. Place 1 sandwich in a hot, large skillet over medium heat. Place a heavy skillet on top of sandwich. Cook 2 to 3 minutes on each side or until cheese is melted and sandwich is flat. Repeat with remaining sandwich. Cut each sandwich in half, and serve immediately.
*⅓ lb. thinly sliced Slow-Cooker Pork Butt Roast may be substituted.

Barbecue Sandwiches

fast fixin's

MAKES 8 SERVINGS; **PREP:** 10 MIN.,
COOK: 10 MIN., **BAKE:** 6 MIN.

These quick sandwiches get a boost from store-bought barbecue sauce. We used a spicy sauce, but use regular if you prefer. (Pictured on page 7)

1½ lb. thinly sliced Baked Pork Loin Roast
    (about 36 slices)*
1 (18-oz.) bottle spicy barbecue sauce
8 French hamburger buns**
Creamy Slaw

1. Preheat oven to 375°. Stir together roast and barbecue sauce in a large skillet over medium-low heat. Cook, stirring occasionally, 8 to 10 minutes or until thoroughly heated.
2. Meanwhile, place buns on a baking sheet. Bake at 375° for 6 to 8 minutes or until golden brown. Cut buns in half lengthwise. Layer pork on bottom halves of buns. Top each with 1 heaping tablespoonful Creamy Slaw; cover with top halves of buns. Serve with remaining slaw.
*1½ lb. thinly sliced Slow-Cooker Pork Butt Roast may be substituted.
**French rolls may be substituted.

Creamy Slaw:

fast fixin's • make ahead

MAKES 4 CUPS; **PREP:** 5 MIN.

1 cup mayonnaise
¼ cup sugar
2 Tbsp. cider vinegar
1 tsp. horseradish
⅛ tsp. salt
⅛ tsp. coarsely ground pepper
1 (16-oz.) package shredded coleslaw mix

1. Stir together mayonnaise, sugar, and next 4 ingredients. Stir in coleslaw mix, stirring until blended. Cover and chill coleslaw until ready to serve. Store in an airtight container in refrigerator up to 4 days.

Fancy Without the Fuss

For a fun presentation of typical barbecue sandwich ingredients, make a sundae—a barbecue "sundae," that is. These individual treats are pretty as well as delicious, which makes them perfect for parties and casual get-togethers. Set up a station for guests to make their own sundaes, or layer the ingredients yourself in individual glasses. Simply spoon chopped or shredded Baked Pork Butt Roast evenly into 12-oz. glasses. Top each glass with desired amounts of shredded cheese. Add Creamy Coleslaw or your favorite store-bought deli slaw and chopped fresh cilantro. Dollop each serving with sour cream. Serve sundaes with tortilla wedges, lime wedges, and pickle slices, if desired. Garnish with fresh cilantro sprigs, if desired.

Italian-Style Sandwiches

fast fixin's

MAKES 4 SERVINGS; **PREP:** 15 MIN.
(Pictured on page 7)

1 (5.3-oz.) container spreadable goat cheese
2 Tbsp. refrigerated pesto with basil
1 (12-oz.) package ciabatta rolls
1 lb. thinly sliced Baked Pork Loin Roast
    (about 24 slices)*
1⅓ cups firmly packed arugula
½ cup jarred roasted red bell pepper strips
¼ small red onion, thinly sliced

1. Stir together goat cheese and pesto. Spread goat cheese-and-pesto mixture on cut sides of rolls. Layer pork roast, arugula, and remaining ingredients on bottom halves of rolls. Cover with top halves of rolls.
*1 lb. thinly sliced Slow-Cooker Pork Butt Roast may be substituted.
Note: For testing purposes only we used Buitoni Pesto With Basil and Cobblestone Mill Ciabatta Rolls.

Fruit Salad

Test Kitchen Favorite

MAKES 6 SERVINGS; **PREP:** 5 MIN.

1 (11-oz.) can mandarin oranges, drained
1 (20-oz.) can pineapple chunks, drained
1 cup seedless green grapes
3 bananas, sliced
⅔ cup vanilla yogurt
2 Tbsp. orange marmalade
¼ tsp. ground ginger

1. Combine mandarin oranges and next 3 ingredients.
2. Stir together yogurt, orange marmalade, and ground ginger, and toss with fruit mixture.
3. Chill salad until ready to serve.

Creative Cornbread

This steaming golden treat gets a makeover. Add a bit of flair to the humble pone; each recipe can double as an entrée.

The down-home simplicity of a steaming golden wedge of cornbread makes it an enjoyable addition to any meal. But even this venerable Southern staple can benefit from a makeover. These recipes lend flair to the humble pone, and each can double as an entrée should you choose.

Crawfish Cornbread

MAKES 8 TO 10 SERVINGS; **PREP:** 20 MIN.,
COOK: 5 MIN., **BAKE:** 45 MIN.

2 Tbsp. butter
1 small onion, finely chopped
½ cup finely chopped green bell pepper
2 jalapeño peppers, seeded and minced
1 cup milk
½ cup vegetable oil
3 large eggs
1 (14.75-oz.) can cream-style corn
1½ cups grated Cheddar cheese
¾ cup chopped green onion
2 cups plain yellow cornmeal
1 Tbsp. baking powder
2 tsp. Cajun seasoning
1 tsp. salt
½ tsp. baking soda
¼ tsp. ground red pepper
1 lb. frozen, peeled crawfish tails, thawed
    and drained

1. Preheat oven to 400°. Heat a 10- to 12-inch (1½-inch deep) cast-iron skillet in oven 15 minutes.
2. Meanwhile, melt butter in a large skillet over medium heat. Add onion and bell pepper; sauté 5 minutes or until onion is tender. Remove from heat. Stir in seeded and minced jalapeños.
3. Stir together milk, oil, and eggs in a large bowl. Stir in corn, cheese, onion mixture, and chopped green onion.

4. Stir together cornmeal and next 5 ingredients just until blended. Stir in milk mixture, stirring just until dry ingredients are moistened. Stir in crawfish. Pour into hot cast-iron skillet.
5. Bake at 400° for 45 minutes or until golden brown. Serve immediately.

—**DARLENE WILLIAMS**, COVINGTON, LOUISIANA

Note: To make cornbread in a baking dish, prepare recipe as directed, beginning with Step 2. Pour batter into a well greased 13- x 9-inch baking dish. Proceed with recipe as directed, increasing bake time to 50 minutes.

Shrimp Cornbread: Substitute 1 lb. unpeeled, medium-size raw shrimp (31/35 count), peeled, deveined, and coarsely chopped, for crawfish. Proceed with recipe as directed.

Cornbread Focaccia

MAKES 8 SERVINGS; **PREP:** 20 MIN.,
STAND: 20 MIN., **RISE:** 45 MIN.,
BAKE: 20 MIN., **COOL:** 5 MIN.

This pizza-like flatbread makes a light meal when paired with a hearty salad or alongside a bowl of your favorite soup.

1 (¼-oz.) envelope rapid-rise yeast
1 cup warm water (100° to 110°)
1 Tbsp. sugar
2 cups all-purpose flour
½ cup plain yellow cornmeal
1 Tbsp. chopped fresh rosemary
1 tsp. salt
3 Tbsp. olive oil, divided
1 Tbsp. balsamic vinegar
1 (14.5-oz.) can fire-roasted diced tomatoes,
    drained
⅓ cup shredded Parmesan cheese
½ tsp. kosher salt
¼ tsp. freshly ground pepper

1. Combine rapid-rise yeast, warm water, and sugar in a small bowl, and let stand 5 minutes or until mixture bubbles.
2. Stir together 2 cups flour and next 3 ingredients in a large bowl; stir in yeast mixture and 2 Tbsp. oil until well blended (dough will be sticky). Turn dough out onto a well-floured surface, and knead until smooth and elastic (about 3 to 5 minutes). Place in a well-greased bowl, turning to grease top. Cover with plastic wrap, and let stand 15 minutes.
3. Sprinkle cornmeal onto a baking sheet. Place dough on baking sheet, and roll into a 12-inch square, sprinkling with flour as needed to prevent sticking (about 1 Tbsp.). Cover with plastic wrap, and let rise in a warm place (85°), free from drafts, 45 minutes.
4. Preheat oven to 400°. Brush dough with balsamic vinegar. Gently press end of a wooden spoon into top of dough, forming indentations. Top with tomatoes and cheese. Sprinkle with salt and pepper. Drizzle with remaining 1 Tbsp. oil.
5. Bake at 400° for 20 minutes or until golden and cheese is melted. Cool 5 minutes, and cut into squares.

—**INSPIRED BY ANGIE NELSON**,
LEDBETTER, KENTUCKY

TIP

Cornmeal gives crunch and Southern flavor to the easy yeast dough that bakes up as Cornbread Focaccia.

Healthy Living®

Try our collection of kid-friendly weeknight dinners. And keep your hunger at bay with our nutrient-packed snack mix.

Together in the Kitchen

This busy family cooks almost every night of the week, and so can you with these simple and delicious meals.

Time in the kitchen together is top priority for this busy Georgia family. Dunwoody resident Sue Spann recalls happy memories of cooking with her mother and grandmother when she was growing up. "Almost every family picture we have is of us in the kitchen," says Sue, as she reminisces with her mother, Marion. "That's how much we love to cook," Sue adds.

Now her 16-year-old daughter, Sophie, is learning the important life lesson of cooking and eating well. "Mom and I go to the grocery store together on weekends," explains Sophie. "We cook during the week, and I usually bring leftovers to school for lunch."

One of Sue's parenting philosophies is to cook together and always taste new things. "Kids are more willing to try any type of food if they've helped prepare it," she says. Chances are, even your picky eaters will love this collection of family favorites, from hot and hearty Skillet-Grilled Burritos to Thai Pesto Shrimp over zesty Coconut-Lime Rice. Give them a try, and see what your family thinks.

Healthy Benefits

- Cooking together can help open up the lines of communication between parents and kids. It also inspires an appreciation for new tastes.
- Eating fish daily, such as omega-3-rich halibut, can reduce the risk of stroke and heart attack by more than 50%. Just two servings a week can help lower triglycerides, improving cardiovascular health.

Thai Pesto Shrimp
family favorite
MAKES 6 SERVINGS; PREP: 30 MIN.,
COOK: 5 MIN.
(Pictured on page 162)

1½ lb. unpeeled, large raw shrimp (16/20 count)
Coconut-Lime Rice
1 cup loosely packed fresh cilantro leaves
3 Tbsp. fresh lime juice
2 Tbsp. unsalted dry-roasted peanuts
2 Tbsp. minced fresh ginger
2 garlic cloves, minced
1 tsp. kosher or ¾ tsp. regular salt
2 tsp. honey
½ tsp. dried crushed red pepper
¼ cup olive oil, divided

1. Peel shrimp; devein, if desired. Prepare Coconut-Lime Rice.
2. Meanwhile, process cilantro, next 7 ingredients, and 3 Tbsp. olive oil in a food processor 15 to 20 seconds or until smooth, stopping to scrape down sides.
3. Sauté shrimp in remaining 1 Tbsp. hot oil in a large skillet over medium-high heat 3 to 5 minutes or just until shrimp turn pink. Stir in cilantro mixture. Serve over rice.

Per serving (including rice): Calories 300; Fat 13.9g (sat 3.7g, mono 7.6g, poly 2.2g); Protein 21g; Carb 23.9g; Fiber 0.7g; Chol 168.1mg; Iron 3.2mg; Sodium 719mg; Calc 41mg

Coconut-Lime Rice:
MAKES 6 SERVINGS; PREP: 10 MIN.,
COOK: 25 MIN.

1 cup light coconut milk
½ tsp. salt
1½ cups uncooked jasmine rice
1 tsp. lime zest
1½ Tbsp. fresh lime juice

1. Bring coconut milk, salt, and 2 cups water to a boil in a saucepan over medium heat. Stir in rice; cover, reduce heat to low, and simmer, stirring occasionally, 20 to 25 minutes or until liquid is absorbed and rice is tender. Stir in lime zest and juice.

Per serving: Calories 104; Fat 2g (sat 1.9g, mono 0g, poly 0g); Protein 2g; Carb 19.8g; Fiber 0.3g; Chol 0mg; Iron 0.4mg; Sodium 204mg; Calc 0.7mg

Skillet-Grilled Burritos
family favorite
MAKES 8 SERVINGS; **PREP:** 20 MIN., **COOK:** 8 MIN. PER BATCH

Dip these flavorful burritos into the creamy sauce or your favorite salsa. (Pictured on page 162)

2 cups chopped cooked chicken breast
1 (15-oz.) can black beans, rinsed and drained
1 (11-oz.) can yellow corn with red and green bell peppers, drained
1 cup (4 oz.) shredded 2% reduced-fat Cheddar cheese
Creamy Cilantro-Jalapeño Sauce
8 (8-inch) soft taco-size whole wheat flour tortillas, warmed
Vegetable cooking spray
Salsa

1. Toss together first 4 ingredients and ½ cup Creamy Cilantro-Jalapeño Sauce. Spread ¾ cup chicken mixture just below center of each tortilla. Fold opposite sides of tortillas over filling, and roll up. Coat burritos with cooking spray.
2. Coat a hot griddle or nonstick skillet with cooking spray. Cook burritos, in batches, on hot griddle over medium heat, pressing gently with a spatula, 3 to 4 minutes on each side or until golden brown and cheese is melted. Serve with salsa and remaining Creamy Cilantro-Jalapeño Sauce.

Per serving (including 2½ Tbsp. sauce): Calories 342; Fat 10.3g (sat 4.4g, mono 0.6g, poly 0.5g); Protein 23.2g; Carb 37.2g; Fiber 4.6g; Chol 40mg; Iron 2.3mg; Sodium 612mg; Calc 119mg

Creamy Cilantro-Jalapeño Sauce:
make ahead
MAKES ABOUT 1¼ CUPS; **PREP:** 10 MIN., **CHILL:** 30 MIN.

1 cup light sour cream
½ cup loosely packed fresh cilantro leaves, chopped
2 Tbsp. diced pickled jalapeño peppers
2 tsp. chopped yellow onion
2 tsp. Dijon mustard
1 tsp. lime zest

1. Stir together all ingredients in a small bowl. Cover and chill 30 minutes. Store in an airtight container up to 2 days.

Per 2½ Tbsp.: Calories 43; Fat 2.5g (sat 2g, mono 0g, poly 0g); Protein 2.1g; Carb 2.6g; Fiber 0.1g; Chol 0mg; Iron 0mg; Sodium 56mg; Calc 1mg

● TIP ●

Simply spread the chicken mixture just below the center of each tortilla, and fold the left and right sides of the tortillas while rolling up. Then place the burritos, seam-side down, onto a hot griddle or skillet, and brown on each side for a crispy, melt-in-your-mouth main dish.

Test Kitchen Notebook

- Buy frozen fish in bulk. Wholesale clubs carry a variety of frozen meats, including fish. It's usually cheaper per pound and tastes just as good.
- Have leftovers for lunch the next day. Take them to work, or send the kids to school with a hearty meal.

Seared Halibut With Herbed Tomato Sauce
MAKES 4 SERVINGS; **PREP:** 10 MIN., **COOK:** 21 MIN.
(Pictured on page 163)

4 (6-oz.) halibut fillets (½-inch thick)*
½ tsp. salt, divided
¼ tsp. pepper
2 tsp. extra virgin olive oil
½ medium onion, chopped
2 garlic cloves, minced
1 Tbsp. drained capers
¼ tsp. dried basil
¼ tsp. dried oregano
1 (14.5-oz.) can petite diced tomatoes

1. Pat fish dry with paper towels. Season fish with ¼ tsp. salt and ¼ tsp. pepper. Cook fish in hot oil in a large skillet over medium-high heat 3 to 4 minutes on each side or until fish flakes with a fork and is opaque throughout. Transfer fish to a serving platter, and keep warm.
2. Add onion and garlic to skillet, and sauté 1 to 2 minutes or until onion is tender. Stir in capers, basil, oregano, and remaining ¼ tsp. salt; cook 1 minute. Reduce heat to low, add tomatoes, and cook, stirring occasionally, 10 minutes. Top fish with tomato sauce.
*Frozen halibut or fresh or frozen cod may be substituted.

Per serving: Calories 199; Fat 5.5g (sat 0.8g, mono 2.7g, poly 1.3g); Protein 29.5g; Carb 6.9g; Fiber 2.1g; Chol 43.6mg; Iron 1.6mg; Sodium 559mg; Calc 91mg

Roasted Cauliflower With Pine Nuts and Raisins

MAKES 4 SERVINGS; **PREP:** 20 MIN.,
STAND: 5 MIN., **BAKE:** 20 MIN.,
BROIL: 2 MIN.

¼ cup golden raisins
1 head cauliflower (about 2 lb.)
¼ cup pine nuts
2 Tbsp. olive oil
1 tsp. chopped fresh or ½ tsp. dried thyme
½ tsp. salt
¼ tsp. pepper
1 Tbsp. butter
1 large garlic clove, pressed
¼ cup Japanese breadcrumbs (panko)

1. Preheat oven to 400°. Cover raisins with hot water in a small bowl; let stand 5 minutes or until plump. Drain.
2. Cut cauliflower into equal-size florets. Toss together florets, pine nuts, olive oil, and thyme in a jelly-roll pan. Spread in single layer, and season with salt and pepper.
3. Bake at 400° for 20 minutes or until edges of cauliflower are caramelized and nuts are toasted. Remove from oven. Increase oven temperature to broil.
4. Microwave butter with garlic in a small glass bowl at HIGH 30 seconds. Stir in raisins and breadcrumbs. Toss raisin mixture with cauliflower mixture in jelly-roll pan, and spread mixture in a single layer.
5. Broil 6 inches from heat 2 minutes or just until golden. Serve immediately.

Per serving: Calories 221; Fat 16g (sat 3.3g, mono 7.4g, poly 4.1g); Protein 4.9g; Carb 18.8g; Fiber 4.5g; Chol 7.5mg; Iron 1.3mg; Sodium 366mg; Calc 42mg

Game-Day Munchies

An energizing, nutrient-rich snack mix is always good to have on hand, especially on Super Bowl Sunday. Instead of fattening treats with empty calories, serve this delicious and nutrient-rich one at your next gathering. Simply toast the nuts, and toss them with the rest of the ingredients. For personalized portions, roll up kraft paper into cone shapes, staple the sides, and let guests help themselves.

Easy Party Snack Mix

MAKES ABOUT 10 CUPS; **PREP:** 10 MIN.,
BAKE: 7 MIN.

Nutritious snacking throughout the day can prevent overeating at each meal. If you can't find rye chips, you can use your favorite pretzel sticks.

½ Tbsp. butter
1 cup salted almonds
1 (9.9-oz.) can wasabi peas
2 cups garlic rye chips
1 (8.5-oz.) package sesame sticks

1. Preheat oven to 350°. Melt butter in a 9-inch cake pan in a 350° oven. Add nuts, tossing to coat. Bake 7 minutes or until lightly toasted; remove from oven.
2. Toss together nuts, wasabi peas, garlic rye chips, and sesame sticks in a large bowl. Store in an airtight container up to 1 week.

—ELIZABETH GRIFFIN, LITTLE ROCK, ARKANSAS

Note: For testing purposes only, we used Hapi Snacks Wasabi Peas, Gardetto's Special Request Roasted Garlic Rye Chips, and Pepperidge Farm Baked Naturals Toasted Sesame Snack Sticks.

Per ½ cup: Calories 197; Fat 10g (sat 2.1g, mono 2.4g, poly 0.9g); Protein 5.5g; Carb 21.3g; Fiber 2.3g; Chol 1mg; Iron 0.3mg; Sodium 268mg; Calc 18mg

Healthy Benefits

Wasabi (WAH-sah-bee), the Japanese version of horseradish, has many benefits. Not only does it have antibacterial properties against dental cavities and common types of foodborne illness, but it can also inhibit the growth of cancer cells.

Chocolate!

Tips, tricks, and tempting Valentine treats.

Cheap Thrills Cocoa powder is pure chocolate with most of the cocoa butter removed. It's loaded with flavor and nutritional benefits and is surprisingly low in fat and calories. Cocoa is a favorite pantry ingredient, and one we use often in hot chocolate, mocha lattes, and baked goods.

There are two types of cocoa: regular (or natural) cocoa and more delicately flavored Dutch-processed (or European-style) cocoa, which has been treated with an alkali to neutralize the acidity. Both are unsweetened and may be used interchangeably *except* in recipes, such as chocolate cake or quick bread, that call for a chemical leaven. While regular cocoa (an acid) reacts with baking soda, Dutch-processed cocoa must be paired with baking powder (unless another acidic ingredient is present in the recipe).

Special Cuts ~

Chopping chocolate into small pieces allows it to melt quickly and evenly. To avoid scorching, melt chocolate over indirect heat in the top of a double boiler or in a heatproof bowl set in a shallow pan of hot water. Or microwave chocolate at MEDIUM (50% power), stirring at 10- to 15-second intervals until melted.

A luscious drift of **chocolate shavings** transforms the simplest dessert into an elegant offering. Run a vegetable peeler over the narrow side of a thick bar of chocolate, and you'll have a beautiful garnish ready in minutes. For quick clean up, catch the shavings on a sheet of wax paper.

By warming the chocolate and applying more pressure with the vegetable peeler, **chocolate curls** are made with the same technique used for shavings. A 5-second zap at MEDIUM (50% power) in the microwave softens a thick bar of chocolate just enough to remove long strips that curl naturally. Rewarm as needed.

Bittersweet Decisions

- The fewer the ingredients in a recipe, the more pronounced the chocolate flavor, so splurge on premium brands when making special treats such as truffles or ganache.

- **Here's how you get that luscious chocolate** flavor. Cacao is a thick paste of pure chocolate made from ground cacao beans. When pressed, the paste separates into cocoa solids and cocoa butter. Finely ground cocoa solids become cocoa powder. The percentage of cacao printed on a label represents the combined weight of cocoa solids and cocoa butter. A higher percentage of cacao means less sugar and more intense chocolate flavor.

- **Unsweetened chocolate** is pure chocolate (100% cacao) without added sugar. **Sweet baking chocolate** has added cocoa butter and sugar. **Milk chocolate** is pure chocolate with added cocoa butter, sugar, and milk solids. **White chocolate** is made with cocoa butter, sugar, milk solids, and flavoring.

- **Store chocolate in a cool, dark pantry** or cupboard, away from aromatic herbs and spices. (Chocolate, like butter, absorbs strong odors.) Overly warm temperatures cause the cocoa butter in chocolate to separate and rise to the surface, creating a powdery white film called "fat bloom." When chocolate is exposed to high humidity or moisture, condensation forms on the surface, leaving behind crystals of "sugar bloom" as it evaporates. Both types of bloom affect the texture of chocolate, but it's still safe to eat or use for baking.

March 59

No Fuss Allowed

Pull on your dark denim and slip into your favorite heels for fresh food and fun with the girls.

Casual Lunch

SERVES 12

Spicy Boiled Shrimp With Creamy Buttermilk-Avocado Sauce

Chicken Caesar Salad Bites

Blue Cheese-Walnut Finger Sandwiches

Corn-and-Lima Bean Salad (double recipe)

Mustard-Dill Tortellini Salad Skewers

Vanilla-Champagne Soaked Fruit

Follow our lead for a bash that's sure to be the buzz for weeks to come. Graze on Chicken Caesar Salad Bites that transform familiar flavors into chic little nibbles, or try Blue Cheese-Walnut Finger Sandwiches. They bring new flair to the standard cream cheese version. In a time crunch? No worries. Many of the recipes offer flexibility, so look for time-saving tips sprinkled throughout. Choose a seasonal color for the table, but be sure to keep it easy by pulling in lighter and darker hues, from plants to plates, for simple sophistication.

Spicy Boiled Shrimp With Creamy Buttermilk-Avocado Sauce

MAKES 12 SERVINGS; **PREP:** 25 MIN., **COOK:** 5 MIN., **CHILL:** 1 HR.

Tip: To ensure that shrimp stay chilled, place half out when guests arrive, and replenish the platter as needed.

2 lb. peeled and deveined large cooked shrimp with tails (26/30 count)
2 lemons
4 tsp. hot sauce
2 tsp. Creole seasoning
1 (5-oz.) package mixed baby greens, thoroughly washed
Creamy Buttermilk-Avocado Sauce

1. Bring 2 qt. water to a boil in a Dutch oven. Add shrimp, and cook 30 seconds. Drain, rinse under cool running water, and place in a small bowl.
2. Fill a medium bowl with ice. Place bowl containing shrimp in ice. Cover and chill 1 to 24 hours.
3. Squeeze juice from lemons through a small strainer over shrimp in a large bowl, drizzle with hot sauce, and toss to coat. Sprinkle with Creole seasoning, and toss to coat. Serve shrimp over mixed greens with Creamy Buttermilk-Avocado Sauce.

Creamy Buttermilk-Avocado Sauce:

MAKES ABOUT 1²/₃ CUPS; **PREP:** 10 MIN.

Process 1 cup buttermilk, 1 chopped ripe avocado, 2 Tbsp. chopped fresh parsley, 2 finely chopped green onions, and 2 Tbsp. fresh lemon juice in a food processor 30 seconds or until smooth. Season with kosher salt and freshly ground pepper to taste. Store in refrigerator covered with plastic wrap directly on surface (to prevent discoloration) up to 2 days.

Chicken Caesar Salad Bites

MAKES 4 DOZEN; **PREP:** 30 MIN., **BAKE:** 10 MIN., **COOL:** 15 MIN.

Time-saver tip: Bake Parmesan cheese rounds up to 3 days before your get-together, and store in an airtight container.

1 (5-oz.) package shredded Parmesan cheese
Parchment paper
2 cups finely chopped cooked chicken
½ cup arugula, chopped
¼ cup Caesar dressing
2 Tbsp. fresh lime juice
Freshly ground pepper to taste
2 Tbsp. crushed Parmesan pita chips

1. Preheat oven to 350°. Spoon Parmesan cheese by rounded teaspoonfuls, 1 inch apart, onto parchment paper-lined baking sheets, forming mounds. Bake 10 to 12 minutes or until melted, bubbly, and golden brown. Cool on baking sheets 15 minutes.
2. Stir together chicken and next 3 ingredients. Stir in freshly ground pepper to taste. Spoon mixture onto Parmesan cheese rounds. Top with crushed pita chips.
Note: For testing purposes only, we used Sargento Artisan Blends Parmesan Shredded Cheese.

Blue Cheese-Walnut Finger Sandwiches

MAKES ABOUT 7 DOZEN; **PREP:** 30 MIN., **BAKE:** 6 MIN., **COOL:** 20 MIN.

Time-saver tip: Instead of preparing sandwiches, mix spread as directed and serve it with preserves on crackers. (Pictured on page 164)

¾ cup chopped walnuts or pecans
1 (8-oz.) package cream cheese, softened
5 oz. creamy blue cheese, rind removed
1 Tbsp. chopped fresh parsley
2 (14-oz.) whole grain bread loaves (22 slices)
¼ cup fig, cherry, or apricot preserves

1. Preheat oven to 350°. Bake walnuts in a single layer in a shallow pan 6 to 8 minutes or until toasted and fragrant, stirring after 5 minutes. Cool completely (about 20 minutes).

2. Stir together walnuts and next 3 ingredients. Spread on 1 side of each bread slice. Spread fig preserves on half of bread slices; top with remaining bread slices, cheese sides down. Chill sandwiches in airtight zip-top plastic bags up to 24 hours, if desired. Cut crusts from sandwiches. Cut each sandwich into 8 pieces.

Note: For testing purposes only, we used Saga blue cheese and Pepperidge Farm Whole Grain 15 Grain Bread.

Corn-and-Lima Bean Salad

test kitchen favorite

MAKES 6 SERVINGS; **PREP:** 15 MIN., **COOK:** 5 MIN., **COOL:** 10 MIN., **CHILL:** 1 HR.

3 cups fresh corn kernels (6 ears)
1 tablespoon olive oil
1 cup fresh baby lima beans*
¼ cup diced roasted red bell pepper
1 tablespoon fresh basil leaves, cut into
    thin strips
1 tablespoon lemon juice
¾ teaspoon salt
¼ teaspoon dried crushed red pepper

1. Sauté corn kernels in hot oil in a large skillet over medium-high heat 3 minutes or until tender; add lima beans, and cook 2 minutes. Remove from heat, and let cool 10 minutes.

2. Toss together lima bean mixture, bell pepper, and next 4 ingredients in a large bowl. Cover and chill 1 hour.

*1 cup frozen baby lima beans, thawed, may be substituted.

Mustard-Dill Tortellini Salad Skewers

make ahead

MAKES 12 SERVINGS; **PREP:** 25 MIN., **COOK:** 5 MIN., **STAND:** 2 MIN., **CHILL:** 4 HR.

Time-saver tip: Nix the skewers, and toss salad with ½ cup of dressing just before serving. Spoon into a pretty bowl, and garnish with a dill sprig. (Pictured on page 165)

1 (9-oz.) package refrigerated cheese
    tortellini
1 (8-oz.) package frozen sugar snap peas
68 (4-inch) wooden skewers
1 pt. grape tomatoes, cut in half
Mustard-Dill Vinaigrette*

1. Cook tortellini according to package directions. Rinse under cold running water.

2. Place sugar snap peas in a small bowl; cover with plastic wrap. Microwave at HIGH 2 minutes. Let stand, covered, 2 minutes. Rinse under cold running water.

3. Thread each skewer with 1 sugar snap pea, 1 tortellini, and 1 tomato half. Place skewers in a 13- x 9-inch baking dish. Pour Mustard-Dill Vinaigrette over skewers, turning to coat. Cover and chill 4 hours. Transfer skewers to a serving platter; discard any remaining vinaigrette.

*1 (12-oz.) bottle light Champagne vinaigrette may be substituted. For testing purposes only, we used Girard's Light Champagne Dressing.

Mustard-Dill Vinaigrette:

MAKES 1¾ CUPS; **PREP:** 10 MIN.

Whisk together ½ cup white wine vinegar, 2 Tbsp. chopped fresh dill, 3 Tbsp. Dijon mustard, 2 pressed garlic cloves, and 2 tsp. sugar. Add 1¼ cups olive oil in a slow, steady stream, whisking constantly until thoroughly combined. Whisk in kosher salt and pepper to taste.

Vanilla-Champagne Soaked Fruit

make ahead

MAKES 12 SERVINGS; **PREP:** 15 MIN., **COOK:** 15 MIN., **STAND:** 5 MIN., **CHILL:** 3 HR.

Time-saver tip: Substitute 1 (11-oz.) can mandarin orange segments for the fresh orange.

1 (750-milliliter) bottle Champagne or
    sparkling wine
¾ cup sugar
1 vanilla bean, split*
1 (1-oz.) package fresh mint, chopped
1 cantaloupe, halved
1 pt. fresh raspberries
1 large orange, peeled and sectioned
½ honeydew melon, peeled and chopped
    (about 4 cups)
Garnishes: chopped fresh mint,
    vanilla bean pod

1. Bring first 3 ingredients to a boil in a 3-qt. saucepan over high heat; boil, stirring occasionally, until sugar is dissolved (about 4 to 5 minutes). Reduce heat to medium, and cook 10 minutes or until mixture is reduced by half. Remove from heat, and stir in mint. Let stand 5 minutes.

2. Pour mixture through a fine wiremesh strainer into a bowl, discarding mint. Scrape seeds from vanilla bean into bowl; whisk until blended. Reserve vanilla bean pod for garnish.

3. Cut 1 cantaloupe half into 10 thin wedges. Cut 2 thin wedges from remaining half of cantaloupe; reserve remaining cantaloupe for another use. Place cantaloupe, raspberries, orange sections, and honeydew in a 13- x 9-inch baking dish; pour warm syrup over fruit. Cover and chill 3 to 24 hours. Remove fruit from syrup using a slotted spoon. Arrange on a serving platter. Serve syrup with fruit. Garnish, if desired.

*1 Tbsp. vanilla extract may be substituted. Stir in with mint.

Note: Be sure to scrub cantaloupe rind with a vegetable brush before cutting into wedges.

Our Easiest Layer Cakes Ever

It's all about a hip presentation and updated flavor combinations. We've taken the fear out of baking; you'll never need that box of cake mix again.

Basic Vanilla Cake Batter

MAKES ABOUT 6 CUPS; **PREP:** 20 MIN.

Add an additional ¼ tsp. vanilla extract if you do not have almond extract.

2 cups sugar
1 cup butter, softened
3 large eggs
1 tsp. vanilla extract
¼ tsp. almond extract
3 cups cake flour
1½ tsp. baking powder
¼ tsp. salt
1 cup buttermilk

1. Beat sugar and butter at medium speed with a heavy-duty electric stand mixer until creamy and fluffy (about 5 minutes). Add eggs, 1 at a time, beating until yellow disappears after each addition. Beat in vanilla and almond extracts.

2. Whisk together flour, baking powder, and salt in a small bowl; add to sugar mixture alternately with buttermilk, beginning and ending with flour mixture. Beat at medium-low speed just until blended after each addition. (Batter will be thick.) Use immediately.

Ultimate Vanilla Cake Batter: Substitute 2 tsp. vanilla bean paste for vanilla extract. Proceed with recipe as directed.

Chocolate Cake Batter: Reduce cake flour to 2 cups. Proceed with recipe as directed in Step 1. Whisk ¾ cup unsweetened cocoa into flour mixture in Step 2; proceed with recipe as directed. Beat ⅓ cup hot water into batter just until smooth.

Pick a Pan

These batters can be baked in many different pans. Follow our guide below for perfect layers every time. As usual, be sure to test the cakes for doneness by inserting a wooden pick into the center. It should come out clean.

- Bake at 350° in 2 greased and floured (9-inch) round cake pans 32 to 36 minutes. Cool as directed.
- Bake at 350° in 2 greased and floured (8-inch) square pans 30 to 34 minutes. Cool as directed.
- Bake at 350° in 2 lightly greased parchment paper-lined (15- x 10-inch) jelly-roll pans 15 to 17 minutes. Cool in pans on wire racks 30 minutes.

Basic Layer Cake

MAKES 10 TO 12 SERVINGS; **PREP:** 10 MIN.;
BAKE: 34 MIN.; **COOL:** 1 HR., 10 MIN.
(Pictured on page 8)

Vanilla, Ultimate Vanilla, or Chocolate Cake Batter
Desired Buttercream Frosting
Garnishes as desired

1. Preheat oven to 350°. Pour desired batter into 2 greased and floured 8-inch round (2-inch-deep) cake pans, spreading to edges. Bake 34 to 38 minutes or until a wooden pick inserted in center comes out clean. Cool in pans on a wire rack 10 minutes. Remove from pans to wire rack, and cool completely (about 1 hour). Spread desired buttercream on top and sides of cake. Garnish, if desired.

Vanilla Cupcakes: Prepare Basic Vanilla Cake Batter* as directed through Step 2. Place paper baking cups in muffin pans, and coat with vegetable cooking spray; spoon batter into cups, filling three-fourths full. Bake at 350° for 20 to 25 minutes or until a wooden pick inserted in center comes out clean. Cool in pans on a wire rack 10 minutes. Remove from pans to wire rack, and cool completely (about 1 hour). Spread tops of cupcakes with desired buttercream frosting. Makes 24 cupcakes. Prep: 20 min., Bake: 22 min., Cool: 1 hr.
*Ultimate Vanilla Cake Batter or Chocolate Cake Batter may be substituted.

Vanilla Petits Fours

MAKES 32 CAKES; **PREP:** 45 MIN.,
FREEZE: 1 HR.

For a creative presentation idea for these pretty cakes, turn to page 74.

Basic Vanilla Cake Batter
¾ cup apricot spreadable fruit*
Vanilla Buttercream Frosting
1 to 2 drops red food coloring
1 to 2 drops yellow food coloring

Baking Tips and Suggestions

- Allow butter and eggs to sit at room temperature 30 to 45 minutes.
- Add extracts to butter-and-sugar mixture instead of at the end to fully incorporate into the batter.
- Cooking spray with flour works like a charm to keep cakes from sticking to pans.
- Bake cakes on the same oven rack, but be sure to leave 2 inches of space between pans so heat can circulate freely.
- Slowly add milk to buttercream, 1 Tbsp. at a time, to ensure a proper consistency.
- Use ½ cup seedless jam spread instead of buttercream between layers for amped-up fruit flavor and contrast.

1. Prepare Basic Vanilla Cake Batter as directed.

2. Pour batter into 2 lightly greased parchment paper-lined 15- x 10-inch jelly-roll pans.

3. Bake and cool as directed in "Pick a Pan" box on opposite page. Do not remove cakes from pans.

4. Spread top of 1 cooled cake (in pan) with spreadable fruit. Invert remaining cake onto fruit-covered cake. Remove top pan. Remove and discard top piece of parchment paper. Cover and freeze cake 1 to 2 hours.

5. Run an offset spatula under and around sides of cake to release from pan. Invert cake onto a cutting board. Remove and discard remaining piece of parchment paper. Trim and discard edges of cake. Cut cake into 32 squares.

6. Tint Vanilla Buttercream Frosting with desired amount of food coloring, and beat until blended. Place in a zip-top plastic freezer bag (do not seal). Snip 1 corner of bag to make a small hole. Pipe frosting onto each cake square. Garnish, if desired.

*Seedless jam may be substituted.

Vanilla Buttercream Frosting

MAKES ABOUT 2¾ CUPS; **PREP:** 10 MIN.

½ cup butter, softened
1 tsp. vanilla extract
⅛ tsp. salt
1 (16-oz.) package powdered sugar
3 to 5 Tbsp. milk

1. Beat first 3 ingredients at medium speed with an electric mixer until creamy.

2. Gradually add powdered sugar alternately with 3 Tbsp. milk, 1 Tbsp. at a time, beating at low speed until blended and smooth after each addition. Beat in up to 2 Tbsp. additional milk for desired consistency.

Ultimate Vanilla Buttercream Frosting: Substitute 2 tsp. vanilla bean paste for vanilla extract. Proceed with recipe as directed. Makes about 2 cups.

Vanilla Latte Buttercream Frosting: Increase vanilla extract to 2 tsp. Proceed with recipe as directed, beating in 1 Tbsp. instant espresso with butter. Makes about 2¼ cups.

Chocolate Buttercream Frosting: Increase milk to 5 to 7 Tbsp. Prepare recipe as directed in Step 1. Whisk together ⅔ cup unsweetened cocoa and powdered sugar. Proceed with recipe as directed. Makes about 2¼ cups.

Mint Chocolate Chip Buttercream Frosting: Reduce milk to 1 to 2 Tbsp. Prepare recipe as directed, beating in 3 Tbsp. peppermint schnapps with butter. Proceed with recipe as directed. Beat in 1 (4-oz.) finely chopped bittersweet chocolate baking bar. Makes about 2½ cups.
Note: For testing purposes only, we used Ghirardelli 60% Cocoa Bittersweet Chocolate Baking Bar.

Chocolate-Malt Buttercream Frosting: Increase milk to 5 to 7 Tbsp. Prepare recipe as directed in Step 1. Whisk together ½ cup unsweetened cocoa, ½ cup malted milk powder, and powdered sugar. Proceed with recipe as directed.

Key Lime Buttercream Frosting: Reduce milk to 1 to 2 Tbsp. Prepare recipe as directed in Step 1. Beat in 1½ tsp. Key lime zest. Proceed with recipe as directed in Step 2, beating in 3 Tbsp. Key lime juice with milk.

Raspberry Buttercream Frosting: Omit milk. Proceed with recipe as directed, beating in ½ cup fresh raspberries with butter. Makes about 2½ cups.
Note: Be sure to wash and thoroughly dry raspberries before adding to frosting.

Blackberry Buttercream Frosting: Omit milk. Prepare recipe as directed in Step 1, beating in ½ cup fresh blackberries and 1 tsp. lemon zest with butter. Proceed with recipe as directed, beating in an additional 1 cup powdered sugar. Makes about 2½ cups.
Note: Be sure to wash and thoroughly dry blackberries before adding to frosting.

Butterscotch-Caramel Buttercream Frosting: Reduce milk to 1 to 3 Tbsp. Proceed with recipe as directed, beating in ⅓ cup butterscotch-caramel topping with butter. Makes about 2¼ cups.
Note: For testing purposes only, we used Smucker's Special Recipe Butterscotch Caramel Flavored Topping.

Speedy Pork Chops

Easy prep. Few ingredients. Little fuss.

Good food doesn't have to be complicated. Enjoy this terrific menu that can be on the table in 40 minutes. Grilled Basil-and-Garlic Pork Chops, seasoned with common pantry spices, deliver Italian-inspired flavor with little effort.

Countdown to Dinner

40 minutes ahead:
• Preheat grill and start the rice.

20 minutes ahead:
• Prep veggies for Okra-Tomato Sauce.

15 minutes ahead:
• Begin grilling pork chops.

10 minutes ahead:
• Cook Okra-Tomato Sauce while chops are grilling.

Unbeatable Southern Supper

SERVES 6

Grilled Basil-and-Garlic Pork Chops

Basmati Rice and Peas

Okra-Tomato Sauce

Grilled Basil-and-Garlic Pork Chops

fast fixin's

MAKES 6 SERVINGS; PREP: 5 MIN., GRILL: 14 MIN.

While the meat is grilling, cook the Okra-Tomato Sauce, a mild blend of fire-roasted tomatoes and vegetables. Serve over Basmati Rice and Peas, or use as a topping over greens.

1 tsp. salt
1 tsp. pepper
1 tsp. dried basil
½ tsp. garlic powder
6 (6- to 8-oz.) bone-in pork loin chops

1. Preheat grill to 350° to 400° (medium-high) heat. Combine first 4 ingredients; sprinkle over pork chops.
2. Grill pork, covered with grill lid, over 350° to 400° (medium-high) heat 5 to 7 minutes on each side or until done.

Basmati Rice and Peas

MAKES 6 SERVINGS (4 CUPS); PREP: 10 MIN., COOK: 25 MIN., STAND: 5 MIN.

Popcorn-scented basmati is a flavorful alternative to long-grain rice. You can find it on the same aisle as regular rice.

2 cups low-sodium chicken broth
1 Tbsp. butter
½ tsp. salt
1 cup uncooked basmati rice
1 (15½-oz.) can black-eyed peas, rinsed and drained
1½ tsp. lemon zest
2 green onions, thinly sliced

1. Bring broth, butter, and salt to a boil over medium-high heat in a large saucepan. Stir in rice; cover, reduce heat to low, and simmer 20 minutes or until broth is absorbed and rice is tender. Remove from heat, and stir in peas and zest using a fork. Cover and let stand 5 minutes. Sprinkle with onions.
Note: For testing purposes only, we used Mahatma Basmati Rice.

Basmati Rice and Pigeon Peas: Substitute 1 (15-oz.) can green pigeon peas for black-eyed peas. Proceed with recipe as directed.

Okra-Tomato Sauce

fast fixin's

MAKES 6 SERVINGS; PREP: 10 MIN., COOK: 8 MIN.

1 Tbsp. butter
½ yellow bell pepper, chopped
½ medium-size sweet onion, chopped
1 (14.5-oz.) can fire-roasted diced tomatoes
2 cups frozen cut okra
¼ cup low-sodium chicken broth
1 tsp. sugar
¼ tsp. salt

1. Melt butter in a large skillet over medium-high heat; add bell pepper and onion, and sauté 3 minutes. Stir in remaining ingredients, and cook, stirring occasionally, 5 minutes.

Soups for Spring

Greet the season and your company with these refreshing starters. The fresh ingredients burst with flavor.

Blueberry Soup

MAKES 5 CUPS; **PREP:** 10 MIN.,
COOK: 10 MIN., **COOL:** 5 MIN., **CHILL:** 4 HR.

Dress up this cool and colorful soup with a garnish of Sweet Treat Croutons or a sprig of fresh lavender.

4½ cups fresh blueberries*
1 (12-oz.) can frozen lemonade concentrate, thawed
½ cup cold water
1 tsp. dried lavender
1 tsp. vanilla extract
1½ cups vanilla yogurt
Sweet Treat Croutons

1. Stir together fresh blueberries, lemonade concentrate, and ½ cup cold water in a 3-qt. saucepan. Bring to a boil; reduce heat, stir in dried lavender, and simmer, stirring occasionally, 5 minutes or until blueberries burst. Remove from heat, and cool 5 minutes. Stir in vanilla extract.
2. Press mixture through a fine wire-mesh strainer into a large bowl, using back of a spoon to squeeze out juice. Discard pulp. Stir in yogurt. Cover and chill 4 to 24 hours. Serve with Sweet Treat Croutons.
*2 (12-oz.) packages frozen blueberries may be substituted.

Sweet Treat Croutons:

MAKES ABOUT 2 CUPS; **PREP:** 10 MIN.,
BAKE: 10 MIN., **COOL:** 30 MIN.

You can make toasty crouton bites with homemade pound cake too. They're also a grand addition to fondue, your favorite ice cream, or as a topping on fresh fruit salad.

½ (10.75-oz.) package frozen butter pound cake, thawed
3 Tbsp. butter, melted
1 Tbsp. chopped fresh mint

1. Preheat oven to 400°. Cut butter pound cake into ½-inch cubes, and place in a large bowl. Add butter and chopped fresh mint, and toss gently to coat. Place cubes in a single layer on a baking sheet. Bake for 10 minutes or until lightly toasted. Cool completely (about 30 minutes).

Test Kitchen Notebook

Try cool Blueberry Soup served from an Ice Bowl for a sensational recipe that will wow friends and family.

Ice Bowl

MAKES 1 BOWL; **PREP:** 15 MIN.;
COOK 15 MIN.; **COOL:** 1 HR., 10 MIN.;
FREEZE: 8 HR.; **STAND:** 10 MIN.

We boiled the water twice so the bowl will be clear when frozen, making an attractive serving bowl.

1 (4-cup) glass or stainless
    steel bowl with rim
1 (6-cup) glass or stainless
    steel bowl with rim
Freezer tape

1. Bring 6 cups water to a boil in a 2-qt. saucepan over medium-high heat. Remove from heat, and cool 10 minutes. Return to heat, and bring to a boil. Remove from heat, and cool completely (about 1 hour).
2. Fill 1 (6-cup) bowl halfway with cooled water. Place 1 (4-cup) bowl inside 6-cup bowl. Using 4 (5-inch) pieces of freezer tape, tape rims of bowls together so that there is an equal amount of space between bowls (about ½ inch to 1 inch). (photo 1)

3. Gradually pour remaining cooled water into space between bowls, filling to just below rims of bowls. (photo 2) Freeze bowls 8 to 24 hours.
4. Place frozen bowls on a tray, and let stand at room temperature 8 to 10 minutes or until bowls separate easily. Remove tape and smaller bowl. Invert larger bowl, releasing Ice Bowl. (photo 3) Freeze Ice Bowl until ready to serve. Place on a small tray or charger plate to serve.
Note: You may use 6 cups distilled water and omit Step 1.

Asparagus, Lemon, and Dill Soup

MAKES 7 CUPS; **PREP:** 20 MIN.,
COOK: 25 MIN.

1 lb. fresh asparagus
1 medium leek
3 Tbsp. butter
2 celery ribs, finely chopped
1 small onion, chopped
5 cups vegetable broth
½ cup uncooked orzo pasta
3 egg yolks
¼ cup lemon juice
1 to 1½ Tbsp. finely chopped fresh dill
¾ tsp. salt

1. Snap off and discard tough ends of asparagus; remove scales with a vegetable peeler, if desired. Cut asparagus into 1-inch pieces.
2. Remove root, tough outer leaves, and tops from leek, leaving 2 inches of dark leaves. Finely chop leek; rinse well, and drain.
3. Melt butter in a large Dutch oven over medium heat; add leek, celery, and onion; sauté 4 to 5 minutes or until tender. Stir in broth, and bring to a boil over medium-high heat. Cover, reduce heat to low, and simmer 10 minutes. Stir in asparagus and orzo. Cover and simmer 10 minutes or until vegetables and orzo are tender.
4. Whisk egg yolks until thickened and pale. Gradually stir about 2 cups hot soup mixture into yolks; add yolk mixture to remaining hot soup mixture, stirring constantly 2 to 3 minutes or until thickened. Stir in lemon juice, dill, and salt, and serve immediately, or if desired, cover and chill.

Zucchini-Potato Soup
make ahead

MAKES 7 CUPS; **PREP:** 20 MIN.,
COOK: 40 MIN., **COOL:** 5 MIN.

Inspired by the classic potato-and-leek vichyssoise (vihsh-ee-SWAHZ), we added zucchini and gave this recipe our Southern twist with the addition of crisp, crumbled bacon. Prepare the soup the day before you want to serve it. Just pour into chilled bowls for guests.

1 medium leek
4 bacon slices
½ cup chopped celery
1 garlic clove, minced
4 cups low-sodium fat-free chicken broth
1 lb. zucchini, sliced (about 3 small squash)
½ lb. small new potatoes, quartered
1 cup half-and-half
⅓ cup chopped fresh parsley
¼ tsp. kosher salt
¼ tsp. pepper

1. Remove root, tough outer leaves, and tops from leek, leaving 2 inches of dark leaves. Thinly slice leek; rinse well, and drain.
2. Cook bacon in a large Dutch oven over medium-high heat 8 to 10 minutes or until crisp; remove bacon, and drain on paper towels, reserving 2 Tbsp. drippings in Dutch oven. Crumble bacon.
3. Sauté leek, celery, and garlic in hot drippings 3 to 4 minutes or until tender. Add chicken broth, zucchini, and potatoes, and simmer 20 to 25 minutes. Stir in half-and-half, parsley, salt, and pepper. Remove from heat, and cool 5 minutes.
4. Process potato mixture, in batches, in a blender or food processor until smooth, stopping to scrape down sides as needed. Sprinkle with crumbled bacon, and serve immediately, or if desired, cover and chill 4 to 6 hours.

Ready-To-Cook Veggies

Start with bagged vegetables from the produce section for fabulous recipes.

We know that eating more vegetables is the *right* thing to do, but it's not always a convenient thing to do. With precut veggies from the supermarket produce department, healthful sides can become a daily occurrence. Take advantage of their practicality in these superfast recipes.

Curried Cauliflower
fast fixin's

Golden-hued Curried Cauliflower gets a kick from dried crushed red pepper and pairs beautifully with flank steak and couscous.

MAKES 4 SERVINGS; **PREP:** 5 MIN.,
COOK: 14 MIN.

1 tsp. curry powder
¼ tsp. dried crushed red pepper
2 Tbsp. vegetable oil
2 (10-oz.) packages fresh cauliflower florets
1 medium onion, chopped
¾ tsp. salt

1. Cook curry powder and red pepper in hot oil in a large skillet over medium heat, stirring often, 1 minute. Add cauliflower, onion, and salt, and cook, stirring constantly, 2 to 3 minutes or until onion is crisp-tender. Reduce heat to low; add 6 Tbsp. water. Cover and cook, stirring occasionally, 8 to 10 minutes or just until cauliflower is tender.

Grilled Flank Steak With Curried Cauliflower and Couscous: Rub 1 (1-lb.) flank steak with 1 Tbsp. olive oil; sprinkle with 1 tsp. salt and ¼ tsp. pepper. Cook flank steak in a grill pan over medium-high heat 8 minutes on each side or to desired degree of doneness. Remove from pan, cover loosely with aluminum foil, and let stand 10 minutes before slicing. Prepare 1 (10-oz.) box plain couscous according to package directions, stirring ¼ cup golden raisins into water just before couscous. Cut flank steak diagonally across the grain into slices, and serve over couscous with Curried Cauliflower. Makes 4 servings; Prep: 15 min., Cook: 16 min., Stand: 10 min.

Creamy Broccoli Bake

MAKES 4 TO 6 SERVINGS; **PREP:** 15 MIN., **COOK:** 8 MIN., **BAKE:** 30 MIN.

2 (12-oz.) packages fresh broccoli florets
1 Tbsp. salt
2 Tbsp. butter
2 Tbsp. all-purpose flour
1½ cups milk
1 (3-oz.) package cream cheese, softened
1 (4-oz.) package crumbled blue cheese
¼ tsp. salt
⅓ cup finely crushed saltine crackers (about 10 crackers)

1. Preheat oven to 350°. Coarsely chop broccoli. Cook broccoli and 1 Tbsp. salt in a Dutch oven in boiling water to cover 3 minutes or until crisp-tender; drain.
2. Melt butter in a medium-size heavy saucepan over low heat; whisk in flour until smooth. Cook, whisking constantly, 1 minute. Gradually whisk in milk; cook over medium heat, whisking constantly, until mixture is thickened and bubbly. Stir in cheeses and ¼ tsp. salt until melted. Stir in broccoli.
3. Place in a lightly greased 11- x 7-inch baking dish; sprinkle with crackers.
4. Bake at 350° for 30 minutes or until golden and bubbly.

— **LINDA PINKERTON**, ODESSA, FLORIDA

So Southern

Instant Gourmet

Elevate a bowl of ramen noodles to uptown Southern fare. This recipe, featuring shrimp from the Gulf, couldn't be quicker, easier, or more delicious.

Noodle Bowl

1. Stir together flavor packet from 1 (3-oz.) package Oriental-flavored ramen noodle soup mix, 2 cups water, 1 chopped green onion, and 2 Tbsp. chopped fresh cilantro in a medium saucepan. Bring to a boil; add noodles and ½ cup fresh trimmed snow peas. Cook 1 minute, and stir in 6 peeled and deveined, medium-size raw shrimp (26/30 count). Cook 2 minutes. Transfer to a bowl, and top with ¼ cup shredded napa cabbage and 1 to 2 Tbsp. chopped peanuts. Makes 1 serving. Prep: 10 min., Cook: 5 min.
Note: You can substitute ½ cup chopped cooked chicken for the shrimp.

Creamy Broccoli Bake With Chicken: Prepare recipe as directed through Step 2. Stir in 1 lb. chopped cooked chicken breast. Proceed with recipe as directed.

Sesame Green Beans

family favorite • fast fixin's
MAKES 3 SERVINGS; **PREP:** 10 MIN., **COOK:** 7 MIN.

1 (12-oz.) package fresh green beans
1 garlic clove, chopped
2 tsp. toasted sesame oil
2 Tbsp. lite soy sauce
1 Tbsp. toasted sesame seeds (optional)

1. Cook green beans in boiling salted water to cover 5 minutes or to desired degree of doneness. Drain; cover and keep warm.
2. Cook garlic in hot sesame oil in a small skillet over medium heat 1 minute. Stir in soy sauce. Add beans, and cook 1 minute or until thoroughly heated. Sprinkle with sesame seeds, if desired. Serve immediately.

Sesame Shrimp-and-Green Beans Over Rice: Increase toasted sesame oil to 3 tsp. Prepare 1 cup uncooked long-grain rice according to package directions. Peel and devein 1 lb. large, raw shrimp (21/25 count).

Cook shrimp in 1 tsp. hot toasted sesame oil in a medium skillet over medium- high heat, stirring often, 2 to 3 minutes or just until shrimp turn pink. Remove shrimp from skillet; proceed with recipe as directed, stirring in shrimp with green beans in Step 2. Serve shrimp mixture over hot cooked rice. Makes 4 servings; Prep: 20 min., Cook: 10 min.

Quick Honey Carrots

family favorite •fast fixin's
MAKES 4 SERVINGS; **PREP:** 15 MIN.

1 (1-lb.) bag baby carrots
1 Tbsp. honey
2 tsp. cider vinegar
1½ tsp. olive oil
½ tsp. salt
½ tsp. chopped fresh or ¼ tsp. dried thyme
⅛ tsp. pepper

1. Toss together all ingredients in a microwave-safe bowl. Cover and microwave at HIGH 6 to 7 minutes or to desired degree of doneness.

— **INSPIRED BY MITZI CRAWFORD,**
EAST BEND, NORTH CAROLINA

Breakfast With Friends

Welcome the weekend with our leisurely menu. Champagne flutes filled with fruit juice and a quick casserole spooned into ramekins add the finishing touches.

Weekend Brunch

SERVES 8 TO 10

Brown Sugar-Bourbon Baked Ham

Sweet-and-Spicy Mustard Sauce

Baked Grits and Greens

Pink-and-White Grapefruit Salad

Morning Glory Muffin Bread

Favorite biscuits

Brown Sugar-Bourbon Baked Ham

family favorite

MAKES 8 TO 10 SERVINGS; **PREP:** 15 MIN.;
BAKE: 2 HR., 30 MIN.; **STAND:** 20 MIN.

Delicious warm or cold, this Southern Living favorite is the ultimate make-ahead main dish. Basting delivers big flavor and a beautiful glaze with little effort.

1 (6- to 8-lb.) fully cooked, bone-in ham
48 whole cloves
1 (16-oz.) package light brown sugar
1 cup spicy brown mustard
1 cup cola soft drink
¾ cup bourbon
Garnish: fresh bay leaves

1. Preheat oven to 350°. Remove skin from ham, and trim fat to ¼-inch thickness. Make shallow cuts in fat ¾ inch apart in a diamond pattern. Insert cloves in centers of diamonds. Place ham in a lightly greased 13- x 9-inch pan.
2. Stir together brown sugar and next 3 ingredients; spoon mixture over ham.
3. Bake at 350° on lowest oven rack 2 hours and 30 minutes, basting with pan juices every 15 to 20 minutes. Remove ham from oven, and let stand 20 minutes before slicing. Garnish, if desired.

Sweet-and-Spicy Mustard Sauce

make ahead

MAKES 1¼ CUPS; **PREP:** 10 MIN.,
COOK: 7 MIN., **COOL:** 15 MIN.

This snappy sauce is a natural with hot biscuits and ham and also makes a terrific sandwich spread for grilled chicken or turkey.

½ cup sugar
2 egg yolks
2 Tbsp. dry mustard
2 Tbsp. all-purpose flour
1 cup evaporated milk, divided
¼ cup vinegar

1. Whisk together first 4 ingredients and ⅓ cup evaporated milk in a small bowl.
2. Cook remaining ⅔ cup milk in a small heavy saucepan over medium heat, stirring often, 1 to 2 minutes or just until bubbles appear. (Do not boil.) Whisk in mustard mixture, and cook, whisking constantly, 3 to 5 minutes or until smooth and thickened. Remove from heat, and let cool 15 minutes; whisk in vinegar. Serve immediately, or cover and chill until ready to serve. Store in an airtight container in refrigerator up to 1 week.

—EMILY SHELTON,
HOLLY SPRINGS, NORTH CAROLINA

Baked Grits and Greens

make ahead

MAKES 8 TO 10 SERVINGS; **PREP:** 20 MIN.,
COOK: 8 MIN., **BAKE:** 30 MIN.

Prepare through Step 2 up to a day ahead; cover and chill. Remove from the fridge, add the buttered crushed croutons, and let stand 30 minutes before baking.

1 tsp. garlic salt
1 cup uncooked quick-cooking grits
⅓ cup finely chopped red onion
5 Tbsp. butter, divided
2 large eggs
1 (10-oz.) package frozen chopped spinach, thawed and drained
1½ cups (6 oz.) shredded Parmesan cheese
½ cup bottled creamy Caesar dressing
½ tsp. freshly ground pepper
1¼ cups coarsely crushed garlic-flavored croutons

1. Preheat oven to 350°. Bring garlic salt and 4 cups water to a boil in a large saucepan over medium-high heat; gradually stir in grits. Reduce heat to medium, and cook, stirring often, 5 minutes or until thickened. Remove from heat, and stir in onion and 3 Tbsp. butter.
2. Whisk together eggs and next 4 ingredients in a large bowl. Stir about

one-fourth of grits mixture gradually into egg mixture; add remaining grits mixture, stirring constantly. Pour into a lightly greased 13- x 9-inch baking dish.

3. Melt remaining 2 Tbsp. butter, and toss with coarsely crushed croutons; sprinkle over grits mixture.

4. Bake at 350° for 30 to 35 minutes or until mixture is set and croutons are golden brown.

Baked Grits and Greens With Bacon: Prepare recipe as directed, stirring 1 (3-oz.) package bacon bits into egg mixture.

—JANET F. GILBERT, DANIELSVILLE, GEORGIA

Note: For testing purposes only, we used Oscar Mayer Real Bacon Bits.

Pink-and-White Grapefruit Salad

MAKES 8 TO 10 SERVINGS; PREP: 25 MIN.

3 large pink grapefruit, peeled
2 large white grapefruit, peeled
Fresh Citrus Sauce
¼ cup chopped pistachios
Garnish: baby lettuces

1. Cut grapefruit into ½-inch-thick slices. Arrange pink and white grapefruit slices alternately on a platter. Just before serving, drizzle grapefruit slices with ⅔ cup Fresh Citrus Sauce, and sprinkle with pistachios. Serve with remaining Fresh Citrus Sauce. Garnish, if desired.

Fresh Citrus Sauce:

make ahead

MAKES ABOUT 1¾ CUPS; PREP: 10 MIN.,
COOK: 5 MIN., COOL: 10 MIN., CHILL: 2 HR.

This versatile dressing pairs well with almost any medley of fresh fruit.

½ cup sugar
1½ Tbsp. cornstarch
1½ cups fresh orange juice
1 tsp. lemon zest
¼ cup fresh lemon juice

1. Combine sugar and cornstarch in a small saucepan; whisk in orange juice. Bring to a boil over medium heat, whisking constantly; boil 1 minute. Remove from heat, and whisk in lemon zest and juice. Cool 10 minutes, stirring occasionally. Transfer to an airtight container; place heavy-duty plastic wrap directly on warm sauce (to prevent a film from forming); chill 2 hours before serving. Store in refrigerator, with plastic wrap on surface of sauce, up to 1 week.

—MARLENE SPEARS, ATHENS, ALABAMA

Morning Glory Muffin Bread

freezeable • make ahead

MAKES 12 TO 16 SERVINGS; PREP: 20 MIN.;
BAKE: 1 HR.; COOL: 1 HR., 20 MIN.

Lightly spiced with the rich, moist flavor of carrot cake, these muffins are a tasty match for cream cheese and ginger preserves.

1 cup chopped pecans
3 cups all-purpose flour
1 tsp. salt
1 tsp. baking soda
1 tsp. ground cinnamon
½ tsp. ground nutmeg
2 cups sugar
¾ cup canola oil
3 large eggs
2½ tsp. vanilla extract
1 (8-oz.) can crushed pineapple, undrained
2 large carrots, finely grated (1 cup)
1 cup golden raisins

1. Preheat oven to 350°. Bake pecans in a single layer on a baking sheet 5 to 7 minutes or until lightly toasted and fragrant. Cool completely on a wire rack (about 15 minutes).

2. Meanwhile, combine flour, salt, baking soda, ground cinnamon, and nutmeg in a large bowl; make a well in center of mixture.

3. Whisk together sugar, canola oil, eggs, and vanilla extract; fold in crushed pineapple and carrots. Add to flour mixture, stirring just until dry ingredients are moistened. Fold in toasted pecans and raisins. Spoon into 2 greased and floured 8- x 4-inch loaf pans.

4. Bake at 350° for 55 to 60 minutes or until a wooden pick inserted in center comes out clean. Cool in pans on a wire rack 15 minutes. Remove from pans to wire rack, and cool completely (about 50 minutes).

—GEORDYTH SULLIVAN, MIAMI, FLORIDA

Morning Glory Muffins: Prepare batter as directed. Spoon into lightly greased muffin pans, filling two-thirds full. Bake at 350° for 23 to 25 minutes or until a wooden pick inserted in center comes out clean. Cool in pans on wire rack 5 minutes. Remove from pans to wire rack, and cool completely (about 30 minutes). Makes 2 dozen muffins. Prep: 30 min., Bake: 23 min., Cool: 50 min.

Note: Bread and muffins may be made ahead and frozen in a zip-top plastic freezer bag up to 1 month, if desired. Remove from bag, and let thaw at room temperature.

In Season: Artichokes

Brush off any hesitation, and give this vegetable a try. Our Test Kitchen experts offer steaming and grilling tips that dispel the bad rap. We even included a recipe for fried artichokes—coated in cornmeal, of course.

Grilled Fresh Artichokes

MAKES 4 TO 8 SERVINGS; **PREP:** 20 MIN., **COOK:** 45 MIN., **COOL:** 15 MIN., **GRILL:** 10 MIN.

To grill artichokes, you have to steam them first. **Table talk:** *We tested a fancy steaming mixture that had about 10 ingredients, including wine, but found this simple mixture that calls for lemon and garlic imparts great flavor for a lower cost.*

1 lemon, thinly sliced
5 fresh parsley sprigs
3 garlic cloves
2 tsp. salt
4 fresh artichokes (about ¾ lb. each)
3 Tbsp. olive oil
Salt and pepper
Buttery Dipping Sauces or Mayo Mixtures
Garnish: fresh flat-leaf parsley sprigs

1. Combine lemon, next 3 ingredients, and 2½ cups water in large Dutch oven. Place a steamer basket in Dutch oven.
2. Wash artichokes by plunging up and down in cold water. Cut off stem ends; trim about 1 inch from top of each artichoke, using a serrated knife. Remove any loose bottom leaves. Trim one-fourth off top from each outer leaf, using kitchen shears.
3. Arrange artichokes in steamer basket. Bring to a boil; cover, reduce heat, and simmer 35 to 40 minutes or until stem end is easily pierced with a long wooden pick. Remove artichokes from Dutch oven. Let cool 15 minutes.
4. Preheat grill to 350° to 400° (medium-high). Carefully cut artichokes in half lengthwise; remove and discard choke. Liberally brush cut sides of artichokes with olive oil, and sprinkle with desired amount of salt and pepper.

5. Grill artichokes, covered with grill lid, over 350° to 400° (medium-high) heat 5 minutes on each side. Serve with Buttery Dipping Sauces or Mayo Mixtures. Garnish, if desired.

Steamed Fresh Artichokes:

Prepare recipe as directed through Step 3. (Do not cool.) Carefully pull open center leaves of artichokes. Remove and discard choke using a long spoon. Serve with Buttery Dipping Sauces or Mayo Mixtures. Makes 4 servings; Prep: 15 min., Cook: 45 min.

Buttery Dipping Sauces

Our Food staff especially liked these with the Steamed Fresh Artichokes. You can also brush either sauce on steamed artichoke halves in place of olive oil, salt, and pepper before grilling.

Peppy Basil Butter: Microwave ⅓ cup butter in a microwave-safe glass bowl at HIGH 30 to 45 seconds or until melted and hot. Stir in 3 Tbsp. chopped fresh basil, ½ tsp. salt, and ¼ tsp. dried crushed red pepper. Let stand 10 minutes before serving. Makes about ⅓ cup; Prep: 5 min., Stand: 10 min.

Balsamic-Apricot Butter: Microwave ⅓ cup butter in a microwave-safe glass bowl at HIGH 30 to 45 seconds or until melted and hot. Stir in 2 Tbsp. apricot preserves* and 1 Tbsp. balsamic vinegar. Season with salt and pepper to taste. Makes about ⅓ cup; Prep: 5 min. *2 Tbsp. peach preserves may be substituted.

Q&A

What is an artichoke? It's the flowering bud of a thistle plant.
How do you select a good one? Top-quality artichokes are heavy for their size, bright, almost shiny green with a purple tinge, cold but not wet feeling, and have tightly compacted leaves.
Is there nutritional value? Yes. A 12-oz. artichoke is high in vitamin C and potassium.
What is the peak season? Artichokes are more plentiful and flavorful between March and May. They are also cheaper.
How do you eat artichoke leaves? Slide leaves between your teeth to remove the tender, nutty-tasting portion. Cut the artichoke heart into bites with a knife and fork and plunge into sauce before popping into your mouth.

Cornmeal-Fried Artichokes

MAKES 3 TO 4 SERVINGS; **PREP:** 30 MIN., **FRY:** 5 MIN. PER BATCH

These are worth the time. You really do remove all the leaves. This is based on the Italian fritto misto, or mixed fry, that includes small pieces of battered and fried meats, fish, and vegetables, especially artichokes. Keep fried artichokes warm between batches on a rack in a jelly-roll pan in a 225° oven for up to 30 minutes.

4 fresh artichokes (about ¾ lb. each)
Canola oil
1½ cups plain yellow cornmeal
2 tsp. kosher salt
1½ tsp. fresh ground pepper
¾ cup buttermilk
1 large egg
¾ cup all-purpose flour
Mayo Mixtures

1. Cut 3 inches from top of each artichoke, using a serrated knife. Discard top portion. Remove and discard leaves from bottom portions of artichokes.

Test Kitchen Know-How

Once you've prepped a couple of artichokes, you'll pick up speed. You will need a serrated (aka bread) knife, kitchen shears, and a steamer basket. Steamer baskets are typically sold in grocery stores for less than $5.

Cut off the top one-third of the artichoke using a serrated knife in a sawing motion. (A chef's knife tends to drag through the tough leaves, loosening them from the stem.) Clip off the prickly leaf tips with kitchen shears.

Artichokes are tender and done when a wooden skewer firmly but easily slides into the stem end.

For grilling, steam first, and then cut artichoke in half. During testing, we noticed that when cut right side up, many leaves broke away. To keep the leaves attached, flip the artichoke upside down and use a serrated knife.

Pop the inedible fuzzy choke away from the heart, or base of the artichoke, using a teaspoon or grapefruit spoon.

Trim green skin from sides and stems, using a paring knife, being careful to leave stem ends intact. Cut each artichoke lengthwise into fourths. Remove and discard chokes.

2. Pour oil to a depth of 3 inches into a Dutch oven; heat over medium-high heat to 350°.

3. Combine cornmeal, salt, and pepper in a shallow bowl. Whisk together buttermilk and egg in another bowl.

4. Toss artichokes in flour. Dip in egg mixture, and dredge in cornmeal mixture, shaking off excess.

5. Fry artichokes, in batches, in hot oil 5 minutes or until tender and golden brown. Drain on a wire rack over paper towels. Serve with Mayo Mixtures.

Fast Fried Artichokes: Substitute 2 (14-oz.) cans artichoke bottoms, rinsed and drained, for fresh artichokes. Reduce salt to 1 tsp. Pat artichokes dry with paper towels; cut each into fourths. Proceed with recipe as directed, beginning with Step 2. Makes 4 to 6 servings; Prep: 15 min., Fry: 5 min. per batch

Mayo Mixtures

Try these with grilled, steamed, or Cornmeal-Fried Artichokes. They're also great as sandwich spreads; tossed with cooked pasta for pasta salad; as sauces for vegetables; or slathered on fresh, cooked corn on the cob.

Pepperoncini Mayo: Stir together ⅔ cup mayonnaise, 3 Tbsp. chopped pepperoncini peppers, and 1 tsp. lemon zest. Season with salt and pepper to taste. Makes about ¾ cup. Prep: 5 min.

Garlic-Lemon Mayo: Stir together ⅔ cup mayonnaise, 1 pressed garlic clove, 2 tsp. lemon zest, 1 Tbsp. lemon juice, and ⅛ tsp. ground red pepper. Season with salt to taste. Makes about ¾ cup; Prep: 5 min.

Herb-Shallot Mayo: Stir together ⅔ cup mayonnaise, 2 Tbsp. finely chopped fresh flat-leaf parsley, 1 Tbsp. Dijon mustard, and 1 minced shallot*. Season with salt and pepper to taste. Makes about ¾ cup; Prep: 5 min. *2 Tbsp. minced sweet onion may be substituted.

Chipotle-Lime Mayo: Stir together ⅔ cup mayonnaise, 1 Tbsp. minced canned chipotle pepper in adobo sauce, 1 tsp. lime zest, and 2 tsp. lime juice. Season with salt and pepper to taste. Makes about ¾ cup; Prep: 5 min.

Make the most of spring with our tips for nutritious and colorful salads that can't be beat.

Power Up Your Salad

Color your plate with everyday ingredients for delicious meals that energize.

Salads make a nutritious meal. Or do they? We all know that eating colorful veggies and greens is a delicious way to pack in powerful antioxidants, but some toppings and dressings can add up to a lot of wasted calories and fat if you don't watch out. Your choices in lettuce and other greens can also affect the good-for-you factor. Choose your ingredients wisely, and include lots of color.

The Darker, The Better

Lettuce and greens vary in levels of nutrients. Though paler lettuces, such as iceberg, have some nutritional value and are typically less expensive, it's best to choose the deeper, brighter ones—that's where you'll find more of the cancer-fighting antioxidants. Avoid dark spots, wilted leaves, and yellowing. Mix and match a variety of colors and textures, such as crunchy romaine tossed with soft, nutrient-rich spinach leaves or peppery arugula with frilly red leaf lettuce.

Very Clean Veggies

Thoroughly wash all greens and vegetables, even prepackaged fresh produce. While rinsing under running water offers some protection against unsafe bacteria, we recommend these alternatives.

- **Prepackaged greens:** Make a solution of 1⅓ cups 3% hydrogen peroxide (it's perfectly safe and has no aftertaste) and 2⅔ cups distilled water; keep it in a spray bottle. Spritz the greens with the solution, rinse with distilled water, and then spin or pat them dry. Replace the solution once a week.
- **Fresh greens:** Soak and rinse several times with distilled water to remove dirt and grit. Make a double batch of peroxide mixture, and soak the greens in it. Rinse and pat dry.
- **Fresh vegetables:** Purchase a vegetable brush (used only for cleaning produce). Gently scrub the veggies with the peroxide solution, and rinse.

Keep Dressings Light

You don't have to go completely fat free. In fact, we prefer light and reduced-fat dressings over fat-free ones, which tend to contain more sugar and other additives to boost flavor. Newman's Own and Girard's, for example, each have a great line of light salad dressings that taste just as good as the full-fat versions. If you want your bottled dressing creamier, add some nonfat or low-fat plain yogurt to thicken it, which also gives you an extra dose of dairy. Or come up with your own creative combinations. Choose monounsaturated salad oils, such as olive and nut oils, when making your own dressing.

Healthy Benefits

- Red and purple grapes and juice contain flavonoids that help reduce cholesterol, protect against heart disease, and promote lung health.
- A small handful of nuts or seeds on your salad can make your meal more filling, helping to reduce hunger pangs and overeating throughout the day.

Spinach-Grape Chopped Salad

editor's pick

MAKES 4 SERVINGS; **PREP:** 10 MIN., **COOK:** 5 MIN.

2 Tbsp. pine nuts
1 (6-oz.) package fresh baby spinach, thoroughly washed
1 cup seedless red grapes, sliced
¼ cup crumbled reduced-fat feta cheese
¼ cup light raspberry-walnut vinaigrette

1. Heat pine nuts in a small skillet over medium-high heat, stirring constantly, 5 minutes or until toasted and fragrant.
2. Coarsely chop spinach. Toss together spinach, grapes, feta cheese, and vinaigrette in a serving bowl. Sprinkle with pine nuts, and serve immediately.

—**KERRI RAY**, ALPHARETTA, GEORGIA

Note: For testing purposes only, we used Newman's Own Light Raspberry & Walnut Dressing.

Per serving: Calories 106; Fat 6.5g (sat 1.4g, mono 0.8g, poly 1.5g); Protein 3.4g; Carb 10.6g; Fiber 1.6g; Chol 2.5mg; Iron 1.7mg; Sodium 273mg; Calc 65mg

Tasty Toppings

- Grate some carrots to sprinkle over your salad for an extra boost of beta-carotene, a strong antioxidant known to reduce the risk of heart disease, help prevent cancer, and promote good vision.
- Nuts and seeds not only add extra flavor and crunch (especially when toasted), but they also contain heart-healthy fat and are rich in protein and fiber. Choose a small handful of almonds, pecans, peanuts, sunflower seeds, pine nuts, walnuts, or flaxseed.
- Our staff loves adding edamame (green soybeans) to salads. Look for frozen edamame in the freezer section. You can also find them fully cooked and ready to eat.

QUICK & EASY

Our Favorite Bargain

Budget-friendly cuts of turkey are fast and flavorful options anytime.

Speedy doesn't have to be bland. These tasty main-dish recipes deliver tons of bold flavor. With a variety of cuts available at the supermarket, turkey makes a great choice for everyday meals. It's low in fat, loaded with protein, and fast-cooking. You'll have supper on the table in no time.

Spice-Rubbed Grilled Turkey Tenderloins

MAKES 4 TO 6 SERVINGS; **PREP:** 10 MIN., **GRILL:** 20 MIN., **STAND:** 10 MIN.

2 Tbsp. light brown sugar
1 tsp. salt
1 tsp. ground cumin
¼ to ½ tsp. ground red pepper
⅛ tsp. ground ginger
⅛ tsp. ground coriander
1½ lb. turkey tenderloin
2 Tbsp. olive oil

1. Preheat grill to 350° to 400° (medium-high) heat. Stir together first 6 ingredients. Brush turkey tenderloin with olive oil, and rub with brown sugar mixture.
2. Grill turkey, covered with grill lid, over 350° to 400° (medium-high) heat 10 minutes on each side or until a meat thermometer inserted into thickest portion registers 165°. Let stand 10 minutes before serving.

Mini Apple-Cheddar Turkey Meatloaves

MAKES 4 TO 6 SERVINGS; **PREP:** 15 MIN., **BAKE:** 21 MIN.

Shred the apple and onion using the large holes of a box grater. Cheese grits and a salad make the perfect complements for this dish.

1 to 1½ lb. ground turkey
¼ cup Japanese breadcrumbs (panko)*
1 medium onion, shredded
1 medium-size Granny Smith apple, peeled, cored, and shredded
1 large egg, lightly beaten
1 tsp. salt
¾ tsp. pepper
1¼ cups (5 oz.) freshly shredded Cheddar cheese, divided

1. Preheat oven to 375°. Gently combine ground turkey, next 6 ingredients, and ½ cup cheese just until combined, using hands. Spoon turkey mixture into 12 lightly greased muffin cups.

2. Bake at 375° for 16 minutes. Sprinkle with remaining ¾ cup cheese. Bake 5 minutes or until cheese is melted and a meat thermometer inserted into centers of meatloaves registers 165°.
*Fine, dry breadcrumbs may be substituted.

Mini Pesto-Turkey Meatloaves:

Omit apple and pepper. Substitute mozzarella cheese for Cheddar cheese. Proceed with recipe as directed, stirring 2 Tbsp. chopped fresh basil and 3 Tbsp. refrigerated pesto into meat mixture in Step 1.
Note: For testing purposes only, we used Buitoni Pesto With Basil.

Turkey Parmesan

family favorite • fast fixin's
MAKES 4 SERVINGS; **PREP:** 10 MIN., **COOK:** 12 MIN.

Serve this tasty dish with angel hair pasta and marinara sauce.

1 lb. boneless turkey breast cutlets (8 cutlets)
2 Tbsp. fresh lemon juice
⅓ cup all-purpose flour
¼ cup grated Parmesan cheese
2 tsp. dried basil
1 tsp. pepper
¾ to 1 tsp. salt
3 Tbsp. butter

1. Rinse turkey cutlets, and pat dry. Brush turkey with lemon juice.
2. Combine flour and next 4 ingredients in a shallow dish. Dredge turkey in flour mixture, shaking off excess.
3. Melt 2 Tbsp. butter in a large non-stick skillet over medium-high heat. Cook turkey, in 2 batches, 2 to 3 minutes on each side or until golden brown, adding remaining 1 Tbsp. butter to skillet as needed. Keep turkey warm on a wire rack in a jelly-roll pan in a 200° oven.

Bake Up Success

Your layer cakes are ready for an encore with our secrets, tips, and a favorite tool.

About the Tool

The Test Kitchen loves this handy gadget called an **offset spatula.** The angled steel blade is flexible enough to keep your hands free of frosting and is perfect for spreading batter in a pan. They range in length from 6 to 14 inches. Our best advice is to use one that feels the most comfortable in your hand. Prices range from less than $10 to more than $30. This useful utensil is also called a bent icing knife.

Frost It Right

We strongly believe that if something tastes great, it should look great too. Follow these easy steps for presentation perfection.

Step 1: Place one cake layer on a plate or cake stand. Gently slide pieces of parchment paper under edges of cake. Spoon about ½ cup buttercream frosting onto the bottom layer; push to edge leaving a ½-inch border. A swiveling cheese board is a great substitute if you don't have a revolving cake stand.

Step 2: Place second layer on top of frosted cake. Spoon a good amount of frosting on the top of the cake.

Step 3: Spread frosting to the edge and down the sides of cake with a spatula or knife using a sweeping motion. Before serving, remove and discard parchment paper.

Under Glass Try this clever serving idea for petits fours at your next party. Place each little cake in a shallow bowl or on a small plate, and then cover it with a clear wineglass turned upside down. The glass will keep the cake moist all during dinner, and the effect is guaranteed to draw as many rave reviews as the recipe itself (see page 62). Match bowl colors to icing for a coordinated look.

Flour Power

Cake flour is soft wheat flour with low protein content. What does this mean to a novice baker? It's more forgiving than all-purpose flour. If you accidentally overmix the batter, the cake's texture won't be tough after baking. Less gluten is developed, and for cakes this is a critical factor—it means a soft, tender crumb. Cake flour also is bleached, which explains its very bright, white appearance.

If you use all-purpose flour instead of cake flour, reduce the amount of flour called for by 2 Tbsp. per cup. Or make your own version of cake flour by whisking together ¾ cup all-purpose flour plus 2 Tbsp. cornstarch for each cup of cake flour.

April

A Farm-Fresh Easter

Cooking with local produce is the hallmark of chef Amy Tornquist, one of North Carolina's brightest culinary stars. Join her family and friends for a down-home Easter dinner that celebrates the best of what's in season.

W e bet, as a child, Amy Tornquist made her *parents* finish their vegetables. Follow her around for more than a minute, especially at the Carrboro Farmers' Market just outside of Chapel Hill, North Carolina, and you can easily imagine her happily encouraging her mom to try one more forkful of "yummy" cauliflower or "awesome" carrots. This gifted chef, busy mother of two, and longtime champion of local food is passionate about produce.

With the coffee finally kicking in, Amy wipes the sleep from her eyes and hits the early-morning market in full stride. She shows off two handfuls of just-picked, dew-damp lettuces, cradling the tender greens as if she's holding a Fabergé egg. "If that's not the definition of beautiful, I don't know what is," she coos. But there's no time to linger. Amy purposefully fills sturdy wicker baskets with the most pristine nature-built goodies this side of the Garden of Eden.

The chilly morning blossoms into a gorgeous spring afternoon as Amy applies the finishing touches to a big ol' Easter dinner she's prepared for family and friends. This year everyone gathers at Elodie Farms in Rougemont, home to Dave Artigues and his farmstead goat cheese-making facility. (Amy features his cheeses at Watts Grocery, her critically acclaimed Durham restaurant.)

"It's so great to finally see something green. I feel like I've done nothing but stare at sweet potatoes all winter," jokes Amy, tossing vibrant asparagus into Asparagus-New Potato Hash.

"Everyone just gets happy when the farmers market opens, but it always seems to be about two weeks later than I want it to be. But, hey, I'm not complaining," she adds with a big laugh.

Out on the front porch, Dave, helped by Amy's husband, Jeremy, serves the adults tall glasses of ice-cold limeade to wash down the rich Shrimp-and-Blue Cheese Spread. Conversation quickly turns to wagering on whose child will win the annual egg roll. Meantime, the kids work up an appetite playing leapfrog on the soft grass, occasionally trying to steal a predinner cupcake or cookie off the dessert table positioned under a large shade tree.

By day's end, everyone's filled with great food and fun. As Dave's older son, Will, basks in the glory of his first-ever egg roll victory (happily accepting high-fives all the way around), Amy offers a toast in honor of the new season's bounty and the pleasure of sharing a meal with loved ones. Glass raised high, Amy turns to Jeremy and whispers, "What a perfect day."

Gather for a Feast

SERVES 8

Shrimp-and-Blue Cheese Spread

Pork Roast With Carolina Gravy

Asparagus-New Potato Hash

Watts Grocery Spoon Bread

Lemon Curd-Filled Angel Food Cake
or Easter Cookies

Shrimp-and-Blue Cheese Spread

chef recipe • make ahead

MAKES 5½ CUPS; PREP: 25 MIN.,
COOK: 7 MIN., STAND: 15 MIN., CHILL: 4 HR.

2½ lb. unpeeled, large raw shrimp
    (21/25 count)*
¼ cup diced sweet onion
2 Tbsp. olive oil
½ (8-oz.) package cream cheese, softened
4 green onions, finely chopped
1 celery rib, finely chopped
1 cup crumbled blue cheese
1 cup mayonnaise
½ cup sour cream
2 Tbsp. chopped fresh parsley
2 tsp. lemon juice
1 tsp. Dijon mustard
½ tsp. salt
½ tsp. pepper
Assorted fresh vegetables
French bread baguette slices

Shop Like a Chef

Follow Amy's expert advice for navigating the farmers market like a pro.
- **Go early.** It's hard to shop, especially if you're a newcomer, when the market is crowded. Plus, early birds have a better selection and get more attention.
- **Ask questions.** Amy says the idea is to build relationships. Farmers care about regulars, so don't be afraid to ask something as simple as how to cook a new vegetable or whether or not they can cut a deal. They might even set aside some of their best stuff if they know you're a repeat customer and expect your visit.

Whether you're at home or traveling, find a market near you with the help of the *Southern Living* Local Market Listing by visiting southernliving.com/local markets.

1. Peel shrimp; devein, if desired.
2. Sauté onion in hot oil in a skillet over medium-high heat 3 minutes or until onion is tender. Stir in shrimp, and cook, stirring occasionally, 3 to 4 minutes or just until shrimp turn pink. Transfer to a bowl, and let stand 15 minutes. Chop shrimp, and return to bowl.
3. Stir in cream cheese and next 10 ingredients. Cover and chill 4 hours. Store in an airtight container up to 2 days. Serve with vegetables and bread slices.
*2½ lb. frozen unpeeled, large raw shrimp (21/25), thawed according to package directions, may be substituted.

—AMY TORNQUIST, DURHAM, NORTH CAROLINA

Pork Roast With Carolina Gravy
chef recipe

MAKES 8 SERVINGS; PREP: 25 MIN., COOK: 53 MIN., BAKE: 3 HR., STAND: 20 MIN.

If you don't own an instant-read thermometer, it's worth purchasing one for this recipe. Cooking this budget-friendly roast to between 180° and 185° ensures incredibly tender slices for a pretty presentation.

4 medium leeks
1 (5- to 6-lb.) bone-in pork shoulder roast (Boston butt)
Kitchen string
2 tsp. salt
2 tsp. pepper
3 thick bacon slices, chopped
1 Tbsp. vegetable oil
10 garlic cloves, halved
3 medium onions, halved and sliced
2½ cups low-sodium chicken broth
½ cup dry white wine
10 fresh thyme sprigs
4 bay leaves
1 Tbsp. butter

1. Preheat oven to 350°. Remove and discard root ends and dark green tops of leeks. Thinly slice leeks; rinse well, and drain.

2. Tie pork roast with kitchen string, securing at 2-inch intervals. Season with salt and pepper.
3. Cook bacon in hot oil in an ovenproof Dutch oven or large, deep cast-iron skillet over medium-high heat 3 minutes. Add leeks, garlic, and onion, and cook, stirring frequently, 15 to 17 minutes or until mixture is golden brown; transfer to a bowl.
4. Add pork roast, fat side down, to Dutch oven, and cook 2 minutes on all sides or until browned. Remove pork.
5. Return leek mixture to Dutch oven; top with pork. Add broth and next 3 ingredients. Reduce heat to medium, and bring to a light boil. Remove from heat, and cover with heavy-duty aluminum foil.
6. Bake at 350° for 3 to 3½ hours or until a meat thermometer inserted into thickest portion registers 180° to 185°. Remove pork from Dutch oven, cover with foil, and let stand 20 minutes before slicing.
7. Meanwhile, pour pan juices through a wire mesh strainer into a saucepan to equal 4 cups, discarding solids (add equal parts broth and white wine to pan juices to equal 4 cups, if necessary). Let stand 5 minutes; skim fat from surface of pan juices.
8. Bring to a boil over medium-high heat, and cook 20 to 25 minutes or until liquid is reduced to 1 cup and slightly thickened. Remove from heat, and stir in butter until melted. Serve with pork.

—AMY TORNQUIST, DURHAM, NORTH CAROLINA

Shredded Pork With Carolina Gravy:
Prepare recipe as directed through Step 5. Bake at 350° for 4 to 5 hours or until a meat thermometer inserted into thickest portion registers 195°. Remove pork from Dutch oven, cover with foil, and let stand 20 minutes. Shred pork with two forks. Proceed with recipe as directed.

Asparagus-New Potato Hash
chef recipe

MAKES 8 SERVINGS; PREP: 20 MIN., COOK: 25 MIN., COOL: 15 MIN.

The crisp texture and bright flavors of this dish complement the pork roast. Small red potatoes, which hold their shape when cooked, are the key to this recipe. Crumbled farmer's cheese adds some tang.

1 lb. small red potatoes
1 lb. fresh asparagus
2 shallots, minced
2 Tbsp. olive oil
1 tsp. chopped fresh thyme
1 tsp. salt
½ tsp. pepper
2 tsp. fresh lemon juice
⅓ cup crumbled farmer's cheese or queso fresco
Garnish: lemon slices

1. Bring potatoes and salted water to cover to a boil in a Dutch oven over medium-high heat. Cook 15 minutes or just until tender; drain well. Cool 15 minutes; cut into quarters.
2. Snap off and discard tough ends of asparagus. Cut asparagus into ½-inch pieces.
3. Sauté shallots in hot oil in a large nonstick skillet 1 minute. Add asparagus, thyme, salt, pepper, and lemon juice; sauté 2 to 3 minutes or until asparagus is crisp-tender. Add potatoes, and sauté 3 minutes or until mixture is thoroughly heated. Remove from heat, and sprinkle with cheese. Garnish, if desired.

—AMY TORNQUIST, DURHAM, NORTH CAROLINA

Note: For testing purposes only, we used Chapel Hill Creamery farmer's cheese.

Watts Grocery Spoon Bread
chef recipe

MAKES 8 SERVINGS; PREP: 20 MIN.,
COOK: 5 MIN., COOL: 5 MIN., BAKE: 45 MIN.

We streamlined Amy Tornquist's version while still maintaining its wonderful fluffy texture by whisking whole eggs with the other liquid ingredients. Don't worry if the Carolina Gravy from the Roast ends up over the spoon bread—the pan sauce adds scrumptious flavor.

1 Tbsp. butter, softened
2 Tbsp. plain white cornmeal
1¼ cups plain white cornmeal
¾ cup all-purpose flour
2 Tbsp. sugar
2 tsp. salt
2 Tbsp. butter
4 large eggs
1 cup buttermilk
1 cup whipping cream
2 tsp. baking soda
1 tsp. chopped fresh thyme
⅛ to ¼ tsp. ground red pepper

1. Preheat oven to 375°. Grease a 2½-qt. soufflé dish with 1 Tbsp. butter. Dust with 2 Tbsp. cornmeal. (Tap dish lightly to remove excess cornmeal.)
2. Combine 1¼ cups cornmeal and next 3 ingredients in a large bowl; make a well in center of mixture.
3. Bring 3 cups water to a boil in a saucepan over medium-high heat. Remove from heat, and whisk into cornmeal mixture, whisking until smooth. Add 2 Tbsp. butter, whisking until butter is melted. Cool 5 minutes.
4. Whisk together eggs and next 5 ingredients; whisk into cornmeal mixture. Pour cornmeal mixture into prepared baking dish.
5. Bake at 375° for 45 to 50 minutes or until golden brown and center is almost set. Serve immediately.

—AMY TORNQUIST, DURHAM, NORTH CAROLINA

Buy Local

"Even in this economy, it still pays to buy local," insists Amy. The majority of the dairy and vegetables she uses at her restaurant, Watts Grocery, come from within a two-hour radius of Durham, and she has been recognized for her commitment to sustainable agriculture. Amy also understands the real-life financial pressures facing consumers.

"When it comes to feeding my family, I get the most bang for my buck with local or organic produce. That's my top priority," Amy reveals. After that, she considers eggs and then dairy the best values. "Having said that, if it's a decision between buying organic at the grocery store or fresh from your local farmers' market, always go with local first," she recommends. But at the end of the day, Amy says one of the simplest ways to save money and still eat well is to buy in season.

Lemon Curd-Filled Angel Food Cake
chef recipe • make ahead

MAKES 12 SERVINGS; PREP: 30 MIN.;
BAKE: 34 MIN.; COOL: 1 HR., 30 MIN.;
CHILL: 1 HR.

An angel food cake pan looks similar to a traditional tube pan, but it has a removable bottom and three or four metal "feet" attached to the top rim. The feet allow the pan to be inverted while cooling, which yields a light and fluffy cake texture. Be sure to let the cake cool completely (1½ hours) before cutting horizontally into three equal rounds. (Pictured on page 9)

1¾ cups plus 2 Tbsp. sugar
1⅓ cups all-purpose flour
¼ tsp. salt
2 tsp. lemon juice
½ tsp. vanilla extract
½ tsp. light rum
¼ tsp. orange extract
1¾ cups egg whites (about 13 to
    15 eggs)
¾ tsp. cream of tartar
Lemon Curd Filling
Cream Cheese Frosting
Garnishes: lemon slices, lavender sprigs

1. Preheat oven to 375°. Sift together sugar, flour, and salt in a bowl. Combine lemon juice, vanilla extract, rum, and orange extract.

2. Beat egg whites and cream of tartar at high speed with a heavy-duty electric stand mixer until stiff peaks form; gently transfer egg white mixture to a large bowl.
3. Gradually fold in sugar mixture with a large spatula, ⅓ cup at a time, folding just until blended after each addition. Fold in lemon juice mixture.
4. Spoon batter into an ungreased 10-inch angel food pan with feet.
5. Bake at 375° for 34 to 38 minutes or until a long wooden pick inserted in center comes out clean. Invert cake, and let cool in pan 1 hour. Remove cake from pan to a wire rack, and let cool completely (about 30 minutes). Cut cake horizontally into 3 equal rounds.
6. Spread Lemon Curd Filling between layers, leaving a ½-inch border. Cover and chill 1 hour.
7. Spread Cream Cheese Frosting on top and sides of cake. Garnish, if desired.

Lemon Curd Filling:
MAKES 1¼ CUPS; PREP: 5 MIN.

1 (10-oz.) jar lemon curd
⅓ cup sour cream

1. Stir together all ingredients until blended. Cover and chill until ready to use.
Note: For testing purposes only, we used Dickinson's Lemon Curd.

Cream Cheese Frosting:

MAKES ABOUT 3 CUPS; **PREP:** 10 MIN.

Purchase two boxes of powdered sugar to get the 5 cups called for in this recipe.

1 (8-oz.) package cream cheese, softened
3 Tbsp. butter, softened
1 Tbsp. fresh lemon juice
1½ tsp. vanilla extract
5 cups powdered sugar

1. Beat cream cheese and butter at medium speed with an electric mixer until creamy; add lemon juice and vanilla, beating just until blended. Gradually add powdered sugar, beating at low speed until blended.

Lemon Curd-Filled Angel Food Cupcakes: Prepare recipe as directed through Step 3. Arrange 12 (2½- x 2-inch) muffin-size paper baking molds* on an aluminum foil-lined baking sheet; spoon batter into baking molds, filling almost completely full. Bake at 375° for 17 to 19 minutes or until a long wooden pick inserted in centers comes out clean. Transfer to a wire rack, and cool completely (about 1 hour). Make a small hole in top of each cupcake using the handle of a wooden spoon. Spoon Lemon Curd Filling into a zip-top plastic freezer bag. Snip 1 corner of bag to make a tiny hole. Pipe a generous amount of filling into each cupcake. Spread Cream Cheese Frosting on tops of cupcakes. Garnish, if desired. Makes 12 cupcakes; Prep: 30 min., Bake: 17 min., Cool: 1 hr.
*15 jumbo aluminum foil baking cups may be substituted. Place baking cups directly on an aluminum foil-lined baking sheet; fill cups, and proceed as directed.
Note: For testing purposes only, we used mini round pans and Reynolds Jumbo Baking Cups.

SO SOUTHERN

Nesting Instinct

Decorate your Easter table with a speckled surprise. For an authentic robin's egg look, use a toothbrush to add delicate markings with brown craft paint.

For tea-stained eggs, add 2 tea bags to a glass of hot water, and allow to steep. Lower egg into water for several minutes until desired color is reached. Set aside to dry.

For blue eggs, combine 1 drop of blue food coloring with 1 drop of green food coloring in a glass of water. Feel free to play with different amounts of food coloring to adjust the color. Lower egg into water and set aside to dry.

To speckle eggs, we used one bottle of brown craft paint and a toothbrush. Dip brush into paint and lightly splatter and dab around the egg to achieve a random, lightly dotted pattern. Allow to dry.

Easter Cookies

chef recipe • make ahead

MAKES ABOUT 2 DOZEN (3½-INCH) COOKIES; **PREP:** 25 MIN.; **CHILL:** 2 HR., 15 MIN.; **BAKE:** 14 MIN. PER BATCH; **COOL:** 35 MIN.; **STAND:** 1 HR.

Make this dough up to three days ahead.

1½ cups butter, softened
1 cup powdered sugar
¼ tsp. salt
1 tsp. vanilla extract
2¾ cups all-purpose flour, sifted
Simple Icing

1. Beat butter, sugar, and salt at medium speed with a heavy-duty electric stand mixer until creamy. Add vanilla; beat until well blended. Gradually add flour, beating at low speed until blended. (Dough will be very soft.)
2. Divide dough into 2 equal portions; wrap each with plastic wrap, and flatten into a disc. Chill 2 to 24 hours.
3. Preheat oven to 350°. Unwrap 1 dough disc on a well-floured surface. Cover with a large piece of plastic wrap, and roll to ¼-inch thickness; cut into desired shapes with 3½-inch cookie cutters. Place 1 inch apart on ungreased baking sheets. Chill 15 minutes. Repeat procedure with remaining dough disc.
4. Bake at 350° for 14 to 17 minutes or just until edges are lightly browned. Cool on baking sheets 5 minutes. Transfer to wire racks, and let cool completely (about 30 minutes). Decorate cookies with Simple Icing. Let stand 1 hour or until icing is firm.

Simple Icing:

MAKES ABOUT 2¼ CUPS; **PREP:** 10 MIN.

6 cups powdered sugar
2 Tbsp. meringue powder
½ tsp. lemon juice
Food coloring paste or drops

1. Whisk together first 3 ingredients and 6 to 8 Tbsp. water until smooth. Divide mixture into 5 to 6 small bowls; tint icing in each bowl with desired food coloring paste or drops, stirring until blended.
Note: For testing purposes only, we used Wilton Meringue Powder. Meringue powder and food coloring paste can be found at crafts and cake-decorating stores.

Pasta We Love

Put back that jar of spaghetti sauce, and check out these smart ideas for your favorite noodles.

Let's be honest, pasta and red sauce are about as cozy as iced tea and lemon. There's nothing wrong with either combo, but both are fairly predictable. We gave the subject a flavor-filled makeover using colorful veggies. Fettuccine-Vegetable Toss and Chicken Tortellini With Asparagus and Olives are easy to make in less than 30 minutes. Serve either of these dishes with mixed greens tossed with a light vinaigrette for a pasta-perfect meal any night of the week.

Fettuccine-Vegetable Toss
fast fixin's

MAKES 6 SIDE-DISH OR 4 MAIN-DISH SERVINGS; **PREP:** 15 MIN., **COOK:** 13 MIN.

Fettuccine-Vegetable Toss is an uptown spin on classic Alfredo that doubles as a meatless main dish or hearty side. We think it's best using refrigerated fettuccine, but dried noodles will work just fine too.

1 (9-oz.) package refrigerated fettuccine*
2 carrots, cut into ¼-inch pieces (about 1 cup)
2 Tbsp. olive oil
½ (8-oz.) package sliced fresh mushrooms
1 Tbsp. finely chopped green onion
1 garlic clove, minced
2 (6-oz.) packages fresh baby spinach, thoroughly washed
1 (16-oz.) jar Alfredo sauce
¼ cup grated Asiago or Parmesan cheese
¼ cup chopped fresh basil
Salt and pepper to taste
Garnishes: chopped fresh basil, grated Asiago or Parmesan cheese, carrot ribbons

1. Prepare fettuccine according to package directions.
2. Sauté carrots in hot oil in a Dutch oven over medium-high heat 3 to 4 minutes. Stir in mushrooms, onion, and garlic, and sauté 3 to 4 minutes or until mushrooms are tender. Add spinach, and cook 2 to 3 minutes or until wilted. Stir in Alfredo sauce, cheese, basil, and hot cooked pasta, stirring just until blended. Cook 1 to 2 minutes or just until thoroughly heated. Season with salt and pepper to taste. Serve immediately. Garnish, if desired.
*½ (16-oz.) package fettuccine may be substituted.

Chicken Tortellini With Asparagus and Olives
fast fixin's

MAKES 4 TO 6 SERVINGS; **PREP:** 15 MIN., **COOK:** 11 MIN.

1 (20-oz.) package refrigerated herb-and-chicken tortellini
1 lb. fresh asparagus
¼ cup chopped green onions (about 2 onions)
2 Tbsp. olive oil
1 medium-size red bell pepper, cut into thin strips
1 (10-oz.) jar sun-dried tomato pesto
¼ cup (1 oz.) shredded Parmesan cheese
2 to 3 Tbsp. sliced ripe black olives (optional)

1. Prepare tortellini according to package directions.
2. Meanwhile, snap off and discard tough ends of asparagus. Cut asparagus into 2-inch pieces.
3. Sauté onions in hot oil in a large skillet over medium heat 1 to 2 minutes or until softened. Increase heat to medium-high, add asparagus and bell pepper, and sauté 5 to 6 minutes.
4. Stir in pesto. Cook, stirring occasionally, 2 to 3 minutes or until thoroughly heated. Remove from heat; stir in pasta, and sprinkle with Parmesan cheese and, if desired, sliced black olives. Serve immediately.

Chicken and Pasta With Vegetables: Substitute ½ (16-oz.) package farfalle (bow-tie pasta) for tortellini. Cut 1 lb. chicken breast tenders into bite-size pieces, and sprinkle with 1 tsp. salt and ½ tsp. freshly ground pepper. Sauté chicken in 2 Tbsp. hot oil in a large skillet over medium-high heat 6 to 7 minutes or until done. Proceed with recipe as directed, stirring in chicken with pasta in Step 4. Prep: 15 min., Cook: 18 min.

—**SUSAN BROWN,** STATESBORO, GEORGIA

Fizzy Drinks

Make more than you think you'll need. That's our advice for these fizzy and fabulous drinks. All you do is add a carbonated beverage, such as ginger ale or sparkling white wine, to lemonade, tea, or fruit juice mixtures. Their not-too-sweet flavors make them lovely for showers, brunches, or lazy afternoon get-togethers on the porch.

Sparkling Wine-Fruit Refresher

fast fixin's

MAKES 6 SERVINGS; **PREP:** 10 MIN.

Keep this recipe handy for your next brunch. It's a great alternative to mimosas. Another idea: Add a diced kiwifruit to your favorite mixed berries in this versatile light cocktail.

1 cup lemon-lime soft drink, chilled
1 cup assorted berries
1 (6-oz.) can frozen limeade concentrate, thawed
¼ cup loosely packed fresh mint or basil leaves, torn
1 (750-milliliter) bottle sparkling white wine or Champagne, chilled

1. Combine first 4 ingredients in a large pitcher. Gently stir in sparkling wine. Serve immediately.

— CYNTHIA GIVAN, FORT WORTH, TEXAS

Sparkling Fruit Refresher: Substitute 3 (12-oz.) cans orange-flavored sparkling water, chilled, for sparkling white wine. Proceed with recipe as directed.

Sparkling Grape Juice-Lemonade

MAKES 4 SERVINGS; **PREP:** 10 MIN.,
FREEZE: 4 HR.

Freeze grapes in clusters as purchased. This is not a girl's-only punch; it's a hit with men too.

1 bunch seedless grapes (about ⅓ lb.)
1 (750-milliliter) bottle sparkling white grape juice, chilled
¼ cup thawed frozen lemonade concentrate

1. Place grapes in a zip-top plastic freezer bag; seal bag. (Do not remove grapes from stems.) Freeze completely (about 4 hours).
2. Gently stir together grape juice and lemonade concentrate in a large pitcher. Add frozen grapes to pitcher. Serve immediately.

— JAYNE HARRINGTON, MESA, ARIZONA

Note: Grapes may be stored in freezer up to 1 week.

Party Anytime

Keep Sparkling Grape Juice-Lemonade cold with frozen grapes—they add pizzazz without diluting the flavor. Green, red, or black grapes all look great, so buy what's on sale. The freshest grapes hold tightly to the stems. To check before purchasing, very gently shake the bunch—the more grapes that fall away, the older the fruit.

White Grape-and-Orange Cooler

test kitchen favorite

MAKES: 6½ CUPS; **PREP:** 5 MIN.,
COOK: 3 MIN., **CHILL:** 2 HR.

⅓ cup sugar
1 cup white grape juice
½ cup orange juice
1 (1-liter) bottle ginger ale, chilled

1. Bring sugar and 1 cup water to a boil over medium-high heat, and cook, stirring often, 3 minutes or until sugar dissolves. Remove from heat, and cool.
2. Stir in juices, and chill 2 hours. Stir in ginger ale just before serving. Serve over ice.

Test Kitchen Idea

Ice Pop Spritzers: Place ice pops in glasses and add a carbonated beverage—that's it. For a party, offer a variety of ice-pop flavors, lemon-lime soft drinks, and sparkling fruit drinks. Let guests mix and match. Our Food staff especially liked strawberry-kiwi ice pops with lemon-lime soft drink, lime pops with blackberry-flavored sparkling fruit drink, and tropical fruit bars with clementine-flavored sparkling fruit drink.

Healthy Living®

Take advantage of longer days and warmer evenings to cook dinner outside.
And discover some great recipes that use nature's most perfect sweetener on page 84.

Good-for-You Grilling

Get outside and enjoy this lightened menu that begins and ends on the grill.

Guilt-Free Supper

SERVES 6

Flank Steak With Radish Salsa

Balsamic Grilled Veggies

Italian-Herb Bread

Slightly Sweet Tea

Grilled Banana Splits

Flank Steak With Radish Salsa

fast fixin's

MAKES 6 SERVINGS; **PREP:** 5 MIN.,
GRILL: 16 MIN., **STAND:** 5 MIN.

1 (2-lb.) flank steak
1 Tbsp. Montreal steak seasoning
Radish Salsa
Garnishes: lime wedges, fresh cilantro
    sprigs, radish quarters, cucumber slices

1. Preheat grill to 350° to 400° (medium-high) heat. Sprinkle both sides of steak with seasoning. Grill steak, covered with grill lid, 8 minutes on each side or to desired degree of doneness. Remove from grill, and cover steak with aluminum foil; let stand 5 minutes. Uncover and cut steak diagonally across the grain into thin slices. Serve with Radish Salsa. Garnish, if desired.

Note: For testing purposes only, we used McCormick Grill Mates Montreal Steak Seasoning.

Per serving (including ⅓ cup salsa, not garnishes): Calories 236; Fat 10.6g (sat 4.3g, mono 4.2g, poly 0.4g); Protein 31.4g; Carb 1.7g; Fiber 0.5g; Chol 57mg; Iron 2.2mg; Sodium 501mg; Calc 31mg

---

Radish Salsa:

MAKES ABOUT 2 CUPS; **PREP:** 10 MIN.,
CHILL: 2 HRS.

This recipe easily doubles. Serve it over grilled burgers, spoon it into tacos, or offer it as an appetizer with baked chips.

6 large radishes, grated
1 large cucumber, peeled, seeded, and
    chopped
¼ cup chopped fresh cilantro
1 garlic clove, pressed
1 Tbsp. fresh lime juice
¼ tsp. salt

1. Toss together all ingredients. Cover and chill up to 2 hours. Season with salt to taste.

Per ⅓ cup (not including salt to taste): Calories 9; Fat 0.1g (sat 0g, mono 0g, poly 0g); Protein 0.4g; Carb 1.7g; Fiber 0.5g; Chol 0mg; Iron 0.2mg; Sodium 102mg; Calc 11mg

---

Eco-Friendly Grilling

- When lighting a charcoal grill, use natural coals free of chemicals, such as Wild Oats or Cowboy brands found at major supermarkets and home-improvement centers. Your food will taste better, and you'll be protecting the environment.
- Lighting natural charcoal is a breeze when you use a charcoal chimney, found at most hardware stores. Instead of newspaper, we used Weber FireStarter lighter cubes for faster flames, which are smokeless and environmentally safe. Simply place them on the bottom grill rack, light them, and place the charcoal-filled chimney over them. Once the coals heat up and turn ashy in color, they're ready for grilling. Look for lighter cubes at home-improvement stores, or visit www.weber.com.

Balsamic Grilled Veggies

MAKES 6 SERVINGS; **PREP:** 20 MIN.,
GRILL: 25 MIN.

2 Tbsp. olive oil
1 Tbsp. dried or ¼ cup chopped fresh basil
1 Tbsp. balsamic vinegar
2 tsp. kosher or 1½ tsp. table salt
1 tsp. pepper
1 fennel bulb
1 large red onion, cut into 1-inch pieces
1 (8-oz.) package fresh mushrooms
1 pt. cherry tomatoes
2 medium zucchini, cut into 1-inch pieces
4 small yellow squash, cut into 1-inch pieces

1. Preheat grill to 350° to 400° (medium-high) heat. Stir together olive oil and next 4 ingredients in a small bowl.
2. Rinse fennel thoroughly. Trim and discard root end of fennel bulb. Trim stalks from bulb, reserving fronds for another use. Cut bulb in half vertically, and remove core. Cut bulb into ½-inch-thick slices.
3. Toss fennel, onion, and mushrooms with half of olive oil mixture, and place in a grill wok or metal basket.
4. Grill, covered with grill lid, 10 minutes over 350° to 400° (medium-high) heat. Toss tomatoes, zucchini, and yellow squash with remaining olive oil mixture. Add to grill wok or basket. Grill, covered with grill lid, stirring occasionally, 10 to 15 minutes or until vegetables are tender. Serve vegetables immediately.

Per serving: Calories 110; Fat 5.2g (sat 0.7g, mono 3.6g, poly 0.6g); Protein 4.5g; Carb 14.4g; Fiber 4.6g; Chol 0mg; Iron 1.5mg; Sodium 680mg; Calc 68mg

Italian-Herb Bread

family favorite • fast fixin's

MAKES 6 SERVINGS; PREP: 10 MIN.,
GRILL: 5 MIN.

6 (1-inch-thick) Italian bread slices
2 Tbsp. olive oil
1 tsp. dried Italian seasoning
½ tsp. kosher or table salt
½ tsp. freshly ground pepper

1. Preheat grill to 350° to 400° (medium-high) heat. Brush 1 side of each bread slice with olive oil; sprinkle with Italian seasoning, salt, and pepper. Grill bread slices, seasoned sides down, covered with grill lid, 4 to 5 minutes or until toasted.

Per slice: Calories 97; Fat 5.4g (sat 0.8g, mono 3.8g, poly 0.7g); Protein 1.8g; Carb 10.3g; Fiber 0.7g; Chol 0mg; Iron 0.7mg; Sodium 277mg; Calc 21mg

Slightly Sweet Tea

MAKES ABOUT 2 QT.; PREP: 10 MIN.,
COOK: 5 MIN., STEEP: 10 MIN.

4 cups water
7 green tea bags
½ cup honey
4 cups cold water
1 navel orange, cut into wedges
1 lime, cut into wedges

1. Bring 4 cups water to a boil in a medium saucepan; add tea bags. Boil 1 minute; remove from heat. Cover and steep 10 minutes. Remove and discard tea bags.
2. Stir in honey. Pour into a 2-qt. pitcher; stir in 4 cups cold water and orange and lime wedges. Serve over ice.
Note: For testing purposes only, we used Bigelow Green Tea.

Per cup: Calories 68; Fat 0g (sat 0g, mono 0g, poly 0g); Protein 0.1g; Carb 18.6g; Fiber 0.3g; Chol 0mg; Iron 0.1mg; Sodium 1mg; Calc 4mg

Grilled Banana Splits

MAKES 6 SERVINGS; PREP: 15 MIN.,
BAKE: 7 MIN., GRILL: 8 MIN.

Choose baby bananas (also known as Oritos, Lady Fingers, and Manzanos) or small bananas that are just ripe and still firm so they'll hold their shape on the grill.

Vegetable cooking spray
¼ cup chopped pecans
¼ cup sweetened flaked coconut
6 unpeeled baby or small bananas with green tips*
6 fresh pineapple slices**
1 pt. fat-free vanilla ice cream
1 pt. low-fat chocolate frozen yogurt
Chocolate Sauce
Garnish: maraschino cherries

1. Coat cold cooking grate of grill with cooking spray. Preheat grill to 300° to 350° (medium) heat.
2. Preheat oven to 350°. Place pecans in a single layer in a shallow pan. Place coconut in a single layer in another shallow pan. Bake pecans and coconut 7 to 8 minutes or until toasted and pecans are fragrant, stirring occasionally.
3. Peel bananas, and cut in half lengthwise. Coat bananas with cooking spray. Grill pineapple slices, covered with grill lid, over 300° to 350° (medium) heat 4 minutes on each side or until lightly caramelized. Grill banana halves 1 to 2 minutes on each side or until lightly caramelized.
4. Chop grilled pineapple. Arrange 2 grilled banana halves in each of 6 (8-oz.) banana-split dishes or other serving bowls. Scoop ¼ cup vanilla ice cream and ¼ cup chocolate frozen yogurt into each dish between banana slices. Top each with 1 Tbsp. Chocolate Sauce, 1 chopped pineapple slice, 2 tsp. pecans, and 2 tsp. coconut. Garnish, if desired. Serve immediately.
*3 regular bananas, peeled and quartered, may be substituted. Increase grilling time to 4 minutes on each side.
**Canned pineapple slices in juice, drained, may be substituted.
Note: If using a charcoal grill, place banana slices around the outer edge of grill to prevent burning. Watch them carefully as they will cook fast.

Per serving (including about 1 Tbsp. Chocolate Sauce, not garnish): Calories 336; Fat 8.5g (sat 3.5g, mono 2.5g, poly 1.2g); Protein 7.9g; Carb 63.4g; Fiber 3.8g; Chol 5mg; Iron 1.2mg; Sodium 74mg; Calc 187mg

Chocolate Sauce:

MAKES ABOUT ⅓ CUP; PREP: 5 MIN.

2 (0.78-oz.) dark chocolate bars, broken into pieces
¼ cup 1% low-fat milk

1. Microwave chocolate and milk in a small microwave-safe bowl at HIGH 30 to 45 seconds or until chocolate is melted. Stir until mixture is smooth.
Note: For testing purposes only, we used CocoaVia Original Chocolate Bars.

Per serving (about 1 Tbsp.): Calories 41; Fat 2.6g (sat 1.5g, mono 0g, poly 0g); Protein 0.7g; Carb 5.1g; Fiber 0.4g; Chol 1.3mg; Iron 0.3mg; Sodium 5mg; Calc 23mg

Nature's Sugar Substitute

It's not just for biscuits anymore. Stir up these recipes to take advantage of honey's powerful benefits.

Not all sugars are created equal. Honey may be nature's most perfect. Not only does it sweeten our lives, but unprocessed honey (the kind you find from a beekeeper at your local farmers market) is also packed with powerful cancer-fighting antioxidants that help protect cells.

Zesty Honey-Lemon Dressing

fast fixin's • make ahead

MAKES ABOUT ¾ CUP; **PREP:** 10 MIN.

Serve this dressing over fresh garden greens or drizzle over steamed green beans, asparagus, or broccoli.

1 Tbsp. chopped fresh parsley
3 Tbsp. honey
1 tsp. lemon zest
4 Tbsp. fresh lemon juice
2 tsp. Dijon mustard
1 garlic clove, pressed
½ tsp. salt
½ tsp. pepper
⅓ cup olive oil

1. Whisk together chopped fresh parsley and next 7 ingredients in a small bowl. Add oil in a slow, steady stream, whisking constantly until smooth. Use immediately, or store in an airtight container in refrigerator up to 5 days. If chilled, let stand at room temperature 15 minutes. Whisk before serving.

Per 1 Tbsp.: Calories 75; Fat 6.2g (sat 0.9g, mono 4.8g, poly 0.6g); Protein 0.1g; Carb 5.1g; Fiber 0.1g; Chol 0mg; Iron 0.1mg; Sodium 117mg; Calc 2mg

Sweet-'n'-Salty Honey Cheese Spread

fast fixin's

MAKES 10 APPETIZER SERVINGS;
PREP: 10 MIN.

1 (10.5-oz.) goat cheese log
½ cup roasted, salted sunflower seeds
⅓ cup honey
1 pt. fresh raspberries, blackberries, or blueberries
Garnish: fresh mint leaves
Assorted crackers

A Toast to Local Honey

Like wine, there are many varieties of honey. The color, flavor, and texture all depend on the type of flower nectar the bees use to make the honey. Tupelo is a Southern favorite, produced only in Northwest Florida, while clover, alfalfa, heather, and acacia are among the more common flavors. But bees will visit almost any nearby blooming plants, including herbs. Also like wine, when it comes to color, the deeper the hue, the deeper the flavor. Colors range from clear to amber to almost black. Taste some from your area. You'll reap the health rewards while supporting the ecosystem. Get started at www.honeylocator.com.

1. Press or roll goat cheese log in sunflower seeds, thoroughly covering cheese, including ends. Arrange cheese on a serving platter with any remaining sunflower seeds. Drizzle with honey. Sprinkle with berries. Garnish, if desired. Serve immediately with assorted crackers.

—**BUFFY HARGETT**, BIRMINGHAM, ALABAMA

Per serving (with raspberries): Calories 197; Fat 12.6g (sat 6.5g, mono 2.7g, poly 2.7g); Protein 8.4g; Carb 14.4g; Fiber 2.4 g; Chol 24mg; Iron 1.2mg; Sodium 154mg; Calc 104mg

Beekeeper's Jezebel Sauce

MAKES ABOUT 1½ CUPS; **PREP:** 10 MIN.,
COOK: 4 MIN.

This sweet-and-spicy sauce is delicious served with pork tenderloin and grilled chicken or as a dipping sauce for fried shrimp. It also makes a great savory spread for biscuits or roast beef and turkey sandwiches.

1 (15.25-oz.) jar apricot preserves
¼ cup fat-free chicken broth*
¼ cup honey
3 Tbsp. horseradish
1 Tbsp. chopped fresh parsley
2 Tbsp. Dijon mustard
1 tsp. chopped fresh thyme
¼ tsp. dried crushed red pepper

1. Whisk together all ingredients in a small saucepan. Cook over medium heat, whisking frequently, 3 to 4 minutes or until thoroughly heated and sauce is a pourable consistency. Use immediately, or store in an airtight container in refrigerator up to 1 week.

—**ROSE MARIE CROWE**, TRUSSVILLE, ALABAMA

*Vegetable broth may be substituted.
Note: For testing purposes only, we used Polaner All Fruit Apricot Spread.
Note: To make a spread, prepare recipe as directed, omitting chicken broth. Use immediately, or store in an airtight container up to 1 week.

Per ¼ cup: Calories 232; Fat 0.1g (sat 0g, mono 0g, poly 0g); Protein 0.2g; Carb 60.4g; Fiber 0.3g; Chol 0mg; Iron 0.2mg; Sodium 165mg; Calc 7mg

Strawberries: They're Here!

One taste of April's debut fruit, and we're ready to get in the kitchen. How about you?

Sneak one from the carton, take a bite, and imagine them topping pillow-soft Cornmeal Shortcakes, tossed in a delicate salad paired with cheese and fresh basil, or dipped in a salty-sweet caramel mixture.

Strawberry-Fruit Toss With Cornmeal Shortcakes
family favorite

MAKES 6 SERVINGS; **PREP:** 30 MIN., **STAND:** 15 MIN.

Shortcut: Bake frozen biscuits to use in place of the shortcakes. The fruit mixture is also a great topper for ice cream or pound cake. (Pictured on page 167)

1 (16-oz.) container fresh strawberries, sliced
1 cup chopped fresh pineapple
2 kiwifruit, peeled and chopped
¼ cup sugar
1 Tbsp. chopped fresh mint
½ tsp. lime zest
1 Tbsp. fresh lime juice
½ cup whipping cream
1 tsp. sugar
Cornmeal Shortcakes, warm

1. Combine first 7 ingredients; let mixture stand 15 minutes, gently stirring after 7 minutes.
2. Beat whipping cream and 1 tsp. sugar at medium speed with an electric mixer until soft peaks form. Use immediately, or cover and chill up to 2 hours.
3. Place warm Cornmeal Shortcakes on dessert plates, and spoon strawberry mixture over shortcakes. Serve immediately with whipped cream. Or, if desired, split shortcakes, and place one half on each dessert plate. Spoon strawberry mixture over shortcake halves; top with whipped cream and remaining shortcake halves. Serve immediately.

Cornmeal Shortcakes:

MAKES 6 SERVINGS; **PREP:** 15 MIN., **BAKE:** 18 MIN.

One Test Kitchen staffer who's an avid baker proclaimed she was "in love with this dough." It's easy to work with, stays moist, and melts in your mouth. We give a range on bake time because oven temperatures vary.

1¾ cups all-purpose flour
¼ cup plain yellow cornmeal
6 Tbsp. cold butter, cut into pieces
1½ tsp. baking powder
½ tsp. salt
¼ tsp. lemon zest
2 Tbsp. sugar, divided
1 large egg, lightly beaten
⅔ cup whipping cream
1 Tbsp. butter, melted
1½ tsp. sugar

1. Preheat oven to 425°. Combine first 7 ingredients in a food processor. Process mixture 20 seconds or until mixture resembles coarse sand. Transfer mixture to a large bowl.
2. Whisk together egg and cream; add to flour mixture, stirring just until dry ingredients are moistened and a dough forms.
3. Turn dough out onto a lightly floured surface, and knead 3 to 4 times.
4. Transfer dough to a lightly greased baking sheet. Pat or roll dough into a 6-inch circle. Cut into 6 wedges; gently separate wedges by 1 inch. Brush tops with melted butter. Sprinkle with 1½ tsp. sugar.
5. Bake at 425° for 18 to 23 minutes or until golden and firm to touch.

• TIPS •

Buy the best strawberries and keep them fresh with these pointers from our Test Kitchen pros.

Selection:
- A ripe berry will have a shiny, deep red color from the tip of the berry to beneath the green cap. It will be sweeter and juicier than those with white or green beneath the cap.
- Check the carton from top to bottom for any damaged or moldy fruit. They'll cause the others to deteriorate quickly.

Storing:
- Sort when you get home. Remove and discard any bruised berries you didn't see when purchasing. Don't wash. Return berries to the carton or place in a colander, uncovered. You want air to circulate around the fruit.
- Flavor starts to fade after two days of refrigeration

Cleaning:
- Wash just before using. Don't remove the green caps before washing. (Water will seep into the berry, softening the texture and weakening the flavor.) Pat dry with paper towels.

Prep Step

Before you slice, cut in half, puree, or chop strawberries for a recipe you should "hull." This term means removing the leaves and tiny core beneath the cap of the berry. A paring knife will do it, but be careful not to remove too much fruit. To use a tweezer-like strawberry huller (available at kitchen shops), pinch the berry right beneath the cap and twist.

Strawberry-Turkey-Brie Panini

MAKES 4 SERVINGS; **PREP:** 15 MIN.,
COOK: 3 MIN. PER BATCH

1 (8-oz.) Brie round
8 Italian bread slices
8 oz. thinly sliced smoked turkey
8 fresh basil leaves
½ cup sliced fresh strawberries
2 Tbsp. red pepper jelly
2 Tbsp. butter, melted
Garnish: strawberry halves

1. Trim and discard rind from Brie. Cut Brie into ½-inch-thick slices. Layer 4 bread slices evenly with turkey, basil leaves, strawberries, and Brie.
2. Spread 1½ tsp. pepper jelly on 1 side of each of remaining 4 bread slices; place bread slices, jelly sides down, on top of Brie. Brush sandwiches with melted butter.
3. Cook sandwiches, in batches, in a preheated panini press 2 to 3 minutes or until golden brown. Garnish, if desired.
Note: For testing purposes only, we used Braswell's Red Pepper Jelly. To prepare sandwiches without a panini press, cook in a preheated grill pan over medium-high heat 2 to 3 minutes on each side or until golden.

Tangy Berries-and-Cheese Salad

fast fixin's

MAKES 4 SERVINGS; **PREP:** 10 MIN.,
BAKE: 5 MIN.

Strawberries available early in the season are often small ones from Florida. Leave them whole in this salad. Later in the season, the berries will be bigger. Cut those in half.

¼ cup slivered almonds
2 Tbsp. olive oil
2 Tbsp. white balsamic vinegar
¼ tsp. salt
⅛ tsp. coarsely ground pepper
1 Tbsp. thinly sliced fresh basil
1 (5-oz.) package mâche (about 4 cups), thoroughly washed*
1½ cups fresh strawberries, cut in half
½ cup crumbled farmer's cheese**

1. Preheat oven to 350°. Bake almonds in a single layer in a shallow pan 5 to 7 minutes or until toasted and fragrant.
2. Whisk together oil and next 3 ingredients in a bowl; stir in basil. Add mâche; toss to combine. Top with strawberries, farmer's cheese, and toasted almonds. Serve immediately.
*4 cups Bibb lettuce may be substituted.
**Queso fresco may be substituted.

Salted Caramel Strawberries

fast fixin's • make ahead

MAKES 20; **PREP:** 15 MIN., **STAND:** 15 MIN.

Once washed, pat strawberries dry with paper towels. Caramel mixture will not stick to wet strawberries.

20 large fresh strawberries
40 caramels
3 Tbsp. whipping cream
¼ tsp. salt
1¼ cups coarsely chopped mixed nuts
Wax paper

1. Pat strawberries completely dry with paper towels.
2. Microwave caramels, 3 Tbsp. whipping cream, and ¼ tsp. salt in a 1-qt. microwave-safe bowl at MEDIUM (50% power) 3½ minutes or until smooth, stirring at 1-minute intervals.
3. Dip each strawberry halfway into caramel mixture. Roll in nuts, and place on lightly greased wax paper. Let stand 15 minutes. Serve immediately, or cover and chill up to 8 hours.
Note: For testing purposes only, we used Kraft Caramels and Planters NUTrition Heart Healthy Mix.

Strawberries Romanoff Pancakes With Brown Sugar-Sour Cream Sauce

MAKES 4 SERVINGS; **PREP:** 20 MIN.,
CHILL: 30 MIN., **STAND:** 30 MIN.

"Romanoff" is defined as a dessert of strawberries soaked in orange juice and liqueur and topped with whipped cream. Our spin is a sauce inspired by the simple idea of dipping berries in sour cream, then brown sugar, and eating immediately.

2 (16-oz.) containers fresh strawberries, sliced (about 6 cups)
⅓ cup granulated sugar
2 Tbsp. orange liqueur*
1 cup sour cream
3 Tbsp. brown sugar
Angela's Pancakes

1. Stir together first 3 ingredients. Cover and let stand 30 minutes.
2. Meanwhile, stir together sour cream and brown sugar. Cover and chill 30 minutes.
3. Stack pancakes on individual plates. Top with strawberry mixture, and dollop with sour cream mixture. Serve immediately.
*Orange juice may be substituted.

Reinvent leftovers: To make a wonderful shake, puree remaining strawberry mixture in a blender. Add vanilla ice cream and milk, and blend to desired thickness.

Angela's Pancakes:
MAKES ABOUT 18 (2½-INCH) PANCAKES; PREP: 15 MIN., STAND: 3 MIN., COOK: 4 MIN. PER BATCH

Stand time allows the pancake mixture to thicken and activates the baking soda for light, fluffy results.

1 cup cake flour
1 tsp. baking soda
1 tsp. sugar
1 tsp. orange zest
½ tsp. salt
¾ cup buttermilk
¼ cup milk
1 large egg, lightly beaten
2 Tbsp. butter, melted

1. Combine first 5 ingredients in a large bowl. Whisk together buttermilk, milk, egg, and melted butter; whisk into flour mixture just until blended. Let stand 3 minutes.
2. Pour about ⅛ cup batter for each pancake onto a hot (350°) lightly greased griddle or large nonstick skillet over medium heat. Cook pancakes 2 minutes or until tops are covered with bubbles and edges look dry and cooked. Turn and cook 2 more minutes. Keep pancakes warm in a 200° oven up to 30 minutes.

Free-form Strawberry Cheesecake
family favorite • fast fixin's
MAKES 6 SERVINGS; PREP: 20 MIN.

Powdered sugar dissolves almost instantly when stirred into berries, while granulated sugar needs stand time. We chose powdered for this quick-to-put-together recipe. (Pictured on page 166)

2 cups fresh strawberries, sliced
4 Tbsp. powdered sugar, divided
1½ cups ready-to-eat cheesecake filling
1 tsp. lime zest
1 Tbsp. lime juice
6 crisp gourmet cookies, crumbled
Garnishes: crisp gourmet cookies, lime slices

1. Stir together strawberries and 2 Tbsp. powdered sugar.
2. Stir together cheesecake filling, lime zest, lime juice, and remaining 2 Tbsp. powdered sugar.
3. Spoon cheesecake mixture into 6 (6-oz.) glasses or ramekins. Sprinkle with crumbled cookies. Top with strawberries. Garnish, if desired. Serve immediately.
Note: For testing purposes only, we used Philadelphia Ready-To-Eat Cheesecake Filling and Biscoff cookies.

Grown-up Ground Beef

We paired deliciously bold tastes with a kitchen staple to come up with these creative combinations.

Parmesan-and-Mushroom-Stuffed Meatloaf
family favorite • make ahead
MAKES 6 SERVINGS; PREP: 30 MIN., COOK: 5 MIN., BAKE: 1 HR., STAND: 10 MIN.

2 Tbsp. butter
1 (8-oz.) package sliced fresh mushrooms
1 shallot, finely chopped
1 garlic clove, minced
1½ lb. ground round
½ cup Italian-seasoned breadcrumbs
½ cup grated Parmesan cheese
¼ cup milk
1 large egg, beaten
1 tsp. salt
¼ tsp. freshly ground pepper
Wax paper
1½ cups (6 oz.) shredded Italian six-cheese blend
¾ cup sun-dried tomatoes in oil, well drained
1 (10½-oz.) container refrigerated bruschetta topping

1. Preheat oven to 350°. Melt butter in a nonstick skillet over medium heat; add mushrooms, shallot, and garlic, and sauté 5 minutes or until tender.
2. Gently stir together ground round and next 6 ingredients in a large bowl just until combined. Shape mixture into a 14- x 10-inch rectangle on a sheet of wax paper. Top with mushroom mixture, cheese, and tomatoes, leaving a 1½-inch border on all sides. Roll up, jelly-roll fashion, starting at 1 long side and using wax paper as a guide. Place meatloaf roll, seam side down, in a lightly greased 15- x 10-inch jelly-roll pan.
3. Bake at 350° for 1 hour or until center is no longer pink. Remove from oven, and top with bruschetta topping. Let stand 10 minutes before slicing.

— JENELLE PICKETT, LOCUST GROVE, ARKANSAS

Note: For testing purposes only, we used Buitoni Refrigerated Classic Bruschetta topping. To make ahead, prepare recipe as directed through Step 2. Cover and chill 8 hours. Let stand at room temperature 15 minutes. Proceed with recipe as directed.

Tomato 'n' Beef Casserole With Polenta Crust

MAKES 6 SERVINGS; **PREP:** 20 MIN.,
COOK: 35 MIN., **BAKE:** 30 MIN.
(Pictured on page 173)

1 tsp. salt
1 cup plain yellow cornmeal
½ tsp. Montreal steak seasoning
1 cup (4 oz.) shredded sharp Cheddar
    cheese, divided
1 lb. ground chuck
1 cup chopped onion
1 medium zucchini, cut in half lengthwise
    and sliced (about 2 cups)
1 Tbsp. olive oil
2 (14½-oz.) can petite diced tomatoes, drained
1 (6-oz.) can tomato paste
2 Tbsp. chopped fresh flat-leaf parsley

1. Preheat oven to 350°. Bring 3 cups
water and 1 tsp. salt to a boil in a 2-qt.
saucepan over medium-high heat. Whisk
in cornmeal; reduce heat to low, and
simmer, whisking constantly, 3 minutes
or until thickened. Remove from heat,
and stir in steak seasoning and ¼ cup
Cheddar cheese. Spread mixture into a
lightly greased 11- x 7-inch baking dish.
2. Brown ground chuck in a large nonstick skillet over medium-high heat,
stirring often, 10 minutes or until meat
crumbles and is no longer pink; drain
and transfer to a bowl.
3. Sauté onion and zucchini in hot oil
in skillet over medium heat 5 minutes
or until crisp-tender. Stir in beef, tomatoes, and tomato paste; simmer, stirring
often, 10 minutes. Pour beef mixture
over cornmeal crust. Sprinkle with
remaining ¾ cup cheese.
4. Bake at 350° for 30 minutes or until
bubbly. Sprinkle casserole with parsley
just before serving.

— **KATHY GIZZI**, ROTONDA WEST, FLORIDA

**Italian Beef Casserole With
Polenta Crust:** Substitute Italian
sausage for ground chuck and Italian
six-cheese blend for Cheddar cheese.
Prepare recipe as directed, sautéing 1 medium-size green bell pepper,
chopped, with onion in Step 3.

Celebrate With Style

This family's popular menu for Passover is ideal for your
spring get-together.

Festive gatherings around the
table, highlighted by great
food and lively conversation,
are a Southern tradition.
Reader Marlene Shapiro's
Passover brunch is no exception. This
Birmingham resident was delighted to
open her door and share a few updated
favorites served at the annual event. So
treat your family to these creative gems.
They'll make any occasion special.

Passover Menu

SERVES 8 TO 10

Mini Salmon Croquettes

Thin Potato Kugel

Flourless Peanut Butter-Chocolate
Cookies

Chocolate-Pecan Meringues

Mini Salmon Croquettes
make ahead

MAKES 14 CROQUETTES; **PREP:** 25 MIN.,
COOK: 12 MIN.

2 (14.75-oz.) cans pink salmon
½ cup finely chopped yellow onion
2 Tbsp. chopped fresh parsley
1 Tbsp. lemon zest
2 tsp. fresh lemon juice
1 tsp. salt
1 tsp. pepper
2 large eggs, lightly beaten
½ cup unsalted matzo meal
¾ cup olive oil
Kosher salt (optional)
Mixed baby salad greens
Lemon-Dill Sauce
Thin Potato Kugel (optional)

1. Drain salmon, remove skin and
bones, and flake. Place salmon in a
large bowl. Add onion and next 5 ingredients. Stir in eggs and matzo meal.
(Batter will be wet.)
2. Shape salmon mixture into
14 (1-inch-thick, 2-inch-wide) patties.
3. Cook, in 2 batches, in hot oil in
a large skillet over medium-high
heat 2 to 3 minutes on each side
or until golden brown and crispy.
Drain on a paper towel-lined wire rack.
Sprinkle with kosher salt, if desired.
Serve immediately over mixed baby
salad greens with Lemon-Dill Sauce
and, if desired, Thin Potato Kugel.

— **MARLENE SHAPIRO**, BIRMINGHAM, ALABAMA

To Make Ahead: Prepare recipe as
directed through Step 2. Place patties
in a lightly greased aluminum foil-lined
pan. Cover and chill 24 hours. Let
stand at room temperature 10 minutes.
Proceed with recipe as directed.

Lemon-Dill Sauce:

MAKES ABOUT 1 CUP; PREP: 10 MIN.

½ cup sour cream
½ cup mayonnaise
2 Tbsp. drained capers
4 tsp. chopped fresh dill
1½ tsp. lemon zest
4 tsp. fresh lemon juice
1 tsp. white wine vinegar
Kosher salt to taste

1. Pulse first 7 ingredients in a food processor 2 to 3 times or until smooth, stopping to scrape down sides as needed. Season with salt to taste.

—MARLENE SHAPIRO, BIRMINGHAM, ALABAMA

Thin Potato Kugel
make ahead

MAKES 8 TO 10 SERVINGS; PREP: 20 MIN.,
BAKE: 30 MIN., COOL: 5 MIN.

We recommend thoroughly washing and scrubbing potatoes before peeling to remove any dirt or grit.

4 medium-size baking potatoes
    (about 2 lb.), peeled
1 medium onion, peeled
2 large carrots, peeled
1 Tbsp. lemon juice
2 Tbsp. olive oil
3 large eggs
1¼ tsp. salt
¼ tsp. ground white pepper
¼ tsp. paprika
⅓ cup unsalted matzo meal

1. Preheat oven to 425°. Grate potato, onion, and carrot through large holes of a box grater; toss with lemon juice. Spread mixture onto layers of paper towels or a cloth towel. Roll up towel, starting at 1 short side. Squeeze towel to absorb excess liquid. Place potato mixture in a large bowl.
2. Brush olive oil on bottom and up sides of a 15- x 10-inch jelly-roll pan. Heat pan in 425° oven 5 minutes.
3. Meanwhile, whisk together eggs and next 3 ingredients in a small bowl. Place

matzo meal in a fine wire-mesh strainer. Rinse matzo meal under running water, shaking strainer gently until mixture forms a ball. Whisk into egg mixture.
4. Stir egg mixture into potato mixture until well combined. Carefully spoon potato mixture into hot jelly-roll pan. Press mixture in an even layer, using a spatula.
5. Bake at 425° for 30 to 35 minutes or until golden brown and crisp. Remove from oven to wire rack, and let cool 5 minutes. Cut into pieces before serving.

—MARLENE SHAPIRO, BIRMINGHAM, ALABAMA

Note: Thin Potato Kugel can be made ahead. Prepare as directed, and cover and chill up to 2 days.

Thin Sweet Potato Kugel:

Substitute 4 medium-size sweet potatoes (about 2 lb.) for baking potatoes. Omit lemon juice. Proceed with recipe as directed, whisking ¼ tsp. ground thyme into eggs in Step 3.

Flourless Peanut Butter-Chocolate Cookies

MAKES 2 DOZEN; PREP: 10 MIN.,
BAKE: 12 MIN. PER BATCH, COOL: 20 MIN.

1 cup creamy peanut butter
¾ cup sugar
1 large egg
½ tsp. baking soda
¼ tsp. salt
1 cup semisweet chocolate morsels
Parchment paper

1. Preheat oven to 350°. Stir together first 5 ingredients in medium bowl until well blended. Stir in chocolate morsels.
2. Drop dough by rounded tablespoonfuls 2 inches apart onto parchment paper-lined baking sheets.
3. Bake at 350° for 12 to 14 minutes or until puffed and lightly browned. Cool on baking sheets on a wire rack 5 minutes. Remove to wire rack, and let cool 15 minutes.

—MINDI SHAPIRO LEVINE, BIRMINGHAM, ALABAMA

Chocolate-Pecan Meringues
make ahead

MAKES ABOUT 3 DOZEN; PREP: 20 MIN.;
BAKE: 1 HR., 45 MIN.; COOL: 30 MIN.

4 egg whites
¼ tsp. cream of tartar
¼ tsp. vanilla extract
1 cup sugar
¼ tsp. salt
⅓ cup semisweet chocolate morsels
⅓ cup finely chopped pecans
Parchment paper

1. Preheat oven to 225°. Beat first 3 ingredients at high speed with an electric mixer until foamy. Gradually add sugar and salt, beating until stiff peaks form. Gently fold in chocolate morsels and pecans.
2. Drop meringue mixture by tablespoonfuls 1 inch apart onto 2 parchment paper-lined baking sheets.
3. Bake at 225° for 1 hour, placing 1 pan on middle oven rack and other on lower oven rack. Switch pans, and bake 45 minutes or until meringues are dry but not browned. Cool completely on baking sheets on a wire rack (about 30 minutes). Store in an airtight container up to 1 week.

— MINDI SHAPIRO LEVINE, BIRMINGHAM, ALABAMA

Fix It Fast

Tips and tricks for fabulous fish.

Flash in the Pan When you're in the mood for a great-tasting meal, but short on time, pick up some fish fillets. They're as quick and easy to cook as boneless chicken breasts and almost as versatile. In fact, many of the same cooking methods and dry seasoning blends used for chicken work equally well with fish.

It takes just 3 to 4 minutes to sauté thin fillets in a hot skillet. (A general rule is to cook fish about 7 to 10 minutes per inch of thickness.) Use a well-seasoned cast-iron or nonstick skillet, and turn the pieces only once—the first side down gets the crispest. Baked or broiled fillets don't need to be turned at all. To check for doneness, slip a small knife under the fish and gently lift. When fully cooked, the fillet will begin to flake and break open, changing in color from translucent to opaque.

The Perfect Catch

Truly fresh fish smells only faintly of the sea. A little salt and coarsely ground pepper along with a drizzle of olive oil are the only things needed to bring out the fabulous flavor. A sprinkling of fresh herbs is purely optional.

- **Rather than shop for a specific type of fish, see what looks the freshest.** Similar types of fish can usually be substituted in a recipe. If the ingredient list calls for a mild-flavored white fish such as cod, for example, you can easily substitute orange roughy or snapper. Bolder-flavored fish, such as tuna and swordfish, are often interchangeable.

- **Fresh fish should be stored on ice in the display counter and well drained so that water doesn't pool around it.** Fillets should look moist and firm, with no discoloration or dryness around the edges. Whole fish should have clear, shiny eyes; moist red gills; and scales that cling tightly to the skin.
- **High-tech methods of freezing lock in fresh flavor, providing a quality selection of fish year-round.** Look for packages that are clean and tightly sealed, with no signs of freezer burn. Allow 24 hours to thaw a 1-pound package of frozen fish in the refrigerator. Speeding up the process by thawing at room temperature or under running water drains the moisture and breaks down the texture of the fish.

Grate Expectations

If you've never tried grilling fish, you're in for a treat. Start with a clean, lightly greased grate, and be sure to preheat the grill. Lightly brush both sides of the fillets with oil or coat with vegetable cooking spray. Delicate fish or fillets that flake easily (such as cod or halibut) need to be grilled in a hinged wire fish basket. Firm-textured fish, such as tuna, salmon, and swordfish, can be grilled directly on the grate.

May

Burgers You Won't Believe

Shrimp, beef, and pork paired with zesty, lip-smacking spreads: Check out our coolest Southern updates on everyone's favorite cookout food.

Grab a cold one, and get the grill going—we have the coolest (and tastiest) twists around for this outdoor-season icon. Test Kitchen Pro Kristi Michele Crowe and Associate Food Editor Shirley Harrington went a tad burger crazy—moseying beyond ground beef—as they tried out shrimp and ground pork too. (Don't worry, we stayed grounded in reality, so the ingredients are easy to find.) Proof was on the platter after our burger-tasting sessions: Not even an itty-bitty bite was left! Yep, these are so flavorful and fun-loving they'll knock your flip-flops off. Cheers to bare feet in lush grass and a good-looking burger in hand.

Test Kitchen Tips: Burgers

- **Take it easy.** Overworking the beef or pork and seasonings when blending or shaping can toughen the meat. "Think like you would when making biscuits," says Kristi, "delicate and quick handling is best." Kristi divides the mixture roughly into portions. (If the recipe makes four burgers, create four portions.) Cuddle each portion in one hand while using fingertips on the other hand to gently press and flatten into a patty.
- **No slip? Then don't flip.** If a spatula doesn't easily slide under the very out-side edge of the burger, it's not ready to turn. Back off and wait until the sides of the burger start to appear cooked and try again.
- **Skip the squish.** Don't press patties or repeatedly flip them over. This will push the juices out of the meat, leaving it dry and less flavorful. The dripping juices cause grill flare-ups too.

Shrimp Burgers With Sweet 'n' Spicy Tartar Sauce

freezeable • make ahead

MAKES 4 SERVINGS; **PREP:** 25 MIN., **CHILL:** 1 HR., **FREEZE:** 30 MIN., **GRILL:** 12 MIN.

Recipes for shrimp burgers, a favorite food of Southern shrimping towns, are often big secrets. Here we divulge our version, which is chunky and spicy with some Cajun flair. (Pictured on page 169)

1¼ lb. unpeeled, medium-size raw shrimp
    (31/40 count)
Vegetable cooking spray
1 large egg, lightly beaten
1 Tbsp. mayonnaise
2 tsp. lemon juice
½ tsp. salt
⅛ tsp. ground red pepper
3 Tbsp. finely chopped celery
2 Tbsp. chopped green onion
1 Tbsp. chopped fresh parsley
1¼ cups crushed cornbread crackers
    (about 1 sleeve or 24 crackers)
4 Kaiser rolls with poppy
    seeds, split
Sweet 'n' Spicy Tartar Sauce
4 Bibb lettuce leaves
Garnish: grilled lemon halves

1. Peel shrimp; devein, if desired. Cut each shrimp into thirds.

2. Line a 15- x 10-inch jelly-roll pan with aluminum foil. Coat with cooking spray.
3. Stir together egg and next 4 ingredients until blended; stir in celery, green onion, and parsley. Fold in shrimp and cracker crumbs (mixture will be very thick). Shape into 4 (4-inch-wide, 1-inch-thick) patties. Place patties on prepared pan. Cover and chill 1 to 24 hours. Transfer to freezer, and freeze 30 minutes.
4. Coat cold cooking grate of grill with cooking spray, and place on grill. Preheat grill to 350° to 400° (medium-

TIP

To make our chunky-style Shrimp Burgers With Sweet 'n' Spicy Tartar Sauce, cut each medium-size shrimp into three pieces.

high) heat. Grill burgers, covered with grill lid, 4 to 5 minutes or until burgers lift easily from cooking grate using a large spatula. Turn burgers, and grill 4 to 5 minutes or until shrimp turn pink and burgers are cooked through and lightly crisp.

5. Grill buns, cut sides down, 1 to 2 minutes or until lightly toasted. Serve burgers on buns with Sweet 'n' Spicy Tartar Sauce and lettuce. Garnish, if desired.

Note: For testing purposes only, we used Keebler Town House Bistro Corn Bread Crackers.

• TIP •

Freeze Shrimp Burger patties before grilling. That's our Test Kitchen trick to ensure they hold together on the grill. Top with our special tartar sauce and a good squeeze of lemon.

Sweet 'n' Spicy Tartar Sauce:
make ahead
MAKES ABOUT 1 CUP; **PREP:** 5 MIN., **CHILL:** 30 MIN.

1 cup mayonnaise
2 Tbsp. chopped fresh parsley
2 Tbsp. horseradish
1½ tsp. Cajun seasoning
1½ tsp. lemon juice
¼ tsp. paprika

6. Stir together all ingredients in a bowl. Cover and chill 30 minutes to 24 hours.

Note: For testing purposes only, we used McCormick Cajun Seasoning.

Pecan-Crusted Pork Burgers With Dried Apricot-Chipotle Mayonnaise
MAKES 4 SERVINGS; **PREP:** 15 MIN., **GRILL:** 18 MIN.

These nut-crusted pork burgers grill up crispy on the outside and juicy on the inside. Ground pork is becoming more common in the meat case. You can also ask your butcher to grind it. Usually the lean-to-fat ratio is similar to ground chuck. We find French hamburger buns at Publix grocery stores.

Vegetable cooking spray
1½ lb. lean ground pork
2 Tbsp. reserved mayonnaise mixture from Dried Apricot-Chipotle Mayonnaise
1 Tbsp. butter, melted
½ cup finely chopped pecans
½ tsp. salt
¼ tsp. pepper
4 French hamburger buns, split
4 Bibb lettuce leaves
Dried Apricot-Chipotle Mayonnaise

1. Coat cold cooking grate of grill with cooking spray, and place on grill. Preheat grill to 350° to 400°(medium-high) heat.

2. Gently combine pork and reserved 2 Tbsp. mayonnaise mixture until blended, using hands. Shape into 4 (4-inch-wide, 1-inch-thick) patties.

3. Stir together butter and next 3 ingredients in a small bowl until well blended. Sprinkle each patty with about 2 Tbsp. pecan mixture (about 1 Tbsp. on each side), gently pressing to adhere.

4. Grill pecan-covered pork patties, covered with grill lid, over 350° to 400° (medium-high) heat 6 to 8 minutes on each side or until a meat thermometer inserted into centers registers 155°.

5. Grill buns, cut sides down, 1 to 2 minutes or until lightly toasted. Serve burgers on buns with lettuce and Dried Apricot-Chipotle Mayonnaise.

• TIP •

There's only enough pecan mixture to lightly sprinkle on the pork patties. You may be tempted to add more pecans. Don't—the burgers will be too sweet.

Dried Apricot-Chipotle Mayonnaise:
fast fixin's
MAKES ABOUT 1 CUP; **PREP:** 10 MIN., **STAND:** 15 MIN.

Don't shortcut the soak time for the apricots. The tart lime juice balances the concentrated sweetness of this dried fruit.

½ cup dried apricots
¼ cup hot water
2 Tbsp. fresh lime juice
½ cup mayonnaise
1 canned chipotle chile pepper in adobo sauce, chopped
2 Tbsp. finely chopped green onion
1 Tbsp. adobo sauce from can

1. Stir together dried apricots, hot water, and lime juice in a small bowl. Let stand 15 minutes; drain. Pat apricots dry, and coarsely chop.

2. Stir together mayonnaise and next 3 ingredients; reserve 2 Tbsp. mixture for Pecan-Crusted Pork Burgers. Stir apricots into remaining mayonnaise mixture. Cover and chill until ready to serve.

Dixie Beef Burgers With Chowchow Spread

MAKES 4 SERVINGS; **PREP:** 30 MIN.,
GRILL: 16 MIN.

We loved the slightly sweet Chowchow Spread and the tangy Banana Pepper Spread on these burgers. Make both and let guests choose. (Pictured on page 168)

1 (13.5-oz.) package frozen onion rings
1 cup grape tomatoes, quartered
1 Tbsp. honey
½ tsp. cider vinegar
½ cup finely chopped sweet onion, divided
¾ tsp. salt, divided
1½ lb. ground chuck
½ tsp. coarsely ground pepper
1 (8-oz.) package country ham biscuit slices
4 sourdough hamburger buns, split
4 green leaf lettuce leaves
Chowchow Spread or Banana Pepper Spread

1. Prepare onion rings according to package directions; keep warm on a wire rack in a jelly-roll pan at 200° up to 20 minutes.
2. Stir together tomatoes, honey, cider vinegar, ¼ cup onion, and ¼ tsp. salt.
3. Preheat grill to 350° to 400° (medium-high) heat. Gently combine beef, pepper, and remaining ¼ cup onion and ½ tsp. salt in a large bowl until blended, using hands. Shape mixture into 4 (4-inch-wide, ¾-inch-thick) patties.
4. Grill, covered with grill lid, over 350° to 400° (medium-high) heat 5 to 6 minutes on each side or until beef is no longer pink in center. Grill ham slices 1 to 2 minutes on each side or until lightly crisp. Grill buns, cut sides down, 1 to 2 minutes or until lightly toasted.
5. Layer each of 4 bun halves with lettuce, burger, Chowchow or Banana Pepper Spread, grilled ham slices, and an onion ring. Spoon tomato mixture into centers of each onion ring. Top with remaining bun halves. Serve with remaining onion rings.

—**JANICE ELDER,** CHARLOTTE, NORTH CAROLINA

Note: For testing purposes only, we used Alexia Onion Rings with panko coating.

Chowchow Spread:
make ahead
MAKES ABOUT ⅔ CUP; **PREP:** 5 MIN.

Chowchow is a spicy mixture of chopped and pickled vegetables usually including green tomatoes, onions, and sweet and hot peppers. Look for it on the pickle aisle, or use homemade.

1. Stir together ½ cup chowchow and 3 Tbsp. mayonnaise in a small bowl. Serve immediately, or cover and chill up to 2 days.
Note: For testing purposes only, we used Braswell's Mild Chow Chow.

Banana Pepper Spread:
MAKES ABOUT ½ CUP; **PREP:** 5 MIN.

1. Stir together ¾ cup jarred mild banana pepper rings, drained and chopped; 3 Tbsp. mayonnaise; and ⅛ tsp. paprika in a small bowl. Serve immediately, or cover and chill up to 2 days.

Made for Each Other

Shrimp and grits are one of the hottest culinary duos in town. Once a hearty breakfast for coastal fishermen, the pairing is now a popular dish in roadside cafes and upscale restaurants across the South. Here, several chefs share their secrets.

Test Kitchen Notebook

Try a Little Tenderness

There's nothing quite like the rich-and-creamy texture of slowly simmered stone-ground grits. More perishable than regular grits, which have the germ removed, stone-ground grits are best stored in the freezer. Flavor and cook times vary with the blend of corn used by different brands, so check out the package directions. We think they're well worth the effort, but when you're pressed for time, the variation with quick-cooking (not instant!) grits is a mighty fine substitute.

Creamy Cheddar Cheese Grits
chef recipe
MAKES 8½ CUPS; **PREP:** 10 MIN.;
COOK: 1 HR., 45 MIN.

4 Tbsp. butter, divided
5 cups milk
2 tsp. salt
½ tsp. hot sauce
1 garlic clove, pressed
1½ cups uncooked stone-ground white grits
1 (10-oz.) block sharp white Cheddar cheese, grated

1. Bring 2 Tbsp. butter, next 4 ingredients, and 5 cups water to a boil in a medium-size Dutch oven over medium-high heat. Gradually whisk in grits, and bring to a boil. Reduce heat to medium-low, and simmer, stirring occasionally, 1½ hours or until thickened. Stir in cheese and remaining 2 Tbsp. butter until melted. Serve immediately.

—**INSPIRED BY EMERIL LAGASSE**

Quick-Cooking Creamy Cheddar Cheese Grits: Substitute 2 cups uncooked quick-cooking grits for stone-ground grits. Decrease water and milk to 4½ cups each. Prepare recipe as directed, cooking grits 10 to 15 minutes or until thickened.

Hominy Grill's Shrimp and Grits

chef recipe

MAKES 6 SERVINGS; **PREP:** 30 MIN.,
COOK: 19 MIN.

Easy to make for company, this dish is irresistible any time of day.

2 lb. unpeeled, medium-size raw shrimp
   (31/40 count)
2 Tbsp. all-purpose flour
5 bacon slices, chopped
1 (8-oz.) package sliced fresh mushrooms
3 garlic cloves, minced
⅓ cup fresh lemon juice
½ cup thinly sliced green onions
2 tsp. hot sauce
½ tsp. salt
Creamy Cheddar Cheese Grits

1. Peel shrimp; devein, if desired. Toss shrimp with flour until lightly coated, shaking to remove excess.
2. Cook bacon in a medium skillet over medium-high heat 8 to 10 minutes or until crisp. Remove bacon, and drain on paper towels, reserving drippings in skillet.
3. Sauté mushrooms in hot drippings 4 minutes or just until mushrooms begin to release their liquid. Add shrimp, and sauté 3 to 3½ minutes or just until shrimp turn pink. Add garlic, and sauté 1 minute (do not brown garlic). Add lemon juice and next 3 ingredients; serve immediately over Creamy Cheddar Cheese Grits. Sprinkle with bacon.

—**HOMINY GRILL**, CHARLESTON, SOUTH CAROLINA

Standard Bistro's Shrimp and Grits

chef recipe

MAKES 6 TO 8 SERVINGS; **PREP:** 40 MIN.,
COOK: 22 MIN.

We make this tasty dish year-round and substitute Roma tomatoes and frozen green beans when fresh are past their peak.

½ lb. fresh green beans, cut into 1-inch
   pieces
2 lb. unpeeled, medium-size raw shrimp
   (31/40 count)
½ cup chopped bacon (about 3 slices)
1 large shallot, chopped
4 garlic cloves, minced
1 cup dry white wine
1 medium tomato, chopped (about
   ¾ cup)
3 Tbsp. chopped green onions
2 Tbsp. butter
¾ tsp. salt
½ tsp. pepper
Creamy Cheddar Cheese Grits

1. Cook beans in boiling salted water to cover 3 to 4 minutes or until crisp-tender; drain. Plunge into ice water to stop the cooking process; drain.
2. Peel shrimp; devein, if desired.
3. Cook bacon in a large skillet over medium-high heat 5 minutes or until crisp; remove bacon, and drain on paper towels, reserving 1 Tbsp. drippings in skillet. Reduce heat to low; add shallot, and sauté 1 minute or until tender. Add garlic, and sauté 30 seconds. Add wine, and cook 5 minutes or until reduced to ¼ cup, stirring occasionally to loosen particles from bottom of skillet.
4. Stir in green beans, tomato, and green onions; cook 3 minutes. Add butter, salt, pepper, and shrimp; cook 3 minutes or just until shrimp turn pink.
5. Spoon shrimp mixture over Creamy Cheddar Cheese Grits; sprinkle with bacon, and serve immediately.

—**STANDARD BISTRO**, BIRMINGHAM, ALABAMA

Cajun Sausage Shrimp and Grits

chef recipe • editor's pick

MAKES 6 TO 8 SERVINGS; **PREP:** 30 MIN.,
COOK: 35 MIN.

1½ lb. unpeeled, medium-size raw shrimp
   (31/40 count)
3 Tbsp. butter
2 Tbsp. all-purpose flour
1 medium onion, chopped
½ cup chopped green bell pepper
2 celery ribs, chopped
1 lb. andouille or smoked sausage, cut into
   ¼-inch-thick slices
1 (14-oz.) can chicken broth
½ tsp. salt
¼ tsp. ground red pepper
⅓ cup heavy cream
¼ cup chopped green onions
Creamy Cheddar Cheese Grits

1. Peel shrimp; devein, if desired.
2. Melt butter in a large skillet over medium heat; gradually whisk in flour, and cook, whisking constantly, until flour is a light caramel color (about 6 minutes).
3. Add onion, bell pepper, and celery, and cook 8 to 10 minutes or until tender. Add sausage, and cook 2 minutes. Stir in chicken broth, salt, and pepper, stirring to loosen particles from bottom of skillet. Bring to a light boil over medium-high heat. Reduce heat to medium, and simmer 8 to 10 minutes or until slightly thickened.
4. Stir in shrimp, cream, and green onions, and cook, stirring occasionally, 3 minutes or just until shrimp turn pink. Serve over Creamy Cheddar Cheese Grits.

—**INSPIRED BY EMERIL LAGASSE**

Spring's Biggest Star

One of the South's favorite ingredients—the Vidalia onion—is at its peak.

It's one of the world's sweetest onions, with a name that's a delicious drawl—va-dale'yah, syllables that hang like Spanish moss in South Georgia's thick humidity. It's that very climate that gives birth to an onion so mild and juicy you could almost eat it like an apple. If you don't know about caramelizing onions, you simply must read on. We wondered what it would be like to pair some of the season's freshest fruits with golden Vidalia onions. The result? Sweet Onion 'n' Fruit Salad, so rich in flavor you'll forget it's on the light side. For a melt-in-your-mouth treat, check out our Editor's Pick, Rustic Vidalia Onion Tart.

Caramelized Sweet Onions

freezeable • make ahead

MAKES ABOUT 2 CUPS; **PREP:** 15 MIN., **COOK:** 40 MIN.

Georgia's Vidalia and Texas's 1015 sweet onions are available in spring and summer, but sweet onions are now available just about all year long. In fall and winter months, look for the South American OSO sweet onion.

4 lb. sweet onions, chopped
   (about 12 cups)
1 tsp. chopped fresh or ½ tsp. dried thyme
2 Tbsp. olive oil
½ tsp. salt

1. Cook onion and thyme in hot oil in a large deep skillet over medium heat, stirring often, 35 to 40 minutes or until caramel colored (a deep golden brown). Remove from heat; stir in salt.
Note: Store cooked onions in a zip-top plastic freezer bag or an airtight container in refrigerator up to 1 week or freeze up to 2 months.

Did You Know?

By law, it can only be called a Vidalia onion if it is grown in one of 20 counties in southeast Georgia. Harvesting usually occurs in late April and goes through mid-June. Stock up now while they are in season. Store onions in a cool, dry place for optimum flavor. These sweet, pale yellow onions were first grown in the 1930s near Vidalia, Georgia. The flavor is due to the low amounts of sulfur in the sandy soil where they are grown.

Sweet Onion 'n' Fruit Salad

fast fixin's

MAKES 4 SERVINGS; **PREP:** 20 MIN. (NOT INCLUDING CARAMELIZING ONIONS)

3 Tbsp. apple cider vinegar
1 tsp. Dijon mustard
2 tsp. honey
¼ tsp. salt
¼ cup olive oil
1 (5-oz.) package gourmet mixed salad
   greens, thoroughly washed
1 fresh mango, peeled and sliced
1 fresh papaya, peeled and sliced
½ cup Caramelized Sweet Onions
Garnish: fresh cherries

Good, Better, Best

One taste of these caramelized onions and you'll want them in soups, grits, mashed potatoes, and more.

Start with chopped or sliced raw onions.

After about 20 minutes, the onions will begin to turn golden.

As you continue to cook, they will deepen in color to a golden brown.

1. Whisk together apple cider vinegar, Dijon mustard, honey, and salt. Gradually add olive oil in a slow, steady stream, whisking until blended.
2. Arrange greens on salad plates; top with mango slices, papaya slices, and Caramelized Sweet Onions. Drizzle with vinaigrette. Garnish, if desired.

Rustic Vidalia Onion Tart

editor's pick

MAKES 6 SERVINGS; **PREP:** 15 MIN.,
COOK: 8 MIN., **BAKE:** 17 MIN., **STAND:** 5 MIN.

Don't worry about being exact when folding the piecrust. It's meant to look organic and free-form, allowing the filling to show through.

2 Tbsp. butter
4 medium-size Vidalia onions, thinly sliced
    (about 6½ cups)
1½ tsp. chopped fresh rosemary
¾ tsp. salt
½ tsp. pepper
½ (15-oz.) package refrigerated piecrusts
Parchment paper
1 egg white, lightly beaten
¾ cup (3 oz.) shredded Gruyère cheese

1. Preheat oven to 425°. Melt butter in a large nonstick skillet over medium-high heat; add onion and next 3 ingredients. Cook, stirring occasionally, 8 minutes or until tender.
2. Unroll piecrust onto a lightly floured surface. Pat or roll into a 12-inch circle. Place piecrust on a parchment paper-lined baking sheet. Brush with egg white. Sprinkle ½ cup cheese in center of crust. Spoon onion mixture over cheese, leaving a 2½-inch border. Sprinkle remaining ¼ cup cheese over onion. Fold piecrust border up and over onion, pleating as you go and leaving a 4-inch-wide opening in center. Brush crust with egg white.
3. Bake at 425° on bottom oven rack 17 to 19 minutes or until crust is golden. Let stand 5 minutes before serving.

Rustic Vidalia Onion Tart With Thyme: Substitute chopped fresh thyme for rosemary. Proceed with recipe as directed.

Vidalia-Cheddar-Pecan Muffins

MAKES 1 DOZEN; **PREP:** 10 MIN.,
BAKE: 20 MIN., **COOL:** 8 MIN.

¾ cup chopped pecans
3 Tbsp. butter
1 large Vidalia onion, chopped
    (1½ to 1¾ cups)
2½ cups all-purpose baking mix
1½ cups (6 oz.) shredded Cheddar cheese
¾ cup milk
2 large eggs

1. Preheat oven to 350°. Bake pecans in a single layer in a shallow pan 6 to 8 minutes or until lightly toasted and fragrant, stirring once halfway through.
2. Meanwhile, melt 3 Tbsp. butter in a medium-size nonstick skillet over medium-high heat; add Vidalia onion, and sauté 6 to 8 minutes or until onion is tender and begins to caramelize.
3. Remove pecans from oven; increase oven temperature to 425°.
4. Combine baking mix and cheese in a large bowl; make a well in center of mixture. Whisk together milk and eggs; add to cheese mixture, stirring just until moistened. Stir in onion and pecans. Spoon into a lightly greased muffin pan, filling almost completely full.
5. Bake at 425° for 14 to 16 minutes or until golden. Let cool in pan on a wire rack 2 minutes. Remove from pan to wire rack, and let cool 6 to 8 minutes. Serve warm.

Vidalia-Cheddar-Apple Muffins: Omit pecans. Preheat oven to 425°. Toss 1 peeled and chopped Granny Smith apple with 2 tsp. sugar in a small bowl. Prepare recipe as directed, stirring apple into batter with onion in Step 4. Bake: 14 min.

Vidalia Onion Side Dish

test kitchen favorite

MAKES 2 SERVINGS; **PREP:** 5 MIN.,
COOK: 10 MIN.

2 medium onions
1 beef bouillon cube
½ Tbsp. butter
Garnishes: fresh parsley sprig, pepper

1. Peel 2 medium onions, and cut a thin slice from bottom and top of each one. Scoop out a 1-inch-deep hole from the top of each onion. Place onions, top sides up, in a 2-qt. microwave-safe dish with a lid. Add 1 beef bouillon cube and ½ Tbsp. butter to shallow hole in each onion; cover with lid. Microwave, covered, at HIGH for 8 to 10 minutes or until onion is tender. Garnish each serving with fresh parsley sprig and pepper, if desired.
Note: We recommend only Vidalia or Texas Sweets for this recipe. Be sure to use a microwave-safe lid only; plastic wrap will melt.

Grilled Vidalia Onion Side Dish: If you'd rather grill, wrap each filled-and-topped onion in heavy-duty aluminum foil (or a double layer of regular aluminum foil). Grill over high heat (400° to 450°) 15 to 20 minutes or until tender. Let stand 10 minutes.

Out on the Chesapeake

Family and friends celebrate the legacy of the Seafarers Yacht Club of Annapolis, Maryland. Come along as they cruise the Bay and gather for great food.

As sunlight sparkles on the indigo waters of the Chesapeake Bay, there is a hint of dampness in the air and the faint scent of the marina—seafood, saltwater, and old wood. Boats bob restlessly, tugging at moorings at docks all along the coastline of this enormous sound. Members of the Seafarers Yacht Club of Annapolis, Maryland, with boats docked in Eastport and along the South River, gather for a day brimming with emotion and camaraderie, as well as a kingly spread of good food to mark the boaters' 50th anniversary season.

Charter members of the club came together over a passion for boating and for continuing the African American watermen in the Bay community Through the years, the Seafarers have gathered each May to kick off the season with an official flag-raising ceremony, and this month's event celebrated the beginning of this very special anniversary year. After the flag raising, this gathering becomes increasingly festive as the Seafarers offer a sample of the club's warmth and genuine friendliness. All in attendance are welcome to buckle into safety vests and board boats for a brief outing on the Bay. Once they return to the dock, they'll relish a cruise-worthy buffet featuring signature recipes such as spicy Jerk Chicken, sides, and crab-stuffed fish—a real delicacy when locally caught rockfish are available. Two scrumptious desserts round out the feast.

Spring Chesapeake Picnic

SERVES 6 TO 8

Jerk Chicken

Cornbread-and-Crab-Stuffed Fish

Jean's Potato Salad

Rice and Peas

Lemon Chess Pie

Seafarers' Cherries Jubilee

Jerk Chicken

MAKES 8 SERVINGS; **PREP:** 15 MIN.; **CHILL:** 8 HR.; **STAND:** 30 MIN.; **GRILL:** 1 HR., 10 MIN.

A cousin of one of the club members created this recipe after sampling jerk-flavored foods in Haiti and Jamaica.

1½ tsp. seasoned salt
1 tsp. garlic powder
1 tsp. lemon pepper
1 tsp. paprika
2 (2½- to 3-lb.) cut-up whole chickens
1 fresh lime, cut in half
1 (11-oz.) jar Jamaican jerk seasoning*
Garnish: lime slices

1. Stir together first 4 ingredients. Arrange chicken pieces, skin sides down, in an aluminum foil-lined roasting pan. Sprinkle both sides of chicken with seasoned salt mixture. Squeeze juice from lime over chicken.

Spread jerk seasoning on both sides of chicken. Cover with plastic wrap, and chill 8 to 24 hours. Let stand at room temperature 30 minutes.

2. Light one side of grill, heating to 350° to 400° (medium-high) heat; leave other side unlit. Arrange chicken over unlit side, and grill, covered with grill lid, 1 hour and 10 minutes or until a meat thermometer inserted into thickest portion registers 170°. Garnish, if desired.

—CASSANDRA AUPONT, CHICAGO, ILLINOIS

*1 (8-oz.) bottle liquid Jamaican jerk marinade may be substituted.
Note: For testing purposes only, we used Walkerswood Traditional Jamaican Jerk Seasoning.

Cornbread-and-Crab-Stuffed Fish

MAKES 6 SERVINGS; **PREP:** 30 MIN., **COOL:** 30 MIN., **COOK:** 10 MIN., **BAKE:** 45 MIN.

Crab-stuffed seafood is a menu tradition on the Chesapeake Bay, and in season you may substitute rockfish, a Bay-area favorite, for the bass or snapper called for in the recipe.

1 (6-oz.) package buttermilk cornbread mix
1 cup fresh lump crabmeat, drained (about ½ lb.)
2 Tbsp. butter
¼ cup chopped celery
¼ cup chopped onion
1 tsp. Old Bay seasoning, divided
2 white bread slices, toasted and cut into cubes (about 1 cup)
1 Tbsp. chopped fresh parsley
¼ tsp. lemon zest
½ cup chicken broth
1 (3- to 5-lb.) striped bass or red snapper, dressed
Kitchen string

1. Preheat oven to 350°. Prepare cornbread mix according to package directions. Let cool 30 minutes; crumble into a large bowl.

2. Meanwhile, pick crabmeat, removing any bits of shell.

3. Melt butter in a large skillet over medium heat; add celery and onion, and sauté 10 to 12 minutes or until tender. Stir in ½ tsp. Old Bay seasoning. Stir celery mixture, crab, bread cubes, parsley, and lemon zest into crumbled cornbread, stirring gently until blended. Add broth, and stir gently until moistened.

4. Sprinkle cavity of fish with remaining ½ tsp. Old Bay seasoning. Spoon stuffing mixture into fish, and secure with kitchen string. Place fish in a large, lightly greased roasting pan.

5. Bake at 350° for 45 to 50 minutes or until fish flakes with a fork.

So Southern

Unexpected Twist

Here's a centerpiece idea that comes straight from your pantry. Save vegetable and soup cans, sans labels, and use them as containers running down the center of a table. A surprising mix of flowers and fruit makes these arrangements modern. Lush hydrangeas and sculptural succulents pair perfectly with fresh blackberries and colorful apricots.

Jean's Potato Salad

make ahead

MAKES 8 SERVINGS; **PREP:** 20 MIN.; **COOK:** 20 MIN.; **STAND:** 15 MIN.; **CHILL:** 1 HR., 30 MIN.

The cool, creamy taste of this dish complements spicy-hot Jerck Chicken and Rice and Peas. The flavors of the chicken and potato salad go together like barbecue and coleslaw.

6 medium-size baking potatoes, peeled and cut into ¾-inch cubes (4 lb.)
1½ tsp. salt, divided
6 large eggs
4 green onions, white and light green parts only
1 medium-size green bell pepper, diced
4 celery ribs, diced (about 1¼ cups)
1 large carrot, shredded
1 cup mayonnaise
½ tsp. pepper
Garnishes: Bibb lettuce leaves, green onions

1. Bring potato, ½ tsp. salt, and water to cover to a boil in a large Dutch oven over medium heat, and cook 10 to 15 minutes or just until tender; drain.

2. Place eggs in a single layer in a stainless-steel saucepan. (Do not use nonstick.) Add water to a depth of 3 inches. Bring to a boil; cover, remove from heat, and let stand 15 minutes.

3. Meanwhile, chop green onions. Drain eggs, and return to pan. Fill pan with cold water and ice. Tap each egg firmly on the counter until cracks form all over the shell. Peel under cold running water. Chop eggs.

4. Stir together eggs, green onions, bell pepper, celery, and carrot in a large bowl; add potato, stirring gently to combine.

5. Stir together mayonnaise, pepper, and remaining 1 tsp. salt; add to potato mixture, stirring gently to coat. Season with salt to taste. Cover and chill 1½ to 24 hours before serving. Garnish, if desired.

—JEAN ROBINSON, WASHINGTON, D.C.

Rice and Peas

MAKES 12 SERVINGS; **PREP:** 10 MIN., **COOK:** 30 MIN.

Scotch bonnet chiles range in color from yellow to red and are very hot. Wear rubber gloves to protect your hands when handling these or any chile pepper.

¾ cup finely chopped onion
1 Tbsp. olive oil
2 garlic cloves, minced
2 tsp. fresh thyme leaves
½ tsp. ground allspice
½ tsp. freshly ground pepper
½ cup unsweetened coconut milk
2 cups uncooked long-grain rice
2 (15.8-oz.) cans pigeon or crowder peas, drained
1½ tsp. kosher salt
1 tsp. light brown sugar
1 Scotch bonnet chile (optional)
Garnish: lime slices

1. Sauté onion in hot oil in a Dutch oven over medium-high heat 3 to 4 minutes or until tender. Stir in garlic and next 3 ingredients, and sauté 2 minutes. Stir in coconut milk and 4 cups water, and bring to a boil. Stir in rice, next 3 ingredients, and, if desired, Scotch bonnet chile; cover, reduce heat to low, and simmer 15 to 20 minutes or until liquid is absorbed and rice is tender. Remove and discard Scotch bonnet chile. Garnish, if desired. Serve immediately.

—ALICE MAHAN, BOWIE, MARYLAND

Lemon Chess Pie

editor's pick

MAKES 8 SERVINGS; **PREP:** 10 MIN.;
BAKE: 31 MIN.; **COOL:** 1 HR., 30 MIN.

1 (6-oz.) ready-made shortbread piecrust
1 egg white, lightly beaten
4 large eggs, separated
¾ cup sugar
¼ cup melted butter
½ cup fresh lemon juice
Garnishes: whipped cream, fresh
   raspberries

1. Preheat oven to 350°. Brush piecrust
with beaten egg white. Bake 6 minutes.
Remove from oven, and cool completely
on a wire rack (about 30 minutes).
2. Beat 4 egg whites at high speed with
an electric mixer until stiff peaks form.
3. Whisk together 4 egg yolks, sugar,
and melted butter in a large bowl until
blended. Stir in lemon juice. Fold in
egg whites. Pour mixture into cooled
piecrust, and place pie on a baking sheet.
4. Bake at 350° for 25 to 30 minutes
or until set, shielding edges with aluminum foil after 20 minutes to prevent
excessive browning. Remove from oven
to wire rack, and cool completely (about
1 hour). Garnish, if desired.

—**DR. WILLIAM WOODWARD, JR.**,
ANNAPOLIS, MARYLAND

Note: For testing purposes only, we
used Keebler Ready Crust Shortbread
piecrust.

Seafarers' Cherries Jubilee

fast fixin's

MAKES 6 SERVINGS; **PREP:** 10 MIN.,
COOK: 5 MIN.

1 (15-oz.) can pitted Bing cherries in syrup
1 (14.5-oz.) can pitted tart cherries
   in water
2 Tbsp. cornstarch
¼ cup sugar
½ tsp. ground allspice
¼ cup black raspberry liqueur
¼ cup brandy
6 Tbsp. chocolate liqueur
1 qt. vanilla ice cream
12 chocolate fudge cream-filled rolled
   wafers

1. Combine Bing cherries in a heavy
nonaluminum 3-qt. saucepan; reserve
6 Tbsp. syrup. Stir together cornstarch
and reserved syrup.
2. Stir together sugar and allspice;
add to cherries, and bring to a boil over
medium heat. Reduce heat to low;
add cornstarch mixture, and cook,
stirring constantly, 2 to 3 minutes or
until mixture is thickened and slightly
clear. Remove from heat. Stir in raspberry liqueur and brandy; return to
heat, and cook over medium heat,
stirring constantly, 1 minute.
3. Place 1 Tbsp. chocolate liqueur in
each of 6 (6-oz.) serving dishes, and top
with ice cream. Pour cherry mixture
over ice cream in each dish, and serve
with chocolate wafers.

—**TANYA MORRIS**, MITCHELLVILLE, MARYLAND

Note: For testing purposes only, we
used Chambord Black Raspberry
Liqueur, Godiva Original Chocolate
Liqueur, and Pepperidge Farm
Chocolate Fudge Créme-Filled
Pirouette Rolled Wafers.

Triple Crown Cocktails

These signature drinks score a
trifecta with us.

The Kentucky Derby is one
of the grandest sporting
events in the South, and
the mint julep is as synony-
mous with the race as are
distinctive hats. But the Derby is not
the only leg of the Triple Crown with a
signature drink. We found that Black-
eyed Susan Cocktails are often served
at the Preakness. At the Belmont Stakes
it's Long Island Iced Tea. Here are our
versions of each.

Long Island Iced Tea

fast fixin's

MAKES 2 SERVINGS; **PREP:** 5 MIN.

*Serve this stiff drink in a martini glass
to encourage sipping. Sweet-and-sour
mix is sold in bottles similar to Bloody
Mary mix. (Pictured on page 171)*

6 Tbsp. sweet-and-sour mix
3 Tbsp. vodka
3 Tbsp. gin
3 Tbsp. orange liqueur
3 Tbsp. light rum
3 Tbsp. tequila
Crushed ice
6 Tbsp. cola soft drink
Garnish: lemon slices

1. Combine first 7 ingredients in a
cocktail shaker or martini shaker.
Cover with lid, and shake 30 seconds
or until thoroughly chilled. Remove lid,
and strain into 2 chilled martini glasses.
Pour 3 Tbsp. cola into each glass.
Garnish, if desired. Serve immediately.

So SOUTHERN

Basil Julep

Yes, we know it's usually made with mint. And yes, we know it's a Derby sin to serve it in glass, so maybe we should just call this Basil and Bourbon on Ice. Whatever it is, you can celebrate the South's most famous horse race (and fashion show) by donning a hat and mixing up a batch of this cocktail that offers a fresh take on a beloved tradition. For the recipe and tips on making juleps, see opposite page and below.

Fresh Basil Julep

MAKES 1 SERVING; **PREP:** 10 MIN.

A cocktail straw is placed near the basil sprig garnish so you sniff the fragrance of mint as you take a sip. (Pictured on page 171)

3 fresh basil leaves
1 Tbsp. Basil Simple Syrup
Crushed ice
2 Tbsp. (1 oz.) bourbon
1 (4-inch) cocktail straw
1 fresh basil sprig
Powdered sugar (optional)

1. Place basil leaves and Basil Simple Syrup in a julep cup or an 8- to 10-oz. glass. Gently press leaves against sides of cup with back of a spoon to release flavor. Pack cup tightly with crushed ice; pour bourbon over ice. Insert straw, and place basil sprig directly next to straw. Sprinkle with powdered sugar, if desired.
Note: For testing purposes only, we used Woodford Reserve Distiller's Select Bourbon.

Fresh Mint Julep: Prepare recipe as directed, substituting mint leaves for basil leaves, Mint Simple Syrup for Basil Simple Syrup, and 1 small fresh mint sprig for basil sprig.

Basil Simple Syrup:
make ahead

MAKES ABOUT 1½ CUPS; **PREP:** 5 MIN., **COOK:** 5 MIN., **COOL:** 1 HR., **CHILL:** 24 HR.

Make this the day before your Kentucky Derby party. Once basil is discarded, keep the syrup in the fridge for up to two weeks. It is delicious with unsweetened iced tea.

1 cup sugar
1 cup firmly packed fresh basil sprigs

1. Bring sugar and 1 cup water to a boil in a medium saucepan. Boil, stirring often, 1 minute or until sugar is dissolved. Remove from heat; add basil, and cool completely (about 1 hour). Pour into a glass jar. Cover and chill 24 hours. Remove and discard basil.

Mint Simple Syrup: Prepare recipe as directed, substituting fresh mint sprigs for basil sprigs.

Black-eyed Susan Cocktail
fast fixin's
MAKES 2 SERVINGS; **PREP:** 5 MIN.

This cocktail's name is taken from the flowers used to make the blanket that drapes the winning horse at the Preakness. (Pictured on page 171)

¾ cup orange juice
½ cup pineapple juice
3 Tbsp. vodka
3 Tbsp. light rum
2 Tbsp. orange liqueur
Crushed ice
Garnishes: lime slices, fresh cherries

1. Stir together first 5 ingredients. Fill 2 (12-oz.) glasses with crushed ice. Pour orange juice mixture over ice. Garnish, if desired. Serve immediately.
Note: For testing purposes only, we used Grand Marnier orange liqueur.

Test Kitchen Tips: Juleps

- **Term to know:** "muddle," to crush or mash ingredients with a spoon to release flavor. A bar tool called a "muddler" can be used instead of a spoon. Its shape reminds us of a mini baseball bat.
- **Use crushed ice,** and pack into the cup tightly to keep the drink very cold, causing the cup to frost evenly. (Hold the cup at the rim while making to avoid fingerprints on the frosted cup.)
  To make crushed ice: Fill a 1-gal. heavy-duty zip-top plastic bag half full with ice; seal. Crush ice using a rolling pin or heavy skillet.

Invite some friends over to enjoy the warm weather and
this menu of delicious little bites.

Small-Plate Party

This bite-size but hearty menu offers big flavor with little fuss.

Light Bites

SERVES 6

Orange-Basil Ice

Melon, Mozzarella, and Prosciutto
Skewers

Fresh Herb-Tomato Crostini

Mini Crab Cakes With Garlic-Chive
Sauce

Everyone needs a place to relax. Food Editor Shannon Sliter Satterwhite's porch is her sanctuary, where she can people-watch and just hang out. It's even better with friends, especially later in the evening when it's not too sticky outside. Wherever you choose to be, round up the group for good food and girl talk. This light menu of small delicious bites—pan-fried crab cakes, prosciutto-fruit skewers, and tomato-topped toasts—will leave you satisfied, not stuffed. Plus, you can make most of these ahead, including Orange-Basil Ice. Turn it into a frozen mimosa by topping it off with extra-dry Champagne or sparkling wine just before serving.

Orange-Basil Ice
make ahead

MAKES 6 SERVINGS (3 CUPS); **PREP:** 15 MIN.,
FREEZE: 6 HR., **STAND:** 10 MIN.

Out of all the orange juices to choose from at the grocery store, we prefer Valencia varieties for this recipe. It has a rich, vibrant color. Regular orange juice will work, but expect a greenish tint. You can turn this ice into a frozen mimosa by topping it off with extra-dry Champagne or sparkling wine just before serving.

3 cups Valencia orange juice
½ cup loosely packed fresh basil
    leaves
1 Tbsp. honey*
Garnish: fresh basil leaves

1. Process ½ cup orange juice and basil leaves in a blender or food processor 10 seconds. Pour mixture through a fine wire-mesh strainer into a 4-cup glass measuring cup; add remaining 2½ cups orange juice. Stir in honey.
2. Divide mixture between 2 zip-top plastic freezer bags. Place bags on a jelly-roll pan. Freeze 6 hours or until firm. Remove bags from freezer, and let stand 10 minutes. Break mixture into small chunks using hands.
3. Process chunks, in batches, in a blender or food processor until smooth. Garnish, if desired. Serve immediately.
*1 Tbsp. (3 packets) no-calorie sweetener, such as Splenda, may be substituted.

Note: For testing purposes only, we used Tropicana Pure Valencia Orange Juice.

Per serving: Calories 68; Fat 0g (sat 0g, mono 0g, poly 0g); Protein 0.1g; Carb 16.5g; Fiber 0.1g; Chol 0mg; Iron 0.1mg; Sodium 13mg; Calc 3mg.

Pineapple-Basil Ice: Substitute pineapple juice for Valencia orange juice. Proceed with recipe as directed.

Per serving: Calories 77; Fat 0.2g (sat 0g, mono 0 g, poly 0.1g); Protein 0.5g; Carb 19g; Fiber 0.3g; Chol 0mg; Iron 0.5mg; Sodium 3mg; Calc 19mg

Fresh Orange-Basil Ice: Substitute fresh orange juice for Valencia orange juice. Omit honey. Proceed with recipe as directed.

Per serving: Calories 56; Fat 0.3g (sat 0g, mono 0.1 g, poly 0.1g); Protein 0.9g; Carb 13g; Fiber 0.3g; Chol 0mg; Iron 0.3mg; Sodium 1mg; Calc 16mg

White Grape-Mint Ice: Substitute white grape juice for orange juice and fresh mint leaves for basil leaves. Omit honey. Proceed with recipe as directed.

Per serving: Calories 50; Fat 0.1g (sat 0g, mono 0g, poly 0g); Protein 0.7g; Carb 11.7g; Fiber 0.4g; Chol 0mg; Iron 0.7mg; Sodium 2mg; Calc 19mg

Melon, Mozzarella, and Prosciutto Skewers
fast fixin's

MAKES 20 SKEWERS; **PREP:** 20 MIN.

Put out half of the skewers, and keep the remaining skewers chilled until ready to serve.

20 (1-inch) cantaloupe or honeydew cubes
    (about 2½ cups)
20 thin slices prosciutto (about ½ lb.)
20 fresh small mozzarella cheese balls
    (about 1 [8-oz.] tub)
20 (4-inch) wooden skewers
Freshly cracked pepper

1. Thread 1 melon cube, 1 prosciutto slice, and 1 mozzarella ball onto each of 20 (4-inch) wooden skewers. Sprinkle with cracked pepper.

Note: For testing purposes only, we used Il Villaggio Mozzarella Fior di Latte Ciliegine cheese for mozzarella cheese balls.

Per skewer: Calories 64; Fat 3.7g (sat 2g, mono 0g, poly 0g); Protein 5.4g; Carb 2.3g; Fiber 0g; Chol 15mg; Iron 0.3mg; Sodium 222mg; Calc 67mg

Fresh Herb-Tomato Crostini

make ahead

MAKES ABOUT 20 APPETIZER SERVINGS; **PREP:** 30 MIN., **BAKE:** 10 MIN.

Prepare tomato topping up to two days ahead; cover and store in the refrigerator. Toast bread slices one day ahead; store at room temperature in an airtight container.

¼ cup olive oil
2 garlic cloves, pressed
1 (8.5-oz.) French bread baguette, cut into
    ¼-inch-thick slices
3 Tbsp. fresh lemon juice
2 Tbsp. olive oil
¼ tsp. salt
⅛ tsp. pepper
1 large tomato, finely chopped
¾ cup finely chopped green
    onions
½ cup chopped fresh parsley
1 Tbsp. chopped fresh mint
⅓ cup crumbled feta cheese

1. Preheat oven to 350°. Stir together olive oil and garlic; brush on 1 side of each bread slice. Place bread slices, garlic sides up, on a baking sheet. Bake 10 to 12 minutes or until lightly toasted.

2. Whisk together lemon juice and next 3 ingredients in a large bowl. Add tomato and next 3 ingredients; gently toss to coat.

3. Top each bread slice with tomato mixture (about 2 rounded teaspoonfuls each). Sprinkle with cheese.

—**ANITA EMBRY**, VINCENT, ALABAMA

Per serving: Calories 87; Fat 5.1g (sat 1g, mono 3.4g, poly 0.6g); Protein 1.6g; Carb 7.4g; Fiber 0.6g; Chol 2.2mg; Iron 0.6mg; Sodium 116mg; Calc 28mg

Green Tomato-Fresh Herb Crostini: Substitute 1 finely chopped large green tomato for red tomato. Proceed with recipe as directed.

Fresh Herb-Tomato Tabbouleh Salad: Omit first 3 ingredients. Decrease feta cheese to ¼ cup. Prepare tomato mixture as directed in Step 2; drain. Reserve seasoning packet from 1 (5.25-oz.) tabbouleh salad mix for another use. Pour tabbouleh mix into a large bowl; stir in 1 cup boiling water. Cover and chill 30 minutes. Stir in tomato mixture. Cover and chill 1 hour. Top with feta cheese, and season with salt to taste. MAKES 6 SERVINGS. PREP: 10 MIN; CHILL: 1 HR., 30 MIN.

Note: For testing purposes only, we used Near East Taboule Wheat Salad Mix.

Per serving: Calories 93; Fat 6.1g (sat 1.6g, mono 3.9g, poly 0.5g); Protein 2.1g; Carb 8.7g; Fiber 2.4g; Chol 6mg; Iron 0.9mg; Sodium 243mg; Calc 53mg

Mini Crab Cakes With Garlic-Chive Sauce

MAKES 16 CAKES; **PREP:** 10 MIN., **COOK:** 8 MIN. PER BATCH
(Pictured on page 170)

1 (8-oz.) package fresh lump crabmeat,
    drained
3 whole grain white bread slices
⅓ cup light mayonnaise
3 green onions, thinly sliced
1 tsp. Old Bay seasoning
1 tsp. Worcestershire sauce
2 large eggs, lightly beaten
Vegetable cooking spray
Salt to taste
Garlic-Chive Sauce
Garnish: lemon slices

1. Pick crabmeat, removing any bits of shell. Pulse bread slices in a blender or food processor 5 times or until finely crumbled. (Yield should be about 1½ cups.)

2. Stir together mayonnaise and next 4 ingredients in a large bowl. Gently stir in breadcrumbs and crabmeat. Shape mixture into 16 (2-inch) cakes (about 2 Tbsp. each).

3. Cook cakes, in batches, on a hot, large griddle or nonstick skillet coated with cooking spray over medium-low heat 4 minutes on each side or until golden brown. Season with salt to taste. (Keep cakes warm in a 200° oven for up to 30 minutes.) Serve with Garlic-Chive Sauce. Garnish, if desired.

Note: For testing purposes, we used Sara Lee Soft & Smooth Whole Grain White Bread.

Per cake and 1 Tbsp. sauce (not including salt to taste): Calories 67; Fat 3.7g (sat 1.3g, mono 0.2g, poly 0.1g); Protein 4.2g; Carb 4.3g; Fiber 0.4g; Chol 41mg; Iron 0.3mg; Sodium 238mg; Calc 12mg

Garlic-Chive Sauce:

MAKES 1 CUP; **PREP:** 10 MIN., **CHILL:** 30 MIN.

¾ cup light sour cream*
1 garlic clove, minced
1 Tbsp. chopped fresh chives
¾ tsp. lemon zest
1½ Tbsp. fresh lemon juice
¼ tsp. salt
⅛ tsp. pepper

1. Stir together all ingredients in a small bowl. Cover and chill 30 minutes before serving.

—**SHERRY LITTLE**, SHERWOOD, ARKANSAS

*Light mayonnaise may be substituted.

Per 1 Tbsp.: Calories 16; Fat 0.9g (sat 0.7g, mono 0g, poly 0g); Protein 0.8g; Carb 1g; Fiber 0g; Chol 0mg; Iron 0mg; Sodium 46mg; Calc 1mg

Cool Beans

As soybeans, they're totally boring. But as edamame, they rock.

The first time Executive Editor Scott Jones' teeth slid across the salty, green skin of an edamame pod, it was a little like eating boiled peanuts. Edamame (eh-dah-MAH-meh) are young, green soybeans with a mild, nutty flavor and crisp texture. The beans are also packed with fiber and protein. Most people enjoy them boiled in their pods and salted. He also loves to keep bags of frozen shelled edamame on hand to add to casseroles, pastas, soups, or salads. Look for them in the freezer case at the supermarket. Ready-to-eat edamame are sometimes found in the produce section.

Kid Approved

My chicken-finger-loving 9-year-old, Tallulah, may be the pickiest eater on the planet (a real bummer for her "foodie" dad). The one bright spot? She goes crazy for edamame. For Tallulah, it's all about the fun factor. "I love popping them out of their shells into my mouth. Plus, they're not as mushy as carrots or peas," she says with a smile.

—FOOD EXECUTIVE EDITOR **SCOTT JONES**

Roasted Garlic-Edamame Spread

editor's pick • make ahead

MAKES ABOUT 2½ CUPS; **PREP:** 15 MIN., **BAKE:** 30 MIN., **COOL:** 5 MIN.

This spread is a delicious alternative to hummus. It pairs well with fresh-cut vegetables and is also delicious on toasted crostini and topped with fresh basil. It also works well as a sandwich spread and can be made up to three days ahead.

1 garlic bulb
1 Tbsp. olive oil
2 cups fully cooked, shelled edamame
   (green soybeans)*
½ cup ricotta cheese
¼ cup chopped fresh basil
2 Tbsp. lemon juice
¼ cup olive oil
1 tsp. kosher salt
½ tsp. freshly ground pepper
Assorted fresh vegetables

1. Preheat oven to 425°. Cut off pointed end of garlic; place garlic on a piece of aluminum foil, and drizzle with 1 Tbsp. olive oil. Fold foil to seal. Bake 30 minutes; let cool 5 minutes. Squeeze pulp from garlic cloves into a bowl.
2. Process edamame in a food processor 30 seconds or until smooth, stopping to scrape down sides. Add roasted garlic, ricotta, basil, and lemon juice; pulse 2 to 3 times or until blended.
3. With processor running, pour ¼ cup oil through food chute in a slow, steady stream, processing until smooth. Stir in salt and pepper. Serve with assorted fresh vegetables.
*2 cups uncooked, frozen, shelled edamame (green soybeans) may be substituted. Prepare edamame according to package directions. Plunge into ice water to stop the cooking process; drain. Proceed with recipe as directed. **Note:** For testing purposes only, we used Marjon Shelled Fully Cooked Edamame.

Roasted Garlic-Lima Bean Spread: Substitute 2 cups frozen lima beans for edamame. Prepare lima beans according to package directions. Proceed with recipe as directed.

Crunchy Edamame Slaw

make ahead

MAKES 8 SERVINGS; **PREP:** 30 MIN., **BAKE:** 5 MIN., **CHILL:** 1 HR.

¼ cup chopped lightly salted cashews
¾ cup reduced-fat mayonnaise
1 Tbsp. sesame seeds
2 Tbsp. white wine vinegar
1 Tbsp. soy sauce
2 tsp. sesame oil
2 tsp. honey
4 cups shredded red cabbage (about ½
   head)
2 cups fully cooked, frozen, shelled
   edamame (green soybeans), thawed
1½ cups grated carrots (3 medium carrots)
1 cup peeled, seeded, and diced
   cucumber (about 1 medium cucumber)
¼ cup chopped fresh cilantro
3 Tbsp. thinly sliced green onions
   (2 green onions)
Salt and pepper to taste

1. Preheat oven to 350°. Bake cashews in a single layer in a shallow pan 5 to 6 minutes or until lightly toasted and fragrant, stirring occasionally.
2. Whisk together mayonnaise and next 5 ingredients in a large bowl. Add cabbage, next 5 ingredients, and toasted cashews, tossing to coat. Stir in salt and pepper to taste. Cover and chill 1 to 4 hours.

Let's Talk Turkey

Just because the days are longer doesn't mean you have to spend more time in the kitchen. Check out this speedy approach to tonight's meal.

Speedy Supper

SERVES 4

Mediterranean Turkey Cutlets and Pasta

Green vegetable or tossed salad

Blueberry-Pecan Cobbler (following page)

Iced tea or lemonade

Here are Assistant Food Editor Natalie Kelly Brown's requirements for a perfect main dish: fast prep and cook times, few ingredients, and enticing enough to satisfy hungry appetites. Speedy Mediterranean Turkey Cutlets and Pasta meets her demands. Add a green vegetable or tossed salad, and you're good to go. Blueberry-Pecan Cobbler with its buttery bread-and-sugar topping makes a delightful finale. Put it in the oven before you start the pasta—it will be ready to serve by the end of the meal.

Mediterranean Turkey Cutlets and Pasta

family favorite •fast fixin's

MAKES 4 SERVINGS; **PREP**: 10 MIN., **COOK**: 16 MIN.

Feta cheese and black olives have a wonderful naturally salty flavor our staff loves. Both are assertive, so you won't need to add extra salt. Feel free to substitute your favorite canned tomato blend.

½ (16-oz.) package fettuccine
1 lb. turkey cutlets
1 tsp. Greek seasoning, divided*
¼ cup all-purpose flour
5 Tbsp. olive oil, divided
½ cup chopped red onion
1 (14.5-oz.) can diced tomatoes with balsamic vinegar, basil, and olive oil, undrained
1 (3.8-oz.) can sliced pitted black olives, drained
½ cup crumbled feta cheese
Garnish: chopped fresh parsley

1. Prepare pasta according to package directions.
2. Meanwhile, sprinkle cutlets with ¾ tsp. Greek seasoning. Dredge in flour.
3. Cook half of cutlets in 1½ Tbsp. hot oil in a large nonstick skillet over medium-high heat 3 minutes on each side or until done. Repeat procedure with remaining cutlets and 1½ Tbsp. oil. Remove from skillet, reserving drippings in skillet.
4. Heat remaining 2 Tbsp. oil in skillet with drippings; add onion and remaining ¼ tsp. Greek seasoning, and sauté over medium heat 2 to 3 minutes or until tender. Stir in tomatoes and olives, and cook 1 minute or until thoroughly heated. Remove from heat, and toss in hot cooked pasta until blended.
5. Transfer pasta mixture to a large serving bowl, and sprinkle with half of feta cheese. Top with cutlets and remaining feta cheese. Garnish, if desired. Serve immediately.
*Dried Italian seasoning may be substituted.

Mom's Know-How

I'll let you in on a secret—seasoned canned tomatoes are my friend. They add explosive flavor and take recipes a step beyond ordinary. And the fire-roasted ones can't be beat. Do as I do, and stock up when your local grocer has them on sale. You won't regret it.

—**NATALIE KELLY BROWN**,
ASSISTANT FOOD EDITOR

Blueberry-Pecan Cobbler

MAKES 6 SERVINGS; **PREP:** 15 MIN.,
BAKE: 40 MIN., **STAND:** 10 MIN.

*If you're lucky enough to have leftovers,
reheat and spoon over yogurt for a
luscious breakfast.*

3 (12-oz.) packages frozen blueberries,
    thawed and drained
½ tsp. ground cinnamon
½ tsp. vanilla extract
¾ cup sugar, divided
5 Tbsp. all-purpose flour, divided
5 white bread slices
5 Tbsp. butter, melted
1 large egg
½ cup pecans, finely chopped

1. Preheat oven to 350°. Stir together
first 3 ingredients, ¼ cup sugar, and
3 Tbsp. flour in a lightly greased
11- x 7-inch baking dish.
2. Trim crusts from bread slices; cut
each slice into 5 strips. Arrange strips
over blueberry mixture. Stir together
butter, egg, and remaining ½ cup sugar
and 2 Tbsp. flour. Drizzle over bread
slices. Sprinkle with pecans.
3. Bake at 350° for 40 to 45 minutes
or until golden and bubbly. Let stand
10 minutes. Serve warm.

Pretty Sugar Cookies

Stir up a flutter of compliments with these springtime sweets.

Bring instant smiles with our
glittery butterfly cookies.
The quick-to-mix dough
is a cinch to prepare and,
once baked, even more fun
to decorate. Dip cookies in a three-
ingredient glaze for a sweet pop of color,
and if you like, add a light sprinkle of
sugary sparkle. Perfectly paired with a
glass of lemonade or a cup of tea, these
delightful treats are sure to make any
afternoon special.

Find It

We used a mix of vintage cookie
cutters and others that can be
found on the Internet. Large
and medium butterfly cutters
can be purchased from
www.cakesnthings.com and
www.sugarcraft.com. Look for
other similar butterfly shapes at
www.coppergifts.com.

Chocolate Sugar Cookies
editor's pick

MAKES ABOUT 3 DOZEN (3-INCH) COOKIES
OR 12 (4½-INCH) COOKIES;
PREP: 1 HR., **CHILL:** 10 MIN.,
BAKE: 10 OR 15 MIN. PER BATCH,
COOL: 35 MIN.

*Feel free to use several butterfly cutters in
different sizes. Because bake times vary,
place cutouts of similar sizes on the same
cookie sheet.*

1 cup butter, softened
1 cup sugar
1 large egg
2¼ cups all-purpose flour
¾ cup unsweetened cocoa
¼ tsp. salt

1. Preheat oven to 350°. Beat butter and
sugar at medium speed with an electric
mixer until fluffy. Add egg, beating
until blended.
2. Combine flour, cocoa, and salt;
gradually add to butter mixture, beating
just until blended.
3. Divide dough into 2 equal portions;
flatten each portion into a disk. Cover
and chill 10 minutes.
4. Place 1 portion of dough on a lightly
floured surface, and roll to ⅛-inch
thickness. Cut with a 3- or 4½-inch
butterfly-shaped cutter. Place cookies
2 inches apart on lightly greased baking
sheets. Repeat procedure with remaining dough portion.
5. Bake, in batches, at 350° for 10 to
12 minutes (for 3-inch cookies) and
15 to 17 minutes (for 4½-inch cookies) or until edges are lightly browned.
Let cool on baking sheets 5 minutes;
remove to wire racks, and let cool
30 minutes or until completely cool.
Decorate baked cookies as desired.

Don't Be a Reluctant Baker

Repeat after us: Cookie decorating is a breeze. Glazing the cookies is the easiest way to get bakery-quality beauty, or you can pipe on a design of your choice. Use these helpful tips as a guide.

- Dip tops of cookies in Colorful Vanilla Glaze, and place, glazed side up, on wax paper. Let stand one hour or until glaze is set.
- Use a No. 4 tip on a disposable decorating bag to add pizzazz to cookies. Or try our easy way: Spoon Royal Icing into a zip-top plastic freezer bag. (Do not seal.) Snip one corner of bag to make a small hole. Pipe on Royal Icing, and sprinkle with colored sugar, if desired. Tilt cookies to remove excess sugar. Let stand two hours.
- Brush cooled cookies with Clear Edible Glue, and sprinkle with colored sugar. Tilt cookies to remove excess sugar. Let stand 30 minutes.

Vanilla Sugar Cookies: Omit unsweetened cocoa. Increase flour to 3 cups. Beat in 1 tsp. vanilla extract with butter in Step 1. Proceed with recipe as directed.

Clear Edible Glue

MAKES 2 TBSP. (ENOUGH FOR ABOUT 1½ DOZEN [3-INCH] OR 8 TO 12 [4½-INCH] COOKIES); **PREP:** 3 MIN.

1. Whisk together 2 Tbsp. water and 2 tsp. meringue powder until blended. **Note:** Purchase meringue powder at cake-supply and crafts stores or supercenters.

Colorful Vanilla Glaze

MAKES ABOUT 1 CUP; **PREP:** 5 MIN.

We tinted our frostings with Wilton's cornflower blue and violet food coloring pastes (also called icing colors).

1 (16-oz.) package powdered sugar
Food coloring paste

1. Stir together powdered sugar and 6 Tbsp. water. Tint with desired amount of food coloring paste, stirring until blended. **Note:** Purchase food coloring paste at cake-supply and crafts stores or supercenters.

Royal Icing

MAKES ABOUT 1¾ CUPS; **PREP:** 5 MIN.

2 Tbsp. meringue powder
3 cups powdered sugar
¼ cup cold water
Food coloring paste

1. Beat meringue powder, powdered sugar, and ¼ cup cold water at high speed with a heavy-duty electric stand mixer, using a whisk attachment, until glossy and stiff peaks form. Tint with desired amount of food coloring paste, and beat until blended. Place a damp cloth directly on surface of icing (to prevent a crust from forming) while icing cookies.

Cooking Fresh

Tips, tricks, and flat-out fast frittatas.

Garden Variety Long warm days usher in a wildly delicious season of local farmers markets and roadside produce stands. And Test Kitchen Professional Angela Sellers is sure to be cooking something wonderful with her finds. This month, she shares a recipe for a feather-light frittata and a few insider tips for shopping.

- Smooth-skinned, round potatoes are low in starch and perfect for boiling or roasting. Cook extra to add to frittatas, salads, and breakfast dishes.
- Crisp Kirby cucumbers (also known as pickling cucumbers) are a top choice for sandwiches and salads. Store unwashed in a perforated bag.
- Sweet onions are the buried treasure of early summer. Look for dry, shiny, paper-thin skins. Any hint of odor indicates bruising.
- Freshly picked sweet corn has moist, green husks with straight rows of plump, shiny, evenly formed kernels.
- Fragrance rather than color is the best sign of a good tomato.
- Slender, crisp, bright-colored green beans and firm summer squash with glossy skins are the most tender.

Create a Stir Angela keeps a blender handy for quickly mixing omelets and frittatas. This kitchen essential can also grind coffee beans and whole spices, make breadcrumbs, whip up instant puddings, and reconstitute frozen fruit juice. Don't spend a fortune—less expensive options often perform quite well. However, lightweight plastic blender jars are less stable than glass, scratch easily, and sometimes absorb odors.

Angela's Vegetable Frittata

MAKES 6 TO 8 SERVINGS; **PREP:** 15 MIN.,
COOK: 21 MIN., **BAKE:** 10 MIN.

2 large leeks
2 Tbsp. olive oil
1 cup diced, cooked potato
1 lb. summer squash, sliced
2 Tbsp. chopped fresh parsley
½ tsp. chopped fresh thyme
½ tsp. freshly ground pepper
¾ tsp. salt, divided
8 large eggs
½ cup milk
¾ cup (3 oz.) shredded Parmesan cheese

1. Preheat oven to 450°. Remove and discard root ends and dark green tops of leeks. Cut in half lengthwise, and rinse thoroughly under cold running water to remove grit and sand. Thinly slice leeks.
2. Sauté leeks in 1 Tbsp. hot oil in a 10-inch ovenproof skillet over medium-high heat 4 to 5 minutes or until tender. Remove from skillet. Sauté potato in remaining 1 Tbsp. oil in skillet 3 to 4 minutes or until golden. Add squash, and sauté 10 minutes. Stir in leeks, parsley, thyme, pepper, and ½ tsp. salt until blended.
3. Process eggs, milk, ½ cup Parmesan cheese, ¼ cup water, and remaining ¼ tsp. salt in a blender until blended; pour over leek mixture in skillet. Cook over medium heat, without stirring, 2 minutes or until edges of frittata are set. (Edges should appear firm when pan is gently shaken; the top layer should appear wet.) Sprinkle with remaining ¼ cup cheese.
4. Bake at 450° for 10 to 12 minutes or until center is set.

June

Take Your Pick

Celebrate this month's arrival of Southern blackberries and peaches with 15 all-too-easy recipes—from coffee cake to chicken salad.

Sweet and still warm from the sun, Southern peaches are as close as you will ever get to tasting heaven on earth. In full glory, our blackberries are no less divine. Baskets of these luscious fruits line the stalls at local farmers markets, but if you really want to fill your heart with joy, head down a county road one Saturday morning.

Blackberry-Peach Coffee Cake

MAKES 8 SERVINGS; **PREP:** 20 MIN.;
BAKE: 1 HR., 10 MIN.; **COOL:** 1 HR., 30 MIN.
(Pictured on page 177)

Streusel Topping
½ cup butter, softened
1 cup granulated sugar
2 large eggs
2 cups all-purpose flour
2 tsp. baking powder
½ tsp. salt
⅔ cup milk
2 tsp. vanilla extract
2 cups peeled and sliced fresh firm, ripe
    peaches (about 2 large peaches,
    7 oz. each)
1 cup fresh blackberries
Powdered sugar
Garnishes: fresh blackberries, sliced
    peaches

1. Preheat oven to 350°. Prepare Streusel Topping.
2. Beat butter at medium speed with an electric mixer until creamy; gradually add granulated sugar, beating well. Add eggs, 1 at a time, beating until blended after each addition.
3. Combine flour, baking powder, and salt; add to butter mixture alternately with milk, beginning and ending with flour mixture. Beat at low speed until blended after each addition. Stir in vanilla. Pour batter into a greased and floured 9-inch springform pan; top with sliced peaches and blackberries. Pinch off 1-inch pieces of Streusel Topping, and drop over fruit.
4. Bake at 350° for 1 hour and 10 minutes to 1 hour and 20 minutes or until center of cake is set. (A wooden pick inserted in center will not come out clean.) Cool completely on a wire rack (about 1½ hours). Dust with powdered sugar. Garnish, if desired.
Note: We found that using a shiny or light-colored pan gave us the best results. If you have a dark pan, wrap the outside of the pan with heavy-duty aluminum foil to get a similar result.

Peach Coffee Cake: Omit blackberries. Increase peaches to 3 cups sliced (about 3 large peaches, 7 oz. each). Proceed with recipe as directed.
—AURA LEIGH BORRETT,
OREGON, WISCONSIN

Streusel Topping:
MAKES 1½ CUPS; **PREP:** 10 MIN.

½ cup butter, softened
½ cup granulated sugar
½ cup firmly packed light brown sugar
⅔ cup all-purpose flour
1 tsp. ground cinnamon
½ tsp. ground nutmeg

1. Beat butter at medium speed with an electric mixer until creamy; gradually add granulated sugar and brown sugar, beating well. Add flour, cinnamon, and nutmeg; beat just until blended.

Peach-Blackberry-Yogurt Fruit Cups
fast fixin's
MAKES 4 SERVINGS; **PREP:** 20 MIN.

Peel and slice 2 ripe peaches. Stir together 1½ cups Greek yogurt and 3 Tbsp. honey. Divide peaches, ¾ cup blackberries, yogurt mixture, and ¼ cup granola among 4 glass bowls. Drizzle with additional honey, if desired. Serve immediately.
Note: For testing purposes only, we used Big Sky Bread Company granola.

Where to pick 'em

Here are some great markets to bring home fresh blackberries and peaches. Or you can visit *southernliving.com/localmarkets* for more choices. Please check with vendors before driving long distances, as weather can affect the quantities available.

Blackberries
- **Carrboro Farmers' Market,** Carrboro, North Carolina; www.carrborofarmersmarket. com or (919) 280-3326
- **Nashville Farmers' Market,** Nashville, Tennessee; www.nashvillefarmersmarket.org or (615) 880-2001
- **Petals from the Past,** Jemison, Alabama; www.petalsfromthepast.com or (205) 646-0069

Peaches
- **Cooley Brothers' Peach Farm,** Chesnee, South Carolina; (864) 461-7225
- **Durbin Farms,** Clanton, Alabama; (205) 755-1672
- **Psencik Peach Farm,** Fredericksburg, Texas; www.texaspeaches.com or (830) 990-0152

Georgia Peach Buttercream Frosting

MAKES 4⅓ CUPS; **PREP:** 15 MIN.

This delicately flavored frosting makes just the right amount for a 2-layer, 9-inch cake or a 13- x 9-inch sheet cake.

1 large fresh peach, peeled and chopped (about 8 oz.)
¾ cup butter, softened
1 (32-oz.) package powdered sugar

1. Process peach in a blender or food processor until pureed. (Puree should measure about ½ cup.)
2. Beat butter at medium speed with an electric mixer until creamy; gradually add powdered sugar alternately with pureed peach, beating until well blended after each addition.

—INSPIRED BY **SUSAN C. RICHARDSON**, VIENNA, GEORGIA

Cobbler Custard Cups

MAKES 8 SERVINGS; **PREP:** 15 MIN., **BAKE:** 20 MIN., **COOL:** 40 MIN.

Premium ice cream gives the custard an extra-rich texture, but other brands can also be used in this recipe. The addition of flour eliminates the need for a troublesome water bath.

1½ cups fresh blackberries
1½ cups peeled and chopped fresh peaches (about 2 large)
1 pt. premium vanilla ice cream, melted
¼ cup all-purpose flour
3 large eggs, lightly beaten
1 (5.25-oz.) package sugar cookies, coarsely chopped

1. Preheat oven to 350°. Divide blackberries and peaches between 8 lightly greased 6-oz. custard cups (about ⅓ cup per custard cup).
2. Pour melted ice cream into flour in a slow, steady stream, whisking constantly until smooth; whisk in eggs. Pour mixture over fruit in custard cups. Top

with sugar cookies. Place custard cups on a 15- x 10-inch jelly-roll pan.
3. Bake at 350° for 20 to 25 minutes or until custard is set. Cool on pan 40 minutes.
Note: For testing purposes only, we used Häagen-Dazs Vanilla Ice Cream and Pepperidge Farm Sugar Home Style Cookies. We also tested with Blue Bell Homemade Vanilla Ice Cream.

Blackberry Cornbread

MAKES 8 TO 10 SERVINGS; **PREP:** 15 MIN., **BAKE:** 30 MIN.

We also tested this recipe using ½ cup melted butter in place of the canola oil and loved the rich, pound cake-like flavor it gave to this sweet cornbread.

2 cups self-rising white cornmeal
½ cup sugar
5 large eggs
1 (16-oz.) container sour cream
½ cup canola oil
2 cups fresh blackberries

1. Preheat oven to 450°. Stir together cornmeal and sugar in a large bowl; make a well in center of mixture. Whisk together eggs, sour cream, and oil; add to cornmeal mixture, stirring just until dry ingredients are moistened. Fold in blackberries. Spoon batter into a lightly greased 12-inch cast-iron skillet.
2. Bake at 450° for 30 minutes or until a wooden pick inserted in center comes out clean, shielding with aluminum foil after 25 minutes to prevent excessive browning, if necessary.

—**ALLEN CARTER**, LEXINGTON, KENTUCKY

Blackberry Cornbread Muffins: Prepare batter as directed. Coat 2 muffin pans with vegetable cooking spray; spoon batter into muffin pans, filling three-fourths full. Bake at 450° for 15 to 17 minutes or until tops are golden brown. Cool in pan on a wire rack 5 minutes. Remove from pan to wire rack. Makes 2 dozen muffins; Bake: 15 min. Cool: 5 min.

Three-Cheese Blackberry Quesadillas With Pepper-Peach Salsa

MAKES 4 SERVINGS; **PREP:** 20 MIN., **COOK:** 4 MIN. PER BATCH

You may shy away from the thought of a blackberry quesadilla, but don't, especially when it's paired with a fiery peach salsa. Just imagine a Rio Grande version of cream cheese and pepper jelly sandwiched between the crispness of a pan-fried tortilla.

1 (4-oz.) goat cheese log, softened
½ (8-oz.) package cream cheese, softened
½ cup freshly grated Parmesan cheese
8 (7-inch) soft taco-size flour tortillas
1⅔ cups fresh blackberries, halved
Pepper-Peach Salsa

1. Stir together softened goat cheese, softened cream cheese, and Parmesan cheese until blended. Spread cheese mixture on 1 side of each tortilla; top with blackberries. Fold in half.
2. Cook tortillas, in batches, in a lightly greased large nonstick skillet over medium-high heat 1 to 2 minutes on each side or until golden brown. Cut into wedges, and serve with Pepper-Peach Salsa.

Two-Cheese Blackberry Quesadillas: Omit goat cheese. Increase cream cheese to 1 (8-oz.) package. Proceed with recipe as directed.

Pepper-Peach Salsa:

MAKES ABOUT 1½ CUPS; **PREP:** 15 MIN., **COOK:** 3 MIN.

2 large fresh peaches, diced (about 1½ cups)
½ cup peach jam
1 tsp. lime zest
2 tsp. fresh lime juice
½ tsp. dried crushed red pepper

1. Stir together all ingredients in a small saucepan, and cook over medium heat, stirring often, 2 to 3 minutes or until thoroughly heated.

—INSPIRED BY **MICHAELA ROSENTHAL**, WOODLAND HILLS, CALIFORNIA

Ham Sausage With Fresh Peach Chutney

MAKES 6 SERVINGS; **PREP:** 20 MIN., **COOK:** 12 MIN.

1 lb. chopped cooked ham
½ (16-oz.) package hot ground pork
    sausage
1 large egg, lightly beaten
¾ cup lightly packed soft, fresh
    breadcrumbs (about 2 sandwich bread
    slices)
12 fully cooked bacon slices
Wooden picks
Fresh Peach Chutney

1. Pulse ham in a food processor 4 to 5 times or until finely ground.
2. Stir together ham and next 3 ingredients in a large bowl just until combined. Shape ham mixture into 6 (3¼-inch) patties. Wrap each patty with 2 bacon slices, and secure with wooden picks.
3. Cook patties in a large lightly greased skillet over medium heat 5 to 6 minutes on each side or until done. Remove wooden picks. Serve with Fresh Peach Chutney.
Note: For testing purposes only, we used Oscar Mayer Fully Cooked Bacon.

—**CHRISTIE BURNS**, VILONIA, ARKANSAS

Ham Sausage and Biscuits: Omit bacon. Proceed with recipe as directed, shaping ham mixture into 12 (2¾-inch) patties. Serve with hot biscuits and Fresh Peach Chutney. Makes 12 servings.

Fresh Peach Chutney:

MAKES 1¼ CUPS; **PREP:** 15 MIN., **COOK:** 6 MIN.

1 Tbsp. butter
⅓ cup finely chopped sweet onion
1½ cups chopped fresh peaches
    (about 2 large peaches)
3 Tbsp. light brown sugar
2 Tbsp. balsamic vinegar
½ tsp. Jamaican jerk seasoning

1. Melt butter in a small skillet over medium heat; add onion and sauté 2 to 3 minutes or until tender. Add peaches and remaining ingredients, and cook, stirring often, 2 to 3 minutes or until thoroughly heated.

—**CHRISTIE BURNS**, VILONIA, ARKANSAS

Party Chicken Salad

MAKES 6 SERVINGS; **PREP:** 20 MIN., **BAKE:** 5 MIN., **COOL:** 15 MIN., **CHILL:** 2 HR.

The juice from the peaches adds a sweet note to this luncheon favorite. Serve on a bed of baby lettuces tossed with blackberries. (Pictured on page 176)

1 cup chopped pecans
½ cup mayonnaise
¼ cup minced sweet onion
2 Tbsp. chopped fresh basil
½ tsp. salt
½ tsp. freshly ground pepper
4 cups chopped cooked chicken breast
4 small fresh, firm, ripe peaches, peeled and
    diced
Garnishes: fresh basil sprigs, fresh
    blackberries

1. Preheat oven to 350°. Bake pecans in a single layer on a baking sheet 5 to 7 minutes or until lightly toasted and fragrant. Cool completely in pan on a wire rack (about 15 minutes).
2. Stir together mayonnaise and next 4 ingredients in a large bowl. Fold in pecans, chicken, and peaches; cover and chill 2 hours. Garnish, if desired.

—INSPIRED BY **JUDY FARRINGTON AUST**, TUCKER, GEORGIA

BBQ 101: the art of low & slow

World champion pitmaster Chris Lilly shares his top three tips—and secret recipes—in this look at his new cookbook.

Chris Lilly, author of *Big Bob Gibson's BBQ Book* (Clarkson Potter, 2009), is the Muhammad Ali of competitive barbecue, having won multiple categories at the circuit's Big Three contests: the Memphis in May World Championship Barbeque Cooking Contest (Memphis, Tennessee), the American Royal Open (Kansas City, Missouri), and the Jack Daniel's World Championship Invitational Barbecue (Lynchburg, Tennessee). Chris loves nothing more than talking shop and sharing his tricks of the trade with everyone from the seasoned pro to what he calls "the barbecue beginner."

Championship Pork Butt

MAKES 10 TO 12 SERVINGS; **PREP:** 20 MIN., **GRILL:** 9 HR., **STAND:** 15 MIN.
(Pictured on page 174)

1 (6- to 8-lb.) bone-in pork shoulder roast
    (Boston butt)
Pork Butt Injection Marinade
Pork Butt Dry Rub

1. Rinse pork roast, and pat dry. Inject top of roast at 1-inch intervals with Pork Butt Injection Marinade.
2. Coat roast with Pork Butt Dry Rub, pressing gently to adhere rub to pork.
3. Light one side of grill, heating to 250° (low) heat; leave other side unlit. Place roast over unlit side, and grill,

Here's how to get started.

1. "Overseasoning or overmarinating is a rookie mistake," Chris says. The secret is not in a rub or sauce, but mastering the art of "low and slow" (low heat and slow cooking). Only then are you ready to create your signature flavors.
2. Start with a two-zone fire. Create two different cooking zones by piling hot coals on only one side of the grill (leaving the other side unlit). This approach creates an area for both direct and indirect cooking, increasing the versatility of your grill. The hot (direct) zone is used to sear or grill meats at a high temperature, while the cooler (indirect) zone is used for low-temperature barbecuing.
3. Think of wood as a seasoning rather than a fuel source. Start with a combination of charcoal and a few wet wood chips. The more your confidence and experience grow, the more wood you can use. Chris recommends fruitwoods such as apple, peach, and apricot for pork and chicken; oak, mesquite, and hickory work well for beef.

covered with grill lid, 7 to 9 hours or until a meat thermometer inserted into thickest portion registers 190°, maintaining temperature inside grill between 225° and 250°. Let stand 15 minutes. Slice, shred, or chop roast.

Pork Butt Injection Marinade:
MAKES ABOUT ⅔ CUP; PREP: 5 MIN.

⅓ cup apple juice
⅓ cup white grape juice
¼ cup sugar
1½ Tbsp. salt

1. Stir together all ingredients in a medium bowl. Store in an airtight container in refrigerator up to 2 weeks.

Pork Butt Dry Rub:
MAKES ABOUT 3½ TBSP.; PREP: 10 MIN.

4 tsp. seasoned salt
2 tsp. dark brown sugar
1½ tsp. granulated sugar
1½ tsp. paprika
¼ tsp. garlic powder
¼ tsp. pepper
⅛ tsp. dry mustard
⅛ tsp. ground cumin
1/16 tsp. ground ginger

1. Stir together all ingredients. Store in an airtight container up to 1 month.

Apricot-Pineapple Sweet Ribs
MAKES 4 TO 6 SERVINGS; PREP: 20 MIN.; GRILL: 3 HR., 30 MIN.

The supercharged Rib Liquid Seasoning used to baste Apricot-Pineapple Sweet Ribs takes the South's favorite finger food to new heights. (Pictured on page 175)

2 slabs baby back ribs (about 2 lb. each)
Rib Dry Rub
Rib Liquid Seasoning
Sweet Barbecue Glaze

1. Remove thin membrane from back of each slab by slicing into it and then pulling it off. (This will make ribs more tender.) Generously apply Rib Dry Rub on both sides of ribs, pressing gently to adhere.
2. Light one side of grill, heating to 250° (low) heat; leave other side unlit. Place slabs, meat sides up, over unlit side, and grill, covered with grill lid, 2 hours and 15 minutes, maintaining temperature inside grill between 225° and 250°.
3. Remove slabs from grill. Place each slab, meat side down, on a large piece of heavy-duty aluminum foil. (Foil should be large enough to completely wrap slab.) Pour ½ cup of Rib Liquid Seasoning over each slab. Tightly wrap

each slab in foil. Return slabs to unlit side of grill. Grill, covered with grill lid, 1 hour.
4. Remove slabs; unwrap and discard foil. Brush Sweet Barbecue Glaze on both sides of slabs. Grill slabs, covered with grill lid, on unlit side of grill 15 minutes or until caramelized.

Rib Dry Rub:
MAKES ABOUT ½ CUP; PREP: 5 MIN.

¼ cup firmly packed dark brown sugar
4 tsp. garlic salt
4 tsp. chili powder
2 tsp. salt
1 tsp. ground black pepper
½ tsp. celery salt
¼ tsp. ground white pepper
¼ tsp. ground red pepper
¼ tsp. ground cinnamon

1. Stir together all ingredients. Store in an airtight container up to 1 month.

Rib Liquid Seasoning:
MAKES ABOUT 1 CUP; PREP: 5 MIN.

½ cup pineapple juice
½ cup apricot nectar
1 Tbsp. Rib Dry Rub
1½ tsp. balsamic vinegar
1½ tsp. minced garlic

1. Stir together all ingredients. Store in airtight container in refrigerator up to 2 weeks.

Sweet Barbecue Glaze:
MAKES ABOUT 1½ CUPS; PREP: 5 MIN.

1¼ cups premium tomato-based barbecue sauce
¼ cup honey

1. Stir together all ingredients. Store in an airtight container in refrigerator up to 2 weeks.
Note: For testing purposes only, we used Big Bob Gibson Bar-B-Q Championship Red Sauce.

Season Like a Pro

Follow Chris Lilly's simple, four-step method (adapted from his cookbook) to create your own signature dry rub. The key to building a rub, he says, is understanding how the various seasonings work together.

Step 1: Salts and Sugars

The first thing to consider is the ratio of salt to sugar. A higher ratio of salt works best in rubs for beef, fish, and wild game, while those with more sugar are better suited for pork.

Salt—Refined, fine grained (included in Big Bob's secret pork shoulder seasoning)

Kosher salt—Additive-free, coarse grained

Sea salt—From evaporated seawater; usually very fine grained

Seasoned salt—Regular salt combined with flavoring ingredients (e.g., garlic salt, onion salt, celery salt)

White sugar—Highly refined cane or beet sugar; will scorch at hotter temperatures

Brown sugar—White sugar combined with molasses; adds color and flavor to barbecue

Step 2: Pepper

Dry rubs need to be balanced not only in flavor but also in heat. Add ground pepper to the salt-sugar mix in small increments until your ideal blend of heat and flavor is reached. Adding more pepper is always an option, but you can't remove it, so go slow.

Cayenne pepper—Also called ground red pepper. This hot powder provides instant, or front-end, heat.

White pepper—With a lighter color and a milder flavor, it provides gentle heat and background warmth.

Black pepper—It has a stronger flavor than white or cayenne. Fine- or coarse-ground, both work great.

Chile pepper—Not to be confused with chili (with an "i") powder.

Flavors vary from very hot to mild. Smoked chile powders such as ground chipotle are also widely available.

Step 3: Transition Spices

Transition spices unite the rub's sugars, salts, and peppers. These spices are not as dominant as other spices, so they can be added with a heavier hand.

Chili powder—Has a pungent earthy flavor. Use with beef, lamb, pork, and wild game.

Cumin—Aromatic with a nutty, light peppery flavor. Use with beef, poultry, fish, pork, and seafood.

Paprika—Hungarian paprika has a deeper, heartier flavor, while Spanish paprika has a milder flavor. Use with beef, poultry, fish, pork, and seafood.

Step 4: Signature Flavors

This is the time to stamp your name on your backyard offerings.

Coriander—Use with pork, lamb, poultry, and beef.

Dill—Use with chicken and fish.

Garlic powder—Use with pork, beef, lamb, poultry, seafood, and wild game.

Ginger—Use with wild game, fish, seafood, pork, and poultry.

Onion powder—Use with pork, lamb, poultry, beef, seafood, and wild game.

Oregano—Use with lamb, beef, and fish.

Mustard powder—Use with beef, lamb, poultry, pork, and wild game.

Rosemary—Use with fish and poultry.

Thyme—Use with beef, fish, pork, and poultry.

Grilled Potato Salad

MAKES 4 TO 5 SERVINGS;
PREP: 20 MIN., **COOK:** 10 MIN. PER BATCH,
GRILL: 30 MIN.

Chris created this sensational recipe especially for our story. It was such an enormous hit, he decided to include a version in his cookbook. (Pictured on page 10)

8 bacon slices
4 medium-size red potatoes, cut into ¾-inch cubes (about 5 cups cubed)
1 large white onion, cut into ½-inch-thick strips
Potato Salad Dry Rub
Potato Salad Dressing
Garnish: chopped fresh parsley

1. Preheat grill to 350° to 400° (medium-high) heat. Cook bacon, in batches, in a large skillet over medium-high heat 8 to 10 minutes or until crisp; remove bacon, and drain on paper towels, reserving drippings in skillet. Crumble bacon.
2. Add potatoes, onion, and Potato Salad Dry Rub to hot drippings in skillet, tossing to coat. Remove potato mixture with a slotted spoon.
3. Grill potato mixture, covered with grill lid, over 350° to 400° (medium-high) heat in a grill wok or metal basket 30 minutes or until tender, stirring every 5 minutes. Transfer mixture to a large bowl. Add Potato Salad Dressing, and toss to coat. Stir in bacon. Garnish, if desired. Serve warm.

Potato Salad Dry Rub:
MAKES ABOUT 2 TBSP.; **PREP:** 5 MIN.

2 tsp. salt
1¼ tsp. pepper
1 tsp. paprika
1 tsp. garlic powder
¼ tsp. dried thyme
¼ tsp. dried crushed rosemary
⅛ tsp. celery seeds

1. Stir together all ingredients. Store in an airtight container up to 1 month.

Potato Salad Dressing:

fast fixin's • make ahead

MAKES ABOUT ½ CUP; **PREP:** 5 MIN.

5½ Tbsp. mayonnaise
2 Tbsp. Dijon mustard
2 tsp. Worcestershire sauce

1. Stir together all ingredients. Store in an airtight container in refrigerator up to 2 weeks.

Update a Summer Classic

No need to get heavy with the ingredients. Let squash and zucchini shine with light and simple flavors.

At their seasonal peak now, tender yellow squash and zucchini always catch our eye. But much too often, these summer delicacies are smothered by cheese and tucked away somewhere in the depths of a casserole dish. While we love such traditional treatments, there's so much more to these delicious vegetables.

Summer Squash Stacks With Roasted Red Bell Pepper Sauce

fast fixin's

MAKES 4 SERVINGS; **PREP:** 20 MIN.,
BAKE: 5 MIN.

1 medium-size yellow squash, cut
   diagonally into 8 (¼-inch-thick) slices
   (about ¾ lb.)
2 medium zucchini, cut diagonally into
   16 (¼-inch-thick) slices (about 1 lb.)
2 Tbsp. olive oil
¼ tsp. salt
¼ tsp. pepper
1 (8.8-oz.) package fresh mozzarella cheese
16 basil leaves
Roasted Red Bell Pepper Sauce
Garnish: freshly shaved Parmesan cheese

1. Preheat oven to 350°. Brush squash and zucchini with oil; place in a single layer in a jelly-roll pan. Sprinkle with salt and pepper. Bake 5 minutes or until crisp-tender.
2. Cut mozzarella into 8 (¼-inch-thick) slices. Cut each slice in half. Place half of zucchini on a serving platter. Layer with half each of mozzarella and basil. Top with yellow squash. Layer with remaining mozzarella, basil, and zucchini. Top with Roasted Red Bell Pepper Sauce. Garnish, if desired.

Roasted Red Bell Pepper Sauce:

MAKES ¾ CUP; **PREP:** 5 MIN.

1 (7-oz.) jar roasted red bell peppers,
   drained
2 Tbsp. chopped fresh basil
1 Tbsp. olive oil
1 tsp. salt
2 tsp. lemon juice
½ tsp. pepper
¼ tsp. sugar

1. Process all ingredients in a blender or food processor until smooth, stopping to scrape down sides as needed.

Zucchini Ribbons With Feta and Mint

editor's pick

MAKES 6 SERVINGS; **PREP:** 20 MIN.

Make thin strips of zucchini with a vegetable peeler to create this striking summer salad. Narrow zucchini work best for this recipe so the peeler won't rip the edges of the ribbons. A wide peeler, such as a Y-shaped version, is ideal.

4 medium zucchini (about 2½ lb.)
2 shallots, minced (about ¼ cup)
¾ cup crumbled feta cheese
2 Tbsp. chopped fresh mint
2 to 3 Tbsp. fresh lemon juice
2 Tbsp. olive oil
1 tsp. salt
½ tsp. pepper
Arugula

1. Using a Y-shaped vegetable peeler, cut zucchini lengthwise into very thin strips just until seeds are visible.
2. Toss zucchini ribbons with shallots and next 6 ingredients. Serve immediately over arugula.

Squash Ribbons With Feta and Mint: Substitute yellow squash for zucchini. Proceed with recipe as directed.

Grilled Zucchini With Feta and Mint: Increase olive oil to ¼ cup. Preheat grill to 350° to 400° (medium-high) heat. Cut zucchini lengthwise into ¼-inch-thick slices. Brush with 2 Tbsp. olive oil. Grill zucchini, without grill lid, 2 to 3 minutes on each side or until tender. Proceed with recipe as directed in Step 2. Prep: 20 min.; Grill: 6 min.

Fried Green Goodness

Bet you can't resist chef Linton Hopkins's version of this iconic Southern dish.

At Restaurant Eugene in Atlanta, chef/owner Linton Hopkins puts his stamp on fried green tomatoes by serving them with a rémoulade sauce brightened by house-made bread-and-butter pickles. We substituted chopped purchased pickle slices with outstanding results. These recipes will make you glad you're a Southerner.

Fried Green Tomatoes With Bread-and-Butter Pickle Rémoulade
chef recipe • editor's pick
MAKES 6 TO 8 SERVINGS; PREP: 15 MIN.,
FRY: 6 MIN. PER BATCH

Linton prefers to fry in peanut oil because of its higher smoke point. (Pictured on page 11)

4 large green tomatoes
2 tsp. salt
1 tsp. pepper
1½ cups buttermilk
1 cup plain white cornmeal
1 Tbsp. Creole seasoning
2 cups all-purpose flour, divided
Vegetable or peanut oil
Bread-and-Butter Pickle
    Rémoulade
Garnishes: bread-and-butter pickles, fresh
    parsley sprig

1. Preheat oven to 200°. Cut tomatoes into ¼-inch-thick slices. Sprinkle both sides of tomatoes evenly with salt and pepper.
2. Pour buttermilk into a shallow dish or pie plate. Stir together cornmeal, Creole seasoning, and 1 cup flour in another shallow dish or pie plate.
3. Dredge tomatoes in remaining 1 cup flour. Dip tomatoes in buttermilk, and dredge in cornmeal mixture.
4. Pour oil to a depth of 2 inches in a large cast-iron skillet; heat over medium heat to 350°. Fry tomatoes, in batches, 2 to 3 minutes on each side or until golden. Drain on paper towels. Transfer to a wire rack; keep warm in a 200° oven until ready to serve. Sprinkle with salt to taste. Serve with Bread-and-Butter Pickle Rémoulade. Garnish, if desired.

Bread-and-Butter Pickle Rémoulade:
chef recipe • fast fixin's
MAKES ABOUT 1 CUP; PREP: 15 MIN.

This will keep in the refrigerator for about a week. Serve any left over on sandwiches or with boiled shrimp.

¾ cup mayonnaise
¼ cup Creole mustard
1 Tbsp. chopped fresh chives
1 Tbsp. chopped fresh parsley
1 Tbsp. finely chopped bread-and-butter
    pickles
1 tsp. lemon zest
1 Tbsp. lemon juice
½ tsp. hot sauce
¼ tsp. filé powder
⅛ tsp. salt
⅛ tsp. pepper

1. Stir together all ingredients.
—CHEF LINTON HOPKINS,
RESTAURANT EUGENE, ATLANTA, GEORGIA

Lightened Bread-and-Butter Pickle Rémoulade: Substitute ¾ cup light mayonnaise for regular mayonnaise.

Smart Tomatoes

Each oven-fried slice has two-thirds less calories and seven fewer fat grams than the original.

Oven-Fried Green Tomatoes With Lightened Bread-and-Butter Pickle Rémoulade
MAKES 8 SERVINGS; PREP: 15 MIN.,
BAKE: 18 MIN.

4 large green tomatoes
2 tsp. salt
1 tsp. pepper
Vegetable cooking spray
Parchment paper
1½ cups buttermilk
2 cups Japanese breadcrumbs (panko)
1 Tbsp. Creole seasoning
1 tsp. paprika
1 cup all-purpose flour
Lightened Bread-and-Butter Pickle
    Rémoulade

1. Preheat oven to 400°. Cut tomatoes into ¼-inch-thick slices. Sprinkle both sides of tomatoes evenly with 2 tsp. salt and 1 tsp. pepper.
2. Place a wire rack coated with cooking spray in a parchment paper-lined 15- x 10-inch jelly-roll pan.
3. Pour buttermilk into a shallow dish or pie plate. Stir together panko, Creole seasoning, and paprika in another shallow dish or pie plate.
4. Dredge tomatoes in flour. Dip tomatoes in buttermilk, and dredge in panko mixture. Lightly coat tomatoes on each side with cooking spray; arrange on wire rack.
5. Bake at 400° for 18 to 20 minutes or until golden brown, turning once after 10 minutes. Serve with Lightened Bread-and-Butter Pickle Rémoulade.

Herbs Make an Impact

From garden pot to cooktop, fresh herbs transform the simplest dish into something spectacular.

Trust Assistant Food Editor Marion McGahey: she is no gardener. But she cannot imagine cooking without her fresh herbs. She lines her front steps with terra-cotta pots spilling over with her fragrant favorites. Herbs couldn't be easier to grow (even for the brownest of thumbs) and brighten up everything from pasta to olive oil to veggies.

Lemon-Mint Vinaigrette
editor's pick• make ahead
MAKES 1½ CUPS; **PREP:** 10 MIN.

Drizzle this vinaigrette over salad greens topped with fish or chicken, green peas, and shredded carrots. We doubled the reader's original recipe because this dressing is so flavorful and versatile. If you don't have any extra virgin olive oil on hand, you may use all olive oil. Don't, however, use all extra virgin; the flavor will overpower the other ingredients.

½ cup olive oil
½ cup extra virgin olive oil
2 Tbsp. finely chopped fresh mint
2 Tbsp. finely chopped fresh parsley
6 Tbsp. fresh lemon juice
1 Tbsp. Dijon mustard
1 tsp. sugar
½ tsp. salt
½ tsp. pepper

1. Whisk together all ingredients. Store in an airtight container in the refrigerator up to 2 weeks. Let chilled vinaigrette come to room temperature before serving.

—INSPIRED BY **JAN MENNELL**, MIDDLETON, WISCONSIN

Herbed Breadcrumbs
fast fixin's
MAKES 2¼ CUPS; **PREP:** 15 MIN.,
COOK: 8 MIN.

These breadcrumbs quickly dress up vegetables such as green beans, asparagus, or sliced tomatoes. You can also sprinkle them over a simple broiled fish or your favorite pasta dish to add a flavorful crunch.

½ (12-oz.) sourdough French bread loaf, cut into cubes (about 3½ to 4 cups cubed)
1 tsp. minced garlic
3 Tbsp. olive oil
3 Tbsp. chopped fresh parsley
2 tsp. chopped fresh thyme
2 tsp. chopped fresh rosemary
¼ cup grated Parmesan cheese
Salt and pepper to taste

1. Process bread in a food processor 20 seconds or until coarsely ground.
2. Cook breadcrumbs and garlic in hot oil in a large nonstick skillet, stirring often, 5 to 7 minutes or until lightly browned. Stir in parsley, thyme, and rosemary, and cook 30 seconds. Remove from heat, and stir in Parmesan cheese. Season with salt and pepper to taste.
Note: Breadcrumbs can be frozen for up to 1 month. Sauté frozen breadcrumbs in a lightly greased skillet 3 to 4 minutes or until crisp.

Test Kitchen Notebook

- One of our favorite ways to use fresh herbs is to stir them into ground lamb or beef for Greek-style burgers. Serve in pitas, and top with thick Greek yogurt, arugula, and crumbled feta cheese. For every 1 pound of ground lamb or beef, stir in 1 Tbsp. chopped fresh mint, 1 Tbsp. chopped fresh parsley, and ¾ tsp. Greek seasoning. Grill burgers over 350° to 400° (medium-high) heat with grill lid closed until centers are no longer pink.
- Herb Ice Cubes are a quick and easy way to preserve an abundance of fresh herbs. Keep these convenient cubes onhand to stir into sauces or—in the case of mint—add style and flavor to iced tea and Mojitos.

Herb Ice Cubes: Process 2 cups firmly packed fresh herb leaves (such as basil, parsley, or cilantro) and 1 cup water or chicken broth in a food processor 20 seconds or until leaves are finely chopped. Divide mixture among compartments of 1 ice cube tray. Freeze 8 hours or until firm. Transfer ice cubes to a large zip-top plastic freezer bag. Store in the freezer up to 2 months. **Makes** about 12 ice cubes..

—**MARION MCGAHEY**, ASSISTANT FOOD EDITOR

Host a summer get-together with delicious Texas comfort food that's lower in fat and calories.

Texas Taco Queen

Maria Corbalan, owner of Austin's Taco Xpress, shows us how to get Texas-size flavor without the guilt.

You don't have to be raised in the South to be called a Southerner. Argentina-born Maria Corbalan, owner and creator of Taco Xpress in Austin, Texas, exemplifies Southern hospitality. "I don't shake hands, honey. I give hugs," says Maria as she welcomes customers with open arms and a rich South American accent. Her personality is warm and flavored with a little spice, just like her tacos.

But these aren't just any tacos. They're the real deal, with authentic ingredients that melt in your mouth and leave you wanting more. After one trip

Food Editor Shannon Sliter Satterwhite was hooked. Thankfully, Maria, an honorary Southerner, shared some of her unforgettable recipes with us. Did we mention they're also good for you? You wouldn't expect this from hearty comfort food, but all have fewer calories and fat than typical tacos. Though nothing compares to being at Maria's restaurant, where you can sip fresh margaritas and enjoy live music, these slightly modified recipes come pretty close to what's delivered to your table.

Don't take our word for it. Try them yourself. And if you get the pleasure of dining at Taco Xpress, give Maria a hug.

There's Something About Maria

The minute you meet Maria Corbalan, you feel like you've always known her. Maybe it's her life experiences and down-to-earth nature that make her so relatable. After living what she describes as a meandering hippie lifestyle from the age of 16, surviving rough times and overcoming addiction, this free spirit eventually found peace in Austin. Maria also found her professional calling—tacos. With $500 in her pocket and a little help from friends, she began a simple business out of a tiny converted trailer. Little did she know that her runty restaurant on wheels, known as Taco Xpress, would soon be embraced by hungry regulars who would happily wait in long lines to place their orders.

Maria has returned the favor by giving back and helping others. "I don't take anything for granted," she says. "The choices in my past keep me humble and human, and today I am thankful for my community." Now, three locations later, Taco Xpress on South Lamar is much larger than the original one but still serves some of the best tacos on the planet.

Picadillo Tacos
MAKES 8 TACOS; **PREP:** 15 MIN., **COOK:** 16 MIN.

This meaty mixture is also great served as a taco salad or wrapped in enchiladas and burritos.

1 lb. ground round
1 Tbsp. vegetable oil
2 carrots, diced
1 small onion, diced
½ tsp. salt
2 plum tomatoes, diced
1 to 2 canned chipotle peppers in adobo sauce, minced
8 (8-inch) soft taco-size corn or flour tortillas, warmed
Garnish: fresh cilantro sprigs

1. Cook ground round in hot oil in a large skillet over medium-high heat, stirring often, 7 minutes or until meat crumbles and is no longer pink. Stir in carrots, onion, and salt; sauté 5 minutes. Add tomatoes and chipotle peppers, and cook, stirring occasionally, 3 to 4 minutes or until tomatoes begin to soften. Serve mixture with warm tortillas. Garnish, if desired.

Per taco with flour tortilla and ½ cup beef mixture (not including garnish): Calories 165; Fat 5.8g (sat 1.5g, mono 1.1g, poly 1.2g); Protein 11.1g; Carb 16.8g; Fiber 1g; Chol 23mg; Iron 1.8mg; Sodium 395mg; Calc 48mg

Vegetarian Picadillo Tacos:
Substitute 1 (12-oz.) package frozen meatless burger crumbles for ground round. Proceed with recipe as directed, sautéing crumbles in hot oil 3 to 4 minutes. Prep: 15 min., Cook: 13 min.

Per taco with flour tortilla and ½ cup meatless mixture (not including toppings): Calories 173; Fat 6g (sat 0.8g, mono 0.8g, poly 2.7g); Protein 9.7g; Carb 20.6g; Fiber 2.5g; Chol 0mg; Iron 2.2mg; Sodium 548mg; Calc 63mg

Tacos Verdes

vegetarian

MAKES 16 TACOS; **PREP:** 20 MIN.,
COOK: 25 MIN.

Save the leftover vegetable mixture in the broth, and simply reheat in a saucepan. Serve with a slotted spoon over rice and beans for another hearty main dish.

½ lb. fresh green beans, trimmed and cut
    into 1-inch pieces
1 (8-oz.) package sliced fresh mushrooms
2 medium zucchini, diced
2 medium tomatoes, chopped
1 large red bell pepper, chopped
½ small eggplant, diced
1 small white onion, chopped
1 Tbsp. lime juice
1 Tbsp. vegetable oil
1¼ tsp. salt
¾ tsp. garlic powder
¾ tsp. ground cumin
¾ tsp. pepper
16 (8-inch) soft taco-size corn or flour
    tortillas, warmed
Toppings: shredded cabbage, crumbled
    queso fresco (fresh Mexican cheese)

1. Bring first 13 ingredients and 1 cup water to a boil in a large Dutch oven over medium-high heat. Reduce heat to medium-low, and cook, stirring occasionally, 20 minutes or until vegetables are tender. Serve vegetable mixture using a slotted spoon with warm tortillas and desired toppings.

Per taco with flour tortilla and ½ cup vegetable mixture (not including toppings): Calories 112; Fat 3.4g (sat 0.7g, mono 0.2g, poly 0.7g); Protein 3g, Carb 18.2g; Fiber 2g; Chol 0mg; Iron 1.2mg; Sodium 373mg; Calc 55mg

Taco Toppings

Take your pick of
nutritious toppings:

- carrots
- avocado
- mango
- onions
- queso fresco
- red cabbage
- jalapeños
- Salsa Roja (recipe
  on following page)

Tacos Al Pastor

MAKES 6 TACOS; **PREP:** 15 MIN.,
CHILL: 4 HR., **COOK:** 10 MIN.

1 lb. pork tenderloin, cut into ½-inch cubes
1 (8-oz.) can pineapple tidbits in juice,
    drained
1 medium onion, chopped
¼ cup chopped fresh cilantro
1 Tbsp. Mexican-style chili powder
1 tsp. ground cumin
1 tsp. dried oregano
1 tsp. pepper
1 tsp. chopped garlic
¾ tsp. salt
1 Tbsp. canola oil
6 (8-inch) soft taco-size corn or flour
    tortillas, warmed
Toppings: chopped radishes, fresh
    cilantro leaves, crumbled queso fresco,
    chopped onions, chopped jalapeño

1. Combine pork and next 9 ingredients in a large zip-top plastic freezer bag. Seal and chill 4 to 24 hours.

2. Cook pork mixture in hot oil in a large nonstick skillet over medium-high heat, stirring often, 10 minutes or until pork is done. Serve mixture with warm tortillas and desired toppings.

Note: For testing purposes only, we used McCormick Gourmet Collection Mexican-Style Chili Powder.

Per taco with flour tortilla and ½ cup pork mixture (not including toppings): Calories 221; Fat 8.1g (sat 1.9g, mono 2.8g, poly 1g); Protein 18.2g; Carb 17.7g; Fiber 0.8g; Chol 50mg; Iron 1.9mg; Sodium 552mg; Calc 58mg

Spicy Chicken-Pineapple Tacos:
Substitute 1 lb. skinned and boned chicken thighs, chopped, for pork tenderloin. Proceed with recipe as directed.

Per taco with flour tortilla and ½ cup chicken mixture (not including toppings): Calories 230; Fat 10.4g (sat 2.3g, mono 3.5g, poly 1g); Protein 15.5g; Carb 17.7g; Fiber 0.8g; Chol 50mg; Iron 1.8mg; Sodium 564mg; Calc 62mg

Migas Tacos

MAKES 2 TACOS; **PREP:** 15 MIN.,
COOK: 8 MIN.

⅓ cup lightly crushed tortilla chips
¼ cup chopped onion
¼ cup diced tomatoes
2 Tbsp. chopped jalapeño peppers
1 tsp. vegetable oil
2 large eggs, lightly beaten
Pinch of salt and pepper
2 (8-inch) soft taco-size flour tortillas, warmed
½ cup (2 oz.) shredded 2% reduced-fat
　　Mexican four-cheese blend

1. Sauté first 4 ingredients in hot oil
in a medium-size nonstick skillet over
medium heat 3 to 4 minutes or just until
onion is translucent.
2. Whisk together eggs, salt, and pepper.
Add to skillet, and cook, without stirring,
1 to 2 minutes or until eggs begin to set on
bottom. Gently draw cooked edges away
from sides of pan to form large pieces.
Cook, stirring occasionally, 2 minutes or
until eggs are thickened and moist. (Do
not overstir.) Spoon egg mixture into
warm tortillas, and sprinkle with cheese;
serve immediately.

Per taco with flour tortilla: Calories 256; Fat 13.8g (sat 5.7g, mono 2g,
poly 1.9g); Protein 10.7g; Carb 25g; Fiber 2g; Chol 21.8mg; Iron 1.3mg;
Sodium 384mg; Calc 280mg

Chimichurri

MAKES ¾ CUP; **PREP:** 10 MIN.,
COOK: 45 SEC., **STAND:** 5 MIN.

*This sauce is nothing like Maria's fiery
version. We toned down the heat, but we
loved her method of soaking the
pepper flakes. The bright green will
eventually darken if you make it ahead,
but it's just as good. Serve with any taco
or on grilled meats.*

1 Tbsp. dried crushed red pepper
3 Tbsp. red wine vinegar
2 large bunches fresh cilantro, coarsely
　　chopped (about 3 cups)
¼ cup vegetable oil
2 tsp. dried oregano
¼ tsp. ground black pepper
¼ tsp. salt

1. Microwave ¼ cup water at HIGH
45 seconds. Add crushed red pepper,
and let stand 5 minutes. Pour through
a fine wire-mesh strainer into a bowl,
discarding liquid.
2. Process vinegar, next 5 ingredients,
and 2 Tbsp. water in a food processor
5 to 10 seconds or until cilantro is finely
chopped. Stir in crushed red pepper.
Store in an airtight container up to
3 days.

Per Tbsp.: Calories 44; Fat 4.8g (sat 0.7g, mono 1g, poly 3g);
Protein 0.2g; Carb 0.6g; Fiber 0.4g; Chol 0mg; Iron 0.3mg;
Sodium 51mg; Calc 8mg

Salsa Roja

make ahead

MAKES 2½ CUPS; **PREP:** 10 MIN.

Add more peppers if you like yours spicy.

1 (28-oz.) can whole tomatoes, drained
3 jalapeño peppers, seeded and coarsely
　　chopped
⅓ cup coarsely chopped sweet onion
¼ cup loosely packed fresh cilantro leaves
1 garlic clove, minced
Salt to taste

1. Pulse first 5 ingredients in a blender
or food processor 5 to 6 times or just until
chopped and combined. Season with salt
to taste. Store in an airtight container in
refrigerator up to 3 days.

Per ¼ cup: Calories 17; Fat 0g (sat 0g, mono 0g, poly 0g); Protein 0.7g;
Carb 3g; Fiber 0.8g; Chol 0mg; Iron 0.4mg; Sodium 119mg; Calc 13mg

WHAT'S FOR SUPPER?

Three Layers of Flavor

Sausage, fluffy mashed potatoes, and crunchy onions
make a delicious meal.

Comfort Supper

SERVES 4

Onion-Topped Sausage 'n' Mashed
Potato Casserole

Green Beans With
Tangy Mustard Sauce

Raspberry-Lemonade Pie

Iced tea

Surprise your family with this
comforting combination of
textures and flavors. Plus,
you'll be impressed by how
fuss-free this supper really
is. It's perfect for busy moms. Hearty
Onion-Topped Sausage 'n' Mashed
Potato Casserole is packed with a rich,
meaty tomato sauce and refrigerated
mashed potatoes and topped with
crunchy, kid-approved fried onions.
When Assistant Food Editor Natalie
Kelly Brown does this at home, she stirs
together the green beans while the casserole bakes so everything's ready to go
on the table at the same time.

Mom's Memory Bank Tip

In one of her frenzied moments, a lightbulb went off in Natalie's head, and she discovered a time-saving and less messy method for removing sausage casings. Simply freeze the sausage overnight, and then let it partially thaw in the refrigerator. Cut a slit down one side of the partially frozen sausages, and peel the casings right off.

Onion-Topped Sausage 'n' Mashed Potato Casserole
family favorite

MAKES 6 SERVINGS; **PREP:** 15 MIN.,
COOK: 13 MIN., **BAKE:** 40 MIN.,
STAND: 5 MIN.

This hearty dish uses a few of our favorite convenience products.

1 (19.5-oz.) package sweet ground turkey sausage, casings removed*
2 (14.5-oz.) cans diced tomatoes in sauce
¼ cup loosely packed fresh basil leaves, chopped**
1 shallot, chopped
1 tsp. salt-free garlic-and-herb seasoning
1 (24-oz.) package refrigerated garlic-flavored mashed potatoes
1 (8-oz.) package shredded Italian five-cheese blend
¼ tsp. dried Italian seasoning
1 cup French fried onions

1. Preheat oven to 350°. Brown sausage in a large skillet over medium-high heat, stirring often, 6 to 8 minutes or until meat crumbles and is no longer pink; drain.
2. Stir in tomatoes and next 3 ingredients, and cook, stirring occasionally, 5 minutes. Transfer sausage mixture to a lightly greased 11- x 7-inch baking dish.
3. Stir together mashed potatoes, cheese, and Italian seasoning in a large bowl. (Mixture will be dry.) Spread potato mixture over sausage mixture in baking dish.
4. Bake at 350° for 35 to 40 minutes or until bubbly. Top with fried onions, and bake 5 more minutes. Let stand 5 minutes before serving.
*1 (1¼-lb.) package ground chicken sausage may be substituted.
**½ tsp. dried basil may be substituted.
Note: For testing purposes only, we used Bob Evans Garlic Mashed Potatoes and Mrs. Dash Garlic & Herb Seasoning Blend.

Green Beans With Tangy Mustard Sauce
fast fixin's

MAKES 4 SERVINGS; **PREP:** 15 MIN.

Store any remaining Tangy Mustard Sauce in refrigerator for up to five days. Toss sauce with your favorite mixed greens.

¼ cup olive oil
1 Tbsp. country-style Dijon mustard
1 Tbsp. balsamic vinegar
1 Tbsp. honey
¼ tsp. salt
¼ tsp. pepper
1 (12-oz.) package fresh green beans*

1. Whisk together first 6 ingredients in a small bowl until well blended.
2. Prepare green beans according to package directions. Toss green beans with desired amount of dressing.
*1 (12-oz.) package frozen cut green beans may be substituted. For testing purposes only, we used Birds Eye Steamfresh Frozen Cut Green Beans.

Kitchen Express: Omit olive oil, vinegar, and next 3 ingredients. Stir together mustard and ½ cup bottled balsamic vinaigrette. Proceed with recipe as directed in Step 2.

Raspberry-Lemonade Pie
test kitchen favorite

MAKES 8 SERVINGS; **PREP:** 10 MIN.,
FREEZE: 4 HR.

1 (14-oz.) can sweetened condensed milk
1 (6-oz.) can frozen lemonade concentrate, partially thawed
3 Tbsp. seedless raspberry preserves
1 (8-oz.) container frozen whipped topping, thawed
1 (6-oz.) ready-made prepared graham cracker crust
Garnishes: fresh raspberries, fresh mint sprigs

1. Whisk together first 3 ingredients in a large bowl until smooth. Fold in whipped topping.
2. Pour into crust; freeze 4 hours or until firm. Garnish, if desired.

Pink Lemonade Pie: Substitute pink lemonade concentrate for lemonade concentrate and omit raspberry preserves. Prepare as directed.

Easy Entertaining

An insider's guide to serving designer cheese on the cheap.

High Style Cheese trays are fast, easy, and always a hit, whether you need a standout appetizer on the spur of the moment or a special offering for a casual get-together. Stacking a trio of cheeses on a colorful cake stand adds a new dimension to the traditional party tray. Trimmed with fresh rosemary and thyme, the festive tiers yield double dividends as a clever centerpiece for an afternoon tea or bridal shower.

We chose wheels of Brie, Muenster, and goat cheese, but almost any assortment of cheeses in graduated sizes will make an attractive presentation. You can even shape and chill your favorite cheese spreads in small cake pans and ramekins lined with plastic wrap. When selecting unfamiliar cheeses, make sure the flavors and textures partner well. Stronger-tasting cheeses are best served separately. Many stores offer samples and recommendations.

Tray Chic A few quick cuts turn a sheet of frozen puff pastry into a stylish serving tray. Top with several decorative wedges of cheese or a selection of sliced cheeses cut into various shapes and sizes. (Allow 2 to 3 ounces of cheese per person, and serve at room temperature.) Add a basket of warm bread and some hot soup, and you're ready for a fun evening with friends.

Puff Pastry Cheese Tray:
Preheat oven to 400°. Whisk together 1 large egg and 2 tsp. water. Unfold 1 thawed puff pastry sheet (from 1 [17.3-oz.] package) on an ungreased baking sheet; brush with egg mixture. Cut 4 (½-inch-wide) strips from 1 side of pastry, cutting parallel to seam of pastry. Place strips along outer edges of pastry, overlapping and trimming ends of strips as needed. Prick bottom of pastry generously with a fork. Sprinkle bottom of pastry with 1 tsp. of your favorite seasoning blend. If desired, gently press fresh herb sprigs onto bottom of pastry. Bake for 6 minutes. Prick bottom of pastry generously with fork again (to prevent center from rising). Bake 6 more minutes or until lightly brown. Let cool on pan 2 minutes; transfer to a wire rack, and let cool 45 minutes or until completely cool. Makes 1 tray. Prep: 10 min., Bake: 12 min., Cool: 47 min.

Fee, Fie, Faux, Yum!
Impressively rich and creamy, this Gourmet Cheese Spread delivers all the luscious taste and texture of a mild-flavored goat cheese for less than half the price.

Gourmet Cheese Spread:
editor's pick
Beat 1 (8-oz.) package softened cream cheese and 2 (4-oz.) packages softened, crumbled feta cheese at medium speed with an electric mixer until smooth. Shape cheese mixture into 2 (5- x 2-inch) logs. Roll 1 log in 1½ tsp. coarsely ground pepper; roll remaining log in 2 tsp. chopped fresh parsley. Wrap in plastic wrap; chill 4 hours. Serve with crackers or crusty French bread. Makes 8 servings. Prep: 5 min., Chill: 4 hr.

July

This Summer's Best Outdoor Menu

The grill and a little prep work (but only just a little, we promise) are the secrets to these 16 easy, delicious recipes. Our tips and tricks give you the confidence to pull off this party.

Southern Cookout

SERVES 6

Herb-Marinated Flank Steak

Flank Steak Sandwiches With Blue Cheese

Baked Bean Crostini

Peppery Grilled Okra With Lemon-Basil Dipping Sauce

Double Peanut Butter Candy Bites With Granola

Lemonade Iced Tea

So SOUTHERN

Try a Summer Place Setting

Fashion a wedge of melon into a boat shape. Then use a wooden skewer, twine, and thick card stock for a sail. Cut paper into a curved triangle, and use a pen to personalize. Cut a hole at the top and bottom of the paper, and feed onto a wooden skewer. Fix into place with a small piece of knotted twine at each end.

Herb-Marinated Flank Steak

MAKES 6 SERVINGS; **PREP:** 15 MIN., **CHILL:** 30 MIN., **GRILL:** 18 MIN., **STAND:** 10 MIN.

½ small sweet onion, minced
3 garlic cloves, minced
¼ cup olive oil
2 Tbsp. chopped fresh basil
1 Tbsp. chopped fresh thyme
1 Tbsp. chopped fresh rosemary
1 tsp. salt
½ tsp. dried crushed red pepper
1¾ lb. flank steak
1 lemon, halved

1. Place first 8 ingredients in a 2-gal. zip-top plastic bag, and squeeze bag to combine. Add steak; seal bag, and chill 30 minutes to 1 hour and 30 minutes.

Remove steak from marinade, discarding marinade.
2. Preheat grill to 400° to 450° (high) heat. Grill steak, covered with grill lid, 9 minutes on each side or to desired degree of doneness. Remove from grill; squeeze juice from lemon over steak. Let stand 10 minutes. Cut across the grain into thin slices.

Herb-Marinated Chicken Breasts: Substitute 1¾ lb. skinned and boned chicken breasts for flank steak. Proceed with recipe as directed, grilling chicken 7 minutes on each side or until done. Prep: 15 min., Chill: 30 min., Grill: 14 min.

Flank Steak Sandwiches With Blue Cheese

MAKES 6 SERVINGS; **PREP:** 20 MIN., **GRILL:** 22 MIN., **STAND:** 10 MIN.
(Pictured on page 179)

2 large sweet onions
4 Tbsp. olive oil, divided
½ tsp. salt
½ tsp. freshly ground pepper
3 red bell peppers
6 (2- to 3-oz.) ciabatta or deli rolls, split*
5 oz. soft ripened blue cheese
1½ cups loosely packed arugula
Herb-Marinated Flank Steak
6 Tbsp. mayonnaise

1. Preheat grill to 400° to 450° (high) heat. Cut onion into ¼-inch-thick slices. Brush with 1 Tbsp. olive oil, and sprinkle with ¼ tsp. salt and ¼ tsp. pepper. Cut bell peppers into 1-inch-wide strips. Place pepper strips in a large bowl, and drizzle with 1 Tbsp. olive oil. Sprinkle with remaining ¼ tsp. salt and ¼ tsp. pepper; toss to coat.
2. Grill onion and bell pepper strips, covered with grill lid, over 400° to 450° (high) heat 7 to 10 minutes on each side or until lightly charred and tender.
3. Brush cut sides of rolls with remaining 2 Tbsp. olive oil, and grill, cut sides down, without grill lid, over 400° to

450° (high) heat 1 to 2 minutes or until lightly browned and toasted.

4. Spread blue cheese on cut sides of roll bottoms; top with arugula, bell pepper strips, steak, and onion. Spread mayonnaise on cut sides of roll tops. Place roll tops, mayonnaise sides down, on top of onion, pressing lightly.

*French hamburger buns may be substituted. We tested with Publix French Hamburger Buns.

Note: We tested with Saga Classic Soft-Ripened Blue-Veined Cheese.

Flank Steak Sandwiches With

Brie: Substitute 5 oz. Brie, rind removed, for blue cheese. Proceed with recipe as directed.

Herb Chicken Sandwiches:

Substitute Herb-Marinated Chicken Breasts for flank steak. Proceed with recipe as directed.

Herb Chicken Sandwiches With

Grilled Peaches: Reduce onions to 1 and red bell peppers to 2. Cut 2 large peaches into ¼-inch-thick rounds, cutting through stem and bottom ends. Proceed with recipe as directed, grilling peach slices, covered with grill lid, over 350° to 400° (medium-high) heat 3 to 5 minutes on each side or until grill marks appear. Assemble sandwiches as directed, topping onion with peach slices. Prep: 20 min., Grill: 32 min., Stand: 10 min.

Double Grilled Cheese Sandwiches

1. Preheat grill to 400° to 450° (high) heat. Spread ¼ cup softened butter on 1 side of 12 bread slices. Layer 2 white American cheese slices and 1 mild Cheddar cheese slice on unbuttered sides of each of 6 bread slices. Top with remaining bread slices, buttered sides up. Grill 1 to 2 minutes on each side or until grill marks appear and cheese melts. Makes 6 servings; Prep: 10 min., Grill: 4 min.

Test Kitchen Notebook

7 Tips for a Flawless Party

1. **Just say "Yes!"** Southerners are always asking what they can bring to a party. Make it easy on yourself, and let your guests help out by delegating recipes or tasks.
2. **Get a game plan.** Read over all the recipes to see what can be made ahead, do your shopping early, and make a to-do list. (Lemon-Basil Dipping Sauce, Herb-Marinated Flank Steak, and Lemonade Iced Tea can all be made the day before.)
3. **Keep it real.** When it comes to decorating, you don't have to spend a fortune. Find creative ways to use what you already have. Senior Photo Stylist Buffy Hargett uses an old colander with potted plants for a centerpiece (page 179) and rubber bands to keep silverware together.
4. **Turn up the tunes!** Nothing gets the party going like good music. Encourage your guests to make their own party playlists for your get-together (assuming everyone has great taste in music, of course).
5. **Take 10.** Test Kitchen Professional Marian Cooper Cairns recommends taking 10 minutes to sit down, relax, and compose yourself before your guests arrive.
6. **Loosen 'em up.** Setting up an activity for guests is a great way to get people to relax, whether it's a game (such as croquet or boccie) or just helping out at the grill.
7. **Have fun!** Remember it's a party and no one likes an uptight hostess. Enjoy it.

Baked Bean Crostini

MAKES 8 TO 10 SERVINGS; **PREP:** 20 MIN., **GRILL:** 2 MIN., **COOK:** 18 MIN.

(Pictured on page 179)

1 (8.5-oz.) French bread baguette
Vegetable cooking spray
5 thick hickory-smoked bacon slices
½ cup diced sweet onion
1 (28-oz.) can baked beans
3 Tbsp. apple cider vinegar
1 Tbsp. grated fresh ginger
1 Tbsp. yellow mustard
2 tsp. diced pickled jalapeño peppers
¼ tsp. salt
Toppings: chopped fresh rosemary, queso fresco (fresh Mexican cheese), spicy barbecue sauce, pickled jalapeño pepper slices, hot sauce

1. Preheat grill to 400° to 450° (high) heat. Cut bread into 40 (¼-inch-thick) slices, discarding ends. Coat 1 side of each bread slice with cooking spray. Grill bread slices, without grill lid, 1 to 2 minutes on each side.

2. Cook bacon in a large skillet over medium-high heat 8 to 10 minutes or until crisp; remove bacon, and drain on paper towels, reserving 2 Tbsp. drippings in skillet. Crumble bacon.

3. Sauté onion in hot drippings 5 minutes or until tender. Stir in beans and next 5 ingredients; cook over medium heat, stirring occasionally, 5 minutes or until thoroughly heated and slightly thickened. Spoon bean mixture onto grilled bread slices. Sprinkle with crumbled bacon. Serve with desired toppings.

Note: We tested with Bush's Best Country Style Baked Beans. Instead of grilling, bread slices may be baked on a baking sheet at 350° for 8 minutes or until lightly toasted.

Peppery Grilled Okra With Lemon-Basil Dipping Sauce

MAKES 8 SERVINGS; PREP: 15 MIN.,
CHILL: 24 HR., GRILL: 6 MIN., COOL: 5 MIN.
(Pictured on page 179)

Cheesecloth or coffee filter
1 (32-oz.) container plain low-fat yogurt
¼ cup chopped fresh basil
2 Tbsp. lemon juice
½ tsp. minced garlic
¼ tsp. sugar
1½ tsp. salt, divided
1¼ tsp. freshly ground pepper,
    divided
2 lb. fresh okra, trimmed
2 Tbsp. olive oil
Garnish: freshly ground pepper

1. Line a wire-mesh strainer with 3 layers of cheesecloth or 1 (12-cup) coffee filter. Place strainer over a bowl. Spoon yogurt into strainer. Cover and chill 24 hours. Remove yogurt, discarding strained liquid.
2. Preheat grill to 400° to 450° (high) heat. Combine strained yogurt, basil, next 3 ingredients, ½ tsp. salt, and ¼ tsp. pepper. Cover and chill until ready to serve.
3. Toss together okra, olive oil, and remaining 1 tsp. salt and 1 tsp. pepper in a large bowl.
4. Grill okra, covered with grill lid, over 400° to 450° (high) heat 2 to 3 minutes on each side or until tender. Cool 5 minutes.
5. Transfer okra to a serving dish, and serve with dipping sauce. Garnish, if desired.

Double Peanut Butter Candy Bites With Granola

1. Preheat oven to 350°. Shape 1 (16.5-oz.) package refrigerated peanut butter cookie dough into 24 (1-inch) balls, and place in cups of lightly greased miniature muffin pans. Bake 15 to 18 minutes or until edges are lightly browned. Remove from oven, and press 1 miniature peanut butter cup candy into each cookie.

SO SOUTHERN

Make Watermelon Agua Frescas

Maria Corbalan, owner of Taco Xpress in Austin, Texas, shared this refreshing recipe with us. Process 4 cups cubed seedless watermelon, cantaloupe, or honeydew melon and ¼ cup sugar in a blender until smooth, stopping to scrape down sides as needed. Pour mixture through a fine wire-mesh strainer into a pitcher, discarding solids. Stir in 2 cups cold water. Cover and chill until ready to serve. Serve over ice. MAKES ABOUT 5 CUPS; PREP: 10 MIN.

Sprinkle cookies with ¼ cup granola cereal (½ tsp. each). Makes 2 dozen. Prep: 20 min., Bake: 15 min.
Note: We tested with Reese's Peanut Butter Cups and Quaker Natural Granola cereal.

Double Peanut Butter Candy Bites With Peanuts: Substitute chopped peanuts for granola. Proceed with recipe as directed.

Peanut Butter-Caramel Candy Bites With Granola: Substitute 24 bite-size chocolate-covered caramel-peanut nougat bars for miniature peanut butter cup candies. Proceed with recipe as directed.
Note: We tested with Snickers.

Peanut Butter-Caramel Candy Bites With Colorful Candies: Substitute 24 bite-size chocolate-covered caramel-peanut nougat bars for miniature peanut butter cup candies. Substitute 72 candy-coated chocolate pieces for granola. Proceed with recipe as directed.
Note: We tested with Snickers and M & M's.

Lemonade Iced Tea

MAKES 8 CUPS; PREP: 10 MIN.,
COOK: 5 MIN., STEEP: 10 MIN.
(Pictured on page 178)

3 cups water
2 family-size tea bags
1 (1-oz.) package fresh mint leaves (about
    1 cup loosely packed)
½ cup sugar
4 cups cold water
1 (6-oz.) can frozen lemonade concentrate,
    thawed
Garnish: fresh citrus slices

1. Bring 3 cups water to a boil in a 2-qt. saucepan. Remove from heat, add tea bags, and stir in fresh mint. Cover and steep 10 minutes.
2. Remove and discard tea bags and mint. Stir in sugar until dissolved.
3. Pour tea into a 3-qt. container, and stir in 4 cups cold water and lemonade concentrate. Serve over ice. Garnish, if desired.

Bourbon-Lemonade Iced Tea: Prepare recipe as directed, and stir in 1 cup bourbon. Makes 9 cups.

Spiced Dark Rum-Lemonade Iced Tea: Prepare recipe as directed, and stir in 1 cup spiced dark rum. Makes 9 cups.

Quick, Cool Salads

Easy picnic dishes plus great new ways to serve them

I t's the season for carefree entertaining, and simple-to-fix salads are perfect picnic fare—whether it's a backyard barbecue, Sunday lunch in the park, or a romantic getaway just for the two of you.

Tuna Salad With Lemon Aïoli

make ahead

MAKES 8 SERVINGS; **PREP:** 10 MIN., **CHILL:** 2 HR.

3 (12-oz.) cans solid white tuna in spring water, drained and flaked
½ English cucumber, cut into half-moon-shaped slices
1 large Granny Smith apple, diced
¼ cup minced red onion
Lemon Aïoli

1. Stir together all ingredients; cover and chill 2 hours.

Lemon Aïoli:

MAKES ABOUT ⅔ CUP; **PREP:** 5 MIN.

½ cup mayonnaise
2 Tbsp. chopped fresh parsley
2 tsp. lemon zest
2 Tbsp. fresh lemon juice
1 garlic clove, pressed
½ tsp. freshly ground pepper

1. Stir together all ingredients.

—NANCY HAJECK, FAIRVIEW, TENNESSEE

Clever Picnic Ideas

- Hollow a crusty loaf of artisan bread, and spoon in Tuna Salad With Lemon Aïoli.
- Cranberry-Almond Chicken Salad looks cool in an insulated ice bucket lined with lettuce leaves.
- Slipcover lightweight, disposable cooler bags with colorful canvas totes.
- Look for retro-chic finds, such as a vintage gardening tray, at flea markets and garage sales.
- Stock up on vinyl tablecloths. Jewel-bright and dirt cheap, these gems are the ultimate in waterproof ground covers.
- Check out garden shops for outdoor tableware. A pretty planter filled with low-maintenance bedding plants makes a festive centerpiece all summer.

Cranberry-Almond Chicken Salad

make ahead

MAKES 6 SERVINGS; **PREP:** 15 MIN., **BAKE:** 5 MIN., **COOL:** 15 MIN.

Serve in a lettuce-lined bowl.

⅔ cup slivered almonds
3 cups chopped cooked chicken
¾ cup sweetened dried cranberries
2 celery ribs, diced
½ small sweet onion, diced
¾ cup mayonnaise
1 Tbsp. Greek seasoning
2 Tbsp. fresh lemon juice

1. Preheat oven to 350°. Bake almonds in a single layer in a shallow pan 5 to 7 minutes or until lightly toasted and fragrant. Cool completely in pan on a wire rack (about 15 minutes).
2. Stir together almonds, chicken, dried cranberries, and remaining ingredients; serve immediately, or cover and chill up to 24 hours.

—DEANNE ANTHONY, POTEAU, OKLAHOMA

Artichoke-Pecan Chicken Salad: Substitute 1 cup coarsely chopped pecans for almonds and 1 (14-oz.) can artichoke hearts for cranberries. Drain artichokes, and pat dry with paper towels. Coarsely chop artichokes. Proceed with recipe as directed.

Hoppin' John Salad

make ahead

MAKES 8 SERVINGS; **PREP:** 10 MIN., **COOK:** 30 MIN., **CHILL:** 2 HR.

½ cup uncooked long-grain rice
2 cups fresh or frozen black-eyed peas
2 tsp. salt, divided
¼ cup fresh lemon juice
2 Tbsp. olive oil
1 jalapeño pepper, seeded and minced
1 garlic clove, pressed
¼ tsp. pepper
½ cup chopped celery
½ cup loosely packed fresh parsley leaves, chopped
¼ cup loosely packed fresh mint leaves, chopped

1. Prepare rice according to package directions. Meanwhile, cook peas and 1 tsp. salt in water to cover in a large saucepan over medium-high heat, stirring often, 30 minutes or until tender; drain.
2. Whisk together lemon juice, next 4 ingredients, and remaining 1 tsp. salt in a large bowl. Stir in peas, rice, celery, parsley, and mint until blended. Cover and chill 2 hours. Season with salt to taste.

—ADELYNE SMITH, DUNNVILLE, KENTUCKY

It's Scalloping Season

The time is now—catch your dinner in Florida's shallow waters from July 1 to September 10.

The scallop eyes did it for Associate Travel/Livings Editor Annette Thompson. She's always been a sucker for bright blue eyes. And the sight of 40 of them staring back at her from the wrinkled edges of a 3-inch shell is charming—and downright comical. That's just one of the unexpected pleasures of spending a day hunting for the succulent morsels.

Her family scheduled a day with an outfitter on Florida's Steinhatchee River to scoot out to the Gulf's rich sea grass beds. Their guide, Jim Henley, instructed them to explore the 6-inch-tall grasses that give the clear water its green hue. "Look for their eyes," Jim said. "When the scallop sees you, it will try to swim away." She could handle being watched by a scallop's neon blue eyes. But being outswum by the 3-inch bivalve? No way!

Annette and her 17-year-old son, Russell, quickly made a game of catch and show. After diving in the 6-foot-deep water, they'd meet on the surface, clear their snorkels, and shout, "Look at this one!" Her husband often popped up with stories about his scallops playing hide-and-seek in the grass beds. Within the first hour, they'd each filled their mesh bags with their catch.

Nearby, dozens of other boats congregated on the flat water. Onboard, folks played stereos, slathered on sunscreen, and picnicked like a Saturday tailgate where everyone's team wins the game.

The Freshest Sashimi

During one of their breaks, Jim brought out a scallop knife. "Let's taste them," he said. Annette may belly up to sushi bars at home, but the thought of plopping a fresh-from-the-sea scallop in her mouth was daunting.

But she's a mom. With Russell watching her reaction, she agreed. Jim quickly opened the shell and separated the meat from the viscera. "Try a bite," he said, holding out the white bay scallop. She did. A perfectly seasoned surprise.

The light salt taste turned the bay scallop into a wonderful delicacy. They all ate a few—even Russell—and then they realized that they would have to catch some more for dinner. No problem. By now, they were old pros.

Scallop Sauté
fast fixin's

MAKES 4 SERVINGS;
PREP: 15 MIN., COOK: 15 MIN.

1 red bell pepper, cut into strips
1 green bell pepper, cut into strips
1 medium onion, sliced
3 garlic cloves, minced
3 Tbsp. vegetable oil, divided
1 lb. fresh bay scallops, drained*
3 Tbsp. lite soy sauce
1 tsp. orange zest
3 Tbsp. fresh orange juice
1 Tbsp. dry white wine
¼ tsp. dried crushed red pepper
2 Tbsp. butter

1. Sauté first 4 ingredients in 2 Tbsp. hot oil in a large skillet over medium-high heat until tender. Remove from pan, and keep warm.
2. Sauté scallops in remaining 1 Tbsp. oil in skillet over medium heat 5 minutes or until done. Remove scallops from pan, and keep warm.
3. Add 2 Tbsp. soy sauce, orange zest, and next 3 ingredients to skillet. Bring mixture to a boil, and cook over high heat about 2 minutes. Gradually whisk in butter and remaining 1 Tbsp. soy sauce until well blended. Serve immediately over vegetable mixture and scallops.
*Sea scallops may be substituted. Cook in remaining 1 Tbsp. oil in skillet over medium heat 5 to 6 minutes; turn over, and cook 3 to 5 minutes or until golden brown.

Tips for Catching Scallops

- Bring a mask, snorkel, and swim fins. If you don't have a boat, book a day with an outfitter who also provides your saltwater fishing license and mesh bag to collect scallops. We like Capt. Jim Henley, www.saltwaterfishn.com.
- Search for the 3-inch shells tucked between grasses in 4 to 6 feet of water. Gently pick them up and place in your mesh bag.
- Store your catch on ice.
- Count on a pound of scallops in the shell per person for a meal.
- Most folks wait till they are at the dock to clean. Use a scallop knife to open the shells, and a spoon for cleaning. Separate the dark viscera from the white meat, and discard.

Great Recipes for the Beach

Pimiento cheese creates easy lunch options; fresh shrimp anchors a casual supper.

Don't forget about the food this summer when loading up the family for a weekend at the beach. To make these recipes away from home, tuck a few pantry items in a canvas bag, and then buy the rest of the ingredients once you get there. (Make the Bacon Pimiento Cheese ahead, and pack it in a cooler.) The best part? Restaurant-quality meals at a fraction of the cost.

Barbecue Shrimp
make ahead

MAKES 6 TO 8 SERVINGS; **PREP:** 10 MIN.,
BAKE: 35 MIN.

You'll want to be sure to serve lots of extra bread for sopping up the rich, spicy sauce of this New Orleans classic.

2 lemons, cut into wedges
1 cup butter, melted
1 cup ketchup
½ cup Worcestershire sauce
4 garlic cloves, chopped
2 bay leaves
3 Tbsp. Old Bay seasoning
1 tsp. dried rosemary
1 tsp. dried thyme
4 lb. unpeeled, large raw shrimp
    (21/25 count)
French bread
Smoked Gouda Grits (optional)

1. Preheat oven to 400°. Stir together first 9 ingredients. Place shrimp in a broiler pan; pour lemon mixture over shrimp.

2. Bake at 400° for 35 minutes or just until shrimp turn pink, stirring every 10 minutes. Discard bay leaves. Serve with lemon wedges, French bread, and, if desired, Smoked Gouda Grits.
Note: To make ahead, stir together first 9 ingredients. Cover and chill up to 5 days. Proceed with recipe as directed.

Smoked Gouda Grits
fast fixin's

MAKES 6 TO 8 SERVINGS; **PREP:** 10 MIN.,
COOK: 10 MIN.

6 cups low-sodium chicken
    broth*
2 cups milk
2 tsp. salt
½ tsp. pepper
2 cups uncooked quick-cooking grits
8 oz. smoked Gouda cheese, shredded
3 Tbsp. butter

1. Bring chicken broth, milk, salt, and pepper to a boil in a medium saucepan over medium-high heat; gradually whisk in grits. Cover, reduce heat to medium-low, and simmer, whisking occasionally, 5 minutes or until thickened. Stir in cheese and butter until melted.
*Water may be substituted.
Note: We tested with Frico Smoked Gouda.

Bacon Pimiento Cheese
MAKES ABOUT 3½ CUPS; **PREP:** 15 MIN.,
COOK: 10 MIN.

4 bacon slices
2 (8-oz.) blocks sharp Cheddar cheese,
    shredded
1 (4-oz.) jar diced pimiento, rinsed and
    drained
½ cup mayonnaise
2 Tbsp. finely chopped onion
1 Tbsp. Worcestershire sauce
¼ tsp. salt
⅛ tsp. ground red pepper
⅛ tsp. black pepper

1. Cook bacon in a large skillet 4 to 5 minutes on each side or until crisp; remove bacon, and drain on paper towels. Crumble bacon. Stir together bacon, cheese, and remaining ingredients just until blended. Store cheese mixture in an airtight container in refrigerator up to 1 week.

Bacon Pimiento Cheeseburgers
MAKES 6 SERVINGS; **PREP:** 20 MIN.,
GRILL: 16 MIN.

2¼ lb. ground chuck
1 tsp. freshly ground pepper
1 tsp. Worcestershire sauce
1 tsp. salt
1⅓ cups Bacon Pimiento Cheese
Hamburger buns
Toppings: tomato slices, red onion
    slices, lettuce leaves, mustard,
    mayonnaise, ketchup

1. Preheat grill to 350° to 400° (medium-high) heat.
2. Combine first 3 ingredients in a large bowl until blended. (Do not overwork meat mixture.) Shape mixture into 6 (4-inch) patties. Sprinkle with salt.
3. Grill, covered with grill lid, over 350° to 400° (medium-high) heat 7 to 8 minutes on each side or until beef is no longer pink. Top with Bacon Pimiento Cheese, and serve on buns with desired toppings.

Almond Sand Dollar Cookies

test kitchen favorite

MAKES 4 DOZEN; **PREP:** 25 MIN.,
CHILL: 1 HR., **BAKE:** 8 MIN. PER BATCH

1 cup butter, softened
2 cups sifted powdered sugar
2 large eggs
1 large egg, separated
3⅓ cups all-purpose flour
½ tsp. baking powder
¼ cup granulated sugar
1 tsp. ground cinnamon
Sliced almonds

1. Preheat oven to 350°. Beat 1 cup softened butter at medium speed with an electric mixer until creamy; gradually add 2 cups sifted powdered sugar, beating until well blended. Add 2 eggs and 1 egg yolk, beating until blended.
2. Combine flour and baking powder. Add to butter mixture, beating at low speed until blended. Shape dough into a ball, and wrap in plastic wrap. Chill 1 hour.
3. Roll dough to an ⅛-inch thickness on a lightly floured surface; cut with a 3-inch round cutter. Place on lightly greased, parchment paper-lined baking sheets; brush with lightly beaten egg white.
4. Stir together granulated sugar and ground cinnamon, and sprinkle evenly over cookies. Gently press 5 almond slices in a spoke design around center of each cookie.
5. Bake at 350° for 4 minutes; remove pan from oven, and gently press almonds into cookies again. Bake 4 more minutes or until edges are lightly browned. Remove cookies to wire racks to cool.

Cooking With Tortilla Chips

For the crunchiest coating ever

Tortilla chips are our Test Kitchen's go-to coating when baking or pan-frying. They turn a gorgeous golden brown when cooked and create a crisp crust that won't get soggy. Plus, it's a great way to make use of the crumbs in the bottom of the bag. (And let's be honest, you've always wondered what to do with those crumbs, right?)

Lime Tortilla-Crusted Chicken Tenders

fast fixin's

MAKES 6 SERVINGS; **PREP:** 15 MIN.,
BAKE: 15 MIN.

Pair this with salsa verde and rice.

2 large eggs
1 (2-lb.) package frozen chicken tenderloins, thawed
¾ tsp. salt
¾ tsp. pepper
¼ cup all-purpose flour
2¾ cups finely crushed lime-flavored tortilla chips
Garnishes: fresh cilantro sprigs, lime wedges

1. Preheat oven to 425°. Whisk together eggs and 1 Tbsp. water until blended.
2. Sprinkle chicken with salt and pepper. Dredge in flour; dip in egg mixture, and dredge in crushed tortilla chips. Place chicken on a lightly greased wire rack on an aluminum foil-lined baking sheet.
3. Bake at 425° for 15 to 20 minutes or until done. Garnish, if desired.
Note: We tested with Tostitos Hint of Lime Tortilla Chips.

Crispy Eggplant With Tomatoes and Mozzarella

editor's pick

MAKES 8 SERVINGS; **PREP:** 20 MIN.,
COOK: 8 MIN. PER BATCH

Use smaller eggplants, which are less bitter. Look for eggplants with a small, round dimple versus the deep, long groove in the bottom.

3 large eggs
3 medium tomatoes
1 small eggplant, cut into ¼-inch-thick rounds (about 1 lb.)
2 cups crushed tortilla chips
1 cup vegetable oil
Salt and pepper to taste
1 (8-oz.) package fresh mozzarella cheese, cut into 8 (¼-inch-thick) rounds
¼ cup firmly packed fresh basil leaves, torn
Balsamic vinegar

1. Whisk together eggs and 1 Tbsp. water until blended.
2. Cut tomatoes into 16 (⅛-inch-thick) slices. Place tomatoes in a single layer on paper towels.
3. Dredge eggplant in ½ cup crushed tortilla chips; dip in egg mixture, and dredge in remaining 1½ cups crushed tortilla chips.
4. Cook eggplant, in batches, in hot oil in a 10-inch (3-inch-deep) skillet over medium heat 3 to 4 minutes on each side or until golden brown. Place on a wire rack, and sprinkle with salt and pepper to taste.
5. Cut cheese rounds in half. Arrange eggplant, cheese, and tomatoes on a serving platter; sprinkle with basil, and drizzle with balsamic vinegar. Sprinkle with salt and pepper to taste.

Healthy Living.

Enjoy some favorite recipes made with local produce.
Plus, try a lighter version of a Southern classic.

Eat Local, Eat Fresh

Oklahoma City chef and organic gardener Kamala Gamble
takes a fresh approach to food and shares her tips for
healthy eating.

Kamala Gamble talks faster than an auctioneer, but when it comes to food, this trained chef and organic gardener wants the world to slow down. The cofounder of Slow Food Oklahoma City, Kamala believes that meals made from naturally produced local vegetables, fruits, meats, and dairy products are good for your health, good for the local economy, and good for your taste buds.

Slower Is Better "Slow food" began as a reaction to a McDonald's opening in Rome's Piazza di Spagna in 1986. Today, it's a worldwide movement dedicated to promoting local artisans who grow, market, prepare, and serve wholesome and fresh traditional foods.

Kamala (rhymes with "Pamela") bought into the movement while cooking at Chicago's famed Frontera Grill, where nearly every ingredient is locally produced. When she and her husband, Lance, moved back to Oklahoma in 2001 and bought a house with a big backyard, the next step seemed obvious. "I said, 'Oh, I'll just start a garden,'" she recalls incredulously. "That's like saying, 'Oh, I'll just have a root canal without anesthesia.'"

Her soil, unfortunately, was "horrid, black clay." She learned to loosen and enrich the soil by tilling in copious amounts of composted cow and horse manure, green manure cover crops like clover and alfalfa, and even worm castings. Mulching with hay each year also adds organic matter as it breaks down.

Today, the 1½-acre plot, called Guilford Gardens, is a highly productive Community Supported Agriculture (CSA) farm that sells fresh, organic produce to approximately 80 local subscribers. Each week for 8 to 12 weeks, subscribers pick up a basket of vegetables. The contents change every time. Kamala grows more than 15 kinds of tomatoes, 20 kinds of peppers, 4 varieties of potatoes, 4 kinds of onions, and 6 kinds of eggplant. (For suggestions on planting a small family garden, see "Easy Starter Plants" on the following page.)

Terrific Tomatoes Most of Kamala's tomatoes are heirloom types she chooses for flavor, color, shape, and variety. She won't eat mass-produced tomatoes that are picked green and "taste like cardboard."

"Heirlooms aren't as productive as hybrids (genetic crosses) you find at the grocery store," she admits, "but for the average home gardener, that's not a big deal, as long as you grow at least eight tomato plants. Grow 'Sweet Baby Girl,' 'Sun Gold,' 'Juliet,' and 'Early Girl,' and we promise you'll get huge production."

Find Locally Grown Produce Near You

Want that you-pick flavor without gardening? Consider these options.

- **Join Community Supported Agriculture (CSA)**—These programs connect farmers directly with the public. CSA members buy subscriptions and in return receive weekly or monthly boxes of harvested goods. www.nal.usda.gov/afsic/pubs/csa/csa.shtml
- **Farmers Markets**—To find one near you, visit www.localharvest.org or search online, key words "farmers market" plus your state's name.
- **You-Pick**—If you pick it yourself, then you know it's fresh. Find what's available in your area at www.pickyourown.org.

Healthy Living

Easy Starter Plants

Kamala says the following are great for beginners embarking on a first vegetable garden. She starts her garden with both transplants and seeds. Favorite sources include Seed Savers Exchange (www.seedsavers.org), Johnny's Selected Seeds (www.johnnyseeds.com), and Peaceful Valley Farm & Garden Supply (www.groworganic.com).

WHAT TO PLANT	WHEN TO PLANT	WHY SHE LOVES IT
Basil	Plant in spring for summer harvest.	Very productive; essential for pesto; "ridiculously pricey in the store."
Cucumber	Plant in spring for summer harvest.	Loves the flavor of 'Lemon' and 'National Pickling' varieties; "[they] give you phenomenal production."
Sweet Pepper	Plant in spring for summer and fall harvest.	Let a green pepper turn red for sweeter flavor and more vitamins; " 'Giant Marconi' produces like nobody's business."
Leaf lettuce	Plant in early spring for spring harvest or late summer for fall harvest.	"At the store, baby greens cost an arm and a leg, but if you sprinkle a packet of lettuce seed over the soil, in two weeks you'll have baby greens and save $10 a pound."
Spinach	Plant in early spring for spring harvest or early fall for fall harvest.	Great in salads; very nutritious; a quick grower that builds confidence.
Tomato	Plant in spring for summer harvest or midsummer for fall harvest.	Tremendous number of types; "they give you the most flavor 'pow' from your garden."

How To Chiffonade

Here, Kamala teaches a simple technique for creating thin shreds of herbs and lettuces. Use the tiny pieces as pretty garnishes for soups, salads, and desserts.

Step 1: Stack several basil leaves together; roll the stacked leaves lengthwise.

Step 2: Slice the roll into thin strips.

Tomato-Cucumber Bread Salad

MAKES 6 SERVINGS; **PREP:** 25 MIN.,
BAKE: 5 MIN., **COOL:** 10 MIN.

3 crusty artisan sourdough bread slices
3 cups mixed salad greens
1 cup halved grape tomatoes
1 medium cucumber, peeled, seeded, and chopped
½ cup loosely packed fresh basil leaves, thinly sliced (see how-to above)
½ cup thinly sliced red onions
Red Wine Vinaigrette

1. Preheat oven to 425°. Cut bread into 1-inch cubes (about 2½ cups), and place on a jelly-roll pan. Bake 5 to 7 minutes or until lightly toasted. Transfer bread to a wire rack, and cool completely (about 10 minutes).

2. Toss bread cubes with salad greens and next 4 ingredients. Serve with Red Wine Vinaigrette.

Per serving (including about 1½ Tbsp. vinaigrette): Calories 219; Fat 13.3g (sat 2g, mono 9g, poly 2.1g); Protein 4.8g; Carb 21.8g; Fiber 2.1g; Chol 0mg; Iron 1.8mg; Sodium 413mg; Calc 41mg

Marinated Tomato-Cucumber Bread Salad: Omit salad greens. Increase bread slices to 6, and toast as directed in Step 1. Increase grape tomatoes to 1 pt., halved. Toss together 4 medium-size ripe tomatoes, chopped; grape tomato halves; and next 3 ingredients in a large bowl. Toss in ⅓ cup Red Wine Vinaigrette. Let stand 10 minutes. Toss in bread cubes. Let stand 15 minutes. Makes 8 servings. Prep: 25 min., Bake: 5 min., Stand: 25 min., Cool: 10 min.

Per serving (including about 1 Tbsp. vinaigrette): Calories 249; Fat 10.6g (sat 1.6g, mono 6.9g, poly 1.9g); Protein 6.8g; Carb 33.3g; Fiber 2.7g; Chol 0mg; Iron 2.4mg; Sodium 468mg; Calc 34mg

Red Wine Vinaigrette:

make ahead

MAKES ABOUT ⅔ CUP; **PREP:** 5 MIN.

¼ cup red wine vinegar
½ tsp. salt
½ tsp. freshly ground pepper
⅓ cup olive oil

1. Whisk together first 3 ingredients in a small bowl. Add oil in a slow, steady stream, whisking constantly until smooth.

2. Use immediately, or store in an airtight container in refrigerator up to 1 week. If chilled, let stand at room temperature 15 minutes, and whisk before serving.

Per Tbsp.: Calories 65; Fat 7.5g (sat 1.1g, mono 5.3g, poly 1.1g); Protein 0g; Carb 0g; Fiber 0g; Chol 0mg; Iron 0mg; Sodium 117mg; Calc 0.6mg

Potato Salad's Light Side

This updated Southern classic is made with a creamy herb mixture that has fewer fat grams but still all the flavor of the heavier traditional recipes.

Herbed Potato Salad

MAKES 4 SERVINGS; **PREP:** 15 MIN.,
COOK: 25 MIN., **COOL:** 30 MIN.,
CHILL: 1 HR.

2 lb. red potatoes, cubed
1 (14-oz.) can fat-free chicken broth
1 garlic clove, minced
½ cup nonfat plain yogurt
1 Tbsp. chopped fresh dill
1 Tbsp. chopped fresh oregano
2 Tbsp. light mayonnaise
2 Tbsp. olive oil
2 Tbsp. white wine vinegar
1 tsp. salt
Garnishes: fresh dill sprig, chopped toasted pecans

1. Bring first 3 ingredients and 2 cups water to a boil in a large saucepan over medium-high heat, and cook 20 minutes or until tender. Drain and let cool 30 minutes.

2. Whisk together yogurt and next 6 ingredients in a large bowl until combined.

3. Gently fold potatoes into yogurt mixture. Cover and chill 1 to 12 hours. Garnish, if desired.

—SUSAN CONLEY, NATCHEZ, MISSISSIPPI

Per cup (not including garnishes): Calories 274; Fat 10.4g (sat 1.6g, mono 5.3g, poly 1.3g); Protein 7.7g; Carb 40.7g; Fiber 3.9g; Chol 3.3mg; Iron 1.9mg; Sodium 702mg; Calc 71mg

New Ways With Tomato Pie

Noble tomatoes of all colors combine with squash, cucumbers, and herbs for today's take on the South's favorite summer comfort food.

Mention the words "tomato pie" to a Southerner this time of year, and you'll likely get a big grin, followed by: "I wish I had a slice right now." For those of y'all who don't know, this rich, savory treat is like a supercharged tomato, mayo, and cheese sandwich—only better. That's what made our search to update this classic such a challenge. Tomato-Leek Pie, submitted by reader Kelly Rudat of Lake St. Louis, Missouri, takes the building blocks of a traditional pie but amps up the whole affair with a sweet leek and a tart green tomato. Yum!

On these pages, you'll find a few forward-thinking interpretations on the theme, such as the deliciously ingenious Tomato-Rosemary Tart from Test Kitchen Professional Angela Sellers. These recipes received rave reviews from the Food staff, and we're sure they will have your taste buds dancing the two-step.

Tomato-Leek Pie

MAKES 6 SERVINGS; **PREP:** 15 MIN.,
BAKE: 38 MIN., **COOL:** 5 MIN.,
STAND: 30 MIN., **COOK:** 5 MIN.

½ (15-oz.) package refrigerated
   piecrusts
2 medium-size red tomatoes
2 medium-size yellow tomatoes
1 green tomato
½ tsp. kosher salt
1 medium leek
2 Tbsp. butter
¼ tsp. pepper
½ cup grated Parmesan cheese
½ cup light mayonnaise
1 large egg, lightly beaten
Garnish: fresh flat-leaf parsley sprigs

1. Preheat oven to 450°. Fit piecrust into a 9-inch pie plate according to package directions; fold edges under, and crimp.
2. Bake at 450° for 8 to 10 minutes or until golden brown. Remove from oven, and let cool 5 minutes. Reduce oven temperature to 375°.
3. Cut tomatoes into ¼-inch slices. Place tomatoes on a paper towel-lined wire rack. Sprinkle tomatoes with kosher salt. Let stand 20 minutes. Pat dry with paper towels. (See photos below.)

Step 1: Place tomato slices on paper towels on a wire rack. Sprinkle tomatoes with kosher salt. Let stand 20 minutes.

Step 2: Pat dry with paper towels to absorb liquid.

4. Remove and discard root end and dark green top of leek. Cut in half lengthwise, and rinse thoroughly under cold running water to remove grit and sand. Thinly slice leek.
5. Melt butter in a large skillet over medium heat; add leek, and sauté 3 to 5 minutes or until tender.
6. Layer leek on bottom of prepared crust. Top with tomato slices, and sprinkle with pepper. Stir together cheese, mayonnaise, and egg in a medium bowl until blended. Spread cheese mixture over top of tomatoes.
7. Bake at 375° for 30 minutes or until thoroughly heated. Let stand 10 minutes. Garnish, if desired.

—**KELLY RUDAT**, ST. LOUIS, MISSOURI

Tomato Tips

- Ripen tomatoes, stem side up, in a cool spot away from direct sunlight to help prevent bruising and rotting.
- Never refrigerate whole, uncut tomatoes. The cold stops the ripening process, rendering them tasteless and mealy.
- Save time when peeling lots of tomatoes by giving them a quick dip in boiling water, followed by a plunge in ice water. The process loosens their skins.

Southern Tomato Vegetable Pie

MAKES 6 SERVINGS; **PREP:** 20 MIN., **STAND:** 30 MIN., **COOK:** 10 MIN., **BAKE:** 50 MIN.

4 plum tomatoes
½ tsp. kosher salt
6 thick bacon slices
1 (10-oz.) package frozen chopped spinach, thawed
1 cup (4 oz.) shredded Italian six-cheese blend
¾ cup light mayonnaise
½ cup canned artichoke hearts, drained and chopped
½ cup chopped fresh basil
2 green onions, thinly sliced
1 garlic clove, chopped
½ tsp. dried crushed red pepper
1 (9-inch) frozen unbaked deep-dish piecrust shell, thawed

1. Cut tomatoes into ½-inch slices. Place on a paper towel-lined wire rack. Sprinkle tomatoes with salt. Let stand 20 minutes. Pat dry with paper towels.
2. Preheat oven to 375°. Cook bacon in a large skillet over medium-high heat 8 to 10 minutes or until crisp; remove bacon, and drain on paper towels. Crumble bacon.
3. Drain spinach well, pressing between paper towels. Combine crumbled bacon, spinach, and next 7 ingredients in a large bowl until well blended.
4. Spread ¼ cup spinach mixture on bottom of piecrust.
5. Layer with half of tomato slices; top with half of remaining spinach mixture. Repeat layers once. Cover loosely with aluminum foil.
6. Bake pie, covered, at 375° for 30 minutes. Uncover and bake 20 to 25 minutes. Let stand 10 minutes. Serve warm or at room temperature.

—CYNTHIA MESSENGER,
MOUNT PLEASANT, SOUTH CAROLINA

Tomato-Rosemary Tart

MAKES 4 SERVINGS; **PREP:** 15 MIN., **STAND:** 20 MIN., **BAKE:** 24 MIN.

Serve this savory pie as a starter for a ladies gathering, or have it as a light supper with a tossed salad. Lemon zest provides a lovely counterpoint to this tart. (Pictured on page 180)

3 plum tomatoes
½ tsp. kosher salt
½ (17.3-oz.) package frozen puff pastry sheets, thawed
¼ cup (1 oz.) shredded mozzarella cheese
1 tsp. lemon zest
1 tsp. fresh rosemary
½ tsp. freshly ground pepper
1 Tbsp. chopped fresh parsley (optional)

1. Preheat oven to 400°. Cut tomatoes into ¼-inch slices, and place on a paper towel-lined wire rack. Sprinkle tomatoes with salt. Let stand 20 minutes. Pat dry with paper towels.
2. Unfold 1 puff pastry sheet on a lightly greased baking sheet. Arrange tomato slices in a single layer on pastry. Stir together cheese and next 3 ingredients in a small bowl. Sprinkle cheese mixture over tomatoes.
3. Bake tart at 400° for 24 to 27 minutes or until pastry is puffed and golden brown. Sprinkle with parsley, if desired.

Grilled Tomato-Rosemary Tart:
Prepare recipe as directed through Step 2, unfolding pastry sheet onto a lightly floured baking sheet. Preheat grill to 350° to 400° (medium-high) heat. Turn 1 side of grill off; leave other side lit. Transfer tart from baking sheet to unlit side of grill, and grill, covered with grill lid, 20 to 22 minutes or until pastry is puffed and golden brown. Prep: 15 min., Stand: 20 min., Grill: 22 min.

Cherry Tomato-Cucumber Salad Tartlets

fast fixin's

MAKES 6 TO 8 APPETIZER SERVINGS; **PREP:** 15 MIN., **BAKE:** 10 MIN.

This easy-to-prepare dish makes an irresistible pickup hors d'oeuvre. Fill the tiny shells just before serving. (Pictured on page 181)

½ cup Cherry Tomato-Cucumber Salad
⅓ cup crumbled feta cheese
1 (9-oz.) package frozen mini-phyllo pastry shells
Garnish: crumbled feta cheese

1. Preheat oven to 350°. Finely chop ½ cup Cherry Tomato-Cucumber Salad.
2. Divide feta cheese among pastry shells. Place on a baking sheet.
3. Bake shells at 350° for 10 minutes or until feta is melted. Spoon 1 heaping teaspoonful finely chopped salad mixture into each pastry shell. Garnish, if desired. Serve immediately.

Cherry Tomato-Cucumber Salad:

MAKES 6 SERVINGS; **PREP:** 15 MIN.

1 pt. cherry tomatoes, halved
1 medium cucumber, peeled, seeded, and thinly sliced
¼ cup thinly sliced sweet onion
¼ cup chopped fresh parsley
2 Tbsp. olive oil
1 Tbsp. lemon juice
1 tsp. salt
½ tsp. pepper

1. Toss together all ingredients in a medium bowl to combine.

Cherry Tomato-Cucumber-Cheese Salad: Prepare recipe as directed. Gently stir in 1 (8-oz.) package fresh mozzarella, cubed. Serve immediately, or cover and chill 1 hour.

Herb Vinegars

Instantly add refreshing flavor to marinades, salad dressings, and more.

Thyme in a Bottle Herb-infused vinegars are simple to make and easy to improvise. No time-consuming chopping or tricky techniques required—just snip a handful of 1- to 3-inch-long sprigs, and get ready for some fun.

Pat Conlee teaches a workshop on making herb vinegars at Petals From the Past in Jemison, Alabama (www.petalsfromthepast.com), and shares her recipes with us here. The same method of preparation works with any combination of fresh herbs and vinegar—so don't be timid about creating your own favorites after you've experimented with these. Each recipe yields about 2 cups and takes around 15 minutes to prepare.

Italian Herbal Vinegar:
¼ cup each of basil, oregano, marjoram, chives (or chive blossoms), and thyme; 2 garlic cloves, smashed; 1 cup white wine vinegar; and 1 cup red wine vinegar

Classic Tarragon Vinegar: 1 cup tarragon and 2 cups Champagne vinegar

Basil, Garlic, and Chive Vinegar:
1 cup basil; ½ cup chives (or 6 chive blossoms); 2 garlic cloves, smashed; and 2 cups red wine vinegar

Peppercorn Vinegar:
1 Tbsp. black peppercorns, 1 Tbsp. white peppercorns, 2 (6-inch-long) strips lemon zest, ¼ cup thyme, and 2 cups white wine vinegar

Helpful Hints To make your own herb vinegars, you'll need about 1 cup of fresh herbs for every 2 cups of vinegar. White wine vinegar pairs well with almost any herb; red wine vinegar is best with stronger herbs such as rosemary and oregano. Rice wine vinegar is a great match for delicately flavored herbs and flowers such as chive blossoms. Don't use *distilled* vinegar—it's a natural for household cleaning, but the harsh acidity overpowers the flavor of herbs. Quart-size canning jars with plastic storage caps make the best containers for steeping flavored vinegars. If you use metal lids, place plastic wrap over the top of the jar before adding the lid to prevent the vinegar from turning dark.

1. **Gather herbs in the morning,** after the dew has dried. Wash, remove excess moisture in a salad spinner, and pat dry with a clean kitchen towel. Bruise or crumple herbs to release maximum flavor.
2. **Fill dry, sterilized jars** with desired herbs and seasonings. (A quick run through the dishwasher sterilizes jars— just be sure to dry with the heat cycle on. Plastic lids are top-rack safe.)
3. **Heat vinegar in a nonaluminum saucepan** over medium heat 10 minutes or just until bubbles appear (do not boil); remove from heat, and pour into prepared jars, making sure herbs are totally submerged. Cool completely (about two hours). Cover and chill one week. (The longer the herbs and vinegar stand, the more intense the flavor.)
4. **Line a fine wire-mesh strainer** with a paper coffee filter. Pour vinegar mixture through strainer into a large measuring cup, discarding herbs and seasonings.
5. **Fill dry, sterilized glass bottles** with fresh herb sprigs, if desired, and add strained vinegar. Tightly seal the bottles with nonmetallic lids or corks; store in the refrigerator up to one month.

August

Summer Is Served!

Fresh from the farm: 11 recipes bring delicious entrées and sides to the table in under 30 minutes.

It's peak season for fast flavor. Skillets sizzle with fragrant medleys of sweet corn and fork-tender okra. Perfectly ripe tomatoes team up with tiny, cream-colored field peas for an irresistible salad. When it comes to the grill, anything goes—from speedy, spice-rubbed chicken to fingerling potatoes. With recipes this good and easy, there's no need to fuss with fancy extras or elaborate cooking techniques. A little chopping here, a dice or two there, and you're set.

Shrimp-and-Pasta Salad

MAKES 4 SERVINGS; **PREP:** 10 MIN., **COOK:** 10 MIN.

Light and lemony, this recipe easily doubles for dinner with friends. (Pictured on page 12)

8 oz. uncooked medium-size shell pasta
Lemon-Herb Dressing With Mint and Tarragon (recipe below)
1 lb. peeled, medium-size cooked shrimp (31/40 count)
1 large nectarine, cut into thin wedges
1 cup chopped seedless cucumber
Garnishes: fresh raspberries, arugula

1. Cook pasta according to package directions; drain. Plunge into ice water to stop the cooking process; drain and place in a large bowl. Add ½ cup dressing, tossing to coat. Stir in shrimp, nectarine, and cucumber. Serve with remaining ¼ cup dressing. Garnish, if desired.

—RECIPE INSPIRED BY ROGER MCGAUGH, WEBSTER GROVES, MISSOURI

Grilled Fingerling Potato Salad

fast fixin's

MAKES 4 SERVINGS; **PREP:** 10 MIN., **COOK:** 10 MIN., **GRILL:** 8 MIN.

Low in starch with a creamy texture and paper-thin skin, fingerling potatoes don't need to be peeled. Parboiling jump-starts the cooking process for the grill. Prep the dressing and other ingredients while the potatoes simmer. (Pictured on page 13)

Vegetable cooking spray
2 lb. fingerling potatoes, halved
Lemon-Herb Dressing With Chives and Tarragon (recipe at left)
½ cup crumbled Gorgonzola or feta cheese
⅓ cup chopped lightly salted roasted almonds

1. Coat cold cooking grate of grill with cooking spray, and place on grill. Preheat grill to 350° to 400° (medium-high) heat.

2. Bring potatoes and water to cover to a boil in a large Dutch oven over medium-high heat; cook 10 minutes or until crisp-tender. Drain. Coat potatoes with cooking spray.

3. Place potatoes on cooking grate of grill, and grill, covered with grill lid, 8 to 10 minutes or until tender, turning occasionally. Remove from grill, and gently toss warm potatoes with dressing. Transfer to a serving platter, and sprinkle with cheese and almonds.

One Dressing, Three Ways

This versatile dressing is a favorite for summer salads. We used the original recipe in Shrimp-and-Pasta Salad, the chive-and-tarragon variation in Grilled Fingerling Potato Salad, and the basil variation in Heirloom Tomato Salad With Fresh Lady Peas.

Lemon-Herb Dressing With Mint and Tarragon

fast fixin's

MAKES ¾ CUP; **PREP:** 10 MIN.

⅓ cup canola oil
3 Tbsp. chopped fresh mint
1 Tbsp. chopped fresh tarragon
1 Tbsp. honey mustard
1 tsp. lemon zest
¼ cup fresh lemon juice
1 tsp. salt
½ tsp. dried crushed red pepper

1. Whisk together all ingredients until blended.

—RECIPE INSPIRED BY ROGER MCGAUGH, WEBSTER GROVES, MISSOURI

Lemon-Herb Dressing With Chives and Tarragon: Substitute chopped fresh chives for mint. Proceed with recipe as directed.

Lemon-Herb Dressing With Basil: Substitute ⅓ cup chopped fresh basil for mint and tarragon. Proceed with recipe as directed. Season with salt to taste.

Southern Favorite

Also known as lady peas and white acre peas, cream peas are oblong and pale green-and-cream-colored. Smaller and sweeter in flavor than other field peas, these tender legumes cook in half the time. If you can't find them, look for fresh purple hull or pink-eyed peas.

Heirloom Tomato Salad With Fresh Lady Peas

fast fixin's

MAKES 6 SERVINGS; **PREP:** 10 MIN.,
COOK: 8 MIN.

Cool and refreshing, Heirloom Tomato Salad With Fresh Lady Peas is the perfect partner for anything grilled. (Pictured on page 13)

1 cup fresh lady peas
Lemon-Herb Dressing With Basil, divided
    (recipe on opposite page)
2 lb. assorted heirloom tomatoes, cut into
    ¼-inch-thick slices
4 fresh basil leaves, thinly sliced
1 (4-oz.) package soft goat cheese,
    crumbled
Salt and freshly ground pepper to taste

1. Cook peas in boiling salted water to cover in a large saucepan 8 to 10 minutes or just until tender. Drain and rinse until completely cool. Drizzle ¼ cup Lemon-Herb Dressing With Basil over peas, and toss to coat.
2. Arrange tomato slices on a platter or individual serving plates. Spoon peas over tomatoes; sprinkle with basil, goat cheese, and salt and pepper to taste. Serve with remaining dressing.

Maque Choux

fast fixin's

MAKES 6 SERVINGS; **PREP:** 10 MIN.,
COOK: 20 MIN.

This Louisiana favorite (pronounced "mock shoe") is delicious on its own or topped with barbecued pork.

1 medium-size sweet onion, chopped
1 green bell pepper, chopped
1 garlic clove, minced
1 jalapeño pepper, minced
2 Tbsp. canola oil
4 cups fresh corn kernels (about 8 ears)
2 tomatoes, chopped
2 tsp. Creole seasoning

1. Sauté onion, bell pepper, garlic, and jalapeño pepper in hot oil in a Dutch oven over medium-high heat 10 minutes or until tender. Stir in corn, tomatoes, and seasoning; reduce heat to low. Cover and cook 10 minutes, stirring occasionally.

—RECIPE INSPIRED BY SUSAN E. DOLLAR,
NATCHITOCHES, LOUISIANA

Parmesan Okra

MAKES 4 SERVINGS; **PREP:** 10 MIN.,
COOK: 8 MIN.

This quick-to-fix side delivers the flavor of fried okra without the fuss. Pair it with grilled Italian sausage, or try Creole Okra With Smoked Sausage for an all-in-one skillet supper.

1 lb. fresh okra, cut into ½-inch-thick slices
2 Tbsp. olive oil
¼ cup Italian-seasoned breadcrumbs
2 tsp. Greek seasoning
¼ cup freshly shaved Parmesan cheese

1. Sauté okra in hot oil in a large skillet over medium-high heat 5 to 6 minutes or until crisp-tender. Sprinkle with breadcrumbs and seasoning, and cook, stirring often, 3 minutes. Sprinkle with Parmesan cheese, and serve immediately.

—RECIPE FROM ANNE DEDERT, QUINCY, ILLINOIS

Creole Okra With Smoked Sausage: Omit Parmesan cheese. Substitute 1 tsp. Creole seasoning for 2 tsp. Greek seasoning. Cut 1 lb. smoked sausage diagonally into ¼-inch-thick slices, and sauté in a large skillet over medium-high heat 7 to 8 minutes or until golden brown. Remove sausage from skillet, and wipe skillet clean. Proceed with recipe as directed; stir in sausage. Serve immediately. Prep: 10 min., Cook: 15 min.

Caramelized Cajun Chicken

fast fixin's

MAKES 4 SERVINGS; **PREP:** 10 MIN.,
GRILL: 8 MIN.

Pounding the chicken breasts trims the time on the grill and ensures even cooking. Boneless chicken thighs and pork chops cook as quickly as chicken breasts and make great substitutes.

4 skinned and boned chicken breasts
2 Tbsp. light brown sugar
2 Tbsp. Cajun seasoning
Salt to taste

1. Preheat grill to 350° to 400° (medium-high) heat. Place chicken between 2 sheets of heavy-duty plastic wrap; flatten to ½-inch thickness using a rolling pin or flat side of a meat mallet.
2. Stir together brown sugar and Cajun seasoning; rub mixture over chicken.
3. Grill chicken, covered with grill lid, 4 minutes on each side or until done. Season with salt to taste.

Caramelized Cajun Pork Chops: Substitute 4 (½-inch-thick) boneless pork loin chops for chicken breasts. Proceed with recipe as directed.

Cook Brisket Like a Pro

We give a thumbs-up to Fiesta Brisket, which blends Tex-Mex flavors with the Lone Star State's most popular beef cut. Sauce the meat, grab an icy longneck, and you're good to go.

No, you don't need to be from the Lone Star State to cook brisket in the best Texas tradition. Here's proof: Floridian Elisa Tacher sent us her recipe for Texas-style brisket, and we loved it. Test Kitchen Professional Norman King tried it out on a gas grill and an oven. Both methods are shown here. But no matter how you cook it, you'll get credit for delicious brisket—deep in the heart of…your own dining room.

•TIP•

When buying brisket look for some fat (also called marbling) throughout the meat, which helps make it moist and tender.

Fiesta Brisket
editor's pick

MAKES 8 SERVINGS; **PREP:** 30 MIN.,
COOK: 5 MIN., **STAND:** 30 MIN.,
CHILL: 2 HR., **SOAK:** 30 MIN., **GRILL:** 5 HR.

Don't shy away from this slow-cooked, robust brisket because of the long ingredients list—you'll love it.

4 guajillo chiles
4 cups boiling water
½ cup cider vinegar
½ cup low-sodium chicken broth
8 garlic cloves
1 medium onion, chopped
3 fresh thyme sprigs
2 tsp. dried Mexican oregano leaves*
1½ tsp. ground cumin
½ tsp. ground cloves
½ tsp. ground allspice
3 tsp. salt, divided
2 tsp. ground pepper
1 (4- to 5-lb.) beef brisket flat
8 cups hickory wood chips
2 large limes, cut into wedges
Garnish: fresh cilantro sprig

1. Cook chiles in a skillet over high heat 5 minutes or until fragrant, turning often. Remove stems and seeds from chiles. Place chiles in a large bowl; add 4 cups boiling water, and let stand 20 minutes. Drain.

2. Process chiles, vinegar, next 8 ingredients, and ¾ tsp. salt in a blender or food processor until smooth, stopping to scrape down sides as needed.

3. Sprinkle pepper and remaining 2¼ tsp. salt over brisket. Place brisket in an extra-large zip-top plastic freezer bag or a large shallow dish. Pour chile mixture over brisket; rub brisket with chile mixture. Seal or cover, and chill 2 to 24 hours.

4. Soak wood chips in water 30 minutes. Prepare gas grill by removing cooking grate from 1 side of grill. Close grill lid, and light side of grill without cooking grate, leaving other side unlit. Preheat grill to 250° to 300° (low) heat.

5. Spread 4 cups soaked and drained wood chips on a large sheet of heavy-duty aluminum foil. Cover with another sheet of heavy-duty foil, and fold edges to seal. Poke several holes in top of pouch with a fork. Place pouch directly on lit side of grill. Cover with cooking grate.

6. Remove brisket from marinade, discarding marinade. Place brisket, fat side up, in a 12- x 10-inch disposable foil roasting pan. Place pan on unlit side of grill; cover with grill lid.

Trim excess fat, leaving only about ⅛ inch on the meat.

Place brisket in a zip-top plastic bag and pour chile mixture over meat. Rub chile mixture into brisket.

7. Grill brisket, maintaining internal temperature of grill between 225° and 250°, for 1½ hours. Carefully tear open foil pouch with tongs, and add remaining 4 cups soaked and drained wood chips to pouch.

8. Cover with grill lid, and grill, maintaining internal temperature of grill between 225° and 250°, until a meat thermometer inserted into thickest portion of brisket registers 165° (about 1½ hours).

9. Remove brisket from grill. Place brisket on a large sheet of heavy-duty aluminum foil, and pour ½ cup pan drippings over brisket; wrap with foil, sealing edges.

10. Return brisket to unlit side of grill, and grill, covered with grill lid, until meat thermometer registers 195° (about 2 hours). Remove from grill, and let stand 10 minutes. Cut brisket across the grain into thin slices. Squeeze juice from limes over brisket before serving. Garnish, if desired.

— **RECIPE FROM ELISA LEVY TACHER,**
TALLAHASSEE, FLORIDA

Note: Guajillo chiles and Mexican oregano may be found on the spice aisle of specialty grocery stores or in Mexican markets.
*Dried oregano may be substituted for Mexican oregano.

Grill Fiesta Brisket until a meat thermometer registers 195°.

Upgrade Your Favorite Bottled Sauce

Dress up any store-bought barbecue sauce with a few extra ingredients for a homemade taste. Try either of these options on Fiesta Brisket.

Curry-Apricot Barbecue Sauce

MAKES ABOUT 1 CUP; **PREP:** 5 MIN.

1. Stir together 1 cup barbecue sauce, 3 Tbsp. apricot preserves, 1 Tbsp. fresh lime juice, and 1 tsp. curry powder in a small bowl. Store in an airtight container in refrigerator up to 5 days.
Note: We tested with Stubb's Original Bar-B-Q Sauce.

Cilantro-Lime Barbecue Sauce

MAKES ABOUT 1 CUP; **PREP:** 5 MIN.

1. Stir together 1 cup barbecue sauce, 2 Tbsp. chopped fresh cilantro, 1 tsp. lime zest, and 1 Tbsp. fresh lime juice in a small bowl.
2. Store in an airtight container in refrigerator up to 5 days.
Note: We tested with Bull's-Eye Original Barbecue Sauce.

Oven-Roasted Fiesta Brisket:
Prepare recipe as directed through Step 3. Preheat oven to 350°. Remove brisket from marinade, discarding marinade. Wrap brisket with heavy-duty aluminum foil, and place in a jelly-roll pan. Bake 3 hours or until a meat thermometer inserted into thickest portion registers 195° and brisket is very tender. Remove from oven, and let stand 10 minutes. Cut brisket across the grain into thin slices. Prep: 30 min., Cook: 5 min., Stand: 30 min., Chill: 2 hr., Bake: 3 hr.

Chipotle Barbecue Sauce

MAKES 2⅔ CUPS; **PREP:** 15 MIN., **COOK:** 30 MIN.

Our Food staff liked this sauce prepared with root beer, but you can substitute cola soft drink too.

1 (10¾-oz.) can tomato puree
1½ cups root beer
1 medium-size sweet onion, finely chopped
¼ cup firmly packed light brown sugar
2 Tbsp. fresh lemon juice
1 tsp. ground chipotle chile powder
1 tsp. salt
¼ tsp. ground cumin
¼ tsp. dried oregano
⅛ tsp. dried crushed red pepper

1. Stir together tomato puree and remaining ingredients in a 2-qt. saucepan over medium heat. Bring to a boil, stirring frequently. Cover, reduce heat to low, and simmer 25 to 30 minutes or until sauce thickens.

The Summer Sidekick

These pickles take only minutes of your time.

Flirting with puttin' up pickles but don't want the hassle? Find 10 minutes to slice, sugar, and season store-bought pickles. After a stint in the fridge, they're hot, sweet, and homemade.

Test Kitchen Tip

Make sure you store these pickles in glass bowls or containers. Plastic will absorb odors, and metal will turn dark and result in off-flavors of the food.

Sweet-Hot No-Cook Pickles
make ahead
MAKES 1 QT.; **PREP:** 10 MIN.,
STAND: 1 HR., **CHILL:** 8 HR.

Wear plastic gloves when working with the chiles. For equally great taste without the hotness, make the Sweet No-Cook Pickles variation. Enjoy the pickles from the jar or serve them with fried fish or burgers.

1 (46-oz.) jar dill pickles, drained
18 Thai chile peppers*
2 cups sugar
1 Tbsp. white wine vinegar

1. Cut pickles into ¼-inch-thick slices. Make 4 lengthwise slits in each chile pepper, keeping stem end intact. Layer pickle slices alternately with peppers in pickle jar.
2. Gradually add sugar, tapping bottom of jar gently on a flat surface to allow sugar to settle in jar. Add vinegar. Cover with lid, and let stand at room temperature 1 hour, shaking jar occasionally. Chill 8 hours, shaking jar occasionally to ensure even chile pepper heat distribution. Store in refrigerator up to 2 weeks.
*2 large jalapeño peppers, sliced, may be substituted.
Note: For testing purposes only, we used Mt. Olive Kosher Dill Pickles.

Sweet No-Cook Pickles: Omit peppers. Cut pickles as directed in Step 1; return to pickle jar. Proceed with recipe as directed.

— **RECIPE FROM ANITA WILBANKS,**
CANTON, GEORGIA

A Taste of Old Florida

Follow Florida's County 365 to Spring Creek Restaurant, where the Lovel family offers old-Panhandle hospitality, the secret to mullet backbone, and these classic family recipes.

Seafood Supper

SERVES 6

Fried Soft-Shell Crab with Florida Cocktail Sauce and Stone Crab Sauce

Crispy Hush Puppies

Heavenly Key Lime Pie

Wine and beer

If Spring Creek, Florida, population 50, had a director of tourism, it would surely be Leo Lovel. The fisherman, restaurateur, author, and raconteur reels you in as he talks about this peaceful hammock at the end of County 365, some 30 miles south of Tallahassee.

"This place is really special," he says. "It's one of the few undeveloped areas on the coast, pretty much the same as it was 30 years ago." Carved out of St. Marks National Wildlife Refuge, Spring Creek is a community of mostly low-lying cinder block homes surrounded by lush vegetation. There is not a high-rise within 10 miles.

Leo and his son, Clay, run Spring Creek Restaurant, serving local seafood and homemade pies. (Leo has also written two volumes of stories about the area, which Clay, a coastal artist, illustrated.) The restaurant offers warm greetings and retro style. Bottles of wine on the counter offer the only clue that it isn't 1977, the year Leo's parents bought the place. "I think we're the last restaurant on this coast that adheres to local fish and old Southern-style seafood," Leo says. It's surely one of the few that are family run, with cooks and servers whose parents, aunts, and even grandparents worked here.

Clay, whose meticulously detailed drawings and oil paintings decorate the restaurant, is the current proprietor. He and his brother, Ben, grew up in the restaurant, a tradition that's continuing with their children, Margo, Katie, and Marybel.

Local Flavor Let us be clear: You won't find fussy fare at Spring Creek. What you will find is really fresh seafood, simply prepared and seasoned with a taste of Florida as it used to be. "We can tell you the name of the person who caught everything we sell," Leo says.

The restaurant is one of a dwindling number that still serves mullet. The Lovels serve it fried, with the favored portion—the backbone—on the side. Leo says with a chuckle, "Some customers come in and say, 'I want a backbone dinner.' But people who've never had mullet hold up the backbone and say, 'Why is this on my plate?'"

Do Try This at Home Senior Writer Donna Florio talked the family out of some of their prized recipes. For a taste of the real thing, head down there yourself. Tell them Donna sent you— they may put an extra backbone on your plate. Ask Leo, and he'll tell you how to eat it. Maybe even who caught it.

Fried Soft-Shell Crab

MAKES 6 SERVINGS; **PREP:** 15 MIN., **FRY:** 4 MIN. PER BATCH
(Pictured on page 185)

Vegetable oil
1 (12-oz.) can evaporated milk
1 large egg
6 soft-shell crabs
1½ tsp. seasoned salt
1½ cups self-rising flour

1. Pour oil to a depth of 3 inches into a Dutch oven; heat to 360°. Whisk together milk, egg, and ¼ cup water in a large bowl.
2. Rinse crabs, and pat dry. Sprinkle crabs with seasoned salt. Dredge crabs in flour; dip in milk mixture, and dredge in flour again. Fry crabs, in batches, in hot oil 2 to 3 minutes on each side or until golden brown. Drain on a wire rack over paper towels.

Fried Shrimp: Substitute 2 lb. peeled, large raw shrimp with tails (21/25 count) for soft-shell crab. Prepare recipe as directed, heating oil to 325° and frying shrimp, in batches, 3 to 4 minutes or until golden brown. Prep: 20 min., Fry: 3 min. per batch

Fried Grouper: Substitute 2 lb. grouper, cut into 2-inch fillets, for soft-shell crab. Prepare recipe as directed, heating oil to 350° and frying grouper, in batches, 3 minutes on each side or until golden brown. Prep: 10 min., Fry: 6 min. per batch.

Fried Oysters: Substitute 2 pt. fresh oysters, drained, for soft-shell crab. Prepare recipe as directed, frying oysters, in batches, 2 to 3 minutes or until golden brown. Serve immediately. Prep: 10 min., Fry: 2 min. per batch

Florida Cocktail Sauce

MAKES ABOUT 1¼ CUPS; **PREP:** 5 MIN.
Stir together 1 cup ketchup, 2 Tbsp. horseradish, 1 Tbsp. fresh lemon juice, ½ tsp. worcestershire sauce, and ⅛ tsp. hot sauce. Cover and chill until ready to serve.

Stone Crab Sauce

MAKES ABOUT 1 CUP; **PREP:** 5 MIN.
Stir together 1 cup mayonnaise, 2 tsp. horseradish, 1 tsp. yellow mustard, 1 tsp. fresh lemon juice, and ⅛ tsp. seasoned salt. Cover and chill until ready to serve.

Crispy Hush Puppies

MAKES ABOUT 40; **PREP:** 15 MIN., **CHILL:** 1 HR., **FRY:** 4 MIN. PER BATCH

Clay suggests using a melon baller dipped in hot water for shaping the hush puppies. Be careful to shake off excess water so it won't drip into the grease and splatter.

2 cups self-rising flour
1¼ cups plain yellow cornmeal
¼ cup sugar
¼ tsp. granulated garlic
¼ tsp. salt
⅛ tsp. baking soda
1 large egg, beaten
⅔ cup buttermilk Ranch dressing
⅔ cup buttermilk
½ cup chopped green bell pepper
½ cup finely chopped onion
Vegetable oil

1. Stir together flour and next 5 ingredients in a medium bowl.
2. Stir together egg and next 4 ingredients in a large bowl; stir in flour mixture just until moistened. (Batter will be thick.) Cover and chill 1 hour.
3. Pour oil to a depth of 2 inches into a Dutch oven; heat to 360°. Drop batter by rounded teaspoonfuls, in batches, into hot oil. Fry 2 to 3 minutes on each side or until hush puppies are golden and a wooden pick inserted into center comes out clean. Drain on a wire rack over paper towels; keep warm in a 250° oven.

Heavenly Key Lime Pie
family favorite

MAKES 6 TO 8 SERVINGS; **PREP:** 15 MIN., **BAKE:** 15 MIN., **COOL:** 1 HR., **CHILL:** 1 HR.

This pie is wonderful with fresh or bottled Key lime juice. (Pictured on page 184)

1 (14-oz.) can sweetened condensed milk
3 egg yolks
2 tsp. Key lime zest*
½ cup Key lime juice
1 (9-inch) graham cracker piecrust
1 cup whipping cream
3 Tbsp. powdered sugar
Garnish: fresh Key lime slices*

1. Preheat oven to 350°. Whisk together condensed milk and next 3 ingredients until well blended. Pour mixture into piecrust.
2. Bake at 350° for 15 minutes or until pie is set. Cool completely on a wire rack (about 1 hour). Chill 1 hour before serving.
3. Beat whipping cream at high speed with an electric mixer 2 to 3 minutes or until soft peaks form, gradually adding powdered sugar. Top pie with whipped cream. Garnish, if desired.
*Regular lime zest and slices may be substituted.
Note: We tested with Nellie & Joe's Famous Key West Lime Juice.

The Best Brownies

Take our favorite go-to brownie recipe and upgrade it with six easy stir-ins and toppings.

Everyone knows what they like and don't like in a brownie. So when our entire Food staff approved So Good Brownies at first bite, we were in shock. The usual bantering among those who like cake-textured brownies versus lovers of gooey ones was set aside in favor of requests for more until the pan was empty. Now *that's* a great brownie.

Test Kitchen Notebook

Worth the Splurge If you like brownies cut from the outside edges of the pan over those in the center, try the Edge Brownie Pan, about $35, bakersedge.com. Its design will remind you of a maze. When cut, each brownie has two crusty edges. So Good Brownies do work in this pan, however they will be thinner. Reduce baking time to 30 to 32 minutes.

So Good Brownies

MAKES 16 SERVINGS; **PREP:** 10 MIN., **COOK:** 1½ MIN., **BAKE:** 40 MIN., **COOL:** 1 HR.

This is our adaptation of a recipe many of our foodies use from Baker's Chocolate. After a few bites of our luscious treats, you'll be saying "bye-bye" to box mixes.

4 (1-oz.) unsweetened chocolate baking squares
¾ cup butter
1½ cups granulated sugar
½ cup firmly packed brown sugar
3 large eggs
1 cup all-purpose flour
1 tsp. vanilla extract
⅛ tsp. salt

1. Preheat oven to 350°. Line bottom and sides of an 8-inch pan with aluminum foil, allowing 2 to 3 inches to extend over sides; lightly grease foil.
2. Microwave chocolate squares and butter in a large microwave-safe bowl at HIGH 1½ to 2 minutes or until melted and smooth, stirring at 30-second intervals. Whisk in granulated and brown sugars. Add eggs, 1 at a time, whisking just until blended after each addition. Whisk in flour, vanilla, and salt.
3. Pour mixture into prepared pan.
4. Bake at 350° for 40 to 44 minutes or until a wooden pick inserted in center comes out with a few moist crumbs. Cool completely on a wire rack (about 1 hour). Lift brownies from pan, using foil sides as handles. Gently remove foil, and cut brownies into 16 squares.

Test Kitchen Secret: Fast Stir-ins

Prepare So Good Brownies as directed through Step 2. Add a few ingredients, tweak the baking times, and get ready to experience brownies unlike any we've discovered.

Caramel-Macchiato Brownies:

Coffee fiends: Go with 1 Tbsp. espresso powder. Be advised—these are sticky! Avoid them if you wear braces.

Stir 1 cup miniature marshmallows, ½ cup caramel bits*, and 1½ tsp. to 1 Tbsp. instant espresso into batter. Increase bake time to 44 to 46 minutes.
*12 caramels, quartered, may be substituted.
Note: Be sure to insert wooden pick into brownie, not marshmallow, when testing for doneness. (Marshmallows will rise to the top when baking.) We tested with Kraft Caramel Bits.

White Chocolate-Blueberry Brownies:

A taste of chocolate-covered blueberries gave our Food staff this idea.

Stir 1 (3.5-oz.) package dried blueberries and 1 (4-oz.) white chocolate bar, coarsely chopped, into batter. Increase bake time to 44 to 46 minutes.
Note: We tested with Sunsweet Dried Blueberries and Ghirardelli White Chocolate Baking Bar.

Toasted Coconut-Cashew Brownies:

editor's pick
This spicy, nutty brownie got our top rating.

Spread 1 cup sweetened flaked coconut into a single layer on a baking sheet. Bake at 350° for 8 minutes or until lightly toasted, stirring every 2 minutes. Let cool 10 minutes. Stir toasted coconut; ½ cup cashews, chopped; and 2 Tbsp. finely chopped crystallized ginger into batter. Increase bake time to 44 to 46 minutes.

Test Kitchen Secret: Easy Topping Upgrades

For indulgent and family-friendly double-decker brownies, prepare So Good Brownies as directed through Step 3. Add a topping layer and adjust the baking times slightly.

Peanut Butter Streusel Brownies: Stir together ½ cup all-purpose flour, 2 Tbsp. light brown sugar, 2 Tbsp. granulated sugar, ⅓ cup chunky peanut butter, 2 Tbsp. melted butter, and ⅛ tsp. salt until blended and crumbly. Sprinkle peanut butter mixture over batter. Increase bake time to 50 to 54 minutes.

Candy-and-Pretzel Brownies: Sprinkle 1 cup pretzel sticks, broken into pieces, and 2 (3.7-oz.) king-size chocolate-coated caramel-peanut nougat bars, coarsely chopped, over batter. Increase bake time to 52 to 54 minutes.
Note: Be sure to insert wooden pick into brownies, not candy bar pieces, when testing for doneness. We tested with Snickers King Size candy bars.

Spicy Pecan Brownies: Whisk together 1 Tbsp. ancho chile powder, 2 Tbsp. maple syrup, ¼ tsp. ground cinnamon, ⅛ tsp. salt, and ⅛ tsp. freshly cracked pepper in a medium bowl. Stir in 1½ cups chopped pecans. Sprinkle pecan mixture over batter. Increase bake time to 42 to 46 minutes, shielding with aluminum foil during last 15 minutes of baking to prevent excessive browning, if necessary.

Southern Classic You don't have to turn on the stove to make one of summer's simple pleasures—the tomato sandwich. Thick slices of juicy red tomatoes pair with basic white bread, a hefty layer of mayo (we love Duke's, a Southern staple), salt, pepper, and few sprigs of basil for a taste of heaven.

Quick-and-Easy Beans

They're convenient, filling, good for you, and cheap. Need we say more?

We love canned beans. They're indispensable for tossing into pasta, casseroles, salads, and soups. They also make great dips and spreads that you can put together in no time. Do as we do, and keep a few cans on hand. Try them in these recipes for a delicious meal when time is short.

Pasta With White Beans And Arugula

fast fixin's

MAKES 8 SERVINGS; **PREP:** 15 MIN., **COOK:** 15 MIN.

Crumbled feta cheese and sun-dried tomatoes make this pasta dish super flavorful.

1 (16-oz.) package farfalle (bow-tie) pasta
1 (19-oz.) can cannellini beans, rinsed and drained
1 (8.5-oz.) jar sun-dried tomatoes with herbs in oil, drained and chopped
1 (5-oz.) package fresh arugula, thoroughly washed
1 (4-oz.) package crumbled feta cheese
¼ cup chopped fresh basil
2 Tbsp. fresh lemon juice
2 Tbsp. olive oil
½ tsp. salt

1. Cook pasta according to package directions; drain. Stir together beans and next 7 ingredients in a large bowl. Stir in hot cooked pasta until blended.

Pasta With Chickpeas, Tuna, and Arugula: Substitute 1 (16-oz.) can chickpeas, rinsed and drained, for cannellini beans. Stir in 3 (5-oz.) cans solid white tuna in water, drained.

Bean-and-Sausage Cornbread Casserole

taste of the south

MAKES 6 TO 8 SERVINGS; **PREP:** 20 MIN., **COOK:** 10 MIN., **BAKE:** 25 MIN.

1 (1-lb.) package mild ground pork sausage
½ cup chopped red onion
½ cup chopped green bell pepper
4 (16-oz.) cans pinto beans, rinsed and drained
1 (14.5-oz.) can diced tomatoes with zesty green chiles, drained
½ tsp. salt
1 (8-oz.) package shredded Mexican four-cheese blend
1 cup buttermilk
1 cup self-rising white cornmeal mix

1. Preheat oven to 425°. Brown sausage in a large skillet over medium heat, stirring often, 7 minutes or until sausage crumbles and is no longer pink. Add onion and bell pepper, and sauté 3 minutes or until vegetables are tender. Drain. Stir in beans, tomatoes, and salt.
2. Pour sausage mixture into a lightly greased 13- x 9-inch baking dish. Sprinkle with 1½ cups cheese. Stir together buttermilk and cornmeal mix, and spoon over cheese; sprinkle with remaining ½ cup cheese.
3. Bake at 425° for 25 to 30 minutes or until browned.

—RECIPE FROM BRENDA MILLER,
HUNTSVILLE, ALABAMA

Black Bean-and-Chicken Cornbread Casserole: Substitute 1 lb. skinned and boned chicken breasts, chopped, for sausage, and 4 (15.5-oz.) cans black beans, rinsed and drained, for pinto beans. Stir ½ cup chopped fresh cilantro into chicken mixture with beans.

Easy Enchiladas

Fiesta night! A deli-roasted chicken helps make short work of this classic Mexican entrée. Luscious? Absolutely. In fact, we guarantee your family will clamor for seconds.

Fiesta Night

SERVES 4 TO 6

Chicken-and-Green Chile Enchiladas

Avocado-Tomato Toss

Lemonade or Classic Margarita

Chicken-and-Green Chile Enchiladas

MAKES 4 TO 6 SERVINGS; **PREP:** 20 MIN., **BAKE:** 30 MIN.

Substitute leftover roast beef or your favorite shredded barbecued pork as a tasty alternative to chicken.

3½ cups chopped cooked chicken
⅔ cup Onion-and-Garlic Mixture
2 (4-oz.) cans chopped green
 chiles
1 Tbsp. chopped fresh cilantro
3 (10-oz.) cans enchilada sauce,
 divided
2 cups (8 oz.) shredded Mexican four-cheese
 blend, divided
8 (9-inch) burrito-size flour tortillas

1. Preheat oven to 425°. Stir together first 4 ingredients, 1½ cups enchilada sauce, and 1 cup cheese.

2. Spoon about ½ cup chicken mixture down center of each tortilla; roll tortillas up, and place, seam sides down, in a lightly greased 13- x 9-inch baking dish. Pour remaining enchilada sauce over tortillas. Sprinkle with remaining 1 cup cheese.

3. Bake, covered, at 425° for 20 minutes; uncover and bake 10 minutes or until cheese is melted and golden brown.

Onion-and-Garlic Mixture:

MAKES ABOUT 1⅓ CUPS; **PREP:** 5 MIN., **COOK:** 10 MIN.

This recipe has lots of uses. It's great as a base for French onion soup, spread on toast topped with your favorite cheese, stirred into mashed potatoes or hash browns, or mixed into hamburger patties.

2 cups chopped onion (1 large onion)
1 Tbsp. vegetable oil
3 garlic cloves, chopped

1. Sauté onion in hot oil in a 3½-qt. saucepan over medium heat 8 minutes or until tender; add garlic, and sauté 2 minutes. Store in an airtight container in refrigerator up to 5 days.

Avocado-Tomato Toss

fast fixin's
MAKES 6 SERVINGS; **PREP:** 15 MIN.

⅓ cup chopped fresh cilantro
¼ cup olive oil
2 Tbsp. red wine vinegar
2 Tbsp. fresh lime juice
½ tsp. salt
2 cups halved cherry tomatoes
⅓ cup thinly sliced red onion
2 medium avocados, halved and cut into
 chunks
4 large romaine lettuce leaves, shredded

1. Whisk together first 5 ingredients in a large bowl. Add tomatoes, red onion, and avocados, gently stirring to coat. Serve over shredded romaine lettuce.

Classic Margarita

test kitchen favorite
MAKES: 1 SERVING; **PREP:** 10 MIN.

Make any size batch of this recipe by simply multiplying the ingredient measurements by the desired number of servings. For larger batches, stir together all ingredients in a pitcher until powdered sugar is dissolved. Chill and serve over ice. For a sweeter drink, use ½ cup powdered sugar instead of ⅓ cup.

Fresh lime wedge (optional)
Margarita salt (optional)
Ice
⅓ cup fresh lime juice*
3 tablespoons orange liqueur
2 tablespoons tequila
⅓ to ½ cup powdered sugar
Garnish: lime slice

1. Rub rim of a chilled margarita glass with lime wedge, and dip rim in salt to coat, if desired.

2. Fill cocktail shaker half full with ice. Add lime juice, liqueur, tequila, and powdered sugar; cover with lid, and shake until thoroughly chilled. Strain into prepared glass. Garnish, if desired, and serve immediately.

*⅓ cup thawed frozen limeade concentrate may be substituted for fresh lime juice. Omit powdered sugar, and proceed with recipe as directed.

Note: For testing purposes only, we used Cointreau for orange liqueur and Jose Cuervo Especial for tequila.

Celebrate summertime by indulging in a cool treat.
You'll be surprised to learn some refreshing ways to serve this Southern favorite.

Guilt-Free Ice Cream

Our favorite light brands from the freezer section (yes, we sampled a grocery cart full) inspired seven delicious ways to enjoy the South's coolest summer treat.

Just a few figure-friendly bites of these luscious treats will satisfy your craving, and who can resist when they look so tasty.

The average American consumes about 15 quarts of ice cream per year, and Southerners especially are known to be ice-cream lovers. Southerners are known to be ice cream lovers. And, Americans consume about 15 quarts of ice cream per year. Low-calorie ice cream that tastes like cardboard is a thing of the past. Newer manufacturing processes make for great-tasting flavors that won't make you feel guilty. Now you can indulge and still look great in your swimsuit.

Mini Mocha Ice-Cream Scoops

MAKES 4 SERVINGS; **PREP:** 10 MIN., **FREEZE:** 30 MIN.

1. Line a baking sheet with wax paper, and place in freezer. Process ½ cup chocolate-covered espresso beans in a food processor 30 seconds or until finely chopped. Pour espresso crumbs into a shallow dish. Scoop 1¼ cups low-fat coffee or chocolate ice cream into small balls using a 1¼-inch ice-cream scoop, and roll ice cream in espresso crumbs. Arrange on prepared baking sheet in freezer. Freeze 30 minutes to 24 hours. Serve in Dipped Sugar Cones, if desired.

Per serving: Calories 126; Fat 5.5g (sat 2.8g, mono 0g, poly 0g); Protein 2.3g; Carb 20g; Fiber 1.1g; Chol 4.9mg; Iron 0.2mg; Sodium 41mg; Calc 50mg

Mini Nutty Ice-Cream Scoops:

Substitute ½ cup finely chopped mixed nuts for chocolate-covered espresso beans and low-fat vanilla bean ice cream for coffee ice cream. (Do not process nuts.)

Per serving: Calories 169; Fat 9.5g (sat 1.3g, mono 5.2g, poly 2g); Protein 4.7g; Carb 17g; Fiber 2.5g; Chol 3mg; Iron 0.7mg; Sodium 31.4mg; Calc 103mg

Mini Berry Ice-Cream Scoops:

Substitute dried mixed berries for chocolate-covered espresso beans and low-fat vanilla ice cream for coffee ice cream. Finely chop berries (do not process).

Per serving: Calories 114; Fat 1.4 g (sat 0.6g, mono 0g, poly 0g); Protein 1.9g; Carb 22.9g; Fiber 1.4g; Chol 3.1mg; Iron 0.1mg; Sodium 28mg; Calc 63mg

Mini Double-Chocolate Ice-Cream Scoops:

Substitute ⅓ cup grated dark chocolate for chocolate-covered espresso beans, and low-fat chocolate ice cream for coffee ice cream. (Do not process chocolate.)

Per serving: Calories 133; Fat 6g (sat 3.3g, mono 0g, poly 0g); Protein 1.9g; Carb 20.7g; Fiber 0.7g; Chol 5mg; Iron 0.8mg; Sodium 34mg; Calc 50mg

Mini Tropical Ice-Cream Scoops:

Substitute ½ cup sweetened flaked coconut for chocolate-covered espresso beans and pineapple sherbet for coffee ice cream. Preheat oven to 350°. Bake coconut in a single layer in a shallow roasting pan 8 to 10 minutes or until toasted. Let cool 10 minutes. (Do not process coconut.)
Prep: 10 min., Bake: 8 min., Cool: 10 min., Freeze: 30 min.

Per serving: Calories 117; Fat 3.5g (sat 3.1g, mono 0.1g, poly 0g); Protein 0.9g; Carb 21.1g; Fiber 0.9g; Chol 3.1mg; Iron 0.1mg; Sodium 48mg; Calc 26mg

Dipped Sugar Cones

MAKES 4 CONES; **PREP:** 10 MIN., **COOK:** 1 MIN.

1. Microwave 1 extra-dark chocolate square in a microwave-safe glass measuring cup at HIGH 1 minute or until melted, stirring at 30-second intervals. Dip top edges of 4 sugar cones into melted chocolate. Dip into 1 Tbsp. shaved chocolate or chopped mixed nuts.

Per serving with nuts: Calories 75; Fat 2.9g (sat 0.8g, mono 0.7g, poly 0.3g); Protein 1.4g; Carb 11.7g; Fiber 0.5g; Chol 1mg; Iron 0.4mg; Sodium 16mg; Calc 8mg

Note: We tested with Hershey's All Natural Extra Dark Chocolate (60% Cacao) squares and Keebler Sugar Cones.

Test Kitchen Taste Test

We went on an ice-cream run and discovered the lighter side of the freezer section. After sampling nearly 20 gallons of creamy goodness, here are a few of our favorites.

- **Breyers Natural Vanilla:** all-natural ingredients; vanilla bean really comes through
- **Edy's Slow Churned Vanilla Bean:** super-rich and creamy; tastes like homemade
- **The Skinny Cow Low Fat Vanilla Ice Cream Sandwiches:** taste like they're from the ice-cream truck; satisfy chocolate and creamy cravings

• TIP •

Serve Mini Mocha Ice-Cream Scoops at your next ice-cream social. Keep your cones upright by surrounding them with heart-healthy chopped nuts. (If you want to splurge on a splash of color, jelly beans work just as well.)

Ice-Cream Crêpes
test kitchen favorite

MAKES 6 SERVINGS; **PREP:** 10 MIN.

This recipe makes 3 crêpes to be shared by 6 people. Scoop ice cream into ⅓ cupfuls, and freeze on a baking sheet until ready to assemble.

3 Tbsp. light hot fudge topping
3 (7-inch) prepared French crêpes
1 cup low-fat chocolate ice cream
½ cup raspberries
1 Tbsp. powdered sugar

1. Warm fudge topping according to package directions; set aside.
2. Microwave French crêpes at HIGH 10 seconds.
3. Spoon ⅓ cup chocolate ice cream in center of 1 crêpe, and wrap sides of crêpe around ice cream. Place, seam side down, on a serving dish. Repeat procedure with remaining ice cream and crêpes. Drizzle 1 Tbsp. warm fudge topping over each crêpe, and top evenly with raspberries; sprinkle evenly with powdered sugar. Serve immediately.
Note: We tested with Smucker's Toppings Light Hot Fudge and Frieda's French Style Crêpes.

Per serving: Calories 80; Fat 1g (sat 0.3g, mono 0.0g, poly 0.0g); Protein 1.8g; Carb 16.8g; Fiber 1.2g; Chol 4mg; Iron 0.4mg; Sodium 67mg; Calc 39mg

Skinny Ice-Cream Sandwich Sundaes

MAKES 12 SERVINGS; **PREP:** 20 MIN., **COOK:** 1 MIN., **FREEZE:** 30 MIN.

Wax paper
6 reduced-fat ice-cream sandwiches
4 extra-dark chocolate squares, coarsely chopped
¼ cup chopped lightly salted peanuts*
Strawberry Sauce
Toppings: diced fresh pineapple, diced kiwifruit

1. Line a baking sheet with wax paper; top with ice-cream sandwiches.
2. Microwave chocolate in a microwave-safe glass measuring cup at HIGH 1 to 1½ minutes or until melted and smooth, stirring at 30-second intervals. Immediately spoon 1 tsp. melted chocolate onto each ice-cream sandwich, and sprinkle with nuts; lightly press nuts into chocolate. Lightly cover with plastic wrap, and freeze sandwiches 30 minutes.
3. Cut each sandwich into quarters, and place 2 pieces in each of 12 small bowls. Drizzle with 1 Tbsp. Strawberry Sauce, and sprinkle with desired toppings. Serve immediately.
*Toasted pecans may be substituted. Preheat oven to 350°. Bake ¼ cup chopped pecans in a single layer in a shallow pan 7 to 8 minutes or until toasted and fragrant, stirring occasionally.
Note: We tested with Hershey's All Natural Extra Dark Chocolate (60% Cacao) squares and The Skinny Cow Low Fat Vanilla Ice Cream Sandwiches.

Per serving with 1 Tbsp. Strawberry Sauce (not including toppings): Calories 112; Fat 3.4g (sat 1.5g, mono 0.7g, poly 0.5g); Protein 3.1g; Carb 19.8g; Fiber 2.4g; Chol 1mg; Iron 0mg; Sodium 72mg; Calc 4mg

Strawberry Sauce:

1. Process 1 (16-oz.) container fresh strawberries, hulled; ½ tsp. lime zest; 1 Tbsp. fresh lime juice; and 2½ Tbsp. honey in a blender or food processor 1 minute or until smooth, stopping to scrape down sides as needed. Makes 1⅔ cups. Prep: 5 min.

Per Tbsp.: Calories 10; Fat 0g (sat 0g, mono 0g, poly 0g); Protein 0.1g; Carb 2.4g; Fiber 0.3g; Chol 0mg; Iron 0.1mg; Sodium 0mg; Calc 2mg

Creamy Strawberry-Mint Pie

MAKES 10 SERVINGS; **PREP:** 30 MIN., **BAKE:** 10 MIN., **COOL:** 30 MIN., **STAND:** 35 MIN., **FREEZE:** 3 HR.

This scrumptious pie has a frozen yogurt filling and a reduced-fat chocolate cookie crust. It's delicious with or without Strawberry Sauce.

½ (18-oz.) package reduced-fat cream-filled chocolate sandwich cookies (about 22 cookies)
2 Tbsp. butter, melted
1 qt. fat-free strawberry frozen yogurt
1 (16-oz.) package fresh strawberries, hulled
2 Tbsp. powdered sugar
2 Tbsp. chopped fresh mint
Garnishes: edible flowers, fresh strawberries slices, Strawberry Sauce

1. Preheat oven to 350°. Process cookies and butter in a food processor until finely chopped. Firmly press mixture on bottom and up sides of a lightly greased 9-inch springform pan. Bake 10 minutes. Cool completely on a wire rack (about 30 minutes).
2. Let frozen yogurt stand at room temperature 20 minutes or until slightly softened. (See "Ice-Cream Tips" box.)
3. Process strawberries, powdered sugar, and mint in food processor until strawberries are pureed, stopping to scrape down sides as needed.

4. Place frozen yogurt in a large bowl; cut into large (3-inch) pieces. Fold strawberry mixture into yogurt until smooth. Spoon mixture into prepared crust. Freeze 3 hours or until firm. Let stand at room temperature 15 minutes before serving. Garnish, if desired.
Note: We tested with Publix Low Fat Strawberry Frozen Yogurt and Reduced Fat Oreo cookies.

Per serving: Calories 262; Fat 6g (sat 2.2g, mono 2.4g, poly 0.9g); Protein 5.8g; Carb 48.9g; Fiber 1.7g; Chol 8mg; Iron 1.5mg; Sodium 172mg; Calc 129mg

Ice-Cream Tips

- Premium ice creams and frozen yogurts typically soften more evenly than budget brands. Low-fat products also tend to soften faster.
- You want to achieve the consistency of self-serve ice cream. Too-soft or melted ice cream may soak into the crust or leak from the bottom of the spring-form pan. Return the ice cream to the freezer if you think it's getting too soft.

September

Six New Ways With Corn Bread

Take your pick from six weeknight-easy recipes that showcase the South's ultimate quick bread. Tweak the basic stir-and-bake batter, and you can make a fast skillet focaccia or crostini by the dozen. And that's just for starters. For breakfast, try Cornbread Omelets with spicy chorizo and cheese. Need a little comfort? Ham-and-Greens Pot Pie fills the bill. Peppered with Creole seasoning, Shrimp-and-Okra Hushpuppies are perfect with catfish. And don't shy away from stirring up a big batch of our Skillet Cornbread. You'll love the leftovers. Split, toasted, and glistening with the salty sweetness of melted butter, day-old cornbread is like a really good pound cake—you can eat it for days and never get tired of it. Totally effortless, totally fun.

Cornbread Crostini

MAKES 5 DOZEN; PREP: 15 MIN.,
BAKE: 15 MIN.
PER BATCH

Small, thin rounds of cornbread baked in muffin pans replace baguette slices as a tasty base for Southern-style crostini. (Pictured on page 15)

2 cups self-rising white cornmeal mix
2 cups buttermilk
½ cup all-purpose flour
2 large eggs, lightly beaten
¼ cup butter, melted
2 Tbsp. sugar

1. Preheat oven to 400°. Stir together all ingredients just until moistened. Spoon batter into greased muffin pans (about 1 Tbsp. per cup). Bake, in batches, 15 minutes or until golden brown. **Note:** Cool completely, and freeze in zip-top plastic freezer bags up to 1 month, if desired. To serve, arrange desired number of cornbread rounds on a baking sheet, and bake at 350° for 5 to 6 minutes or until thoroughly heated.

Quick Crostini Toppers

Cornbread Crostini make a crisp start for all sorts of delicious toppings—from soft cheeses and chutneys to fresh figs and country ham. Here are a few of our favorite combos.

- Boursin cheese, finely chopped red and yellow bell peppers, and chives
- Gorgonzola cheese, sliced apples, parsley, and freshly ground black pepper
- Goat cheese, cranberry chutney, watercress, and freshly ground pepper

We also serve Cornbread Crostini with hot toppings—just assemble, place on a baking sheet, and broil 5 inches from heat one minute or until the cheese is melted.

- Shredded barbecue pork, shredded pepper Jack cheese, diced sweet-hot pickles, and finely chopped fresh cilantro
- Plum tomato slices, shredded Cheddar cheese, crumbled bacon, and a dollop of mayonnaise

3 Tasty Tricks With Crostini Cornbread Batter

We knew the recipe we used for Cornbread Crostini could also make a fabulous skillet cornbread and some pretty terrific waffles. The big surprise? We loved the delicious results we got when we poured the batter into a slow cooker. No—it doesn't get cast-iron crisp around the edges, but the crust does turn a deep golden brown.

- **Slow-Cooker Cornbread:** Pour batter into a lightly greased 6-qt. slow cooker. Cover and cook on LOW 2 hours or until a wooden pick inserted in center comes out clean. Makes 8 to 10 servings. Prep: 10 min., Cook: 2 hr.
- **Skillet Cornbread:** Preheat oven to 425°. Heat a well-greased 10-inch cast-iron skillet in oven 5 minutes. Pour batter into hot skillet. Bake for 25 to 30 minutes or until golden brown. Makes 8 to 10 servings. Prep: 10 min., Bake: 25 min.
- **Cornbread Waffles:** Cook batter in a preheated, oiled waffle iron until done. Makes 8 servings. Prep: 15 min., Cook: 3 min. per batch.

Cornbread Focaccia

MAKES 8 TO 10 SERVINGS; **PREP:** 15 MIN., **BAKE:** 30 MIN.

A sprinkling of yeast is stirred into the batter—but there's no rise time or kneading. (Pictured on page 14)

2 cups self-rising white cornmeal mix
2 cups buttermilk
½ cup all-purpose flour
1 (¼-oz.) envelope rapid-rise yeast
2 large eggs, lightly beaten
¼ cup butter, melted
2 Tbsp. sugar
1 cup crumbled feta cheese
1 cup coarsely chopped black olives
¾ cup grape tomatoes, cut in half
1 Tbsp. coarsely chopped fresh rosemary

1. Preheat oven to 375°. Heat a well-greased 12-inch cast-iron skillet in oven 5 minutes. Stir together cornmeal mix and next 6 ingredients just until moistened; pour into hot skillet. Sprinkle with feta cheese, olives, tomatoes, and rosemary. Bake 30 minutes or until golden brown.

Beer-Cheese Cornbread

MAKES 8 TO 10 SERVINGS; **PREP:** 10 MIN., **BAKE:** 25 MIN.

2 cups self-rising white cornmeal mix
1 cup (4 oz.) shredded sharp Cheddar
    cheese
1 cup buttermilk
½ cup all-purpose flour
½ cup beer
2 large eggs, lightly beaten
¼ cup butter, melted
2 Tbsp. sugar

1. Preheat oven to 425°. Heat a well-greased 10-inch cast-iron skillet in oven 5 minutes. Stir together all ingredients just until moistened; pour into hot skillet.
2. Bake at 425° for 25 to 30 minutes or until golden brown.

Cornbread Omelets

MAKES 5 SERVINGS; **PREP:** 20 MIN., **COOK:** 20 MIN.

A feather-light cornbread batter takes the place of eggs in these fun omelets.

¾ lb. chorizo sausage, casings removed
    (about 3 links)
6 Tbsp. butter, divided
3 green onions, chopped
1 small red bell pepper, chopped
2 jalapeño peppers, minced
1 cup self-rising white cornmeal mix
½ cup buttermilk
½ cup milk
¼ cup all-purpose flour
1 large egg, lightly beaten
Vegetable cooking spray
1 cup (4 oz.) shredded Mexican cheese blend

1. Sauté chorizo in an 8-inch nonstick omelet pan or skillet with sloped sides 7 to 10 minutes or until browned. Remove from skillet, and drain on paper towels. Wipe skillet clean.
2. Melt 1 Tbsp. butter in skillet, and sauté green onions, bell pepper, and jalapeño peppers over medium-high heat 3 to 5 minutes or until tender. Transfer to a bowl; stir in chorizo. Wipe skillet clean.
3. Whisk together cornmeal mix, buttermilk, milk, all-purpose flour, and 1 large egg.
4. Coat skillet with cooking spray; melt 1 Tbsp. butter in skillet over medium-high heat, rotating pan to coat bottom evenly. Pour about ⅓ cup cornmeal mixture into skillet. Tilt pan so uncooked portion flows around to coat bottom of pan, cooking until almost set, bubbles form, and edges are dry (about 1½ minutes). Gently flip with a spatula.
5. Sprinkle 1 side of omelet with about ½ cup onion mixture and about 3 Tbsp. cheese. Fold omelet in half; cook 30 seconds or until cheese is melted. Transfer to a serving plate; keep warm. Repeat procedure 4 times with remaining butter, cornmeal mixture, onion mixture, and cheese. Serve immediately.

Shrimp-and-Okra Hushpuppies

MAKES 8 SERVINGS (ABOUT 2½ DOZEN); **PREP:** 10 MIN., **STAND:** 5 MIN., **FRY:** 4 MIN. PER BATCH

1 cup self-rising yellow cornmeal mix
½ cup self-rising flour
1 cup peeled medium-size raw shrimp
    (21/25 count), chopped
1 tsp. Creole seasoning
½ cup frozen diced onion, red and green bell
    peppers, and celery, thawed
½ cup frozen cut okra, thawed and chopped
1 large egg, lightly beaten
¾ cup beer
Canola oil

1. Stir together cornmeal mix and flour in a large bowl until combined.
2. Sprinkle shrimp with Creole seasoning. Add shrimp, onion mixture, and okra to cornmeal mixture. Stir in egg and beer just until moistened. Let stand 5 to 7 minutes.
3. Pour oil to depth of 4 inches into a Dutch oven; heat to 350°. Drop batter by level tablespoonfuls into hot oil, and fry, in batches, 2 to 2½ minutes on each side or until golden brown. Drain on a wire rack over paper towels; serve immediately.
Note: Keep fried hushpuppies warm in a 225° oven up to 15 minutes. We tested with McKenzie's Seasoning Blend for diced onion, red and green bell peppers, and celery.

Ham-and-Greens Pot Pie With Cornbread Crust

MAKES 8 TO 10 SERVINGS; **PREP:** 10 MIN., **COOK:** 30 MIN., **BAKE:** 20 MIN.

Pouring the cornbread batter over a hot filling helps cook the crust from the bottom.

4 cups chopped cooked ham
2 Tbsp. vegetable oil
3 Tbsp. all-purpose flour
3 cups low-sodium chicken broth
1 (16-oz.) package frozen diced onion, red and green bell peppers, and celery
1 (16-oz.) package frozen chopped collard greens
1 (16-oz.) can black-eyed peas, rinsed and drained
½ tsp. dried crushed red pepper
Cornbread Crust Batter

1. Preheat oven to 425°. Sauté ham, in batches, in hot oil in a Dutch oven over medium-high heat 5 minutes or until lightly browned. Return ham to Dutch oven; add flour, and cook, stirring constantly, 1 minute. Gradually add chicken broth, and cook, stirring constantly, 3 minutes or until broth begins to thicken.
2. Bring mixture to a boil; stir in frozen onion, peppers, and celery and collard greens. Return to a boil; cover and cook, stirring often, 15 minutes. Stir in black-eyed peas and red pepper, and spoon hot mixture into a lightly greased 13- x 9-inch baking dish. Pour Cornbread Crust Batter over hot mixture.
3. Bake at 425° for 20 to 25 minutes or until cornbread is golden brown and set.
Note: We tested with McKenzie's Seasoning Blend for frozen diced onion, red and green bell peppers, and celery.

Cornbread Crust Batter:

MAKES 1 (13- X 9-INCH) CRUST; **PREP:** 5 MIN.

1½ cups self-rising white cornmeal mix
½ cup all-purpose flour
1 tsp. sugar
2 large eggs, lightly beaten
1½ cups buttermilk

1. Combine first 3 ingredients; make a well in center of mixture. Add eggs and buttermilk, stirring just until moistened.

Simple Shrimp Supper

Here's the plan: Pick up a pound of shrimp, and prepare this inspiring recipe for an easy meal. On another night, prepare the same shrimp base again, and turn it into a tasty salad.

Tempura Shrimp Tacos

MAKES 6 SERVINGS; **PREP:** 25 MIN., **STAND:** 5 MIN., **FRY:** 2 MIN. PER BATCH

Make coleslaw up to 24 hours in advance to jump-start this recipe.

1 lb. unpeeled, large raw shrimp (31/35 count)
1 cup tempura batter mix
¾ cup cold light beer
2 tsp. fajita seasoning mix
Vegetable oil
12 (6-inch) fajita-size flour tortillas, warmed
Mexi-Coleslaw Mix
Toppings: chopped tomatoes, diced avocados, chopped fresh cilantro

1. Peel shrimp; devein, if desired.
2. Whisk together tempura batter mix, beer, and fajita seasoning in a large bowl; let stand 5 minutes.
3. Pour oil to depth of 2 inches into a Dutch oven; heat to 325°. Dip shrimp in tempura batter, shaking off excess. Fry shrimp, in batches, 1 to 2 minutes on each side or until golden; drain on a wire rack over paper towels.
4. Serve in warm tortillas with Mexi-Coleslaw Mix and desired toppings.
Note: We tested with McCormick Golden Dipt Tempura Seafood Batter Mix.

Tempura Shrimp Salad: Omit tortillas. Prepare 2 batches of Mexi-Coleslaw Mix as directed. Proceed with Tempura Shrimp Tacos recipe as directed through Step 3. Place Mexi-Coleslaw Mix in a serving bowl; top with shrimp. Serve with desired toppings.

Mexi-Coleslaw Mix:

MAKES 6 SERVINGS ; **PREP:** 10 MIN., **CHILL:** 30 MIN.

1. Stir together 2 Tbsp. chopped fresh cilantro, 3 Tbsp. mayonnaise, 1 Tbsp. fresh lime juice, and ½ tsp. fajita seasoning in a large bowl; add ½ (16-oz.) package shredded coleslaw mix, stirring to coat. Season with salt to taste. Cover and chill 30 minutes to 24 hours.

3 Quick-and-Easy Rice Upgrades

It takes only some simple stir-ins, such as fresh herbs, citrus zest, and coconut milk, to brighten up this basic side.

Brown Rice With Feta, Pistachios, and Mint

fast fixin's • family favorite

MAKES 8 SERVINGS; **PREP:** 15 MIN., **COOK:** 15 MIN.

If you're not a fan of brown rice, try our long-grain variation at right.

2 Tbsp. butter
2 shallots, minced
1 tsp. salt
2 cups uncooked quick-cooking brown rice
1/4 cup crumbled feta cheese
1/4 cup chopped pistachios
3 Tbsp. chopped fresh mint
1/2 tsp. lemon zest
1/2 tsp. pepper

1. Melt butter in a medium saucepan over medium-high heat. Add shallots, and sauté 1 minute. Stir in salt and 3 1/4 cups water; bring to a boil. Stir in brown rice; cover, reduce heat to low, and cook 10 minutes or until water is absorbed and rice is tender. Stir in feta cheese and next 4 ingredients.
Note: We tested with Uncle Ben's Whole Grain Fast & Natural Instant Brown Rice.

Long-Grain Rice With Feta, Pistachios, and Mint: Substitute 1 cup uncooked long-grain rice for 2 cups quick-cooking brown rice. Reduce water to 2 cups. Cook, covered, 20 minutes or until water is absorbed and rice is tender. Prep: 15 min., Cook: 25 min.

Coconut Rice With Fresh Ginger and Cilantro

family favorite

MAKES 4 SERVINGS; **PREP:** 10 MIN., **COOK:** 25 MIN.

1 1/4 cups vegetable broth
1/2 cup coconut milk
1 Tbsp. grated fresh ginger
1 tsp. salt
1 cup uncooked basmati rice
3 Tbsp. fresh cilantro, chopped

1. Stir together first four ingredients in a large saucepan; bring to a boil over high heat. Stir in basmati rice; cover, reduce heat to low, and cook 20 minutes or until liquid is absorbed and rice is tender. Stir in cilantro.

Citrus-Scented Rice With Fresh Basil

family favorite

MAKES 4 SERVINGS; **PREP:** 10 MIN., **COOK:** 25 MIN.

Citrus-Scented Rice With Fresh Basil pairs perfectly with chicken, fish, or pork.

2 cups chicken broth
2 Tbsp. butter
1 Tbsp. orange zest
2 Tbsp. fresh orange juice
1 tsp. lemon zest
1 cup uncooked basmati rice
3 Tbsp. fresh basil, chopped
Orange and lemon zest (optional)
Orange and lemon slices (optional)

Stir together first five ingredients in a large saucepan; bring to a boil over high heat. Stir in basmati rice; cover, reduce heat to low, and cook 20 minutes or until liquid is absorbed and rice is tender. Stir in chopped fresh basil. Garnish with orange and lemon zest and orange zest and lemon slices, if desired.

Test Kitchen Secrets

How can you tell when your rice is cooked?
Look for steam holes on the surface of the rice. These little holes indicate that all the water has evaporated. Let the rice rest off the heat for another minute or two; then fluff with a fork.

Looking for more flavor?
Cook rice in low-fat chicken broth instead of water.

Got a pan with stuck-on rice?
Let it soak in warm water for at least 30 minutes; then scrape it with a metal or plastic spatula. If necessary, heat the pan of water over low heat to help loosen the rice.

What We're Cooking At Home

Southern Living Food pros Natalie, Marian, and Norman share a few of their favorite easy weeknight recipes. Whether you're a busy mom, working spouse, or living the single life, they give you solutions for getting supper on the table pronto.

For the Working Mom

Recipes from Assistant Food Editor, Natalie Kelly Brown

"My husband and girls love fish, and I cook it often because it's so easy. I can have dinner on the table in an hour."

Natalie's Cajun-Seasoned Pan-Fried Tilapia

family favorite • fast fixin's

MAKES 4 SERVINGS; **PREP:** 10 MIN., **COOK:** 6 MIN.

4 (4- to 6-oz.) tilapia fillets
1½ tsp. Cajun seasoning*
3 Tbsp. self-rising flour
½ cup plain yellow cornmeal
1 Tbsp. butter
2 Tbsp. olive oil
Lemon (optional)
Garnish: fresh parsley sprig

1. Sprinkle fillets with 1 tsp. seasoning. Combine remaining seasoning, flour, and cornmeal. Dredge fillets in flour mixture, shaking off excess.
2. Melt butter with oil in a large skillet over medium-high heat; add fillets, and cook 3 to 4 minutes on each side or until fish flakes with a fork. Squeeze juice from lemon over fillets, and garnish, if desired. Serve immediately.
*Creole seasoning may be substituted.

Cajun-Seasoned Pan-Fried Chicken Breasts:
Substitute 4 (8-oz.) skinned and boned chicken breasts for tilapia. Proceed with recipe as directed, cooking 8 to 10 minutes on each side or until done. Prep: 10 min., Cook: 16 min.

Cajun-Seasoned Pan-Fried Pork Chops:
Substitute 4 (8-oz.) bone-in center-cut pork chops for tilapia. Proceed with recipe as directed, cooking 8 to 10 minutes on each side or until done. Prep: 10 min., Cook: 16 min.

Sautéed Sugar Snap Peas

MAKES 4 SERVINGS; **PREP:** 5 MIN.
COOK: 5 MIN.

1. Cook 1 lb. fresh sugar snap peas in boiling salted water 2 to 3 minutes or until crisp-tender. Drain and plunge into ice water to stop the cooking process. Drain. Melt 1 Tbsp. butter in a large skillet; stir in peas, 2 tsp. lemon juice, and ½ tsp. salt, and cook 1 minute or until thoroughly heated. Serve immediately.

For Singles

Recipes from Test Kitchen Professional, Norman V. King

"This sauce is so versatile and its flavors play well with just about everything. I make a batch on the weekend, then use it to top baked chicken or as a base for homemade pizza. I also love to stir the sauce into rice and peas."

Norman's Spicy Tomato Sauce

editor's pick

MAKES ABOUT 5¼ CUPS;
PREP: 15 MIN., **COOK:** 50 MIN.

If you'd like a less spicy sauce, use 1 Tbsp. of Italian Seasoning Mix.

½ cup finely chopped onion
2 tsp. minced garlic
1 Tbsp. extra virgin olive oil
1½ Tbsp. Italian Seasoning Mix
1 (28-oz.) can crushed tomatoes
1 (8-oz.) can Spanish-style tomato sauce
1 tsp. kosher salt
1 tsp. honey

1. Sauté onion and garlic in hot oil in a 3-qt. saucepan over medium heat 2 to 3 minutes or until tender. Stir in Italian Seasoning Mix, and cook 1 minute.

Stir in crushed tomatoes, tomato sauce, and 1 cup water; bring to a boil, stirring constantly. Reduce heat to low, and simmer 40 to 45 minutes or until slightly thickened. Stir in salt and honey.

Note: We tested with Goya Tomato Sauce.

Spicy Tomato Sauce With Italian Sausage: Remove casings from ½ lb. mild Italian sausage (about 2 sausages). Cook in a 3-qt. saucepan over medium heat 8 to 10 minutes or until meat is no longer pink, breaking sausage into pieces. Drain; return sausage to pan. Proceed as directed.

Spicy Tomato Sauce With Ground Chuck: Cook ½ lb. ground chuck in a 3-qt. saucepan over medium heat 6 to 8 minutes until meat crumbles and is no longer pink. Drain; return to pan. Proceed as directed.

Spicy Tomato Sauce With Cajun Smoked Sausage: Cook ½ lb. sliced Cajun smoked sausage in a 3-qt. saucepan over medium heat 5 to 6 minutes or until browned. Drain; return to pan. Proceed as directed.

Note: We tested with Conecuh Cajun Smoked Sausage.

Italian Seasoning Mix:
make ahead
MAKES ABOUT ½ CUP; **PREP:** 5 MIN.

Don't want to get out the food processor? Norman uses a mortar and pestle to grind these ingredients.

½ cup dried basil
2 Tbsp. plus 2 tsp. dried oregano
4 tsp. dried crushed red pepper
2 tsp. whole black peppercorns

1. Process basil, oregano, crushed red pepper, and black peppercorns in a food processor 1 minute or until mixture is a fine powder. Store in an airtight container at room temperature up to 4 months.

Baked Ziti With Italian Sausage

MAKES 4 TO 6 SERVINGS; **PREP:** 10 MIN., **BAKE:** 20 MIN., **STAND:** 10 MIN.

1. Preheat oven to 350°. Prepare 1 (16-oz.) package ziti pasta according to package directions. Stir together pasta, Spicy Tomato Sauce With Italian Sausage, and ½ cup (2 oz.) shredded part-skim mozzarella cheese. Spoon mixture into a lightly greased 11- x 7-inch baking dish. Sprinkle with an additional ½ cup cheese. Bake at 350° for 20 to 25 minutes or until cheese is melted. Let stand 10 minutes before serving.

For the Working Spouse

Recipes from Test Kitchen Specialist , Marian Cooper Cairns

"My husband, Lee, loves Savory Vegetable Bread Pudding. I mix and match vegetables I have on hand for this recipe—sometimes it's baked with okra and tomatoes or summer squash and mushrooms."

Marian's Savory Vegetable Bread Pudding

MAKES 4 TO 6 SERVINGS; **PREP:** 20 MIN., **COOK:** 10 MIN., **BAKE:** 35 MIN., **STAND:** 5 MIN.

1 bunch Swiss chard (about 1 lb.)
6 large eggs
1 cup milk
2 tsp. Dijon mustard
1¼ tsp. salt
¾ tsp. pepper
3 cups cubed ciabatta bread
    (about 1-inch cubes)
1½ cups freshly grated Parmesan cheese,
    divided
1 (8-oz.) package sliced fresh mushrooms
1 red bell pepper, chopped
1 small onion, chopped
1 tsp. minced garlic
2 Tbsp. olive oil

1. Preheat oven to 350°. Remove and discard ribs from Swiss chard. Rinse with cold water; drain and coarsely chop.

2. Whisk together eggs and next 4 ingredients in a large bowl; stir in bread and half of cheese.

3. Sauté mushrooms and next 3 ingredients in hot oil in a large skillet over medium-high heat 8 minutes. Stir in Swiss chard, and sauté 2 minutes. Fold vegetable mixture into egg mixture. Pour into a lightly greased 11- x 7-inch baking dish. Sprinkle with remaining cheese.

4. Bake at 350° for 35 to 40 minutes or until center is set. Let stand 5 minutes.

Okra-Tomato Casserole: Omit mushrooms and Swiss chard. Substitute shredded Monterey Jack cheese for Parmesan cheese, 1½ tsp. Cajun seasoning for salt, and green bell pepper for red bell pepper. Reduce pepper to ½ tsp. Prepare recipe as directed in Step 2, adding 2 Tbsp. chopped fresh flat-leaf parsley and 2 medium tomatoes, chopped, with bread. Proceed with recipe as directed, sautéing 2 cups sliced okra with onion 8 to 10 minutes in Step 3.

Cooler days and football bring the opportunity for great outdoor gatherings. Discover some of our best recipes and essentials for tailgating.

Tailgating— Lightened Up

Love tailgating but don't want the fuss—or the fat? These four simple, healthful recipes are so good you may even forget the wings.

Game-Day Menu

SERVES 4

Chopped Chicken Sandwich With Crunchy Pecan Slaw

Tex-Mex Butternut Bisque

Oatmeal-Pecan Snack Cookies

Spiked Arnold Palmer

Chopped Chicken Sandwich With Crunchy Pecan Slaw

fast fixin's

MAKES 4 SERVINGS; PREP: 15 MIN.,
GRILL: 15 MIN.

Get your salad and sandwich in one convenient package with this game-day favorite.

4 hoagie rolls
½ cup grated Swiss cheese, divided
2 cups chopped cooked chicken
¼ cup Sweet-and-Spicy Dressing
Vegetable cooking spray
2 to 3 cups Crunchy Pecan Slaw
Celery salt (optional)

1. Light one side of grill, heating to 350° to 400° (medium-high) heat; leave other side unlit.
2. Split rolls in half horizontally, and hollow out soft bread from tops and bottoms, leaving a ¼-inch-thick shell. Reserve soft bread for another use, if desired. Sprinkle bottom halves of rolls with half of Swiss cheese.
3. Stir together chicken and Sweet-and-Spicy Dressing in a small bowl. Divide chicken mixture among bottom halves of rolls, and top with remaining cheese. Cover with top halves of rolls. Lightly coat each sandwich with cooking spray, and wrap with aluminum foil.
4. Place sandwiches over unlit side of grill, and grill, covered with grill lid, 10 to 12 minutes. Unwrap sandwiches, place over unlit side of grill, and grill 5 minutes or until crust is crisp and cheese is melted. Remove from grill, and cut in half.
5. Remove top halves of rolls from sandwiches. Arrange Crunchy Pecan Slaw over chicken and cheese; lightly sprinkle with celery salt, if desired. Cover with top halves of rolls. Serve immediately.
Per serving: Calories 439; Fat 16g (sat 6.1g, mono 5.8g, poly 3.2g); Protein 33.7g; Carb 38.6g; Fiber 3.4g; Chol 72mg; Iron 2.1mg; Sodium 470mg; Calc 247mg

---

Sweet-and-Spicy Dressing:

fast fixin's • make ahead
MAKES ¾ CUP; PREP: 5 MIN.

¼ cup lemon juice
¼ cup honey
2 Tbsp. hot sauce
2 Tbsp. canola oil
1 tsp. celery salt
¼ tsp. pepper

1. Whisk together all ingredients in a small bowl. Store in refrigerator in an airtight container up to 3 days.
Per (1 Tbsp.) serving: Calories 44; Fat 2.3g (sat 0.2g, mono 1.4g, poly 0.7g); Protein 0g; Carb 6.4g; Fiber 0g; Chol 0mg; Iron 0mg; Sodium 92mg; Calc 1mg

---

Crunchy Pecan Slaw:

fast fixin's • make ahead
MAKES 10 CUPS; PREP: 20 MIN.,
BAKE: 8 MIN.

Hold leftover slaw in the refrigerator until the next day. Try it on hot dogs or add grilled sliced chicken or shrimp for a great salad.

1 cup chopped pecans
1 head napa cabbage, cut into thin strips
1 Braeburn apple, cut into thin strips
½ cup sliced radishes
½ cup Sweet-and-Spicy Dressing
3 green onions, sliced

1. Preheat oven to 350°. Bake pecans in a single layer in a shallow pan 8 to 10 minutes or until toasted and fragrant.
2. Toss together pecans, cabbage, and remaining ingredients in a large bowl until blended.
Per (1 cup) serving: Calories 146; Fat 10.5g (sat 0.9g, mono 6g, poly 3.1g); Protein 2.3g; Carb 12.2g; Fiber 2.9g; Chol 0mg; Iron 0.5mg; Sodium 87mg; Calc 54mg

**Thai Pesto Shrimp
With Coconut-Lime Rice**
(page 55)

Skillet-Grilled Burritos *(page 56)*

Tailgating Essentials

Simplify taking food on the road with these portable containers and serving pieces—must-haves for any fan.

Tiffin Box: Pack food in a large, stacking Tiffin box. You can serve food in the individual compartments or use them as bowls. When you're done, cleanup is easy. Just stack together, bring it home, and toss the trays in the dishwasher. Tiffin food box: $39, from Vivo; *www.vivodirect.com*

Bamboo Plates: Pass on the paper plates and go with bamboo instead. Made for single use, they're fashioned from organic bamboo and are compostable. They look great and are better for the environment than other disposable plates. Bamboo plates: $4.99-$9.99 (set of eight), from Cost Plus World Market; *www.worldmarket.com*

Stainless Steel Thermos: Make taking soup to the game fuss-free. Heat soup the morning before, and store in a large thermos to keep it hot for hours. A good thermos is worth the investment and will get years of use for hot or cold soups, cider, or hot chocolate. Stanley 2.0-qt. classic vacuum bottle: $40, from Stanley; *www.stanley-pmi.com*

Spork: Bringing multiple sets of utensils can be cumbersome. Instead, use this all-in-one knife, fork, and spoon combo. These super-cool tools are also dishwasher safe. Light my fire spork: $9.95 (set of four), from REI; *www.rei.com*

Tex-Mex Butternut Bisque

MAKES 6 (1⅓-CUP) SERVINGS; **PREP:** 15
MIN., **COOK:** 30 MIN., **COOL:** 15 MIN.

*Go ahead and use full-fat half-and-half.
Our tasting table tried this with fat-free
half-and-half and agreed that it doesn't
compare to the real thing.*

1 medium-size sweet onion, chopped
2 garlic cloves, finely chopped
1 Tbsp. canola oil
1½ lb. butternut squash, peeled and cut into
    1-inch cubes
1 tsp. chili powder
1 tsp. ground cumin
1 tsp. salt
1 (32-oz.) container low-sodium vegetable
    broth
1 (4.5-oz.) can chopped green chiles
3 (6-inch) fajita-size corn tortillas, torn into
    small pieces
½ cup half-and-half
Garnish: thinly sliced root vegetable chips

1. Sauté onion and garlic in hot oil in a
Dutch oven over medium-high heat 2 to
3 minutes or until tender. Add squash
and next 3 ingredients, and cook 1
minute; stir in broth and chiles. Cover
and bring to a boil. Reduce heat to low,
and simmer 20 to 25 minutes or until
squash is fork-tender.
2. Remove from heat, and stir in tortilla
pieces. Let cool 15 minutes. Process
mixture, in batches, in a blender or food
processor until smooth, stopping to
scrape down sides as needed. Return
squash mixture to Dutch oven.
3. Stir in half-and-half, and cook over
medium heat 2 to 3 minutes or until
thoroughly heated. Garnish, if desired.

—TAMMY VARCOE, BROOKLYN, NEW YORK

Note: Soup may also be processed with
a hand-held blender directly in Dutch
oven. We tested with Terra Stix for
thinly sliced root vegetable chips.

Per serving (not including garnish): Calories 158; Fat 5.3g (sat 1.6g,
mono 2.1g, poly 0.8g); Protein 3g; Carb 27.6g; Fiber 5.8g; Chol 7mg;
Iron 1mg; Sodium 879mg; Calc 133mg

Oatmeal-Pecan Snack Cookies

test kitchen favorite

MAKES 4 DOZEN; **PREP:** 20 MIN.,
BAKE: 13 MIN. PER BATCH, **COOL:** 10 MIN.

*These nutritious cookies are great with a
cup of cold low-fat milk for breakfast on
the go. Store them in zip-top plastic freezer
bags in the freezer for up to one month.*

1¾ cups all-purpose flour
1¾ tsp. pumpkin pie spice
½ tsp. salt
½ tsp. baking soda
¼ cup butter, softened
6 oz. reduced-fat cream cheese, softened
1½ cups firmly packed dark brown sugar
½ cup egg substitute
1 tsp. vanilla extract
3 cups uncooked regular oats
¾ cup dried cherries
Vegetable cooking spray
½ cup chopped pecans

1. Preheat oven to 350°. Combine flour,
pumpkin pie spice, salt, and baking
soda.
2. Beat butter, cream cheese, and
sugar at medium speed with an electric
mixer until fluffy. Add egg substitute
and vanilla, beating until blended.
Gradually add flour mixture, beating at
low speed just until blended. Stir in oats
and dried cherries.
3. Drop dough by rounded tablespoonfuls onto baking sheets coated with
cooking spray; gently flatten dough into
circles. Sprinkle about ½ tsp. chopped
pecans onto each dough circle, gently
pressing into dough.
4. Bake, in batches, at 350° for 13 to 14
minutes or until a wooden pick inserted
in centers comes out clean. Remove
cookies from baking sheets to wire
racks, and let cool 10 minutes.

Per cookie: Calories 99; Fat 2.7g (sat 1.3g, mono 0.9g, poly 0.5g);
Protein 2.1g; Carb 16.1g; Fiber 1g; Chol 5mg; Iron 0.7mg; Sodium 70mg;
Calc 18mg

Spiked Arnold Palmer

MAKES ABOUT 10 CUPS; **PREP:** 10 MIN.,
STEEP: 5 MIN., **CHILL:** 30 MIN.

*To make this tea a day ahead, follow rec-
ipe as directed, omitting ice and garnish.
Store in the refrigerator in a pitcher.
When you are ready to serve, stir in ice
cubes and lemon slices.*

4 cups boiling water
5 regular-size tea bags
¾ cup sugar
1 tsp. lemon zest
4 cups cold water
1 cup bourbon
½ cup fresh lemon juice
Garnish: lemon slices

1. Pour boiling water over tea bags,
sugar, and lemon zest in a large bowl.
Stir until sugar is dissolved; cover and
steep 5 minutes.
2. Pour mixture through a fine wire-
mesh strainer into a large pitcher,
discarding tea bags and zest. Stir in 4
cups cold water and next 2 ingredients.
Cover and chill 30 minutes to 12 hours.
Serve over ice. Garnish, if desired.

Per (1-cup) serving: Calories 113; Fat 0g (sat 0g, mono 0g, poly 0g);
Protein 0.1g; Carb 16.1g; Fiber 0.1g; Chol 0mg; Iron 0mg; Sodium 6mg;
Calc 7mg

Southwestern Soup *(page 29)*

Seared Halibut With Herbed Tomato Sauce *(page 56)*

Blue Cheese-Walnut Finger Sandwiches *(page 60)*

**Mustard-Dill Tortellini
Salad Skewers** *(page 61)*

Free-form Strawberry Cheesecake
(page 87)

166

Strawberry-Fruit Toss With Cornmeal Shortcakes *(page 85)*

**Dixie Beef Burgers With
Chowchow Spread** *(page 94)*

Shrimp Burgers With Sweet 'n' Spicy Tartar Sauce *(page 92)*

Mini Crab Cakes With Garlic-Chive Sauce *(page 103)*

**Black-eyed Susan Cocktail, Long Island
Iced Tea, and Fresh Basil Julep** *(pages 100-101)*

Chicken Tetrazzini With Prosciutto and Peas *(page 32)*

**Tomato 'n' Beef Casserole
With Polenta Crust** *(page 88)*

Championship Pork Butt
(page 112)

Apricot-Pineapple Sweet Ribs *(page 113)*

Party Chicken Salad *(page 112)*

Blackberry-Peach Coffee Cake *(page 110)*

Lemonade Iced Tea *(page 126)*

Pick up summer flowers (only a few bucks), and place in an old colander.

Flank Steak Sandwiches With Blue Cheese *(page 124)*

Baked Bean Crostini *(page 125)*

Peppery Grilled Okra With Lemon-Basil Dipping Sauce *(page 126)*

Tomato-Rosemary Tart *(page 135)*

Cherry Tomato-Cucumber Salad Tartlets *(page 135)*

Grilled Apple Salad *(page 197)*

Praline-Apple Bread
(page 196)

Heavenly Key Lime Pie *(page 144)*

Fried Soft-Shell Crab *(page 143)*

Natalie's Cajun-Seasoned Pan-Fried Tilapia *(page 156)*

Roasted Dry-Rub Turkey With Gravy, Sautéed Green Beans, Smoky Cranberry-Apple Sauce, Cornbread Yeast Rolls *(pages 243-244)*

Crab Crostini and Whiskey Sours *(page 242)*

Peanut Butter-Banana Sandwich Bread Puddings With Dark Caramel Sauce *(page 244)*

Scallops in Orange-Butter Sauce *(page 289)*

Clementine-Cranberry Salsa *(page 288)*

Mississippi Mud Fondue *(page 257)*

Sour Cream Coffee Cake Muffins *(page 260)*

Brandy Alexander Cheesecake *(page 256)*

Great Grits and More

Bet you've never had grits like these. In *Glorious Grits: Fresh, Flavorful Recipes for Grits, Cornmeal & Polenta*, (Oxmoor House, 2009), author Susan McEwen McIntosh offers recipes that'll change your thinking about this Southern staple. One taste of her dishes, and you may never go back to plain old grits again.

Easy Pork Grillades Over Panko-Crusted Grits Patties

MAKES 6 SERVINGS; **PREP:** 30 MIN., **COOK:** 25 MIN.

Panko-Crusted Grits Patties
1¼ lb. boneless pork loin chops
¼ cup all-purpose flour
2 tsp. Old Bay seasoning
4 Tbsp. olive oil, divided
1 cup chopped celery
½ cup chopped green bell pepper
½ cup chopped red bell pepper
2 cups sliced baby portobello mushrooms
1 (14.5-oz.) can diced tomatoes
    with garlic and onion
½ cup low-sodium chicken broth
1½ tsp. chopped fresh or ½ tsp.
    dried thyme
¾ tsp. chopped fresh or ¼ tsp.
    dried oregano
¼ to ½ tsp. dried crushed red pepper
¼ tsp. salt

1. Prepare Panko-Crusted Grits Patties; keep warm.
2. Trim fat from pork chops, and cut pork crosswise into thin strips. Combine flour and Old Bay seasoning; dredge pork in flour mixture.
3. Cook half of pork in 2 Tbsp. hot oil in a large skillet over medium-high heat 3 minutes on each side or until browned.
4. Repeat procedure with 1 Tbsp. oil and remaining pork. Remove pork from skillet.
5. Sauté celery and bell peppers in remaining 1 Tbsp. oil in skillet 30 seconds. Add mushrooms, and sauté 2 minutes. Add tomatoes and next 5 ingredients; cook over medium heat 5 minutes. Add pork; cover, reduce heat, and simmer 5 minutes. Serve over Panko-Crusted Grits Patties.

Panko-Crusted Grits Patties:

MAKES 6 SERVINGS; **PREP:** 20 MIN., **COOK:** 25 MIN., **COOL:** 15 MIN., **CHILL:** 2 HR., **BAKE:** 25 MIN.

2 cups uncooked stone-ground grits
2 tsp. salt
1 cup freshly grated Parmesan cheese
1 large egg, lightly beaten
1½ cups Japanese breadcrumbs (panko)
¼ to ½ tsp. ground red pepper (optional)
Vegetable cooking spray

1. Bring grits, salt, and 6 cups water to a boil in a large heavy saucepan over medium heat, stirring constantly. Reduce heat to low; simmer, stirring frequently, 20 to 25 minutes or until very thick. Remove from heat; stir in Parmesan cheese until melted.
2. Spoon grits into a 13- x 9-inch pan lined with heavy-duty plastic wrap; spread in an even layer. Cool 15 minutes. Place a dry paper towel over grits, and cover with plastic wrap. Chill 2 hours or until very firm.
3. Preheat oven to 425°. Turn chilled grits out onto a cutting board; remove plastic wrap and paper towel, and cut grits into 12 squares.
4. Whisk together egg and 2 Tbsp. water in a bowl. Combine panko and, if desired, ground red pepper in a shallow dish. Dip grits patties into egg wash; dredge in panko mixture. Place grits patties on a baking sheet coated with cooking spray.
5. Bake at 425° for 25 minutes or until lightly browned.

Huevos Rancheros on Cilantro Grits Cakes
test kitchen favorite

MAKES 4 SERVINGS; **PREP:** 20 MIN.,
COOK: 48 MIN., **COOL:** 15 MIN., **CHILL:** 2 HR.,
BROIL: 12 MIN.

Poach eggs in a zesty tomato sauce instead of water for this Southwestern brunch favorite. It's a delicious twist on a dish that's typically served over tortillas.

1 cup uncooked stone-ground grits
1¼ tsp. salt
⅓ cup finely chopped onion
2 Tbsp. olive oil, divided
1 cup (4 oz.) shredded Monterey Jack cheese
½ cup minced fresh cilantro
Vegetable cooking spray
1 cup chopped green bell pepper
1 Tbsp. all-purpose flour
1 (8-oz.) can tomato sauce
1 (14.5-oz.) can diced tomatoes with green chiles, undrained
½ cup canned black beans, rinsed and drained
4 large eggs
Chopped fresh cilantro

1. Bring grits, salt, and 3¼ cups water to a boil in a medium saucepan over high heat, stirring constantly. Reduce heat to low, and simmer, stirring frequently, 20 to 25 minutes or until very thick.
2. Sauté onion in 1 Tbsp. hot oil in a small skillet over medium heat 4 to 5 minutes or until tender. Add cheese, minced cilantro, and sautéed onion to hot cooked grits, stirring until cheese melts. Spoon mixture into an 8-inch square pan lined with heavy-duty plastic wrap; spread into an even layer. Let cool 15 minutes. Place a dry paper towel over grits, and cover with plastic wrap. Chill 2 hours or until very firm.
3. Preheat broiler with oven rack 5½ inches from heat. Cut grits into 4 squares. Coat tops of grits cakes with cooking spray, and place in a lightly greased broiler pan. Broil 5 minutes. Remove from oven, and flip grits cakes; broil 7 to 9 minutes or until lightly browned.
4. Sauté bell pepper in remaining 1 Tbsp. hot oil in a large skillet over medium heat 5 minutes or until tender. Gradually whisk in flour until blended. Cook 1 minute, whisking constantly. Gradually stir in tomato sauce and tomatoes; cook 5 minutes. Stir in beans, and bring mixture to a light simmer. Break eggs, and slip into tomato mixture 1 at a time, as close as possible to surface of tomato mixture. Cover and cook just below a simmer 8 minutes or to desired degree of doneness.
5. Place 1 grits cake on each of 4 individual serving plates. Top each cake with 1 egg and about ¾ cup sauce; sprinkle with fresh cilantro.
Note: We tested with Del Monte Diced Tomatoes With Zesty Mild Green Chilies.

The Season's Best Salads

Take advantage of fall's fresh produce with these simple and elegant salads.

Beet, Goat Cheese, and Avocado Salad

MAKES 6 SERVINGS; **PREP:** 25 MIN.,
COOK: 30 MIN., **COOL:** 25 MIN.

A tangy vinaigrette plays perfectly with the sweet, nutty flavors of Beet, Goat Cheese, and Avocado Salad. Wear gloves to prevent beets from staining your hands.

3 large beets (about 1½ lb.)
1 tsp. orange zest
¼ cup fresh orange juice
2 Tbsp. raspberry vinegar
1 Tbsp. maple syrup
¼ cup olive oil
1 (4-oz.) package watercress, thoroughly washed*
2 small avocados, sliced
½ (4-oz.) goat cheese log, crumbled
⅓ cup thinly sliced red onion
Freshly ground pepper to taste

1. Trim beet stems to 1 inch; gently wash, and place in a 3½-qt. saucepan with water to cover. Bring to a boil over medium-high heat. Reduce heat to medium-low, and simmer 25 to 30 minutes or until tender. Remove beets from heat; drain, rinse, and cool completely (about 25 to 30 minutes). Peel and cut beets into eighths.

Test Kitchen Secrets

Flavored oils and vinegars offer endless possibilities for creating your own salad dressings.

- The ratio for a classic vinaigrette is three parts oil to one part vinegar or fresh lemon juice, but you can adjust the proportions according to taste.
- Substitute fruit preserves or jam for a portion of the oil. Fresh herbs, minced shallots or garlic, and fresh ginger are also great additions.
- Nut oils can be strongly flavored and overpower a dressing, so combine them with a little olive oil when preparing a vinaigrette. Check the sell-by date, and refrigerate after opening.
- White balsamic vinegar has the same sweet taste as the traditional version, but it won't discolor foods.

2. Whisk together orange zest and next 3 ingredients. Gradually add olive oil in a slow, steady stream, whisking until blended.

3. Line a serving platter with watercress. Arrange beets and avocado slices in alternating rows (2 each) on top of watercress. Sprinkle with goat cheese, onion, and freshly ground pepper to taste. Serve with orange vinaigrette.

—JANICE HELLMANN, ATLANTA, GEORGIA

*1 (6-oz.) package fresh baby spinach may be substituted.

Autumn Salad With Maple-Cider Vinaigrette
test kitchen favorite
MAKES 8 SERVINGS; **PREP:** 10 MIN.

Place pear in a paper sack to speed up ripening. The dressing and nuts can be made ahead.

1 (10-oz.) bag baby spinach
1 ripe Bartlett pear, cored and thinly
   sliced
1 small red onion, thinly sliced
1 (4-oz.) package crumbled blue cheese
Sugared Curried Walnuts
Maple-Cider Vinaigrette

1. Combine first 5 ingredients in a large bowl. Drizzle with Maple-Cider Vinaigrette, gently tossing to coat.

Sugared Curried Walnuts:
MAKES 1½ CUPS; **PREP:** 5 MIN.,
BAKE: 10 MIN.

1 (6-oz.) package walnut halves
2 Tbsp. butter, melted
3 Tbsp. sugar
¼ tsp. ground ginger
⅛ tsp. curry powder
⅛ tsp. kosher salt
⅛ tsp. ground red pepper

1. Preheat oven to 350°. Toss walnuts in melted butter. Stir together sugar and next 4 ingredients in a medium bowl; sprinkle over walnuts, tossing to coat. Spread in a single layer on a nonstick aluminum foil-lined pan.

2. Bake at 350° for 10 minutes. Cool in pan on a wire rack; separate walnuts with a fork. Store in an airtight container for up to 1 week.

Maple-Cider Vinaigrette:
MAKES 1⅓ CUPS; **PREP:** 5 MIN.

⅓ cup cider vinegar
2 Tbsp. pure maple syrup
1 Tbsp. Dijon mustard
¼ tsp. salt
¼ tsp. pepper
⅔ cup olive oil

1. Whisk together first 5 ingredients. Gradually whisk in oil until completely blended. Cover and refrigerate up to 3 days.

Harvest Wild Rice Salad With Pumpkin Vinaigrette
editor's pick
MAKES ABOUT 4 CUPS; **PREP:** 25 MIN.,
BAKE: 8 MIN., **COOL:** 25 MIN., **CHILL:** 2 HR.

For a quick-and-easy meal, serve over a bed of greens and top with sautéed or grilled chicken.

½ cup chopped pecans
1 (6-oz.) package long-grain and wild
   rice mix
½ cup sweetened dried cranberries
1 cup finely chopped celery
¾ cup chopped green onions
¼ cup canned pumpkin
¼ cup white wine vinegar
1 Tbsp. honey
½ tsp. salt
¼ tsp. dried thyme
¼ tsp. pepper
⅓ cup olive oil

1. Preheat oven to 350°. Bake pecans in a single layer in a shallow pan 8 to 10 minutes or until toasted and fragrant.
2. Prepare rice according to package directions; let cool completely (about 25 minutes). Stir in cranberries, celery, green onions, and toasted pecans.
3. Whisk together canned pumpkin, next 5 ingredients, and 2 Tbsp. water. Gradually whisk in olive oil in a slow, steady stream, whisking until blended.
4. Pour pumpkin vinaigrette over rice mixture; stir gently to coat. Cover and chill 2 to 24 hours. Serve at room temperature.

Fresh Ideas for Apples

You know what they say about apples and temptation, right? Fall's favorite fruit is awfully hard to resist...and these original dishes are, well, sinfully delicious.

Praline-Apple Bread

freezeable • make ahead

MAKES 1 LOAF; **PREP:** 20 MIN.;
BAKE: 1 HR., 6 MIN.; **COOL:** 1 HR., 10 MIN.;
COOK: 5 MIN.

Sour cream is the secret to the rich, moist texture of this bread. There's no butter or oil in the batter—only in the glaze. This bread is even decadent enough to serve as dessert. (Pictured on page 183)

1½ cups chopped pecans, divided
1 (8-oz.) container sour cream
1 cup granulated sugar
2 large eggs
1 Tbsp. vanilla extract
2 cups all-purpose flour
2 tsp. baking powder
½ tsp. baking soda
½ tsp. salt
1½ cups finely chopped, peeled Granny
    Smith apples (about ¾ lb.)
½ cup butter
½ cup firmly packed light brown sugar

1. Preheat oven to 350°. Bake ½ cup pecans in a single layer in a shallow pan 6 to 8 minutes or until toasted and fragrant, stirring after 4 minutes.
2. Beat sour cream and next 3 ingredients at low speed with an electric mixer 2 minutes or until blended.
3. Stir together flour and next 3 ingredients. Add to sour cream mixture, beating just until blended. Stir in apples and ½ cup toasted pecans. Spoon batter into a greased and floured 9- x 5-inch loaf pan. Sprinkle with remaining 1 cup chopped pecans; lightly press pecans into batter.
4. Bake at 350° for 1 hour to 1 hour and 5 minutes or until a wooden pick

inserted into center comes out clean, shielding with aluminum foil after 50 minutes to prevent excessive browning. Cool in pan on a wire rack 10 minutes; remove from pan to wire rack.
5. Bring butter and brown sugar to a boil in a 1-qt. heavy saucepan over medium heat, stirring constantly; boil 1 minute. Remove from heat, and spoon over top of bread; let cool completely (about 1 hour).

—RECIPE FROM DEBBIE GRUSSKA,
HOBART, INDIANA

Note: To freeze, cool bread completely; wrap in plastic wrap, then in aluminum foil. Freeze up to 3 months. Thaw at room temperature.

Apple Upside-Down Pie

family favorite

MAKES 8 SERVINGS; **PREP:** 25 MIN.;
BAKE: 1 HR.; **COOL:** 1 HR., 10 MIN.

A buttery mix of brown sugar and pecans caramelizes as it bakes beneath the bottom crust of this pie.

1 cup chopped pecans
½ cup firmly packed light brown
    sugar
⅓ cup butter, melted
1 (15-oz.) package refrigerated piecrusts,
    divided
4 medium-size Granny Smith apples,
    peeled and cut into 1-inch chunks
    (about 1¾ lb.)
2 large Jonagold apples, peeled and cut into
    1-inch chunks (about 1¼ lb.)
¼ cup granulated sugar
2 Tbsp. all-purpose flour
1 tsp. ground cinnamon
½ tsp. ground nutmeg

1. Preheat oven to 375°. Stir together first 3 ingredients, and spread onto bottom of a 9-inch pie plate. Fit 1 piecrust over pecan mixture in pie plate, allowing excess crust to hang over sides.
2. Stir together Granny Smith apples and next 5 ingredients. Spoon mixture into crust, packing tightly and mounding in center. Place remaining piecrust over filling; press both crusts together, fold edges under, and crimp. Place pie on an aluminum foil-lined jelly-roll pan. Cut 4 to 5 slits in top of pie for steam to escape.
3. Bake at 375° on lower oven rack 1 hour to 1 hour and 5 minutes or until juices are thick and bubbly, crust is golden brown, and apples are tender when pierced with a long wooden pick through slits in crust. Shield pie with aluminum foil after 50 minutes, if necessary, to prevent excessive browning. Cool on wire rack 10 minutes. Place a serving plate over top of pie; invert pie onto serving plate. Remove pie plate, and replace any remaining pecans in pie plate on top of pie. Let cool completely (about 1 hour).

Test Kitchen Notebook

Apples are available year-round, but some, such as the McIntosh and Honeycrisp, are here only for a short time so enjoy them now. When choosing apples, keep in mind that different types work best for different uses. Fuji and Gala apples that taste great eaten out of hand are perfect for salads, but they don't always hold their shape well when baked. Granny Smith gets top honors for best all-around apple—the tartness, flavor, and texture make it excellent for cooking. Other good choices are the Cortland, Empire, and Jonagold.

MARY ALLEN PERRY,
SENIOR FOOD EDITOR

Test Kitchen Secrets

Save those apple peels, and brew up a bottle of Brown Sugar-Apple Simple Syrup. It adds a trendy twist to tea, but you can also serve it in place of maple syrup with pancakes, oatmeal, or a warm baked apple.

Brown Sugar-Apple Simple Syrup:

Bring 2 cups firmly packed apple peels, 2 cups firmly packed light brown sugar, and 2 cups water to a boil in a large saucepan over medium-high heat. Boil, stirring constantly, 1 minute or until sugar is dissolved. Reduce heat to low, and cook 5 minutes or until slightly thickened. Remove from heat, and cool completely (about 1 hour). Pour mixture through a wire-mesh strainer into a large bowl; discard apple peels. Pour syrup into glass jars. Store in an airtight container in refrigerator up to 3 weeks. Makes about 2⅓ cups. Prep: 10 min., Cook: 10 min., Cool: 1 hr.

Grilled Apple Salad

MAKES 8 SERVINGS; **PREP:** 10 MIN., **BAKE:** 6 MIN., **GRILL:** 4 MIN.

A quick cook time leaves the apples crisp-tender; for more caramelization, go an extra few minutes on each side. Serve with crackers. (Pictured on page 182)

1 cup pecan halves
Vegetable cooking spray
4 Gala apples (about 1½ lb.)
1 (6-oz.) package baby spinach, thoroughly washed
1 (5-oz.) package spring greens mix, thoroughly washed
3 oz. extra-sharp white Cheddar cheese, shaved
Salt and pepper to taste
Brown Sugar-Cider Vinaigrette

1. Preheat oven to 350°. Bake pecans in a single layer in a shallow pan 6 to 8 minutes or until toasted and fragrant, stirring after 4 minutes.
2. Coat cold cooking grate of grill with cooking spray, and place on grill. Preheat grill to 350° to 400° (medium-high) heat. Cut apples crosswise into ¼-inch-thick rings, cutting from one side through the other.
3. Grill apple rings, covered with grill lid, 2 to 3 minutes on each side or until crisp-tender. Arrange spinach and spring greens mix on a serving platter; top with apples, cheese, and toasted pecans. Season with salt and pepper to taste. Serve with Brown Sugar-Cider Vinaigrette.

Brown Sugar-Cider Vinaigrette:

MAKES ABOUT 1 CUP; **PREP:** 10 MIN.

⅔ cup canola oil
⅓ cup apple cider vinegar
2 green onions, minced
3 Tbsp. light brown sugar
3 Tbsp. chopped fresh basil
1 Tbsp. Dijon mustard
½ tsp. dried crushed red pepper
¼ tsp. salt

1. Whisk together all ingredients until blended.

Skillet Fried Apples
fast fixin's
MAKES 4 SERVINGS; **PREP:** 10 MIN., **COOK:** 15 MIN.

Serve this versatile side dish with baked ham and cheese grits, or spoon over hot buttered biscuits. Balsamic vinegar and onion give the variation a savory note that's perfect with grilled chicken or pan-fried pork chops. Both versions are delicious sprinkled with lightly salted, roasted pecans.

3 Tbsp. butter
5 large Granny Smith apples, peeled and sliced (about 2¼ lb.)
⅔ cup firmly packed light brown sugar
1 tsp. apple pie spice

1. Melt butter in a 12-inch skillet over medium-high heat; add apples and remaining ingredients. Sauté 15 to 20 minutes or until apples are tender.

Skillet-Fried Balsamic Apples and Sweet Onion: Omit apple pie spice. Melt butter in a large skillet over medium-high heat; add 2 large sweet onions, sliced, and sauté 5 minutes. Add apples, brown sugar, and ¼ cup balsamic vinegar, and sauté 15 to 20 minutes or until apples are tender. Makes 6 servings. Prep: 15 min., Cook: 20 min.

Superfast Appetizers

Think parties are too much trouble for weeknights? Not with these easy starters. You'll have them ready quicker than you can say "come on over after work."

Salt-and-Pepper Oven Fries

family favorite

MAKES 8 TO 10 SERVINGS; **PREP:** 5 MIN., **BAKE:** 27 MIN.

Serve these with any of our dipping sauces or just plain ketchup, but be sure to try them the French way at least once—with Lemon-Garlic Mayo.

1 (26-oz.) package frozen extra-crispy French fried potatoes
¾ tsp. freshly ground black pepper
½ tsp. kosher salt

1. Preheat oven to 425°. Arrange potatoes in a single layer on 2 lightly greased 15- x 10-inch jelly-roll pans. Bake 15 minutes, placing 1 pan on middle oven rack and other on lower oven rack. Switch pans, and bake 12 to 15 more minutes or until lightly browned. Sprinkle with pepper and salt, tossing lightly. Serve immediately.

Note: We tested with Ore-Ida Extra Crispy Fast Food Fries.

Italian Oven Fries: Prepare recipe as directed. Sprinkle potatoes with ⅔ cup grated Parmesan cheese and ½ tsp. garlic powder, tossing lightly. Serve with warm marinara sauce.

Barbecue Oven Fries: Omit salt and pepper. Sprinkle baked fries with 1 Tbsp. barbecue seasoning and desired amount of salt, tossing lightly. Serve with Spicy Mustard-Barbecue Sauce.

Jerk Oven Fries: Omit salt and pepper. Sprinkle baked fries with 1 Tbsp. jerk seasoning, tossing lightly. Serve with Sweet-and-Tangy Ketchup.

Southwest Oven Fries: Omit salt and pepper. Stir together 1 tsp. chili powder, ½ tsp. ground cumin, ½ tsp. ground black pepper, ¼ tsp. salt, and ¼ tsp. ground red pepper. Sprinkle baked fries with chili powder mixture, tossing lightly. Serve with Chipotle Ranch Dip.

Lemon-Garlic Mayo

MAKES ABOUT 1 CUP; **PREP:** 5 MIN., **STAND:** 5 MIN.

1. Combine 1 Tbsp. lemon juice and 2 garlic cloves, minced, in a small bowl; let stand 5 minutes. Stir in 1 cup mayonnaise and 2 Tbsp. chopped fresh parsley. Season with salt and pepper to taste.

Spicy Mustard-Barbecue Sauce

MAKES ABOUT 1 CUP; **PREP:** 5 MIN.

1. Stir together 1 cup spicy barbecue sauce, 2 Tbsp. Dijon mustard, and 1 Tbsp. honey.

Sweet-and-Tangy Ketchup

MAKES ABOUT 1¼ CUPS; **PREP:** 10 MIN.

1. Stir together 1 cup ketchup, 1 Tbsp. brown sugar, 1 tsp. lime zest, and 5 tsp. lime juice.

Chipotle Ranch Dip

MAKES ABOUT 1 CUP; **PREP:** 5 MIN.

1. Stir 1 Tbsp. chopped fresh cilantro and ½ tsp. chipotle powder into 1 cup Ranch dressing.

• TIPS •

Serve Salt-and-Pepper Oven Fries in votive holders for a fun look. Dip fries in Lemon-Garlic Mayo.

Brie-and-Fig Mini Tarts
fast fixin's

MAKES 15 TARTS; **PREP:** 10 MIN.,
BAKE: 6 MIN.

½ (8-oz.) Brie round, rind removed
1 (1.9-oz.) package frozen mini-phyllo
    pastry shells
2 Tbsp. fig preserves
1 Tbsp. minced candied ginger
Freshly ground pepper to taste

1. Preheat oven to 375°. Cut Brie into 15 pieces. Place 1 piece into each phyllo shell, and top each with a rounded ¼ teaspoonful fig preserves. Place on a baking sheet, and bake 6 minutes. Sprinkle with candied ginger and pepper to taste.

Goat Cheese-and-Olive Mini Tarts: Preheat oven to 375°. Place 1 tsp. softened goat cheese into each of 15 frozen mini-phyllo pastry shells. Top each with ½ tsp. olive tapenade. Place on a baking sheet, and bake 6 minutes. Sprinkle with 1 tsp. fresh thyme leaves and freshly ground pepper to taste.

Cheddar-Chutney Mini Tarts: Preheat oven to 375°. Stir together 2 oz. softened cream cheese and ½ cup (2 oz.) shredded extra-sharp Cheddar cheese. Divide cream cheese mixture among 15 frozen mini-phyllo pastry shells; top each with ½ tsp. mango chutney. Place on a baking sheet, and bake 6 minutes.

Monte Cristo Mini-Tarts: Preheat oven to 375°. Divide 2 oz. shaved ham among 15 frozen mini-phyllo pastry shells. Sprinkle with ½ cup (2 oz.) shredded Swiss cheese, and top each with ¼ tsp. strawberry jam. Place on a baking sheet, and bake 6 minutes.

SO SOUTHERN

Taste the Harvest
Create an easy appetizer using fresh muscadine jelly made from grapes grown in Jemison, Alabama, paired with two wheels of Brie cheese. Sandwiched with the jelly and served with crackers, it's a sweet sample of fall. To order Bronze Muscadine Jelly ($6.95 for 8 ounces) from Petals from the Past, visit www.petalsfromthepast.com.

Kentucky Lemonade
fast fixin's

MAKES 18 CUPS; **PREP:** 10 MIN.

1 (12-oz.) can frozen lemonade
    concentrate, thawed
2 cups orange juice
1 (7.5-oz.) container frozen lemon juice from
    concentrate, thawed
1 pt. bourbon, chilled
1 (2-liter) bottle lemon-lime soft drink,
    chilled
1 (1-liter) bottle club soda, chilled
Garnish: lemon slices

1. Stir together first 4 ingredients in a large pitcher. Slowly add soft drink and club soda. Serve immediately over ice. Garnish, if desired.

Screwdriver Punch: Substitute 2 (12-oz.) cans frozen orange juice concentrate, thawed, for first 3 ingredients, and 1 pt. vodka for bourbon.

One + One = Wonderful

The Spanish love these tiny nibbles they call *pinchos*. Skewer any two items on a pick, and serve a colorful assortment on a tray. Try our combinations, or experiment with some of your own.

- Cube of salami + small gherkin pickle
- Cube of fontina cheese + dried Mission fig quarter
- Quartered marinated artichoke heart + 1 boiled medium-size shrimp
- ½ small fresh mozzarella ball + rolled-up roasted red bell pepper strip
- ½ pickled okra + one piece of country ham

Our Favorite Spices

Update your spice rack with a flavor makeover for fall.

When the heat of September gives way to cravings for cool-weather comfort foods, we start restocking the pantry with fresh jars of dried herbs and spices. Anything more than six months old gets tossed, and a few new finds are added to the mix. Here, Test Kitchen Specialist/Food Stylist Marian Cooper Cairns shares her list of favorites for fall cooking.

Chili powder: A combo of ground chile peppers, cumin, garlic, and oregano, this Tex-Mex favorite amps up the flavor of foods from beef stew and barbecue sauce to cornbread and quesadillas. Heat levels vary depending on the peppers used.

Cinnamon: Ground cinnamon moves front and center on the spice rack for fall baking. Whole sticks add a subtle infusion of flavor to hot beverages as well as savory stews and braises. Saigon cinnamon has a stronger kick than cassia or Ceylon.

Cumin: It's a signature ingredient in Southwestern dishes, but cumin is also used in Mediterranean and Indian cooking—especially in curries. Toasting whole seeds in a dry sauté pan brings out the rich nutty flavor of this aromatic spice.

Granulated garlic: Okay— dehydrated ground garlic is not exactly the same as fresh, but it does have advantages as a speedy alternative to minced garlic. Here's the exchange: 1 garlic clove = 1 tsp. chopped fresh garlic = ½ tsp. minced fresh garlic = ¼ tsp. granulated garlic = ⅛ teaspoon garlic powder.

Gray salt: Hand-harvested from coastal areas of France, this trendy sea salt is used to enhance the flavor and finish of everything from grilled endive to caramel-frosted cupcakes. Unlike table salt, the granules are moist and unrefined.

Nutmeg: Like cinnamon, this familiar spice warms up both sweet and savory dishes. Sprinkle over roasted root vegetables or sautéed spinach just before serving, or stir a pinch or two into your favorite macaroni and cheese. 1 whole nutmeg = 2 to 3 tsp. ground.

Poultry seasoning: If you bottled up the aromatic essence of cornbread dressing, this would be it. Most brands of poultry seasoning are heavy on sage and thyme, but when it comes to secondary herbs and spices, each company offers its own unique blend. Some even add ginger, lemon zest, or ground allspice. Use poultry seasoning in chicken and dumplings, pot pies, or as a tasty salt-free rub for pork.

Seasoning blends: Quicker than marinades, these creative combos add instant flavor. Choose versatile blends, such as Creole seasoning or a Montreal or Chicago steak seasoning, that work well with meat, poultry, and seafood. Flavor profiles and salt content vary with brands, so check the label. Ingredients are always listed in descending order according to weight.

Turkish bay leaves: Steeped in long-simmered soups and stews or tucked into a zip-top plastic freezer bag with a marinating pot roast, bay leaves add a rich depth of flavor. Use in moderation—one leaf is plenty for a family-size recipe. Oval-shaped Turkish bay leaves are milder and less expensive than the slender California variety.

Vanilla: Cheap imitations are no substitute for the real thing here—so go ahead and splurge on pure vanilla extract. If you're a fan of whole vanilla beans and the gourmet look of those lovely little seeds they leave behind, pick up a jar of vanilla bean paste (1 Tbsp. = 1 whole vanilla bean, so it's a thrifty exchange).

Southern Living
Food for Today

Try some of these great *Southern Living* kitchen-tested recipes featuring some of your favorite brands.

Bertolli Sauce

Use a jar of tomato-basil sauce and a host of other prepackaged ingredients to quickly prepare cannelloni that your family will love.

Tomato-Basil Chicken Cannelloni

MAKES 6 TO 8 SERVINGS; **PREP:** 20 MIN., **BAKE:** 35 MIN.

1 (8-oz.) package manicotti shells
3 cups chopped cooked chicken
2 (8-oz.) containers chive-and-onion cream cheese
1 (10-oz.) package frozen chopped spinach, thawed and well drained
2 cups (8 oz.) shredded mozzarella cheese, divided
½ cup Italian-seasoned breadcrumbs
¾ tsp. garlic salt
½ tsp. freshly ground pepper
1½ (24-oz.) jars BERTOLLI Tomato-Basil Sauce
Garnish: chopped fresh basil

1. Preheat oven to 350°. Prepare pasta according to package directions.
2. Meanwhile, stir together chicken, cream cheese, spinach, 1 cup mozzarella cheese, and next 3 ingredients in a large bowl.
3. Cut pasta shells in half through 1 side. Fill each shell with chicken mixture, gently pressing cut sides together around filling. Place, cut sides down, in 2 lightly greased 11- x 7-inch baking dishes. Pour sauce over shells.
4. Bake, covered, at 350° for 25 minutes. Uncover and sprinkle with remaining 1 cup mozzarella cheese. Bake, uncovered, 10 to 15 minutes or until cheese is melted and cannelloni are thoroughly heated. Garnish, if desired.
Note: You can make this in a 13- x 9-inch baking dish if you don't have 2 (11- x 7-inch) dishes. Bake, covered, 30 minutes. Uncover, sprinkle with cheese, and bake 15 to 20 minutes or until cheese is melted and cannelloni are thoroughly heated.

Campbell's

Soup is the secret ingredient in all these delectable recipes that help solve the dinner dilemma.

Beef Stroganoff Meatballs

MAKES 6 TO 8 SERVINGS; **PREP:** 10 MIN., **COOK:** 29 MIN.

1 medium-size sweet onion, diced
1 (4.5-oz.) jar sliced mushrooms, drained
2 cups beef broth
2 (10¾-oz.) cans CAMPBELL'S Cream of Mushroom Soup
1 Tbsp. Worcestershire sauce
½ tsp. freshly ground pepper
1 (28-oz.) package frozen Italian-style meatballs
½ (16-oz.) package wide egg noodles
¼ cup sour cream
Garnishes: fresh parsley sprigs, freshly cracked pepper

1. Sauté onion in a lightly greased large saucepan over medium heat 2 minutes. Add mushrooms, and sauté 2 to 3 minutes or until onion is tender.
2. Whisk together beef broth and next 3 ingredients in a medium bowl until smooth. Add soup mixture and meatballs to onion mixture in pan. Cook meatballs according to time on package directions, stirring occasionally.
3. Meanwhile, prepare noodles according to package directions.
4. Remove meatball mixture from heat; stir in sour cream until smooth and blended. Serve meatball mixture over hot cooked noodles. Garnish, if desired.

Buttermilk Baked Chicken

MAKES 4 TO 6 SERVINGS; **PREP:** 10 MIN.,
BAKE: 45 MIN.

*Serve this delicious main-dish recipe
with creamy mashed potatoes and green
beans for an easy weeknight meal.*

¼ cup butter
4 bone-in chicken breasts (about
    2½ lb.)
1½ cups buttermilk, divided
½ tsp. freshly ground pepper
¾ cup all-purpose flour
1½ cups sliced baby portobello mushrooms
1½ tsp. chopped fresh thyme
1 (10¾-oz.) can CAMPBELL'S Cream of
    Mushroom Soup

1. Preheat oven to 425°. Melt butter in
oven in a lightly greased 13- x 9-inch
baking dish (about 3 minutes).
2. Meanwhile, dip chicken in ½ cup
buttermilk; sprinkle with pepper, and
dredge in flour.
3. Remove baking dish from oven. Add
mushrooms and thyme. Arrange chicken,
breast sides down, in baking dish.
4. Bake at 425° for 25 minutes. Turn
chicken, and bake 10 minutes.
5. Stir together soup and remaining
1 cup buttermilk. Pour over chicken,
and bake 10 minutes or until a meat
thermometer inserted into thickest portion registers 165°, shielding chicken
with aluminum foil to prevent excessive
browning, if necessary.
6. Transfer chicken to a serving platter. Whisk soup mixture in baking dish
until blended, and drizzle over chicken.

Slow-Cooker Chili

MAKES ABOUT 16 CUPS; **PREP:** 10 MIN.;
COOK: 4 HR., 12 MIN.

*Freeze any leftovers for a great make-
ahead cold-weather comfort dish. Omit
the beans, if desired.*

3¼ lb. ground chuck
1 medium-size green bell pepper, chopped
3 (14½-oz.) cans diced tomatoes with garlic
    and onion, undrained
3 (10¾-oz.) cans CAMPBELL'S Tomato Soup
1 (16-oz.) can light red kidney beans, rinsed
    and drained
1 (6-oz.) can tomato paste
5 Tbsp. chili powder
1 tsp. freshly ground pepper
½ tsp. paprika
Toppings: sour cream, shredded Cheddar
    cheese, chopped green onions, sliced
    black olives, corn chips

1. Cook ground chuck in a large
nonstick skillet over medium-high heat
12 to 14 minutes or until meat crumbles and is no longer pink; drain.
2. Place meat in a 6-qt. slow cooker;
stir in ½ cup water, green bell pepper,
and next 7 ingredients. Cover and
cook on HIGH 4 hours. Serve with
desired toppings.

Zesty King Ranch Chicken Casserole

MAKES 8 SERVINGS; **PREP:** 10 MIN.,
COOK: 4 MIN., **BAKE:** 25 MIN.,
STAND: 10 MIN.

*For a zestier version of this casserole, use
original diced tomatoes and green chiles.*

2 Tbsp. butter
½ (10-oz.) package frozen diced onion, red
    and green bell peppers, and celery
2 (10¾-oz.) cans CAMPBELL'S Cream of
    Chicken Soup
2 (10-oz.) cans mild diced tomatoes and
    green chiles
1 tsp. Mexican-style chili powder*
3 cups shredded deli-roasted chicken
3 cups freshly grated sharp Cheddar cheese
3 cups coarsely crumbled lime-flavored
    white corn tortilla chips
Garnishes: fresh cilantro sprigs, lime
    wedges

1. Preheat oven to 400°. Melt butter in
a large skillet over medium-high heat.
Add frozen vegetables, and sauté 4 to
5 minutes or until tender. Transfer to a
medium bowl; stir in soup, diced tomatoes, and chili powder.
2. Layer half of chicken in a lightly
greased 13- x 9-inch baking dish. Top
with half of soup mixture and 1 cup
Cheddar cheese. Sprinkle with 1½ cups
tortilla chips. Repeat layers once. Top
with remaining 1 cup cheese.
3. Bake at 400° for 25 to 30 minutes
or until bubbly. Let stand 10 minutes
before serving. Garnish, if desired.
*1 tsp. chili powder and ⅛ tsp. ground
red pepper may be substituted.

Bush's Beans

Discover the great taste and nutrition that beans can add to these family-favorite dishes.

Chili-Cheeseburger Mac-and-Cheese

MAKES 4 TO 6 SERVINGS; **PREP:** 15 MIN., **COOK:** 9 MIN.

1 (12-oz.) box shells and cheese
1 lb. ground beef
1 (16-oz.) can BUSH'S Chili Beans - Mild
1 (14.5-oz.) can diced tomatoes with zesty mild green chiles
1 tsp. chili powder
½ tsp. salt
¼ tsp. ground cumin

1. Prepare shells and cheese according to package directions.
2. Meanwhile, cook beef in a 12-inch (2½-inch-deep) nonstick skillet or Dutch oven over medium-high heat, stirring often, 8 minutes or until meat crumbles and is no longer pink; drain and rinse under hot running water. Return beef to skillet. Stir in beans and next 4 ingredients.
3. Cook over medium-high heat 7 to 9 minutes or until two-thirds of liquid has evaporated. Stir prepared pasta into beef mixture. Serve immediately.

Creamy Black Bean Soup

MAKES 6 CUPS; **PREP:** 10 MIN., **COOK:** 15 MIN., **COOL:** 5 MIN.

Spread warmed leftover soup over crispy tostadas and layer with chopped rotisserie chicken, shredded lettuce, chopped tomatoes, and avocado for a quick supper or snack. For a thinner soup, use only 2 cans of black beans.

1 cup medium onion, diced
1 garlic clove, minced
1 Tbsp. olive oil
3 cups chicken broth
3 (15-oz.) cans BUSH'S Black Beans, rinsed and drained
1 (14.5-oz.) can diced tomatoes with zesty mild green chiles, undrained
½ tsp. chili powder
½ tsp. ground cumin
1 Tbsp. chopped fresh cilantro
1 Tbsp. lime juice
Toppings: sour cream, shredded Cheddar cheese, diced tomatoes, chopped fresh cilantro, lime wedges, tortilla chips

1. Sauté onion and garlic in hot oil in a Dutch oven over medium-high heat 4 to 6 minutes or until tender.
2. Stir in broth and next 4 ingredients, stirring to loosen particles from bottom of Dutch oven; cover and bring to a boil. Uncover, reduce heat to medium-low, and simmer, stirring occasionally, 8 minutes. Remove from heat; stir in cilantro and lime juice. Let cool 5 minutes.
3. Process soup, in batches, in a blender or food processor 30 seconds or until smooth. Return to Dutch oven, and stir until blended. Serve with desired toppings.

Chicken-and-Rice Casserole

MAKES 6 SERVINGS; **PREP:** 10 MIN., **BAKE:** 15 MIN., **STAND:** 5 MIN.

Pick up a deli rotisserie chicken from the grocery store for a timesaving step. One 2-pound chicken equals approximately 3 cups chopped.

1 (8.8-oz.) pouch ready-to-serve long grain and wild rice mix
1 (15.8-oz.) can BUSH'S Great Northern Beans, rinsed and drained
1 (10¾-oz.) can cream of chicken soup
3 cups chopped cooked chicken
1 cup milk
1 Tbsp. chopped fresh parsley
¼ tsp. freshly ground pepper
1 cup freshly shredded Cheddar cheese
¼ cup fine, dry breadcrumbs
Garnish: fresh flat-leaf parsley sprigs

1. Preheat oven to 425°. Prepare rice according to package directions.
2. Stir together beans, next 5 ingredients, and rice in a large bowl. Pour mixture into a lightly greased 11- x 7- inch baking dish. Sprinkle with cheese and breadcrumbs.
3. Bake at 425° for 15 to 18 minutes or until thoroughly heated and cheese is melted. Let stand 5 minutes before serving. Garnish, if desired.

Hellmann's

This creamy pantry staple adds moistness and flavor to a variety of dishes.

Roasted Potato Wedges With Tarragon Mayonnaise

MAKES 6 SERVINGS; **PREP:** 10 MIN., **COOK:** 18 MIN.

1 (20-oz.) package frozen roasted potato wedges
1¼ cups HELLMANN'S or BEST FOODS Real Mayonnaise
4 tsp. chopped fresh tarragon
1½ tsp. horseradish
1 tsp. white balsamic vinegar
¼ tsp. freshly ground pepper
¼ tsp. salt
Garnishes: freshly ground pepper, chopped fresh tarragon

1. Prepare potato wedges according to package directions.
2. Meanwhile, stir together mayonnaise and next 5 ingredients in a small bowl. Serve with potato wedges. Garnish, if desired.

Fried Shrimp Skewers With Creole Sauce

MAKES 8 APPETIZER SERVINGS; **PREP:** 10 MIN., **COOK:** 20 MIN.

This Cajun-inspired appetizer can also be served on a platter with Creole sauce.

1¼ cups HELLMANN'S or BEST FOODS Real Mayonnaise
2 Tbsp. chopped fresh parsley
3 Tbsp. Creole mustard
1½ tsp. fresh lemon juice
3½ tsp. Cajun seasoning, divided
Vegetable oil
½ (12-oz.) package seasoned fish fry batter mix
1 lb. peeled, medium-size raw shrimp with tails (31/40 count)
¾ cup buttermilk
16 (4-inch) wooden skewers
Garnish: fresh parsley sprigs

1. Whisk together mayonnaise, next 3 ingredients, and ½ tsp. Cajun seasoning in a small bowl.
2. Pour oil to depth of 3 inches into a Dutch oven; heat to 325°. Stir together batter mix and remaining 3 tsp. Cajun seasoning. Toss shrimp and buttermilk together in a large bowl. Dredge shrimp in batter mixture, shaking off excess. Arrange on a baking sheet.
3. Fry shrimp, in batches, 1½ minutes on each side or until golden brown. Drain on wire racks over paper towels.
4. Thread 2 shrimp onto each skewer. Serve with Creole sauce. Garnish, if desired.

Lemon-Blueberry Muffins

MAKES 12 SERVINGS; **PREP:** 10 MIN., **COOK:** 18 MIN., **COOL:** 15 MIN.

4 cups plus 2 Tbsp. all-purpose baking mix, divided
¾ cup plus 3 Tbsp. sugar, divided
¼ tsp. ground cinnamon, divided
¾ cup HELLMANN'S or BEST FOODS Real Mayonnaise
½ cup milk
2 large eggs
2 tsp. lemon zest
2 Tbsp. fresh lemon juice
1¼ cups fresh or frozen blueberries
1 Tbsp. melted butter

1. Preheat oven to 400°. Whisk together 4 cups baking mix, ¾ cup sugar, and ⅛ tsp. cinnamon in a large bowl; reserve 2 Tbsp. mixture. Make a well in center of remaining sugar mixture in bowl.
2. Whisk together mayonnaise and next 4 ingredients; add to sugar mixture in large bowl, stirring just until moistened.
3. Toss blueberries with reserved 2 Tbsp. sugar mixture. Carefully fold blueberries into batter. Spoon into a lightly greased muffin pan, filling almost completely full.
4. Stir together 1 Tbsp. melted butter and remaining 2 Tbsp. baking mix, 3 Tbsp. sugar, and ⅛ tsp. cinnamon until mixture is crumbly; sprinkle over batter in pan.
5. Bake at 400° for 18 to 20 minutes or until a wooden pick inserted in center comes out clean. Cool in pan on a wire rack 5 minutes. Remove from pan to wire rack, and cool 10 minutes.

Uncle Ben's

You can count on rice for healthy main and side dishes.

Savory Citrus-Asparagus Brown Rice

MAKES 4 TO 6 SERVINGS; **PREP:** 10 MIN.

1 (1-lb.) fresh asparagus, trimmed and
    cut into 1-inch pieces
¾ tsp. salt
2 (8.8-oz.) packages UNCLE BEN'S Whole
    Grain Brown Ready Rice
1 lemon
¼ tsp. freshly ground pepper
¼ cup freshly shaved Parmesan
    cheese

1. Combine asparagus, 2 Tbsp. water, and salt in a medium-size microwave-safe bowl. Cover tightly with plastic wrap; fold back a small edge to allow steam to escape. Microwave at HIGH 2½ minutes or until crisp-tender.
2. Prepare rice according to package directions.
3. Grate zest from lemon to equal 1 tsp., and squeeze juice from lemon to equal 1 Tbsp.
4. Add rice, lemon zest, juice, and pepper to asparagus, tossing to combine. Sprinkle with Parmesan cheese. Serve immediately.

Sesame-Cilantro Chicken-and-Rice Salad

MAKES 6 TO 8 SERVINGS; **PREP** 5 MIN.,
COOK: 10 MIN.

Serve this recipe with lime wedges over a bed of fresh tender greens for an easy main-dish salad.

2 (8.8-oz.) packages UNCLE BEN'S Whole
    Grain Brown Ready Rice
2 limes
¼ cup sweet chili sauce
2 tsp. sesame oil
½ tsp. salt
5 tsp. chopped fresh cilantro,
    divided
3 cups chopped cooked chicken
Toppings: sliced green onions, toasted
    sesame seeds

1. Prepare rice according to package directions.
2. Grate zest from limes to equal 1 tsp., and squeeze juice from limes to equal 2 Tbsp. Whisk together lime zest, juice, chili sauce, sesame oil, salt, and 3 tsp. cilantro.
3. Combine rice, chicken, and chili sauce mixture in a large bowl, tossing to coat. Sprinkle with remaining 2 tsp. chopped fresh cilantro. Serve with desired toppings.

Quick Dirty Rice

MAKES 6 SERVINGS; **PREP:** 5 MIN.,
COOK: 15 MIN.

1 (1-lb.) package ground pork
    sausage
2 (8.8-oz.) packages UNCLE BEN'S Whole
    Grain Brown Ready Rice
½ (10-oz.) package frozen diced onion, red
    and green bell peppers, and celery
½ cup chicken broth
½ tsp. Cajun seasoning
½ tsp. salt
¼ tsp. freshly ground pepper
2 Tbsp. chopped fresh parsley
Toppings: fresh parsley sprigs,
    hot sauce

1. Cook sausage in a large nonstick skillet over medium-high heat, stirring often, 8 to 10 minutes or until sausage crumbles and is no longer pink. Remove sausage from skillet using a slotted spoon; reserve drippings in skillet. Drain sausage on paper towels.
2. Prepare rice according to package directions.
3. Sauté frozen vegetables in hot drippings over medium-high heat 3 minutes or until vegetables are tender and begin to brown. Add chicken broth, Cajun seasoning, salt, and pepper; bring to a boil. Stir in rice and sausage. Cook 1 minute or until thoroughly heated. Stir in 2 Tbsp. parsley. Serve with desired toppings.

Mahatma Rice and Success Rice

This pantry staple is the star ingredient in these wonderful weeknight dishes.

Shrimp and Veggie Fried Rice

MAKES 4 SERVINGS; **PREP:** 15 MIN., **COOK:** 20 MIN.

1 lb. unpeeled, medium-size raw shrimp (31/40 count)
1 (1½-inch) piece fresh ginger, peeled
3 to 4 Tbsp. lite soy sauce
2 (3.5-oz.) bags SUCCESS Brown Rice, uncooked
1 (8-oz.) package fresh sugar snap peas
2 Tbsp. sesame oil, divided
6 green onions, cut into 2-inch pieces
¾ cup matchstick carrots
2 large eggs, lightly beaten
Toppings: chopped green onions, chopped peanuts, lite soy sauce

1. Peel shrimp; devein, if desired.
2. Grate ginger using the large holes of a box grater. Squeeze juice from grated ginger into a small bowl to equal about 1 tsp.; discard solids. Stir in soy sauce.
3. Prepare rice and peas according to package directions.
4. Meanwhile, sauté shrimp in 1 tablespoon hot oil in a large nonstick skillet over medium-high heat 4 to 5 minutes or just until shrimp turn pink. Remove from skillet; keep warm.
5. Sauté green onions and carrots in remaining 1 tablespoon hot oil in skillet over medium-high heat 2 minutes or until crisp-tender. Add rice and peas, and cook, stirring frequently, 2 minutes or until thoroughly heated. Push rice mixture to sides of pan, making a well in center of mixture.
6. Add eggs to center of mixture, and cook, stirring occasionally, 1 to 2 minutes or until set. Stir eggs into rice mixture. Stir in soy sauce mixture and shrimp. Cook 1 minute or until thoroughly heated. Serve with desired toppings.

Panko-Crusted Rice Cakes With Lemon-Basil Sauce

MAKES 8 SERVINGS; **PREP:** 25 MIN., **COOK:** 32 MIN., **COOL:** 10 MIN.

Top these rice cakes with fresh crab meat or shrimp for an easy, elegant appetizer.

1⅓ cups MAHATMA Enriched Thai Fragrant Long Grain Jasmine Rice, uncooked
¾ tsp. salt, divided
1½ cups Italian-style Japanese breadcrumbs (panko), divided
5 Tbsp. chopped fresh basil, divided
3 large eggs, lightly beaten
1 cup grated Parmesan cheese
1 garlic clove, pressed
¼ tsp. freshly ground pepper
1 cup mayonnaise
1 Tbsp. Creole mustard
2 tsp. lemon zest
1 Tbsp. fresh lemon juice
1 cup vegetable oil
Garnishes: lemon slices, fresh basil leaves, fresh lettuce leaves

1. Bring 2⅔ cups water to a boil in a large saucepan over medium-high heat; add rice and ½ tsp. salt. Cover, reduce heat to low, and simmer 20 minutes or until liquid is absorbed and rice is tender. Let cool 10 minutes.
2. Stir together rice, ½ cup breadcrumbs, 2 tablespoons chopped fresh basil, and next 4 ingredients.
3. Shape rice mixture into 16 (¾-inch-thick) patties. Dredge in remaining 1 cup breadcrumbs.
4. Pulse mayonnaise, next 3 ingredients, and remaining ¼ tsp. salt and 3 Tbsp. chopped fresh basil in a food processor or blender 4 to 5 times or until well blended, stopping to scrape down sides as needed. Season with freshly ground pepper to taste.
5. Cook rice cakes, in 2 batches, in hot oil in a large nonstick skillet over medium-high heat 2 to 3 minutes on each side or until golden brown and crispy. Drain on a paper towel-lined wire rack. Serve with lemon-basil sauce. Garnish, if desired.

Herb-and-Pepper Brown Rice Salad

MAKES 4 TO 6 SERVINGS; **PREP:** 20 MIN., **COOK:** 40 MIN., **STAND:** 5 MIN., **BAKE:** 6 MIN.

If you chill this salad, consider adding the full amount of lemon juice (four tablespoons). The acidity will fade the longer the dish chills.

2¼ cups low-sodium chicken broth
1 cup MAHATMA Natural Whole Grain Brown Rice, uncooked
¼ cup pine nuts
¾ cup chopped jarred roasted red bell peppers, drained
1 cup peeled and diced English cucumber (about 1 small)
1 Tbsp. chopped fresh dill
1 Tbsp. chopped fresh parsley
1 tsp. lemon zest
3 to 4 Tbsp. fresh lemon juice
1 shallot, finely chopped
1¼ Tbsp. sugar
½ tsp. salt
½ Tbsp. freshly ground pepper
½ cup extra virgin olive oil
⅓ cup crumbled feta cheese

1. Bring broth to a boil in a 2-qt. saucepan; stir in brown rice. Cover, reduce heat, and simmer 40 minutes or until rice is tender. Remove from heat; let stand, covered, 5 minutes. Drain well.
2. Preheat oven to 350°. Bake pine nuts in a jelly-roll pan 6 to 8 minutes or until lightly toasted and fragrant, stirring after 4 minutes.
3. Stir together hot cooked rice, roasted red bell peppers, and next 3 ingredients in a large bowl.
4. Whisk together lemon zest and next 5 ingredients in a small bowl. Add olive oil in a slow, steady stream, whisking constantly until blended. Drizzle over rice mixture; toss to coat. Sprinkle with toasted pine nuts and crumbled feta

cheese. Serve immediately, or cover and chill up to 24 hours. If chilled, let stand at room temperature 15 minutes before serving.

Southern Succotash With Rice

MAKES 6 TO 8 SERVINGS; **PREP:** 10 MIN., **COOK:** 35 MIN.

1 (16-oz.) package frozen baby lima beans
1 (16-oz.) package frozen corn kernels
2 (3.5-oz.) bags SUCCESS White Rice, uncooked
4 bacon slices
2 small onions, chopped
¾ cup chopped jarred roasted red bell peppers, drained
2 garlic cloves, minced
¼ cup whipping cream
1¾ tsp. salt
1 tsp. freshly ground pepper
½ tsp. hot sauce

1. Cook lima beans according to package directions, adding corn to beans during last 5 minutes of cooking. Drain bean mixture, reserving ½ cup cooking liquid.
2. Meanwhile, prepare rice according to package directions. Cook bacon in a large skillet over medium-high heat 7 to 8 minutes or until crispy; remove bacon, and drain on paper towels, reserving 1 tablespoon drippings in skillet. Crumble bacon.
3. Sauté onion in hot drippings over medium-high heat 7 to 8 minutes or until tender. Add bell pepper and garlic; sauté 1 minute. Stir in bean mixture, hot cooked rice, reserved ½ cup cooking liquid, whipping cream, and next 3 ingredients. Reduce heat to medium, and cook, stirring often, 5 to 7 minutes or until thoroughly heated. Top with crumbled bacon.

Swanson

Broth adds rich and delicious flavor to everyday dishes.

Beef and Mushrooms With Egg Noodles

MAKES 4 TO 6 SERVINGS; **PREP:** 10 MIN., **COOK:** 4 HR.

1 (10 ¾-oz.) can CAMPBELL'S Cream of Mushroom Soup
1 cup SWANSON Beef Stock
⅓ cup dry red wine
1 (1-oz.) envelope dry onion soup mix
½ tsp. freshly ground pepper
1 (8-oz.) package sliced baby portobello mushrooms
1 (2-lb.) boneless chuck roast, trimmed
½ (16-oz.) package extra-wide egg noodles
3 Tbsp. chopped fresh parsley, divided

1. Whisk together first 5 ingredients in a lightly greased 5-qt. slow cooker. Stir in mushrooms. Add roast to slow cooker. Cover and cook on HIGH 4 to 4½ hours or until beef is tender and shreddable.
2. Meanwhile, prepare noodles according to package directions. Toss hot cooked noodles with 2 Tbsp. parsley.
3. Spoon beef mixture over hot cooked noodles. Sprinkle with remaining 1 Tbsp. parsley, and serve immediately.

Beefy Vidalia Onion Soup

MAKES ABOUT 6 SERVINGS; **PREP:** 10 MIN., **COOK:** 1 HR.

For an upscale single-serving option, ladle soup into ovenproof bowls. Top each bowl with a French bread slice and Swiss cheese slice. Place bowls on a jelly-roll pan, and broil 5 inches from heat until cheese is melted.

¼ cup butter

6 medium-size Vidalia onions, thinly
    sliced

3 Tbsp. all-purpose flour, divided

1 lb. top sirloin steak, cut into
    ¾-inch cubes

2 Tbsp. vegetable oil

½ cup dry red wine

6 cups SWANSON Beef Broth

6 (¾-inch-thick) French bread slices

1. Melt butter in a large Dutch oven over medium-high heat. Add onions, and sauté 20 to 24 minutes or until onions begin to caramelize and are very tender. Sprinkle with 1 tablespoon flour, and stir gently. Remove from Dutch oven.

2. Toss beef in remaining 2 Tbsp. flour. Cook beef in hot oil in Dutch oven over medium-high heat 6 to 8 minutes or until browned.

3. Add wine and broth, and stir to loosen particles from bottom of Dutch oven. Add onions and any accumulated juices to Dutch oven; bring to a boil. Cover, reduce heat to low, and simmer 30 minutes.

4. Meanwhile, preheat oven to 350°. Bake bread slices on a jelly-roll pan 8 to 10 minutes or until crispy and lightly toasted. Serve with soup.

Tex-Mex Chicken-and-Rice Soup

MAKES ABOUT 8 CUPS; **PREP:** 10 MIN., **COOK:** 28 MIN., **STAND:** 5 MIN.

2 (10-oz.) cans mild diced tomatoes and
    green chiles

7 cups SWANSON Chicken Broth

2 cups shredded cooked chicken

¾ cup uncooked long-grain rice

¾ tsp. ground cumin

¼ tsp. freshly ground pepper

1 to 2 Tbsp. chopped pickled jalapeño
    pepper slices (optional)

2 Tbsp. chopped fresh cilantro

1 Tbsp. lime juice

Toppings: avocado slices, lime wedges,
    fresh cilantro sprigs, tortilla chips

1. Combine first 6 ingredients and, if desired, chopped jalapeño peppers in a Dutch oven. Cover and bring to a boil over medium-high heat. Reduce heat to low, and simmer 18 minutes or until rice is tender. Stir in cilantro and lime juice. Let stand, uncovered, 5 minutes before serving. Serve with desired toppings.

Roast Chicken With Citrus Wild Rice

MAKES 4 TO 6 SERVINGS; **PREP:** 10 MIN.; **BAKE:** 1 HR., 30 MIN.; **STAND:** 10 MIN.

3 shallots, minced

1 Tbsp. chopped fresh thyme

1 Tbsp. chopped fresh sage

1 (12-oz.) can frozen orange juice
    concentrate, thawed

1½ cups SWANSON Chicken Stock

2 Tbsp. honey

½ tsp. freshly ground pepper

Vegetable cooking spray

1 (4- to 5-lb.) whole chicken

2 (6-oz.) packages long-grain and
    wild rice mix

Garnishes: orange slices, fresh thyme sprigs

1. Preheat oven to 425°. Stir together first 3 ingredients in a medium bowl; reserve 2 Tbsp. herb mixture. Whisk orange juice concentrate and next 3 ingredients into remaining herb mixture until blended.

2. Place a wire rack in an aluminum foil-lined roasting pan. Coat wire rack and pan with cooking spray.

3. If applicable, remove giblets from chicken, and reserve for another use. Rinse chicken, and pat dry. Gently loosen and lift skin from breast and drumsticks with fingers. (Do not totally detach skin.) Rub reserved 2 Tbsp. herb mixture underneath skin. Carefully replace skin. Place chicken, breast side up, in prepared pan. Pour orange juice mixture over chicken.

4. Bake at 425° for 30 minutes. Reduce oven temperature to 375°; baste chicken with pan drippings. Bake 1 hour or until a meat thermometer inserted into thigh registers 180°, basting at 30-minute intervals and, if necessary, shielding with foil after 30 minutes to prevent excessive browning. Let stand 10 minutes.

5. Meanwhile, cook rice according to package directions, omitting fat. Serve chicken with hot cooked rice and, if desired, pan drippings. Garnish, if desired.

Oscar Mayer Deli Fresh

These hearty lunch meats are great in everything from sandwiches to quick tostados..

Beef and Blue Crostini

MAKES 4 APPETIZER SERVINGS;
PREP: 12 MIN., **COOK:** 8 MIN.

12 (¼-inch-thick) French bread
    slices
½ cup sour cream
2 tsp. chopped fresh chives
2 tsp. horseradish
2 tsp. Dijon mustard
1 (7-oz.) package OSCAR MAYER Deli Fresh
    Shaved Roast Beef, chopped
¼ cup crumbled blue cheese
Freshly ground pepper
Garnish: fresh chives

1. Preheat oven to 350°. Place bread slices on a baking sheet. Bake 8 to 10 minutes or until toasted.
2. Meanwhile, stir together sour cream and next 3 ingredients in a small bowl.
3. Top each bread slice with chopped roast beef, sour cream mixture, and blue cheese. Sprinkle crostini with freshly ground pepper. Garnish, if desired.

Kentucky Hot Browns With Smoked Turkey

MAKES 5 SERVINGS; **PREP:** 15 MIN.,
COOK: 20 MIN.

1 (1.32-oz.) envelope country gravy mix
1 cup milk
1½ cups (6 oz.) freshly shredded Parmesan
    cheese, divided
Salt and freshly ground pepper to taste
5 (1-oz.) rye or wheat bread slices,
    toasted
Parchment paper
1 (9-oz.) package OSCAR MAYER Deli Fresh
    Shaved Smoked Turkey
6 fully cooked bacon slices
2 plum tomatoes, sliced
Garnishes: freshly cracked pepper, fresh
    flat-leaf parsley

1. Preheat broiler with oven rack 6 inches from heat. Prepare gravy according to package directions, substituting 1 cup milk for water. Remove from heat. Whisk in ½ cup Parmesan cheese; season with salt and pepper to taste. (Sauce will be thick.)
2. Arrange bread slices in a parchment paper-lined 15- x 10-inch jelly-roll pan. Top with turkey and sauce; sprinkle with remaining 1 cup Parmesan cheese.
3. Broil 5 to 6 minutes or until cheese is melted and lightly browned.
4. Meanwhile, microwave bacon according to package directions until crisp; crumble. Top each sandwich with crumbled bacon and tomato slices. Garnish, if desired. Serve sandwiches immediately.

Chicken Tostadas With Avocado Cream

MAKES 5 SERVINGS; **PREP:** 14 MIN.,
COOK: 6 MIN.

5 (6-inch) fajita-size corn tortillas
1 (8-oz.) container sour cream
1 Tbsp. lime juice
¼ tsp. salt
1 medium avocado, halved
2 Tbsp. chopped fresh cilantro, divided
1 (9-oz.) package OSCAR MAYER Deli Fresh
    Shaved Rotisserie Seasoned Chicken,
    chopped
1⅓ cups (5½ oz.) shredded Mexican four-
    cheese blend
2 plum tomatoes, chopped
Toppings: shredded iceberg lettuce,
    chopped pickled jalapeño peppers,
    chopped red onion

1. Preheat broiler with oven rack 4 inches from heat. Arrange tortillas in a single layer on a baking sheet. Broil 5 minutes or until lightly browned, turning after 3 minutes.
2. Pulse sour cream, lime juice, salt, 1 avocado half, and 1 Tbsp. cilantro in a food processor or blender 20 to 30 seconds or until smooth, stopping to scrape down sides as needed. Chop remaining avocado half.
3. Divide chicken among tortillas; sprinkle with cheese. Broil 1 to 2 minutes or until cheese is melted.
4. Top each with avocado-sour cream mixture, chopped avocado, tomatoes, and desired toppings. Sprinkle with remaining 1 Tbsp. cilantro.

Avocados from Mexico

This fresh fruit is a healthy and flavorful addition to salads and appetizers.

Citrus Salad in Avocado Cups

MAKES 4 SERVINGS; **PREP:** 25 MIN.

1 Tbsp. olive oil
4 tsp. honey
2 tsp. lime zest
6 Tbsp. lime juice
2 tsp. lemon juice
½ tsp. salt
2 large grapefruit, peeled and
    sectioned
2 medium-size oranges, peeled and
    sectioned
⅓ cup diced jicama
¼ cup thinly sliced red onion
½ head red leaf lettuce, leaves separated
2 HASS AVOCADOS FROM MEXICO

1. Whisk together first 6 ingredients in a small bowl. Combine grapefruit and next 3 ingredients in a medium bowl. Drizzle with 2 Tbsp. vinaigrette, tossing to coat.
2. Place lettuce on serving plates or a platter. Cut avocados in half; remove and discard seeds. Carefully remove avocado halves from peels, discarding peels. Rub 2 Tbsp. vinaigrette over avocado halves. Top lettuce with avocados, and spoon grapefruit mixture over avocados. Serve with remaining vinaigrette.

Mole-Rubbed Chicken With Mango-Avocado Salsa

MAKES 4 SERVINGS; **PREP:** 18 MIN.,
GRILL: 12 MIN.

2 Tbsp. light brown sugar
1½ tsp. chili powder
1 tsp. unsweetened cocoa
¼ tsp. ground cumin
¼ tsp. freshly ground pepper
1¼ tsp. salt, divided
1½ lb. skinned and boned chicken breasts
2 limes
2 tsp. honey
1 HASS AVOCADO FROM MEXICO,
    chopped
1 cup chopped fresh mango
¾ cup grape tomatoes, quartered
¼ cup finely chopped red onion
4 tsp. chopped fresh cilantro
Garnishes: fresh cilantro sprigs, lime
    wedges

1. Preheat grill to 350° to 400° (medium-high) heat. Stir together brown sugar, next 4 ingredients, and ½ tsp. salt in a small bowl. Rub chicken with sugar mixture, coating well.
2. Grate zest from limes to equal 1 Tbsp.; squeeze juice from limes to equal 2 Tbsp. Whisk together honey, lime zest, and lime juice in a medium bowl. Add avocado, and toss to coat. Stir in mango, next 3 ingredients, and remaining ¾ tsp. salt.
3. Grill chicken, covered with grill lid, 5 to 6 minutes on each side or until a meat thermometer inserted into thickest portion registers 165°. Serve with mango-avocado salsa. Garnish, if desired.

Zesty Guacamole Bites

MAKES 8 TO 10 APPETIZER SERVINGS;
PREP: 20 MIN., **BAKE:** 10 MIN.

For perfect texture, use a pastry blender to mash avocado.

1 (12-oz.) sourdough baguette, cut into
    ¼-inch-thick slices
3 HASS AVOCADOS FROM MEXICO
½ medium-size jalapeño pepper, seeded
    and finely chopped
1 garlic clove, pressed
3 Tbsp. chopped fresh cilantro, divided
2 Tbsp. finely chopped red onion, divided
3 Tbsp. fresh lime juice, divided
1 tsp. salt, divided
1 cup grape tomatoes, quartered
½ cup crumbled queso fresco (fresh
    Mexican cheese)
Garnish: fresh cilantro sprigs

1. Preheat oven to 350°. Place bread slices on a baking sheet. Bake 10 to 12 minutes or until toasted, turning after 8 minutes.
2. Meanwhile, cut avocados in half. Scoop pulp into a bowl, and mash with a pastry blender or fork until slightly chunky. Stir in jalapeño, garlic, 2 Tbsp. chopped fresh cilantro, 1 Tbsp. finely chopped red onion, 2 Tbsp. fresh lime juice, and ¾ tsp. salt. Cover with plastic wrap, allowing plastic wrap to touch mixture, until ready to serve.
3. Toss grape tomatoes with remaining 1 Tbsp. each chopped fresh cilantro, red onion, fresh lime juice, and ¼ tsp. salt.
4. Top each bread round with avocado mixture. Spoon tomato mixture over avocado mixture using a slotted spoon or fork. Sprinkle with crumbled queso fresco. Garnish, if desired.

The Other White Meat® Campaign

It's easy to jazz up your weeknight dinners with these tempting new dishes.

Island Jerk Pork Tenderloin Salad

MAKES 4 SERVINGS; **PREP:** 10 MIN.,
GRILL: 20 MIN.

Serve this dish with in-season fresh fruit for optimum flavor and texture.

4¾ tsp. Caribbean jerk seasoning, divided
¾ tsp. salt, divided
½ tsp. freshly ground pepper, divided
1 lb. PORK Tenderloin
8 tsp. olive oil, divided
1 (20-oz.) container fresh cored pineapple
   in juice, drained and cut into ½-inch-
   thick rings
1 (5-oz.) package mixed salad greens,
   thoroughly washed
1 cup chopped fresh mango (about 1 medium)
Garnishes: fresh cilantro sprigs, fresh
   cracked pepper

1. Preheat grill to 350° to 400° (medium-high) heat. Stir together 4 tsp. jerk seasoning, ¼ tsp. salt, and ¼ tsp. pepper in a bowl.
2. Remove silver skin from tenderloin, leaving a thin layer of fat. Brush pork with 2 tsp. olive oil.
3. Sprinkle 1 tsp. seasoning mixture over pineapple rings. Rub pork with remaining seasoning mixture.
4. Grill pork and pineapple rings at the same time, covered with grill lid. Grill pork 10 to 12 minutes on each side or until a meat thermometer inserted into thickest portion registers 150° to 155°. Grill pineapple 2 minutes on each side or until grill marks appear. Remove pork from grill, and let stand.

5. Meanwhile, puree 2 pineapple rings, 1 Tbsp. water, and remaining 6 tsp. olive oil, ¾ tsp. jerk seasoning, ½ tsp. salt, and ¼ tsp. pepper in a food processor or blender 30 to 60 seconds or until smooth, stopping to scrape down sides as needed.
6. Combine pineapple mixture and salad greens in a large bowl, tossing to coat. Cut pork into slices. Arrange salad greens, sliced pork, pineapple rings, and mango on a large serving platter. Garnish, if desired.

Per serving: Calories 335; Fat 14g (sat 3g, mono 8g, poly 2g); Protein 26g; Fiber: 4g; Chol 75mg; Iron 2mg; Sodium 838mg; Calc 47mg

Sweet 'n' Spicy Braised Pork

MAKES 8 TO 10 SERVINGS; **PREP:** 10 MIN.,;
COOK: 5 HR., 8 MIN.; **STAND:** 10 MIN.

Enjoy this slow-cooked Latin American dish atop black beans and rice with corn tortillas and lime wedges.

3 lb. boneless PORK Shoulder Roast
   (Boston Butt)
½ tsp. salt
½ tsp. freshly ground pepper
1 Tbsp. vegetable oil
2 (14½-oz.) cans diced tomatoes with
   garlic and onion
1 medium-size sweet onion, chopped
1 to 2 chipotle peppers in adobo sauce,
   chopped
2 Tbsp. cider vinegar
2 Tbsp. dark brown sugar
¼ tsp. ground cumin
Garnishes: fresh cilantro sprigs, chopped
   fresh cilantro

1. Sprinkle pork with salt and pepper. Cook pork in hot oil in a large skillet over medium-high heat 2 to 3 minutes on all sides or until pork is browned.
2. Stir together tomatoes and next 5 ingredients in a 5-qt. slow cooker. Add pork, turning to coat.
3. Cover and cook on HIGH 5 hours or until pork is fork-tender. Transfer pork to a cutting board, and let stand 10 minutes. Shred pork with 2 forks. Return shredded pork to slow cooker, and stir until blended. Season with salt and pepper to taste, if desired. Serve immediately with a slotted spoon. Garnish, if desired.

Per serving: Calories 412; Fat 26g (sat 9g,mono 11g,poly 3g); Protein 31g; Chol 109mg; Iron 3.5mg; Sodium 748mg; Calc 59mg

Grilled Pork Chops With Balsamic Syrup

MAKES 4 SERVINGS; **PREP:** 10 MIN.,
COOK: 14 MIN., **GRILL:** 8 MIN.

2 (5-inch) fresh rosemary sprigs, divided
2 cups balsamic vinegar
3 Tbsp. honey, divided
2 Tbsp. Dijon mustard
1 Tbsp. olive oil
1 tsp. salt
½ tsp. freshly ground pepper
4 (¾-inch-thick) Boneless PORK Loin Chops
   (about 1 ½ lb.)

1. Preheat grill to 350° to 400° (medium-high) heat. Remove leaves from 1 rosemary sprig. Chop leaves to equal 1 tsp.
2. Bring balsamic vinegar, 1 Tbsp. honey, and remaining rosemary sprig to a boil in a 2-qt. saucepan over medium-high heat. Cook, stirring occasionally, 14 to 16 minutes or until thick and syrupy (about ⅓ cup).
3. Meanwhile, combine mustard, next 3 ingredients, chopped rosemary, and remaining 2 Tbsp. honey in a large zip-top plastic freezer bag, squeezing

bag to combine ingredients. Add pork, and seal bag, turning to coat. Remove chops from mustard mixture, discarding mixture.

4. Grill pork, covered with grill lid, 4 to 5 minutes on each side or until a meat thermometer inserted into thickest portion registers 150° to 155°. Let stand 5 minutes. Transfer to a serving platter.

5. Remove and discard rosemary sprig from balsamic syrup. Serve syrup with pork.

Per serving: Calories 437; Fat 13g (sat 4g, mono 7g, poly 1g); Protein 35g; Fiber 0g; Chol 100mg; Iron 2.4mg; Sodium 873mg; Calc 67mg

National Peanut Board

Discover some delicious ways to satisfy your cravings for both sweet and savory with this favorite nut.

Nutty Java Mudslides
MAKES 4 TO 6 SERVINGS; **PREP:** 10 MIN.

2 cups ice cubes
2 cups softened chocolate ice cream
3 Tbsp. creamy peanut butter made with USA-GROWN PEANUTS
3 Tbsp. coffee liqueur
2 Tbsp. Irish cream liqueur
2 Tbsp. milk
Garnish: dark chocolate shavings

1. Process ice cubes and next 5 ingredients in a blender or food processor 30 to 45 seconds or until blended and smooth. Serve immediately. Garnish, if desired.

Per serving: Calories 275; Fat 18g (sat 8g, mono 3g, poly 2g); Protein 6g; Chol 30mg; Iron 1mg; Sodium 120mg; Calc 77mg

Peanut Oven-Fried Chicken With Citrus-Ginger Sauce
MAKES 4 SERVINGS; **PREP:** 15 MIN.,
BAKE: 18 MIN

16 saltine crackers
¼ cup USA-GROWN PEANUTS
1 tsp. paprika
½ tsp. salt
½ tsp. pepper
2 egg whites
Vegetable cooking spray
Parchment paper
1¼ to 1½ lb. chicken breast tenders
¼ cup light roast peanut flour made with USA-GROWN PEANUTS
2 Tbsp. grated fresh ginger (about 1 2-inch piece)
⅓ cup orange juice
¼ cup sweet chili sauce
2 Tbsp. creamy peanut butter made with USA-GROWN PEANUTS
1 Tbsp. soy sauce
2 tsp. lime juice
1½ tsp. aromatic peanut oil made with USA-GROWN PEANUTS
Garnish: chopped USA-GROWN PEANUTS

1. Preheat oven to 425°. Process crackers and peanuts in a blender or food processor 30 to 45 seconds or until finely ground. Stir together cracker mixture, paprika, salt, and pepper. Whisk egg whites just until foamy.

2. Place a wire rack coated with cooking spray in a parchment paper-lined 15- x 10-inch jelly-roll pan. Dredge chicken tenders in peanut flour; dip in egg whites, and dredge in cracker mixture. Place chicken on wire rack.

3. Bake at 425° for 18 to 20 minutes or until golden brown and done, turning once after 12 minutes.

4. Meanwhile, squeeze juice from grated ginger into a small bowl; discard solids. Combine ginger juice, orange juice, and next 5 ingredients in a blender or food processor. Pulse 2 to 3 times or until smooth and well blended. Serve immediately with chicken tenders. Garnish, if desired.

Note: We tested with 12% fat light roast peanut flour.

Per serving: Calories 402; Fat 14g (sat 2g, mono 6g, poly 4g); Protein 48g; Fiber 3g; Chol 100mg; Iron 2.4mg; Sodium 1066mg; Calc 28mg

PB&J Snack Bars

MAKES 24 SERVINGS; **PREP:** 20 MIN.,
BAKE: 52 MIN., **COOL:** 1 HR.

Be sure to sprinkle the peanut topping around the edges of the pan to seal in the jelly mixture.

1¼ cups butter, divided
2 cups all-purpose flour
1 cup powdered sugar
1¼ cups grape or strawberry jelly
1 cup creamy peanut butter made with USA-GROWN PEANUTS
¾ cup light roast peanut flour made with USA-GROWN PEANUTS, divided
1 cup salted USA-GROWN PEANUTS, chopped
½ cup uncooked quick-cooking oats
3 Tbsp. light brown sugar
2 Tbsp. granulated sugar
⅛ tsp. salt

1. Preheat oven to 350°. Line bottom and sides of a 13- x 9-inch pan with heavy-duty aluminum foil, allowing 2 to 3 inches to extend over sides; lightly grease foil.
2. Cut 1 cup butter into small pieces. Pulse butter pieces, all-purpose flour, and powdered sugar in a food processor 5 to 6 times or until mixture is crumbly. Press mixture into bottom of prepared pan.
3. Bake at 350° on an oven rack one-third up from bottom of oven 22 to 24 minutes or just until golden brown.
4. Meanwhile, whisk together jelly, peanut butter, and ¼ cup peanut flour in a small bowl until smooth.
5. Microwave remaining ¼ cup butter in a microwave-safe bowl at HIGH 25 seconds or until melted. Stir in peanuts, next 4 ingredients, and remaining ½ cup peanut flour until well blended and crumbly.
6. Spread jelly mixture over crust, leaving a ½-inch border. Sprinkle peanut mixture around edges of pan and over jelly mixture.

7. Bake at 350° for 30 minutes or just until jelly mixture begins to puff. Cool completely in pan on a wire rack (about 1 hour).
8. Carefully and quickly lift baked bars from pan, using foil sides as handles. Place on a cutting board, and cut into 24 bars.
Note: We tested with 12% fat light roast peanut flour.

Per serving: Calories 298; Fat 19g (sat 8g, mono 7g, poly 3g); Protein 6g; Fiber: 2g; Chol 25mg; Iron 1mg; Sodium 149mg; Calc 17mg

Caramelized Plantains With Honey-Peanut Sauce

MAKES 4 SERVINGS; **PREP:** 15 MIN.,
COOK: 6 MIN.

Select black plantains for optimum flavor and tenderness. We do not recommend substituting bananas for plantains.

¼ cup firmly packed light brown sugar
¼ tsp. salt
3 soft black plantains, cut into 1-inch-thick slices (about 3 ½ cups)
⅓ cup aromatic peanut oil made with USA-GROWN PEANUTS
¼ cup honey
2 Tbsp. creamy peanut butter made with USA-GROWN PEANUTS
1 Tbsp. rum
1 tsp. lime zest
¼ tsp. fresh lime juice
⅛ tsp. ground cinnamon
1 Tbsp. butter
Garnishes: chopped USA-GROWN PEANUTS, lime wedges

1. Whisk together brown sugar and salt in a medium bowl. Add plantain slices, tossing to coat.
2. Cook plantains in hot oil in a large nonstick skillet over medium heat 2 minutes on each side or until golden brown. Transfer to serving plates, using a slotted spoon.

3. Combine honey and next 5 ingredients in a small saucepan. Cook over medium heat, whisking constantly, 2 minutes or until thoroughly heated and smooth. Remove from heat; stir in butter until smooth. Spoon sauce over plantains. Serve immediately. Garnish, if desired.

Per serving: Calories 521; Fat 26g (sat 6g, mono 12g, poly 8g); Protein 4g; Fiber 4g; Chol 8mg; Iron 1.3mg; Sodium 217mg; Calc 22mg

M&M'S® Brand

Create some fun with these favorite chocolate candies.

Holiday Power Mix

MAKES ABOUT 7½ CUPS; **PREP:** 5 MIN.

We used a dried fruit mix blend of blueberries, cherries, cranberries, and plums.

2 (5-oz.) packages dried fruit blend
2½ cups pretzel twists
1½ cups M&M'S Dark Chocolate Candies For The Holidays
1 cup roasted, salted almonds
⅓ cup coarsely chopped crystallized ginger

1. Toss all ingredients together in a large bowl. Store in a zip-top plastic freezer bag up to 1 week.

Per ½-cup serving: Calories 254; Fat 9g (sat 3g, mono 3g, poly 1g); Protein 4g; Carb 40g; Fiber 3g; Chol 2mg; Iron 1mg; Sodium 169mg; Calc 32mg

Almond-Shortbread Ice-Cream Cupcakes

MAKES 12 SERVINGS; **PREP:** 20 MIN.;
FREEZE: 1 HR., 30 MIN.; **STAND:** 5 MIN.

You'll need almost an entire 28-oz. container of ice cream for these sweet treats.

12 aluminum foil baking cups
Vegetable cooking spray
1 (7-oz.) package shortbread cookies
1½ cups M&M'S Almond Candies, divided
¼ cup butter, melted
4 cups vanilla ice cream
1½ cups thawed frozen whipped topping

1. Place aluminum foil baking cups in a lightly greased 12-cup muffin pan, and coat with cooking spray.
2. Process cookies in a food processor 30 seconds or until finely ground. (Yield should equal about 1½ cups.) Transfer to a medium bowl. Process 1 cup candies 30 seconds or until finely ground. Stir ground candies and butter into ground cookies until combined. Divide crumb mixture among prepared cups, pressing firmly on bottom and two-thirds up sides of each cup. Freeze 30 minutes.
3. During last 10 minutes of freezing, let ice cream stand at room temperature.
4. Place ice cream in bowl of a heavy-duty electric stand mixer. Beat at low speed, using paddle attachment, 5 to 10 seconds or until just smooth enough to spread.
5. Spoon ice cream into crusts, filling completely full. Freeze 1 hour. Dollop each with about 2 Tbsp. whipped topping, and top with remaining ½ cup candies. Let stand 5 minutes before serving.

Per serving: Calories 335; Fat 20g (sat 9g, mono 5g, poly 1g); Protein 4g; Carb 35g; Fiber 1g; Chol 35mg; Iron 0.5mg; Sodium 147mg; Calc 63mg

Double Chocolate Candy Cookies

MAKES ABOUT 4 DOZEN; **PREP:** 20 MIN.,
BAKE: 15 MIN. PER BATCH,
COOL: 25 MIN. PER BATCH

If you have a heavy-duty electric stand mixer, feel free to beat the oats, baking soda, salt, and candies into the dough (in the order directed in the recipe), instead of stirring. It'll only take a second to be fully incorporated.

½ cup butter, softened
1 cup plus 2 Tbsp. firmly packed
    brown sugar
1 cup granulated sugar
2 cups creamy peanut butter
3 large eggs
1 tsp. light corn syrup
¼ tsp. vanilla extract
4 cups uncooked regular oats
2 tsp. baking soda
¼ tsp. salt
1 cup M&M'S Dark Chocolate Candies
1 cup M&M'S Milk Chocolate Candies

1. Preheat oven to 350°. Beat butter at medium speed with an electric mixer until creamy; gradually add sugars, beating well. Add peanut butter and next 3 ingredients; beat well. Add oats, baking soda, and salt; stir well. Stir in candies. (Dough will be stiff.)
2. Drop dough by heaping tablespoonfuls 3 inches apart onto lightly greased baking sheets.
3. Bake at 350° for 15 minutes or until golden brown. (Centers of cookies will be slightly soft.) Cool on pans on a wire rack 5 minutes; remove from pans to wire racks, and cool completely (about 20 minutes).

Per serving: Calories 187; Fat 10g (sat 3g, mono 3g, poly 2g); Protein 4g; Carb 22g; Fiber 2g; Chol 19mg; Iron 1mg; Sodium 140mg; Calc 14mg

Peanut Butter Brownie Bites

MAKES 16 SERVINGS; **PREP:** 10 MIN.,
BAKE: 53 MIN., **COOL:** 1 HR.

1 (19.27-oz.) package milk chocolate
    brownie mix
½ tsp. vanilla extract
1 (3-oz.) package cream cheese
⅓ cup creamy peanut butter
1 cup M&M'S Peanut Butter Candies

1. Preheat oven to 350°. Line bottom and sides of an 8-inch square pan with aluminum foil, allowing 2 to 3 inches to extend over sides; lightly grease foil.
2. Prepare brownie batter according to package directions for fudgy brownies, stirring vanilla into batter. Pour batter into prepared pan.
3. Place cream cheese in a microwave-safe bowl. Microwave at HIGH 15 seconds. Add peanut butter, and stir until smooth and blended. Drop peanut butter mixture by 16 rounded tsp. onto batter. Sprinkle candies over batter.
4. Bake at 350° for 50 to 53 minutes or until a wooden pick inserted in center comes out with a few moist crumbs. Cool completely on a wire rack (about 1 hour). Lift brownies from pan, using foil sides as handles. Place on a cutting board, and cut into 16 squares.

Per serving: Calories 333; Fat 21g (sat 6g, mono 7g, poly 4g); Protein 6g; Carb 34g; Fiber 2g; Chol 45mg; Iron 1mg; Sodium 175mg; Calc 18mg

Duncan Hines

Bake some moist and delicious treats with red velvet cake mix.

Raspberry-Red Velvet Petits Fours

MAKES 24 SERVINGS; **PREP:** 25 MIN.;
BAKE: 28 MIN.; **COOL:** 1 HR., 10 MIN.

Use a serrated knife to trim top and sides off cake.

1 (18.25-oz.) package DUNCAN HINES Moist
    Deluxe Red Velvet Cake Mix
½ cup seedless raspberry jam
1 (16-oz.) container DUNCAN HINES
    Creamy Homestyle Cream Cheese
    Frosting

1. Preheat oven to 350°. Prepare cake batter as directed. Pour batter into a greased and floured 13- x 9-inch pan.
2. Bake at 350° for 28 to 30 minutes or until a wooden pick inserted in center comes out clean. Cool in pan on a wire rack 10 minutes. Remove from pan to wire rack, and cool completely (about 1 hour).
3. Invert cake onto a cutting board. Cut off rounded top of cake. Trim and discard edges of cake.
4. Cut cake in half crosswise. Cut each piece in half horizontally. Carefully lift top piece off each cake half.
5. Stir jam in a small bowl until smooth and spreadable. Spread jam over bottom halves of cakes. Replace top halves of cakes. Cut each cake half into 12 squares. Transfer petits fours to a serving platter or cake pedestal.

6. Remove lid and foil from frosting. Microwave frosting at HIGH 20 seconds, stirring after 10 seconds. Stir until smooth and spreadable. Transfer frosting to a zip-top plastic freezer bag. Snip 1 corner of bag to make a small hole. Pipe frosting onto top of petits fours, allowing frosting to drip down sides.

Red Velvet Loaf Cakes

MAKES 16 SERVINGS; **PREP:** 25 MIN.;
BAKE: 40 MIN.; **COOL:** 1 HR., 10 MIN.

1 (18.25-oz.) package DUNCAN HINES Moist
    Deluxe Red Velvet Cake Mix
1¼ cups buttermilk
¼ cup butter, melted
2 large eggs
1 tsp. vanilla extract
1½ (16-oz.) containers DUNCAN HINES
    Creamy Homestyle Cream Cheese
    Frosting
Garnishes: white sparkling sugar,
    fresh mint sprigs

1. Preheat oven to 350°. Grease and flour 2 (8½- x 4½-inch) loaf pans.
2. Beat first 5 ingredients at low speed with an electric mixer just until dry ingredients are moistened. Increase speed to medium, and beat 1 minute or until batter is smooth, stopping to scrape down sides of bowl as needed. Pour batter into prepared pans.
3. Bake at 350° for 40 to 45 minutes or until a wooden pick inserted in center comes out clean. Cool in pans on wire racks 10 minutes; remove from pans to wire racks, and cool completely (about 1 hour).
4. Place loaves on a serving plate or cake pedestal. Spread frosting over tops and sides of cakes. Garnish, if desired.

Red Velvet Trifle

MAKES 10 SERVINGS; **PREP:** 25 MIN.,
BAKE: 28 MIN., **CHILL:** 1 HR., **COOL:** 10 MIN.

1 (18.25-oz.) package DUNCAN HINES Moist
    Deluxe Red Velvet Cake Mix
2 (8-oz.) packages cream cheese, softened
2 cups low-fat vanilla yogurt
1 cup powdered sugar
1 tsp. lemon zest
1 pt. fresh raspberries
Garnish: fresh mint sprigs

1. Preheat oven to 350°. Prepare cake batter as directed. Pour batter into a greased and floured 13- x 9-inch pan.
2. Bake at 350° for 28 to 30 minutes or until a wooden pick inserted in center comes out clean.
3. Meanwhile, beat cream cheese at medium speed with a heavy-duty electric stand mixer 1 minute or until creamy. Add yogurt, powdered sugar, and lemon zest. Beat 1 to 2 minutes or until smooth, stopping to scrape down sides of bowl as needed. Cover and chill.
4. Remove cake from oven. Cool in pan on a wire rack 10 minutes. Remove from pan to wire rack, and cool completely (about 1 hour).
5. Invert cake onto a cutting board. Cut rounded top off cake. Trim and discard edges of cake. Cut cake into 32 pieces.
6. Arrange about one-third of cake pieces in a 3-qt. trifle dish. Carefully spread one-third of chilled cream cheese mixture over cake. Repeat layers 2 times, smoothing top layer of cream cheese mixture over cake pieces. Top with raspberries. Cover and chill 1 hour before serving. Garnish, if desired.

Spice Islands

Saigon cinnamon and pure vanilla extract add flavor to this scrumptious cake.

Honey-Cinnamon Tres Leches Cake

MAKES 16 SERVINGS; **PREP:** 30 MIN., **BAKE:** 25 MIN., **STAND:** 2 HR., **CHILL:** 2 HR.

½ cup butter, softened
1 cup sugar
7 large eggs, separated
2½ cups all-purpose flour
1 tsp. baking powder
½ tsp. salt
¾ tsp. SPICE ISLANDS Ground Saigon Cinnamon, divided
1 cup milk
1 tsp. SPICE ISLANDS Pure Vanilla Extract
1 (14-oz.) can sweetened condensed milk
1 (12-oz.) can evaporated milk
1½ cups whipping cream, divided
5 Tbsp. honey, divided

1. Preheat oven to 350°. Beat butter at medium speed with an electric mixer 2 minutes or until creamy. Gradually add sugar, beating until light and fluffy. Add egg yolks, beating just until blended.
2. Whisk together flour, baking powder, salt, and ½ teaspoon cinnamon in a medium bowl. Add to butter mixture alternately with milk, beginning and ending with flour mixture. Beat at low speed just until blended after each addition. Stir in vanilla.
3. Beat egg whites at high speed until stiff peaks form. Fold into batter. Pour batter into a greased and floured 13- x 9-inch pan.
4. Bake at 350° for 25 to 28 minutes or until a wooden pick inserted in center comes out clean.

5. Meanwhile, whisk together sweetened condensed milk, evaporated milk, ½ cup whipping cream, 2 Tbsp. honey, and remaining ¼ tsp. cinnamon in a medium bowl until blended.
6. Pierce top of hot cake generously with the end of a wooden spoon. Gradually pour milk mixture over cake, about ⅓ cup at a time, spreading to edges. (Allow mixture to completely soak into cake between batches.) Let stand 2 hours. Cover and chill 2 hours.
7. Beat remaining 1 cup whipping cream at medium-high speed until foamy; add remaining 3 tablespoons honey, beating until soft peaks form. Spread over top of cake. Serve immediately, or cover and chill until ready to serve.

I Can't Believe It's Not Butter!

Create a mouthwatering dessert that boasts bold flavor with this healthy margarine.

Chocolate-Toffee-Granola Cookies

MAKES 16 SERVINGS; **PREP:** 10 MIN., **BAKE:** 25 MIN., **COOL:** 15 MIN.

Break up large pieces of granola before stirring into batter.

Parchment paper
½ cup I CAN'T BELIEVE IT'S NOT BUTTER! Cooking & Baking Sticks, melted
¾ cup firmly packed light brown sugar
¼ cup granulated sugar
1 large egg
½ tsp. salt
1¼ cups all-purpose flour
1¼ cups granola cereal
¾ cup semisweet chocolate morsels
½ cup toffee bits

1. Preheat oven to 350°. Grease an 8-inch square pan. Line bottom and sides of pan with parchment paper, allowing 2 to 3 inches to extend over sides. Grease parchment paper.
2. Whisk together melted cooking-and-baking sticks and next 4 ingredients in a large bowl until smooth. Whisk in flour; stir in granola, chocolate morsels, and toffee bits until combined. Spread batter into prepared pan.
3. Bake at 350° for 25 to 30 minutes or until a wooden pick inserted in center comes out with a few moist crumbs. Cool in pan on a wire rack 15 minutes. Carefully lift bars from pan, using parchment paper sides as handles. Cut into bars, and serve warm or cool to room temperature.

Eggland's Best

Use these good-for-you eggs to make some great-tasting muffins, cookies, and deviled eggs.

Nutty Peanut Butter Cookies

MAKES 2 DOZEN; **PREP:** 10 MIN., **COOK:** 10 MIN., **COOL:** 10 MIN.

1 cup creamy peanut butter
1 cup firmly packed light brown sugar
1 EGGLAND'S Best Large White Egg
1 tsp. baking soda
¼ cup chopped peanuts
1 tsp. vanilla extract

1. Preheat oven to 350°. Whisk together first 4 ingredients in a medium bowl until smooth. Stir in peanuts and vanilla. Drop by rounded Tbsp. 2 inches apart on lightly greased baking sheets.
2. Bake at 350° for 10 minutes or until puffed and lightly browned. Cool on pan on a wire rack 5 minutes. Remove from pan to wire rack, and cool 5 minutes. Serve warm or cool completely.

Per serving: Calories 110; Fat 6g (sat 1g, mono 3g, poly 2g); Protein 3g; Carb 11g; Fiber 1g; Chol 8mg; Iron 0mg; Sodium: 109mg; Calc 14mg

Apple-Cheddar Muffins

MAKES 12 SERVINGS; **PREP:** 16 MIN., **BAKE:** 14 MIN., **COOL:** 15 MIN.

1 Tbsp. butter
1 medium-size Granny Smith apple, peeled and chopped
½ cup chopped sweet onion
1 Tbsp. sugar
2⅓ cups all-purpose baking mix
1½ cups (6 oz.) shredded extra-sharp Cheddar cheese
¼ cup plain yellow cornmeal
¼ tsp. salt
¾ cup milk
2 EGGLAND'S Best Large White Eggs
⅓ cup chopped pecans

1. Preheat oven to 425°. Melt butter in a small skillet over medium heat. Add apple and next 2 ingredients; sauté 6 minutes or until onion is tender.
2. Combine baking mix and next 3 ingredients in a large bowl; make a well in center of mixture. Whisk together milk and eggs; add to dry ingredients, stirring just until moistened.
3. Stir apple mixture into batter. Spoon batter into a greased muffin pan, filling two-thirds full. Sprinkle batter with chopped pecans.
4. Bake at 425° for 14 minutes or until golden and a wooden pick inserted in center comes out with a few moist crumbs. Let cool in pan on a wire rack 5 minutes. Gently run a knife around edges of muffins to loosen. Remove muffins from pan to wire rack, and let cool 10 minutes. Serve warm.

Per serving: Calories: 208; Fat 10g (sat 4g, mono 2g, poly 1g); Protein 9g; Carb 24g; Fiber 2g; Chol 51mg; Iron 1mg; Sodium 441mg; Calc 255mg

Bacon-Chive Deviled Eggs

MAKES 12 SERVINGS; **PREP:** 30 MIN.

1 dozen EGGLAND'S Best Large White Eggs, hard-cooked and peeled
½ cup mayonnaise
2 tsp. Dijon mustard
1 Tbsp. fresh lemon juice
7 fully cooked bacon slices
2 Tbsp. plus 1 tsp. chopped fresh chives
¾ tsp. freshly ground pepper
¼ tsp. salt
Garnishes: chopped fresh chives; fully cooked, crumbled bacon

1. Slice eggs in half lengthwise; carefully remove yolks, keeping egg white halves intact. Process yolks, mayonnaise, mustard, and lemon juice in a food processor 30 seconds or until smooth, stopping to scrape down sides as needed.
2. Microwave bacon according to package directions until crisp; crumble. Stir bacon, chives, pepper, and salt into yolk mixture.
3. Spoon yolk mixture into a zip-top plastic freezer bag (do not seal). Snip 1 corner of bag to make a small hole. Pipe yolk mixture into egg white halves. Garnish, if desired.
Note: Nutritional analysis does not include garnish.

Per serving: Calories 160; Fat 14g (sat 3g, mono 2g, poly 1g); Protein 7g; Carb 1g; Fiber 0g; Chol 218mg; Iron 1mg; Sodium 234mg; Calc 26mg

Southern Living® BBQ on Tour

Lay's Potato Chips

Grab a bag of chips to whip up a host of dishes from appetizers to entreés to even dessert.

Zesty Spinach-Artichoke Dip and Chips

MAKES ABOUT 3½ CUPS; **PREP:** 15 MIN., **CHILL:** 30 MIN.

1 (14-oz.) can artichoke hearts, drained and chopped
1 (8-oz.) container of sour cream
1 cup mayonaise
3 Tbsp. finely chopped onion
1 tsp. lemon zest
1 Tbsp. fresh lemon juice
1 (1-oz.) envelope vegetable soup mix
1 (10-oz.) package frozen chopped spinach, thawed
Freshly ground pepper to taste
1 (11-oz.) package LAY'S Classic Potato Chips
Garnishes: crushed potato chips, freshly ground pepper

1. Stir together first 7 ingredients in a large bowl.
2. Drain thawed spinach well, pressing between paper towels; stir into artichoke mixture. Season with pepper to taste. Cover and chill 30 minutes to 2 days. Serve with chips. Garnish, if desired.

All-American Squash Casserole With Crispy Potato Chip Topping

MAKES 8 SERVINGS; **PREP:** 15 MIN., **COOK:** 15 MIN., **BAKE:** 35 MIN., **STAND:** 5 MIN.

1½ lb. yellow squash
1 lb. zucchini
1 small sweet onion, chopped
2½ tsp. salt, divided
1 cup grated carrots
1 (10¾-oz.) can cream of chicken soup
1 (8-oz.) container sour cream
1 (8-oz.) can water chestnuts, drained and chopped
2¼ cups crushed LAY'S Classic Potato Chips

1. Preheat oven to 350°. Cut squash and zucchini into ¼-inch-thick slices; place in a Dutch oven. Add chopped onion, 2 tsp. salt, and water to cover. Bring to a boil over medium-high heat, and cook 5 minutes; drain well.
2. Stir together grated carrots, next 3 ingredients, and remaining ½ tsp. salt in a large bowl; fold in squash mixture.
3. Sprinkle 1 cup crushed chips in bottom of a lightly greased 13- x 9-inch baking dish. Spoon squash mixture over crushed chips, and top with remaining chips.
4. Bake at 350° for 35 minutes or until bubbly and golden, shielding with aluminum foil after 20 to 25 minutes to prevent excessive browning, if necessary. Let stand 5 minutes before serving.

Chocolate-Dipped Potato Chips and Ice Cream

MAKES 8 SERVINGS; **PREP:** 20 MIN., **CHILL:** 10 MIN.

1 (7-oz.) container milk or dark-semisweet dipping chocolate
Wax paper
⅓ (11-oz.) package LAY'S Classic Potato Chips (about 4 oz.)
1 qt. vanilla ice cream

1. Prepare chocolate according to package directions.
2. Line a jelly-roll pan with wax paper. Dip potato chips halfway into melted chocolate, gently shaking off excess. Place on prepared pan. Chill 10 to 15 minutes or until chocolate is set. Serve immediately with ice cream, or cover and chill until ready to serve (up to 24 hours).

Salty 'n' Sweet Ice-Cream Truffles

MAKES 2 DOZEN; **PREP:** 20 MIN., **STAND:** 15 MIN., **FREEZE:** 30 MIN.

1 pt. vanilla ice cream
Parchment paper
2 cups crushed LAY'S Classic Potato Chips

1. Let ice cream stand at room temperature 15 minutes to soften.
2. Meanwhile, line a jelly-roll pan with parchment paper, and place in freezer. Pour crushed potato chips into a shallow dish.
3. Scoop ice cream into 24 small balls using a 1¼-inch ice-cream scoop, and roll in crushed potato chips. Arrange on prepared pan in freezer. Freeze truffles 30 minutes. Serve immediately, or place in a zip-top plastic freezer bag, and freeze up to 1 month.

Oscar Mayer Beef Hot Dogs

Try these smart ideas for one of the South's favorite foods.

Quick Skillet Baked Beans and Franks

MAKES 8 TO 10 SERVINGS; **PREP:** 15 MIN.,
COOK: 12 MIN.

Serve this quick one-dish meal with cooked bacon slices and fresh green onions, if desired.

1 (16-oz.) package OSCAR MAYER Premium
    Beef Franks
1 Tbsp. butter
1 small sweet onion, chopped
2 (28-oz.) cans baked beans in tangy sauce
    with brown sugar and bacon
⅓ cup root beer
3 Tbsp. barbecue sauce
3 Tbsp. yellow mustard
2 tsp. cider vinegar
Freshly cracked pepper to taste

1. Cut each hot dog into 6 slices.
2. Melt butter in a large nonstick skillet over medium-high heat; add onion, and sauté 4 minutes or until tender.
3. Add hot dogs, beans, and next 4 ingredients to skillet. Cook, stirring occasionally, 8 to 10 minutes or until thickened. Season with freshly cracked pepper to taste.

Asian Slaw Dogs

MAKES 8 SERVINGS; **PREP:** 20 MIN.,
GRILL: 7 MIN.

Squeezing the juice from grated ginger is easy and adds fresh flavor to this Asian-inspired slaw. To easily release the juice, press the ginger against the back of your measuring spoon using a finger.

Vegetable cooking spray
1 (16-oz.) package OSCAR MAYER Premium
    Jumbo Beef Franks
¼ cup hoisin sauce, divided
8 hot dog buns
1 (4-inch) piece fresh ginger
⅔ cup mayonnaise
2 Tbsp. chopped fresh cilantro
2 Tbsp. lime juice
½ tsp. salt
1 (12-oz.) package broccoli slaw
Toppings: crumbled ramen noodles, fresh
    cilantro sprigs, lime wedges

1. Coat cold cooking grate of grill with cooking spray, and place on grill. Preheat grill to 350° to 400° (medium-high) heat. Brush hot dogs with 2 Tbsp. hoisin sauce.
2. Grill hot dogs, covered with grill lid, 6 to 8 minutes or to desired degree of doneness, turning occasionally. Grill buns, split sides down, covered with grill lid, 1 minute or until grill marks appear.
3. Grate ginger using the large holes of a box grater to equal 2 Tbsp. Squeeze juice from grated ginger into a medium bowl; discard solids. Add mayonnaise, next 3 ingredients, and remaining 2 Tbsp. hoisin sauce, stirring to combine. Add slaw, tossing to coat.
4. Serve grilled hot dogs in buns with slaw mixture and desired toppings.

Layered BBQ Salads With Grilled Hot Dogs

MAKES 8 SERVINGS; **PREP:** 25 MIN.,
GRILL: 6 MIN.

Pick up your favorite deli baked beans and coleslaw for a delicious, easy meal that comes together in minutes.

Vegetable cooking spray
1 (16-oz.) package OSCAR MAYER Premium
    Jumbo Beef Franks
2 Tbsp. barbecue sauce, divided
6 fully-cooked bacon slices
2 cups deli baked beans
1 tsp. cider vinegar
2 cups deli coleslaw
¼ tsp. freshly cracked pepper
1 cup chopped plum tomatoes (about
    3 medium tomatoes)
3 green onions, sliced
Toppings: sliced jalapeño peppers, pickled
    okra, freshly cracked pepper

1. Coat cold cooking grate of grill with cooking spray, and place on grill. Preheat grill to 350° to 400° (medium-high) heat. Brush hot dogs with 1 Tbsp. barbecue sauce.
2. Prepare bacon according to package directions; crumble.
3. Grill hot dogs, covered with grill lid, 6 to 8 minutes or to desired degree of doneness, turning occasionally. Cut hot dogs into bite-size pieces.
4. Stir together baked beans, cider vinegar, and remaining 1 Tbsp. barbecue sauce in a medium bowl. If desired, microwave bean mixture at HIGH 2 minutes or until thoroughly heated, stirring halfway through. Stir together coleslaw and pepper.
5. Divide hot dog slices among 8 (10-oz.) glasses. Top hot dogs evenly with bean mixture, coleslaw mixture, chopped tomatoes, green onions, and crumbled bacon. Serve with desired toppings.

Lea & Perrins

Use Worcestershire sauce to create flavorful marinades for vegetables, meats, and seafood.

Bourbon-Marinated Pork Tenderloin

MAKES 4 TO 6 SERVINGS; **PREP:** 10 MIN., **COOK:** 2 MIN., **GRILL:** 20 MIN., **CHILL:** 2 HR., **STAND:** 10 MIN.

1 (1¼-lb.) pork tenderloin
6 Tbsp. LEA & PERRINS Original
    Worcestershire Sauce
3 Tbsp. bourbon
3 Tbsp. maple syrup
2 Tbsp. honey-Dijon mustard
2 Tbsp. vegetable oil
¼ tsp. freshly ground pepper

1. Remove silver skin from tenderloin, leaving a thin layer of fat covering tenderloin.
2. Whisk together Worcestershire sauce and next 5 ingredients in a small bowl until blended. Pour marinade into a large zip-top plastic freezer bag; add pork, turning to coat. Seal bag, and chill 2 hours, turning occasionally.
3. Preheat grill to 350° to 400° (medium-high) heat. Remove pork from marinade, reserving marinade.
4. Grill pork, covered with grill lid, 10 to 12 minutes on each side or until a meat thermometer inserted into thickest portion registers 150° to 155°. Remove pork from grill, and let stand 10 minutes before slicing.
5. Meanwhile, bring reserved marinade to a boil in a small saucepan over medium-high heat. Boil 2 minutes. Drizzle sauce over pork before serving.

Classic Steak House-Marinated Steaks

MAKES 4 SERVINGS; **PREP:** 20 MIN., **GRILL:** 10 MIN., **CHILL:** 2 HR., **STAND:** 5 MIN.

⅓ cup dark beer
¼ cup LEA & PERRINS Original
    Worcestershire Sauce
1 Tbsp. olive oil
1 Tbsp. honey
1 tsp. lemon zest
¾ tsp. salt, divided
½ tsp. freshly ground pepper, divided
4 (10- to 12-oz.) beef strip steaks
    (1¼ inches thick)
Garnish: freshly ground pepper

1. Whisk together beer, next 4 ingredients, and ¼ tsp. each salt and pepper in a small bowl. Pierce steaks several times with a fork. Pour marinade into a large zip-top plastic freezer bag; add steaks. Seal bag, and chill 2 hours, turning occasionally.
2. Preheat grill to 350° to 400° (medium-high) heat. Remove steaks from marinade, reserving marinade. Sprinkle steaks with remaining ½ tsp. salt and ¼ tsp. pepper.
3. Grill steaks, covered with grill lid, 5 to 6 minutes on each side or to desired degree of doneness. Remove steaks from grill, and let stand 5 minutes before serving.
4. Meanwhile, boil reserved marinade in a small saucepan over medium-high heat 4 minutes or until thickened. Serve with grilled steaks. Garnish, if desired.

Perfect Beach Shrimp

MAKES 6 SERVINGS; **PREP:** 10 MIN., **COOK:** 25 MIN.

1 cup butter, melted
1 cup ketchup
½ cup LEA & PERRINS Original
    Worcestershire Sauce
3 Tbsp. Old Bay seasoning
1 tsp. freshly ground pepper
3 lb. unpeeled, large raw shrimp
    (21/25 count)
Garnish: lemon halves

1. Preheat oven to 400°. Stir together first 5 ingredients. Place shrimp in a broiler pan; pour butter mixture over shrimp.
2. Bake at 400° for 25 minutes or just until shrimp turn pink, stirring every 10 minutes. Garnish, if desired.

Marinated Green Beans

MAKES 6 SERVINGS; **PREP:** 15 MIN., **COOK:** 4 MIN., **CHILL:** 3 HR.

Taste the marinade before adding salt.

1½ lb. fresh green beans, trimmed
¼ cup LEA & PERRINS Original
    Worcestershire Sauce
¼ cup bottled balsamic vinaigrette
1 Tbsp. sugar
¼ tsp. freshly ground pepper
Salt to taste
1 cup thinly sliced red onion
Garnish: freshly cracked pepper

1. Cook beans in boiling water to cover in a large saucepan over medium-high heat 4 minutes or until crisp-tender; drain. Plunge into ice water to stop the cooking process; drain.

2. Whisk together Worcestershire sauce and next 4 ingredients in a small bowl. Pour marinade into a large zip-top plastic freezer bag; add beans and onion. Seal bag, and shake to coat. Chill 3 hours, turning occasionally. Serve with a slotted spoon. Garnish, if desired.

BEEF. It's What's for Dinner.

These recipes are great for a quick weeknight supper or a casual gathering.

Mini Grilled Steak and Gorgonzola Pizzas •

MAKES 4 SERVINGS; **PREP:** 15 MIN., **GRILL:** 15 MIN. (CHARCOAL GRILL) OR 10 MIN. (GAS GRILL), **STAND:** 5 MIN.

1 (1- to 1¼-lb.) BEEF Top Sirloin Steak
   (about ¾-inch thick)
½ tsp. salt
½ tsp. freshly ground pepper
1 red Bartlett pear, thinly sliced
½ cup crumbled Gorgonzola cheese
4 (6- to 7-inch-round) flatbreads
1 Tbsp. white balsamic vinegar
2 tsp. olive oil
2½ cups fresh arugula

1. Preheat a charcoal grill to medium, ash-covered coals or a gas grill to 300° to 350° (medium) heat. Grill steak on a charcoal grill, without grill lid, 13 to 16

minutes, or on a gas grill, covered with grill lid, 8 to 13 minutes. Remove from grill, and sprinkle with salt and pepper. Let stand 5 minutes.

2. Meanwhile, divide pear slices and cheese among flatbreads.

3. Grill flatbreads on a charcoal grill, without grill lid, 2 to 3 minutes or until lightly toasted and cheese begins to melt, or on a gas grill, covered with grill lid, 2 minutes or until lightly toasted and cheese begins to melt.

4. Whisk together vinegar and olive oil in a medium bowl. Add arugula, tossing to coat.

5. Carve steak into thin strips. Divide steak among flatbreads. Top with arugula mixture. Sprinkle with freshly ground pepper to taste, if desired.

Per serving: Calories 505; Fat 20g (sat 7g, mono 7g, poly 4g); Protein 36g; Carb 45g; Fiber 3g; Chol 54mg; Iron 4mg; Sodium 906mg; Calc 210mg

Steak and Grilled Vegetable Panini

MAKES 4 SERVINGS; **PREP:** 15 MIN., **GRILL:** 13 MIN. (CHARCOAL GRILL) OR 8 MIN. (GAS GRILL), **STAND:** 5 MIN., **COOK:** 2 MIN. PER BATCH

Serve these sandwiches with additional red wine vinaigrette on the side for a tasty dipping sauce.

1 large yellow bell pepper, thinly sliced
½ (8-oz.) package sliced baby portobello
   mushrooms
1 small red onion, thinly sliced
2 Tbsp. light red wine vinaigrette, divided
¾ tsp. salt, divided
¾ tsp. freshly cracked pepper, divided
1 (1- to 1¼-lb.) BEEF Top Sirloin Steak
   (about ¾-inch thick)
1 cup firmly packed fresh baby spinach
8 (5½-inch-long, ¼-inch-thick) ciabatta
   bread slices
½ cup (2 oz.) freshly shredded fontina
   cheese

1. Preheat a charcoal grill to medium, ash-covered coals or a gas grill to 300° to 350° (medium) heat. Toss bell pepper, mushrooms, and onion with 1 Tbsp. vinaigrette, ¼ tsp. salt, and ¼ tsp. pepper.

2. Grill steak and vegetables at the same time. Grill steak on a charcoal grill, without grill lid, 13 to 16 minutes, or on a gas grill, covered with grill lid, 8 to 13 minutes. Grill vegetables in a lightly greased grill basket, stirring occasionally, on a charcoal grill, without grill lid, 10 to 12 minutes or until tender, or on a gas grill, covered with grill lid, 8 to 10 minutes or until tender.

3. Remove steak and vegetables from grill. Sprinkle steak with remaining ½ tsp. salt and ½ tsp. pepper. Let steak stand 5 minutes. Carve steak into thin strips.

4. Toss spinach with remaining 1 Tbsp. vinaigrette. Divide spinach among 4 bread slices. Top with cheese, steak, vegetables, and remaining bread slices. (Sandwiches will be very full.)

5. Cook sandwiches, in batches, in preheated panini press 2 to 3 minutes or until light golden brown and grill marks appear.

Per serving: Calories 505; Fat 16g (sat 6g, mono 5g, poly 1g); Protein 33g; Carb 27g; Fiber 3g; Chol 77mg; Iron 3mg; Sodium 974mg; Calc 145mg

Tuscan Beef and Bread Salad

MAKES 6 SERVINGS; **PREP:** 15 MIN.,
GRILL: 10 MIN. (CHARCOAL GRILL) OR
7 MIN. (GAS GRILL), **STAND:** 10 MIN.

8 (½-inch-thick) Italian bread
    slices
2 medium-size sweet onions, cut into
    ¼-inch rounds
6 Tbsp. light balsamic vinaigrette,
    divided
¾ tsp. salt, divided
¾ tsp. freshly ground pepper,
    divided
3 (¾-inch-thick) BEEF Top Loin Steaks
    (about 1½ lb.)
6 medium-size plum tomatoes, chopped
    (about 3½ cups)
⅓ cup chopped fresh basil
¼ cup freshly shaved Parmesan cheese
Garnishes: fresh basil leaves, freshly
    cracked pepper

1. Preheat a charcoal grill to medium, ash-covered coals or a gas grill to 300° to 350° (medium) heat. Brush one side of bread and onion with 2 Tbsp. vinaigrette. Sprinkle onion with ¼ tsp. salt and ¼ tsp. pepper.
2. Grill steaks and onion at the same time. Grill steaks on a charcoal grill, without grill lid, 10 to 12 minutes, or on a gas grill, covered with grill lid, 7 to 10 minutes. Grill onion, on one side only, on a charcoal grill, without grill lid, 8 minutes or until tender and grill marks appear, or on a gas grill, covered with grill lid, 6 minutes or until tender and grill marks appear.
3. Remove steaks and onion from grill. Sprinkle steaks with remaining ½ tsp. salt and ½ tsp. pepper. Let steaks stand 5 minutes.
4. Meanwhile, grill bread on a charcoal grill, without grill lid, 1 to 2 minutes on each side or until lightly browned and grill marks appear, or on a gas grill, covered with grill lid, 1 to 2 minutes on each side or until lightly browned and grill marks appear.
5. Carve steaks into thin strips. Cut strips into bite-size pieces. Coarsely chop onion. Cut bread into 1-inch cubes.
6. Toss steak pieces, onion, bread, tomatoes, and basil with remaining 4 Tbsp. vinaigrette. Season with salt and pepper to taste. Sprinkle with cheese. Let stand 5 minutes before serving. Garnish, if desired.

Per serving: Calories 335; Fat 11g (sat 4g,mono 3g,poly 1g); Protein 30g; Carb 27g; Fiber 3g; Chol 51mg; Iron 3mg; Sodium 875mg; Calc 110mg

Tri-Tip Roast With Green Peppercorn Sauce

MAKES 6 SERVINGS; **PREP:** 10 MIN.,
GRILL: 35 MIN. (CHARCOAL GRILL) OR
25 MIN. (GAS GRILL), **STAND:** 10 MIN.

We recommend grilling the roast until a meat thermometer inserted into thickest portion registers 140°. Serve this dish with mashed potatoes and green beans for a special dinner with friends or a weeknight family supper.

1 (1½- to 2-lb.) BEEF Tri-Tip Roast
2 tsp. olive oil (optional)
2 Tbsp. green peppercorns in brine,
    drained
1 (14-oz.) can low-sodium beef broth
¼ cup dry red wine
1 (1-oz.) envelope dry onion soup mix
½ tsp. cornstarch
½ tsp. Dijon mustard
½ tsp. salt
½ tsp. freshly ground pepper

1. Preheat a charcoal grill to medium, ash-covered coals or a gas grill to 300° to 350° (medium) heat. If desired, brush roast with oil.
2. Grill roast, turning occasionally, on a charcoal grill, without grill lid, 35 to 45 minutes, or on a gas grill, covered with grill lid, 25 to 30 minutes.
3. Meanwhile, bring peppercorns and next 3 ingredients to a boil in a large skillet over medium-high heat. Cook, stirring occasionally, 12 to 14 minutes or until mixture is reduced by half.
4. Whisk together cornstarch and 2 Tbsp. water until smooth. Add cornstarch mixture and mustard to skillet. Cook, stirring constantly, 2 minutes or until slightly thickened.
5. Transfer roast to a serving platter, sprinkle with salt and pepper, and let stand 10 minutes. Carve roast into thin slices. Serve with warm peppercorn sauce.

Per serving: Calories 238; Fat 10g (sat 4g,mono 4g,poly 0g); Protein 29g; Carb 5g; Fiber 1g; Chol 46mg; Iron: 2mg; Sodium 721mg; Calc 37mg

October

A Fall Harvest Dinner Party

This sophisticated yet easy-to-make menu is perfect for celebrating a cool, crisp October evening with friends.

Autumn Menu

SERVES 6

Roasted Grape Chutney with cheese and crackers

Rosemary-Garlic Pork With Roasted Vegetables & Caramelized Apples

Hearts of Romaine Salad

Caramelized Onion Flatbread

Rich Chocolate Tart

The South seems to breathe a collective sigh of relief when October rolls around. There's a welcomed reprieve from steamy summer days. The onset of football season. (Go team!) And the delicious aromas of hearty, cool-weather food pouring out of the oven. These unforgettable seasonal recipes are made for entertaining. From warm brie topped with delicious Roasted Grape Chutney to a mouthwatering Rosemary-Garlic Pork With Roasted Vegetables & Caramelized Apples, this menu will leave you and your guests craving more cool autumn nights.

Roasted Grape Chutney

make ahead

MAKES 1⅓ CUPS
HANDS-ON TIME: 10 MIN.
TOTAL TIME: 1 HR.

1 cup seedless red grapes, halved
1 cup seedless green grapes, halved
1 Tbsp. olive oil
1 Tbsp. red wine vinegar
1 tsp. dried thyme
½ tsp. kosher salt
¼ tsp. pepper

1. Preheat oven to 425°. Stir together all ingredients. Spread grape mixture on an aluminum foil-lined baking sheet. Bake 20 minutes or until grapes begin to shrivel. Remove from oven, and let cool 30 minutes. Store in refrigerator up to 3 days.

Rosemary-Garlic Pork With Roasted Vegetables & Caramelized Apples

MAKES 6 SERVINGS
HANDS-ON TIME: 41 MIN.
TOTAL TIME: 2 HR., 24 MIN. (INCLUDING CARAMELIZED APPLES)

1 lb. carrots, peeled and cut into
   2-inch pieces
1 lb. parsnips, peeled and cut into
   2-inch pieces
2 medium-size sweet onions, quartered
3 tsp. salt, divided
1½ tsp. freshly ground pepper, divided
⅓ cup olive oil, divided
3 Tbsp. fresh rosemary leaves, divided
1 (4-lb.) boneless pork loin roast
Kitchen string
2 Tbsp. Dijon mustard
4 garlic cloves, coarsely chopped
6 large garlic bulbs
¼ cup apple cider vinegar
Caramelized Apples

1. Preheat oven to 425°. Combine first 3 ingredients in a large bowl; sprinkle with 1 tsp. salt and ½ tsp. pepper.
2. Sauté vegetables in 3 Tbsp. hot oil in a 7½-qt. roasting pan over medium-high heat 8 minutes or until caramelized. Remove from heat, and stir in 1 Tbsp. rosemary.
3. Tie pork with kitchen string, securing at 1-inch intervals. Sprinkle pork with remaining 2 tsp. salt and 1 tsp. pepper, and place on top of vegetables in pan. Stir together mustard, chopped garlic, 2 Tbsp. olive oil, and remaining 2 Tbsp. rosemary; spread over pork.
4. Cut off pointed ends of garlic bulbs. Drizzle with remaining 1 tsp. oil. Arrange garlic bulbs, cut sides down, around pork in pan.
5. Bake at 425° for 1 hour and 10 minutes or until a meat thermometer inserted into thickest portion of pork registers 160°. Let stand 10 minutes.
6. Transfer pork and vegetables to a serving platter, reserving drippings in pan. Add apple cider vinegar to pan, and bring to a boil over medium-high heat; reduce heat to medium, and

simmer, stirring often, 3 minutes or until thickened. Pour over vegetables. Slice pork, and serve with roasted vegetables, garlic bulbs, and Caramelized Apples.

Caramelized Apples:

MAKES 6 SERVINGS

HANDS-ON TIME: 10 MIN.

TOTAL TIME: 18 MIN.

¼ cup firmly packed dark brown sugar
4 Pink Lady apples, quartered
4 Granny Smith apples, quartered
Salt and pepper
2 Tbsp. olive oil

1. Rub brown sugar on cut sides of apples; sprinkle with desired amount of salt and pepper.
2. Cook apples in hot oil in a 12-inch skillet over medium-high heat 8 minutes or until caramelized and crisp-tender.

Hearts of Romaine Salad

MAKES 8 SERVINGS

HANDS-ON TIME: 15 MIN.

TOTAL TIME: 45 MIN.

¼ cup extra virgin olive oil
¼ cup Champagne vinegar or white wine vinegar
2 Tbsp. minced shallots
1 Tbsp. whole-grain Dijon mustard
2 tsp. honey
¾ tsp. salt
¼ tsp. freshly ground pepper
4 romaine lettuce hearts
8 radishes, halved and thinly sliced
Garnishes: freshly shaved Parmesan cheese, chopped fresh chives

1. Whisk together first 7 ingredients until blended. Cover and chill 30 minutes. (Dressing may be stored in refrigerator up to 3 days.)
2. Cut romaine hearts in half lengthwise, keeping leaves intact. Arrange halves on individual serving plates. Sprinkle with radishes. Drizzle with vinaigrette. Season with salt and pepper to taste. Garnish, if desired.

Top Fall Reds for $12 or less

Food Executive Editor Scott Jones shares his top red wines to pair with this festive menu.

Hogue: Cabernet/Merlot, Washington
Meridian Vineyards: Pinot Noir, California
Columbia Crest: Grand Estates Shiraz, Washington
Concha y Toro: Carménère, Chile
Bogle Vineyards: Petite Sirah, California

Caramelized Onion Flatbread

MAKES 8 SERVINGS

HANDS-ON TIME: 25 MIN.

TOTAL TIME: 45 MIN.

1 large sweet onion, sliced
3 Tbsp. olive oil, divided
1 lb. bakery pizza dough
1¼ tsp. kosher salt
1 tsp. chopped fresh rosemary

1. Preheat oven to 425°. Sauté onion in 1 Tbsp. hot oil over medium-high heat 15 minutes or until golden brown.
2. Press dough into a 15- x 10-inch jelly-roll pan, pressing to about ¼-inch thickness. Press handle of a wooden spoon into dough to make indentations at 1-inch intervals; drizzle with remaining 2 Tbsp. oil, and sprinkle with salt, rosemary, and caramelized onions.
3. Bake at 425° on lowest oven rack 20 minutes or until lightly browned.

Kitchen Express: Substitute 1 (13.8-oz.) can refrigerated pizza crust dough for bakery pizza dough. Reduce salt to ¾ tsp. Reduce bake time to 10 minutes or until lightly browned.

Rich Chocolate Tart

make ahead

MAKES 12 TO 16 SERVINGS

HANDS-ON TIME: 25 MIN.

TOTAL TIME: 4 HR., 5 MIN.

1½ cups gingersnap crumbs (about 39 cookies)
6 Tbsp. butter, melted
3 Tbsp. powdered sugar
1¾ cups heavy cream
15 oz. bittersweet chocolate, chopped*
1 tsp. vanilla extract
Garnishes: sweetened whipped cream, dried fig halves

1. Preheat oven to 350°. Stir together first 3 ingredients. Firmly press on bottom and up sides of a 9-inch tart pan. Bake 8 to 9 minutes or until fragrant. Cool on a wire rack 30 minutes.
2. Bring cream to a boil in a 3-qt. saucepan over medium-high heat.
3. Process chocolate in a food processor or blender until finely ground. With processor running, pour hot cream and vanilla through food chute in a slow, steady stream, processing until smooth, stopping to scrape down sides as needed.
4. Pour mixture into cooled crust. Chill, uncovered, 3 hours. Garnish, if desired.
*Semisweet chocolate may be substituted.

It's the Great Pumpkin!

Sure, you know it makes a classic holiday pie. But this grand gourd is sensational in soup, bread pudding, cakes, and more.

Pumpkin is a star. It transported Cinderella to the ball in style, was a smash in *The Legend of Sleepy Hollow,* and kept "Peanuts'" Linus awake on Halloween. But pumpkin is more than just a matinee idol—it's one of autumn's favorite flavors. Try these recipes, and you'll agree that Linus was right: The pumpkin is indeed great.

Pumpkin-Acorn Squash Soup

MAKES ABOUT 8 CUPS
HANDS-ON TIME: 45 MIN.
TOTAL TIME: 1 HR., 55 MIN.

Enjoy the hints of ginger and nutmeg in this scrumptious soup.

1 medium-size pumpkin pie (about 3½ lb.)
1 medium-size acorn squash (about 2 lb.)
4 Tbsp. butter, divided
2 Tbsp. honey, divided
½ tsp. salt, divided
1 medium-size sweet onion, chopped
4 tsp. chopped fresh thyme
4½ cups chicken broth
¼ cup half-and-half
1 tsp. cider vinegar
⅛ tsp. ground ginger
⅛ tsp. ground nutmeg
Freshly ground pepper to taste

1. Preheat oven to 400°. Cut pumpkin and squash in half lengthwise, cutting through stem and bottom ends. Reserve seeds for another use. Place pumpkin and squash halves, cut sides up, in an aluminum foil-lined shallow pan.
2. Microwave 2 Tbsp. butter in a microwave-safe bowl at HIGH 25 seconds or until melted; stir in 1 Tbsp. honey and ¼ tsp. salt. Brush cut sides of pumpkin and squash with butter mixture.
3. Bake pumpkin and squash at 400° for 45 minutes or until tender. Let cool completely (about 15 minutes). Scoop out pulp, discarding shells.
4. Melt remaining 2 Tbsp. butter in a Dutch oven over medium heat. Add onion, and sauté 5 minutes or until tender. Add thyme; sauté 1 minute or until fragrant.
5. Stir in broth and pumpkin and squash pulp. Increase heat to medium-high; bring to a boil. Reduce heat to low, and simmer 10 minutes. Remove from heat, and let cool 10 minutes.
6. Process soup, in batches, in a food processor or blender until smooth. Return soup to Dutch oven. Stir in half-and-half, next 4 ingredients, and remaining 1 Tbsp. honey and ¼ tsp. salt. Cook over low heat, stirring often, 3 minutes or until thoroughly heated. Serve immediately.

Kitchen Express Roasted Pumpkin-Acorn Squash Soup: Substitute 1 (15-oz.) can pumpkin for fresh pumpkin pie and 2 (12-oz.) packages frozen cooked pureed squash, thawed, for fresh acorn squash. Decrease butter to 2 Tbsp. Omit Steps 1, 2, and 3. Proceed with Steps 4 through 6, simmering 6 minutes in Step 5 and stirring in 2 Tbsp. honey and ½ tsp. salt with half-and-half in Step 6. Hands-on time: 30 min.; Total time: 55 min.
Note: We tested with Publix Cooked Squash. Be sure to use unsweetened squash puree for best results.

Caramel-Pecan-Pumpkin Bread Puddings
editor's favorite
MAKES 11 SERVINGS
HANDS-ON TIME: 27 MIN.
TOTAL TIME: 9 HR., 22 MIN.

Bread Puddings:

4 large eggs
2 (15-oz.) cans pumpkin
1½ cups milk
1 cup half-and-half
1 cup granulated sugar
1 tsp. ground cinnamon
½ tsp. salt
½ tsp. ground nutmeg
½ tsp. vanilla extract
1 (12-oz.) French bread loaf, cut into
    1-inch pieces (about 10 cups)

Caramel-Pecan Sauce:

1 cup pecans, chopped
1 cup firmly packed light brown sugar
½ cup butter
1 Tbsp. light corn syrup
1 tsp. vanilla extract

1. Prepare Bread Puddings: Whisk together eggs and next 8 ingredients in a large bowl until well blended. Add bread pieces, stirring to thoroughly coat. Cover with plastic wrap, and chill 8 to 24 hours.
2. Preheat oven to 350°. Spoon bread mixture into 11 (6-oz.) lightly greased ramekins. (Ramekins will be completely full, and mixture will mound slightly.) Place on an aluminum foil-lined jelly-roll pan.
3. Bake at 350° for 50 minutes, shielding with foil after 30 minutes.
4. During last 15 minutes of baking, prepare Caramel-Pecan Sauce: Heat pecans in a medium skillet over medium-low heat, stirring often, 3 to 5 minutes or until lightly toasted and fragrant.
5. Cook brown sugar, butter, and corn syrup in a small saucepan over medium heat, stirring occasionally, 3 to 4 minutes or until sugar is dissolved. Remove from heat; stir in vanilla and pecans.

6. Remove bread puddings from oven; drizzle with Caramel-Pecan Sauce. Bake 5 minutes or until sauce is thoroughly heated and begins to bubble.

RECIPE FROM STEPHANIE BYWATER

HOLLADAY, UTAH

One-Dish Caramel-Pecan-Pumpkin Bread Pudding: Prepare recipe as directed in Step 1. Spoon chilled bread mixture into a lightly greased 13- x 9-inch baking dish. Cover with aluminum foil. Bake, covered, at 350° for 35 minutes. Uncover and bake 15 minutes. Proceed with recipe as directed in Steps 4 through 6.

Mini Pumpkin Cakes

MAKES 8 PUMPKINS
HANDS-ON TIME: 30 MIN.
TOTAL TIME: 1 HR., 44 MIN. (INCLUDING CARAMEL-RUM GLAZE)

¾ cup butter, softened
1 (8-oz.) package cream cheese, softened
2 cups sugar
2 large eggs
1½ cups canned pumpkin
½ tsp. vanilla extract
3 cups all-purpose flour
1 tsp. pumpkin pie spice
½ tsp. baking powder
½ tsp. baking soda
½ tsp. salt
Caramel-Rum Glaze*

1. Preheat oven to 350°. Beat butter and cream cheese at medium speed with an electric mixer until creamy. Gradually add sugar, beating until light and fluffy. Add eggs, 1 at a time, beating just until blended after each addition. Stir in pumpkin and vanilla.
2. Combine flour and next 4 ingredients; gradually add to butter mixture, beating at low speed just until blended. Spoon batter into 2 lightly greased pumpkin-shaped muffin pans, filling three-fourths full.
3. Bake at 350° for 24 to 26 minutes or until a wooden pick inserted in center comes out clean. Cool in pans on wire racks 5 minutes. Remove from pans to wire racks, and cool completely (about 30 minutes).
4. Cut rounded tops off muffins to make them flat. Invert top muffins onto bottom muffins, forming pumpkins. Drizzle Caramel-Rum Glaze over pumpkins. Decorate with Caramel Stems, Leaves, and Vines (see page 230), if desired.
*Vanilla Glaze may be substituted.
Note: We tested with Wilton Dimensions Multi-Cavity Mini Pumpkin Pans. Only have one pan? Bake batter in two batches, washing and drying pan between batches.

Caramel-Rum Glaze:

MAKES ABOUT 1½ CUPS
HANDS-ON TIME: 15 MIN.
TOTAL TIME: 15 MIN.

1 cup firmly packed brown sugar
½ cup butter
¼ cup evaporated milk
1 cup powdered sugar, sifted
1 Tbsp. rum

1. Bring first 3 ingredients to a boil in a 2-qt. saucepan over medium heat, whisking constantly; boil, whisking constantly, 1 minute. Remove from heat; gradually whisk in powdered sugar and rum until smooth. Whisk gently 3 to 5 minutes or until mixture begins to cool and thickens slightly. Use immediately.

Vanilla Glaze:

MAKES 1 CUP
HANDS-ON TIME: 5 MIN.
TOTAL TIME: 5 MIN.

2 cups powdered sugar, sifted
1 tsp. vanilla extract
3 to 4 Tbsp. milk

1. Stir together first 2 ingredients and 3 Tbsp. milk, adding up to 1 Tbsp. additional milk for desired consistency. Use immediately.

Test Kitchen Favorite

Find this decorative baking pan at wilton.com. The pumpkin tops are at each corner.

top

bottom

Here's how to get the October cover look

- **Caramel Stem:** Press 1 caramel between fingers, lengthening to 1½ to 2 inches to form a stem. Curl stem gently.
- **Caramel Leaves:** Roll caramels into 2-inch squares on a flat surface, using a rolling pin. Cut into leaves using a paring knife. Gently press tips of leaves to flatten, if desired. Score leaves, using a paring knife. Pinch bottoms of leaves together.
- **Caramel Vines:** Cut 1 caramel into 3 equal pieces. Squeeze each piece gently to flatten, and roll between hands or on a flat surface into a long thin rope. Twist ends to curl.

Mini Pumpkin-Molasses Cakes

MAKES 4 PUMPKINS
HANDS-ON TIME: 20 MIN.
TOTAL TIME: 1 HR., 34 MIN. (INCLUDING CARAMEL-RUM GLAZE)

½ cup butter, softened
¾ cup firmly packed brown sugar
1 large egg
1 cup canned pumpkin
¼ cup molasses
1¾ cups all-purpose flour
1 Tbsp. baking soda
¾ tsp. ground ginger
¼ tsp. salt
Caramel-Rum Glaze* (see page 229)

1. Preheat oven to 375°. Beat butter at medium speed with an electric mixer until creamy; gradually add brown sugar, beating well. Add egg, beating until blended. Add canned pumpkin and molasses, beating well.

2. Combine flour and next 3 ingredients; gradually add to pumpkin mixture, beating at low speed just until blended. Spoon into a lightly greased pumpkin-shaped muffin pan, filling three-fourths full.

3. Bake at 375° for 24 to 26 minutes or until a wooden pick inserted in center comes out clean. Cool in pan on wire rack 5 minutes. Remove from pan to wire rack, and cool completely (about 30 minutes).

4. Cut rounded tops off muffins to make them flat. Invert top muffins onto bottom muffins, forming pumpkins. Drizzle glaze over pumpkins. Decorate with Caramel Stems, Leaves, and Vines, if desired.

*Vanilla Glaze may be substituted.
Note: We tested with Wilton Dimensions Multi-Cavity Mini Pumpkin Pan.

Pumpkin Crisp

test kitchen favorite

MAKES 8 TO 10 SERVINGS
HANDS-ON TIME: 15 MIN.
TOTAL TIME: 1 HR., 25 MIN.

One of our Food staffers, who shall remain anonymous, ate half a pan of this easy and fabulous dessert.

1 (15-oz.) can pumpkin
1 cup evaporated milk
1 cup sugar
1 tsp. vanilla extract
½ tsp. ground cinnamon
1 (18.25-oz.) package butter-flavored yellow cake mix
1 cup chopped pecans
1 cup butter, melted
Whipped cream (optional)
Ground nutmeg (optional)

1. Preheat oven to 350°. Stir together first 5 ingredients. Pour into a lightly greased 13- x 9-inch baking dish. Sprinkle cake mix evenly over pumpkin mixture; sprinkle evenly with pecans. Drizzle butter evenly over pecans.

2. Bake at 350° for 1 hour to 1 hour and 5 minutes or until golden brown. Remove from oven, and let stand 10 minutes before serving. Serve warm or at room temperature with Whipped cream, if desired. Sprinkle with nutmeg, if desired.
Note: We tested with Betty Crocker Super Moist Butter Recipe Yellow Cake Mix.

Roasted Pumpkin Seeds

MAKES ABOUT 1 CUP
HANDS-ON TIME: 5 MIN.
TOTAL TIME: 40 MIN.

Roasted Pumpkin Seeds make a healthy topping for salads or soup. Also known as "pepitas," pumpkin seeds are a great source of many vitamins. You can also roast acorn squash seeds using this method.

1 cup shelled, raw pumpkin seeds*
2 tsp. olive oil
¼ tsp. ground thyme
¼ tsp. salt
⅛ tsp. pepper

1. Preheat oven to 350°. Rinse seeds, and pat dry. Toss together seeds and remaining ingredients in a bowl. Spread in a single layer on an aluminum foil-lined or parchment paper-lined baking sheet. Bake 20 to 25 minutes or until toasted. Cool completely in pan (about 15 minutes).
*Fresh pumpkin seeds may be substituted.

Can't-Miss Veggie Combos

One vegetable is a lowly, lonely side dish. Two or more together? A delicious, healthful hit.

From Our Kitchen

Perfect Roasted Vegetables

Coat cut-up vegetables with oil, and sprinkle with salt and seasonings of your choice. Spread on a baking sheet or broiler pan, leaving plenty of space between veggies so they'll caramelize, not steam. Bake at 425° until crisp-tender, about 15 to 20 minutes, depending on the size and density of the vegetables.

Glazed Fall Vegetables

MAKES 6 SERVINGS
HANDS-ON TIME: 20 MIN.
TOTAL TIME: 1 HR., 20 MIN.

2 sweet potatoes (about 2 lb.)
1 medium-size baking potato (8 oz.)
1 medium-size acorn squash (about 2 lb.)
3 carrots, cut into ½-inch slices
⅓ cup firmly packed brown sugar
2 Tbsp. maple syrup
2 Tbsp. melted butter
1 tsp. vanilla extract
½ tsp. ground cinnamon
Salt to taste

1. Preheat oven to 425°. Peel sweet potatoes and baking potato; cut into 1-inch cubes. Halve, peel, and seed acorn squash; cut into 1-inch cubes. Combine potatoes, squash, and carrots in a large bowl.
2. Stir together brown sugar, maple syrup, and next 3 ingredients in a small bowl; pour over vegetable mixture, and toss well. Pour into a lightly greased roasting pan.
3. Bake at 425° for 1 hour or until vegetables are tender and lightly browned, stirring every 20 minutes. Season with salt to taste.

—**KAREN C. GREENLEE,** LAWRENCEVILLE, GEORGIA

Crumb-Topped Brussels Sprouts and Cauliflower

MAKES 6 SERVINGS
HANDS-ON TIME: 16 MIN.
TOTAL TIME: 26 MIN.

This dish showcases the complementary colors and flavors of the vegetables.

2 Tbsp. butter
1 garlic clove, pressed
¼ cup Italian-seasoned breadcrumbs
½ tsp. salt, divided
2¼ cups trimmed Brussels sprouts (about 1 lb.), halved
2 (10-oz.) packages fresh cauliflower florets (about 3 cups)
1 tsp. fresh lemon juice
¼ tsp. freshly ground pepper

1. Melt butter in a small skillet over medium heat; add garlic, and sauté 1 minute. Stir in breadcrumbs and ¼ tsp. salt, and cook, stirring occasionally, 3 to 4 minutes or until lightly toasted. Remove from heat.
2. Arrange Brussels sprouts in a steamer basket over boiling water. Cover and steam 8 minutes or until crisp-tender. Add cauliflower. Cover and steam 2 to 3½ minutes or just until tender. Transfer Brussels sprouts and cauliflower to a serving dish; sprinkle with lemon juice, pepper, and remaining ¼ tsp. salt, and toss to combine. Sprinkle with breadcrumb mixture; serve immediately.

Our staff is hooked on frozen steam-in-the-bag microwaveable vegetables. We also love budget-friendly steamer bags for fresh veggies. Look for them on the grocery store aisle with aluminum foil and plastic wrap.

HALF-HOUR HOSTESS

Your Easy Halloween Party

This ghostly pumpkin, a blood orange martini, and BBQ sliders get a party going in 30 minutes or less.

Festive Fall Get-together

SERVES 12

The Great White Pumpkin Cheese Ball

Easy Barbecue Sliders

Blood Orange Martinis

Grilled Ratatouille
family favorite

MAKES 4 SERVINGS;
HANDS-ON TIME: 33 MIN.,
TOTAL TIME: 1 HR., 3 MIN.

Serve this as a light, fresh side, or incorporate it into other dishes.

1 medium zucchini
1 small eggplant
2 tsp. salt, divided
2 Tbsp. olive oil
2 garlic cloves, chopped
1 tsp. chopped fresh thyme leaves
¼ tsp. pepper
1 red or green bell pepper, cut into 1-inch
    pieces
1 medium onion, coarsely chopped
1 cup grape tomatoes, halved
Garnishes: chopped fresh basil, fresh thyme
    sprigs

1. Cut zucchini in half lengthwise; cut lengthwise into ¼-inch-thick slices. Peel eggplant, and cut into 1-inch cubes. Sprinkle eggplant with 1 tsp. salt, and let stand 30 minutes.
2. Meanwhile, stir together olive oil, next 3 ingredients, and remaining 1 tsp. salt. Let stand 20 minutes. Rinse eggplant, and pat dry.
3. Preheat grill to 300° to 350° (medium) heat. Combine eggplant, zucchini, bell pepper, onion, and olive oil mixture in a large bowl, tossing to combine. Grill vegetable mixture in a lightly greased grill wok or metal basket, stirring occasionally, 15 minutes. Stir in tomatoes, and grill 3 more minutes or until tomatoes are tender. Garnish, if desired.

Ratatouille Quesadillas
family favorite

MAKES 2 SERVINGS;
HANDS-ON TIME: 13 MIN.,
TOTAL TIME: 1 HR., 16 MIN. (INCLUDING RATATOUILLE)

1. Spoon ⅓ cup coarsely chopped Grilled Ratatouille onto 2 (8-inch) soft taco-size flour tortillas. Sprinkle each with ⅓ cup grated pepper Jack cheese, and top each with a tortilla. Cook quesadillas, in batches, in a lightly greased nonstick skillet over medium heat 2 to 3 minutes on each side or just until cheese melts and outside browns.

Mediterranean Orzo

MAKES 4 TO 6 SERVINGS;
HANDS-ON TIME: 15 MIN.,
TOTAL TIME: 1 HR., 18 MIN. (INCLUDING RATATOUILLE)

1. Prepare 8 oz. uncooked orzo pasta according to package directions. Stir in ¼ cup chopped pitted kalamata olives; ¼ cup chopped fresh parsley; 2 Tbsp. olive oil; ½ tsp. lemon zest; and 2 tsp. fresh lemon juice. Transfer to a serving platter. Spoon warm Grilled Ratatouille over orzo mixture; sprinkle with ½ (8-oz.) package feta cheese with basil and tomato, crumbled.

Recipe Note

For our photo, we used one block each of Cracker Barrel Extra-Sharp Cheddar and Extra-Sharp White Cheddar cheese.

The Great White Pumpkin Cheese Ball

fast fixin's • make ahead

MAKES 12 APPETIZER SERVINGS
TOTAL TIME: 15 MIN.

2 (10-oz.) blocks extra-sharp white Cheddar cheese, shredded*
1 (8-oz.) package cream cheese, softened
2 (4-oz.) goat cheese logs, softened
½ tsp. pepper
Braided pretzel
Muscadine vine and leaf
Crackers and assorted vegetables

1. Stir together first 4 ingredients. Shape mixture into a ball to resemble a pumpkin. Smooth pumpkin's entire surface with metal spatula or table knife. Make vertical grooves in ball, if desired, using fingertips. Press pretzel into top of cheese ball to resemble a pumpkin stem; place muscadine vine and leaf beside pretzel. Serve with crackers and assorted vegetables.
*Extra-sharp Cheddar cheese may be substituted.

Note: We tested with Cracker Barrel Extra-Sharp Cheddar Cheese.
To make ahead, wrap cheese ball in plastic wrap, without stem, vine, or leaf, and store in refrigerator up to two days. Attach stem, vine, and leaf before serving.

Easy Barbecue Sliders
Ready in about 10 minutes.

1. Bake 2 (12-oz.) packages French rolls, split, according to package directions. Serve 1½ lb. shredded barbecued pork on rolls with barbecue sauce and coleslaw. Makes 18 appetizer servings. Total Time: 10 min.
Note: We tested with Pepperidge Farm Hot & Crusty French Rolls.

Blood Orange Martinis

1. Combine 1 cup chilled vodka, 1 cup chilled blood orange juice,* 1 cup chilled apple juice, ½ cup chilled orange liqueur, and, if desired, red liquid food coloring; pour over ice into chilled martini glasses. Makes 3½ cups. Total Time: 5 min.
*Pomegranate or orange juice may be substituted.

TIP

We used Grand Marnier as the orange liqueur in our Blood Orange Martinis.

MAMA'S WAY OR YOUR WAY?

Apple Dumplings: Quick or Classic

One is from scratch, capturing apples at their peak. The other is easy enough for your busiest day.

RECIPES FROM PEGGY BAKER AND ANNE LIVINGSTON
BIRMINGHAM, ALABAMA

Why We Love Mama's Way

Recipe from Peggy Baker

- Tender, homemade dough
- Rich spiced syrup
- 40-minute bake time

Why We Love Your Way

Recipe from Anne Livingston

- Only 6 ingredients
- Uses a refrigerated piecrust
- 20-minute bake time

Peggy's Classic Apple Dumplings

MAKES 6 SERVINGS
HANDS-ON TIME: 30 MIN.
TOTAL TIME: 1 HR., 15 MIN.

1½ cups sugar
½ tsp. ground cinnamon, divided
½ tsp. ground nutmeg, divided
2 Tbsp. butter
2¼ cups all-purpose flour
2 tsp. baking powder
½ tsp. salt
⅔ cup shortening
6 small Rome apples (about 1¾ lb.)
½ cup milk
⅓ cup sugar
¼ cup butter, cut into 6 equal pieces
½ cup chopped pecans, toasted

1. Preheat oven to 375°. Combine 1½ cups sugar, ¼ tsp. cinnamon, and ¼ tsp. nutmeg in a saucepan. Stir in 1½ cups water; bring to a boil. Reduce heat; simmer, stirring occasionally, 5 minutes. Remove from heat; stir in 2 Tbsp. butter. Combine flour, baking powder, and salt. Cut in shortening with a pastry blender until crumbly. Cover and chill. Meanwhile, peel and core apples.
2. Stir milk into flour mixture until moistened. Turn out onto a lightly floured surface, and knead 3 to 4 times. Roll into an 18- x 12-inch rectangle. Cut into 6 (6-inch) squares. Place 1 apple in center of each square.
3. Combine ⅓ cup sugar and remaining ¼ tsp. cinnamon and ¼ tsp. nutmeg; sprinkle over apples. Press 1 piece of butter into each apple center. Moisten edges of dough with water; fold dough over apples, pinching edges to seal. Place dumplings in a lightly greased 13- x 9-inch baking dish. Pour sugar syrup over dumplings.
4. Bake at 375° for 40 minutes or until golden brown. Sprinkle with pecans.

Anne's Quick Apple Dumpling Bundles

MAKES 4 SERVINGS
HANDS-ON TIME: 20 MIN.
TOTAL TIME: 40 MIN.

Test Kitchen Secret: Toasting pecans deepens their natural buttery sweetness. Keep them on hand by refrigerating shelled pecans (toasted or untoasted) in an airtight container for up to three months or freeze up to six months.

½ cup chopped pecans
½ (15-oz.) package refrigerated piecrusts
1 (12-oz.) package frozen spiced apples, thawed
1 egg white, lightly beaten
Sugar
1 (12-oz.) jar caramel topping, warmed

1. Preheat oven to 350°. Bake pecans in a single layer in a shallow pan 5 to 6 minutes or until toasted and fragrant. Remove from oven; increase oven temperature to 425°.
2. Unroll piecrust on a lightly floured surface. Cut piecrust into fourths. Divide apples among each fourth, placing in center. Pull corners together over apples, pinching edges to seal. Place on a lightly greased aluminum foil-lined baking sheet; brush with egg white, and sprinkle with sugar.
3. Bake at 425° for 20 to 22 minutes or until golden. Serve apple bundles with caramel topping. Sprinkle with pecans.
Note: We tested with Stouffer's Harvest Apples and Smucker's Caramel Flavored Topping.

Mac and Cheese From Scratch

It takes only three simple steps to make the rich sauce for this melt-in-your-mouth mainstay.

Classic Baked Macaroni and Cheese

MAKES 6 TO 8 SERVINGS
HANDS-ON TIME: 22 MIN.
TOTAL TIME: 47 MIN.

Whisk warm milk into the flour mixture to ensure a lump-free sauce. We also recommend shredding your own cheese for a creamier texture. We tested with Cracker Barrel Extra-Sharp Cheddar.

2 cups milk
2 Tbsp. butter
2 Tbsp. all-purpose flour
½ tsp. salt
¼ tsp. freshly ground black pepper
1 (10-oz.) block extra-sharp Cheddar cheese, shredded
¼ tsp. ground red pepper (optional)
½ (16-oz.) package elbow macaroni, cooked

Three Easy Steps

1. Whisk Flour into Butter Preheat oven to 400°. Microwave milk at HIGH for 1½ minutes. Melt butter in a large skillet or Dutch oven over medium-low heat; whisk in flour until smooth. Cook, whisking constantly, 1 minute.

2. Whisk in Warm Milk Gradually whisk in warm milk, and cook, whisking constantly, 5 minutes or until thickened.

3. Whisk in Cheese Whisk in salt, black pepper, 1 cup shredded cheese, and, if desired, red pepper until smooth; stir in pasta. Spoon pasta mixture into a lightly greased 2-qt. baking dish; top with remaining cheese. Bake at 400° for 20 minutes or until golden and bubbly.

Healthy Living.

This busy Houston mom and chef shares her secrets for getting her entire family to eat well.

Staying Healthy On the Go

Houston mom and chef Domenica Catelli shows that eating well is easier than you think—no matter how busy you are.

Domenica Catelli was born to love good food. From strong Italian roots and growing up in the family restaurant business, this health-minded chef developed a knack for cooking early on. "By age 3, I was helping my grandmother roll out fresh pasta dough like a pro," she says. "At age 11, I threw my first dinner party."

Now, this seasoned chef is raising her own family. "Other moms are costantly asking me for fast and fresh recipes that their families will love," says Domenica, "so I decided to reach out to them with a cookbook, *Mom-a-licious* (Waterside Productions, 2007), geared toward busy moms just like me."

Basic Tomato Sauce

chef recipe • fast fixin's

MAKES 2⅔ CUPS
HANDS-ON TIME: 30 MIN.
TOTAL TIME: 30 MIN.

Domenica's spicy Basic Tomato Sauce inspired a supper favorite—Hawaiian Pizza. Reduce or omit the dried crushed red pepper for a milder sauce.

4 to 5 garlic cloves, minced
½ tsp. dried crushed red pepper
2 Tbsp. extra virgin olive oil
1 (28-oz.) can crushed tomatoes
½ tsp. salt

1. Sauté garlic and crushed pepper in hot oil in a large saucepan over medium heat 1 minute. (Do not brown garlic.) Stir in tomatoes and salt. Bring sauce to a boil, reduce heat to low, and simmer, stirring occasionally, 15 minutes.

ADAPTED FROM *MOM-A-LICIOUS*,
BY **DOMENICA CATELLI**

Per ⅓ cup: Calories 65; fat 3.8g (sat 0.6g, mono 2.6g, poly 0.6g); Protein 1.8g; Carb 7.9g; Fiber 2g; Chol 0mg; Iron 1.3mg; Sodium 277mg; Calc 38mg

TIP

Use a pasta shape that will capture your sauce, such as penne rigate.

Hawaiian Pizza: Preheat oven to 450°. Spread 3 Tbsp. Basic Tomato Sauce over each of 4 small individual prebaked pizza crusts (2 [7-oz.] packages). Top each with ¼ cup diced smoked ham, ¼ cup chopped fresh pineapple, and 1 Tbsp. diced green bell pepper. Sprinkle each with 2 Tbsp. shredded part-skim mozzarella cheese. Bake on middle oven rack 10 to 12 minutes. Makes 4 servings. Hands-On Time: 10 min., Total Time: 50 min. (including Basic Tomato Sauce)
Note: We tested with Natural Gourmet Kabuli Pizza Crust.

Per pizza: Calories 420; fat 7.7g (sat 2.9g, mono 3.6g, poly 0.7g); Protein 22.8g; Carb 65g; Fiber 6g; Chol 40mg; Iron 2.1mg; Sodium 607mg; Calc 151mg

TIP

Use smaller prebaked crusts for individual pizzas or large rounds to serve a crowd.

Shrimp Creole: Sauté 1 small onion, chopped, and ½ cup each of chopped green bell pepper and celery in 2 tsp. hot olive oil in a large nonstick skillet 5 to 7 minutes. Stir in Basic Tomato Sauce, ¼ cup water, and ½ tsp. Creole seasoning. Bring to a boil; reduce heat, and simmer 20 minutes. Stir in 1 lb. peeled, large raw shrimp (21/25 count). Cover and simmer 5 to 6 minutes or just until shrimp turn pink. Serve over hot cooked rice. Makes 6 servings. Hands-on Time: 25 min., Total Time: 1 hr., 35 min. (including Basic Tomato Sauce)

Per serving (including 1 cup cooked rice): Calories 226; fat 8g (sat 1.2g, mono 4.7g, poly 1.6g); Protein 18.8g; Carb 21.5g; Fiber 3.4g; Chol 115mg; Iron 4.1mg; Sodium 545mg; Calc 102mg

Domenica loves to cook easy recipes that are also good for you

Between TV appearances, book signings, and the planned 2010 re-opening of her family restaurant, Catelli's, in Geyserville, California, Domenica still manages to feed her family well. We spent some quality time with the busy mom and learned a few of her tips on healthy cooking, smart shopping, and looking forever twentysomething. Her real age? Read on.

How do you stay in shape for those skinny jeans? (Really)

I believe that the type of food I eat (nonprocessed, natural, organic) really helps me maintain my health and weight. Exercise is a struggle, but I force myself to do it. I don't eat many sweets nor do I snack late.

I have to ask, how old are you?

My mom always said, "If you are going to lie about your age, lie up." So, with that I would say "50" and the response is, "Wow! You look great for 50!" But in reality—39.

What is your favorite satisfying snack when you know you have a long day ahead?

Hummus with ice-cold salted cucumbers. They give me a boost of energy, I do not feel weighted down, and I get work done!

What is something quick you make for supper that doesn't require a trip to the grocery store or a lot of time in the kitchen?

Pasta! You can create a delicious and satisfying dish with virtually anything in your pantry or fridge.

What's your advice for moms with picky eaters?

Don't give up. Studies suggest that it takes kids up to seven tries to change their picky ways.

What is the number one thing you've learned about food from your mother that you've passed down to your own daughter?

My mother introduced very different foods to me at an early age, so I evolved a multicultural palate. Now, my daughter, Chiara, eats diverse foods—Indian, Japanese, Vietnamese, anything.

What is your best beauty secret that every woman should know?

Water. Always stay hydrated. Also, I don't cake my face or body with petroleum-based products, which can clog pores.

If you could share one ultimate piece of advice with other working moms, what would it be?

Connect! Sometimes moms need an outlet to recharge. A girls' night out lets you share your joys as well as sorrows.

Guiltless French Toast

chef recipe • fast fixin's

MAKES 4 SERVINGS
HANDS-ON TIME: 16 MIN.
TOTAL TIME: 16 MIN.

8 egg whites
¼ cup fresh orange juice
1 Tbsp. vanilla extract
1 tsp. ground cinnamon
4 whole grain bakery bread slices
1 Tbsp. butter
¼ cup maple syrup
Fresh blueberries and kiwi slices

1. Whisk together first 4 ingredients in a shallow dish. Dip bread slices in egg mixture, coating both sides.
2. Melt butter on a griddle or in a large nonstick skillet over medium heat. Place bread slices on hot griddle, and pour remaining egg mixture over bread slices. Cook 3 to 4 minutes on each side or until golden. Drizzle with maple syrup, and top with fruit.

ADAPTED FROM *MOM-A-LICIOUS*,
BY **DOMENICA CATELLI**

Per serving: Calories 220; fat 4.3g (sat 2.1g, mono 1.3g, poly 0.5g); Protein 10.8g; Carb 33.9g; Fiber 2.8g; Chol 8mg; Iron 1.7mg; Sodium 290mg; Calc 58mg

The Tastiest Tailgate Ever

Four easy recipes help you set the perfect game-day party.

In the South, tailgating and football go together like ice and tea. To minimize the pre-party prep and stress—and maximize praise from your guests—try these delicious, make-ahead recipes. Then combine them with a few snacks from your local grocery store or deli, such as a tray of chicken tenders and an assortment of chips and cookies. We guarantee your party will be as much fun as the game!

Game-Day Gathering

SERVES 6 TO 8

Smoky "Pimiento" Cheese Sandwiches

Make-Ahead Muffuletta Party Sandwich

Bacon-Onion Dip

Simple Scotch Shortbread

Southern Sweet Tea

Smoky "Pimiento" Cheese Sandwiches
fast fixin's

MAKES 7 SERVINGS
HANDS-ON TIME: 10 MIN.
TOTAL TIME: 15 MIN.

Cut into smaller sandwiches for easy pickup.

1 (3-oz.) package cream cheese, softened
½ cup mayonnaise
1 tsp. paprika
¼ tsp. salt
2 cups (8 oz.) shredded smoked Cheddar cheese
2 cups (8 oz.) shredded smoked Gouda cheese
½ (8.5-oz.) jar sun-dried tomatoes in oil, drained and chopped
14 bread slices (sourdough and dark wheat)

1. Stir together cream cheese and next 3 ingredients in a large bowl until blended. Stir in shredded cheeses and sun-dried tomatoes until combined.
2. Spread cheese mixture on half of bread slices (about ⅓ cup on each); top with remaining bread slices.

—LORIE ROACH, BUCKATUNNA, MISSISSIPPI

Test Kitchen Notebook

Tailgate Essentials
We never leave home without these:

- Tailgate tent or canopy
- Outdoor chairs and folding table
- Tablecloth
- Packed coolers (soft drinks, beer, wine, bottled water)
- Ice
- Bottle opener and corkscrew
- Drink huggers/koozies
- Paper towels, napkins, and wet wipes
- Hand sanitizer
- Paper or plastic plates, cups, and plastic utensils
- Trash bags
- Your tickets!

—MARION MCGAHEY,
ASSISTANT FOOD EDITOR

Make-Ahead Muffuletta Party Sandwich
make ahead

MAKES 8 SERVINGS
HANDS-ON TIME: 15 MIN.
TOTAL TIME: 8 HR., 15 MIN.

1 cup jarred mixed pickled vegetables, rinsed and finely chopped
¼ cup sliced pimiento-stuffed Spanish olives
2 Tbsp. olive oil
½ tsp. dried crushed red pepper
1 (20-oz.) round Italian bread loaf
⅓ lb. sliced salami
⅓ lb. sliced provolone cheese
⅓ lb. sliced pepperoni

1. Stir together first 4 ingredients.
2. Cut round bread loaf in half horizontally; scoop out bottom, leaving a ½-inch-thick shell.
3. Spoon half of olive mixture into bread shell. Layer with salami, cheese, pepperoni, and remaining olive mixture. Cover with bread top. Wrap loaf tightly with plastic wrap, and chill 8 to 24 hours. Cut loaf into wedges.

Bacon-Onion Dip

fast fixin's • make ahead

MAKES 1¾ CUPS;
HANDS-ON TIME: 10 MIN.,
TOTAL TIME: 10 MIN.

Serve with assorted fresh vegetables.

1 (8-oz.) container sour cream
½ cup cooked and crumbled bacon
2 Tbsp. green onions, sliced
3 Tbsp. buttermilk
1 Tbsp. horseradish
2 tsp. fresh lemon juice
¼ tsp. pepper
½ tsp. salt
Garnish: chopped fresh chives, black pepper

1. Stir together first 8 ingredients. Cover and chill until ready to serve (up to 24 hours). Garnish, if desired.

Try this twist: Blue Cheese-Bacon-Onion Dip: Stir in 1 (4-oz.) package crumbled blue cheese.

Simple Scotch Shortbread

family favorite

MAKES 35 BARS
HANDS-ON TIME: 15 MIN.
TOTAL TIME: 45 MIN.

2 cups butter
1 cup sugar
4 cups all-purpose flour
2 Tbsp. sugar (optional)

1. Preheat oven to 375°. Beat butter at medium speed with an electric mixer until creamy. Gradually add 1 cup sugar, beating until mixture is smooth; add flour, beating until dough forms a ball.
2. Press dough into a 14- x 10-inch jelly-roll pan with floured hands.
3. Bake at 375° for 30 to 35 minutes or until golden brown. Cut immediately into 35 (2-inch) bars. Sprinkle with 2 Tbsp. sugar, if desired

RECIPE FROM RACHEL REED
DEL MAR BEACH, CALIFORNIA

Southern Sweet Tea

test kitchen favorite

MAKES 2 ½ QT.
HANDS-ON TIME: 5 MIN.
TOTAL TIME: 20 MIN.

If you like tea that's really sweet, add the full cup of sugar.

3 cups water
2 family-size tea bags
½ to 1 cup sugar
7 cups cold water

1. Bring 3 cups water to a boil in a saucepan; add tea bags. Boil 1 minute; remove from heat. Cover and steep 10 minutes.
2. Remove and discard tea bags. Add desired amount of sugar, stirring until dissolved.
3. Pour into a 1-gal. container, and add 7 cups cold water. Serve over ice.

Peach Iced Tea: Stir together 1½ qt. Southern Sweet Tea made with ½ cup sugar; add 1 (33.8-oz.) bottle peach nectar and ¼ cup lemon juice. Stir well. Serve over ice. Makes about 2 ½ qt.

Tea 'n' Lemonade: Stir together 2 qt. Southern Sweet Tea made with ½ cup sugar; add 1 cup thawed lemonade concentrate, and stir well. Serve over ice. Makes 2¼ qt.

BEST OF THE SOUTH

MoonPies: What a Hoot!

Easy Owl-ween Treats: Open-faced Oreos, M & M's, candy corn, and sprinkles bring a convenience store treat—a MoonPie—to life. Secure cookies and candy to your MoonPie with melted chocolate candy coating. Then insert a 12- x ¼-inch dowel, available at craft stores, into marshmallow center and secure with more chocolate for an eye-popping, kid-friendly surprise.

"I have a slow cooker. Can you recommend some recipes?"

The answer: two delicious meals for your busy schedule.

Slow-cooker Turkey Chili

MAKES 4 TO 6 SERVINGS
HANDS-ON TIME: 20 MIN.
TOTAL TIME: 6 HR., 20 MIN.

1¼ lb. lean ground turkey
1 large onion, chopped
1 garlic clove, minced
1 (1.25-oz.) envelope chili seasoning mix
1 (12-oz.) can beer
1½ cups frozen corn kernels
1 red bell pepper, chopped
1 green bell pepper, chopped
1 (28-oz.) can crushed tomatoes
1 (15-oz.) can black beans, drained and rinsed
1 (8-oz.) can tomato sauce
¾ tsp. salt
Toppings: shredded Cheddar cheese, finely
    chopped red onion, sliced fresh jalapeños

1. Cook first 4 ingredients in a large skillet over medium-high heat, stirring often, 8 minutes or until turkey crumbles and is no longer pink. Stir in beer, and cook 2 minutes, stirring occasionally. Spoon mixture into a 5½-qt. slow cooker; stir in corn and next 6 ingredients until well blended. Cover and cook on LOW 6 hours. Serve with desired toppings.

Chicken Thighs With Carrots and Potatoes

MAKES 6 SERVINGS
HANDS-ON TIME: 20 MIN.
TOTAL TIME: 6 HR., 20 MIN.

1 medium onion
4 medium-size new potatoes (about 1 lb.)
2 cups baby carrots
¼ cup chicken broth
¼ cup dry white wine or chicken broth
1 tsp. minced garlic
½ tsp. dried thyme
1¼ tsp. salt, divided
½ tsp. pepper, divided
1 tsp. paprika
6 skinned, bone-in chicken thighs

1. Halve onion lengthwise, and cut into ¼-inch-thick slices. Cut potatoes into ¼-inch-thick slices. Place onion in a lightly greased 6-qt. slow cooker; top with potatoes and carrots.
2. Combine broth, next 3 ingredients, ¾ tsp. salt, and ¼ tsp. pepper. Pour over vegetables.
3. Combine paprika and remaining ½ tsp. salt and ¼ tsp. pepper; rub over chicken. Arrange chicken on top of vegetables.
4. Cover and cook on LOW 6 hours or until chicken is done and vegetables are tender.

Tips on buying a slow cooker

Prices range from $25 for a basic, two-temperature-setting (Low/High) model to $125 or more for a programmable, multi-temperature model.

1. Look for a stoneware insert. This dishwasher-, oven-, and microwave-safe insert makes cooking and cleaning a snap.
2. Choose the right size: A standard 2.5-qt. model is fine for two; 3.5- to 5-qt. serves a family of four; larger families need at least a 6-qt. capacity.
3. Determine what's best for your schedule. Programmable models generally let you select a 4- to 6-hour cook time or 8- to 10-hour cycle. A warm setting comes on at the end, and keeps food warm until you're ready.

Y'all Ask Us

Whether you need fresh ideas for your favorite ingredient or have a cooking problem, we're happy to share our Test Kitchen expertise. Ask questions and see answers: southernliving.com/ask-the-tk.

November

This Thanksgiving, Blend New With Tradition

Put the spark back in Thanksgiving with seven fresh recipes we promise will mingle beautifully with your family's time-honored dishes.

Dressed-Up Holiday Dinner

SERVES 8 TO 10

Whiskey Sours

Crab Crostini

Roasted Dry-Rub Turkey With Gravy

Sautéed Green Beans

Smoky Cranberry-Apple Sauce

Cornbread Yeast Rolls

Peanut Butter-Banana Sandwich Bread Puddings With Dark Caramel Sauce

---

Whiskey Sour
fast fixin's
MAKES 1 SERVING
HANDS-ON TIME: 5 MIN.
TOTAL TIME: 5 MIN.

Fresh lemon juice is the key to making a flavorful Whiskey Sour. (Pictured on page 187)

1 lemon half
¼ cup whiskey
1 to 2 Tbsp. powdered sugar
Crushed ice
Garnishes: orange slices, maraschino cherries

1. Squeeze juice from lemon half into a cocktail shaker. Add whiskey and powdered sugar to cocktail shaker; fill with crushed ice. Cover with lid, and shake 30 seconds. Strain into a chilled glass. Garnish with orange slices and maraschino cherries, if desired.
Note: We tested with Gentleman Jack Whiskey.

Crab Crostini
MAKES 8 TO 12 APPETIZER SERVINGS
HANDS-ON TIME: 35 MIN.
TOTAL TIME: 1 HR., 47 MIN.

Say "welcome" to guests with Crab Crostini and Whiskey Sours. (Pictured on page 187)

1 (11-oz.) French bread baguette
2 Tbsp. butter, melted
1 lb. fresh lump crabmeat, drained
2 Tbsp. dry sherry
1 Tbsp. chopped fresh parsley
1½ tsp. hot sauce
¾ tsp. salt, divided
½ cup sour cream
2 Tbsp. mayonnaise
2 tsp. minced green onion
1 tsp. lemon zest
2 tsp. fresh lemon juice
¼ tsp. pepper
Garnish: green onion curls

1. Preheat oven to 350°. Cut bread diagonally into ¼-inch-thick slices (about 40 slices). Place on a baking sheet. Brush tops with butter. Bake 12 to 14 minutes or until golden brown. (Bread may be stored in an airtight container up to 3 days.)
2. Pick crabmeat, removing any bits of shell. Gently toss crab with sherry, parsley, hot sauce, and ½ tsp. salt in a bowl; cover and chill 1 to 24 hours.
3. Meanwhile, stir together sour cream, next 5 ingredients, and remaining ¼ tsp. salt until blended; cover and chill 1 hour to 3 days.
4. Spoon rounded ½ teaspoonfuls sour cream mixture onto each bread slice; top each bread slice evenly with crab mixture. Garnish, if desired. Serve immediately.

Roasted Dry-Rub Turkey With Gravy

MAKES 8 TO 10 SERVINGS
HANDS-ON TIME: 45 MIN.
TOTAL TIME: 3 HR., 10 MIN.
(INCLUDING RUB)

This recipe, with its Paprika-Brown Sugar Rub, yields a turkey with dark crusty skin, even with aluminum shielding. That's good—it will remind you of the crispy outside pieces of barbe-cued meats. (Pictured on page 186)

¼ cup butter, softened
3 garlic cloves, minced
1 Tbsp. chopped fresh thyme
1 (14-lb.) whole fresh turkey
Wooden picks
Paprika-Brown Sugar Rub
2 Granny Smith apples, quartered
Kitchen string
1 (32-oz.) container low-sodium
    chicken broth
3 Tbsp. butter
5 Tbsp. all-purpose flour
Garnishes: whole collard green leaves,
    green apples, lemon slices

1. Preheat oven to 350°. Combine first 3 ingredients.
2. Remove giblets and neck from turkey; pat turkey dry with paper towels. Loosen and lift skin from turkey breast with fingers without totally detaching skin; rub butter mixture underneath skin. Carefully replace skin; secure skin at both ends using wooden picks to pre-vent skin from shrinking.
3. Sprinkle 2 Tbsp. Paprika-Brown Sugar Rub inside cavity. Place apples inside cavity. Tie ends of legs together with string; tuck wingtips under. Place turkey, breast side up, on a rack in a roast-ing pan. Rub 6 Tbsp. Paprika-Brown Sugar Rub over outside of turkey. Pour chicken broth into roasting pan.
4. Bake turkey at 350°, on lowest oven rack, 2 to 2½ hours or until skin is well browned and a meat thermometer inserted into thickest portion of thigh registers 170°, shielding with aluminum foil during last hour of cooking to prevent excessive browning, if neces-sary. (Do not baste.) Transfer turkey to a serving platter, reserving drippings in roasting pan. Let turkey stand 20 min-utes before carving.
5. Meanwhile, pour pan drippings through a fine wire-mesh strainer into a 4-cup glass measuring cup. Let stand 10 minutes. Skim fat from surface of drippings. (Add chicken broth, if needed, to equal 3 cups.)
6. Melt 3 Tbsp. butter over medium heat in a medium saucepan. Whisk in flour, and cook, whisking constantly, 3 to 4 minutes or until golden. Whisk in 3 cups drippings, and bring to a boil over medium-high heat. Reduce heat to low, and simmer 5 minutes, whisking occasionally. Serve with turkey. Garnish, if desired.

Paprika-Brown Sugar Rub:

MAKES ABOUT 1 CUP
HANDS-ON TIME: 5 MIN.
TOTAL TIME: 5 MIN.

1. Combine ½ cup firmly packed brown sugar, 2 Tbsp. kosher salt, 2 Tbsp. smoked paprika, 2 tsp. dried crushed red pepper, 2 tsp. onion powder, 2 tsp. dry mustard, and 1 tsp. coarsely ground pepper. Store in an airtight container up to 4 weeks.

Sautéed Green Beans

MAKES 8 SERVINGS
HANDS-ON TIME: 16 MIN.
TOTAL TIME: 16 MIN.

Cooktop space at a minimum? This dish is just as good at room temperature as it is warm. (Pictured on page 186)

1. Prepare 2 (12-oz.) packages frozen steam-in-bag whole green beans accord-ing to package directions. Sauté 2 minced shallots in 2 Tbsp. butter in a large skillet over medium-high heat 2 to 3 minutes or until tender. Stir in 2 tsp. balsamic vin-egar, green beans, and 1 cup grape tomato halves. Sprinkle with salt and pepper to taste; sauté 2 more minutes.

Smoky Cranberry-Apple Sauce

MAKES 3½ CUPS
HANDS-ON TIME: 25 MIN.
TOTAL TIME: 25 HR., 3 MIN.

We tested with a variety of barbecue sauces and found a sweet-smoky kind, such as Sweet Baby Ray's, worked best with our menu. Find it at Walmart or click on "Product Finder" at sweetbabyrays.com. (Pictured on page 186)

1 (12-oz.) package fresh cranberries
1 cup sugar
¾ cup apple juice
¼ cup minced red onion
2 Tbsp. butter
2 Granny Smith apples, peeled and coarsely
    chopped
½ cup smoky barbecue sauce
Garnish: fresh parsley sprigs

1. Stir together cranberries and next 4 ingredients in a medium saucepan. Bring to a boil over medium-high heat; reduce heat to low, and simmer, stirring occasionally, 10 minutes or until cranberry skins begin to split and pop and mixture begins to thicken.
2. Stir apples and barbecue sauce into cranberry mixture, and simmer 5 min-utes or just until apples are tender. Let cool 30 minutes. Cover and chill 24 hours before serving. Store in refrigera-tor up to 3 days. Let stand 30 minutes before serving. Garnish, if desired.
Note: We tested with Sweet Baby Ray's Original Barbecue Sauce.

Cornbread Yeast Rolls
make ahead

MAKES 18 ROLLS
HANDS-ON TIME: 45 MIN.
TOTAL TIME: 4 HR., 15 MIN.

Food blogger and former Floridian Julie O'Hara inspired this recipe with one on her site, www.aminglingoftastes.com. (Pictured on page 186)

1 (¼-oz.) envelope active dry yeast
1 cup warm water (105° to 115°)
1 Tbsp. sugar
4 cups bread flour, divided
¼ cup honey
4 Tbsp. butter, melted
2 large eggs
1¼ tsp. salt
¾ cup plain yellow cornmeal
Vegetable cooking spray
Parchment paper
2 Tbsp. plain yellow cornmeal
1 large egg, lightly beaten
1 Tbsp. sesame seeds
½ tsp. freshly ground pepper

1. Stir together yeast, 1 cup warm water, and sugar in a 2-cup glass measuring cup; let stand 5 minutes.
2. Beat yeast mixture and 2 cups flour at low speed with a heavy-duty electric stand mixer, using dough hook attachment, until combined. Add honey, butter, 2 eggs, salt, and ¾ cup cornmeal; beat at medium-low speed until well blended, scraping bowl as needed. Gradually beat in 2 remaining cups flour. Continue beating until a dough forms and begins to pull away from sides of bowl. (Dough will be sticky.) Beat dough 1 minute.
3. Coat a large bowl with cooking spray; place dough in bowl, turning to grease top. Cover with plastic wrap, and let rise in a warm place (85°), free from drafts, 2 hours or until doubled in bulk.
4. Line 2 baking sheets with parchment paper; dust each with 1 Tbsp. cornmeal.
5. Punch dough down; turn out onto a lightly floured surface. Knead 1 minute. Shape dough into 18 balls; place on prepared baking sheets. Cover with a clean kitchen towel, and let rise 1 to 1½ hours or until almost doubled in bulk.

6. Preheat oven to 375°. Gently brush rolls with lightly beaten egg, and sprinkle with sesame seeds and pepper. Bake 18 to 22 minutes or until golden on top, browned on bottom, and sound hollow when tapped on base. Let cool on baking sheets 5 minutes. Serve immediately.
Note: To make ahead, prepare recipe as directed through Step 5; cover loosely with plastic wrap or aluminum foil. Chill 24 hours. Uncover and bake as directed in Step 6.

Peanut Butter-Banana Sandwich Bread Puddings With Dark Caramel Sauce

MAKES 8 SERVINGS
HANDS-ON TIME: 25 MIN.
TOTAL TIME: 3 HR., 56 MIN. (INCLUDING TOPPING AND SAUCE)

These puff much like soufflés, so present to guests right out of the oven. Encourage them to hold off enjoying the desserts for 5 minutes while they cool slightly. (Pictured on page 187)

8 buttermilk bread slices, crusts removed
½ cup creamy peanut butter
2 bananas, thinly sliced
2 large eggs
½ cup granulated sugar
2 Tbsp. brown sugar
1¾ cups whipping cream
Peanut Butter Streusel Topping
Dark Caramel Sauce
Garnish: powdered sugar

1. Spread bread slices with peanut butter. Top 4 bread slices with bananas and remaining bread slices, peanut butter sides down, pressing firmly. Cut sandwiches into 1-inch pieces; place in 8 lightly greased (8-oz.) ramekins.
2. Whisk together eggs and sugars; whisk in whipping cream. Gradually pour mixture over sandwich pieces in ramekins; sprinkle with Peanut Butter Streusel Topping. Place ramekins in a 15- x 10-inch jelly-roll pan. Cover and chill 2 to 24 hours.

3. Preheat oven to 375°. Let puddings stand at room temperature 30 minutes. Bake 20 to 25 minutes or until golden brown, set, and puffed. Serve warm with Dark Caramel Sauce. Garnish, if desired.
Note: We tested with Pepperidge Farm Sweet Buttermilk Farmhouse Bread. Bread pudding mixture may be prepared in an 11- x 7-inch baking dish. Bake at 375° for 35 minutes or until golden brown, set, and puffed.

Peanut Butter Streusel Topping:
MAKES 1 CUP
HANDS-ON TIME: 10 MIN.
TOTAL TIME: 10 MIN.

1. Stir together ¼ cup all-purpose flour and ¼ cup firmly packed brown sugar in a bowl. Cut in 2 Tbsp. butter and 2 Tbsp. creamy peanut butter with pastry blender or fork until mixture resembles small peas. Stir in ¼ cup chopped salted peanuts.

Dark Caramel Sauce:
MAKES 1½ CUPS
HANDS-ON TIME: 16 MIN.
TOTAL TIME: 31 MIN.

If you detect a bitter smell after caramelizing the sugar, you might have burned the sugar and need to start over.

1. Cook 1 cup sugar in a 3-qt. heavy saucepan over medium heat 6 to 8 minutes or until sugar caramelizes, tilting and swirling pan to incorporate mixture. Stir in 1 cup whipping cream. (Mixture will bubble and harden.) Cook, stirring constantly, until mixture melts and begins to boil (about 5 minutes). Quickly pour sauce into a bowl; stir in 1 tsp. vanilla extract, and ⅛ to ¼ tsp. salt. Let cool 15 minutes. Serve warm or cool.
Note: To make ahead, cover and chill up to 3 weeks. To reheat, cook, uncovered, in a microwave-safe glass bowl at MEDIUM LOW (30% power) for 2 minutes or until warm, stirring once.

Make-Ahead Turkey Gravy

Make rich, smooth gravy with just-roasted flavor up to three days before your big turkey dinner. We show you how.

Make-Ahead Turkey Gravy

MAKES 4 CUPS
HANDS-ON TIME: 37 MIN.
TOTAL TIME: 1 HR., 52 MIN.

2¼ lb. turkey drumsticks
3 carrots, cut into pieces
1 large onion, quartered
6 fresh parsley sprigs
⅓ cup vegetable oil
½ cup all-purpose flour
6 cups low-sodium chicken broth
½ tsp. pepper
Salt to taste

To make ahead: Cool gravy 45 minutes. Cover and chill up to 3 days. Add a few tablespoons of broth, and reheat over medium heat.

Four Easy Steps

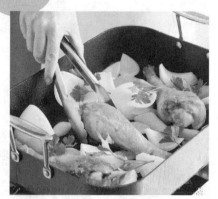

1. Brown drumsticks and veggies. Preheat oven to 400°. Pat drumsticks dry. Cook drumsticks and next 3 ingredients in hot oil in a large roasting pan over medium-high heat. Cook drumsticks 3 minutes on each side; cook vegetables, at the same time, stirring often.

2. Reserve flavorful pan drippings. Bake drumsticks and vegetables in pan at 400° for 30 minutes or until a meat thermometer inserted into thickest portion of drumsticks registers 160°. Remove from oven. Remove and discard vegetables and parsley using a slotted spoon. Reserve drumsticks for another use.

3. Whisk in chicken broth, and stir until smooth. Whisk flour into hot drippings in pan, and cook over medium heat, whisking constantly, 1 minute. Gradually whisk in chicken broth until smooth. Whisk in pepper.

4. Cook gravy to thicken and develop flavor. Bring to a boil over medium-high heat, whisking occasionally. Reduce heat to medium, and gently boil, whisking occasionally, 45 minutes or until thick enough to coat the back of a spoon. Season with salt to taste.

12 New Ways With Pecans

Pecans just say Southern. We coaxed a fresh mix of recipes out of their shells.

1 Turkey-Artichoke-Pecan Salad

Whisk together 5 Tbsp. red wine vinegar, 2 Tbsp. chopped fresh parsley, 2 Tbsp. chopped fresh basil, ½ tsp. salt, and ½ tsp. pepper. Whisk in ¼ cup olive oil until blended. Toss with chopped cooked turkey, coarsely chopped canned artichoke hearts, thinly sliced green onions, chopped toasted pecans, and feta cheese.

2 Pecan-Honey Butter

Stir together ½ cup butter, softened; ½ cup finely chopped toasted pecans; and 2 Tbsp. honey. Store, covered, in refrigerator up to 1 week, or freeze up to 1 month.

Note: Be sure to cool pecans completely after toasting.

3 Pecan-Stuffed Pickled Jalapeños

Cut whole pickled jalapeño peppers in half lengthwise; remove and discard seeds and membranes. Pipe softened spreadable garlic-and-herb cheese into each pepper half. Press peppers, cheese sides down, into chopped toasted pecans. Cover and chill up to 1 day.

4 Chili-Lime Pecans

Stir together 2 Tbsp. lime juice, 1 Tbsp. olive oil, 1 tsp. paprika, 1 tsp. salt, 1 tsp. chili powder, and ½ tsp. ground red pepper. Add 3 cups pecans; toss. Spread in a lightly greased aluminum foil-lined jelly-roll pan. Bake at 350° for 12 to 14 minutes or until pecans are toasted and dry, stirring occasionally. Cool completely.

5 Hot Caramel-Pecan Topping

Cook 1 (19-oz.) jar butterscotch-caramel topping, 1½ cups chopped toasted pecans, 2 Tbsp. whipping cream, 2 Tbsp. maple syrup, and ½ tsp. kosher salt in a saucepan, stirring occasionally, 3 to 5 minutes or until thoroughly heated. Serve warm.

6 Goat Cheese-Pecan Finger Sandwiches

Stir together 4 oz. softened goat cheese, 3 oz. softened cream cheese, ½ cup finely chopped toasted pecans, and 2 Tbsp. chopped fresh parsley. Spread on 7 bread slices. Spread 7 more bread slices with ⅓ cup red pepper jelly; top with cheese-covered bread slices. Remove crusts; cut into desired shapes.

7 Banana-Pecan Smoothies

Process 1½ cups low-fat vanilla yogurt; 2 large ripe bananas, sliced and frozen; 1 cup ice; ½ cup finely chopped toasted pecans; ½ cup milk; 1 Tbsp. honey; and ½ tsp. ground cinnamon in a blender until smooth. Pour into glasses, and serve immediately.

8 Warm Pecan Vinaigrette

Sauté 2 finely chopped shallots in 3 Tbsp. hot oil over medium heat 3 minutes. Stir in ½ cup chopped toasted pecans, 3 Tbsp. apple cider vinegar, 1 Tbsp. Dijon mustard, 1 Tbsp. honey, ¼ tsp. salt, and ¼ tsp. pepper. Reduce heat to low; cook, stirring constantly, until warm.

9 Blue Cheese-Pecan Apples

Arrange 1 thinly sliced Gala apple and 1 thinly sliced Granny Smith apple in overlapping rows on a parchment paper-lined baking sheet. Pinch 1 (5-oz.) soft blue cheese wedge, rind removed, into small pieces; arrange on apples. Bake at 425° for 2 to 3 minutes or just until cheese is melted. Sprinkle with chopped toasted pecans and salt and pepper to taste.

10 Pecan Pesto

Process 4 cups loosely packed fresh basil leaves; 1 cup (4 oz.) freshly shredded Parmesan cheese, 1 cup toasted pecans, 1 cup olive oil, 4 garlic cloves, 2 Tbsp. lemon juice, ½ tsp. salt, and ½ tsp. pepper in a food processor until smooth.

11 Cream Cheese-and-Olive Pecan Bites

Stir together 3-oz. softened cream cheese, ½ cup finely chopped pimiento-stuffed Spanish olives, 1 Tbsp. chopped fresh chives, and ¼ tsp. pepper. Spread onto 40 toasted pecan halves; top with 40 toasted pecan halves, forming sandwiches.

From Our Kitchen

How to Toast Pecans

Toasting pecans brings out even more flavor. Use your sense of smell to judge when they're toasted; the smaller the pieces, the quicker they toast, so don't turn your back!

1. Preheat oven to 350°. Bake pecans in a single layer in a shallow pan until lightly toasted and fragrant, stirring occasionally. (This should take about 8 to 10 minutes.)

12 Croissant French Toast With Pecans

Whisk together ¾ cup half-and-half, 3 large eggs, and 1 tsp. vanilla. Dip 4 day-old croissants, halved, into mixture. Cook ½ cup chopped toasted pecans, ½ cup honey, and 2 Tbsp. butter in a saucepan until hot. Keep warm. Melt 1 Tbsp. butter in a nonstick skillet or griddle over medium heat. Add 4 croissant halves; cook until golden brown. Repeat. Serve with honey mixture. Makes 4 servings. Hands-on time: 20 min., Total time: 20 min.

Four Special Fall Desserts

Showcase the best of autumn with these incredible desserts. Each is delectable and perfect for the holidays, so try them all.

Pumpkin Pie Spectacular

MAKES 8 SERVINGS
HANDS-ON TIME: 20 MIN.
TOTAL TIME: 3 HR., 25 MIN. (INCLUDING STREUSEL AND TOPPING)

Crushed gingersnaps pressed into the crust add a spicy depth of flavor in this fall favorite.

½ (15-oz.) package refrigerated piecrusts
2 cups crushed gingersnaps (about 40 gingersnaps)
1 cup pecans, finely chopped
½ cup powdered sugar
¼ cup butter, melted
1 (15-oz.) can pumpkin
1 (14-oz.) can sweetened condensed milk
2 large eggs, beaten
½ cup sour cream
1 tsp. ground cinnamon
½ tsp. vanilla extract
¼ tsp. ground ginger
Pecan Streusel
7 thin ginger cookies, halved
Ginger-Spice Topping, ground cinnamon

1. Preheat oven to 350°. Fit piecrust into a 9-inch deep-dish pie plate according to package directions; fold edges under, and crimp.
2. Stir together crushed gingersnaps and next 3 ingredients. Press mixture on bottom and ½ inch up sides of piecrust.
3. Bake at 350° for 10 minutes. Let cool completely on a wire rack (about 30 minutes).
4. Stir together pumpkin and next 6 ingredients until well blended. Pour into prepared crust. Place pie on an aluminum foil-lined baking sheet.
5. Bake at 350° for 30 minutes. Sprinkle Pecan Streusel around edge of crust. Bake 40 to 45 minutes or until set, shielding edges with aluminum foil during last 25 to 30 minutes of baking, if necessary. Insert ginger cookies around edge of crust. Let cool completely on a wire rack (about 1 hour). Dollop with Ginger-Spice Topping; dust with cinnamon.
Note: We tested with Anna's Ginger Thins.

Pecan Streusel:

MAKES ABOUT 1 CUP
HANDS-ON TIME: 10 MIN.
TOTAL TIME: 10 MIN.

1. Stir together ¼ cup all-purpose flour; ¼ cup firmly packed dark brown sugar; 2 Tbsp. melted butter; and ¾ cup pecans, coarsely chopped.

Ginger-Spice Topping:

MAKES 3 CUPS
HANDS-ON TIME: 5 MIN.
TOTAL TIME: 5 MIN.

1. Stir together 1 (8-oz.) container frozen whipped topping, thawed; ¼ tsp. ground cinnamon; and ¼ tsp. ground ginger.

—RECIPE FROM VIVIAN CHATEAU, MOBILE, ALABAMA

Upside Down Apple-Pecan-Raisin Pie

MAKES 8 SERVINGS
HANDS-ON TIME: 28 MIN.
TOTAL TIME: 2 HR., 53 MIN.

Sprinkling 1 to 2 tsp. lemon juice over cut apples will help prevent browning.

1 cup pecan halves
4 Tbsp. butter, melted
½ cup firmly packed light brown sugar
1 (15-oz.) package refrigerated piecrusts
½ cup granulated sugar
2 Tbsp. all-purpose flour
½ tsp. ground cinnamon
¼ tsp. freshly grated nutmeg
1½ lb. peeled and sliced Granny Smith or Rome apples (about 3 medium)
1 cup golden raisins
2 Tbsp. butter, cut into pieces

1. Preheat oven to 350°. Bake pecans in a single layer in a shallow pan 8 to 10 minutes or until toasted and fragrant, stirring after 5 minutes. Let cool 30 minutes. Increase oven temperature to 375°.
2. Stir together melted butter and brown sugar. Stir in pecans, and spread mixture on bottom of a lightly greased 9-inch pie plate. Unroll 1 piecrust, and fit into pie plate over top of pecan mixture.
3. Combine granulated sugar and next 3 ingredients in a large bowl. Add apples and raisins, and toss to coat.
4. Spoon apple mixture into prepared crust. Dot butter pieces over apple mixture.
5. Unroll remaining piecrust; place over filling. Fold edges under, and crimp; cut slits in top for steam to escape. Place pie on a baking sheet.
6. Bake at 375° for 50 to 55 minutes, shielding edges with foil during last 30 minutes, if necessary. Cool on a wire rack 5 minutes. Invert pie onto a plate, and let cool 1 hour.

—RECIPE FROM SANDRA PRILL, FRIENDSWOOD, TEXAS

Orange-Sweet Potato Pie With Rosemary-Cornmeal Crust

family favorite

MAKES 8 SERVINGS
HANDS-ON TIME: 35 MIN.
TOTAL TIME: 4 HR., 35 MIN.

Rosemary-Cornmeal Crust:

¾ cup all-purpose flour
½ cup plain white cornmeal
¼ cup powdered sugar
2 tsp. chopped fresh rosemary
¼ tsp. salt
½ cup cold butter, cut into pieces
¼ cup very cold water

Orange-Sweet Potato Filling:

1½ lb. sweet potatoes
3 large eggs
¾ cup granulated sugar
1 cup evaporated milk
3 Tbsp. butter, melted
2 tsp. orange zest
1 Tbsp. fresh orange juice
½ tsp. ground cinnamon
¼ tsp. ground nutmeg
1½ tsp. vanilla extract

1. Prepare Crust: Whisk together first 5 ingredients in a medium bowl until well blended. Cut butter into flour mixture with a pastry blender or fork until mixture resembles small peas and is crumbly.

2. Sprinkle cold water, 1 Tbsp. at a time, over surface of mixture in bowl; stir with a fork until dry ingredients are moistened. Place dough on a plastic wrap-lined flat surface, and shape into a disc. Wrap in plastic wrap, and chill 30 minutes.

3. Unwrap dough, and roll between 2 new sheets of lightly floured plastic wrap into a 12-inch circle. Fit into a 9-inch pie plate. Fold edges under, and crimp. Chill 30 minutes.

4. Preheat oven to 400°. Bake crust 20 minutes, shielding edges with aluminum foil to prevent excessive browning. Cool completely on a wire rack (about 1 hour).

5. Meanwhile, prepare Filling: Bake sweet potatoes at 400° on a baking sheet 50 to 55 minutes or until tender. Let stand 5 minutes. Cut potatoes in half lengthwise; scoop out pulp into a bowl. Mash pulp. Discard skins.

6. Whisk together eggs and granulated sugar until well blended. Add milk, next 6 ingredients, and sweet potato pulp, stirring until blended. Pour mixture into Rosemary-Cornmeal Crust.

7. Bake at 400° for 20 minutes. Reduce heat to 325°, and bake 20 to 25 minutes or until center is set. Let cool completely on a wire rack (about 1 hour).

—RECIPE FROM CRYSTAL DETAMORE-RODMAN,
CHARLOTTESVILLE, VIRGINIA

Kitchen Express: Substitute ½ (15-oz.) package refrigerated piecrusts for cornmeal crust ingredients. Unroll on a lightly floured surface. Sprinkle with 1 Tbsp. plain white cornmeal and 2 tsp. chopped fresh rosemary. Lightly roll cornmeal and rosemary into crust. Fit into a 9-inch pie plate according to package directions. Fold edges under; crimp. Proceed as directed, beginning with Step 5.

Warm and Cozy

Warm Citrus Cider

HANDS-ON TIME: 20 MIN. **TOTAL TIME:** 25 MIN.

This easy cider gets its tangy twist from fresh citrus.

1. Bring 1 gal. apple cider; 2 cups orange juice; ½ cup lemon juice; 1 orange, sliced; 1 lemon, sliced; 1½ tsp. whole cloves; and 3 cinnamon sticks to a boil. Reduce heat; simmer 10 minutes. Discard solids. Garnish with an apple slice, if desired. Serve hot. Makes about 4½ qt.

Caramel-Pecan Bars

MAKES ABOUT 2 DOZEN
HANDS-ON TIME: 25 MIN.
TOTAL TIME: 2 HR., 15 MIN.

3½ cups coarsely chopped pecans
2 cups all-purpose flour
⅔ cup powdered sugar
¾ cup butter, cubed
½ cup firmly packed brown sugar
½ cup honey
⅔ cup butter
3 Tbsp. whipping cream

1. Preheat oven to 350°. Line bottom and sides of a 13- x 9-inch pan with heavy-duty aluminum foil, allowing 2 to 3 inches to extend over sides; lightly grease foil.
2. Arrange pecans in a single layer on a baking sheet. Bake pecans at 350° for 5 to 7 minutes or until lightly toasted and fragrant. Remove from oven to wire rack. Cool completely (about 15 minutes).
3. Pulse flour, powdered sugar, and ¾ cup butter in a food processor 5 to 6 times or until mixture resembles coarse meal. Press mixture on bottom and ¾ inch up sides of prepared pan.
4. Bake at 350° for 20 minutes or until edges are lightly browned. Cool completely on a wire rack (about 15 minutes).
5. Bring brown sugar and next 3 ingredients to a boil in a 3-qt. saucepan over medium-high heat. Stir in toasted pecans, and spoon hot filling into prepared crust.
6. Bake at 350° for 25 to 30 minutes or until golden and bubbly. Remove from oven to wire rack; cool completely (about 30 minutes). Lift baked bars from pan, using aluminum-foil sides as handles. Transfer to a serving plate, and cut into 2-inch squares.

Caramel-Pecan Tart: Prepare recipe as directed, pressing crumb mixture on bottom and up sides of a lightly greased 11-inch tart pan with removable bottom. Makes 12 servings.

MAMA'S WAY OR YOUR WAY?
Collard Greens: Classic or Quick

Simmered with pork or sautéed and meatless, they're a Southern favorite.

RECIPES FROM NANCY TERRELL AND KATIE MORROW
BIRMINGHAM, ALABAMA

Why We Love Mama's Way

Recipe from Nancy Terrell

- Smoky pork flavor
- Tender texture
- Delicious potlikker

Southern-Style Collard Greens

MAKES 10 TO 12 SERVINGS
HANDS-ON TIME: 1 HR., 4 MIN.
TOTAL TIME: 3 HR., 4 MIN.

12 hickory-smoked bacon
    slices, finely chopped
2 medium-size sweet onions, finely
    chopped
¾ lb. smoked ham, chopped
6 garlic cloves, finely chopped
3 (32-oz.) containers chicken broth
3 (1-lb.) packages fresh
    collard greens, washed
    and trimmed
⅓ cup apple cider vinegar
1 Tbsp. sugar
1 tsp. salt
¾ tsp. pepper

1. Cook bacon in a 10-qt. stockpot over medium heat 10 to 12 minutes or until almost crisp. Add onion, and sauté 8 minutes; add ham and garlic, and sauté 1 minute. Stir in broth and remaining ingredients. Cook 2 hours or to desired degree of tenderness.

Why We Love Your Way

Recipe from Katie Morrow

- Speedy preparation
- Better for you
- 26-minute cook time

Sautéed Greens

MAKES 4 TO 6 SERVINGS
HANDS-ON TIME: 26 MIN.
TOTAL TIME: 26 MIN.

½ cup chopped onion
3 garlic cloves, minced
1 Tbsp. chopped fresh ginger
1 serrano pepper, split*
1 Tbsp. sesame oil
1 tsp. salt
½ tsp. pepper
1 (1-lb.) package fresh collard greens,
    washed, trimmed, and coarsely chopped
1 Tbsp. sugar
1 Tbsp. rice vinegar

1. Sauté onion and next 3 ingredients in hot oil in a large skillet or wok 1 minute. Stir in salt and pepper. Add greens; sauté 2 minutes. Add sugar and vinegar; cover and cook 3 minutes or until wilted. Remove and discard serrano pepper before serving.
*½ jalapeño pepper, split, may be substituted.

Sautéed Greens With Pork:
Stir in ½ lb. chopped smoked pork with greens.

Healthy Living®

This time of year it's easy to overindulge. Let these great recipes and tips be your guide to healthier habits during the holidays.

Better-For-You Holiday Sides

Making smart food choices never tasted so good. These three delicious recipes help you keep the carbs and calories in check.

• TIP •

At the Table: Portion size is crucial to limiting calories and fat grams. A good visual cue for a proper side dish serving is a half-full standard size coffee mug.

Cornbread Stuffing With Sweet Potato and Squash

MAKES 10 SERVINGS
HANDS-ON TIME: 47 MIN.
TOTAL TIME: 1 HR., 57 MIN.

Cornbread Stuffing With Sweet Potato and Squash has a hint of sage and is packed with nutrients.

1 cup frozen diced onion, red and green bell peppers, and celery
2 small garlic cloves, pressed
1 Tbsp. canola oil
1½ lb. butternut squash, peeled, seeded, and cut into ¼-inch cubes
2 medium-size sweet potatoes, peeled and cut into ¼-inch cubes
1 Granny Smith apple, peeled and cut into ¼-inch cubes
3 Tbsp. melted butter
2 Tbsp. brown sugar
1 Tbsp. chopped fresh sage
2 tsp. Creole seasoning, divided
2 (14-oz.) cans low-sodium fat-free chicken broth, divided
1 (8-oz.) package cornbread stuffing mix
1 large egg, lightly beaten
⅓ cup chopped pecans
Garnish: fresh or dried sage leaves

1. Preheat oven to 375°. Sauté frozen onion mixture and garlic in 1 Tbsp. hot oil in a large deep skillet over medium-high heat 2 minutes or until vegetables are tender.
2. Stir in squash, next 5 ingredients, 1 tsp. Creole seasoning, and ¼ cup water. Cover, reduce heat to medium, and cook, stirring occasionally, 15 minutes or until squash and potatoes are tender. Stir in 1 can chicken broth.
3. Remove from heat; cool 15 minutes. Stir together stuffing mix, egg, and remaining 1 can chicken broth and 1 tsp. Creole seasoning in a medium bowl. Fold into cooled squash mixture. Spoon mixture into a lightly greased 13- x 9-inch baking dish.
4. Bake, covered with aluminum foil, at 375° for 25 minutes. Uncover, and sprinkle with pecans; bake 20 minutes or until dressing is thoroughly heated and pecans are toasted. Let stand 10 minutes before serving. Garnish, if desired.

—**RECIPE FROM BARBARA ESTABROOK,**

RHINELANDER, WISCONSIN

Per serving: Calories 274; Fat 9.6g (sat 3g, mono 4.1g, poly 1.9g); Protein 6.6g; Carb 42.4g; Fiber 6.9g; Chol 27mg; Iron 1.9mg; Sodium 504mg; Calc 81mg

Israeli Couscous With Roasted Mushrooms

MAKES 8 SERVINGS
HANDS-ON TIME: 10 MIN.
TOTAL TIME: 30 MIN.

Versatile Israeli Couscous With Roasted Mushrooms pairs well with everything from turkey to steak.

2 (4-oz.) packages fresh gourmet mushroom blend, coarsely chopped
2 garlic cloves, thinly sliced
1 Tbsp. olive oil
1 tsp. chopped fresh thyme
1 tsp. kosher salt, divided
½ tsp. freshly ground pepper, divided
2 (6.3-oz.) packages Israeli couscous
2 tsp. Worcestershire sauce
Garnish: fresh thyme sprigs

1. Preheat oven to 400°. Toss together mushrooms, garlic, olive oil, thyme, ½ tsp. salt, and ¼ tsp. pepper in an aluminum foil-lined broiler pan. Spread mushroom mixture in a single layer, and bake 20 minutes.
2. Meanwhile, cook couscous according to package directions.
3. Stir in mushroom mixture, Worcestershire sauce, and remaining salt and pepper. Garnish, if desired.
Note: We tested with Casbah All Natural Original Toasted CousCous.

Per serving: Calories 209; Fat 3.5g (sat 0.5g, mono 2.5g, poly 0.5g); Protein 5.7g; Carb 37.5g; Fiber 2.2g; Chol 0mg; Iron 1.3mg; Sodium 251mg; Calc 9mg

Oven-Roasted Smashed Potatoes

MAKES 6 SERVINGS
HANDS-ON TIME: 10 MIN.
TOTAL TIME: 50 MIN.

A baby or new potato is a young potato of any variety which hasn't yet fully developed its starch. This translates into a waxier texture that's perfect for roasting.

2 (24-oz.) packages baby Yukon gold potatoes
1 medium-size sweet onion, cut into ½-inch pieces
1 Tbsp. olive oil
1 tsp. chopped fresh rosemary
1 tsp. kosher salt
2 tsp. fresh lemon juice
¼ tsp. dried crushed red pepper

1. Preheat oven to 400°. Toss together all ingredients in a broiler pan until well coated. Bake 40 minutes or until tender and browned. Gently smash potatoes with a fork.

Per serving: Calories 218; Fat 2.6g (sat 0.4g, mono 1.7g, poly 0.4g); Protein 5.2g; Carb 45.2g; Fiber 4.2g; Chol 0mg; Iron 1.8mg; Sodium 332mg; Calc 28mg

Test Kitchen Notebook

Norman's Tips for Choosing Side Dishes

Starchy side dishes get a bad repuatation—but carbs aren't necessarily unhealthy. The high-calorie culprits are added oil and butter. When choosing side dishes, look for recipes that have less than ¼ cup of butter or oil. Savory spices, such as cumin and cinnamon, and fresh herbs help maximize flavor without adding fat.

—NORMAN KING,
TEST KITCHEN PROFESSIONAL
AND DIETITIAN

✳ Holiday Dinners

Enjoy our special section of festive food from Southern tables where
you can pass along traditions and make delicious recipes the whole family will love.

Joy! An Easy Party

Need a special supper club menu? Whether you're a novice or a pro, this is it.

Easygoing Entertaining Menu

SERVES 8

Cherry-Pecan Brie, Uptown Figs, or
Bacon-Arugula-Apple Bites

Herbed Pork Roast

Roasted Fall Vegetables

Puffed Mashed Potatoes

Basil-and-Blue Cheese Salad

Brandy Alexander Cheesecake

This is one sit-down supper that's dressy enough to impress yet doable enough to enjoy. Start with one of our super-easy appetizers, and then finish big with rich Brandy Alexander Cheesecake. You'll be relaxed and ready for fun.

3 Super-Easy Appetizers

Complement our menu with any one of these no-fuss party starters.

Cherry-Pecan Brie: Stir together ⅓ cup cherry preserves, 1 Tbsp. balsamic vinegar, ⅛ tsp. freshly ground pepper, and ⅛ tsp. salt in a bowl. Drizzle over 1 (8-oz.) warm Brie round (rind removed from top). Top with chopped toasted pecans. Serve with crackers.

Uptown Figs: Cut a slit in large side of 24 dried figs, cutting to, but not through, stem end. Stir together 1 (3-oz.) package softened cream cheese, 2 tsp. powdered sugar, and 2 tsp. orange liqueur; fill each fig with mixture and 1 roasted, salted almond. Press figs to secure fillings.

Bacon-Arugula-Apple Bites: Toss Red Delicious apple slices in lemon juice; pat dry. Spread each with about 2 tsp. garlic-and-herb spreadable cheese. Top with cooked and crumbled bacon, baby arugula sprigs, and freshly cracked pepper.
Note: We tested with Vermont Gourmet Garlic-and-Herb Spreadable Cheese.

Bacon-Arugula-Apple Bites

⬤ TIP ⬤

Pair modern napkins with traditional plates to relax the mood.

Herbed Pork Roast

MAKES 8 SERVINGS

HANDS-ON TIME: 26 MIN.

TOTAL TIME: 1 HR., 6 MIN.

We loved this roast with gravy. We used Knorr Classic Brown Gravy Mix prepared according to package directions.

1 (4- to 5-lb.) untrimmed pork loin roast
1 tsp. kosher salt
1 tsp. coarsely ground pepper
Kitchen string
5 Tbsp. olive oil, divided
2 Tbsp. chopped fresh sage
2 Tbsp. chopped fresh parsley
2 Tbsp. chopped fresh thyme
1 Tbsp. chopped fresh rosemary

1. Preheat oven to 425°. Sprinkle pork with salt and pepper. Tie pork with kitchen string, securing at 2-inch intervals.

2. Cook pork, fat side down, in 3 Tbsp. hot oil in a stainless-steel skillet over medium-high heat 3 to 5 minutes on each side or until golden brown. Place, fat side up, on a wire rack in an aluminum foil-lined roasting pan. Remove kitchen string; make 5 (½-inch-deep) cuts in pork.

3. Stir together sage, next 3 ingredients, and remaining 2 Tbsp. oil. Stuff herb mixture into slits in pork.

4. Bake at 425° for 30 to 40 minutes or until a meat thermometer inserted into thickest portion registers 150°. Let stand 10 minutes before serving.

Roasted Fall Vegetables

MAKES 8 SERVINGS

HANDS-ON TIME: 20 MIN.

TOTAL TIME: 50 MIN.

Candy cane beets are also known as Chioggia beets. We love this variety because they don't stain like traditional red beets.

8 baby yellow beets
8 baby candy cane beets
10 small carrots with greenery
3 Tbsp. olive oil, divided
1 tsp. kosher salt, divided
½ tsp. pepper, divided

1. Preheat oven to 425°. Cut tops from yellow and candy cane beets, leaving ½-inch stems. Peel beets, and cut in half. Cut tops from carrots, leaving ½ inch of greenery on each.

2. Toss yellow beets and carrots with 2 Tbsp. olive oil in a large bowl; place in a single layer on 1 side of an aluminum foil-lined 15- x 10-inch jelly-roll pan. Sprinkle vegetables in pan with ½ tsp. salt and ¼ tsp. pepper.

3. Toss candy cane beets with remaining 1 Tbsp. olive oil; arrange beets in a single layer on remaining side of jelly-roll pan. Sprinkle with remaining ½ tsp. salt and ¼ tsp. pepper.

4. Bake at 425° for 15 minutes; stir once, and bake 15 minutes or until tender.

Puffed Mashed Potatoes

family favorite • make ahead

MAKES 10 TO 12 SERVINGS

HANDS-ON TIME: 21 MIN.

TOTAL TIME: 1 HR., 6 MIN.

For a pretty presentation out of the oven, spread potato mixture in casserole dish, create swirls with the back of a spoon as you would frost a cake, and then brush with butter. If you like Parmesan cheese, you'll like the Spanish cheese Manchego.

5 lb. Yukon gold potatoes, peeled and cut
    into 2-inch pieces
1 Tbsp. salt, divided
3 Tbsp. butter
¾ cup (3 oz.) shredded Manchego cheese*
¾ cup half-and-half
2 large eggs, lightly beaten
½ tsp. pepper
2 Tbsp. butter, melted

1. Bring potatoes, 2 tsp. salt, and water to cover to a boil in a large Dutch oven over medium-high heat. Boil 20 minutes or until tender; drain. Reduce heat to low. Return potatoes to Dutch oven, and cook, stirring occasionally, 1 to 2 minutes or until potatoes are dry. Remove from heat; mash potatoes with a potato masher to desired consistency.

2. Preheat oven to 400°. Stir butter, next 4 ingredients, and remaining 1 tsp. salt into potatoes. Spread mixture into a lightly greased 2½- to 3-qt. baking dish. Brush with melted butter.

3. Bake at 400° for 20 to 25 minutes or until thoroughly heated and puffed. Serve immediately.

*Shredded Parmesan cheese may be substituted.

Note: To make Puffed Mashed Potatoes ahead, prepare recipe as directed through Step 2. Cover and chill up to 2 days. Remove from refrigerator, and let stand at room temperature for at least 30 minutes. Proceed with recipe as directed.

Basil-and-Blue Cheese Salad

fast fixin's

MAKES 10 TO 12 SERVINGS
HANDS-ON TIME: 20 MIN.
TOTAL TIME: 20 MIN.

It's ideal to slice pears and avocados at the last minute so they won't turn brown. You can do this one hour ahead and toss in a small amount of lemon juice. (Too much will alter the flavor of the vinaigrette.)

⅓ cup olive oil
⅓ cup seasoned rice vinegar
1 tsp. country-style Dijon mustard
½ tsp. salt
¼ tsp. dried crushed red pepper
10 cups mixed salad greens
½ cup firmly packed fresh basil leaves, coarsely chopped
2 ripe pears, thinly sliced
2 fresh navel oranges, sectioned
2 avocados, sliced
1 (4-oz.) package blue cheese, crumbled

1. Whisk together first 5 ingredients. Cover and chill until ready to use (up to 24 hours).
2. Toss together greens and basil. Top with pears, oranges, avocados, and blue cheese; toss. Drizzle with vinaigrette. Serve immediately.

—**RECIPE INSPIRED BY LOUJEAN LAMALFA,**
SANTA ROSA, CALIFORNIA

Brandy Alexander Cheesecake

freezeable • make ahead

MAKES 10 TO 12 SERVINGS
HANDS-ON TIME: 20 MIN.
TOTAL TIME: 11 HR., 8 MIN.

Allowing chill time for a cheesecake is important for developing texture and flavor. To freeze up to 1 month, wrap springform pan tightly with aluminum foil, and slide into a zip-top plastic freezer bag. (Pictured on page 192)

1 (10-oz.) box chocolate-flavored bear-shaped graham crackers, crushed (about 2¼ cups)
6 Tbsp. butter, melted
2 Tbsp. sugar, divided
4 (8-oz.) packages cream cheese, softened
1¼ cups sugar
3 Tbsp. cornstarch
4 large eggs, at room temperature
4 Tbsp. brandy, divided
4 Tbsp. crème de cacao, divided*
1 (16-oz.) container sour cream
Garnishes: blackberries, currants, raspberries, strawberries

1. Preheat oven to 325°. Stir together crushed graham crackers, butter, and 1 Tbsp. sugar. Press mixture on bottom and halfway up sides of a 9-inch spring-form pan. Freeze 10 minutes.
2. Beat cream cheese, 1¼ cups sugar, and cornstarch at medium speed with an electric mixer 2 to 3 minutes or until smooth. Add eggs, 1 at a time, beating at low speed just until yellow disap-pears after each addition. Add 3 Tbsp. brandy and 3 Tbsp. crème de cacao, and beat just until blended. Pour into prepared crust.
3. Bake at 325° for 1 hour or just until center is almost set.
4. During last 2 minutes of baking, stir together sour cream and remaining 1 Tbsp. sugar, 1 Tbsp. brandy, and 1 Tbsp. crème de cacao.
5. Spread sour cream mixture over cheesecake. Bake at 325° for 8 more minutes. Remove cheesecake from oven; gently run a knife along outer edge of cheesecake, and cool completely in pan on a wire rack (about 1½ hours). Cover and chill 8 to 24 hours.
6. Remove sides of springform pan, and place cheesecake on a serving plate. Garnish, if desired.
*Coffee liqueur may be substituted. We tested with Kahlúa.
Note: We tested with Nabisco Teddy Grahams chocolate graham snacks.

—**RECIPE FROM SHANA VERHAGEN,**
ARLINGTON, TEXAS

Fondue Fun

Entertain the easy way. One pot, lots of flavor.

Pull out the warming pot and those funky forks to turn your next gathering into a stylish dip-and-swirl affair. These recipes are all you need. Serve bread cubes with classic Two-Cheese-and-Honey Fondue, and offer Tomato-and-Herb Fondue for dairy-free flavor. For dessert, reinvent the sweet Southern classic, Mississippi Mud. Should there be leftovers of this dreamy delicacy, reheat it the next day and serve over pound cake or ice cream.

Mississippi Mud Fondue

MAKES 4 CUPS
HANDS-ON TIME: 18 MIN.
TOTAL TIME: 18 MIN.
(Pictured on page 190)

Fondue:
1 cup heavy cream
1 (12-oz.) package dark chocolate morsels
1 (7½-oz.) jar marshmallow crème
½ tsp. vanilla extract

Serve with:
Brownies, biscotti, graham crackers, marshmallows, chopped toasted pecans, chopped candied ginger

1. Bring cream to a boil in a large heavy-duty saucepan over medium-high heat; reduce heat to low, and simmer. Add chocolate morsels, and stir until melted and smooth. Stir in marshmallow crème and vanilla, stirring constantly until smooth. Transfer to fondue pot. Keep warm. Serve with desired accompaniments.

Fondue Dos, Don'ts, and Tips

- Allow 20 (1-inch) cubes of bread, 6 to 8 ounces fruit or vegetables, or at least 4 cookies per person.
- Ceramic pots are great for cheese, chocolate, and dessert-based fondues.
- Use metal pots for oil, broth, or beer fondues.
- Be careful with metal dipping forks or skewers; remove meat from skewer before eating.
- Keep portions bite-size.
- If using a wooden table, cover with a thick tablecloth to avoid damage to furniture and catch spills.
- No double dipping.

Two-Cheese-and-Honey Fondue

MAKES 2¾ CUPS
HANDS-ON TIME: 23 MIN.
TOTAL TIME: 23 MIN.

Fondue:
1 cup heavy cream
1 cup chicken broth
1 Tbsp. honey
2 cups (8 oz.) freshly shredded Jarlsberg cheese
½ cup (2 oz.) freshly shredded Swiss cheese
¼ cup all-purpose flour
¼ tsp. dry mustard
¼ tsp. freshly cracked pepper

Serve with:
Cubed ciabatta bread, sliced pears, sliced apples

1. Bring heavy cream, chicken broth, and honey to a boil over medium-high heat; reduce heat to medium-low, and simmer.
2. Meanwhile, combine cheeses, flour, mustard, and pepper in a large bowl. Slowly whisk cheese mixture into simmering broth until melted and smooth. Transfer to fondue pot; keep warm. Serve with desired accompaniments.

Tomato-and-Herb Fondue

MAKES 3 CUPS
HANDS-ON TIME: 21 MIN.
TOTAL TIME: 21 MIN.

Fondue:
1 Tbsp. butter
¼ cup chopped sweet onion
2 garlic cloves, minced
2 (14.5-oz.) cans fire-roasted tomatoes
1 tsp. tomato paste
½ tsp. lemon zest
¼ cup chopped fresh basil

Serve with:
Cubed, lightly toasted French bread; cubed, toasted cheese bread; chopped, cooked chicken tenders; meatballs; tortellini

1. Melt butter in a large saucepan over medium heat; add onion and garlic, and sauté 3 minutes or until vegetables are tender.
2. Add tomatoes, tomato paste, and lemon zest, and cook, stirring occasionally, 8 to 10 minutes. Remove from heat, and stir in basil. Transfer to fondue pot; keep warm. Serve with desired accompaniments.

Sharing a Holiday Tradition

For this Florida family, Hanukkah begins in the kitchen and builds to a celebratory meal. They've shared a few of their favorite recipes.

Hanukkah Celebration

SERVES 6 TO 8

Matzo Ball Soup

Carrot Kugel

Edible Chocolate Dreidels

Jelly Doughnuts
(Sufganiyout)

Hanukkah is a special time when Bill and Cynthia Wigutow pull out all the food stops. A registered dietitian, Cynthia usually cooks lighter meals for her family. But for this occasion, rules are relaxed. The couple's parents and children lend a hand in preparing a festive meal, adding laughter, joy, and wisdom to the day.

Matzo Ball Soup

MAKES ABOUT 3½ QT.
HANDS-ON TIME: 30 MIN.
TOTAL TIME: 4 HR.

Soup:
1 (1-oz.) package fresh dill
1 bunch fresh parsley
Kitchen string
3 skin-on, bone-in chicken breasts
    (about 3 lb.)
1 medium onion, quartered
4 medium carrots, thinly sliced
3 parsnips, thinly sliced
3 celery ribs

Matzo Balls:
2 Tbsp. vegetable oil
4 large eggs, lightly beaten
1 cup matzo meal
1¾ tsp. kosher salt

Seasonings:
1½ to 2 Tbsp. fresh lemon juice
2½ tsp. kosher salt
½ tsp. ground white pepper

Garnish:
Fresh dill sprigs

1. Prepare Soup: Tie half of dill and half of parsley in a bunch with kitchen string. Chop remaining dill and parsley to equal 2 tsp. each.
2. Bring chicken, next 4 ingredients, dill-parsley bunch, and 3½ qt. water to a boil in a large Dutch oven over medium-high heat; skim any foam with a slotted spoon. Cover, reduce heat to medium-low, and simmer, 2½ to 3 hours or until chicken is tender and falls off the bone.
3. Meanwhile, prepare Matzo Balls batter: Whisk together oil, eggs, and ¼ cup water. Add matzo meal and 1¾ tsp. kosher salt; whisk until well blended. Cover and chill 30 minutes.
4. Remove soup from heat. Skim fat from surface of broth. Remove chicken and celery. Pour broth through a fine wire-mesh strainer into a large bowl. Return broth, carrots, and parsnips to Dutch oven, discarding onion and herb bunch. Let chicken, celery, and broth mixture cool 30 minutes.
5. Meanwhile, assemble and cook Matzo Balls: Shape matzo batter into 18 (1-inch) balls (about 1 Tbsp. each), using wet hands. Bring 2½ qt. water to a boil in a large saucepan over medium-high heat. Drop matzo balls into boiling water; return to a boil. Cover, reduce heat to medium-low; simmer 30 minutes. Remove matzo balls from water with a slotted spoon.
6. Squeeze juice from cooled celery ribs into broth. Discard celery ribs. Skin and bone chicken; shred chicken. Add matzo balls, shredded chicken, lemon juice, kosher salt, and pepper to broth. Bring to a boil over medium-high heat. Reduce heat to medium-low; simmer 8 minutes. Stir in reserved dill and parsley; cook 2 minutes. Garnish, if desired.

—RECIPE FROM CYNTHIA WIGUTOW,
HOLLYWOOD, FLORIDA

✳ Holiday Dinners

Carrot Kugel

MAKES 6 TO 8 SERVINGS
HANDS-ON TIME: 10 MIN.
TOTAL TIME: 1 HR., 35 MIN.

This super-simple dish is sweet and soufflé-like. Canned carrots make it easy as pie.

1 cup margarine, melted*
4 (14½-oz.) cans sliced carrots, drained
1½ cups firmly packed brown sugar
1⅓ cups all-purpose flour
4 large eggs, lightly beaten

1. Preheat oven to 350°. Process margarine and carrots in a food processor 30 to 60 seconds or until smooth, stopping to scrape down sides as needed.
2. Whisk together carrot mixture and remaining ingredients in a medium bowl until blended. Spoon carrot mixture into a lightly greased 8-inch square baking dish.
3. Bake at 350° for 1 hour and 20 minutes to 1 hour and 25 minutes or until puffed and edges are lightly browned. Let stand 5 minutes before serving.
—**RECIPE FROM CYNTHIA WIGUTOW,**
HOLLYWOOD, FLORIDA

*Butter or light margarine may be substituted.

Edible Chocolate Dreidels

Edible Chocolate Dreidels

MAKES 12 SERVINGS
HANDS-ON TIME: 15 MIN.
TOTAL TIME: 15 MIN.

12 large marshmallows
12 pretzel sticks
6 tsp. ready-to-spread vanilla frosting
12 milk or dark chocolate kisses
Blue edible-ink marker

1. Decorate outside of 1 large marshmallow with dreidel letters (Nun, Gimel, Hei, Shin) using an edible-ink marker; let dry. Place pretzel stick into flat side of marshmallow, pressing to, but not through, opposite side. Spread ½ tsp. frosting on flat side of 1 chocolate kiss; press onto remaining flat side of marshmallow. Repeat procedure with remaining ingredients.
—**RECIPE FROM CYNTHIA WIGUTOW,**
HOLLYWOOD, FLORIDA
Note: We tested with Wilton FoodWriter Edible Color Marker.

Jelly Doughnuts (Sufganiyout)

MAKES 24 DONUTS
HANDS-ON TIME: 27 MIN.
TOTAL TIME: 2 HR., 42 MIN.

This traditional dessert is made simple by using frozen roll dough in place of homemade yeast dough.

1 (25-oz.) package frozen bread
    roll dough, thawed according to
    package directions
Vegetable oil
½ cup granulated sugar
1¼ tsp. ground cinnamon
½ to 1 cup seedless raspberry jam*
Powdered sugar

1. Place rolls 2 inches apart on 2 lightly greased baking sheets. Cover and let rise in a warm place (85°), free from drafts, according to package directions.
2. Pour oil to a depth of 2 inches into a Dutch oven; heat to 350°. Fry rolls, in batches, 1 to 1½ minutes on each side or until fully cooked and golden brown. Drain on a wire rack over paper towels.
3. Whisk together granulated sugar and cinnamon in a medium bowl. Add warm doughnuts to sugar mixture, tossing to coat. Let cool completely on wire rack (about 15 minutes).
4. Make a small slit in side of each doughnut, using a paring knife. Place jam in a zip-top plastic freezer bag (do not seal). Snip 1 corner of bag to make a small hole. Pipe jam into each doughnut. Dust with powdered sugar.
*Strawberry jelly may be substituted.
Note: We tested with Bridgford Easy to Bake Parkerhouse Style Rolls frozen bread dough.

Bake-and-Take Treats

These warm, sweet recipes are Easy-Bake oven simple.

Sour Cream Coffee Cake Muffins

MAKES 24 MUFFINS
HANDS-ON TIME: 20 MIN.
TOTAL TIME: 52 MIN.
(Pictured on page 191)

1 cup butter, softened
2 cups sugar
2 large eggs
1 cup sour cream
½ tsp. vanilla extract
2 cups all-purpose flour
1 tsp. baking powder
¼ tsp. salt
⅛ tsp. baking soda
24 paper baking cups
1 cup pecan halves, finely chopped
¼ cup sugar
1½ tsp. ground cinnamon

1. Preheat oven to 350°. Beat butter at medium speed with an electric mixer 2 minutes or until creamy. Gradually add 2 cups sugar, beating 2 to 3 minutes. Add eggs, 1 at a time, beating until blended after each addition. Add sour cream and vanilla, beating until blended.
2. Whisk together flour and next 3 ingredients; gradually stir into butter mixture. (Batter will be thick.)
3. Place baking cups in muffin pans. Spoon batter into cups, filling two-thirds full.
4. Stir together pecans, ¼ cup sugar, and cinnamon. Sprinkle pecan mixture over batter.
5. Bake at 350° for 20 to 25 minutes or until a wooden pick inserted in center comes out clean. Remove from pans, and cool completely on wire racks (about 12 to 15 minutes).

—RECIPE FROM NORA HENSHAW,
OKEMAH, OKLAHOMA

GET INSPIRED

Including the muffin pan adds a special touch to this gift.

Be Glad to Give

This holiday season, plan to host a bake sale to fight pediatric cancer. Visit **cookiesforkidscancer.org** to register your own bake sale or purchase all-natural gourmet cookies. The Glad Products Company will match all the money raised by the charity in November and December. For bake sale tips and celebrity chef recipes, visit **gladtogive.com.**

Peanut Butter Cakes

MAKES 7 LOAVES
HANDS-ON TIME: 20 MIN.
TOTAL TIME: 1 HR., 35 MIN.

No time to make frosting? This cake has a baked-on topping.

1 cup creamy peanut butter
½ cup butter, softened
2 cups sugar
4 large eggs
1 cup milk
1½ Tbsp. vanilla extract
2 cups all-purpose flour
1½ tsp. baking powder
½ tsp. salt
Peanutty Topping

1. Preheat oven to 350°. Beat peanut butter and butter at medium speed with an electric mixer until creamy; gradually add sugar, beating well. Add eggs, 1 at a time, beating until blended after each addition. Stir in milk and vanilla.
2. Sift together flour, baking powder, and salt; stir into peanut butter mixture. Pour batter into 7 greased and floured 5- x 3-inch disposable aluminum foil loaf pans, filling each pan half-full. Place pans on a baking sheet; sprinkle with Peanutty Topping.

3. Bake at 350° for 55 to 60 minutes or until a long wooden pick inserted in center comes out clean. Cool completely in pans on wire racks (about 20 minutes). **Chocolate Chip-Peanut Butter Cakes:** Stir 2 cups semisweet chocolate morsels into batter.

Peanutty Topping:

MAKES ABOUT 2 CUPS
HANDS-ON TIME: 10 MIN.

1 cup powdered sugar
1 cup creamy peanut butter
½ cup all-purpose flour
½ cup uncooked regular or
    quick-cooking oats
¼ cup peanuts, chopped
½ tsp. salt

1. Stir together powdered sugar and next 5 ingredients in a medium bowl until thoroughly blended.

—RECIPE FROM **GLENAVE CURTIS,**
JUDSONIA, ARKANSAS

German Chocolate Snack Cakes

MAKES 18 SQUARES
HANDS-ON TIME: 15 MIN.
TOTAL TIME: 2 HR., 20 MIN.

These treats are a snap to prepare. Package them in small boxes with decorative tissue paper for a fun gift idea.

½ cup chopped pecans
1 (18.25-oz.) package German
    chocolate cake mix
4 large eggs, divided
½ cup butter, melted
1 (16-oz.) package powdered sugar
1 (8-oz.) package cream cheese, softened

1. Preheat oven to 350°. Arrange pecans in a single layer in a shallow pan. Bake pecans 5 to 7 minutes or until lightly toasted and fragrant. Remove from oven. Reduce oven temperature to 300°.

2. Stir together cake mix, 1 egg, pecans, and butter; press mixture into bottom of a lightly greased 13- x 9-inch pan.
3. Beat powdered sugar, softened cream cheese, and remaining 3 eggs at medium speed with an electric mixer until smooth. Spoon powdered sugar mixture over batter in pan, spreading to edges.
4. Bake at 300° for 1 hour. Let snack cake cool completely (about 1 hour). Remove cake from pan to a cutting board, and cut into 2½- to 3-inch squares.

Gingerbread

family favorite
MAKES 9 SERVINGS
HANDS-ON TIME: 20 MIN.
TOTAL TIME: 1 HR.

½ cup butter, softened
½ cup granulated sugar
½ cup firmly packed dark brown sugar
1 large egg
⅔ cup molasses
2½ cups all-purpose flour
2 tsp. ground cinnamon
1 tsp. baking soda
1 tsp. ground ginger
½ tsp. salt
½ tsp. ground allspice
½ tsp. ground nutmeg
¼ tsp. ground cloves
⅛ tsp. baking powder
1 cup buttermilk
Whipped cream (optional)
Rum Glaze (optional)

1. Preheat oven to 350°. Beat butter at medium speed with an electric mixer until creamy; gradually add sugars, beating well. Add egg, beating until blended. Add molasses, beating until smooth.
2. Whisk together flour and next 8 ingredients in a large bowl. Add to butter mixture alternately with buttermilk, beginning and ending with flour mixture. Beat at low speed just until blended after each addition. Pour into

9 lightly greased (6-oz.) ramekins.
3. Bake at 350° for 24 to 28 minutes or until a wooden pick inserted in center comes out clean. Let cool on a wire rack 15 minutes. Serve warm with whipped cream, or drizzle with Rum Glaze, if desired.

—RECIPE FROM **VICTORIA PRICE,**
SILVER SPRING, MARYLAND

Note: Gingerbread may be baked in a greased and floured 9-inch square pan. Increase bake time to 50 to 55 minutes.

Rum Glaze:

MAKES ABOUT ½ CUP
HANDS-ON TIME: 10 MIN.
TOTAL TIME: 10 MIN.

We also love this rich glaze drizzled over pound cake slices and ice cream.

½ cup firmly packed dark brown sugar
¼ cup rum
2 Tbsp. butter
1 tsp. molasses

1. Combine brown sugar, rum, butter, and molasses in a small saucepan. Bring to a boil over medium-high heat, stirring constantly. Reduce heat to low, and simmer, stirring occasionally, 3 to 4 minutes or until brown sugar is dissolved and mixture is thickened and bubbly. Serve immediately.
Note: If glaze becomes too thick to pour, return saucepan to cooktop over low heat, and whisk in 1 to 2 Tbsp. water, whisking until glaze thins and becomes a pourable consistency.

Lemon-Poppy Seed Cakes

MAKES 18 MINI BUNDT CAKES
HANDS-ON TIME: 25 MIN.
TOTAL TIME: 1 HR.

Mini Bundt pans (not to be confused with smaller Bundt pans) look like regular muffin pans; however, they have Bundt-shaped cups. The cups in mini Bundt pans can vary in size and shape, so your yield can also vary. For this recipe, we used 2 (12-cup) pans to make 18 miniature Bundt cakes.

½ cup butter, softened
2 oz. cream cheese, softened
1¼ cups granulated sugar
2 large eggs
¾ cup milk
¾ tsp. poppy seeds
¾ tsp. almond extract
2 tsp. lemon zest, divided
1¾ cups all-purpose flour
¾ tsp. baking powder
⅛ tsp. salt
1¼ cups powdered sugar
¼ cup fresh lemon juice

1. Preheat oven to 350°. Beat butter and cream cheese at medium speed with an electric mixer until well blended. Gradually add granulated sugar, beating until creamy and fluffy. Add eggs, 1 at a time, beating just until yellow disappears after each addition. Beat in milk, poppy seeds, almond extract, and 1½ tsp. lemon zest. (Mixture will be slightly lumpy.)
2. Whisk together flour and next 2 ingredients in a large bowl. Gradually add to butter mixture, beating until blended. Spoon batter into 1 greased and floured (12-cup) miniature Bundt pan, filling all cups three-fourths full. Spoon remaining batter into a second pan, filling only 6 cups.
3. Bake lemon-poppy seed cakes at 350° for 24 to 26 minutes or until a wooden pick inserted in centers of

cakes comes out clean. Remove from pans to wire racks, and let cakes cool 10 minutes.
4. Whisk together 1¼ cups powdered sugar, ¼ cup fresh lemon juice, and remaining ½ tsp. lemon zest until smooth. Drizzle glaze over warm cakes. Let cakes stand 4 to 5 minutes or until glaze is set.

—RECIPE FROM MARI MIRANDA,
GLENDALE, CALIFORNIA

Make-Ahead Breakfast Casseroles

Mix up these dishes in 30 minutes the night before for a stress-free meal the next day.

Rise and Shine Menu

SERVES 6 TO 10

One-Dish Blackberry French Toast or Ham-and-Cheese Croissant Casserole

Fresh fruit

Coffee

Orange juice

One-Dish Blackberry French Toast

make ahead

MAKES 8 TO 10 SERVINGS
HANDS-ON TIME: 21 MIN.
TOTAL TIME: 8 HR., 51 MIN.

1 cup blackberry jam
1 (12-oz.) French bread loaf, cut into 1½-inch cubes
1 (8-oz.) package ⅓-less-fat cream cheese, cut into 1-inch cubes
4 large eggs
2 cups half-and-half
1 tsp. ground cinnamon
1 tsp. vanilla extract
½ cup firmly packed brown sugar
Toppings: maple syrup, whipped cream

1. Cook jam in a small saucepan over medium heat 1 to 2 minutes or until melted and smooth, stirring once.
2. Place half of bread cubes in bottom of a lightly greased 13- x 9-inch baking dish. Top with cream cheese cubes, and drizzle with melted jam. Top with remaining bread cubes.
3. Whisk together eggs and next 3 ingredients. Pour over bread mixture. Sprinkle with brown sugar. Cover tightly, and chill 8 to 24 hours.
4. Preheat oven to 325°. Bake, covered, 20 minutes. Uncover and bake 10 to 15 minutes or until bread is golden brown and mixture is set. Serve with desired toppings.

—RECIPE FROM JESSICA MCKINNEY,
CRYSTAL CITY, MISSOURI

Ham-and-Cheese Croissant Casserole
make ahead

MAKES 6 SERVINGS
HANDS-ON TIME: 15 MIN.
TOTAL TIME: 9 HR., 15 MIN.

You can substitute leftover baked ham for chopped ham in this dish. Nutmeg is optional, but adds a subtle touch of spice.

3 (5-inch) large croissants
1 (8-oz.) package chopped cooked ham
1 (5-oz.) package shredded Swiss cheese
6 large eggs
1 cup half-and-half
1 Tbsp. dry mustard
2 Tbsp. honey
½ tsp. salt
½ tsp. pepper
¼ tsp. ground nutmeg (optional)

1. Cut croissants in half lengthwise, and cut each half into 4 to 5 pieces. Place croissant pieces in a lightly greased 10-inch deep-dish pie plate. Top with ham and cheese.
2. Whisk together eggs, next 5 ingredients, and, if desired, nutmeg in a large bowl.
3. Pour egg mixture over mixture in pie plate, pressing croissants down to submerge in egg mixture. Cover tightly, and chill 8 to 24 hours.
4. Preheat oven to 325°. Bake, covered, 35 minutes. Uncover and bake 25 to 30 minutes or until browned and set. Let stand 10 minutes before serving.

—RECIPE FROM KIMBERLY DENNEY,
POMPANO BEACH, FLORIDA

SO SOUTHERN

Salty, Smoky Country Ham
This smokehouse favorite offers flavor and value its city cousins can't beat.

Quality Counts
● Our favorite: Benton's Smoky Mountain Country Hams in Madisonville, Tennessee. Order online from bentonshams.com.

Just Add Water
● Simmer ham slices in water or apple juice to tone down salt. The result will be melt-in-your-mouth tender.

A Little Goes a Long Way
● Use tidbits of country ham to flavor biscuits, black-eyed peas, baked grits, cornbread, scones, red rice, and more.

Pass the Biscuits
● Ham and biscuits go together like peas and cornbread. Slather with pear preserves, spicy mustard, or pepper jelly.

A Smokin' Good Thanksgiving

Join this family in their deliciously untraditional tradition.

Untraditional Feast

SERVES 4 TO 6

Baby Back Ribs With Jackie's Dry Rub

Butter Beans

Smoked Gouda Cheese Grits

Bakery rolls

White Chocolate Ice Cream With Raspberry Sauce

Family and friends are what make Thanksgiving so special, not turkey and dressing. At least that's the philosophy of the McCalla family, who own Jackie M's Catering in Augusta, Georgia. They've transformed their traditional meal into a relaxed, lively cookout complete with ribs, cheese grits, and butter beans. Give their recipes a try—you'll enjoy all the warmth and spirit of the holiday as well as food so good you won't even miss the turkey and dressing.

Jackie's Smoking Tips

Pecan wood is the secret to Jackie's ribs. If pecan wood is not available, feel free to use whole pecans as smoking chips. You can also substitute with mesquite wood, which adds great flavor and is widely available at grocery stores.

Baby Back Ribs With Jackie's Dry Rub

MAKES 4 TO 6 SERVINGS
HANDS-ON TIME: 20 MIN.
TOTAL TIME: 3 HR., 55 MIN.
(INCLUDING RUB)

Baby Back Ribs With Jackie's Dry Rub are cooked without any sauce.

Mesquite wood chips
2 slabs baby back pork ribs (about 4 lb.)
2 Tbsp. mesquite liquid smoke
2 Tbsp. olive oil
3 Tbsp. Jackie's Dry Rub

1. Soak wood chips in water 30 minutes. Prepare smoker according to manufacturer's directions, bringing internal temperature to 225° to 250°; maintain temperature for 15 to 20 minutes.
2. Rinse and pat ribs dry. If desired, remove thin membrane from back of ribs by slicing into it with a knife and then pulling it off. (This will make ribs more tender.) Coat both sides of ribs with liquid smoke and olive oil. Sprinkle ribs with Jackie's Dry Rub, and rub into ribs.
3. Drain mesquite wood chips, and place on coals. Place pork ribs on lower cooking grate; cover with smoker lid.

4. Smoke ribs, maintaining temperature inside smoker between 225° and 250°, for 3 to 4 hours or until tender.

—RECIPE FROM JACQUELINE MCCALLA,
MARTINEZ, GEORGIA

Jackie's Dry Rub:

MAKES ABOUT ½ CUP
HANDS-ON TIME: 5 MIN.
TOTAL TIME: 5 MIN.

1. When grinding the spices it is best to use a mortar and pestle or a small spice grinder. The rub produced by a food processor is too coarse.
2. Combine 2 Tbsp. dried rosemary, 2 Tbsp. dried thyme, 2 Tbsp. kosher salt, and 2 Tbsp. white peppercorns in a mortar bowl or spice grinder; grind using a pestle or grinder until herbs and pepper become a medium-fine powder. Store in an airtight container in a cool, dark place up to 6 months.

—RECIPE FROM JACQUELINE MCCALLA,
MARTINEZ, GEORGIA

Butter Beans

MAKES 4 TO 6 SERVINGS
HANDS-ON TIME: 5 MIN.
TOTAL TIME: 35 MIN.

2 (16-oz.) packages frozen speckled butter beans
2 Tbsp. jarred ham soup base
2 Tbsp. butter, cut up
Salt and pepper to taste

1. Combine beans, ham base, and 4 cups water in a large saucepan. Bring to a boil over medium-high heat. Cover, reduce heat to low, and simmer, 30 to 35 minutes or until beans are tender. Stir in butter, and season with salt and pepper to taste.

—RECIPE FROM JACQUELINE MCCALLA,
MARTINEZ, GEORGIA

Note: We tested with Superior Touch Better Than Bouillon Ham Base.

Smoked Gouda Cheese Grits

MAKES 4 TO 6 SERVINGS
HANDS-ON TIME: 25 MIN.
TOTAL TIME: 25 MIN.

Jackie recommends you try this dish for breakfast or with shrimp for a true Southern-style shrimp and grits. Her secret to perfect shrimp is simple—a quick soak in dry vermouth.

2 cups chicken broth*
1 cup uncooked quick-cooking grits
1 cup freshly grated smoked Gouda cheese
1 Tbsp. butter
½ tsp. salt
Pepper to taste

1. Bring chicken broth and 2½ cups water to a boil in a medium saucepan over medium-high heat. Gradually whisk in grits; reduce heat to low. Cook, stirring occasionally, 10 minutes or until creamy.
2. Gradually stir in cheese, and cook, stirring occasionally, 5 minutes or until cheese is melted and smooth. Stir in butter and salt; season with pepper to taste.
*Vegetable broth may be substituted.

Shrimp and Grits: Soak 1 lb. large peeled raw shrimp (31/40 count) in ⅓ cup dry vermouth 10 minutes; drain. Sauté shrimp in 2 Tbsp. melted butter in a skillet 2 to 3 minutes or until done. Season with salt and ground white pepper to taste. Serve over Smoked Gouda Cheese Grits. Makes 4 to 6 servings. Hands-on time: 10 min., Total time: 35 min. (including grits).

—RECIPE FROM JACQUELINE MCCALLA,
MARTINEZ, GEORGIA

White Chocolate Ice Cream With Raspberry Sauce

MAKES 8 SERVINGS
HANDS-ON TIME: 30 MIN.
TOTAL TIME: 2 HR., 30 MIN. (INCLUDING SAUCE BUT NOT FREEZING TIME, WHICH VARIES)

Make Raspberry Sauce while ice-cream mixture chills. That way they'll both be ready at the same time.

3 (4-oz.) white chocolate baking bars
3¼ cups whole milk, divided
½ cup sugar, divided
3 large eggs
1 tsp. vanilla extract
Raspberry Sauce
Quick Chocolate Sauce (optional)

1. Pour water to depth of 1 inch into bottom of a double boiler over medium heat; bring to a boil. Reduce heat to low, and simmer; place chocolate and ¼ cup milk in top of double boiler over simmering water. Cook, stirring occasionally, 8 to 10 minutes or until melted. Remove from heat, and cool 10 minutes.
2. Meanwhile, cook remaining 3 cups milk and ¼ cup sugar in a heavy non-aluminum saucepan over medium heat, stirring often, 8 minutes or just until it begins to steam (do not boil); remove from heat.
3. Whisk together eggs and remaining ¼ cup sugar in a large bowl. Gradually whisk 1 cup hot milk-sugar mixture into egg mixture; gradually whisk egg mixture into remaining hot milk mixture.
4. Cook over medium heat, stirring constantly, 2 to 3 minutes. (A candy thermometer should register 160° or higher.) Stir in vanilla.
5. Remove from heat, and pour mixture through a non-aluminum fine wire-mesh strainer into a bowl. Whisk in melted chocolate mixture. Cover and chill 2 hours or until cold.

6. Pour mixture into freezer container of a 1-gal. electric ice-cream maker, and freeze according to manufacturer's instructions. (Instructions and times will vary.) Serve with Raspberry Sauce or Quick Chocolate Sauce.
Note: We tested with Ghirardelli White Chocolate Baking Bar.

Raspberry Sauce:

MAKES ABOUT 1 CUP
HANDS-ON TIME: 12 MIN.
TOTAL TIME: 1 HR., 12 MIN.

1 (12-oz.) package frozen raspberries, thawed
⅓ cup sugar
1 tsp. cornstarch
½ tsp. vanilla extract

1. Process berries in a blender or food processor 30 seconds or until smooth. Press through a fine wire-mesh strainer into a saucepan; discard pulp and seeds.
2. Stir together sugar and cornstarch in a small bowl, and add to pureed raspberries; stir in vanilla. Bring raspberry mixture to a boil over medium heat, stirring occasionally. Cook, stirring often, 2 minutes; remove from heat. Pour into a small bowl or cruet; cover and chill 1 hour.

—RECIPE FROM CLINTON MCCALLA, JR.,
MARTINEZ, GEORGIA

Quick Chocolate Sauce:

MAKES ABOUT ¾ CUP
HANDS-ON TIME: 5 MIN.
TOTAL TIME: 5 MIN.

We also love this speedy sauce as a dipper for marshmallows.

1. Microwave ½ cup, plus 2 Tbsp. half-and-half and 1 (4-oz.) semisweet chocolate baking bar, chopped, in a microwave-safe bowl at HIGH 1 to 1½ minutes or until smooth, stirring at 30-second intervals.

At Home With the Pioneer Woman

Ree Drummond is an Internet sensation who charms thousands daily with her honest humor and family-friendly recipes. We got to ride shotgun with her for the day—here's what we learned.

You don't really know "middle of nowhere" until you drive west from Pawhuska, Oklahoma, turn down a long dirt road, and find yourself surrounded by vast stretches of dry grass and rolling hills dotted only with wild horses and roaming cattle. Ree Drummond (aka The Pioneer Woman) calls this place home. Miles from the nearest grocery store, gas station, or strip mall, this place feels wild and free, with space to breathe and time to watch slow sunsets. Ree, her husband ("The Marlboro Man"), and their four children run this working cattle ranch. It's a nonstop job of hard, dirty work from sunrise to sunset, but they love it and do it together, as a family.

Lucky for us, Ree started blogging about her unique world a few years ago. Her site (thepioneerwoman.com) now boasts thousands of devoted followers. She dazzles us daily with her ranch-life confessions, inspiring photography, and mouthwatering recipes—we're still trying to figure out how she does it all. We asked Ree to share recipes and tips that any busy cook will love. Here's what she had to say.

Your top 5 tips for the busy home cook?

• Clean as you go, even if it's against your nature. You'll thank yourself once dinner's over!
• Whenever possible, brown extra ground beef and freeze it, dice extra onions and keep them in the fridge to use all week, grate more cheese than you need and save it for later, etc.
• Roast a large cut of meat (a turkey, for example), and try to see how many meals you can stretch it into! We like turkey enchiladas, turkey and homemade noodles, barbecue turkey pizzas, and turkey Tetrazzini. (You might need to freeze some of it for use later lest your family stages a turkey revolt by week's end.)
• Every once in a while, serve the kids' milk or water in beautiful wineglasses. It makes them feel fancy and special.
• Recruit the kids to set the table, pour water, clear the table, and help do dishes. It's character-building, conveys a powerful message about the importance of contributing to the household, and allows you to curl up on the couch and start watching TV much earlier. That's what kids are for!

5 kitchen tools you can't do without?

• My KitchenAid mixer. I've had mine since the day I got married, and it's my best friend and constant companion.
• My Wüsthof Santoku knife.
• My Cuisinart food processor. It's the best, and it reminds me of my mom cooking in the early eighties.
• Iron skillets. Big, small, old, new.
• Flat whisks. They flatten against the bottom of the skillet and scrape up the good stuff.

How many times a week do you go to the grocery store?

I try to go to the store once a week, but it usually winds up being twice. I keep ground beef in my freezer and a pantry full of staples. I try to fill in the perishables—milk, bread, eggs, fruit—at my local grocery store.

What's your best kitchen trick?

Making homemade buttermilk. I rarely keep store-bought buttermilk on hand, so when I need it (particularly when I make chocolate sheet cake and buttermilk pancakes), I add a tablespoon or so of white vinegar to regular milk and let it sit for five minutes. I pour in the amount of milk the recipe calls for, less a tablespoon or two. Then finish the amount with the vinegar.

Your pantry must-haves?

Canned whole tomatoes. Tons of dried pasta. Pinto beans. Different flour and baking ingredients. Then I have a special shelf where I have jars of sundried tomatoes, prepared pesto, and kalamata olives as well as specialty panini spreads and things I pick up when I visit civilization.

Your favorite splurge ingredient?

Whole beef tenderloin. It's so expensive, but it's just so darned good.

Your favorite convenience product?

When I don't feel like cooking, I send my husband and kids to the store and tell them they can pick out whatever they want. They always come back with Hamburger Helper. I'm not sure how to feel about that, but it sure is easy to whip up!

Cowboy Nachos

MAKES 6 TO 8 SERVINGS
HANDS-ON TIME: 31 MIN.
TOTAL TIME: 29 HR., 21 MIN.
(INCLUDING BRISKET)

Serve Cowboy Nachos (also made from leftover brisket) as a hearty appetizer or one-dish entrée.

2 (16-oz.) cans seasoned pinto beans, drained
2 tsp. hot sauce
1 tsp. minced garlic
½ tsp. freshly ground pepper
3½ cups shredded Braised Beef Brisket
1 Tbsp. canola oil
½ cup taco sauce
¼ cup pan drippings from Braised Beef Brisket*
1 (9-oz.) package round tortilla chips
1 (8-oz.) block Monterey Jack cheese, shredded
Pico de Gallo
Toppings: guacamole, sour cream, pickled jalapeño pepper slices

Use Leftovers—Takes Only 10 Minutes

Cowboy Dip Sandwich

MAKES 4 SERVINGS

1. Leftover Slow-Cooked Mushrooms are great sliced and served in this warm and crusty sandwich.
2. Preheat oven to 400°. Arrange 8 thick bread slices on a baking sheet. Top 4 bread slices with 4 (1-oz.) pepper Jack cheese slices. Bake at 400° for 5 minutes or until bread is toasted and cheese is melted. Top cheese-covered bread slices with warm shredded Braised Beef Brisket and remaining 4 bread slices. Serve sandwiches with warm brisket pan drippings on the side and pickled whole jalapeño peppers.

1. Preheat oven to 425°. Cook first 4 ingredients and ½ cup water in a medium saucepan, stirring occasionally, over medium-low heat 5 to 7 minutes or until thoroughly heated.
2. Cook brisket in hot oil in a skillet over medium heat, stirring often, 4 minutes or until thoroughly heated. Stir in taco sauce and pan drippings; cook 2 minutes.
3. Divide chips, bean mixture, brisket mixture, cheese, and 1 cup Pico de Gallo among 3 pie plates.
4. Bake at 425° for 5 minutes or until cheese is melted. Serve immediately with remaining Pico de Gallo and desired toppings.
*¼ cup beef broth may be substituted.

Pico de Gallo: Stir together 6 plum tomatoes, chopped; ½ cup finely chopped sweet onion; ¼ cup chopped fresh cilantro; 2 Tbsp. fresh lime juice; 1 jalapeño pepper, seeded and minced; 1 garlic clove, minced; and ½ tsp. salt. Makes 3½ cups. Hands-on time: 15 min. Total time: 15 min.
Note: Nachos can be baked as directed in 2 batches on an aluminum foil-lined baking sheet, topping each batch with 1 cup Pico de Gallo.

Braised Beef Brisket

MAKES 16 SERVINGS
HANDS-ON TIME: 15 MIN.
TOTAL TIME: 4 HR., 35 MIN. (PLUS 1 DAY FOR CHILLING)

Can't find a large brisket? Substitute two smaller ones that equal the same weight. This makes a lot, so try one of our other recipes using the leftovers.

2 (14.5-oz.) cans low-sodium beef broth
1 cup low-sodium soy sauce
¼ cup lemon juice
5 garlic cloves, chopped
1 Tbsp. hickory liquid smoke (optional)
1 (7- to 9-lb.) beef brisket
Garnish: fresh parsley sprigs

1. Stir together first 4 ingredients and, if desired, liquid smoke in a large roasting pan. Place brisket in pan, fat side up. Spoon liquid over brisket. Cover tightly with aluminum foil, and chill 24 hours.
2. Preheat oven to 300°. Bake brisket, covered, 4 to 4½ hours or until fork-tender. Uncover and let stand 20 minutes.
3. Transfer brisket to a cutting board. Trim fat from brisket. Cut brisket across the grain into thin slices. (Or cut brisket into large pieces, and shred with two forks.) Pour pan drippings through a wire-mesh strainer, discarding solids. Serve brisket with drippings. Garnish, if desired.

Slow-Cooked Mushrooms

MAKES 12 SERVINGS
HANDS-ON TIME: 10 MIN.
TOTAL TIME: 4 HR., 20 MIN.

We streamlined Ree's recipe to save time—she cooks hers almost 12 hours. Leftovers can be refrigerated up to three days.

4 lb. fresh mushrooms
½ cup butter
1 (750-milliliter) bottle dry red wine
1 Tbsp. Worcestershire sauce
2 chicken bouillon cubes
2 beef bouillon cubes
1 tsp. freshly ground pepper
1 tsp. dill seeds
1 tsp. garlic powder

1. Bring all ingredients to a boil over medium-high heat. Reduce heat to medium-low, maintaining a slow boil. Cook, stirring occasionally, 4 hours or until liquid is reduced to about 1 cup.

Twice-Baked Potatoes

MAKES 16 SERVINGS
HANDS-ON TIME: 30 MIN.
TOTAL TIME: 1 HR., 45 MIN.

8 medium-size baking potatoes (about 4 lb.)
Canola oil
½ cup butter, cut into slices
1 cup sour cream
8 thick-cut peppered bacon slices, cooked
    and crumbled
½ cup milk
½ tsp. seasoned salt
½ tsp. pepper
2 cups grated sharp Cheddar cheese
2 green onions, sliced

1. Preheat oven to 400°. Rub potatoes with oil. Bake on a baking sheet 45 to 50 minutes or until potatoes are tender and skins are crisp.
2. Meanwhile, stir together butter and next 5 ingredients in a large bowl.
3. Remove potatoes from oven, and let cool 15 minutes. Reduce oven temperature to 300°. Cut warm potatoes in half lengthwise; carefully scoop out pulp into bowl with butter mixture, leaving shells intact.
4. Mash pulp and butter mixture together using a potato masher. Stir in 1 cup cheese, green onions, and seasoned salt and pepper to taste. Spoon mixture into potato shells; place on baking sheet. Sprinkle with remaining 1 cup cheese.
5. Bake at 300° for 15 to 20 minutes or until cheese is melted and potatoes are thoroughly heated.

Scrumptious Apple Pie

MAKES 8 SERVINGS
HANDS-ON TIME: 30 MIN.
TOTAL TIME: 1 HR., 55 MIN.

We found the best way to serve Scrumptious Apple Pie is to spoon it right over a big scoop of vanilla ice cream.

7 cups peeled and sliced Granny Smith
    apples (about 5 medium)
½ cup granulated sugar
2 tsp. lemon juice
¾ cup all-purpose flour, divided
½ tsp. salt, divided
¾ cup butter
1 cup firmly packed brown sugar
½ cup uncooked quick-cooking oats
½ (15-oz.) package refrigerated piecrusts
½ cup chopped pecans
Jarred caramel topping, vanilla ice cream

1. Preheat oven to 375°. Stir together first 3 ingredients, ¼ cup flour, and ¼ tsp. salt until well blended.
2. Cut butter into remaining ½ cup flour with a pastry blender or fork until mixture resembles small peas. Stir in brown sugar, oats, and remaining ¼ tsp. salt.
3. Fit piecrust into a 9-inch pie plate according to package directions; fold edges under, and crimp. Place apple mixture in piecrust, and top with brown sugar mixture, pressing gently to adhere. Shield edges of crust with aluminum foil. Place pie on a foil-lined baking sheet.
4. Bake at 375° for 25 minutes. Remove foil from crust, and bake 25 minutes or until golden brown. Sprinkle with pecans, and bake 5 to 7 minutes or until pecans are toasted. Let pie stand 30 minutes to 2 hours before serving. Serve with caramel topping and ice cream.

HALF-HOUR HOSTESS

Host a Shopping Day Drop-In

In 30 minutes or less, a creamy coffee, easy olive spread, and fun tabletop idea help kick off the year's biggest shopping season.

Come by for Coffee

MAKE AS MANY SERVINGS FOR THE NUMBER OF GUESTS YOU PLAN TO INCLUDE

Caramel-Cream
Macchiato Coffee

Cream Cheese-Olive Spread

Assorted bakery cookies
and brownies

Caramel-Cream Macchiato Coffee

A caramel-and-vanilla whipped cream is the base for our rich coffee.

1. Beat 1 cup whipping cream, 3 Tbsp. jarred caramel topping, and ½ tsp. vanilla extract at low speed with an electric mixer until stiff peaks form. Spoon whipped cream into mugs, and pour hot brewed coffee over caramel whipped cream. Makes about 2 cups whipped cream. Hands-on time: 5 min. Total time: 5 min.

Cream Cheese-Olive Spread

This spread doubles as a filling for finger sandwiches.

1. Stir together 1 (8-oz.) package softened cream cheese, ½ cup finely chopped pimiento-stuffed Spanish olives, and 1 Tbsp. mayonnaise in a bowl. Shape cream cheese mixture into 2 (6-inch) logs, and roll in ½ cup toasted chopped pecans and ¼ cup chopped fresh chives. Makes 2 (6-inch) logs. Hands-on time: 10 min. Total time: 10 min. **Note:** We tested with Town House FlipSides Original Pretzel Crackers.

• T I P •

Don't throw out over-whipped cream—it's easy to rescue. Add a few table-spoons of additional whipping cream, then mix on low with an electric mixer until perfect peaks appear.

15-Minute Tabletop Decoration

Caramel Shopping Bag

1. Press together 12 caramel squares, and press a thin strip of chewy chocolate candy around them to hide the center seams. Stud edges with chocolate sprinkles. Roll small pieces of chewy chocolate candies into balls, and press onto bottom for "feet." Press "handles" made from small pieces of rolled caramel squares onto top.

"I have Thanksgiving leftovers.
Any ideas for turkey, rice, and shrimp?"

Combination Fried Rice
southern favorite

MAKES 4 SERVINGS; **HANDS-ON TIME:** 26 MIN.,
TOTAL TIME: 26 MIN.

Use a mix of whatever meat you have on hand. Spicy chili-garlic sauce adds a kick and, once opened, it keeps indefinitely in the refrigerator.

3 Tbsp. vegetable oil, divided
2 large eggs, lightly beaten
½ cup diced onion
½ cup diced bell pepper
1 cup chopped cooked meat, poultry, or shrimp
½ cup frozen English peas
3 cups cooked rice
¼ cup soy sauce
1 tsp. Asian chili-garlic sauce
Garnish: sliced green onions

1. Heat 1 Tbsp. oil in a large skillet or wok over medium-high heat 1 to 2 minutes; add eggs, and gently stir 1 minute or until softly scrambled. Remove eggs from skillet; chop.
2. Heat remaining 2 Tbsp. oil in skillet; add onion and bell pepper, and stir-fry 3 minutes. Add chopped cooked meat and peas; stir-fry 2 minutes. Add rice, soy sauce, and chili-garlic sauce; stir-fry 5 minutes or until thoroughly heated. Stir in eggs. Garnish, if desired.

Easy Egg Rolls
MAKES 16 TO 18; **HANDS-ON TIME:** 36 MIN.,
TOTAL TIME: 36 MIN.

All sorts of delicious leftovers can be tucked inside an egg roll wrapper—and they're a cinch to assemble. Coleslaw mix adds fresh crunch to the filling.

1 (16-oz.) package shredded coleslaw mix
1 cup chopped cooked meat, poultry, or shrimp
1½ Tbsp. minced fresh ginger
2 garlic cloves, pressed
1 tsp. seasoned pepper
½ tsp. salt
1 (16-oz.) package egg roll wrappers
Vegetable oil

1. Stir together first 6 ingredients.
2. Brush water around outer edge of each egg roll wrapper. Spoon ⅓ cup filling in center of each egg roll wrapper. Fold bottom corner over filling, tucking tip of corner under filling; fold left and right corners over filling. Tightly roll filled end toward remaining corner; gently press to seal.
3. Pour oil to depth of 3 inches in a Dutch oven; heat to 375°. Fry egg rolls, in batches, 3 to 4 minutes or until golden brown; drain on paper towels. Serve immediately.

Sweet & Sour
Cranberry Dipping Sauce

1. Bring 1 (16-oz.) can whole-berry cranberry sauce, ⅓ cup firmly packed light brown sugar, ⅓ cup rice wine vinegar, ¼ cup soy sauce, and 1½ Tbsp. grated fresh ginger to a boil in a small saucepan over medium heat. Cook, stirring often, 2 to 3 minutes or until cranberry sauce is melted and sugar is dissolved. Remove from heat, and cool completely (about 30 minutes). Makes 2 cups. Hands-on time: 10 min., Total time: 40 min.

December

Christmas Feast in Fayetteville

For artist and set designer Meredith Boswell, all roads lead back to her beloved Arkansas. This year, we joined the festivities at her annual Christmas dinner, where fun and delicious food abound.

Meredith Boswell loves to entertain in her self-described "funky casualness." Sprinkle in her delightful mix of spunkiness and razor-sharp wit, and laughter is always on the menu. "I learned how to be a hostess from my Aunt Joyce, who was unflappable even in the midst of absolute and inevitable chaos," she says while whipping up a batch of Buttermilk Panna Cotta. "But I learned to cook while living in New Orleans after college. I didn't have a studio, so cooking replaced the same impulse to make things."

Much of Meredith's time is spent away from her Fayetteville home creating the look of some of Hollywood's biggest movies, everything from *Apollo 13* to *How the Grinch Stole Christmas* (she was nominated for Academy Awards for both). As a result, reconnecting with friends as often as possible is extremely important. "I spend a lot of time living in hotels, so having a comfortable home base is essential to me. My house certainly isn't grand, but it has a great kitchen and feels perfect to me," says Meredith, who always looks forward to relaxing with friends during Christmas.

This mostly make-ahead menu reflects Meredith's knack for mixing traditional recipes with updated Southern classics without losing a lick of their delectable essence. Whatever your style, you'll find these recipes suit it perfectly.

Deviled Ham Terrine
make ahead
MAKES 4¾ CUPS
HANDS-ON TIME: 20 MIN.
TOTAL TIME: 8 HR., 50 MIN.

Use the best quality ham you can find. For a great serving idea, simply line a 5-cup serving piece or 2 (2½-cup) serving pieces with plastic wrap, spoon in deviled ham, cover, and chill. When ready to serve, unmold onto a serving plate, discarding plastic wrap. This recipe can easily be halved.

1½ lb. smoked ham, coarsely chopped (about 4 cups)
½ cup finely chopped fresh parsley
½ cup mayonnaise
6 Tbsp. butter, softened
¼ cup whole-grain Dijon mustard
3 Tbsp. dry white wine
1 celery rib, finely chopped
2 green onions, finely chopped
1 tsp. lemon zest
¾ tsp. black pepper
¼ tsp. ground red pepper
Crackers and Quick Winter Pickled Veggies
Garnish: sliced pickled okra

1. Pulse ham, in batches, in a food processor 4 to 6 times or until shredded. (Do not overprocess.)
2. Stir together parsley and next 9 ingredients. Stir in ham until well blended. Cover and chill 8 hours. Store in an airtight container in refrigerator up to 3 days. Let stand at room temperature 30 minutes before serving. Serve with crackers and Quick Winter Pickled Veggies. Garnish, if desired.

• T I P •

Pickle any of these seasonal fall and winter vegetables: cauliflower florets, Swiss chard stalks, carrot sticks, sliced parsnips, halved Brussels sprouts, radishes, sliced fennel, green beans, or bell pepper rings

Quick Winter Pickled Veggies

make ahead

MAKES ABOUT 8 CUPS
HANDS-ON TIME: 35 MIN.
TOTAL TIME: 2 HR., 5 MIN. PLUS 1 DAY FOR CHILLING

Serve alongside Deviled Ham Terrine or add to your favorite martini or Bloody Mary. Make extra as a take-away for your guests. Pickles may seem summery but you can enjoy them using seasonal fall and winter produce.

2 cups apple cider vinegar
⅔ cup sugar
¼ cup kosher salt
3 garlic cloves
1 tsp. yellow mustard seeds
1 tsp. fennel seeds
1 tsp. black peppercorns
½ tsp. dried crushed red pepper
8 cups assorted cut vegetables

1. Bring first 8 ingredients and 2½ cups water to a boil in a large non-aluminum saucepan over medium-high heat, stirring until sugar is dissolved; boil 1 minute. Let stand 30 minutes.

2. Meanwhile, cook vegetables, in batches, in boiling water to cover 1 to 2 minutes or until crisp-tender; drain. Plunge into ice water to stop the cooking process; drain.

3. Transfer vegetables to a large bowl or 2½-qt. container. Pour vinegar mixture over vegetables. Let stand 1 hour. Cover and chill 1 day before serving. Store in an airtight container in refrigerator up to 1 week.

Test Kitchen Secrets

A standing rib roast is always associated with special occasions. ("Standing" means the rib bones are included.) This hearty cut makes an impressive presentation and feeds a crowd. "It's so much easier than roasting a whole turkey or ham. All you do is pop the roast in the pan and let it go until it reaches 120° (for medium-rare). No need to baste or shield," says Test Kitchen Pro Marian Cooper Cairns. Here are a few tips for first-timers:

- This recipe calls for a four-rib roast (a full roast has 7 ribs). One rib provides two generous servings.
- Ask the grocery store butcher to "French," or trim, the meat around the bones for a classic presentation.
- We recommend roasting to an internal temperature of 120°. This may seem low, but once out of the oven, the roast's temperature continues to rise, ensuring a perfect medium-rare in the center, and ends which are more medium to medium-well.
- Look for rib roasts on special during the holidays (as reasonable as $5.99/lb.). While it's definitely a splurge, an on-sale standing rib roast is about the same price as a premium turkey or ham.

Fennel-Crusted Rib Roast

MAKES 8 SERVINGS
HANDS-ON TIME: 20 MIN.
TOTAL TIME: 3 HR., 5 MIN.

1 (7- to 9-lb.) 4-rib prime rib roast, trimmed
2 tsp. black peppercorns
2 tsp. fennel seeds
1½ tsp. coriander seeds
1 Tbsp. olive oil
4 tsp. kosher salt
Garnishes: fresh cranberries, oranges, grey sea salt

1. Preheat oven to 400° Let roast stand at room temperature 30 minutes.

2. Pulse peppercorns, fennel, and coriander in a spice grinder 5 times or until coarsely ground. (Or, place spices in a zip-top plastic freezer bag, and crush using a rolling pin or skillet.) Rub roast with oil, and sprinkle with salt. Press spice mixture onto all sides of roast. Place on a rack in a roasting pan.

3. Bake at 400° for 2 hours or until a meat thermometer inserted into thickest portion registers 120° to 125° (medium-rare) or to desired degree of doneness. Let stand 15 minutes to 1 hour before slicing. If desired, reserve pan drippings for Roasted Asparagus. Garnish, if desired.

Roasted Asparagus: Preheat broiler with oven rack 3 inches from heat. Snap off and discard tough ends of 2 lb. fresh asparagus; toss with 2 Tbsp. pan drippings from Fennel-Crusted Rib Roast* and 1 lemon, thinly sliced. Arrange in a single layer in a 17- x 12-inch jelly-roll pan. Broil 4 to 9 minutes or until browned. Makes 8 servings. Hands-on Time: 15 min. Total Time: 20 min.

*2 Tbsp. olive oil and salt and pepper to taste may be substituted.

This Season's Best Wines for $15 or Less

Executive Food Editor Scott Jones shares his top wine picks to pair with this delicious menu.

White:
- **Clif Family Winery,** The Climber, California
- **Snap Dragon,** Chardonnay, California
- **Waterbrook,** Chardonnay, Washington
- **Penfolds,** Koonunga Hill Chardonnay, Australia

Red:
- **Redtree,** Pinot Noir, California
- **d'Arenberg,** The Stump Jump Shiraz, Australia
- **Fetzer,** Cabernet Sauvignon, California
- **Castle Rock,** Pinot Noir, Washington

Warm Greens With Cornbread Croutons

MAKES 8 SERVINGS
HANDS-ON TIME: 22 MIN.
TOTAL TIME: 37 MIN.

Reserve and freeze a large wedge of cornbread when you make your Thanksgiving dressing. It will save time in making the delicious cornbread croutons. Warm salad not your speed? Try the Baby Greens With Molasses Vinaigrette version.

4 cups (¾-inch) cornbread cubes
2 Tbsp. melted butter
1 tsp. kosher salt, divided
1 tsp. coarsely ground pepper, divided
1 medium-size red onion, halved and sliced
1 garlic clove, minced
¼ cup olive oil
⅓ cup apple cider vinegar
2 Tbsp. molasses
1 Tbsp. coarse-grained Dijon mustard
4 bunches frisée, torn*

1. Preheat oven to 400°. Gently toss cornbread cubes with melted butter, ¼ tsp. salt, and ½ tsp. pepper. Arrange on a baking sheet in a single layer. Bake 15 to 25 minutes or until toasted.
2. Sauté onion and garlic in hot oil in a Dutch oven over medium heat 5 minutes. Stir in vinegar, molasses, mustard, and remaining ¾ tsp. salt and ½ tsp. pepper; cook 1 minute. Add frisée, and toss to coat. Cook, stirring constantly, 1 to 2 minutes or until frisée just begins to wilt. Transfer to a serving dish, and sprinkle with cornbread croutons; serve immediately.
*2 bunches curly endive may be substituted.

Baby Greens With Molasses Vinaigrette

MAKES 8 SERVINGS
HANDS-ON TIME: 15 MIN.
TOTAL TIME: 15 MIN.

1. Whisk together ⅓ cup olive oil, ¼ cup apple cider vinegar, 2 Tbsp. molasses, 1 Tbsp. coarse-grained Dijon mustard, 1 minced garlic clove, ¾ tsp. kosher salt, and ½ tsp. pepper. Toss desired amount of dressing with 1 (5-oz.) package thoroughly washed spring greens mix. Top with ¼ red onion, thinly sliced, and cornbread croutons. Serve with remaining dressing.

Root Vegetable Gratin

make ahead
MAKES 8 SERVINGS
HANDS-ON TIME: 42 MIN.
TOTAL TIME: 1 HR., 52 MIN.

Slice the Yukon golds last to prevent them from browning. Parsnips or carrots can be added to the mix as well; you just need 3½ lb. vegetables total. Rutabagas have a heavy wax coating but will peel easily with a standard vegetable peeler.

2 white bread slices
¼ cup firmly packed fresh flat-leaf parsley leaves
1 (4-oz.) goat cheese log, crumbled
3 Tbsp. butter
3 shallots, minced
3 garlic cloves, minced
5 Tbsp. all-purpose flour
2½ cups milk
1 cup heavy cream
2 tsp. kosher salt
½ tsp. pepper
½ tsp. dried thyme
1½ cups (6 oz.) freshly shredded Parmesan cheese
1 lb. sweet potatoes, peeled and thinly sliced
1 lb. rutabagas, peeled and thinly sliced
1 lb. Yukon gold potatoes, peeled and thinly sliced
½ lb. turnips, peeled and thinly sliced

1. Pulse bread and parsley in a food processor 5 to 7 times or until coarsely chopped. Stir in goat cheese; cover and chill.

2. Preheat oven to 400°. Melt butter in a Dutch oven over medium heat; add shallots and garlic, and cook, stirring often, 3 minutes. Whisk in flour, and cook, whisking constantly, 1 minute. Gradually whisk in milk and next 4 ingredients. Cook, whisking often, 8 to 9 minutes or until mixture thickens. Remove from heat; whisk in cheese until melted and smooth.

3. Layer half each of sliced vegetables in a lightly greased 13- x 9-inch baking dish; pour 2 cups sauce over vegetables. Repeat layers once.

4. Bake at 400° for 45 minutes; sprinkle with breadcrumb mixture, and bake 15 to 20 minutes or until golden brown and potatoes are fork tender. Remove from oven, and let stand 10 minutes.

Note: To make ahead, prepare recipe as directed through Step 3. Cover with plastic wrap, and chill. Preheat oven to 400°. Remove plastic wrap, and let stand at room temperature 30 minutes. Proceed with recipe as directed in Step 4.

Buttermilk Panna Cotta With Zinfandel Poached Figs

make ahead

MAKES 8 SERVINGS
HANDS-ON TIME: 22 MIN.
TOTAL TIME: 8 HR. (INCLUDING FIGS)

Panna cotta, an eggless custard, is generally served unmolded on a serving plate. We serve it in juice glasses for casual flair and ease, plus you can catch every last drop of the spiced Zinfandel syrup. Serve with crisp ginger cookies or almond biscotti.

2 cups heavy cream
½ vanilla bean, split
1 envelope unflavored gelatin
½ cup plus 2 Tbsp. sugar
2½ cups buttermilk
Zinfandel Poached Figs
Garnish: freshly grated nutmeg

1. Combine cream and vanilla bean in a small saucepan; sprinkle gelatin over cream, and let stand 10 minutes. Cook cream mixture over medium-low heat, stirring constantly, 5 minutes or until gelatin is dissolved. Increase heat to medium; add sugar, and stir until sugar is dissolved (about 2 to 3 minutes).

2. Remove from heat. Scrape seeds from vanilla bean into cream mixture with back of a knife; discard vanilla bean. Whisk in buttermilk. Divide mixture among 8 (10-oz.) glasses. Cover and chill 6 hours to 2 days. Spoon 2 to 3 Tbsp. Zinfandel Poached Figs into each glass just before serving. Garnish, if desired.

Zinfandel Poached Figs:

MAKES ABOUT 1½ CUPS
HANDS-ON TIME: 25 MIN.
TOTAL TIME: 1 HR., 25 MIN.

The remaining Zinfandel wine is the perfect companion for the succulent standing rib roast, rich gratin, and warm greens.

1 cup halved dried Mission figlets
1 cup Zinfandel wine*
½ cup chopped dried apricots
⅓ cup honey
½ vanilla bean, split**
⅛ tsp. ground cinnamon
Pinch of salt and pepper

1. Combine all ingredients in a small saucepan. Bring to a boil over medium-high heat; reduce heat to medium-low, and simmer, stirring occasionally, 10 to 12 minutes or until slightly thickened. Scrape seeds from vanilla bean into fig mixture; discard vanilla bean. Cool 1 hour. Serve immediately, or cover and chill until ready to serve. Store in an airtight container in refrigerator up to 2 weeks. If chilled, let stand at room temperature 30 minutes before serving.
*1 cup cranberry-grape juice cocktail and 2 tsp. apple cider vinegar may be substituted.
**½ tsp. vanilla extract may be substituted. (Stir extract into figs after removing saucepan from heat.)

Kumquat Martini

fast fixin's

MAKES 1 SERVING
HANDS-ON TIME: 10 MIN.
TOTAL TIME: 15 MIN. (INCLUDING SYRUP)

Get in the cheer with this sipping cocktail. It's a cross between a mint julep and a classic martini. Take the pressure off the hostess: Prep the ingredients separately in small bowls and let guests muddle and shake their drinks to order.

2 kumquats, sliced
5 fresh mint leaves
1 to 2 Tbsp. Super Simple Syrup
Crushed ice
¼ cup vodka

1. Combine first 3 ingredients in a cocktail shaker. Press leaves and kumquat slices against bottom of shaker using a muddler or back of a wooden spoon to release flavors; add ice and vodka. Cover with lid, and shake vigorously until thoroughly chilled (about 30 seconds). Strain into a chilled martini glass. Serve immediately.

Super Simple Syrup: Microwave 1 cup water in a microwave-safe 4-cup glass measuring cup at HIGH 1 minute and 30 seconds or until very hot. Stir in 2 cups sugar. Stir 20 seconds. Microwave at HIGH 45 seconds; stir until sugar is dissolved and mixture is clear. Cover and chill until ready to use. Store in an airtight container in refrigerator up to 1 month. Makes about 2½ cups. Hands-on Time: 5 min., Total Time: 5 min.

Essential Guide to Christmas

Within these pages, we share some of our best easygoing recipes to help make the season magical.

The Crowd-Pleasing Appetizer

For the perfect low-stress starter, try this rich and creamy baked dip with a hint of blue cheese.

Permission Slip

In a hurry? Try these Test Kitchen-approved ready-made dips available from wholesale clubs and grocery stores.

- Sabra Hummus With Roasted Pine Nuts
- Chef Solutions Heat & Eat Spinach Artichoke Dip
- Garden Fresh Gourmet Jack's Special Salsa
- Gournay Cheese Boursin
- Hannah Tzatziki Yogurt Dip
- Wholly Guacamole

Blue Cheese-Bacon Dip

MAKES 12 TO 15 SERVINGS
HANDS-ON TIME: 36 MIN.
TOTAL TIME: 56 MIN.

Make and bake Blue Cheese-Bacon Dip in four small baking dishes. Arrange each on a tray with grapes and crackers, and scatter throughout the party area.

3 Tbsp. chopped walnuts
7 bacon slices, chopped
2 garlic cloves, minced
2 (8-oz.) packages cream cheese, softened
⅓ cup half-and-half
4 oz. crumbled blue cheese
2 Tbsp. chopped fresh chives
Grape clusters, assorted crackers
Garnish: chopped fresh chives

1. Preheat oven to 350°. Bake walnuts in single layer in a shallow pan 6 to 8 minutes or until toasted and fragrant, stirring after 3 minutes.
2. Cook bacon in a skillet over medium-high heat, stirring often, 10 minutes or until crisp. Remove bacon, and drain on paper towels, reserving 1 Tbsp. drippings in skillet. Add minced garlic to hot drippings, and sauté 1 minute.
3. Beat cream cheese at medium speed with an electric mixer until smooth. Add half-and-half, beating until combined. Stir in bacon, garlic, blue cheese, and chives. Spoon mixture into 4 (1-cup) baking dishes or 1 (1-qt.) baking dish.
4. Bake at 350° for 20 minutes or until golden and bubbly. Sprinkle with chopped walnuts, and serve with grape clusters and assorted crackers. Garnish, if desired.

Goat Cheese-Bacon Dip:
Substitute pecans for walnuts, goat cheese for blue cheese, and 2 tsp. chopped fresh thyme for 2 Tbsp. chives. Serve with pear slices, toasted baguette slices, and assorted crackers.

Cheddar Cheese-Bacon Dip:
Substitute pecans for walnuts, shredded sharp Cheddar cheese for blue cheese, and chopped fresh parsley for chives. Add ⅛ to ¼ tsp. ground red pepper, if desired. Serve with apple slices and assorted crackers.

The Perfect Party Dish

Serve this statement-making salad at your next get-together. Better still, it's make-ahead and easy to tote, ideal for a neighborhood potluck too.

Spinach-Apple Salad With Maple-Cider Vinaigrette

make ahead

MAKES 8 SERVINGS
HANDS-ON TIME: 20 MIN.
TOTAL TIME: 50 MIN.

Pecans seasoned with ginger, curry, and salt top this festive salad.

Sugared Curried Pecans

1 (6-oz.) package pecan halves
2 Tbsp. butter, melted
3 Tbsp. sugar
¼ tsp. ground ginger
⅛ tsp. curry powder
⅛ tsp. kosher salt
⅛ tsp. ground red pepper

Maple-Cider Vinaigrette

⅓ cup cider vinegar
2 Tbsp. pure maple syrup
1 Tbsp. Dijon mustard
¼ tsp. kosher salt
¼ tsp. pepper
⅔ cup olive oil

Salad

1 (10-oz.) package fresh baby spinach, thoroughly washed
1 Gala apple, thinly sliced
1 small red onion, thinly sliced
1 (4-oz.) package crumbled goat cheese

1. Prepare Pecans: Preheat oven to 350°. Toss pecans in butter. Stir together sugar and next 4 ingredients in a bowl; add pecans, tossing to coat. Spread in a single layer in a nonstick aluminum foil-lined pan. Bake 10 minutes. Cool in pan on a wire rack 20 minutes; separate pecans with a fork.
2. Prepare Vinaigrette: Whisk together cider vinegar and next 4 ingredients. Gradually whisk in oil until well blended.
3. Prepare Salad: Combine spinach and next 3 ingredients in a bowl. Drizzle with desired amount of Maple-Cider Vinaigrette; toss to coat. Sprinkle with pecans. Serve with any remaining vinaigrette.

Note: Pecans may be made up to 1 week ahead. Store in an airtight container. Vinaigrette may be made up to 3 days ahead. Cover and chill until ready to serve.

Spinach-Pear Salad With Sugared Curried Walnuts:

Substitute walnuts for pecans, 1 ripe Bartlett pear for apple, and crumbled blue cheese for goat cheese.

The Best Seasonal Sippers

Celebrate in style with these holiday beverages. Choose from a party-starting cocktail to the perfect sparkling wine to toast the New Year.

● QUICK IDEAS ●

Add garnishes to match or complement the preserve flavor you choose. Fresh blackberries and mint sprigs look great on glasses of Blackberry-Bourbon Sours, while lemon and kiwifruit slices are fancy touches to Ginger-Bourbon Cocktails.

Peach-Bourbon Sours

fast fixin's

MAKES 6 SERVINGS
HANDS-ON TIME: 10 MIN.
TOTAL TIME: 10 MIN.

½ cup peach preserves
½ cup hot water
1 cup plus 2 Tbsp. bourbon or whiskey
3 Tbsp. lemon juice
Garnishes: lemon slices, fresh basil sprigs

1. Whisk together peach preserves and hot water in a glass pitcher until preserves are dissolved. Whisk in bourbon and lemon juice.
2. Fill a cocktail shaker with ice. Add one-third of bourbon mixture; cover with lid, and shake until thoroughly chilled. Pour over ice into 2 (8- to 12-oz.) glasses. Repeat procedure with remaining bourbon mixture. Garnish, if desired. Serve immediately.
*Seedless blackberry, apricot, or ginger preserves may be substituted.

Holiday Beverages

White Wine: Pepperwood Grove, Viognier, California ($9)

Red Wine: Concha y Toro, Casillero del Diablo, Carmenère, Chile ($12)

Champagne: Brut, Veuve Clicquot, Yellow Label, France ($45)
"Worth the splurge"

Beer: 90 Minute IPA, Dogfish Brewery, Milton, Delaware ($11, 4-pack)

The Christmas Eve Main Dish

It's one of the busiest days of the season, but take time for this comforting lasagna. Best of all, it can be made a day (or up to a month) ahead.

Classic Lasagna

freezeable • make ahead

MAKES 8 TO 10 SERVINGS
HANDS-ON TIME: 31 MIN.
TOTAL TIME: 2 HR., 30 MIN.

The homemade Italian Meat Sauce for Classic Lasagna takes time, but is worth the effort. Make extra sauce and freeze to enjoy later over spaghetti.

Italian Meat Sauce

2 medium onions, chopped
1 Tbsp. olive oil
4 garlic cloves, minced
1 lb. lean ground beef
1 (14.5-oz.) can basil, garlic, and oregano diced tomatoes
2 (6-oz.) cans tomato paste
1 (8-oz.) can basil, garlic, and oregano tomato sauce
1 bay leaf
1 tsp. dried Italian seasoning
1 tsp. salt
½ tsp. pepper

Lasagna

12 uncooked lasagna noodles
8 cups boiling water
1 Tbsp. olive oil
1 (16-oz.) container ricotta cheese
2 large eggs, lightly beaten
¼ cup grated Parmesan cheese
¼ tsp. salt
¼ tsp. pepper
18 thin part-skim mozzarella cheese slices, divided

1. Prepare Sauce: Sauté onions in hot oil in a 3-qt. skillet over medium-high heat 5 minutes or until tender. Add garlic, and sauté 1 minute. Add beef, and cook, stirring occasionally, 10 minutes or until beef crumbles and is no longer pink. Stir in diced tomatoes and next 6 ingredients; bring to a boil. Cover, reduce heat, and simmer, stirring occasionally, 30 minutes.

2. Meanwhile, prepare Lasagna: Place lasagna noodles in a 13- x- 9-inch pan. Carefully pour 8 cups boiling water and 1 Tbsp. olive oil over noodles. Let stand 15 minutes.

3. Stir together ricotta cheese and next 4 ingredients until blended.

4. Preheat oven to 350°. Remove and discard bay leaf from meat sauce. Spoon 2 cups meat sauce into a lightly greased 13- x 9-inch baking dish.

Shake excess water from 4 noodles, and arrange over meat sauce; top with one-third ricotta mixture (about ¾ cup) and 6 mozzarella cheese slices. Repeat layers twice.

5. Bake, covered, at 350° for 55 minutes. Uncover and bake 15 to 20 minutes or until bubbly. Let lasagna stand 10 minutes before serving.

Test Kitchen Secrets

- Meat sauce can be made ahead. Let cool 30 minutes. Cover and chill up to 24 hours, or freeze up to 1 month.

- To make lasagna the day before: Prepare as directed though Step 4. Cover and chill up to 24 hours. Let stand 30 minutes before baking.

- To make lasagna up to 1 month ahead: Wrap unbaked lasagna, in baking dish, with heavy-duty aluminum foil. Freeze up to 1 month. Thaw 12 hours in refrigerator. Let stand 30 minutes; unwrap, and bake as directed.

The Keep On-Hand Cookie

Stock your freezer with these two simple doughs for sweet cookies and savory cheesy crisps. You'll be ready to slice and bake in minutes.

Slice-and-Bake Shortbread Cookies

freezeable • make ahead

MAKES 4 DOZEN
HANDS-ON TIME: 15 MIN.
TOTAL TIME: 5 HR. 15 MIN.

1 cup butter, softened
¾ cup powdered sugar
2 tsp. vanilla extract
½ tsp. almond extract
2 cups all-purpose flour
¼ tsp. baking powder
⅛ tsp. salt
Wax paper

1. Beat butter at medium speed with an electric mixer until creamy. Gradually add powdered sugar, beating until smooth. Stir in extracts. Stir together flour, baking powder, and salt. Gradually add to butter mixture, beating at low speed until blended.
2. Shape dough into 2 (7-inch) logs; wrap each log in wax paper, and chill 4 hours, or freeze in zip-top plastic freezer bags up to 1 month.
3. Preheat oven to 350°. If frozen, let logs stand 10 minutes. Cut each log into 24 slices, and place slices 1 inch apart on lightly greased or parchment paper-lined baking sheets.
4. Bake at 350° for 10 to 12 minutes or until edges are golden. Remove from baking sheets to wire racks, and cool completely (about 20 minutes).

Cranberry-Orange Shortbread Cookies: Stir in ½ cup chopped dried cranberries and 1 Tbsp. orange zest with extracts in Step 1.

Toffee-Espresso Shortbread Cookies: Omit almond extract. Stir in ½ cup almond toffee bits and 1 Tbsp. espresso powder with vanilla in Step 1.

Pecan Shortbread Cookies: Omit almond extract. Stir in 1 cup finely chopped toasted pecans with vanilla in Step 1.

Coconut-Macadamia Nut Shortbread Cookies: Omit almond extract. Stir in 1 cup toasted coconut, ½ cup finely chopped macadamia nuts, and ¼ tsp. coconut extract with vanilla in Step 1.

Slice-and-Bake Parmesan Cookies

freezeable • make ahead

MAKES ABOUT 2½ DOZEN
HANDS-ON TIME: 10 MIN.
TOTAL TIME: 9 HR.

1⅓ cups all-purpose flour
⅔ cup freshly grated Parmesan cheese
¼ tsp. ground red pepper
½ cup cold butter, cut up
Wax paper
2 Tbsp. milk

1. Stir together first 3 ingredients in a medium bowl; cut in butter with a pastry blender until crumbly. (Mixture will look very dry.) Gently press mixture together with hands, working until blended and smooth (about 2 to 3 minutes). Shape dough into 1 (8-inch) log. Wrap in wax paper, and chill 8 hours, or freeze in a zip-top plastic freezer bag up to 1 month.
2. Preheat oven to 350°. If frozen, let dough stand 10 minutes. Cut dough into ¼-inch-thick slices, and place 1 inch apart on lightly greased or parchment paper-lined baking sheets. Brush with milk.
3. Bake at 350° for 12 to 14 minutes or until lightly browned. Remove from baking sheet to wire racks and cool completely (about 20 minutes).

Smoky Paprika-Pecan Parmesan Cookies: Stir ½ cup finely chopped toasted pecans and 2 tsp. smoked paprika into flour mixture.

Lemon-Black Pepper Parmesan Cookies: Stir 2 tsp. coarsely ground pepper and 1 tsp. lemon zest into flour mixture.

Basil-Parmesan Cookies: Stir 1 Tbsp. chopped fresh basil into flour mixture.

Orange-Fennel Parmesan Cookies: Stir 2 tsp. orange zest and 1 tsp. crushed fennel seeds into flour mixture.

The Christmas Morning Menu

Take a break from unwrapping gifts to enjoy this updated cheese-and-egg casserole, cornmeal-coated bacon slices, and fresh fruit.

Festive Breakfast

SERVES 6

Texas Toast Breakfast
Bread Pudding

Spicy Cornmeal Bacon

Fresh fruit

Orange juice and coffee

Texas Toast Breakfast Bread Pudding

make ahead

MAKES 6 SERVINGS
HANDS-ON TIME: 15 MIN.
TOTAL TIME: 5 HR., 10 MIN.

5 large eggs*
1 cup milk
1½ tsp. Dijon mustard
¾ tsp. salt
⅛ to ¼ tsp. ground red pepper
1 (9.5-oz.) package frozen mozzarella-
    and-Monterey Jack cheese Texas toast,
    chopped
1 cup grated Cheddar cheese

1. Whisk together first 5 ingredients until blended. Layer half of Texas toast in 6 lightly greased 8-oz. ramekins; sprinkle with half of cheese. Repeat layers once. Pour egg mixture over toast and cheese. Cover and chill 4 to 24 hours.
2. Preheat oven to 325°. Bake 18 to 22 minutes or until centers are set. Let stand 5 minutes before serving.
*1¼ cups egg substitute may be substituted.
Note: We tested with Pepperidge Farm Mozzarella and Monterey Jack Texas Toast. To make one casserole, layer toast, cheese, and egg mixture in a lightly greased 11- x 7-inch baking dish as directed. Bake 50 to 55 minutes or until center is set.

Spicy Cornmeal Bacon

MAKES 8 SERVINGS
HANDS-ON TIME: 10 MIN.
TOTAL TIME: 35 MIN.

Cook the bacon before the breakfast bread pudding. Make sure to cook the bacon on two pans. We tried using one, but the bacon slices were too close to the edge of the pan and grease dripped onto the oven floor.

½ cup plain yellow cornmeal
⅓ cup firmly packed light brown sugar
¼ tsp. salt
¼ to ½ tsp. ground red pepper
1 (16-oz.) package thick hickory-smoked
    bacon slices

1. Preheat oven to 425°. Combine first 4 ingredients in a shallow dish. Dredge bacon in cornmeal mixture, shaking off excess. Place bacon in a single layer on lightly greased wire racks in 2 aluminum foil-lined jelly-roll pans.
2. Bake at 425° for 10 minutes, placing 1 pan on middle oven rack and other on lower oven rack. Switch pans, and bake 10 to 14 more minutes or until edges of bacon slices begin to brown. Cool on wire racks 5 minutes.

—RECIPE INSPIRED BY BARBARA WEDDLE,
OCONTO, WISCONSIN

Spicy Cornmeal-Pecan Bacon:
Stir 3 Tbsp. finely chopped pecans into cornmeal mixture in Step 1.

Cornmeal-Coffee Bacon: Omit ground red pepper. Stir 1 Tbsp. instant espresso into cornmeal mixture in Step 1.

The Easiest Dinner Roll

Our five-ingredient, from-scratch recipe is suited for any level of cook—even first-timers.

Hurry-Up Homemade Crescent Rolls

freezeable • make ahead

MAKES 1 DOZEN
HANDS-ON TIME: 25 MIN.
TOTAL TIME: 1 HR., 40 MIN.

Make life even simpler by baking Hurry-Up Homemade Crescent Rolls ahead and storing in freezer for up to two months.

1 (¼-oz.) envelope active dry yeast
¾ cup warm water (105° to 115°)
3 to 3½ cups all-purpose baking mix
2 Tbsp. sugar
All-purpose flour

1. Combine yeast and warm water in a 1-cup measuring cup; let stand 5 minutes. Combine 3 cups baking mix and sugar in a large bowl; gradually stir in yeast mixture.

2. Turn dough out onto a floured surface, and knead, adding additional baking mix (up to ½ cup) as needed, until smooth and elastic (about 10 minutes).

3. Roll dough into a 12-inch circle; cut circle into 12 wedges. Roll up wedges, starting at wide end, to form a crescent shape; place, point sides down, on a lightly greased baking sheet. Cover and let rise in a warm place (85°), free from drafts, 1 hour or until doubled in bulk.

4. Preheat oven to 425°. Bake 10 to 12 minutes or until golden.

Note: Rolls may be frozen up to 2 months. Bake at 425° for 5 minutes; cool completely (about 30 minutes). Wrap in aluminum foil, and freeze in an airtight container. Thaw at room temperature on a lightly greased baking sheet; bake at 425° for 7 to 8 minutes or until golden. We tested with Bisquick All-Purpose Baking Mix.

Test Kitchen Secret

These rolls can also be made in a heavy-duty electric stand mixer. Prepare as directed in Step 1. Beat dough at medium speed, using dough hook attachment, about 5 minutes, beating in ½ cup additional baking mix, if needed, until dough leaves the sides of the bowl and pulls together, becoming soft and smooth.

Jazz it up with our two flavorful toppings.

- Brush unbaked rolls with ¼ cup melted butter and sprinkle with 2 Tbsp. grated Parmesan cheese and ½ tsp. each kosher salt, coarsely ground pepper, and dried Italian seasoning.

- Brush unbaked rolls with lightly beaten egg white and sprinkle with 1 tsp. each sesame seeds, poppy seeds, and fennel seeds.

The Side Dish

Green beans make almost everyone happy—especially with bacon added. Here's our favorite recipe and a quick lesson on bean buying.

Green Beans With Mushrooms and Bacon
family favorite

MAKES 8 SERVINGS
HANDS-ON TIME: 40 MIN.
TOTAL TIME: 40 MIN.

A dash of dried crushed red pepper perks up Green Beans With Mushrooms and Bacon. But it's still tame enough for the whole family

2 lb. fresh tiny green beans (haricots verts)*
8 bacon slices
3 cups sliced shiitake mushrooms
    (about 7 oz.)
¼ cup chopped shallots
⅛ to ¼ tsp. dried crushed red pepper
½ tsp. freshly ground black pepper
¼ tsp. salt

1. Cook beans in boiling salted water to cover in a Dutch oven over medium-high heat 3 minutes or until crisp-tender; drain. Plunge into ice water to stop the cooking process; drain.
2. Cook bacon in a large skillet over medium-low heat 8 to 10 minutes or until crisp; remove bacon, and drain on paper towels, reserving 1½ Tbsp. drippings in skillet. Crumble bacon.
3. Sauté mushrooms and shallots in hot drippings over medium-high heat 5 minutes or until shallots are tender. Add green beans and crushed red pepper; sauté 1 to 2 minutes or until thoroughly heated. Stir in crumbled bacon, black pepper, and salt.
*Snap (or string) beans may be substituted. Increase cook time in Step 1 to 4 to 5 minutes.

Asparagus With Mushrooms and Bacon: Substitute 2 lb. fresh asparagus for green beans. Snap off and discard tough ends of asparagus. Cut asparagus into 1½ -inch pieces. Proceed with recipe as directed, cooking asparagus pieces 2 to 4 minutes in Step 1.

Sugar Snaps With Mushrooms and Bacon: Substitute 1½ lb. sugar snap peas, trimmed, for tiny green beans. Proceed with recipe as directed, cooking sugar snaps 4 minutes in Step 1.

Green Bean ID

Snap (or string) beans refers to the common green bean. These may need trimming, which means snapping off the end of the bean and pulling the tough "string" away from the bean.

Haricot vert [ah-ree-koh VEHR] is French for green string beans, but generally refers to small, very tender beans. We call them tiny green beans in our ingredient listing. Find them loose in produce bins or in 8-oz. packages.

Pole beans aren't the best choice for this dish—they're tougher and require a longer cook time.

Perfect Mashed Potatoes

Whip out your hand-held mixer, and whirl buttery Yukon golds into a heavenly homemade side dish.

Perfect Mashed Potatoes

MAKES ABOUT 6 CUPS
HANDS-ON TIME: 22 MIN.
TOTAL TIME: 43 MIN.

Yukon gold potatoes yield a texture that's just right for holding a pool of flavorful gravy.

3 lb. Yukon gold potatoes
2 tsp. salt, divided
⅓ cup butter
⅓ cup half-and-half
4 oz. cream cheese, softened
¾ tsp. coarsely ground pepper

Test Kitchen Secret

"Using an electric mixer gives you slightly chunky potatoes," says Lyda Jones Burnette, Test Kitchen Director, "which lets everyone know they're homemade." She adds, "Beat only a few seconds beyond the point where you feel the potatoes release from the beaters."

Three Easy Steps

1. Peel potatoes, and cut into 1-inch pieces. Bring potatoes, 1 tsp. salt, and cold water to cover to a boil in a medium-size Dutch oven over medium-high heat. Reduce heat to medium-low, and cook 16 to 20 minutes or until fork-tender; drain.

2. Return potatoes to Dutch oven. Cook 1 minute or until water is evaporated and potatoes look dry. Mound potatoes on 1 side of Dutch oven; add butter, next 3 ingredients, and remaining 1 tsp. salt to opposite side of pan. Cook 1 to 2 minutes or until butter is melted and mixture boils. Heating liquid ingredients keeps potatoes piping hot..

3. Remove from heat; beat at medium speed with a hand-held electric mixer 30 seconds to 1 minute or to desired degree of smoothness. (Do not overbeat.) Serve immediately.

Crispy Tex-Mex Potato Patties

MAKES 4 TO 5 SERVINGS
HANDS-ON TIME: 30 MIN.
TOTAL TIME: 3 HR., 13 MIN. (INCLUDING MASHED POTATOES)

Chilling helps patties hold together while frying. Serve as a side to steak or pork chops, or turn them into a breakfast main dish by adding ham and fried eggs.

2½ cups warm Perfect Mashed Potatoes
1 jalapeño pepper, seeded and minced
¼ tsp. ground cumin
2 cups yellow corn tortilla chips
1 Tbsp. vegetable oil, divided
Toppings: sour cream, salsa, chopped fresh cilantro

1. Stir together first 3 ingredients. Cover and chill 2 to 24 hours. Shape potatoes into 10 (2½-inch) patties.

2. Crush tortilla chips in a zip-top plastic freezer bag until finely crushed. Dredge patties in tortilla chips.

3. Fry half of patties in 1½ tsp. hot oil in a nonstick skillet over medium-high heat 3 to 4 minutes on each side or until golden. Remove from skillet, and drain on paper towels. Repeat with remaining oil and patties. Serve with desired toppings.

Breakfast Tex-Mex Potato Patties: Prepare recipe as directed, stirring ½ cup diced cooked ham into potato mixture before chilling. Keep patties warm on a wire rack in a jelly-roll pan in a 200° oven. Meanwhile, melt 1 Tbsp. butter in a large nonstick skillet over medium heat. Break 3 eggs into skillet. Cook 2 to 3 minutes on each side or until done. Repeat with 2 more eggs. Serve eggs over potato patties with desired toppings. Makes 5 servings. Hands-on Time: 18 min., Total Time: 3 hr., 30 min. (including Potato Patties)

4 Flavors To Try

Mix up delicious twists on Perfect Mashed Potatoes with these ideas.

Garlic-Parmesan Mashed Potatoes: Substitute ¾ cup grated Parmesan cheese for cream cheese. Prepare recipe as directed through Step 1. Sauté 2 tsp. minced garlic in 1 Tbsp. hot olive oil in Dutch oven 1 minute or until lightly browned. Proceed with recipe as directed. Great with chicken.

Cheddar-Chive Mashed Potatoes: Substitute 1¼ cups (5 oz.) shredded sharp Cheddar cheese for cream cheese. Add 2 Tbsp. thinly sliced fresh chives to potatoes before beating. Serve with beef.

Gruyère-Thyme Mashed Potatoes: Substitute 1¼ cups (5 oz.) shredded Gruyère cheese for cream cheese. Add 1 tsp. finely chopped fresh thyme into potatoes before beating. Ideal with pork.

Tangy Mashed Potatoes: Substitute buttermilk for half-and-half. Pair with pot roast.

Overnight Coffee Cakes

Brown sugar and pecans team up with a sprinkling of holiday spice for a trio of make-ahead breakfast favorites.

Praline Pull-Apart Bread
family favorite • make ahead

MAKES 12 SERVINGS
HANDS-ON TIME: 15 MIN.
TOTAL TIME: 9 HR., 25 MIN.

Super-easy Praline Pull-Apart Bread gets a speedy start from frozen roll dough, then rises overnight in the refrigerator. Don't skip the quick step of whipping the cream before stirring in the brown sugar—that's the secret to the smooth texture of the caramel-flavored sauce.

1 cup granulated sugar
4 tsp. ground cinnamon, divided
1 (2-lb.) package frozen bread roll dough
½ cup butter, melted
1 cup chopped pecans
¾ cup whipping cream
¾ cup firmly packed brown sugar

1. Stir together granulated sugar and 3 tsp. cinnamon. Dip rolls in butter, 1 at a time; roll in sugar mixture. Arrange rolls in a lightly greased 10-inch tube pan; sprinkle with pecans. Cover and chill 8 to 18 hours.

Test Kitchen Tip

Be sure to use a tube pan rather than a Bundt pan for the Praline Pull-Apart Bread. (Tube pans have straight, high sides, while Bundt pans are more shallow and fluted.) Although both may measure 10 inches in diameter, each holds a different amount of batter.

2. Preheat oven to 325°. Beat whipping cream at high speed with an electric mixer until soft peaks form; stir in brown sugar and remaining 1 tsp. cinnamon. Pour mixture over dough. Place pan on an aluminum foil-lined baking sheet.

3. Bake at 325° for 1 hour or until golden brown. Cool on a wire rack 10 minutes; invert onto a serving plate, and drizzle with any remaining glaze in pan. **Note:** We tested with Rhodes White Dinner Rolls.

Christmas Coffee Cake

family favorite • make ahead

MAKES 12 SERVINGS
HANDS-ON TIME: 15 MIN.
TOTAL TIME: 1 HR., 35 MIN.

A crisp buttery crust topped with a layer of tender orange-glazed cake sets this recipe apart from the crowd. It's equally good served warm from the oven or left on the kitchen counter to season overnight.

2 cups all-purpose flour
1¾ cups firmly packed light brown sugar
2 Tbsp. orange zest
¾ tsp. ground allspice
½ tsp. salt
½ cup butter, softened
1 cup sour cream
1 large egg, lightly beaten
1 tsp. baking soda
1 cup pecan halves
1 Tbsp. orange juice
1 Tbsp. honey

1. Preheat oven to 350°. Stir together first 5 ingredients in a large bowl. Cut butter into flour mixture with a pastry blender or two forks until crumbly. Firmly press 2½ cups crumb mixture onto bottom of a lightly greased 9-inch springform pan.

2. Stir together sour cream, egg, and baking soda; add to remaining crumb mixture, stirring just until dry ingredients are moistened. Pour sour cream mixture over crumb crust in pan; arrange pecan halves over batter.

3. Bake at 350° for 1 hour or until a wooden pick inserted in center comes out clean, shielding with aluminum foil after 40 minutes to prevent excessive browning, if necessary. Cool on a wire rack 20 minutes.

4. Stir together orange juice and honey, and brush over top of cake.

—RECIPE FROM SANDRA BRITTON,

MARIETTA, GEORGIA

Overnight Cinnamon-Pecan Coffee Cake

family favorite • make ahead

MAKES 8 TO 10 SERVINGS
HANDS-ON TIME: 15 MIN.
TOTAL TIME: 8 HR., 50 MIN.

Overnight Cinnamon-Pecan Coffee Cake is so easy to make you won't believe you started from scratch—until you taste it the next morning. The batter for this streusel-topped breakfast sheet cake can be prepped and chilled in the pan up to 18 hours before baking.

¾ cup butter, softened
1 cup granulated sugar
2 large eggs
2 cups all-purpose flour
1 tsp. baking powder
1 tsp. baking soda
1 tsp. ground nutmeg
½ tsp. salt
1 cup sour cream
¾ cup firmly packed brown sugar
½ cup chopped pecans
1 tsp. ground cinnamon

1. Beat butter and granulated sugar at medium speed with an electric mixer until light and fluffy. Add eggs, 1 at a time, beating just until blended after each addition.

2. Combine flour and next 4 ingredients; add to butter mixture alternately with sour cream, beginning and ending with flour mixture. Beat at low speed just until blended after each addition. Spread batter into a greased and floured 13- x 9-inch pan. Stir together brown sugar, pecans, and cinnamon; sprinkle over batter. Cover pan with plastic wrap, and chill 8 to 18 hours.

3. Preheat oven to 350°. Bake coffee cake 35 minutes or until a wooden pick inserted in center comes out clean. Serve warm or at room temperature.

—RECIPE FROM CINDY PATTERSON,

OGDEN, UTAH

Sweet Potato Casserole

Whether from scratch or a streamlined update, your Christmas meal isn't complete without this Southern side.

Why We Love Mama's Way

Recipe from Jennifer Reich

- Baked sweet potatoes
- A variety of toppings
- Served family style

Classic Sweet Potato Casserole

MAKES 6 TO 8 SERVINGS
HANDS-ON TIME: 20 MIN.
TOTAL TIME: 2 HR. 40 MIN.

This mouthwatering casserole will satisfy lovers of crunchy pecans and cornflakes as well as marshmallows.

4½ lb. sweet potatoes
1 cup granulated sugar
½ cup butter, softened
¼ cup milk
2 large eggs
1 tsp. vanilla extract
¼ tsp. salt
1¼ cups cornflakes cereal, crushed
¼ cup chopped pecans
1 Tbsp. brown sugar
1 Tbsp. butter, melted
1½ cups miniature marshmallows

1. Preheat oven to 400°. Bake sweet potatoes at 400° for 1 hour or until tender. Let stand until cool to touch (about 20 minutes); peel and mash sweet potatoes. Reduce oven temperature to 350°.
2. Beat mashed sweet potatoes, granulated sugar, and next 5 ingredients at medium speed with an electric mixer until smooth. Spoon potato mixture into a greased 11- x 7-inch baking dish.

3. Combine cornflakes cereal and next 3 ingredients in a small bowl. Sprinkle over casserole in diagonal rows 2 inches apart.
4. Bake at 350° for 30 minutes. Remove from oven; let stand 10 minutes. Sprinkle marshmallows in alternate rows between cornflakes; bake 10 minutes. Let stand 10 minutes before serving.

Why We Love Your Way

Recipe from Paden Reich

- Frozen mashed sweet potatoes
- Stylish presentation
- 10-minute bake time

Maple Sweet Potato Cups

MAKES 8 SERVINGS
HANDS-ON TIME: 15 MIN.
TOTAL TIME: 39 MIN.

2 (24-oz.) packages frozen steam-and-mash sweet potatoes
⅓ cup butter, cut up
⅓ cup firmly packed light brown sugar
⅓ cup pure maple syrup
3 tsp. orange zest
1 tsp. salt
4 egg whites
½ cup granulated sugar

1. Preheat oven to 400°. Steam potatoes according to package directions. Mash together sweet potatoes and next 5 ingredients. Spoon mixture into 8 (6-oz.) custard cups. Place on a baking sheet.
2. Beat egg whites at high speed with an electric mixer until foamy.

Add sugar, 1 Tbsp. at a time, beating until stiff peaks form and sugar is dissolved. Spread meringue over sweet potato mixture.
3. Bake at 400° for 10 minutes or until golden brown.
Note: We tested with Ore-Ida Steam N' Mash Sweet Potatoes.

South Carolina's Own: Pimiento Cheeseburger

Burger by birth, Southern by the grace of pimiento cheese. We sampled 19 of them to bring you the best.

The pimiento cheeseburger is a stroke of culinary genius straight from our state. The hot beef patty with luscious, pimiento-flecked streams of golden cheese dribbling down its side is diet-busting and cholesterol-inducing, but nearly irresistible. Reportedly created in the 1960s at Columbia's long-closed Dairy Bar, the pimiento cheeseburger is now on the menu of nearly every diner, grill, tavern, drive-in, or cafe in the state, as well as lots of other places in the South.

We ate our fill of these stellar sand-wiches, seeking the state's tastiest. We were as objective as possible, but personal tastes and standards always play a role in rating food. These choices reflect the opinions of three tasters—former staffer Patricia Wilens, Associate Travel Editor Jennifer Cole, and Senior Writer Donna Florio.

Southern Living's Classic Pimiento Cheese

make ahead

MAKES 4 CUPS
HANDS-ON TIME: 15 MIN.
TOTAL TIME: 15 MIN.

1½ cups mayonnaise
1 (4-oz.) jar diced pimiento, drained
1 tsp. Worcestershire sauce
1 tsp. finely grated onion
¼ tsp. ground red pepper
1 (8-oz.) block extra-sharp Cheddar cheese, finely shredded
1 (8-oz.) block sharp Cheddar cheese, shredded

1. Stir together first 5 ingredients in a large bowl; stir in cheeses. Store in refrigerator up to 1 week.

Jalapeño Pimiento Cheese: Stir 2 seeded and minced jalapeño peppers in with cheeses.

Our Five Favorites

1. Smoke on the Water, Greenville. In this downtown tavern's burger, all the components shine. The pimiento cheese is homemade, studded with fire-roasted red peppers that give it a sprightly kick. It's slathered on a huge, succulent beef patty, settled on a freshly baked brioche bun, and then layered with lettuce and tomato. This burger is a monster, but you'll nevertheless be tempted to eat every luscious bite. The place is hopping on weekends, so plan to get there early. 1 Augusta Street, 864-232-9091. Rating: 5 napkins

2. Nu-Way Restaurant & Lounge, Spartanburg. This no-frills roadhouse's Redneck Burger is justifiably one of our top choices. The meat offers hints of Worcestershire sauce, while cayenne adds a little heat to the cheese, a combination of Monterey jack and extra-sharp Cheddar made by the restaurant owner's mom, Libba Hammond. Though the bun isn't anything special, the burger was certainly enhanced by a sturdy slice of tomato and crisp lettuce leaf. 375 East Kennedy Street, 864-582-9685. Rating: 4 napkins

3. Desserts and More, Columbia. We were surprised to find a full-bodied burger in this colorful cafe better known for its sweets, but the excellent pimiento cheese with its diced green tomatoes and chiles quickly won us over. Each tasty burger patty weighs in at a half-pound and is topped with 4 ounces of cheese plus generous amounts of lettuce and tomato. This is a dessert shop after all, so each pimiento cheeseburger also comes with a slice of cake. 4611 Hardscrabble Road, 803-699-8800. Rating: 4 napkins

4. Poe's Tavern, Sullivan's Island. Were Edgar Allan Poe still in resi-dence at Ft. Moultrie, he would likely frequent this pleasant tavern where many menu items are named after his famous stories. We sampled the Gold-Bug Plus, a deliciously juicy burger capped with a nice portion of pimiento cheese, featuring ricotta cheese and smoked red pimientos. The Angus beef is aged a minimum of 50 days and ground on the premises daily. 2210 Middle Street, 843-883-0083. Rating: 4 napkins

5. Kinch's, Rock Hill. All the elements of a great PC burger align in this comfy little bistro across from city hall. The pimiento cheese, made from a fam-ily recipe, tastes of slightly nutty sharp Cheddar, while the juicy burger hints at being slow cooked. An added bonus: the crispy thick-cut fries. 123 Elk Avenue, 803-327-4923. Rating 3.5 napkins

Runners Up

- Tanner's Big Orange: 322 South Pleasantburg Drive, Greenville; 864-235-2247
- Corner Grill: 105 South Kings Hwy., Myrtle Beach; 843-902-1261
- Ruth's Drive-In, 659 West Carolina Avenue, Hartsville; 843-332-6771
- Mathias Sandwich Shop, 7235 Saint Andrew's Road, Columbia; 803-781-4002

Try These Fresh Ways With Citrus

Make the most of these sunny fruits while they're at their peak with these deliciously creative recipes. They use oranges, grapefruit, and clementines to lend a bright touch to everything from seafood to salsa. All will bring a tropical boost to the coldest day.

Gingered Oranges

MAKES 4 SERVINGS
HANDS-ON TIME: 25 MIN.
TOTAL TIME: 25 MIN.

4 large navel oranges
¼ cup sugar
2 (¼-inch-thick) fresh ginger slices, peeled
Gingersnaps

1. Peel and section oranges over a bowl, reserving juice; place orange sections on a serving plate.
2. Bring sugar, ginger, 3 Tbsp. water, and reserved juice to a boil in a small saucepan over high heat; cook 2 minutes, stirring occasionally. Remove from heat; discard ginger.
3. Pour syrup over orange sections. Serve with gingersnaps.
—**RECIPE FROM NORA HENSHAW**, OKEMAH, OKLAHOMA

Gingered Clementines: Substitute 4 to 6 peeled and sliced clementines for oranges. Proceed with recipe as directed, beginning with Step 2 (without reserved juice).
Note: Clementines will not have juice to add to the syrup, but there will still be enough syrup at the end of Step 2 to coat fruit.

Green Salad With Orange Vinaigrette

MAKES 4 SERVINGS
HANDS-ON TIME: 10 MIN.
TOTAL TIME: 15 MIN. (INCLUDING VINAIGRETTE)

1. Combine 1 head Bibb lettuce, torn; 2 cups torn green leaf lettuce; 2 green onions, chopped; and ¼ cup thinly sliced red onion in a large bowl. Drizzle with Orange Vinaigrette, and toss to coat.

Orange Vinaigrette:

MAKES ABOUT ½ CUP.
HANDS-ON TIME: 5 MIN.
TOTAL TIME: 5 MIN.

1. Whisk together 1 tsp. orange zest, ¼ cup fresh orange juice, 2 Tbsp. lemon juice, 1 tsp. Dijon mustard, ½ tsp. salt, and ¼ tsp. freshly ground pepper. Gradually whisk in 6 Tbsp. olive oil until well blended.

Grapefruit Vinaigrette: Omit orange zest and lemon juice. Substitute grapefruit juice for orange juice. Proceed as directed, whisking in 1 Tbsp. honey.

Clementine-Cranberry Salsa

make ahead

MAKES ABOUT 2¼ CUPS
HANDS-ON TIME: 15 MIN.
TOTAL TIME: 1 HR., 15 MIN.

Serve this brightly flavored condiment alongside turkey fajitas, grilled chicken, or pork.

4 clementines, peeled and sectioned
½ cup fresh cranberries, coarsely chopped*
⅓ cup finely chopped red onion
1 Tbsp. sugar
1 Tbsp. fresh lime juice
1 Tbsp. olive oil
¼ tsp. salt
1 jalapeño pepper, seeded and finely chopped

1. Cut clementine sections in half. Combine all ingredients; cover and let stand 1 hour.
*Frozen cranberries, thawed, may be substituted.
—**RECIPE FROM STEPHANIE HAWKINS**, CHARLESTON, SOUTH CAROLINA

Orange-Cranberry Salsa:
Substitute 2 navel oranges for clementines. Makes 1½ cups.

A Small, Sweet Package

Clementines are Mandarin oranges that taste like sweet tangerines. They're generally seedless, and are easy to peel. They're packed in small wooden cases available at most supermarkets, but our staff says Costco and Walmart offer the best deals.

What to do with all those citrus rinds?

- Put some down the disposal for a fresh scent.
- Simmer in a pot of water with cloves and cinnamon for all-natural air-freshener.
- Use orange and grapefruit cups to serve mashed sweet potatoes or sorbet.
- Make citrus sugar: Combine 1½ tsp. coarsely grated citrus peel and ½ cup granulated sugar. Press peel with a spoon to release oils. Store in a tightly covered container up to 1 month.

Scallops in Orange-Butter Sauce

MAKES 4 SERVINGS
HANDS-ON TIME: 32 MIN.
TOTAL TIME: 32 MIN.

For a golden crust, pat scallops dry before searing, and cook in a very hot pan, being careful not to crowd them.

1 (16-oz.) package vermicelli
5 Tbsp. butter, softened and divided
12 large sea scallops (about 1½ lb.)
½ tsp. kosher salt
¼ tsp. pepper
1 Tbsp. olive oil
6 Tbsp. fresh orange juice
6 Tbsp. dry white wine
½ tsp. orange zest
Garnish: shredded fresh basil

1. Cook vermicelli according to package directions; drain, toss with 2 Tbsp. butter, and keep warm.
2. Rinse scallops, and pat dry with paper towels; sprinkle with kosher salt and pepper.
3. Melt 1 Tbsp. butter with 1½ tsp. olive oil in a large skillet over medium-high heat; add 6 scallops, and cook 2 to 3 minutes on each side or until golden. Remove from skillet, cover loosely with aluminum foil, and keep warm. Repeat procedure with 1 Tbsp. butter, and remaining 1½ tsp. oil and 6 scallops.
4. Combine orange juice and wine in a small saucepan; cook over medium-high heat 10 minutes or until mixture is reduced by half. Remove from heat; stir in orange zest and remaining 1 Tbsp. butter. Divide vermicelli among 4 plates; top with scallops and sauce. Garnish, if desired.

Scallops in Grapefruit-Butter Sauce: Omit orange zest. Substitute grapefruit juice for orange juice.

Scallops in Clementine-Butter Sauce: Substitute clementine juice and clementine zest for orange juice and orange zest.

Grapefruit Brûlée

fast fixin's
MAKES 4 SERVINGS
HANDS-ON TIME: 10 MIN.
TOTAL TIME: 10 MIN.

These work best with a kitchen torch (Bed Bath and Beyond, $29.99), though you can also prepare them under the broiler. Place grapefruit on a rack in a broiler pan to get them close to the heat; broil until sugar bubbles and begins to brown.

1. Cut 2 grapefruit in half. Carefully cut around each grapefruit segment with a paring knife, leaving segments and shells intact. Place grapefruit, cut sides up, on an ovenproof serving platter; sprinkle with ½ cup sugar. Holding a kitchen torch about 2 inches away from top of grapefruit, heat sugar, moving torch back and forth, until sugar bubbles and begins to brown.

Orange-and-Grapefruit Brûlée With Coconut Pudding

MAKES 8 TO 10 SERVINGS
HANDS-ON TIME: 40 MIN.
TOTAL TIME: 40 MIN.

Portion in ramekins or sherbet glasses for a light dessert.

Coconut Pudding

2 cups milk
1 (14-oz.) can coconut milk
3 large eggs
¾ cup sugar
⅓ cup all-purpose flour
1 Tbsp. butter
1 tsp. vanilla extract

Orange-and-Grapefruit Brûlée

2 grapefruit, peeled and sectioned
2 oranges, peeled and sectioned
¼ cup sugar

Garnish

Toasted sweetened flaked coconut

Prepare Pudding: Whisk together first 3 ingredients in a large saucepan; whisk in sugar and flour. Cook over medium heat, stirring constantly, 20 minutes or until thickened. Remove from heat; stir in butter and vanilla until butter is melted. Keep warm, or cover and chill until ready to serve, placing heavy-duty plastic wrap directly on warm pudding (to prevent film from forming).

Prepare Brûlée: Arrange grapefruit and oranges in an ovenproof baking dish or on a platter. Sprinkle with sugar. Holding a kitchen torch 2 inches away from fruit, heat sugar, moving back and forth, until sugar bubbles and begins to brown. Serve fruit with warm or chilled coconut pudding, and garnish, if desired.

Freeze Ahead for an Easy Party

Christmas parties don't come much easier (or relaxed) than this one. Make and freeze all the food weeks ahead; then thaw, serve, and celebrate!

Beefy Black Bean Stew

MAKES 4 QT.

HANDS-ON TIME: 35 MIN.

TOTAL TIME: 2 HR., 20 MIN.

1 (1¾- to 2-lb.) flank steak
1 (32-oz.) container beef broth, divided
1 medium onion, chopped
1 medium-size green bell pepper, chopped
2 garlic cloves, minced
2 Tbsp. chili powder
1 tsp. ground cumin
1 tsp. dried oregano
1 Tbsp. olive oil
3 (15-oz.) cans black beans, drained and rinsed
1 (28-oz.) can petite diced tomatoes
1 (12-oz.) dark beer
1 (6-oz.) can tomato paste
1½ tsp. salt
Toppings: fresh cilantro sprigs, sour cream, shredded Mexican cheese blend, tortilla chips
Lime wedges

1. Preheat oven to 400°. Cut beef into 1-inch strips. Line bottom and sides of a 13- x 9-inch pan with aluminum foil, allowing 2 to 3 inches to extend over sides. Place beef in a single layer in pan. Pour 1 cup beef broth over beef. Cover tightly with aluminum foil.
2. Bake at 400° 1 hour or until beef is shreddable. Remove beef from pan, reserving drippings. Shred beef with 2 forks.
3. Sauté onion and next 5 ingredients in hot oil in a Dutch oven over medium heat 5 minutes or until onion is tender. Stir in shredded beef, reserved pan drippings, beans, next 4 ingredients, and remaining beef broth. Bring to a boil; cover, reduce heat to medium-low, and cook, stirring occasionally, 45 minutes. Serve with desired toppings and lime wedges.

—INSPIRED BY SUSAN M. RUNKLE, WALTON, KENTUCKY

Lemon-Chicken Soup

MAKES 5½ QT.

HANDS-ON TIME: 30 MIN.

TOTAL TIME: 2 HR., 15 MIN.

You'll want to freeze any leftovers of this soup in small containers—it's perfect for taking to lunch or serving a sick child.

6 skin-on, bone-in chicken breasts
2 large onions, chopped
5 celery ribs, chopped
2 garlic cloves, minced
1 tsp. olive oil
1 (1-lb.) package carrots, sliced
4 tsp. lemon zest
2 bay leaves
2 tsp. salt
½ cup loosely packed fresh flat-leaf parsley leaves
Toppings: cooked barley, cooked green beans

1. Bring chicken and water to cover to a boil in a Dutch oven over medium-high heat; reduce heat to low, and simmer 1 hour.
2. Remove chicken, reserving liquid, and let cool 15 minutes. Shred chicken.
3. Pour reserved cooking liquid through a wire-mesh strainer into a bowl, discarding solids; wipe Dutch oven clean. Add water to cooking liquid to equal 10 cups.
4. Sauté onion, celery, and garlic in hot oil in Dutch oven over medium-high heat 5 to 6 minutes or until tender. Add shredded chicken, cooking liquid, carrots, and next 3 ingredients. Cover, reduce heat to medium, and cook 20 minutes or until carrots are tender. Add parsley. Serve with desired toppings.

Sausage-Tortellini Soup

freezeable • make ahead

MAKES 4 QT.

HANDS-ON TIME: 38 MIN.

TOTAL TIME: 1 HR.

Prepare this soup through Step 1 to freeze. Don't cook and add the tortellini until you've reheated the soup.

1½ lb. hot Italian sausage, casings removed*
1 medium onion, diced
3 garlic cloves, minced
2 (15-oz.) cans Italian-style stewed tomatoes
1 (16-oz.) bag frozen cut green beans
1 (8-oz.) package sliced fresh mushrooms
1 (8-oz.) can tomato sauce
4 beef bouillon cubes
3 carrots, sliced
3 medium zucchini, quartered and sliced
1 cup dry red wine
2 tsp. dried Italian seasoning
1 (20-oz.) package refrigerated cheese-filled tortellini
Freshly grated Parmesan cheese

1. Sauté sausage, onion, and garlic in a Dutch oven over medium heat 8 minutes or until sausage crumbles and is no longer pink; drain. Stir in tomatoes, next 8 ingredients, and 10 cups water; bring to a boil. Cover, reduce heat to low, and cook 20 minutes or until carrots are crisp-tender.
2. Cook tortellini according to package directions; drain. Stir into soup just before serving. Serve with Parmesan cheese.

—RECIPE FROM RYAN POE, SONOMA, CALIFORNIA

*1 lb. turkey Italian sausage may be substituted.

Test Kitchen Secrets

- Freeze soups in plastic containers up to two months ahead. Divide soup into smaller containers for quicker thawing. Place frozen soup in a Dutch oven over very low heat and cover. Cook, stirring occasionally, until hot. Times will vary with amount of soup, but plan to heat at least 30 to 40 minutes before serving.
- Loosely wrap frozen Stir-and-Bake Spoon Rolls in foil to reheat, or make and chill the dough up to a week ahead. Bake just before dinner to fill the house with their mouthwatering aroma.
- Wrap brownies in heavy-duty foil, and place in a plastic freezer bag. Freeze up to two months; thaw at room temperature two hours.

Stir-and-Bake Spoon Rolls

freezeable • make ahead
MAKES 2 DOZEN
HANDS-ON TIME: 15 MIN.
TOTAL TIME: 28 MIN.

Bake these rolls and freeze in zip-top freezer bags. They're absolutely the fastest yeast rolls ever.

1 (¼-oz.) envelope active dry yeast
2 cups warm water (100° to 110°)
4 cups self-rising flour
¾ cup butter, melted
¼ cup sugar
1 large egg, lightly beaten

1. Preheat oven to 400°. Combine yeast and 2 cups warm water in a large bowl; let stand 5 minutes. Stir in flour and remaining ingredients until blended. Spoon batter into 2 greased (12-cup) muffin pans. Bake for 13 minutes or until golden.

—RECIPE FROM LILANN HUNTER TAYLOR,
SAVANNAH, GEORGIA

Miniature Spoon Rolls: Spoon batter into 2 greased (24 cup) miniature muffin pans.* Bake at 400° for 9 minutes or until golden. Makes 4 dozen. Hands-on Time: 15 min., Total Time: 24 min.
*4 (12-cup) miniature muffin pans may be substituted.

Bourbon Slushies

freezeable • make ahead
MAKES ABOUT 4 QT.
HANDS-ON TIME: 10 MIN.
TOTAL TIME: 9 HR., 10 MIN.

Assemble the base mixture for this drink, and pop in the freezer. When serving, don't stir. The cherry juice will drip down to the bottom of the glass, producing colorful layers.

1 (64-oz.) container pineapple juice
1 (12-oz.) can frozen lemonade concentrate, thawed
1 (12-oz.) can frozen limeade concentrate, thawed
1½ cups bourbon*
¼ cup maraschino cherry juice
Garnish: maraschino cherries

1. Stir together first 4 ingredients and 1 cup water. Divide mixture into 2 (1-gal.) zip-top plastic freezer bags; seal and freeze 8 hours or until firm.
2. Remove from freezer, and let stand 1 hour or until softened and beginning to melt. Using hands, squeeze bags until mixture is slushy. Spoon 2 cups mixture into each serving glass. Top each with 2 tsp. cherry juice. (Do not stir.) Serve immediately. Garnish, if desired.
*Lemon-lime soft drink may be substituted.

Espresso-Fudge Truffle Brownies

freezeable • make ahead
MAKES 12 SERVINGS
HANDS-ON TIME: 30 MIN.
TOTAL TIME: 1 HR., 11 MIN.

¾ cup butter
5 (1-oz.) unsweetened chocolate baking squares, chopped
3 large eggs
2 cups sugar
2 Tbsp. instant espresso
1¼ cups all-purpose flour
½ tsp. baking powder
¼ tsp. salt
1 cup semisweet chocolate morsels

1. Preheat oven to 350°. Cook butter and chocolate squares in a 3½-qt. saucepan over low heat, stirring occasionally, until melted and smooth (about 3 minutes). Remove from heat; cool slightly (about 1 to 2 minutes).
2. Whisk eggs into chocolate mixture, 1 at a time, whisking until blended after each addition. Gradually add sugar, whisking until blended. Whisk in instant espresso. Gradually add flour, baking powder, and salt, whisking until blended. Stir in chocolate morsels. Pour batter into a lightly greased aluminum foil-lined 13- x 9-inch pan.
3. Bake at 350° for 30 to 33 minutes or until set (a wooden pick inserted in center will come out with a few moist crumbs). Remove from oven; cool in pan on a wire rack 10 minutes. Lift from pan, using foil sides as handles. Cut into squares.

Espresso-Fudge-Pecan Brownies: Sprinkle 1 cup toasted chopped pecans over batter before baking.

Espresso-Fudge-Walnut Brownies: Sprinkle 1 cup toasted chopped walnuts over batter before baking.

Host an Effortless Open House

These stylishly delicious recipes help get your festive mix-and-mingle started in 30 minutes or less.

Test Kitchen Secret

Don't know where to start? Follow our simple timeline.

1. Prepare simple syrup.
2. Prepare Red Pepper Jelly-Brie Bites
3. Brew coffee.

Holiday Cocktail Party

SERVES 10 TO 15

Red Pepper Jelly-Brie Bites

Cranberry-Orange Simple Syrup and Spiced Apple Simple Syrup with Champagne

Mocha Punch

Red Pepper Jelly-Brie Bites

1. Preheat oven to 350°. Place 2 (1.9-oz.) packages frozen mini phyllo pastry shells, thawed, on a baking sheet. Cut 3 oz. Brie cheese into 30 very small pieces. Spoon rounded ¼ teaspoonfuls red pepper jelly into each shell; top with cheese. Sprinkle with 3 Tbsp. chopped roasted salted almonds. Bake tartlets for 5 to 6 minutes or until cheese is melted. Makes 30 tartlets. Total Time: 15 min. **Note:** Roasted Pistachios may be substituted for roasted salted almonds.

•TIP•

Prepare both simple syrups simultaneously to save time. Freeze 20 minutes.

Cranberry-Orange Simple Syrup: Bring 2 cups sugar, 1 cup cranberries, 1 cup orange juice, and ½ cup water to a boil in a medium saucepan. Cook 2 minutes or until sugar dissolves. Remove from heat, and pour through a wire-mesh strainer, pressing berries with back of a spoon. Discard solids. Stir in ½ cup ice cubes; freeze 20 minutes. Makes about 2½ cups. Total Time: 30 min.

Spiced Apple Simple Syrup: Bring 1½ cups sugar, 1½ cups apple juice, and ⅛ tsp. apple pie spice to a boil in a medium saucepan. Cook 2 minutes or until sugar dissolves. Remove from heat, and stir in ½ cup ice cubes; freeze 20 minutes. Makes about 2½ cups. Total Time: 30 min.

Mocha Punch

test kitchen favorite

MAKES 4½ QT.
HANDS-ON TIME: 10 MIN.
TOTAL TIME: 30 MIN.

Chocolate and coffee make a pleasing punch.

1 qt. chocolate milk
4 cups strong brewed coffee, chilled
1 cup Kahlúa or other coffee-flavored liqueur*
1 (14-oz.) can sweetened condensed milk
1 qt. chocolate ice cream
1 qt. coffee ice cream
Semisweet chocolate shavings

1. Combine first 4 ingredients in a large freezer-proof bowl. Cover and freeze 20 minutes. Pour mixture into a large punch bowl. Scoop chocolate and coffee ice creams into punch; stir gently. Sprinkle with chocolate shavings.
*Substitute amaretto-flavored nondairy liquid creamer for Kahlúa, or increase coffee to 5 cups.

Fast and Festive Sandwich Spreads

Try these eight delicious ways to dress up a sandwich — from sweet and tangy Cranberry Mustard to spicy Creole rémoulade.

1 Cranberry-Cream Cheese Spread: Stir together 1 (8-oz.) package cream cheese, softened; ⅔ cup sweetened dried cranberries; ⅓ cup orange marmalade; and ½ cup chopped walnuts. Chill 4 hours.
*We love it with sliced turkey and fresh arugula on toasted ciabatta bread.

—RECIPE FROM PEGGY CLINE, JONESBORO, GEORGIA

2 Herbed Chèvre Spread: Stir together 1 (10.5-oz.) goat cheese log, softened; ¼ cup chopped fresh basil; ¼ cup plain yogurt; 2 Tbsp. each chopped fresh chives and parsley; and 3 Tbsp. olive oil. Season with salt and freshly ground pepper.
*We love it spread into pita pockets with warm grilled onions, thinly sliced pork tenderloin, and crisp salad greens. It's also wonderful on fresh veggie subs.

—RECIPE FROM MARTHA NEWBERRY, FRANKLIN, TENNESSEE

3 Lemon-Rosemary Mayonnaise: Stir together 2 cups mayonnaise; 2 Tbsp. chopped fresh rosemary; 1½ Tbsp. lemon zest; and 1 garlic clove, pressed.
*We love it with smoked turkey and avocado on black-olive bread.

4 Béarnaise Mayonnaise: Cook ⅓ cup dry white wine, 1 Tbsp. white wine vinegar, and 2 minced shallots in a small saucepan over medium-high heat 5 minutes or until liquid is reduced to 1 Tbsp. Remove from heat, and cool. Stir in 1 cup mayonnaise, 1 Tbsp. chopped fresh tarragon, 1 tsp. lemon zest, and ⅛ tsp. pepper.
*We love it with any type of beef—from grilled burgers to steak sandwiches.

5 White Barbecue Sauce: Stir together 1½ cups mayonnaise, ¼ cup horseradish, 3 Tbsp. cider vinegar, 1 Tbsp. fresh lemon juice, 1 tsp. coarsely ground pepper, and ¼ tsp. salt. Cover and chill 1 hour.
*We love it on grilled chicken sandwiches with fresh tomatoes and basil.

6 Cranberry Mustard: Stir together 1 cup whole-berry cranberry sauce, ⅓ cup Dijon mustard, and ¼ tsp. dried crushed red pepper.
*We love it on grilled sandwiches – especially with ham, white Cheddar, and thinly sliced apple on whole grain bread.

7 Creole Apple-Butter Mustard: Stir together 1 cup apple butter and ¼ cup Creole mustard.
*We love it for breakfast with pan-fried pork chops on hot sweet potato biscuits.

8 Spicy Rémoulade Sauce: Stir together 1 cup mayonnaise; ¼ cup sliced green onions; 1 Tbsp. chopped fresh parsley; 2 Tbsp. Creole mustard; 2 tsp. lemon zest; 2 garlic cloves, pressed; and ½ tsp. ground red pepper.
*We love it with boiled shrimp and shredded iceberg lettuce on toasted sourdough rolls.

Great Food and More

Try these delicious recipes adapted from Matt and Ted Lee's new cookbook, *The Lee Bros. Simple Fresh Southern* (Clarkson Potter, 2009). These self-described Southern food evangelists have packed their book with updated dishes and witty commentary. It's the perfect gift for your favorite foodie.

Cheese Relish

make ahead

MAKES 2 CUPS
HANDS-ON TIME: 15 MIN.
TOTAL TIME: 2 HR., 25 MIN.

Serve this tangy cousin to pimiento cheese spread on crackers or in grilled sandwiches. The secret is to make sure the cheese is well-chilled before grating.

2 Tbsp. capers, drained
10 oz. Swiss cheese, finely grated (about 3½ cups)
1 (12-oz.) jar sliced mild banana peppers, drained and minced
2 Tbsp. minced fresh chives
3 Tbsp. sour cream
¼ tsp. pepper
¼ tsp. dried crushed red pepper
¼ tsp. kosher salt

1. Soak capers in water to cover 10 minutes; drain.
2. Stir together capers and remaining ingredients. Cover and chill 2 hours before serving. Store in refrigerator up to 2 days.

This Just In

Hot off the press is the *Hot and Hot Fish Club Cookbook* (Running Press Books, 2009) by Chris and Idie Hastings. Chris is one of our favorite Southern chefs, and the book captures the farm-to-table philosophy and fresh flavors of the couple's Birmingham, Alabama, restaurant. In stores now, or visit www.hotandhotfishclub.com.

Fig and Bourbon Compote

make ahead

MAKES 1 PT.
HANDS-ON TIME: 15 MIN.
TOTAL TIME: 44 MIN.

This versatile compote is perfect over roasted pork, cheesecake, or pound cake.

1 cup apple cider
⅔ cup bourbon
1 Tbsp. dark brown sugar
10 oz. dried Mission figlets (about 2 cups), halved
½ cup whipping cream
1½ Tbsp. powdered sugar

1. Combine cider, bourbon, and brown sugar in a small saucepan. Stir in figlets, and let stand 10 minutes.
2. Bring fig mixture to a simmer; cook 10 minutes or until figs are soft. Transfer figs to a medium bowl using a slotted spoon. Simmer liquid until thickened and reduced by half (about 4 minutes). Pour liquid over figs. Serve warm, or store in refrigerator up to 1 week.
3. Beat cream at medium speed with an electric mixer until soft peaks form. Add powdered sugar, beating until stiff peaks form. Serve over compote.

Pickled Grapes With Rosemary and Chiles

make ahead

MAKES 4 PT.
HANDS-ON TIME: 10 MIN.
TOTAL TIME: 1 HR., 45 MIN.

We loved these unusual "pickles" with everything from chicken salad to antipasto. They're also delicious straight off a fork.

3 cups seedless green grapes (about 1 lb.)
3 cups seedless red grapes (about 1 lb.)
2 cups white wine vinegar
3 garlic cloves, thinly sliced
2 Tbsp. kosher salt
2 (4-inch-long) fresh rosemary sprigs
2 tsp. sugar
½ tsp. dried crushed red pepper

1. Pack grapes into 4 (1-pt.) canning jars with lids.
2. Bring vinegar, next 5 ingredients, and 1 cup water to a simmer in a medium saucepan. Remove from heat, and pour hot vinegar mixture over grapes. Cover loosely, and let cool to room temperature (about 30 minutes). Seal and chill 1 hour before serving. Store in refrigerator up to 1 week.

Carrot Pickles With Shallots and Dill

make ahead

MAKES 2 PT.
HANDS-ON TIME: 15 MIN.
TOTAL TIME: 2 HR., 50 MIN.

1½ lb. carrots
2 large shallots, thinly sliced
6 fresh dill sprigs
4 garlic cloves, peeled and crushed
2 tsp. black peppercorns
½ tsp. celery seeds
2 cups white wine vinegar
2 tsp. kosher salt
2 tsp. sugar

1. Cut carrots diagonally into ⅛-inch-thick slices. Combine carrots and next 5 ingredients in 2 (1-pt.) canning jars with lids.
2. Bring vinegar and remaining ingredients to a simmer in a medium saucepan. Remove from heat, and pour hot vinegar mixture over carrot mixture. Cover loosely, and let cool to room temperature (about 30 minutes). Seal and chill 2 hours before serving. Store in refrigerator up to 2 weeks.

WHAT'S FOR SUPPER?

No-Fuss Meals

Streamline weeknight cooking with these six delicious main dish ideas paired with simple sides.

Apple-Chicken Sausage With Apricot-Pepper Relish

fast fixin's

MAKES 6 SERVINGS
HANDS-ON TIME: 18 MIN.
TOTAL TIME: 22 MIN.

Serve over hot cooked grits, mashed potatoes, or rice.

½ cup chicken broth
¼ cup apricot preserves
1 Tbsp. apple cider vinegar
2 (12-oz.) packages smoked chicken-and-apple sausage links, cut in half lengthwise
1 Tbsp. olive oil
2 large red bell peppers, cut into thin strips
1 medium onion, thinly sliced

1. Whisk together chicken broth, preserves, and cider vinegar.
2. Cook sausage links, in batches, in hot oil, in a nonstick skillet over medium-high heat 3 to 5 minutes or until browned. Add peppers and onion, and sauté 2 minutes.
3. Add broth mixture, and reduce heat to medium; cover and cook 4 minutes. Serve with a slotted spoon.
Note: We tested with Emeril's Chicken & Apple Gourmet Smoked Sausage.

—INSPIRED BY PENNY NICHOLS,
BATON ROUGE, LOUISIANA

Chicken-Fried Chicken

MAKES 6 SERVINGS
HANDS-ON TIME: 31 MIN.
TOTAL TIME: 31 MIN.

Ask your butcher to cube chicken breasts or pound chicken breasts with spiked side of meat mallet.

6 (6-oz.) skinned and boned cubed chicken breasts
1¾ tsp. salt
½ tsp. pepper
2 large eggs, lightly beaten
¼ cup milk
1 cup all-purpose flour
3 cups vegetable oil

1. Season chicken with salt and pepper. Combine egg and milk in a shallow dish.
2. Dip chicken in egg mixture; dredge in flour, shaking off excess.
3. Fry chicken, in 2 batches, in hot oil in a large skillet over medium heat 4 to 5 minutes on each side or until done. Place chicken on a wire rack in a jelly-roll pan, and keep warm in a 225° oven.

Crunchy Dijon Salmon

MAKES 6 SERVINGS
HANDS-ON TIME: 10 MIN.
TOTAL TIME: 22 MIN.

Serve with ready-to-serve rice and broccolini. Sauté broccolini in 2 tsp. sesame oil until crisp-tender; sprinkle with toasted sesame seeds.

6 (4-oz.) salmon fillets
¾ tsp. salt
¼ tsp. pepper
3 Tbsp. whole-grain Dijon mustard
½ cup Japanese breadcrumbs (panko)

1. Preheat oven to 450°. Sprinkle fillets with salt and pepper; spread mustard over tops and sides of each fillet. Press breadcrumbs onto each fillet. Place fillets on a lightly greased wire rack on an aluminum foil-lined baking sheet. Bake 12 to 15 minutes or until fish flakes with a fork.

Barbecued Pork Quesadillas

fast fixin's

MAKES 4 SERVINGS
HANDS-ON TIME: 26 MIN.
TOTAL TIME: 26 MIN.

Melt butter, minced garlic, and chili powder in a microwave-safe bowl; pour mixture over cooked corn on the cob for a tasty side.

1 lb. chopped barbecued pork (without sauce)
1 cup barbecue sauce
½ cup chopped fresh cilantro
2 green onions, minced
8 (6-inch) fajita-size flour tortillas
1 (8-oz.) package shredded Mexican four-cheese blend
Toppings: sour cream, sliced green onions, barbecue sauce

1. Stir together first 4 ingredients.
2. Place 1 tortilla in a hot lightly greased skillet or griddle. Sprinkle tortilla with ¼ cup cheese, and spoon ⅓ cup pork mixture on half of tortilla. Cook 2 to 3 minutes or until cheese melts. Fold tortilla in half over filling; transfer to a serving plate. Repeat procedure with remaining tortillas, cheese, and pork mixture. Serve with desired toppings.

Beef Lombardi

MAKES 6 SERVINGS
HANDS-ON TIME: 25 MIN.
TOTAL TIME: 50 MIN.

Whisk together ½ cup bottled balsamic vinaigrette dressing, 1 Tbsp. chopped fresh basil, and 1 Tbsp. honey until blended. Serve over mixed greens.

1 (8-oz.) package medium egg noodles
1 lb. lean ground beef
1½ tsp. salt, divided
½ tsp. dried Italian seasoning
1 (6-oz.) can tomato paste
1 (14½-oz.) cans diced fire-roasted tomatoes
1 (3-oz.) package cream cheese, softened
½ cup sour cream
4 green onions, chopped
½ cup (2 oz.) shredded Italian six-cheese blend

1. Preheat oven to 350°. Prepare egg noodles according to package directions.
2. Meanwhile, sprinkle ground beef with 1¼ tsp. salt and Italian seasoning. Cook beef in a large skillet over medium heat, stirring often, 5 to 6 minutes or until meat crumbles and is no longer pink.
3. Stir in tomato paste, and cook 2 minutes; stir in tomatoes, ½ cup water, and remaining ¼ tsp. salt; reduce heat to medium-low, and simmer 8 minutes.
4. Microwave cream cheese in a microwave-safe bowl at HIGH 20 seconds. Stir in sour cream and green onions. Stir cream cheese mixture into hot cooked noodles.
5. Place noodle mixture in bottom of a lightly greased 11- x 7-inch baking dish. Top with beef mixture; sprinkle with cheese.
6. Bake at 350° for 25 minutes or until hot and bubbly.

To lighten: Substitute low-fat or fat-free sour cream and 2% reduced-fat cheese.

Test Kitchen Secret

The trick to a great crust is to use a very hot grill. Have your hood fan on high—there will be some smoke. If you can't find flat-i.ron steak in your local market, a flank, top blade chuck, or sirloin steak will work just fine.

Grilled Flat-Iron Steak

MAKES 8 SERVINGS
HANDS-ON TIME: 25 MIN.
TOTAL TIME: 35 MIN.

For a great accompaniment, prepare couscous according to package directions. Stir in fresh spinach leaves, lemon zest, and cherry tomato halves; toss until combined.

2 (1-lb.) flat-iron steaks*
4 tsp. vegetable oil
3½ tsp. Montreal steak seasoning
½ tsp. kosher salt

1. Rub steaks with oil, steak seasoning, and salt.
2. Cook steaks, in batches, in a grill pan over medium-high heat 5 to 7 minutes on each side or to desired degree of doneness. Let stand 10 minutes. Cut diagonally across the grain into thin strips.
Note: We tested with McCormick Grill Mates Montreal Steak Seasoning.
*2 (1-lb.) flank steaks may be substituted.

The Tastiest Gift

Our velvety chocolate sauce and its three delicious variations make terrific presents for everyone from friends to teachers to neighbors.

Hot Fudge Sauce

fast fixin's • make ahead

MAKES 3¼ CUPS
HANDS-ON TIME: 10 MIN.
TOTAL TIME: 10 MIN.

Hot Fudge Sauce is ready in 10 minutes. When giving as gift, include a reminder to refrigerate.

1 (8-oz.) package unsweetened chocolate
   baking squares
½ cup butter
2 cups sugar
1 cup milk
1 tsp. vanilla extract
⅛ tsp. salt

1. Melt chocolate and butter in a large, heavy saucepan over low heat, stirring constantly. Add sugar, and cook, stirring constantly, 30 seconds or until blended. Add milk, and cook, stirring constantly, 3 minutes or until thoroughly heated and sugar is dissolved. (Do not boil.) Remove from heat. Stir in vanilla and salt. Cover and chill leftover sauce up to 2 weeks.

Note: To reheat, microwave sauce in a microwave-safe bowl, stirring occasionally, at HIGH for 15- to 30-second intervals or until warm.

Espresso-Hot Fudge Sauce: Add 2 Tbsp. instant espresso with sugar.

Whiskey-Hot Fudge Sauce: Stir in 3 Tbsp. Southern Comfort with vanilla and salt.

Brown Sugar-Cinnamon-Hot Fudge Sauce: Substitute 1 cup firmly packed brown sugar for 1 cup granulated sugar. Stir in ½ tsp. ground cinnamon with vanilla and salt.

Hot Fudge Hot Chocolate

MAKES 1 SERVING, **HANDS-ON TIME:** 7 MIN., **TOTAL TIME:** 7 MIN.

1. Stir together 1¼ cups milk and ¼ cup Hot Fudge Sauce in a microwave-safe mug. Microwave at HIGH 1½ minutes or until hot. Stir before serving, and top with 1 marshmallow.

Espresso-Hot Fudge-Hot Chocolate Sauce: Substitute Espresso Hot Fudge Sauce for regular sauce.

Whiskey-Hot Fudge-Hot Chocolate: Substitute Whiskey-Hot Fudge Sauce for regular sauce.

Brown Sugar-Cinnamon Hot Fudge-Hot Chocolate: Substitute Brown Sugar-Cinnamon Hot Fudge Sauce for regular sauce.

Festive Dessert Ideas

Want an impressive yet easy way to end a special occasion dinner? Pair any of our Hot Fudge Sauces with ice cream and more for decadent sundaes. (Add a copy of these ideas when giving the sauce to friends.)

Triple Mint Sundaes: Scoop pink peppermint, mint chocolate chip, and spearmint ice creams into julep cups or dessert glasses. Drizzle with Hot Fudge Sauce. Garnish with fresh mint sprigs and rolled wafer cookies.
Note: We tested with Pepperidge Farm Mint Chocolate Pirouettes.

Cookie Box Sundaes: Scoop coffee ice cream onto a cold jelly-roll pan; freeze 2 hours. Press 4 butter cookies onto sides of each scoop, forming a box. Top each with 1 ice-cream scoop. Freeze up to 2 hours. Serve with Espresso-Hot Fudge Sauce and strawberries.
Note: We tested with Pepperidge Farm Chessmen Cookies.

Cherry Ice-Cream Cordials: Freeze ½ cup maraschino cherries with stems and ¼ cup Southern Comfort in an airtight container 8 hours. Drain; pat cherries dry. (Keep 4 for garnish.) Discard stems from remaining cherries, and coarsely chop cherries. Layer Whiskey-Hot Fudge Sauce, chopped cherries, and cherry-vanilla ice cream in 4 small glasses. Garnish with sweetened whipped cream, chocolate sprinkles, and reserved cherries.

Brownie Bite Sundaes: Drizzle Brown Sugar-Cinnamon-Hot Fudge Sauce on dessert plates. Top with bite-size brownies and caramelized pear-and-toasted pecan ice cream. Garnish with toasted pecans.

Holiday Sweets

Share the magic of Christmas with this decadent cake.

'Tis the season for oven-baked goodies, and this luscious cake is one of our favorites. This layered chocolate cake contains one of our favorite secret ingredients, sour cream, which adds a rich, moist texture that is sure to please. The Whipped Ganache Filling sandwiched between the two layers adds a spectacular taste of chocolate. The snowy white icing topped with candied orange slices, fresh cranberries, and citrus leaves delivers a showy presentation.

Chocolate-Citrus Cake With Candied Oranges

MAKES 16 SERVINGS
HANDS-ON TIME: 1 HR.
TOTAL TIME: 6 HR., 40 MIN. (INCLUDING FILLING, FROSTING, AND ORANGES)

Parchment paper
2 (4-oz.) bittersweet chocolate baking bars, chopped
½ cup butter, softened
1⅔ cups granulated sugar
⅓ cup firmly packed light brown sugar
3 large eggs
2 cups all-purpose flour
1 tsp. baking soda
½ tsp. salt
1 (8-oz.) container sour cream
1 tsp. vanilla extract
1 cup hot brewed coffee
Whipped Ganache Filling
Seven-Minute Frosting
Candied Oranges
Garnish: fresh citrus leaves, cranberries

1. Preheat oven to 350°. Grease and flour 2 (9-inch) round pans. Line bottoms of pans with parchment paper. Lightly grease parchment paper.
2. Melt chocolate in a microwave-safe bowl at HIGH 1½ minutes or until smooth, stirring at 30-second intervals.
3. Beat butter and sugars at medium speed with a heavy-duty electric stand mixer until well blended (about 3 minutes). Add eggs, 1 at a time, beating just until blended after each addition. Add melted chocolate, beating just until blended.
4. Sift together flour, baking soda, and salt. Gradually add to chocolate mixture alternately with sour cream, beginning and ending with flour mixture. Beat at low speed just until blended after each addition. (Mixture will be thick.)
5. Stir vanilla into hot coffee. Gradually add coffee mixture to batter in a slow, steady stream, beating at low speed just until blended. Pour batter into prepared pans.
6. Bake at 350° for 38 to 42 minutes or until a wooden pick inserted in center comes out clean. Cool in pans on a wire rack 10 minutes. Remove from pans to wire rack, and let cool completely (about 1 hour).
7. Spread Whipped Ganache Filling between layers, spreading to edges of cake and leveling with an offset spatula. Gently press top cake layer down, pressing out a small amount of ganache filling from between layers, and spread filling around sides of cake, filling in any gaps between layers. Spread Seven-Minute Frosting over top and sides of cake. Swirl frosting using back of a spoon, if desired. Top with Candied Oranges. Garnish, if desired.
Square Chocolate-Citrus Cake With Candied Oranges: Substitute 2 (8-inch) square pans for 2 (9-inch) round pans. Prepare pans and batter as directed; pour batter into pans. Bake at 350° for 36 to 38 minutes or until a wooden pick inserted in center comes out clean. Cool and assemble as directed.

Cook's Notes

- Ganache is a rich frosting made with melted chocolate and whipping cream. The mixture, which thickens as it cools, should be warm enough to pour, yet thick enough to spread on the cake. Pour the ganache into the center of the cake; spread quickly using a spatula to push the frosting around the cake.
- Ganache can also be used as a filling for cakes, cookies, and tarts. After chilling for several hours, it becomes firm enough to shape into truffles.
- To easily release cakes, be sure to grease and flour the pans. Use a pastry brush to generously coat the bottom and sides of each pan with a solid vegetable shortening such as Crisco. (Margarines with a high liquid-to-fat ratio can cause the cakes to stick to the pans.) Lightly sprinkle with flour, tilting and tapping the pans so the flour completely covers the greased surfaces; invert the pans, and gently tap out any excess flour.

Whipped Ganache Filling:

MAKES ABOUT 3 CUPS
HANDS-ON TIME: 10 MIN.
TOTAL TIME: 2 HR., 10 MIN.

1 (12-oz.) package semisweet chocolate morsels
1½ cups whipping cream
1 Tbsp. orange liqueur

1. Microwave chocolate morsels and whipping cream in a 3-qt. microwave-safe glass bowl at HIGH 2½ minutes or until melted and smooth, stirring at 30-second intervals. Whisk in liqueur until smooth. Cover and chill 2 hours or until mixture is thickened.
2. Beat at medium speed with an electric mixer 20 to 30 seconds or until soft peaks form and ganache lightens in color. (Do not overmix.) Use immediately.

Seven-Minute Frosting:

MAKES ABOUT 4 CUPS
HANDS-ON TIME: 10 MIN.
TOTAL TIME: 10 MIN.

Cover bowl with a damp paper towel or cloth to keep frosting from drying out while you are frosting the cake.

2 egg whites
1¼ cups sugar
1 Tbsp. corn syrup
1 tsp. orange liqueur

1. Pour water to depth of 1½ inches into a 2- to 2½-qt. saucepan; bring to a boil over medium-high heat. Reduce heat to medium, and simmer.
2. Combine egg whites, next 3 ingredients, and ¼ cup water in a 2½-qt. glass bowl; beat at high speed with an electric mixer until blended. Place bowl over simmering water, and beat at high speed 5 to 7 minutes or until soft peaks form; remove from heat. Beat to spreading consistency (about 2 to 3 minutes). Use immediately.

Candied Oranges:

MAKES ABOUT 19 PIECES
HANDS-ON TIME: 10 MIN.
TOTAL TIME: 1 HR., 30 MIN.

Don't skip the first step. It removes the bitterness from the orange piths.

2 large navel oranges, thinly sliced
Parchment paper
2 cups sugar
½ vanilla bean, split

1. Bring 4 cups water to a boil in a 3- to 3½-qt. saucepan over medium-high heat. Add oranges. Return to a boil; cook 5 minutes. Transfer oranges to a parchment paper-lined jelly-roll pan, using a slotted spoon; discard water.
2. Combine sugar and 2 cups water in saucepan. Scrape seeds from vanilla bean into water; add vanilla bean to water. Bring to a boil over medium-high heat, stirring occasionally, until sugar is dissolved. Add orange slices. Return to a boil; cover, reduce heat to medium, and simmer 10 minutes. Uncover and cook, stirring occasionally, 35 to 45 minutes or until orange rinds are softened and translucent.
3. Carefully remove oranges, using tongs, and arrange on parchment paper-lined jelly-roll pan, folding and curling oranges as desired. Blot with paper towels to absorb excess moisture.
4. Pour syrup in saucepan through a fine wire-mesh strainer into a bowl, reserving syrup and vanilla bean for another use. Discard any remaining solids. Let oranges stand 15 minutes.
Note: Cranberries tossed with 2 Tbsp. reserved syrup make for a pretty presentation atop the cake.

—**ROSE MARIE CROWE**, TRUSSVILLE, ALABAMA

Quick & Easy Mac and Cheese Meals

One simple recipe with 7 mouthwatering variations will spice up your weeknight suppers.

We definitely couldn't keep this one a secret—mac-n-cheese from scratch in just 20 minutes! (On a busy night, it doesn't get much better than that.) With tons of flavorful stir-ins such as broccoli, bacon, ham, spinach, asparagus, chicken, and more, this versatile dish will soon be one of your faithful standbys. Serve it up with a simple salad, and you've got a comforting meal on the table in no time at all.

Easy Creamy Mac-n-Cheese

MAKES 4 SERVINGS
HANDS-ON TIME: 20 MIN.
TOTAL TIME: 20 MIN.

½ (16-oz.) package rotini pasta
¼ cup butter
¼ cup all-purpose flour
2½ cups 2% milk
½ tsp. salt
¼ tsp. ground red pepper
⅛ tsp. garlic powder
1 (10-oz.) block 2% sharp Cheddar cheese, shredded

1. Prepare pasta according to package directions.
2. Meanwhile, melt butter in a large saucepan over medium heat. Gradually whisk in flour until smooth; cook, whisking constantly, 1 minute. Gradually whisk in milk and next 3 ingredients; cook, whisking constantly, 8 to 10 minutes or until thickened. Remove from heat.
3. Gradually stir in Cheddar cheese, stirring until cheese is melted and sauce is smooth. Stir in hot cooked pasta. Serve immediately.

Try One of These Twists

1. **Bell Pepper-Green Chile Mac-n-Cheese:** Stir ½ cup chopped, roasted red bell peppers and 1 (4-oz.) can chopped green chiles into cheese sauce with pasta.

2. **Broccoli-Ham Mac-n-Cheese:** Stir 2 cups chopped smoked ham and 1 (12-oz.) package frozen steam-in-bag broccoli florets, cooked according to package directions, into cheese sauce with pasta.

3. **Chicken-Asparagus Mac-n-Cheese:** Stir 2 cups chopped cooked chicken and 1 (9-oz.) package frozen asparagus cuts, cooked according to package directions, into cheese sauce with pasta.

4. **Kitchen Express:** Prepare pasta according to package directions. Cook 2 (10-oz.) containers refrigerated light Alfredo sauce in a large saucepan over medium heat, stirring often, 3 to 4 minutes or until thoroughly heated. Gradually whisk in 1 (10-oz.) block 2% sharp Cheddar cheese, shredded, until smooth. Stir in hot cooked pasta and ¼ tsp. ground red pepper. Hands-on Time: 15 min., Total Time: 15 min.

5. **Pea-Prosciutto Mac-n-Cheese:** Cook ½ cup thinly sliced prosciutto, pancetta, or bacon (about 2 oz.) in a lightly greased skillet until crisp. Stir prosciutto and 1 (12-oz.) package frozen sweet peas, cooked according to package directions, into cheese sauce with pasta.
Note: We tested with Birds Eye Steamfresh Fresh Frozen Sweet Peas.

6. **Southwest Chicken Mac-n-Cheese:** Stir 2 cups chopped cooked chicken and 1 (10-oz.) can mild diced tomatoes and green chiles, drained, into cheese sauce with pasta.

7. **Spinach-Bacon Mac-n-Cheese:** Stir ½ cup chopped cooked bacon (about 6 slices) and 1 (6-oz.) package fresh baby spinach, thoroughly washed, into cheese sauce with pasta.

Eating beans every day is easy with these
good-for-you Southern comfort foods.

Southern-Style Superfood: Beans

Fresh, frozen, or canned, beans add healthy benefits
to these Southern comfort foods.

Repeat after us : A day without a bean is no day at all. That's because beans are better for you than other foods combined. Not only do they help prevent cancer, reduce cholesterol, and maintain gastrointestinal health, but legumes are some of the most satisfying superfoods—they fill you up and prevent overeating. And if you're a Southerner with a craving for comfort food, these deliciously lightened recipes leave no excuse not to eat them.

Chicken-and-White Bean Chili

MAKES 11 CUPS
HANDS-ON TIME: 30 MIN.
TOTAL TIME: 35 MIN. (INCLUDING SEASONING MIX)

We used a rotisserie chicken from our supermarket deli. One chicken generally yields 3 to 4 cups chopped meat.

3 to 4 cups chopped cooked chicken
4 (16-oz.) cans navy beans, drained and rinsed
4 (4.5-oz.) cans chopped green chiles
1 (14-oz.) can low-Sodium fat-free chicken broth
2 Tbsp. Chili Seasoning Mix
Garnishes: sour cream, fresh cilantro sprig

1. Stir together first 5 ingredients in a Dutch oven; bring to a boil over medium-high heat, stirring occasionally. Cover, reduce heat to low, and simmer, stirring occasionally, 15 minutes. Garnish, if desired.

Per cup (not including garnishes): Calories 295; Fat 4.1g (sat 1.1g, mono 1.3g, poly 1.1g); Protein 26.7g; Carb 38.3g; Fiber 9.9g; Chol 38.2mg; Iron 4.3mg; Sodium 700mg; Calc 86mg

Chili Seasoning Mix:

MAKES ABOUT 1⅓ CUPS
HANDS-ON TIME: 5 MIN.
TOTAL TIME: 5 MIN.

This versatile seasoning mix yields big dividends in time-saving suppers. Keep a jar on hand all winter, ready to stir up a delicious batch of tasty chili.

¾ cup chili powder
2 Tbsp. ground cumin
2 Tbsp. dried oregano
2 Tbsp. dried minced onion
2 Tbsp. seasoned salt
2 Tbsp. sugar
2 tsp. dried minced garlic*

1. Stir together all ingredients. Store seasoning mix in an airtight container at room temperature up to 4 months. Shake or stir well before using.
*1 tsp. garlic powder may be substituted.

Per tbsp.: Calories 15; Fat 0g (sat 0g, mono 0g, poly 0g); Protein 0.2g; Carb 2.9g; Fiber 0.7g; Chol 0mg; Iron 0.5mg; Sodium 541mg; Calc 12mg

Anytime Succotash
family favorite

MAKES 6 SERVINGS
HANDS-ON TIME: 23 MIN.
TOTAL TIME: 33 MIN.

We like the richness of whole milk in this recipe, but you can use reduced-fat or fat-free milk, if you wish.

1 (10-oz.) package frozen petite lima beans
1 (16-oz.) package frozen white shoepeg corn
2 Tbsp. butter
2 Tbsp. all-purpose flour
1 tsp. sugar
½ tsp. salt
½ tsp. seasoned pepper
1¼ cups milk
Garnish: cooked and crumbled bacon

1. Cook lima beans according to package directions; drain. Pulse corn in a food processor 8 to 10 times or until coarsely chopped.
2. Melt butter in a large saucepan over medium heat; add flour, stirring until smooth. Cook, stirring constantly, 1 minute; stir in sugar, salt, and seasoned pepper. Gradually add milk, stirring until smooth. Stir in corn, and cook, stirring often, 12 to 15 minutes or until corn is tender and mixture is thickened. Stir in drained lima beans. Garnish, if desired, and serve immediately.

Per serving (not including garnish): Calories 199; Fat 6.2g (sat 3.5g, mono 1.6g, poly 0.6g); Protein 7.6g; Carb 31.7g; Fiber 4.6g; Chol 15.1mg; Iron 1.6mg; Sodium 258mg; Calc 75mg

Tomato, Bean, and Bread Salad

MAKES 6 SERVINGS
HANDS-ON TIME: 20 MIN.
TOTAL TIME: 1 HR., 26 MIN.

Add grilled chicken breast to Tomato, Bean, and Bread Salad for a heartier dish. Marinate the chicken in extra dressing 2 to 8 hours before grilling for more flavor.

4 (2.5-oz.) five-grain hoagie rolls
Vegetable cooking spray
½ cup light Caesar dressing
¼ cup firmly packed fresh basil leaves, cut into thin strips
1 tsp. fresh lemon juice
1 (19-oz.) can cannellini beans, drained and rinsed
1 large tomato, diced
½ medium-size sweet onion, thinly sliced
4 cups chopped romaine lettuce
Garnish: freshly shredded Parmesan cheese

1. Preheat oven to 400°. Cut rolls into 1-inch cubes (about 8 cups). Place bread cubes on a baking sheet, and coat with cooking spray. Bake 6 to 7 minutes or until lightly toasted.
2. Stir together dressing, basil, and lemon juice in a large serving bowl. Add bread cubes, beans, tomato, and onion, tossing to coat. Cover and chill 1 hour.
3. Toss with lettuce just before serving; garnish, if desired.

—INSPIRED BY REBECCA GUFFEY,

APEX, NORTH CAROLINA

Note: We tested with Girard's Light Caesar Dressing.

Per serving: Calories 265; Fat 8.4g (sat 2.4g, mono 0.9g, poly 1.1g); Protein 9g; Carb 39.1g; Fiber 5.4g; Chol 6.7mg; Iron 2.2mg; Sodium 624mg; Calc 99mg

Sour Cream Cornbread

MAKES 8 SERVINGS
HANDS-ON TIME: 10 MIN.
TOTAL TIME: 37 MIN.

1½ cups self-rising cornmeal mix
½ cup all-purpose flour
1 (15-oz.) can low-sodium cream-style corn
1 (8-oz.) container light sour cream
3 large eggs, lightly beaten
2 Tbsp. chopped fresh cilantro
½ cup (2 oz.) 2% reduced-fat shredded Cheddar cheese (optional)

1. Preheat oven to 450°. Heat a 10-inch cast-iron skillet in oven 5 minutes.
2. Stir together cornmeal mix and flour in a large bowl; add corn and next 3 ingredients, stirring just until blended. Pour batter into hot lightly greased skillet.
3. Bake at 450° for 22 to 24 minutes or until golden brown and cornbread pulls away from sides of skillet. If desired, top with cheese, and bake 1 minute or until cheese is melted and bubbly.

Per serving (including cheese topping): Calories 254; Fat 6g (sat 2.9g, mono 1g, poly .8g); Protein 9.7g; Carb 43g; Fiber 2.9g; Chol 92mg; Iron 2.5mg; Sodium 518mg; Calc 158mg

Quick From A Can

Here are three easy and delicious ways to eat more beans. Draining and rinsing canned beans reduces the Sodium by about 40%.

1. **Dress up store-bought salsa:** Stir a can of black beans, drained and rinsed, into your favorite refrigerated salsa. Add lime juice and chopped cilantro to freshen it up. Serve as a dip with chips or as a topping over grilled fish, chicken, or pork.

2. **Make a melt-in-your-mouth quesadilla:** Mash some canned pinto beans, drained and rinsed, and spread over flour tortillas; top with cheese and taco sauce. Fold tortillas in half, and brown on each side on a hot griddle or skillet.

3. **Whip up a tasty sandwich spread:** Process a can of garbanzo beans, rinsed and drained, with a garlic clove, ¼ cup lemon juice, 3 Tbsp. water, 2 Tbsp. light sour cream, and ½ tsp. lemon pepper. Serve in a pita with fresh veggie slices and feta cheese.

Quick Skillet Red Beans and Rice: Substitute 2 (16-oz.) cans light kidney beans, drained and rinsed, for dried beans. Reduce Creole Seasoning to 2 tsp. Cook sausage and next 4 ingredients in a large nonstick skillet over medium heat, stirring often, 5 minutes or until sausage browns. Add garlic; sauté 1 minute. Stir in 2 tsp. seasoning, beans, and 2 cups chicken broth. Bring to a boil; reduce heat to low, and simmer 20 minutes. Serve with hot cooked rice and, if desired, hot sauce. Garnish, if desired. Makes 8 cups. Hands-on Time: 26 min., Total Time: 46 min.

Per cup (with 1 cup rice): Calories 424; Fat 3.2g (sat 1.1g, mono 0.2g, poly 0.4g); Protein 17.21g; Carb 79.5g; Fiber 7.6g; Chol 25.2mg; Iron 4.3mg; Sodium 804mg; Calc 76mg

Slow-Cooker Red Beans and Rice

MAKES 10 CUPS
HANDS-ON TIME: 15 MIN.
TOTAL TIME: 7 HR., 15 MIN.

Slow-Cooker Red Beans and Rice can be prepped in 15 minutes—the rest is all hands-off cooking. No soaking required. Save even more time by purchasing pre-chopped veggies in the produce section.

1 lb. dried red beans
¾ lb. smoked turkey sausage, thinly sliced
3 celery ribs, chopped
1 green bell pepper, chopped
1 red bell pepper, chopped
1 sweet onion, chopped
3 garlic cloves, minced
1 Tbsp. Creole seasoning
Hot cooked long-grain rice
Hot sauce (optional)
Garnish: finely chopped green onions, finely chopped red onion

1. Combine first 8 ingredients and 7 cups water in a 4-qt. slow cooker. Cover and cook on HIGH 7 hours or until beans are tender.
2. Serve red bean mixture with hot cooked rice, and, if desired, hot sauce. Garnish, if desired.

Per cup (with 1 cup rice): Calories 407; Fat 2.1g (sat 0.8g, mono 0.2g, poly 0.2g); Protein 19g; Carb 77g; Fiber 11.7g; Chol 15mg; Iron 5.8mg; Sodium 492mg; Calc 77mg

Vegetarian Red Beans and Rice: Substitute frozen meatless smoked sausage, thawed and thinly sliced, for turkey sausage.

Per cup (with 1 cup rice): Calories 422; Fat 3.5g (sat 0.4g, mono 0.2g, poly 0.2g); Protein 21.5g; Carb 76.4g; Fiber 12.2g; Chol 0mg; Iron 6.1mg; Sodium 530mg; Calc 113mg

"I have leftover eggnog. Can I cook or bake with it?"

It's the secret ingredient in these three delicious treats.

Eggnog Pound Cake

MAKES 12 SERVINGS
HANDS-ON TIME: 15 MIN.
TOTAL TIME: 2 HR., 25 MIN.

1 (16-oz.) package pound cake mix
1¼ cups eggnog
2 large eggs
½ tsp. freshly grated nutmeg
½ tsp. vanilla extract

1. Preheat oven to 350°. Beat all ingredients together at low speed with an electric mixer until blended. Increase speed to medium, and beat 2 minutes. Pour into a lightly greased 9- x 5-inch loaf pan.
2. Bake at 350° for 1 hour to 1 hour and 5 minutes or until a long wooden pick inserted in center comes out clean. Cool in pan on a wire rack 10 minutes. Remove from pan to wire rack, and cool completely (about 1 hour).

Eggnog Cupcakes: Prepare batter as directed. Place 24 paper baking cups in 2 (12-cup) muffin pans; spoon batter into cups, filling two-thirds full. Bake at 350° for 18 to 20 minutes or until a wooden pick inserted in center comes out clean. Remove from pans to wire racks, and let cool completely (about 45 minutes). Meanwhile, beat ½ cup softened butter and 1 (3-oz.) package softened cream cheese at medium speed with an electric mixer until creamy. Gradually add 1 (16-oz.) package powdered sugar alternately with ¼ cup eggnog, beginning and ending with sugar. Beat at low speed just until blended after each addition. Add ½ tsp. freshly grated nutmeg and ½ tsp. vanilla extract; beat until smooth. Spread over cupcakes. Makes 24 cupcakes. Hands-on Time: 25 min.; Total Time: 1 hr., 28 min.

Quick Eggnog-Mocha Latte

MAKES 1 SERVING **HANDS-ON TIME:** 5 MIN.
TOTAL TIME: 5 MIN.

1. Pour 1 (0.71-oz.) envelope instant cocoa mix into a large mug. Stir in ⅓ cup hot strong brewed coffee. Microwave ¼ cup eggnog in a microwave-safe glass measuring cup at HIGH 30 seconds or until hot. Stir into cocoa mixture.

Chai Tea Eggnog Cookies

MAKES 2 DOZEN
HANDS-ON TIME: 20 MIN.
TOTAL TIME: 46 MIN.

1 chai tea bag
1 (17.5-oz.) package sugar cookie mix
½ cup melted butter
1 large egg
4 Tbsp. eggnog, divided
Parchment paper
Cinnamon sugar
1 cup powdered sugar
½ tsp. freshly grated nutmeg

1. Preheat oven to 350°. Remove tea leaves from tea bag; discard bag.
2. Stir together tea leaves, cookie mix, butter, egg, and 2 Tbsp. eggnog until well blended.
3. Drop dough by tablespoonfuls onto parchment paper-lined baking sheets. Flatten dough slightly with bottom of a glass dipped in cinnamon sugar.
4. Bake at 350° for 8 to 10 minutes or until lightly browned. Remove from baking sheet to a wire rack, and cool completely (about 10 minutes).
5. Whisk together powdered sugar, nutmeg, and remaining 2 Tbsp. eggnog until smooth. Drizzle over cooled cookies.
Note: We tested with Tazo Organic Chai Black Tea.

Test Kitchen Secret

Other quick ideas for leftover eggnog: Use as base for French toast, drizzle on butternut squash soup, or use to flavor cheesecake.

5-Ingredient Comfort Food

Party Starters in a Pinch

Your company will never guess that this food for the soul took such little time to prepare.

Meaty Cheese Dip

MAKES 6 CUPS; **PREP:** 3 MIN.,
COOK: 12 MIN.

You'll be amazed at the flavor from these four ingredients. The hot sausage and salsa keep things lively. Want a spicier dip? Substitute 1 (32-oz.) loaf Mexican pasteurized prepared cheese product for the regular loaf of cheese product.

1 lb. ground chuck
½ lb. ground hot pork sausage
1 (32-oz.) loaf pasteurized prepared cheese product, cubed
1 (8-oz.) jar medium salsa

1. Cook ground chuck and sausage in a large skillet, stirring until meat crumbles and is not longer pink.
2. Add cheese and salsa; cook over low heat, stirring constantly, until cheese melts. Serve warm with large corn chips.

Creamy Chipotle-Black Bean Dip

MAKES 1 CUP; **PREP:** 10 MIN.

Adobo sauce is a thick Mexican mixture made from chiles, vinegar, and spices that can be used as a marinade or as a sauce served on the side. Here, it packs a little punch into sour cream and prepared bean dip.

½ cup sour cream
½ cup prepared black bean dip
1 tsp. minced chipotle peppers in adobo sauce
1 tsp. adobo sauce from can
¼ tsp. salt

1. Combine all ingredients; stir well. Cover and chill up to 3 days. Serve with tortilla chips.

Kahlúa-Pecan Brie

MAKES 8 APPETIZER SERVINGS;
PREP: 10 MIN.; **COOK:** 5 MIN.

Crunchy pecans lend a nice texture contrast to the soft creamy Brie. Serve this hot from the oven so the cheese is smooth and creamy alongside gingersnaps or apple slices.

1 (15-oz.) round Brie
½ cup chopped pecans, toasted
2½ Tbsp. Kahlúa or other coffee liqueur
2 Tbsp. brown sugar

1. Preheat oven to 350°. Remove rind from top of cheese, cutting to within ½ inch of edge. Place on an oven-safe dish.
2. Combine pecans, Kahlúa, and brown sugar; spread mixture over cheese. Bake at 350° for 5 minutes or just until softened.

Bacon Appetizers

MAKES 2 DOZEN; **PREP:** 10 MIN.,
COOK: 20 MIN., **BAKE:** 7 MIN.

Only four ingredients, but put together just so, they pack a wallop of first-course pleasure.

1 lb. bacon
1¾ cups (7 oz.) shredded Gouda cheese
1 cup mayonnaise
½ (16-oz.) package cocktail rye bread, lightly toasted
Garnishes: sun-dried tomato slivers, sliced ripe olives, fresh herbs

1. Preheat oven to 350°.
2. Cook bacon in a large skillet over medium-high heat until crisp; remove bacon, and drain on paper towels. Crumble bacon. Combine bacon, cheese, and mayonnaise in a large bowl.
3. Spread mixture on rye bread slices. Place on ungreased baking sheets. Bake at 350° for 7 minutes or until cheese is bubbly. Garnish, if desired. Serve warm.

Tomato Crostini

MAKES 4 SERVINGS; **PREP:** 20 MIN.

Try these light and airy wedges as a simple savory appetizer. This recipe easily doubles or quadruples for a crowd.

¼ cup goat cheese
¼ cup cream cheese, softened
1 (6-inch) prebaked Italian pizza crust
5 plum tomatoes, chopped
1 Tbsp. chopped fresh herbs (parsley, thyme, basil, or rosemary)

1. Stir together goat cheese and cream cheese; spread on pizza crust. Cut into wedges; top evenly with tomatoes and herbs.

Pepperoni Pizza Pinwheels

MAKES 12 SERVINGS; **PREP:** 8 MIN.,
BAKE: 12 MIN.

Kids love to dip these cheesy pizza bites in spaghetti sauce. It's just the perfect thing for little hands, but sure to please all ages.

1 (11-oz.) can refrigerated pizza crust
1 cup (4 oz.) shredded pizza cheese
    blend
½ cup grated Parmesan cheese
1 (3.5-oz.) package sliced pepperoni,
    chopped
½ cup spaghetti sauce, heated

1. Preheat oven to 400°. Unroll pizza crust on a cutting board; roll crust into a 12- x 9-inch rectangle. Sprinkle with cheeses and pepperoni.
2. Roll up, starting with long side; moisten edge with water, and pinch seam to seal. Cut into 1-inch-wide slices, and place 1 inch apart in a lightly greased 15- x 10-inch jelly-roll pan; flatten pinwheels slightly.
3. Bake at 400° for 12 to 14 minutes or until golden. Serve immediately with warm spaghetti sauce.

Mouthwatering Main Dishes

Enjoy these simple and satisfying dishes that can be made in a hurry for busy weeknights or relaxed gatherings.

Ultimate Cheese Pizza

MAKES 4 SERVINGS; **PREP:** 10 MIN.,
BAKE: 12 MIN.

Shred any leftover cheese you find in the fridge for this simple pie.

1 (14.5-oz.) can whole tomatoes, drained
    and chopped
1 tsp. bottled minced garlic
1 (12-inch) prebaked pizza crust
2 cups (8 oz.) mixed shredded cheese

1. Preheat oven to 450°. Stir together tomatoes and garlic. Spread crust with tomato mixture, and sprinkle with cheese.
2. Bake directly on oven rack at 450° for 12 to 14 minutes or until cheese is melted.

Ultimate Cheeseburger Pizza:

Substitute 1½ cups shredded Cheddar cheese for 2 cups mixed shredded cheese. Prepare Ultimate Cheese Pizza as directed, sprinkling 1½ cups cooked and crumbled ground beef (about ½ lb.), ¼ cup chopped green onions, and ½ tsp. salt over tomato mixture. Sprinkle with cheese. Bake as directed. Serve with pickles, if desired.

Ultimate Veggie Pizza: Prepare

Ultimate Cheese Pizza as directed, arranging 2 cups roasted or grilled vegetables over tomato mixture. Sprinkle with cheese. Bake as directed.

Beef Fillets With Orange Cream

MAKES 4 SERVINGS; **PREP:** 5 MIN.,
GRILL: 17 MIN.

The slightly orange-colored sauce and orange zest curls make a pretty presentation and lend a hint to the flavor of these succulent fillets.

4 (6- to 8-oz.) beef tenderloin fillets
½ tsp. cracked pepper (optional)
1 cup whipping cream
2 Tbsp. orange marmalade
1 to 2 Tbsp. prepared horseradish

1. Preheat grill to 350° to 400° (medium-high) heat. Sprinkle fillets with cracked pepper, if desired.
2. Grill, covered with grill lid, over 350° to 400° (medium-high) heat 4 to 6 minutes on each side or to desired degree of doneness.
3. Bring whipping cream, marmalade, and horseradish to a boil over medium-high heat, stirring constantly; reduce heat, and simmer, stirring often, 5 minutes or until thickened. Serve immediately with fillets.

5-Ingredient Comfort Food

The Perfect Burgers

MAKES 6 BURGERS; **PREP:** 10 MIN.,
STAND: 35 MIN., **GRILL:** 13 MIN.

A simple, rustic burger right off the grill is every man's favorite dish. Pair the burgers with the French Fries on page 310.

1½ lb. ground beef (75/25 or 25% fat)
1½ tsp. kosher salt
1½ tsp. coarsely ground pepper
6 (1-oz.) Cheddar cheese slices
6 hamburger buns
Toppings: lettuce leaves, red onion slices, tomato slices

1. Preheat grill to 350° to 400° (medium-high) heat. Gently combine beef, salt, and pepper. Shape into 6 (4-inch) 1-inch-thick patties. Using thumb and forefinger, lightly press middle of patties, pressing in but not completely through, creating an indentation in center of patties. Let stand at room temperature 30 minutes.
2. Grill, covered with grill lid, over 350° to 400° (medium-high heat) heat 6 to 7 minutes on each side or until no longer pink in center. Top each burger with 1 cheese slice, and grill, covered with grill lid, 1 to 2 minutes or until cheese is melted. Remove from grill, and let stand 5 minutes. Serve on hamburger buns with desired toppings.

Country Ham With Redeye Gravy

MAKES 6 SERVINGS; **PREP:** 10 MIN.,
COOK: 29 MIN.

For true redeye gravy, Southerners use caffeinated coffee for its pick-me-up quality.

2 cups hot strong brewed coffee
¼ cup firmly packed brown sugar
2 (12-oz.) slices boneless country ham

1. Stir together coffee and sugar; let mixture cool.
2. Cook ham in a large cast-iron skillet over medium heat 5 to 7 minutes on each side or until browned. Remove ham, and keep warm, reserving drippings in skillet.
3. Add coffee mixture to skillet, stirring to loosen particles from bottom; bring to a boil. Boil, stirring occasionally, until reduced by half (about 15 minutes). Serve with ham.

Baked Ham

MAKES 16 SERVINGS; **PREP:** 5 MIN.,
BAKE: 3 HR., **STAND:** 15 MIN.

1 (10-lb.) smoked ham
1 (13-oz.) jar orange marmalade
¼ cup stone-ground mustard
1 Tbsp. fresh thyme, chopped

1. Preheat oven to 300°. Wrap ham in aluminum foil, and place in a lightly greased 13- x 9-inch pan; bake at 300° for 2 hours.
2. Remove ham from oven, and unwrap. Remove skin and excess fat from ham. Score fat on ham in a diamond pattern.
3. Stir together marmalade and remaining ingredients in a small bowl. Spoon glaze over ham, and bake 1 hour, basting every 15 minutes or until a meat thermometer inserted into the thickest portion registers 140°. Let stand 15 minutes before slicing.

Slow-Cooker BBQ Pork

MAKES 6 SERVINGS; **PREP:** 5 MIN.,
COOK: 7 HR.

This super-simple recipe delivers big flavor. Reduce the fat but not the flavor in this juicy cut of pork by preparing it a day ahead. Cool the barbecue, and refrigerate overnight. Remove and discard any solidified fat before reheating.

1 (3- to 4-lb.) shoulder pork roast
1 (18-oz.) bottle barbecue sauce
1 (12-oz.) can cola soft drink

1. Place pork roast in a 6-qt. slow cooker; pour barbecue sauce and cola over roast.
2. Cover with lid, and cook on HIGH 6 to 7 hours or until meat is tender and shreds easily. Serve on buns with slaw or over hot toasted cornbread.
Note: We tested with Sticky Fingers Memphis Original Barbecue Sauce. If you don't have a slow cooker, place roast in a lightly greased Dutch oven; stir together barbecue sauce and cola, and pour over roast. Before placing lid on top of Dutch oven, cover roast with a double layer of aluminum foil. Bake, tightly covered, at 325° for 3½ hours or until tender.

Pan-Fried Pork Chops

MAKES 6 TO 8 SERVINGS; **PREP:** 10 MIN.,
COOK: 2 MIN. PER BATCH

½ cup all-purpose flour
1 tsp. salt
1 tsp. seasoned pepper
1½ lb. wafer-thin boneless pork chops
¼ cup vegetable oil

1. Combine first 3 ingredients in a
shallow dish; dredge pork chops in
flour mixture.
2. Fry pork chops, in 3 batches, in hot
oil in a large skillet over medium-high
heat 1 minute on each side or until
browned. Drain on paper towels.

Cheesy Chicken Penne

MAKES 4 TO 6 SERVINGS; **PREP:** 10 MIN.,
COOK: 10 MIN.

*The combination of sour cream and
melted cheese makes this pasta creation
incredibly saucy.*

8 oz. uncooked penne
1 (16-oz.) loaf pasteurized prepared cheese
    product, cubed
1 (8-oz.) container sour cream
½ cup milk
2½ cups prepackaged chopped cooked
    chicken

1. Cook pasta according to package
directions, including salt; drain.
2. Meanwhile, cook cubed cheese, sour
cream, and milk over medium-low heat,
stirring constantly, 5 minutes or until
cheese melts. Stir in pasta and chicken,
and cook until thoroughly heated.

Mama's Fried Chicken

MAKES 4 TO 6 SERVINGS; **PREP:** 30 MIN.,
CHILL: 2 HR., **COOK:** 30 MIN. PER BATCH

Fried chicken feeds the soul of the South.

1 (3- to 4-lb.) whole chicken, cut into
    pieces
1 tsp. salt
1 tsp. pepper
2 cups buttermilk
Self-rising flour
Vegetable oil
Salt (optional)

1. Sprinkle chicken with 1 tsp. each
salt and pepper. Place chicken in a shallow dish or zip-top plastic freezer bag,
and add buttermilk. Cover or seal, and
chill at least 2 hours.
2. Remove chicken from buttermilk,
discarding buttermilk. Dredge chicken
in flour.
3. Pour oil to a depth of 1½ inches in a
deep skillet or Dutch oven; heat to 360°.
Add chicken, a few pieces at a time;
cover and cook 6 minutes. Uncover
chicken, and cook 9 minutes. Turn
chicken; cover and cook 6 minutes.
Uncover and cook 5 to 9 minutes, turning chicken the last 3 minutes for even
browning, if necessary. Drain on paper
towels. Sprinkle lightly with salt while
chicken is hot, if desired.

Pecan Chicken

MAKES 4 SERVINGS; **PREP:** 12 MIN.,
BAKE: 15 MIN.

*Using just three ingredients to flavor this
chicken makes a miraculous quick main
dish. Pounding chicken breasts shortens
the time they take to cook.*

4 skinned and boned chicken breast halves
2 Tbsp. honey
2 Tbsp. Dijon mustard
2 Tbsp. finely chopped pecans

1. Preheat oven to 350°. Place chicken
between 2 sheets of heavy-duty plastic
wrap, and flatten to ¼-inch thickness
using a meat mallet or rolling pin.
2. Stir together honey and mustard;
spread on both sides of chicken, and
dredge in pecans; arrange in a lightly
greased 8-inch square baking dish.
3. Bake at 350° for 15 to 18 minutes or
until done.
Note: We tested with Grey Poupon
Dijon Mustard.

Parmesan-Crusted Orange Roughy

MAKES 4 SERVINGS; **PREP:** 5 MIN.,
BAKE: 7 MIN.

4 (6-oz.) orange roughy fillets (1 inch thick)
3 Tbsp. freshly shredded Parmesan cheese
1 tsp. dried dillweed

1. Preheat oven to 450°. Arrange fillets
in a single layer in a lightly greased
15- x 10-inch jelly-roll pan. Combine
Parmesan cheese and dillweed.
Sprinkle evenly over fillets.
2. Bake at 450° for 7 to 9 minutes or until
fish flakes when tested with a fork.

Southern Sides

These homestyle sides might just upstage the entrées.

Buttermilk-Garlic Mashed Potatoes

MAKES 4 SERVINGS; **PREP:** 10 MIN., **COOK:** 6 MIN.

2 Tbsp. butter
3 garlic cloves, chopped
2 cups buttermilk
⅔ cup milk
½ tsp. salt
½ tsp. pepper
1 (22-oz.) package frozen mashed potatoes

1. Melt butter in a Dutch oven over medium heat; add garlic, and sauté 1 minute.
2. Add buttermilk and next 3 ingredients. Cook, stirring constantly, 5 minutes or until thoroughly heated. Stir in potatoes until smooth.
Note: We tested with Ore-Ida Mashed Potatoes. There's no need to thaw them.

Soufflé Potatoes

MAKES 8 SERVINGS; **PREP:** 5 MIN., **BAKE:** 5 MIN.

The instant potato flakes in this recipe make for a super-quick soufflé.

2⅔ cups instant potato flakes
1 large egg, beaten
1 (2.8-oz.) can French fried onion rings
¼ tsp. salt
½ cup (2 oz.) shredded Cheddar cheese

1. Preheat oven to 350°. Prepare potato flakes according to package directions. Add egg, onion rings, and salt, stirring until blended. Spoon mixture into a lightly greased 2-qt. baking dish; sprinkle with cheese. Bake, uncovered, at 350° for 5 minutes or until cheese melts.

Microwave Directions: Prepare potato flakes in microwave according to package directions. Add egg, onion rings, and salt, stirring until blended. Spoon mixture into a lightly greased 2-qt. baking dish. Microwave at HIGH 4 to 5 minutes. Sprinkle with cheese; cover and let stand 2 minutes or until cheese melts.

French Fries

MAKES 6 SERVINGS; **PREP:** 30 MIN., **COOK:** 5 MIN. PER BATCH

These russet strips are twice-fried for extra crispy results. These fries go well with The Perfect Burgers on page 308.

4 lb. russet or Idaho potatoes, peeled
Vegetable oil
Salt to taste

1. Cut potatoes into ¼-inch-wide strips.
2. Pour vegetable oil to a depth of 4 inches in a Dutch oven, and heat to 325°. Fry potato strips, in batches, until lightly golden but not brown, 4 to 5 minutes per batch. Drain strips on paper towels.
3. Heat oil to 375°. Fry strips, in small batches, until golden brown and crisp, 1 to 2 minutes per batch. Drain on clean paper towels. Sprinkle strips with salt, and serve immediately.

Salt-and-Pepper Fries: Prepare French Fries as directed. Grind some fresh pepper over hot fries after you sprinkle them with salt.

Garlic-Butter New Potatoes

MAKES 6 SERVINGS; **PREP:** 6 MIN., **COOK:** 13 MIN.

18 new potatoes, quartered (about 2¾ lb.)
¼ cup butter or margarine
2 garlic cloves, minced
1 Tbsp. chopped fresh parsley
¼ tsp. pepper

1. Combine potatoes and salted water to cover in a large saucepan; cook, covered, 10 minutes or until tender. Drain.
2. Meanwhile, melt butter in a small skillet over medium-high heat; add garlic, and cook, stirring constantly, 3 minutes or until tender. Add parsley and pepper; pour over potatoes, tossing gently to coat.

Rice Pilaf

MAKES 4 SERVINGS; **PREP:** 5 MIN.,
COOK: 30 MIN.

1 Tbsp. olive oil
1 cup uncooked long-grain rice
2½ cups chicken broth
½ cup coarsely chopped walnuts or pecans,
  toasted

1. Heat olive oil in a large skillet over
medium-high heat until hot. Add rice;
sauté 3 to 5 minutes or just until rice is
lightly browned.
2. Meanwhile, bring broth to a boil in
a large saucepan. Gradually add rice to
broth; cover, reduce heat, and simmer 25
minutes or until liquid is absorbed and
rice is tender. Stir in walnuts or pecans.

Lemon Vermicelli

MAKES 4 SERVINGS; **PREP:** 10 MIN.,
COOK: 22 MIN.

*Instead of mashed potatoes or rice, serve
this lemon-kissed buttered pasta topped
with Parmesan cheese. It's especially
good with fish or chicken.*

⅓ cup whipping cream
3 Tbsp. butter
1 (7-oz.) package dried vermicelli
¼ cup fresh lemon juice
⅓ cup freshly grated Parmesan cheese

1. Combine cream and butter in a
small saucepan; cook over medium-low
heat until butter melts. Set aside, and
keep warm.
2. Cook vermicelli according to
package directions; drain. Place in a
bowl, and toss with lemon juice; let
stand 1 minute. Add cheese and warm
cream mixture; toss to coat. Serve
immediately.

Corn Pudding

MAKES 6 SERVINGS; **PREP:** 10 MIN.,
COOK: 20 MIN.

2 cups milk
½ cup yellow cornmeal
1 (16-oz.) package frozen whole kernel corn,
  thawed
½ tsp. salt
2 Tbsp. whipping cream

1. Bring milk to a boil in a heavy saucepan; gradually add cornmeal, stirring
until blended after each addition. Cook,
stirring constantly, just until mixture
begins to boil. Reduce heat, and cook,
stirring constantly, until thickened.
2. Add corn, stirring until mixture is
the consistency of whipped potatoes.
Stir in salt and whipping cream.

Buttermilk Fried Corn

MAKES 2 CUPS; **PREP:** 15 MIN.,
COOK: 15 MIN., **OTHER:** 30 MIN.

*Soaked in buttermilk, floured, and then
fried, corn kernels are a crispy side or
topping for salads, soups, and casseroles.*

2 cups fresh corn kernels
1½ cups buttermilk
⅔ cup all-purpose flour
⅔ cup cornmeal
1 tsp. salt
½ tsp. pepper
Corn oil

1. Combine corn kernels and buttermilk in large bowl; let stand 30 minutes.
Drain.
2. Combine flour and next 3 ingredients in a large zip-top plastic bag. Add
corn to flour mixture, a small amount at
a time, and shake bag to coat corn.

3. Pour oil to a depth of 1 inch in a
Dutch oven; heat to 375°. Fry corn,
a small amount at a time, in hot oil
2 minutes or until golden. Drain on
paper towels. Serve as a side dish, or
sprinkle on salads and soups.

Homemade Applesauce

MAKES ABOUT 6 CUPS; **PREP:** 20 MIN.,
COOK: 20 MIN.

*For the best taste and texture, use a
variety of apples—such as Granny Smith,
Golden Delicious, and Gala—when
making applesauce and apple pie. Stir
in a little chopped rosemary, and serve
this applesauce as a side dish with pork
chops or hash browns.*

12 large apples, peeled and coarsely
  chopped
1 cup sugar
½ lemon, sliced

1. Cook all ingredients in a Dutch
oven over medium heat, stirring often,
20 minutes or until apples are tender
and juices are thickened. Remove and
discard lemon slices. Serve applesauce
warm; or let cool and store in an airtight container in the refrigerator for
up to 1 week.

Spiced Applesauce: Substitute
½ cup firmly packed brown sugar
and ½ cup granulated sugar for 1 cup
sugar. Omit lemon slices, and add
1 tsp. ground cinnamon and ¼ tsp.
ground cloves; prepare as directed.

Bounty of Breads

Whether served as morning foods, alongside dinner, or as an afternoon snack, these gooey, quick homemade treats will please any palate.

Easy Banana Pancakes

MAKES 16 SERVINGS; **PREP:** 5 MIN., **COOK:** 4 MIN. PER BATCH

These airy cakes come together in a flash, thanks to biscuit mix and mashed bananas.

2 cups all-purpose baking mix
1 cup milk
2 ripe bananas, mashed
2 large eggs, lightly beaten
Maple syrup or fruit topping

1. Combine first 4 ingredients in a medium bowl, stirring just until dry ingredients are moistened.
2. Pour about ¼ cup batter for each pancake onto a hot, lightly greased griddle. Cook pancakes 2 minutes or until tops are covered with bubbles and edges look cooked; turn and cook other side. Serve immediately with syrup or fruit topping.
Note: We tested with Bisquick All-Purpose Baking Mix.

Mayonnaise Rolls

MAKES 6 ROLLS; **PREP:** 8 MIN., **BAKE:** 15 MIN.

These moist rolls are a delight thanks to the addition of mayonnaise. Bake for guests, and utilize an entire muffin pan by doubling these four simple ingredients.

1 cup self-rising flour
½ cup milk
3 Tbsp. mayonnaise
¾ tsp. sugar

1. Preheat oven to 425°. Combine all ingredients in a bowl, stirring just until dry ingredients are moistened. Spoon batter into a lightly greased muffin pan, filling three-fourths full. Bake at 425° for 15 minutes.

Caramel-Pecan Rolls

MAKES 8 SERVINGS; **PREP:** 10 MIN., **BAKE:** 14 MIN.

¼ cup caramel syrup
1 (8-oz.) can refrigerated crescent rolls
¼ cup firmly packed brown sugar
2 Tbsp. finely chopped pecans
½ tsp. ground cinnamon

1. Preheat oven to 375°. Spoon in 1½ tsp. syrup into each of 8 muffin cups coated with cooking spray; set aside.
2. Unroll crescent dough, and separate into rectangles. Combine brown sugar, pecans, and cinnamon; sprinkle evenly over each rectangle, pressing gently into dough. Roll up, jelly-roll fashion, starting at long end. Pinch ends of dough to seal. Gently cut each log into 6 slices. Place 3 slices, cut sides down, in prepared muffin cups. Bake at 375° for 14 minutes. Run a knife around edges of cups; invert onto a platter.

Caramel-Nut Pull-Apart Bread

MAKES 12 SERVINGS; **PREP:** 12 MIN., **BAKE:** 30 MIN.

Gooey pull-apart bread goes over well at any breakfast table. This version is certainly no exception.

1 cup plus 2 Tbsp. firmly packed brown sugar
1 cup chopped walnuts
⅔ cup butter, melted
3 (12-oz.) cans refrigerated biscuits
2 Tbsp. cinnamon sugar

1. Preheat oven to 350°. Combine brown sugar and walnuts in a small bowl. Stir in butter. Spoon half of brown sugar mixture in bottom of a greased 12-cup Bundt pan.
2. Cut each biscuit in half (use kitchen scissors for quick cutting), and place in a large bowl. Sprinkle biscuits with cinnamon sugar; toss well to coat. Arrange half of biscuits over brown sugar mixture in Bundt pan. Spoon remaining brown sugar mixture over biscuits in pan; top with remaining biscuits.
3. Bake at 350° for 30 to 35 minutes or until browned. Turn out onto a serving platter immediately, spooning any remaining sauce over bread. Serve warm.
Note: We tested with Pillsbury Golden Layers Flaky Biscuits.

Basic Buttermilk Cornbread

MAKES 8 SERVINGS; **PREP:** 10 MIN., **BAKE:** 38 MIN.

¼ cup butter
1½ cups buttermilk
1 large egg
2 cups self-rising cornmeal

1. Preheat oven to 425°. Melt butter in a 10-inch cast-iron skillet in oven 8 minutes.
2. Whisk together buttermilk and egg in a large bowl; add melted butter from skillet, whisking until blended. Whisk in cornmeal until smooth. Spoon into hot skillet.
3. Bake at 425° for 30 minutes or until golden. Cut into wedges to serve.

Cornmeal Biscuits

MAKES 3 DOZEN; **PREP:** 20 MIN., **COOK:** 13 MIN.

These buttery biscuits blend two Southern bread traditions. They have a slight nutty crunch from the cornmeal, but a texture more like biscuits.

4 cups self-rising flour
½ cup yellow cornmeal
1 cup butter, cut up
2 cups buttermilk
¼ cup milk

1. Preheat oven to 425°.
2. Combine flour and cornmeal in a large bowl; cut in butter with a pastry blender or fork until crumbly. Add buttermilk, stirring just until dry ingredients are moistened.
3. Turn dough out onto a lightly floured surface; knead 2 or 3 times.
4. Pat or roll dough to a ½-inch thickness, and cut with a 2-inch round cutter. Place on lightly greased baking sheets. Reroll remaining dough, and proceed as directed. Brush tops with milk.
5. Bake at 425° for 13 to 15 minutes or until golden.

Easy Pan Biscuits

MAKES 20 BISCUITS; **PREP:** 15 MIN., **COOK:** 15 MIN.

Soft drinks have a long history as ingredients in some deliciously novel recipes for pot roasts, glazed ham, barbecue sauce, sorbets, and granitas. Here, lemon-lime soft drink adds a touch of sweetness and sour cream adds a rich taste to these butter-brushed biscuits in a square pan.

2 cups all-purpose baking mix
½ cup sour cream
6 Tbsp. lemon-lime soft drink or diet lemon-lime soft drink
3 Tbsp. butter, melted and divided

1. Preheat oven to 425°.
2. Combine first 3 ingredients, stirring to form a soft dough; lightly flour hands, and divide dough into 20 equal portions. Shape each portions into a ball, and place in a lightly greased 8-inch square pan. (Dough portions will touch.) Brush evenly with half of butter.
3. Bake at 425° for 15 minutes or until golden brown. Brush evenly with remaining half of butter. Serve immediately.
Note: We tested with Bisquick All-Purpose Baking Mix and Sprite Lemon-Lime Soft Drink.

Blueberry Muffins

MAKES 1 DOZEN; **PREP:** 10 MIN., **COOK:** 15 MIN.

In the early 1800s muffins were so popular that "muffin men" traveled the countryside ringing a bell at tea time to announce their muffins for sale.

2 cups self-rising flour
½ cup sugar
1 cup milk
¼ cup vegetable oil
2 large eggs
1 cup fresh or frozen blueberries

1. Preheat oven to 400°.
2. Combine flour and sugar in a large bowl; make a well in center of mixture. Whisk together milk, oil, and eggs until well blended. Add to flour mixture, and stir just until dry ingredients are moistened. Gently fold in blueberries.
3. Spoon mixture into lightly greased muffin pans, filling two-thirds full.
4. Bake at 400° for 15 to 18 minutes or until golden brown.

Famous Sausage Ball Muffins

MAKES 4 DOZEN; **PREP:** 5 MIN., **COOK:** 13 MIN. PER BATCH

This recipe has been around for years, and every cook has definite opinions and memories related to it. We found the recipe fun to revisit as easy mini muffins and with some flavor variations.

2 cups all-purpose baking mix
1 lb. hot or regular ground pork sausage
2 cups (8 oz.) shredded sharp Cheddar cheese

1. Preheat oven to 400°. Combine all ingredients in a large bowl, pressing together with hands. Spoon rounded tablespoonfuls into lightly greased 1¾-inch miniature muffin pans. Bake at 400° for 13 to 15 minutes or until lightly browned. Remove from pans, and serve warm with desired sauce, such as Ranch dressing, honey mustard, or barbecue sauce.
Note: We tested with Bisquick All-Purpose Baking Mix, Jimmy Dean Pork Sausage, and Cracker Barrel Sharp Cheddar Cheese.

Sweet Endings

Everyone will want to save some room for these homey favorites.

Coconut-Sour Cream Cake

MAKES 12 SERVINGS; **PREP:** 25 MIN.,
COOK: ABOUT 27 MIN., **CHILL:** 9½ HR.

Butter-flavored cake mix gives you a head start on this elegant-looking 4-layer cake. The flavor gets better and the cake more moist the longer it chills.

1 (18.25-oz.) package butter-recipe cake mix
1 (16-oz.) container sour cream
2 cups sugar
4 cups sweetened flaked coconut
1½ cups frozen whipped topping, thawed

1. Prepare cake mix according to package directions, using 2 (9-inch) round cake pans. Slice each cake layer horizontally in half, using a long serrated knife.
2. Combine sour cream, sugar, and coconut in a bowl; stir well. Cover and chill 1½ hours. Reserve 1 cup sour cream mixture. Spread remaining sour cream mixture between layers.
3. Fold whipped topping into reserved sour cream mixture. Spread on top and sides of cake. Place cake in an airtight container. Cover and chill at least 8 hours.
Note: We tested with Pillsbury Butter-Recipe Cake Mix.

Brownie Trifle

MAKES 16 TO 18 SERVINGS; **PREP:** 25 MIN.,
BAKE: 20 MIN., **CHILL:** 8 HR.

Smooth-textured sweet brûlée isn't as hard to prepare as you might think. In this version, white chocolate adds an updated twist to the classic recipe.

1 (19.8-oz.) package fudge brownie mix
¼ cup coffee liqueur (optional)
1 (3.9-oz.) package chocolate fudge instant pudding mix
1 (8.7-oz.) package toffee-flavored candy bars, crushed
1 (12-oz.) container frozen whipped topping, thawed

1. Prepare brownie mix according to package directions in a 13- x 9-inch pan. Prick tops of warm brownies at 1-inch intervals with a wooden pick, and brush with coffee liqueur, if desired. Crumble into small pieces.
2. Prepare pudding mix according to package directions, omitting chilling.
3. Place half of crumbled brownies in bottom of a 3-quart trifle bowl; top with half each of pudding, candy bars, and whipped topping. Repeat layers. Cover and chill at least 8 hours.
Note: We tested with Kahlúa Coffee Liqueur.

Caramel Pie

MAKES 1 (9-INCH) PIE; **PREP:** 4 MIN.,
COOK: 9 HR., **CHILL:** 2 HR.

Wake up to pie? Indeed! This pie is a great candidate to cook while you sleep.

1 (14-oz.) can sweetened condensed milk
1 (9-inch) ready-made graham cracker crust
1 (8-oz.) container frozen whipped topping, thawed
2 (1.4-oz.) chocolate-covered toffee candy bars, coarsely chopped

1. Pour milk into a 2-cup glass measuring cup; cover with aluminum foil.
2. Place measuring cup in a 3½-quart electric slow cooker; carefully pour hot water in slow cooker to reach the level of milk in measuring cup. Cover and cook on LOW 9 hours.
3. Pour caramelized milk into crust; cool completely. Spread whipped topping over pie; sprinkle with chopped candy bars. Cover and chill 2 hours or until ready to serve.
Note: We tested with Skor Chocolate-covered Toffee Candy Bars.

Apple-Gingerbread Cobbler

MAKES 8 SERVINGS; **PREP:** 15 MIN.,
COOK: 5 MIN., **BAKE:** 30 MIN.

Using a packaged gingerbread mix, this easy-to-make cobbler is ready for the oven in 15 minutes.

1 (14-oz.) package gingerbread mix, divided
¼ cup firmly packed light brown sugar
½ cup butter, divided
½ cup chopped pecans
2 (21-oz.) cans apple pie filling
Vanilla ice cream (optional)

1. Preheat oven to 375°. Stir together 2 cups gingerbread mix and ¾ cup water until smooth; set mixture aside.

2. Stir together remaining gingerbread mix and brown sugar; cut in ¼ cup butter until mixture is crumbly. Stir in pecans; set aside.

3. Combine apple pie filling and remaining ¼ cup butter in a large saucepan, and cook, stirring often, 5 minutes over medium heat or until thoroughly heated. Spoon hot apple mixture evenly into a lightly greased 11- x 7-inch baking dish. Spoon gingerbread mixture over hot apple mixture; sprinkle with pecan mixture

4. Bake at 375° for 30 to 35 minutes or until set. Serve cobbler with vanilla ice cream, if desired.

German Chocolate Squares

MAKES 2 DOZEN; **PREP:** 8 MIN.,
COOK: 35 MIN.

1 (21-oz.) package family-style brownie mix
1½ cups chopped pecans
1 (14-oz.) can sweetened condensed milk
1 (14-oz.) package sweet coconut
1 (12-oz.) package semisweet chocolate morsels

1. Preheat oven to 350°. Prepare brownie mix according to package directions using directions for cake-like brownies. Stir in pecans; spread batter evenly into a lightly greased 13- x 9-inch pan. Bake at 350° for 25 minutes or until a wooden pick inserted in center comes out clean.

2. Combine condensed milk and coconut. Spread over baked brownies; sprinkle with chocolate morsels. Bake 10 more minutes or until chocolate morsels are glossy. Cool completely on a wire rack; cut into squares.

Rosemary Shortbread Cookies

MAKES 1½ DOZEN; **PREP:** 15 MIN.,
BAKE: 18 MIN. PER BATCH

1½ cups all-purpose flour
½ cup butter, chilled
¼ cup powdered sugar
2 Tbsp. minced fresh rosemary
2 Tbsp. granulated sugar

1. Preheat oven to 325°. Process first 4 ingredients in a food processor until mixture forms a ball.

2. Roll dough to ¼-inch thickness on a lightly floured surface. Cut with a 2-inch cookie cutter; place on lightly greased baking sheets.

3. Bake at 325° for 18 to 20 minutes or until edges are lightly browned. Sprinkle with granulated sugar. Remove to wire racks to cool completely.

Jam Kolache

MAKES 3½ DOZEN; **PREP:** 16 MIN.,
BAKE: 15 MIN. PER BATCH

½ cup butter, softened
1 (3-oz.) package cream cheese, softened
1¼ cups all-purpose flour
Strawberry jam (about ½ cup)

1. Preheat oven to 375°. Beat butter and cream cheese at medium speed with an electric mixer until creamy. Add flour to butter mixture, beating well.

2. Roll dough to ⅛-inch thickness on a lightly floured surface; cut with a 2½-inch round cookie cutter. Place on lightly greased baking sheets. Spoon ¼ tsp. jam on each cookie. Fold opposite sides to center, slightly overlapping edges; press down lightly on centers.

3. Bake at 375° for 15 minutes. Remove to wire racks to cool.

Chocolate-Almond Macaroons

MAKES 2 DOZEN; **PREP:** 15 MIN.,
BAKE: 15 MIN. PER BATCH

Take time to bake some sweets with your children during the holiday season. Recipes like this for macaroons give kids a chance to take part and create kitchen memories.

¾ cup sweetened condensed milk
1 (14-oz.) package sweetened flaked coconut
¼ to ½ tsp. almond extract
⅛ tsp. salt
24 whole almonds
½ cup dark chocolate morsels (optional)

1. Preheat oven to 350°. Stir together first 4 ingredients. Drop dough by lightly greased tablespoonfuls onto parchment paper-lined baking sheets. Gently press an almond into top of each cookie.

2. Bake at 350° for 15 to 17 minutes or until golden. Remove to wire racks to cool.

3. If desired, microwave chocolate morsels in a microwave-safe bowl on HIGH 1 minute and 15 seconds or until melted and smooth, stirring every 30 seconds. Transfer to a 1-quart zip-top plastic freezer bag; snip a tiny hole in 1 corner of bag. Pipe melted chocolate over cooled cookies by gently squeezing bag.

Chocolate Pudding

MAKES 5 CUPS; **PREP:** 15 MIN.,
COOK: 16 MIN.

*Here's a really rich but simple
homemade pudding. A small
serving will satisfy.*

⅓ cup cornstarch
4 cups whipping cream
1 cup sugar
1 cup semisweet chocolate morsels
1 Tbsp. vanilla extract
⅛ tsp. salt

1. Combine cornstarch and ½ cup
water, stirring until smooth. Bring whipping cream to a simmer in a 2-quart
saucepan over medium heat. Stir in
cornstarch mixture, sugar, and remaining ingredients, stirring constantly until
chocolate melts. Cook pudding, stirring
constantly, 8 minutes or until thick and
creamy. Serve warm or chilled.

Boiled Custard

MAKES 4 CUPS; **PREP:** 15 MIN.,
COOK: 25 MIN.

*Boiled custard conjures up thoughts
of Christmas in many families.
It's a simple delicacy that needs
no adornment.*

4 cups milk
6 large egg yolks
¾ cup sugar
2 Tbsp. cornstarch
Dash of salt
2 tsp. vanilla extract

1. Pour milk into top of a double boiler,
and bring water to a boil. Heat milk
until tiny bubbles begin to appear
around edges of pan. Remove from
heat, and set aside.
2. Beat egg yolks with a wire whisk
until frothy. Add sugar, cornstarch,
and salt, beating until thickened.
Gradually stir about 1 cup hot milk
into yolk mixture; add to remaining
milk, stirring constantly.
3. Cook custard mixture in double
boiler over low heat, stirring occasionally, 25 minutes or until thickened and
candy thermometer registers 180°.
(Do not boil.) Stir in vanilla. Serve
warm or cold.

Mini-Doughnut Stacks

MAKES 8 SERVINGS; **PREP:** 10 MIN.,
BROIL: 4 MIN.

16 miniature powdered sugar
    doughnuts
2 Tbsp. butter, softened
1 pint chocolate-cherry ice cream
Toppings (optional): hot fudge sauce,
    whipped cream, maraschino cherries
    with stems

1. Preheat oven to broil. Cut doughnuts
in half horizontally; spread cut sides
evenly with butter. Place buttered sides
up on a lightly greased baking sheet.
2. Broil doughnut halves 3 inches
from heat 3 to 4 minutes or until
golden brown.
3. Place 1 to 4 doughnut halves on each
serving plate. Top with a small scoop of
ice cream. Serve with desired toppings.
Note: We tested with Ben & Jerry's
Cherry Garcia Ice Cream.

Classic Cola Float

MAKES 1 SERVING; **PREP:** 5 MIN.

*Add cherry syrup or flavored soda to
this kid-friendly quencher. It is even
better topped with a maraschino cherry
with a stem.*

Vanilla ice cream
1 (12-oz.) can cola soft drink
¼ tsp. vanilla extract

1. Scoop ice cream into a tall glass,
filling half full. Top with cola, and
gently stir in vanilla.

Root Beer Float

MAKES 1 SERVING; **PREP:** 5 MIN.

*Use premium root beer and a
high-quality vanilla ice cream to
make the best dessert drink.*

Vanilla ice cream
1 (12-oz.) can root beer

1. Scoop ice cream into a tall glass,
filling half full. Top with root beer, and
gently stir. Serve immediately.

Porter Float

MAKES 1 SERVING; **PREP:** 5 MIN.

*Dark beer gives the ice-cream float a
new dimension.*

Vanilla ice cream
3 to 4 Tbsp. creamy porter or stout beer
Fresh raspberries
Fresh mint sprig

1. Scoop ice cream into a tall glass,
filling two-thirds full. Top with a few
Tbsp. of beer. Top with raspberries and
a mint sprig.
Note: We tested with Samuel Smith
Oatmeal Stout.

Holiday Favorites

Mostly Make-Ahead Holiday Feast

'Tis the season for family gatherings and good food. The plan on page 320 will help you produce a dynamite-tasting meal with time to spare. Take our make-ahead tips and prepare the whole menu, or just pick a recipe or two to add to your traditional meal.

Christmas Dinner

SERVES 8

Crab and Oyster Bisque

Coffee-Crusted Beef Wellingtons

Cast-Iron Herbed Potatoes Anna

Scalloped Greens

Cabbage and Apple Salad
With Roasted Onions

Carrots With Country Bacon

Cardamom-Scented Sweet Potato Pie

Chocolate Tiramisù Charlotte

Wine

Coffee

Crab and Oyster Bisque

MAKES 10 CUPS; **PREP:** 15 MIN.,
COOK: 20 MIN.

This rich seafood soup earned our Test Kitchen's highest rating. Serve the bisque in little cups at the start of your meal.

¼ cup butter or margarine
4 garlic cloves, minced
2 shallots, finely chopped
3 Tbsp. all-purpose flour
1 (8-oz.) bottle clam juice
1 cup dry white wine
1 Tbsp. Worcestershire sauce
1 tsp. Cajun seasoning
¼ tsp. pepper
1 qt. whipping cream
1 (12-ounce) container fresh oysters, drained
1 lb. fresh lump crabmeat

1. Melt butter in a Dutch oven over medium heat; add garlic and shallot, and sauté until tender. Add flour; cook 1 minute, stirring constantly. Add clam juice and wine; cook 2 minutes or until thickened, stirring constantly.
2. Stir in Worcestershire sauce and next 3 ingredients. Cook until thoroughly heated, about 10 minutes. Stir in oysters and crabmeat; cook just until edges of oysters curl.

Coffee-Crusted Beef Wellingtons

freezeable • make ahead
MAKES 8 SERVINGS; **PREP:** 58 MIN.,
COOK: 30 MIN., **BAKE:** 41 MIN.,
CHILL: 8 HR.

Coffee gives classic beef Wellington an intriguing new flavor dimension. For the pastry wrap, we found puff pastry shells easier to work with than sheets. Follow our make-ahead steps that make this fancy entrée easy. You can freeze filets up to a month ahead, and bake them without thawing.

2 tsp. freshly ground coffee
1 tsp. salt
¾ tsp. pepper
¾ tsp. garlic powder
8 (5- to 6-oz.) center-cut filet mignons (1½ inches thick)
1 Tbsp. olive oil or vegetable oil
3 Tbsp. butter or margarine
¼ cup finely chopped onion
¼ cup finely chopped carrot
¼ cup finely chopped celery
2 garlic cloves, minced
¾ cup Madeira
¾ cup freshly brewed coffee
½ cup beef broth
2 Tbsp. butter or margarine
½ lb. fresh mushrooms, minced
2 shallots, minced
½ tsp. salt
½ tsp. pepper
½ cup Madeira
8 frozen puff pastry shells, thawed
1 large egg, lightly beaten
2 large eggs, lightly beaten
2 Tbsp. butter
2½ Tbsp. all-purpose flour
½ cup whipping cream
½ tsp. salt
Garnishes: fresh rosemary, flat-leaf parsley, and thyme

1. Combine first 4 ingredients; stir well. Pat filets dry. Coat both sides of filets

Worry-Free Wellingtons

- You can assemble the pastry-wrapped beef, make the sauce ahead, and freeze both up to 1 month. The sauce freezes well in ice cube trays. Wrap the Wellingtons in press-and-seal plastic wrap and then in zip-top freezer bags.
- We found that preheating a broiler pan for 5 minutes and baking Wellingtons on the lowest oven shelf produced the best baked results with golden, flaky pastry.
- There's no fussy pastry cutout garnish. Before serving, simply tuck fresh herbs into the pastry for each serving.

with spice rub. Heat 1 Tbsp. oil in a large skillet over medium-high heat until skillet is hot. Sear filets, in 2 batches, 1 to 1½ minutes on each side. Remove filets from skillet; place on a plate, and cover and chill until ready to assemble Wellingtons. (Don't clean skillet.)

2. While filets are chilling, melt 3 Tbsp. butter in same skillet over medium-high heat. Add onion, carrot, celery, and garlic; sauté 5 minutes or until very tender. Add ¾ cup Madeira, brewed coffee, and broth; simmer 5 minutes. Remove from heat, and let cool. Transfer sauce to a 4-cup glass measuring cup, and chill overnight, if desired, or pour cooled sauce into ice cube trays and freeze. Once frozen, seal frozen sauce cubes in zip-top freezer bags.

3. Melt 2 Tbsp. butter in same skillet over medium-high heat. Add mushrooms, shallots, ½ tsp. salt, and ½ tsp. pepper; sauté until all liquid evaporates. Add ½ cup Madeira; cook over medium-high heat until all liquid evaporates. Remove from heat, and let cool. Cover and chill until ready to assemble Wellingtons.

4. Roll each of 8 puff pastry shells to about ⅛-inch thick on a lightly floured surface; spoon 1 heaping tablespoonful mushroom filling in center of each pastry. Top each with a chilled filet. Brush edges of each pastry square with 1 beaten egg. Wrap 2 opposite sides of pastry over each filet, overlapping them; seal seam with beaten egg. Wrap remaining 2 sides of pastry over filet, and seal with beaten egg. Seal any gaps with beaten egg and press pastry around filet to enclose completely. Wrap Wellingtons individually in press-and-seal plastic wrap. Place wrapped Wellingtons in large zip-top freezer bags, and freeze overnight or up to 1 month.

5. To bake, place oven rack on lowest oven shelf; preheat oven to 425°. Place a broiler pan on oven rack; heat pan 5 minutes. Brush tops and sides of frozen Wellingtons with 2 beaten eggs. Carefully place frozen Wellingtons, seam side down, on preheated pan. Bake at 425° for 36 minutes.

6. While Wellingtons bake, melt 2 Tbsp. butter in a saucepan over medium heat; add 2½ Tbsp. flour and cook, stirring constantly, 1 minute.

Add reserved Madeira sauce; cook, stirring constantly, over medium heat 6 to 8 minutes or until slightly thickened. (If using frozen Madeira sauce cubes, thaw cubes in a saucepan over medium heat before adding to flour mixture.) Stir in whipping cream; simmer 5 minutes or until desired thickness. Add ½ tsp. salt. Remove from heat.

7. Arrange baked Wellingtons on a serving platter. Cut a small slit in top of each pastry, and tuck several sprigs of fresh herbs into each slit. Serve with Madeira sauce.

Note: You can bake beef Wellingtons the same day they're assembled. After wrapping beef filets in pastry, cover and chill Wellingtons 1 hour. Bake as directed, reducing the baking time to 20 to 25 minutes. We tested with part of 2 Pepperidge Farm 10-oz. packages Frozen Puff Pastry Shells.

Holiday Favorites

The Countdown

It's the biggest holiday celebration of the year. Let our timeline help you organize your meal preparation.

1 week to 1 month ahead:
- Make grocery list. Shop for nonperishables.
- Visit wine shop to select wines.
- Prepare Coffee-Crusted Beef Wellingtons; freeze.
- Plan centerpiece and other table decorations.

2 or 3 days ahead:
- Take inventory of china, serving dishes, and utensils.
- Gather whatever pieces you'll need. Polish silver.

1 day ahead:
- Prepare Chocolate Tiramisù Charlotte; refrigerate overnight.
- Blanch and peel pearl onions, and prepare dressing for salad; refrigerate overnight.
- Peel and slice carrots; refrigerate overnight.
- Prepare Scalloped Greens without breadcrumb topping, and refrigerate unbaked overnight.
- Set the table, complete with centerpiece.

morning of the meal:
- Prepare and bake Cardamom-Scented Sweet Potato Pie.

3 hours before the meal:
- Prepare and bake Cast-Iron Herbed Potatoes Anna.

2 hours before the meal:
- Add breadcrumb topping to Scalloped Greens, and bake; cover with foil to keep warm.
- Prepare Cabbage and Apple Salad with Roasted Onions.
- Prepare Carrots with Country Bacon.

45 minutes before the meal:
- Prepare Crab and Oyster Bisque; keep warm over low heat.
- Bake beef Wellingtons (do not thaw); finish sauce, and keep warm over low heat.

just before serving:
- Reheat side dishes in the oven and on the stovetop as needed.
- Garnish beef Wellingtons with herbs.

just after dinner:
- Brew coffee.
- Set out desserts for guests to sample.

Cast-Iron Herbed Potatoes Anna

make ahead

MAKES 6 TO 8 SERVINGS; **PREP:** 27 MIN.; **BAKE:** 1 HR., 17 MIN.

Last-minute stovetop cooking gets this classic potato dish browned and crispy on the bottom. A well-seasoned cast-iron skillet is the key to unmolding the dish.

⅓ cup butter
6 garlic cloves, finely chopped
1 Tbsp. finely chopped fresh
    rosemary
1 Tbsp. finely chopped fresh
    thyme
2 Tbsp. vegetable oil
2¼ lb. russet potatoes, peeled and thinly
    sliced (about ⅛ inch thick)
¾ tsp. salt, divided
¾ tsp. freshly ground pepper,
    divided

1. Melt butter in a small skillet over medium heat. Add garlic. Cook 2 minutes or just until garlic is lightly browned. Remove from heat, and stir in rosemary and thyme; set aside.

2. Preheat oven to 400°. Brush bottom and sides of a 9-inch cast-iron skillet with 2 Tbsp. oil. Arrange enough potato slices to cover bottom of skillet, overlapping slices; drizzle with ⅓ herbed garlic butter. Sprinkle with ¼ tsp. salt and ¼ tsp. pepper. Repeat procedure twice with remaining potatoes, herbed garlic butter, salt, and pepper. Brush a piece of aluminum foil with melted butter; press foil firmly, buttered side down, onto potato slices.

3. Bake at 400° for 1 hour and 10 minutes. Remove from oven, and using an oven mitt, press down firmly on the aluminum foil-covered potatoes. Remove aluminum foil, and place skillet on stovetop over medium heat. Cook 5 minutes. Remove from heat; let stand 2 minutes. Invert potatoes onto a plate, coaxing potatoes loose from skillet with a spatula.

Make Ahead: Bake potatoes Anna earlier in the day; invert onto an oven-proof plate, and cover loosely with foil. Just before serving, uncover and reheat at 400° for 10 minutes.

Scalloped Greens
make ahead

MAKES 15 SERVINGS; **PREP:** 28 MIN., **COOK:** 3 HR., **STAND:** 15 MIN.

Greens have never tasted as good as they do in this crumb-topped casserole.

1 (1-lb.) bag chopped collard greens
1 (1-lb.) bag chopped turnip greens
½ cup all-purpose flour
¼ cup grated onion
2 large garlic cloves, minced
3 cups milk
2 cups half-and-half
2 large eggs
1¼ tsp. salt, divided
¼ tsp. pepper
2 cups (8 oz.) shredded sharp white Cheddar cheese
2 cups (8 oz.) shredded Havarti cheese
3 cups sourdough breadcrumbs
2 Tbsp. butter or margarine, melted

1. Wash greens; remove coarse stems. Bring greens and 3 cups water to a boil in a large Dutch oven. Cover, reduce heat, and simmer 1 hour and 45 minutes or until tender, stirring occasionally. Drain well. Return greens to pot.
2. Preheat oven to 350°. Whisk together flour, next 5 ingredients, 1 tsp. salt, and pepper. Add flour mixture to greens in pot. Add cheeses; pour into a buttered 13- x 9-inch baking dish.
3. Combine breadcrumbs, 2 Tbsp. melted butter, and remaining ¼ tsp. salt, tossing until crumbs are coated. Sprinkle over greens.

4. Bake, uncovered, at 350° for 1 hour and 15 minutes or until golden. Let stand 15 minutes before serving.
Note: To make 3 cups sourdough breadcrumbs, we used ⅓ (10-oz.) round loaf sourdough bread, torn into pieces, and pulsed in a food processor.
Make Ahead: Cook greens, shred cheese, assemble casserole, and store in refrigerator, without breadcrumb topping, up to a day ahead. Prepare breadcrumb topping, and add just before baking. Bake casserole according to recipe up to 2 hours before serving. Reheat briefly before serving.

Cabbage and Apple Salad With Roasted Onions
make ahead

MAKES: 8 SERVINGS; **PREP:** 38 MIN., **COOK:** 8 MIN., **BAKE:** 30 MIN.

It's worth the time to blanch and peel pearl onions for this salad. We don't recommend using frozen pearl onions.

2 (10-oz.) packages fresh pearl onions
1 head red cabbage, shredded
2 Tbsp. salt
2 Tbsp. olive oil
6 Tbsp. white wine vinegar, divided
6 Tbsp. maple syrup, divided
2 cups chopped pecans, toasted and divided
1 cup sour cream
½ tsp. salt
4 Granny Smith apples, chopped
1 head curly endive, chopped

1. Trim bottom ends of onions. Blanch unpeeled onions, in batches, in rapidly boiling water in a large saucepan 45 seconds. (It's important to blanch in batches so that the water remains at a boil.) Drain and peel onions; place in a large zip-top freezer bag, seal, and refrigerate overnight, if desired.
2. Combine cabbage and 2 Tbsp. salt in a large bowl; let stand 30 minutes,

tossing occasionally. Rinse thoroughly, and drain well.
3. Meanwhile, preheat oven to 450°. Combine onions and oil in a shallow roasting pan or a large cast-iron skillet; toss to coat. Spread onions in a single layer. Roast at 450° for 25 minutes or until browned, stirring after 20 minutes.
4. Combine ¼ cup each vinegar and maple syrup; add to roasted onions. Roast 5 more minutes or until slightly thickened and onions are glazed. Set aside.
5. Combine remaining 2 Tbsp. vinegar, 2 Tbsp. maple syrup, 1 cup chopped pecans, sour cream, and ½ tsp. salt in a food processor or blender; process 1 to 2 minutes or until smooth. Cover and chill dressing overnight, if desired.
6. Toss together chopped apple, cabbage, and endive in a large bowl. Drizzle each serving with dressing, and top with roasted onions; sprinkle with remaining 1 cup pecans.
Make Ahead: Blanch and peel pearl onions a day ahead; store in refrigerator. Prepare dressing up to a day ahead, and store in refrigerator.

Wine Advice

Offer both red and white. Put an assortment of bottles on your sideboard for guests to sample. Consider an Australian Shiraz or French Syrah; the full-bodied flavor of either partners well with this rich meal of beef Wellington. For a white wine, offer Gallo of Sonoma Chardonnay, lightly chilled. Serve wine in fashionable tumblers. They're elegant, yet sturdier than stemmed glasses.

Carrots With Country Bacon

make ahead

MAKES 6 TO 8 SERVINGS; **PREP:** 19 MIN., **COOK:** 35 MIN.

Thick-sliced bacon in this recipe is sometimes labeled country bacon or wood-smoked bacon. Any bacon that cooks up crisply will make a nice topping.

4 thick bacon slices
2 lb. carrots, peeled and diagonally sliced into 1-inch pieces
¼ cup firmly packed light brown sugar
2 Tbsp. butter
2 tsp. chopped fresh thyme

1. Cook bacon in a large skillet over medium heat until crisp. Drain, reserving 1 Tbsp. drippings in skillet. Crumble bacon, and set aside. Add carrots, 2 cups water, sugar, and butter to skillet. Bring to a boil. Cook over medium-high heat 30 to 35 minutes or until liquid is reduced to a glaze and carrots are tender. Sprinkle with thyme and reserved bacon.
Make Ahead: Peel and slice carrots up to a day ahead. Store in a zip-top plastic bag in refrigerator.

Cardamom-Scented Sweet Potato Pie

MAKES 1 (9½-INCH) DEEP PIE;
PREP: 19 MIN.; **COOK:** 20 MIN.;
BAKE: 1 HR., 22 MIN.

This delicately flavored custard pie is accented with freshly ground spices.

1¼ lb. sweet potatoes, peeled and cut into 1½-inch chunks
1 (3-inch) cinnamon stick, broken
¼ tsp. cardamom seeds
4 large eggs
2 cups half-and-half
1 cup sugar
2 tsp. grated orange zest
2 tsp. vanilla extract
¼ tsp. salt
1½ cups all-purpose flour
½ tsp. salt
½ cup chilled shortening
5 to 6 Tbsp. ice water
Garnishes: sweetened whipped cream, ground cinnamon

1. Preheat oven to 425°. Arrange sweet potatoes in a steamer basket over boiling water. Cover and steam 20 minutes or until very tender.
2. While sweet potatoes cook, process cinnamon and cardamom seeds in a coffee grinder or blender until finely ground; set aside, reserving ¼ tsp. for top of pie.
3. When sweet potatoes are done, cool slightly, and process in a food processor until smooth. Whisk together spices (except for ¼ tsp.), sweet potatoes, eggs, and next 5 ingredients in a large bowl.
4. Combine flour and ½ tsp. salt. Cut in shortening with a pastry blender until the size of small peas. Sprinkle ice water, 1 Tbsp. at a time, evenly over surface; stir with a fork until dry ingredients are moistened. Shape dough into a ball. Roll dough to about ¼-inch thickness on a lightly floured surface. Fit into an ungreased 9½-inch deep-

dish fluted tart pan; trim off excess pastry along edges. Line tart shell with aluminum foil, pressing foil into the flutes. Trim foil to within ½ inch of top of pan. Fold foil down over top edge of crust to prevent overbrowning.

5. Bake at 425° for 15 minutes; remove foil, and bake 7 minutes or until pastry is golden. Reduce oven temperature to 350°. With tart pan still on oven rack, pull out rack; pour filling into pastry, and sprinkle with remaining ¼ tsp. spices. Bake at 350° for 1 hour or until set. Cool completely before serving. Garnish, if desired. Store sweet potato pie in refrigerator.

Note: If you don't have a fluted tart pan, you can bake this pie in 2 (9-inch) glass pie plates. Fit each piecrust (from a 15-oz. package refrigerated piecrusts) into a 9-inch pie plate according to package directions; fold edges under, and crimp. (No need to prebake crusts for these smaller pies.) Pour filling evenly into 2 prepared piecrusts. Sprinkle with remaining ¼ tsp. spices. Bake at 450° for 15 minutes. Reduce heat to 350°; bake 30 more minutes or until set. Cool on a wire rack. (Pies will be thin.) Or bake pies using 2 frozen piecrusts.

Tip: Use a meat mallet to break cinnamon stick before placing in coffee grinder. Tap cardamom pods lightly with mallet to release seeds.

Chocolate Tiramisù Charlotte

make ahead ·

MAKES 12 SERVINGS; **PREP:** 1 HR.,
COOK: 14 MIN., **CHILL:** 8 HR.,
STAND: 20 MIN.

Every holiday dinner needs a luscious chocolate dessert. This one can be made ahead and can sit out awhile before serving.

1 round bakery pound cake
2 Tbsp. instant espresso granules
¾ cup boiling water
½ cup Kahlúa or sweet marsala wine, divided
6 large eggs, separated
1¼ cups sugar, divided
2 envelopes unflavored gelatin
½ cup cold water
½ cup whipping cream, divided
1½ (8-oz.) containers mascarpone cheese*
1¼ cups (8 oz.) double chocolate morsels, divided
2 Tbsp. butter
Garnishes: sweetened whipped cream, coarsely chopped chocolate-covered coffee beans

1. Slice enough pound cake to get 18 (⅓-inches) slices. Line sides and bottom of an ungreased 9-inch springform pan with 12 to 14 slices of pound cake. Set remaining pound cake aside. Dissolve espresso in ¾ cup boiling water; stir in ¼ cup Kahlúa. Brush pound cake with ¾ cup espresso mixture, setting aside remaining ¼ cup espresso mixture.

2. Whisk together 6 egg whites and ¾ cup sugar in top of a double boiler; place over simmering water, and cook, whisking often, until mixture reaches 160°. Transfer egg white mixture to a large bowl; beat at high speed with an electric mixer until stiff peaks form. Set aside.

3. Sprinkle gelatin over ½ cup cold water in a saucepan; let soften 1 minute.

Cook over medium heat, stirring until gelatin dissolves. Add ¼ cup whipping cream; set aside.

4. Whisk together 6 egg yolks, remaining ½ cup sugar, and remaining ¼ cup Kahlúa in top of double boiler. Place over simmering water, and cook, whisking often, until mixture reaches 160°. Remove bowl, and beat at medium speed with a handheld electric mixer until thick and pale. Add mascarpone cheese and gelatin mixture, beating until smooth. Fold in about 1 cup meringue; fold in remaining meringue. Spoon half of mascarpone mixture into springform pan. Top with remaining pound cake slices; brush pound cake slices with remaining ¼ cup espresso mixture.

5. Place half of chocolate morsels in a glass bowl. Microwave on HIGH 1½ minutes; stir until smooth and slightly cool. Add ½ cup mascarpone mixture, stirring until smooth; fold into remaining mascarpone mixture. Spoon chocolate mascarpone mixture into springform pan. Chill 20 minutes or until slightly firm on top.

6. Combine remaining chocolate morsels, remaining ¼ cup whipping cream, and butter in a small glass bowl. Microwave on HIGH 1½ minutes. Stir until chocolate melts and mixture is smooth. Spoon chocolate ganache over top of dessert, spreading to edges with a small offset spatula. Cover and chill at least 8 hours.

7. Before serving, run a knife around edge of pan to release sides. Remove Charlotte to a serving plate; let stand 20 minutes. Garnish, if desired.
*Substitute 12 oz. cream cheese for mascarpone cheese.
Note: We tested with Ghirardelli Chocolate Morsels.

Appetizers with Appeal

Each of these hors d'oeuvres is either make ahead or quick & easy—or both.

Asian Curry Dip

make ahead

MAKES ¾ CUP; **PREP:** 6 MIN., **CHILL:** 30 MIN.

This spicy dip is great served with store-bought sweet potato chips, raw vegetables such as sugar snap peas, or boiled shrimp.

½ cup sour cream
2 Tbsp. seasoned rice vinegar
1 Tbsp. soy sauce
1 Tbsp. honey
1 tsp. curry powder
1 tsp. grated fresh ginger
1 tsp. dark sesame oil
¼ tsp. ground red pepper

1. Whisk together all ingredients in a small bowl. Cover and chill at least 30 minutes.
Note: We tested with Terra exotic vegetable chips as dippers.

Smoked Salmon Spread

make ahead

MAKES 3⅓ CUPS; **PREP:** 15 MIN., **CHILL:** 1 HR.

Serve this creamy spread with bagel chips or endive leaves.

2 (8-oz.) packages cream cheese, softened
2 (4-oz.) packages smoked salmon, coarsely chopped
⅔ cup chopped red onion
2 Tbsp. chopped fresh dill or 2 tsp. dried dill
1½ to 2 tsp. freshly ground pepper
½ tsp. grated lemon rind
1 Tbsp. caper juice (from a jar of capers) or fresh lemon juice
Garnish: finely chopped red onion
Capers

1. Process cream cheese and salmon in a food processor until smooth, stopping to scrape down sides. Add ⅔ cup red onion and next 4 ingredients; process just until combined, stopping to scrape down sides. Transfer spread to a bowl. Cover and chill at least 1 hour. Garnish, if desired. Serve capers as an accompaniment.

The Ultimate Party Crab Dip

make ahead

MAKES ABOUT 9 CUPS; **PREP:** 32 MIN.; **COOK:** 2 HRS., 30 MIN.

It's ultimate because it's really rich and will serve a crowd for a holiday open house. Many newer slow cookers have a warm setting, which is perfect for keeping this dip hot throughout a party.

2 Tbsp. butter
6 green onions, chopped
2 garlic cloves, minced
1 cup heavy whipping cream
1 (14-oz.) can quartered artichoke hearts, drained and coarsely chopped
3 (8-oz.) packages cream cheese, softened
1 (8-oz.) can diced water chestnuts, drained
¾ cup chopped ham
½ cup shredded Parmesan cheese
2 Tbsp. minced pickled jalapeño pepper slices or 1 fresh jalapeño, minced
¾ tsp. salt
¼ tsp. pepper
1 lb. fresh lump crabmeat, drained
1 cup (4 oz.) shredded sharp Cheddar cheese

1. Melt butter in a large nonstick skillet over medium heat. Add green onions and garlic; sauté 4 minutes or until tender. Add cream and artichokes. Bring to a boil; reduce heat, and simmer 4 to 5 minutes or until reduced to 2 cups.
2. Beat cream cheese in a large bowl until smooth and creamy. Stir in water chestnuts and next 5 ingredients. Add artichoke cream sauce; stir until well combined. Gently fold in crabmeat.
3. Spoon dip into a lightly greased 3- or 4-quart slow cooker. Sprinkle with Cheddar cheese. Cook, covered, on LOW 2½ hours or until thoroughly heated and cheese melts. Serve with toasted baguette slices or crackers.

Reuben Cheese Ball

make ahead

MAKES 20 SERVINGS; **PREP:** 45 MIN.,
BAKE: 10 MIN., **CHILL:** 1 HR.

*This cheese ball combines the flavors
of a Reuben sandwich into the perfect
party appetizer. Make the cheese mixture
ahead, and roll in breadcrumbs just
before serving. Spread leftovers on a
sandwich.*

1 (8-oz.) package cream cheese, softened
⅓ cup sour cream
2 cups (8 oz.) shredded Swiss cheese
1 cup (4 oz.) shredded extra-sharp Cheddar
    cheese (do not use preshredded)
1 cup chopped deli corned beef
    (6 oz. sliced)
¼ cup chopped sauerkraut, drained and
    squeezed dry
1 Tbsp. spicy brown mustard
1 tsp. caraway seeds, crushed
2 (1-lb.) loaves party pumpernickel or
    rye bread
1 tsp. butter or margarine, melted
¼ cup chopped fresh Italian parsley

1. Combine cream cheese and sour
cream in a large bowl; beat at medium
speed with an electric mixer until
smooth. Add Swiss cheese and next
5 ingredients; beat at low speed until
blended. Cover and chill 1 hour.
2. Preheat oven to 350°. Process
enough bread slices (about 3 or 4) to
make ½ cup crumbs. Combine crumbs
and melted butter; spread crumbs on
a jellyroll pan. Bake at 350° for 5 to 6
minutes or until toasted. Cool completely. Combine toasted breadcrumbs
and chopped parsley.
3. Shape chilled cheese mixture into a
ball; roll in breadcrumbs and parsley.
Cover cheese ball, and chill briefly until
ready to serve.
4. Arrange remaining bread slices on a
baking sheet; bake at 350° for 5 minutes
or until toasted. Serve with cheese ball.

Marinated Goat Cheese and Pine Nuts

make ahead

MAKES 8 SERVINGS; **PREP:** 13 MIN.,
CHILL : 3 HRS., 30 MIN.

*This colorful make-ahead marinated
cheese is ideal for entertaining.*

1 (8-oz.) jar dried tomatoes in oil with herbs
Olive oil
2 garlic cloves, minced
2 Tbsp. chopped fresh rosemary or
    2 Tbsp. dried rosemary
1 tsp. grated lemon rind
½ tsp. dried crushed red pepper
½ tsp. freshly ground black pepper
3 (3-oz.) packages goat cheese
¼ cup pine nuts, toasted

1. Drain tomatoes, reserving oil. Add
enough olive oil to measure ¾ cup oil.
Chop enough tomatoes to yield
½ cup; reserve remaining tomatoes
for other uses.
2. Combine oil, tomatoes, garlic, and
next 4 ingredients in a small bowl.
3. Using a sharp knife, carefully slice
goat cheese in ¼-inch-thick slices. Place
cheese in an 11- x 7-inch dish; pour
marinade over cheese. Cover and chill
several hours. Place marinated cheese
on a serving platter; pour marinade over
cheese, and sprinkle with pine nuts.
Serve with crackers.

Sugar and Spice Pecans

make ahead

MAKES 4 CUPS; **PREP:** 5 MIN.,
BAKE: 45 MIN.

*Package these coated pecans in little gift
bags, or set them out as hors d'oeuvres at
a holiday gathering.*

1 cup sugar
2 tsp. pumpkin pie spice
2 tsp. grated orange rind
¼ tsp. salt
2 egg whites
¼ cup butter, melted
4 cups pecan halves

1. Preheat oven to 250°. Stir together
first 4 ingredients.
2. Beat egg whites at high speed with
an electric mixer until foamy. Gradually
add sugar mixture, beating at high
speed until soft peaks form. Fold in
melted butter and pecan halves. Spread
coated nuts in a single layer on a large
jelly-roll pan lined with nonstick aluminum foil or parchment paper.
3. Bake at 250° for 45 minutes or until
nuts are toasted, stirring every 15 minutes. Remove from oven; let cool completely on pan. Remove from pan. Store
in an airtight container up to 2 weeks.

Red Pepper-Ham Roll-Ups

freezable • make ahead

MAKES ABOUT 4½ DOZEN; **PREP:** 20 MIN., **FREEZE:** 20 MIN.

Get a jump on your holiday party food; make and freeze these roll-ups to 1 month ahead. Slice frozen roll-ups, and let them thaw before serving.

1 (8-oz.) package cream cheese, softened
1 (3-oz.) package cream cheese, softened
2 garlic cloves, finely chopped
⅓ cup finely chopped walnuts, toasted
¼ cup pitted kalamata or pimiento-stuffed olives, chopped
¼ cup roasted red bell peppers from a jar, patted dry and chopped
¼ tsp. pepper
8 (⅛-inch-thick) slices premium deli ham
54 pitted kalamata olives

1. Beat cream cheese at medium speed with an electric mixer until creamy; stir in garlic and next 4 ingredients.
2. Spread about 2 Tbsp. cream cheese mixture over each ham slice. Roll up, jelly-roll fashion, starting with the long side. Place roll-ups, seam side down, on a baking sheet. Fill ends of rolls with remaining cream cheese mixture. Cover and freeze roll-ups 20 minutes.
3. Meanwhile, place olives on small wooden picks.
4. Using a sharp knife, slice each roll-up into 1-inch pieces; secure each with 1 olive pick. Cover and chill until ready to serve.
Note: We tested with Boar's Head Black Forest Ham.

Pizza Bread

fast fixin's

MAKES 4 DOZEN APPETIZERS; **PREP:** 7 MIN., **BAKE:** 15 MIN.

Add your favorite toppings to these kid-friendly pizzas. We liked using both green and black olives.

1 (16-oz.) package twin French bread loaves
1 (8-oz.) package cream cheese, softened
2 Tbsp. mayonnaise
1 tsp. dried Italian seasoning
1 (3.5-oz.) package pepperoni slices, chopped
1 (2¼-oz.) can sliced ripe olives or ½ cup pimiento-stuffed olives, sliced, or both
1 cup (4 oz.) shredded mozzarella cheese

1. Preheat oven to 375°. Slice bread loaves in half horizontally.
2. Combine cream cheese, mayonnaise, and Italian seasoning in a small bowl; stir well. Spread evenly over cut sides of bread; sprinkle evenly with pepperoni and olives. Top with cheese. Place on a baking sheet. Bake at 375° for 12 to 15 minutes or until lightly browned. Cut each loaf half into 12 slices.
Note: We tested with Pepperidge Farm Twin French Bread Loaves and Hormel Pepperoni Slices.

Smoked Sausage Bundles

make ahead

MAKES 3 DOZEN; **PREP:** 15 MIN. , **COOK:** 19 MIN.

1 (16-oz.) package fully cooked smoked sausage
2 (17.3-oz.) packages frozen puff pastry sheets, thawed
½ cup honey mustard dressing
1 large egg, lightly beaten
Additional honey mustard dressing

1. Preheat oven to 400°. Slice sausage into 36 slices; set aside.
2. Cut pastry sheets into 36 (3-inch) squares; spread center of each square with ½ tsp. honey mustard dressing. Place 1 piece sausage on dressing. Bring edges of pastry together; press to seal. Place bundles on lightly greased baking sheets. Whisk together egg and 1 Tbsp. water; brush over bundles.
3. Bake at 400° for 19 minutes or until golden. Remove from baking sheet to a serving platter. Serve with additional dressing, if desired.
Note: We tested with Naturally Fresh Honey Mustard Dressing.

Cheese-Jalapeño Jelly Thumbprints

make ahead

MAKES 3 DOZEN; **PREP:** 39 MIN., **BAKE:** 14 MIN., **CHILL:** 1 HR., **STAND:** 5 MIN.

Adults will love this savory twist on the traditional thumbprint cookie.

1 (8-oz.) block sharp white Cheddar cheese, shredded
⅓ cup butter, softened
⅓ cup freshly grated Parmesan cheese
1 egg yolk
1¼ cups all-purpose flour
¼ tsp. ground red pepper
¼ tsp. salt
1 cup toasted pecan halves, finely ground
⅓ cup jalapeño pepper jelly

1. Process first 4 ingredients in a food processor until blended. Add flour, ground red pepper, and salt; process until dough forms a ball, stopping often to scrape down sides. Shape dough into a disc; cover and chill 1 hour.
2. Preheat oven to 400°. Let dough stand at room temperature 5 minutes. Shape dough into 1-inch balls; roll in ground pecans.

3. Place balls 1 inch apart on ungreased baking sheets. Press thumb in center of each ball to make an indention.

4. Bake at 400° for 14 minutes or until browned. Immediately fill each center with a heaping ¼ tsp. jelly, pressing gently into cookie with back of spoon. Remove from pans to wire racks; cool completely. Store in an airtight container between layers of wax paper up to 2 days.

Jalapeño-Sausage Cheese Squares
make ahead

MAKES ABOUT 4 DOZEN; **PREP:** 8 MIN.,
COOK: 7 MIN., **BAKE:** 35 MIN, **STAND:** 10 MIN.

These spicy bites are great for a brunch buffet.

1 lb. hot or mild ground pork sausage
1 (12-oz.) jar pickled jalapeño slices, drained and patted dry
1½ (8-oz.) blocks Cheddar and Monterey Jack cheese, shredded
6 large eggs, lightly beaten
1 cup milk
1 tsp. garlic powder
¼ tsp. pepper

1. Preheat oven to 350°. Cook sausage in a large skillet over medium-high heat, stirring until sausage crumbles and is no longer pink. Drain.
2. Place jalapeño slices in a lightly greased 13- x 9-inch baking dish. Top with sausage; sprinkle with cheese.
3. Whisk together eggs and next 3 ingredients. Pour over cheese.
4. Bake at 350° for 35 minutes or until set. Let stand 10 minutes. Cut into bite-size squares. Serve warm.
Note: To make this recipe ahead, bake as directed; let cool, cover, and chill up to 1 day. Reheat at 350° for 15 minutes; let stand briefly, and then cut into squares just before serving.

Easy Mushroom Puffs
make ahead

MAKES 40 PUFFS; **PREP:** 32 MIN.,
BAKE: 15 MIN. PER BATCH, **CHILL:** 1 HR.

Simple ingredients come together in a quick and delicious appetizer that will have everyone asking for the recipe.

1 (8-oz.) container garlic-and-herb cream cheese
2 (4.5-oz.) jars sliced mushrooms, drained
½ cup chopped onion
¼ cup grated Parmesan cheese
1 tsp. dried chives
¼ tsp. hot sauce
1 (17.3-oz.) package frozen puff pastry sheets, thawed
1 large egg
Freshly ground pepper (optional)

1. Combine first 6 ingredients in a medium bowl; cover and chill 1 hour.
2. Preheat oven to 400°. Roll 1 sheet puff pastry into a 16- x 10-inch rectangle. Cut pastry in half lengthwise. Spread one-fourth of filling (about ½ cup) down center of each rectangle. Whisk together egg and 1 Tbsp. water, and brush edges of pastry with egg wash. Fold pastry in half lengthwise over filling; seal edges of pastry with a fork. Cut each pastry into 10 pieces, and place on a parchment-lined baking sheet.
3. Repeat procedure with remaining sheet puff pastry and filling. Brush remaining egg wash over top of pastries and, if desired, sprinkle with pepper.
4. Bake at 400° for 15 minutes or until lightly browned.
Make Ahead: Filling can be made up to 2 days ahead and chilled.
Note: We tested with Philadelphia Swirls Garlic-and-Herb Cream Cheese.

Bacon-Wrapped Shrimp and Snow Peas
fast fixin's

MAKES 6 APPETIZER SERVINGS;
PREP: 18 MIN., **COOK:** 12 MIN.,
STAND: 5 MIN.

Leave the tails on the shrimp if you're entertaining.

1 Tbsp. grated lime rind
2 Tbsp. fresh lime juice
1 Tbsp. dark sesame oil
1 tsp. salt
½ to 1 tsp. pepper
2 tsp. hot sauce
12 jumbo shrimp, peeled (about ¾ lb.)
12 fresh snow peas
12 fully cooked bacon slices

1. Preheat broiler. Toss together first 7 ingredients in a large bowl until shrimp are coated; let stand 5 minutes.
2. Trim ends of snow peas. Wrap each slice of bacon around 1 shrimp and 1 snow pea; secure with a wooden pick. Place shrimp on a lightly greased rack of a broiler pan. Repeat procedure with remaining shrimp, snow peas, and bacon.
3. Broil 3 inches from heat 12 minutes or until shrimp turn pink, turning after 6 minutes. Arrange appetizers on a serving platter. Serve hot.
Note: Use round rather than flat wooden picks; they're less likely to burn. Our secret to plump, pretty snow peas after baking is to first soak snow peas in a bowl of cold water 1 hour; then drain before skewering. For testing purposes only, we used Armour Ready Crisp Bacon.

Our Best Casseroles

Here's a casserole collection that boasts a variety of big flavors. Each recipe yields enough for a crowd.

Gumbo Casserole With Creamed Garlic Shrimp

MAKES 8 SERVINGS; **PREP:** 40 MIN.;
COOK: 1 HR., 22 MIN.; **BAKE:** 20 MIN.

A rich brown roux and the signature Cajun culinary trinity (onion, bell pepper, and celery) provide authentic flavors for this hearty dish. It's best served hot from the oven. Call ahead and ask your fishmonger to peel and devein the shrimp for you.

2 lb. unpeeled, medium-size fresh shrimp
1 Tbsp. Creole seasoning
2 Tbsp. bacon drippings
3 Tbsp. all-purpose flour
1 Tbsp. vegetable oil
⅓ cup finely chopped onion
⅓ cup finely chopped green bell pepper
⅓ cup finely chopped celery
2 garlic cloves, minced
1 tsp. dried thyme
1 tsp. dried oregano
¾ tsp. salt
½ tsp. pepper
4 green onions, chopped
½ cup chicken broth or water
2 cups whipping cream
1 lb. uncooked spaghetti, broken in half and
    cooked according to package directions
1 cup freshly grated Parmesan cheese
Garnish: additional chopped green onions

1. Peel and devein shrimp, if desired. Combine shrimp and Creole seasoning in a medium bowl; set aside.
2. Cook bacon drippings, flour, and oil in a large skillet over medium heat, whisking constantly, 20 to 25 minutes or until roux is the dark brown color of pecan shells. Add ⅓ cup onion and next

3 ingredients; cook 5 minutes or until tender. Add thyme and next 3 ingredients; cook 1 minute, stirring constantly. Add shrimp and 4 green onions; cook over medium-high heat 3 minutes or until shrimp are almost done; transfer to a large bowl.
3. Add broth to skillet, scraping bottom of skillet to loosen browned bits. Add whipping cream. Bring to a boil over medium-high heat; reduce heat, and simmer 6 minutes. Add to shrimp. Stir in cooked pasta; toss well to combine. Pour into a lightly greased 13- x 9-inch baking dish. Sprinkle with Parmesan cheese.
4. Bake, uncovered, at 350° for 20 minutes or until thoroughly heated. Garnish, if desired.
Note: We tested with Tony Cachere's Creole Seasoning.

Deep-Dish Spanakopita

MAKES 8 SERVINGS; **PREP:** 44 MIN.,
COOK: 20 MIN., **BAKE:** 36 MIN.

This Greek-flavored casserole starts out on the lowest oven rack to crisp the bottom pastry layer and finishes on the middle rack to ensure a flaky top.

2 Tbsp. olive oil
8 green onions, chopped (1 cup)
3 garlic cloves, minced
3 (6-oz.) packages fresh baby spinach or
    11 cups chopped Swiss chard
1 (8-oz.) package feta cheese,
    crumbled
½ cup freshly grated Parmesan cheese
¼ cup chopped dried tomatoes in oil
1 tsp. dried oregano
¾ tsp. salt, divided
¼ tsp. pepper
½ (16-oz.) package frozen phyllo pastry,
    thawed
⅓ cup butter, melted
1 Tbsp. butter
1 Tbsp. all-purpose flour
1 cup milk
2 oz. cream cheese, cubed and softened

1. Preheat oven to 400°. Heat olive oil in a Dutch oven over medium-high heat until hot. Add green onions and garlic; sauté 3 minutes or until tender. Add spinach and ¼ cup water; cover and cook 8 minutes or until spinach wilts. Cool spinach completely in a colander set over a bowl. Return cooled spinach to pan. Add cheeses, tomatoes, oregano, ½ tsp. salt, and pepper, stirring well to combine.
2. Trim phyllo sheets to 13- x 9-inch, if necessary. Layer 8 sheets of phyllo in a lightly greased 13- x 9-inch baking dish, using half of melted butter to brush between sheets. (Keep remaining phyllo covered with a damp cloth.) Bake at 400° on lowest oven rack for 6 minutes or until lightly browned; set aside.

3. Melt 1 Tbsp. butter in a small saucepan over medium heat. Stir in flour; cook 1 minute. Gradually whisk in milk. Cook over medium heat 2 minutes, whisking constantly. Whisk in cream cheese and remaining ¼ tsp. salt.

4. Spread spinach filling over baked phyllo crust; drizzle with white sauce.

5. Layer remaining phyllo sheets over filling using remaining half of melted butter to brush between sheets. Using a sharp knife, score top layer of phyllo into 8 portions. Bake at 400° on middle oven rack 30 minutes or until pastry is golden. Serve hot.

Note: We tested with Athenos Phyllo Pastry.

Roasted Vegetable Lasagna

MAKES 8 SERVINGS; **PREP:** 34 MIN.;
COOK: 31 MIN.; **BAKE:** 1 HR., 13 MIN.;
STAND: 15 MIN.

This white-sauced meatless lasagna will appeal to a vegetarian crowd.

1 medium butternut squash (about 2 lb.)
½ large sweet potato, cut into ½-inch cubes (about 1 cup)
3 Tbsp. olive oil, divided
3 cups sliced leeks (about 5 medium)
1 red bell pepper, cut into thin strips
4 cups milk
4 garlic cloves, halved
3 Tbsp. butter or margarine
¼ cup all-purpose flour
1 tsp. salt
½ tsp. pepper
9 dried precooked lasagna noodles
1 cup grated Asiago cheese
1 cup whipping cream
½ cup grated Parmesan cheese

1. Preheat oven to 450°. Microwave butternut squash on HIGH 2 minutes (This step softens squash for slicing). Cut squash in half lengthwise; remove and discard seeds. Peel squash, and cut into ½-inch cubes. Set aside 3 cups cubed squash; reserve any remaining squash for another use.

2. Combine 3 cups squash, sweet potato, and 2 Tbsp. olive oil on a large rimmed baking sheet. Bake at 450° for 10 minutes.

3. Meanwhile, combine leeks, bell pepper, and remaining 1 Tbsp. oil in a large bowl. Add to partially roasted squash mixture, stirring gently. Bake at 450° for 20 minutes or until vegetables are tender, stirring after 15 minutes. Return roasted vegetables to bowl; set aside.

4. Combine milk and garlic in a large saucepan; bring just to a boil. Reduce heat, and simmer, uncovered, 10 minutes. Remove and discard garlic.

5. Melt butter in a large saucepan over medium heat; whisk in flour until smooth. Cook 1 minute, whisking constantly. Gradually whisk in warm milk; cook over medium-high heat, whisking constantly, 12 to 13 minutes or until slightly thickened. Remove from heat; stir in salt and pepper. Add to roasted vegetables, stirring gently.

6. Spoon 1 cup vegetable mixture into a lightly greased 13- x 9-inch baking dish. Top with 3 lasagna noodles; spread half of remaining vegetable mixture over noodles, and sprinkle with ½ cup Asiago cheese. Repeat procedure with 3 noodles, remaining vegetable mixture, and remaining Asiago cheese. Break remaining 3 noodles in half and lay on top of casserole. (Breaking the noodles keeps them from curling up.)

7. Beat cream at high speed with an electric mixer until soft peaks form. Spread whipped cream over noodles; sprinkle with Parmesan cheese. Bake, covered, at 350° for 30 minutes. Uncover and bake 13 more minutes or until golden and bubbly. Let stand 15 minutes before serving.

Pizza Strata
make ahead

MAKES 8 to 10 SERVINGS; **PREP:** 21 MIN.;
BAKE: 55 MIN.; **STAND:** 8 HR, 10 MIN.;
CHILL: 8 HR.

As this casserole bakes, the aroma will make you think you've ordered out for pizza.

1 (16-oz.) French or Italian bread loaf, cut into ½-inch cubes (about 20 cups)
1 cup finely chopped prosciutto (about 4 oz.)
¼ cup chopped roasted red bell pepper
¼ cup chopped green onions
½ cup freshly grated Parmesan cheese
1 (14½-oz.) can diced tomatoes, undrained
1 cup coarsely chopped pimiento-stuffed olives
1 cup (4 oz.) shredded mozzarella cheese
6 large eggs
3 cups milk
1 tsp. dried Italian seasoning
½ tsp. salt
½ tsp. pepper
¼ cup chopped fresh flat-leaf parsley

1. Arrange bread cubes in a single layer on large baking sheets. Let stand 8 hours to dry.

2. Spread half of bread cubes in a greased 13- x 9-inch baking dish. Sprinkle prosciutto and next 3 ingredients evenly over bread cubes. Arrange remaining bread cubes evenly over Parmesan. Top with tomatoes, olives, and mozzarella cheese.

3. Whisk together eggs and remaining 5 ingredients. Pour egg mixture evenly over bread cubes, pressing down cubes gently to absorb liquid; cover and chill 8 hours.

4. Preheat oven to 325°. Bake, uncovered, at 325° for 55 minutes or until set and top is browned. Let stand 10 minutes before serving.

Chic Mac and Cheese

MAKES 12 SERVINGS; **PREP:** 35 MIN.,
COOK: 35 MIN., **BAKE:** 30 MIN.,
STAND: 5 MIN.

2 Tbsp. butter
1 large green bell pepper, chopped
1 large red bell pepper, chopped
1 large yellow bell pepper, chopped
4 celery ribs, finely chopped
¼ tsp. salt
½ cup butter or margarine
½ cup all-purpose flour
2 cups whipping cream
2 cups half-and-half
¼ tsp. celery seeds
¼ tsp. ground white pepper
1 lb. blue cheese, crumbled
2 large eggs
½ cup finely chopped fresh celery leaves
1 lb. uncooked penne pasta
1 cup freshly grated Parmesan cheese

1. Melt 2 Tbsp. butter in a large skillet over medium-high heat. Add peppers and celery; sauté 8 to 10 minutes or until crisp-tender. Sprinkle with salt. Set aside.
2. Melt ½ cup butter in a large saucepan over low heat. Add flour, whisking until smooth; cook 1 minute. Gradually add whipping cream and half-and-half; cook over medium heat, stirring constantly, until thickened. Whisk in celery seeds and white pepper. Remove from heat; add blue cheese, whisking until cheese melts.
3. Whisk eggs in a medium bowl until lightly beaten. Gradually whisk about one-fourth of hot white sauce into eggs, whisking constantly. Whisk in celery leaves.
4. Cook pasta according to package directions; drain and return to pan. Stir in vegetables and white sauce. Pour into a lightly greased 13-x 9-inch baking dish. Sprinkle with Parmesan cheese.
5. Bake uncovered, at 400° for 30 minutes or until bubbly and lightly browned. Let stand 5 minutes before serving.
Note: We tested with Maytag Blue Cheese.

Quick Gifts From the Kitchen

Each of these recipes has a time-saving twist—we've added a homemade touch to purchased or packaged foods.

Marinated Cheese and Olives

make ahead

MAKES 8 CUPS; **PREP:** 5 MIN.,
CHILL: 8 HR.

The shortcut here: dressing up cubed cheese and olives.

4 (8-oz.) packages cubed colby-Jack cheese
1 (10-oz.) jar or 2 (7-oz.) jars kalamata olives, drained
1 (16-oz.) bottle olive oil and vinegar dressing
1 Tbsp. dried Italian seasoning
½ tsp. dried crushed red pepper
6 garlic cloves, crushed
6 fresh rosemary sprigs

1. Combine all ingredients except rosemary in a large bowl; stir gently. Cover and chill at least 8 hours or up to 24 hours.
2. Divide cheese and olives into 6 glass containers. Place 1 rosemary sprig in each container. Pour remaining dressing evenly into containers. Cover and refrigerate up to 2 weeks.

Roasted Chili-Cheese Dip

fast fixin's • make ahead

MAKES 5 CUPS; **PREP:** 17 MIN.,
COOK: 8 MIN

We liked this dip served on tacos and burritos.

2 Tbsp. butter
½ cup finely chopped sweet onion
2 large garlic cloves, minced
4 (8-oz.) containers refrigerated Mexican cheese dip
1 (16-oz.) jar fire-roasted red and green chiles, drained and finely chopped
1 tsp. ground cumin

1. Melt butter in a large skillet over medium-high heat. Add onion; sauté 3 minutes or until tender. Add garlic; sauté 1 minute. Reduce heat to medium; stir in cheese dip, chiles, and cumin, stirring constantly until cheese melts. Serve warm with tortilla chips, or spoon dip into small jars or containers. Cover and chill. Give jars of dip as gifts along with reheating instructions.
Note: To reheat 1 cup dip, place in a microwave-safe bowl. Microwave dip on HIGH for 3 minutes, stirring after 1½ minutes. We tested with Olé Mexican Cheese Dip and Melissa's Fire-Roasted Red and Green Chiles.

Chocolate-Covered Cherry Cookies

MAKES 3½ DOZEN; **PREP:** 12 MIN.,
COOK: 10 MIN. PER BATCH

Place these cookies in candy cups, and give them in a gift box.

⅓ cup butter, softened
⅓ cup shortening
1 large egg
1 (17.5-oz.) package chocolate chip cookie
  mix
½ cup unsweetened cocoa
42 assorted chocolate-covered cherries
½ cup powdered sugar
4 to 5 tsp. cherry liqueur or maraschino
  cherry juice

1. Preheat oven to 375°. Beat butter and shortening in a large bowl at medium speed with an electric mixer until fluffy; add egg, beating until blended.
2. Combine cookie mix and cocoa; gradually add to butter mixture, beating well. Shape dough into 1-inch balls. Place balls 2 inches apart on ungreased baking sheets.
3. Bake at 375° for 8 to 10 minutes. Cool 2 minutes. Gently press 1 cherry candy in center of each cookie. Cool completely on baking sheets; transfer to wire racks.
4. Combine powdered sugar and liqueur in a small bowl, stirring until smooth. (Glaze should be thick, yet easy to drizzle.) Place glaze in a small zip-top plastic bag. Snip a tiny hole in 1 corner of bag. Drizzle glaze over cookies. Let stand until set.
Note: Depending on the size candy box you buy, you may need two boxes for these cookies. We tested with Betty Crocker Chocolate Chip Cookie Mix and Russell Stover Hand-Dipped Cherry Cordials.

Chocolate-Almond Croissants

MAKES 1 DOZEN; **PREP:** 28 MIN.,
BAKE: 7 MIN., **STAND:** 3 HR.

Bakery-style croissants or frozen croissants work fine in this recipe. If using frozen croissants, slice them while frozen.

1 (12½-oz.) can almond filling
1 dozen small croissants, split in half
  horizontally
1 cup double chocolate morsels or regular
  semisweet chocolate morsels
1 cup sliced almonds, toasted

1. Preheat oven to 325°. Stir almond filling. Spread each croissant bottom with about 2 Tbsp. almond filling. Cover with tops; place on a large foil-lined baking sheet, and bake at 325° for 7 minutes or until lightly toasted.
2. Place chocolate morsels in a small microwave-safe bowl; microwave on HIGH 1 to 2 minutes or until melted, stirring once. Spread melted chocolate over croissants. Sprinkle almonds over chocolate. Let stand at room temperature 2 to 3 hours or until chocolate is firm.
Note: If you use frozen Sara Lee Petit French Style Croissants, you'll need 2 (6-ounce) packages. We tested with Ghiradelli Double Chocolate Morsels.

Chocolate-Raspberry Petits Fours

MAKES 30 PETITS FOURS; **PREP:** 50 MIN.,
CHILL: 30 MIN.

Place these moist little brownie bites in candy cups for gift giving.

2 (11-oz.) boxes prebaked mini brownies
⅓ cup seedless raspberry jam
1 Tbsp. raspberry liqueur (optional)
1 (15-oz.) container pourable milk
  chocolate frosting
½ cup white chocolate morsels

1. Place brownies on a wire rack set over a baking sheet.
2. Microwave jam in a glass measuring cup on HIGH 10 to 15 seconds or just until slightly melted; stir until smooth. Stir in liqueur, if desired. Pour a small amount of jam into a flavor injector; inject each brownie through the side with a small amount of jam. Refill injector as needed until all brownies are filled.
3. Microwave pourable frosting in original container on HIGH 20 seconds. Pour or spoon frosting over brownies.
4. If additional frosting is needed, scrape off excess frosting from baking sheet, and reheat.
5. Microwave white chocolate morsels in a glass measuring cup on HIGH 1 minute or until melted, stirring after 30 seconds. Place white chocolate in a zip-top freezer bag. Snip a tiny hole in 1 corner of bag; drizzle melted white chocolate over brownies. Chill brownies 30 minutes or until chocolate is firm.
Note: Look for plastic flavor injectors in the kitchen gadget section at Wal-Mart. We tested with Entenmann's Little Bites Brownies and Betty Crocker Pourable Milk Chocolate.

Bittersweet Sugar Cookie Macaroons

MAKES 40 SANDWICH COOKIES;
PREP: 28 MIN, **BAKE:** 12 MIN. PER BATCH,
COOL: 5 MIN.

Sandwich these coconut-covered sugar cookies together with chocolate. The shortcut: portioned cookie dough.

1 (18-oz.) package refrigerated ready-to-bake sugar cookie bar dough
3 cups sweetened flaked coconut
1 (4-oz.) bittersweet chocolate baking bar, chopped
2 Tbsp. whipping cream

1. Preheat oven to 350°. Cut each cookie dough portion into 4 equal pieces.
2. Roll dough pieces in coconut; shape into balls. Place balls 2 inches apart on lightly greased baking sheets.
3. Bake at 350° for 12 to 13 minutes or until edges are golden. Cool on baking sheets 5 minutes; transfer to wire racks to cool completely.
4. Combine chocolate and whipping cream in a small glass bowl. Microwave on HIGH 30 seconds; stir. Spoon melted chocolate into a small zip-top plastic bag. Snip a small hole in 1 corner of bag. Pipe ½ to 1 tsp. chocolate mixture onto center of 40 cookie bottoms.
Top with remaining half of cookies, pressing gently to adhere. Let sandwich cookies stand on wire racks for chocolate to harden.
Note: We tested with Nestlé Refrigerated Ready-to-Bake Sugar Cookie Bar Dough and Ghirardelli Bittersweet Chocolate Baking Bar.

Cook's Notes

Follow these step-by-step instructions for Bittersweet Sugar Cookie Macaroons.

Cut each portion of cookie dough into four pieces.

Pipe chocolate onto flat sides of half the baked cookies.

Sandwich the chocolate with remaining cookies.

Pistachio Pastry Twists

MAKES 10 TWISTS; **PREP:** 28 MIN.,
BAKE: 19 MIN. PER BATCH

Wrap these flaky pastries in cellophane, and tie with ribbon, or deliver them in a vase. Add a monogram sticker to the vase to personalize the gift.

2 egg yolks
⅓ cup sugar
½ tsp. ground cinnamon
½ tsp. ground cardamom
1 (17.3-oz.) package frozen puff pastry sheets, thawed
½ cup finely chopped roasted pistachios
2 Tbsp. butter, melted

1. Whisk together egg yolks and 1 Tbsp. water in a small bowl.
2. Combine sugar, cinnamon, and cardamom.
3. Preheat oven to 400°. Carefully roll each sheet of puff pastry into a 9½-inch square on a lightly floured work surface. Brush each sheet with egg wash, and sprinkle with 2 Tbsp. sugar mixture. Sprinkle chopped pistachios evenly over 1 sheet, leaving a ¼-inch border; top with remaining sheet, sugared side down. Firmly press edges to seal. Brush top of pastry with melted butter; sprinkle with remaining sugar mixture. Cut pastry into ¾-inch-thick strips, using a pizza cutter. Twist each strip 3 times, and place 2 inches apart on lightly greased baking sheets.
4. Bake at 400° for 19 minutes or until golden. Remove from pans immediately, and cool on wire racks.
Note: To reheat pastry twists, bake at 450° for 5 minutes or just until heated. Cool. (As they cool, they crisp up.)

Dried Tomato and Rosemary Flatbread

MAKES 6 TO 8 SERVINGS; **PREP:** 10 MIN., **BAKE:** 10 MIN., **STAND:** 5 MIN.

The key to crispy results here is rolling the dough out really thin.

1 (6½-oz.) package pizza crust mix
½ cup warm water (100° to 110°)
¼ cup minced dried tomatoes packed in oil, drained
2 Tbsp. finely chopped fresh rosemary
Olive oil
2 Tbsp. olive oil
½ cup (2 oz.) shredded Italian five-cheese blend

1. Preheat oven to 425°. Combine first 4 ingredients in a medium bowl; stir well. Cover and let stand at room temperature 5 minutes. Turn dough out onto a heavily floured surface, and knead 1 minute or until dough forms a smooth ball, adding more flour, if necessary. Divide dough in half.
2. Roll each portion of dough into a 12- x 10-inch rectangle; transfer dough to 2 baking sheets brushed with olive oil. (To transfer dough easily, roll dough onto rolling pin, and unroll onto baking sheets.) Roll or press each portion of dough into a 14- x 12-inch rectangle. (Dough should be very thin.) Brush each portion with 1 Tbsp. olive oil; sprinkle evenly with cheese.
3. Bake at 425° for 10 minutes or until crispy and cheese is browned. Remove flatbread to wire racks, and let cool completely. To serve, break flatbread into large pieces. Store in an airtight container.
Note: We tested with Jiffy Pizza Crust Mix.

Saffron and Golden Raisin Breakfast Bread

MAKES 1 LOAF; **PREP:** 1 HR., 42 MIN.; **BAKE:** 32 MIN.; **STAND:** 1 HR.

Put your bread machine to work mixing this dough. We liked the bread best sliced and toasted.

¼ tsp. saffron threads
2 tsp. warm water
3 egg yolks
¾ cup warm water (75° to 85°)
2 Tbsp. butter, softened
2 Tbsp. granulated sugar
1 (12-oz.) package bread machine country white bread mix
½ cup golden raisins
½ cup chopped walnuts
Turbinado sugar

1. Combine saffron and 2 tsp. water in a small bowl; let stand 5 minutes. Place saffron mixture, 2 egg yolks, ¾ cup warm water, and next 5 ingredients, including yeast packet from bread mix) in a bread machine. Set bread machine to "dough" setting according to manufacturer's instructions; start machine.
2. When dough cycle is complete, turn dough out onto a lightly floured surface, and knead several times. Form dough into a loaf, and place in a greased 9- x 5-inch loafpan. Let dough rise in a warm place (85°), free from drafts, for 1 hour or until doubled in size.
3. Preheat oven to 350°. Combine remaining egg yolk with 1 Tbsp. water. Brush tops of loaves with egg wash, and sprinkle with turbinado sugar.
4. Bake at 350° for 32 minutes or until golden. Remove from pan, and cool completely on a wire rack.

Mini Breakfast Breads: Divide dough into 3 portions. Form into 3 small loaves, and place in 3 greased 5¾- x 3¼-inch loafpans. Continue with recipe, letting dough rise 40 minutes and baking mini loaves at 350° for 20 minutes or until golden. Makes 3 loaves.
Note: We tested with Fleischmann's Bread Machine Country White Bread Mix. We recommend cooling this loaf on its side on a wire rack. This helps the loaf maintain its shape.

Gingerbread Fruitcake

MAKES 1 LOAF; **PREP:** 12 MIN., **BAKE:** 55 MIN., **STAND:** 1 HR., **COOL:** 10 MIN.

No one will guess that this brandy-soaked loaf starts with a mix.

1 (7-oz.) package dried fruit bits
¾ cup sweetened dried cranberries
6 Tbsp. apricot brandy, divided
1 (14.5-oz.) package gingerbread cake and cookie mix
1 large egg, lightly beaten
¾ cup chopped pecans, toasted

1. Combine dried fruit bits, cranberries, and ¼ cup brandy in a medium bowl. Let stand 30 minutes.
2. Preheat oven to 350°. Place mix in a large bowl; make a well in center. Add 1¼ cups water and egg, stirring just until blended. Stir in soaked dried fruit and chopped pecans. (Batter is not as thick as typical fruitcake batter.) Pour batter into a greased 9- x 5-inch loafpan.
3. Bake at 350° for 55 to 60 minutes or until a long wooden pick inserted in center comes out clean. Cool in pan on a wire rack 10 minutes; remove from pan. Poke holes in loaf at 1-inch intervals, using a long wooden pick. Brush remaining 2 Tbsp. brandy over loaf. Cool completely on a wire rack. For best results, store in an airtight container 2 to 3 days before serving.
Note: For testing purposes only, we used SunMaid Dried Fruit Bits and Betty Crocker Gingerbread Cake and Cookie Mix.

Seasonal Pantry Favorites

Cranberries, vanilla, and coconut—three holiday pantry staples—are highlighted in these recipes.

Chocolate-Almond-Coconut Macaroons

make ahead

MAKES 2 DOZEN; **PREP:** 18 MIN.,
BAKE: 20 MIN.

1 (14-oz.) package sweetened flaked
    coconut
¾ cup sweetened condensed milk
½ (7-oz.) package almond paste, grated
2 Tbsp. all-purpose flour
½ tsp. vanilla extract
½ tsp. almond extract
½ tsp. grated orange zest
¼ tsp. salt
¼ cup semisweet chocolate
    mini-morsels
1 egg white
Parchment paper
½ cup semisweet chocolate morsels
    (optional)
1 Tbsp. shortening (optional)
¼ cup sliced almonds, toasted (optional)

1. Preheat oven to 325°. Combine coconut and sweetened condensed milk in a large bowl. Add almond paste and next 5 ingredients. Stir in mini-morsels.
2. Beat egg white at high speed with an electric mixer until stiff peaks form; fold into coconut mixture.
3. Drop by heaping tablespoonfuls onto parchment paper-lined baking sheets.
4. Bake at 325° for 20 to 21 minutes or until edges are golden and tops are lightly browned. Cool completely on baking sheets.
5. If desired, microwave chocolate morsels and shortening in a 1-cup glass measuring cup on HIGH 1 minute or until melted, stirring once.
6. Pour melted chocolate into a small zip-top freezer bag. Snip a small hole in 1 corner of bag; drizzle chocolate over macaroons, and sprinkle with toasted almonds, if desired. Let stand until chocolate is firm.
Note: We tested with Odense Almond Paste.

Coconut-Cranberry Trifle

make ahead

MAKES 12 SERVINGS; **PREP:** 23 MIN.;
 COOK: 5 MIN.; **CHILL:** 4 HRS., 45 MIN.

1 (16-oz.) can whole-berry cranberry
    sauce
1 (12-oz.) jar red currant jelly
2 Tbsp. grated orange zest (rind of
    2 oranges)
1 Tbsp. cornstarch
3 (3.4-oz.) packages coconut cream or
    vanilla instant pudding mix
4 cups milk
1 (16-oz.) frozen pound cake, thawed, cut
    into 1-inch cubes, and divided
6 Tbsp. Grand Marnier, divided
1½ cups sweetened flaked coconut, toasted
    and divided
2 cups frozen whipped topping, thawed

1. Combine first 4 ingredients in a medium saucepan. Bring to a boil over medium heat; cook 1 minute or until thickened and bubbly. Chill 45 minutes or until completely cooled, stirring occasionally.
2. Combine pudding mix and milk in a large bowl; whisk 2 minutes or until thickened.
3. Place one-third of pound cake cubes in a 3-quart trifle bowl; drizzle with 2 Tbsp. orange liqueur. Top with one-third of cranberry-orange sauce and one-third of pudding. Sprinkle with ½ cup coconut.
4. Repeat layers twice using remaining cake cubes, orange liqueur, cranberry-orange sauce, pudding, and coconut, reserving last ½ cup coconut for garnish.
5. Spread whipped topping over trifle. Sprinkle with reserved coconut. Cover and chill at least 4 hours.
Note: We tested with Crosse & Blackwell Red Currant Jelly.

Cranberry-Couscous Salad

MAKES 6 SERVINGS; **PREP:** 10 MIN.,
COOK: 4 MIN., **STAND:** 5 MIN.

Pair this cinnamon-scented side with grilled chicken or lamb.

1½ cups chicken broth
½ cup dried cranberries
1 tsp. ground cinnamon
¼ tsp. ground cumin
1 cup uncooked couscous
⅓ cup vegetable or canola oil
2 Tbsp. rice vinegar
½ cup sliced almonds, toasted
⅓ cup chopped green onions
2 Tbsp. chopped fresh mint or
    parsley
Red leaf lettuce leaves

1. Combine first 4 ingredients in a medium saucepan; bring to a boil. Remove from heat, and stir in couscous. Cover and let stand 5 minutes. Fluff with a fork; let cool, uncovered.
2. Whisk oil and vinegar; pour vinaigrette over couscous. Add almonds, green onions, and mint; toss well. Serve at room temperature or chilled over red leaf lettuce.

Appendices

handy substitutions

ingredient	substitution

baking products

Baking powder, 1 teaspoon
- ½ teaspoon cream of tartar plus ¼ teaspoon baking soda

Chocolate
- semisweet, 1 ounce — 1 ounce unsweetened chocolate plus 1 tablespoon sugar
- unsweetened, 1 ounce or square — 3 tablespoons cocoa plus 1 tablespoon fat
- chips, semisweet, 6-ounce package, melted — 2 ounces unsweetened chocolate, 2 tablespoons shortening plus ½ cup sugar

Cocoa, ¼ cup
- 1 ounce unsweetened chocolate (decrease fat in recipe by ½ tablespoon)

Corn syrup, light, 1 cup
- 1 cup sugar plus ¼ cup water
- 1 cup honey

Cornstarch, 1 tablespoon
- 2 tablespoons all-purpose flour or granular tapioca

Flour
- all-purpose, 1 tablespoon
  - 1½ teaspoons cornstarch, potato starch, or rice starch
  - 1 tablespoon rice flour or corn flour
  - 1½ tablespoons whole wheat flour
- all-purpose, 1 cup sifted — 1 cup plus 2 tablespoons sifted cake flour
- cake, 1 cup sifted — 1 cup minus 2 tablespoons all-purpose flour
- self-rising, 1 cup — 1 cup all-purpose flour, 1 teaspoon baking powder plus ½ teaspoon salt

Shortening
- melted, 1 cup — 1 cup cooking oil (don't use cooking oil unless recipe calls for melted shortening)
- solid, 1 cup (used in baking) — 1⅛ cups butter or margarine (decrease salt called for in recipe by ½ teaspoon)

Sugar
- brown, 1 cup firmly packed — 1 cup granulated white sugar
- powdered, 1 cup — 1 cup sugar plus 1 tablespoon cornstarch (processed in food processor)
- granulated white, 1 teaspoon — ⅛ teaspoon noncaloric sweetener solution or follow manufacturer's directions
- granulated white, 1 cup
  - 1 cup corn syrup (decrease liquid called for in recipe by ¼ cup)
  - 1 cup honey (decrease liquid called for in recipe by ¼ cup)

Tapioca, granular, 1 tablespoon
- 1½ teaspoons cornstarch or 1 tablespoon all-purpose flour

dairy products

Butter, 1 cup
- ⅞ to 1 cup shortening or lard plus ½ teaspoon salt
- 1 cup margarine (2 sticks; do not substitute whipped or low-fat margarine)

Cream
- heavy (30% to 40% fat), 1 cup — ¾ cup milk plus ⅓ cup butter or margarine (for cooking and baking; will not whip)
- light (15% to 20% fat), 1 cup
  - ¾ cup milk plus 3 tablespoons butter or margarine (for cooking and baking)
  - 1 cup evaporated milk, undiluted
- half-and-half, 1 cup
  - ⅞ cup milk plus ½ tablespoon butter or margarine (for cooking and baking)
  - 1 cup evaporated milk, undiluted
- whipped, 1 cup — 1 cup frozen whipped topping, thawed

Egg
- 1 large — ¼ cup egg substitute
- 2 large
  - 3 small eggs or ½ cup egg substitute
  - 1 large egg plus 2 egg whites
- 1 egg white (2 tablespoons) — 2 tablespoons egg substitute

Milk
- buttermilk, 1 cup
  - 1 tablespoon vinegar or lemon juice plus whole milk to make 1 cup (let stand 10 minutes)
  - 1 cup plain yogurt
  - 1 cup whole milk plus 1¾ teaspoons cream of tartar
- fat free, 1 cup
  - 4 to 5 tablespoons nonfat dry milk powder plus enough water to make 1 cup
  - ½ cup evaporated skim milk plus ½ cup water
- whole, 1 cup
  - 4 to 5 tablespoons nonfat dry milk powder plus enough water to make 1 cup
  - ½ cup evaporated milk plus ½ cup water

ingredient	substitution

Milk (continued)
    sweetened condensed,
        1 (14-ounce) can (about 1¼ cups)
	• Heat the following ingredients until sugar and butter dissolve: ⅓ cup plus
	    2 tablespoons evaporated milk, 1 cup sugar, 3 tablespoons butter or margarine.
	• Add 1 cup plus 2 tablespoons nonfat dry milk powder to ½ cup warm water.
	    Mix well. Add ¾ cup sugar, and stir until smooth.

Sour cream, 1 cup	• 1 cup plain yogurt plus 3 tablespoons melted butter or 1 tablespoon cornstarch • 1 tablespoon lemon juice plus evaporated milk to equal 1 cup
Yogurt, 1 cup (plain)	• 1 cup buttermilk

miscellaneous

Broth, beef or chicken canned broth, 1 cup	• 1 bouillon cube or 1 teaspoon bouillon granules dissolved in 1 cup boiling water

Garlic
    1 small clove
    garlic salt, 1 teaspoon
	
	• ⅛ teaspoon garlic powder or minced dried garlic
	• ⅛ teaspoon garlic powder plus ⅞ teaspoon salt

Gelatin, flavored, 3-ounce package	• 1 tablespoon unflavored gelatin plus 2 cups fruit juice
Herbs, fresh, chopped, 1 tablespoon	• 1 teaspoon dried herbs or ¼ teaspoon ground herbs
Honey, 1 cup	• 1¼ cups sugar plus ¼ cup water
Mustard, dried, 1 teaspoon	• 1 tablespoon prepared mustard
Tomatoes, fresh, chopped, 2 cups	• 1 (16-ounce) can (may need to drain)
Tomato sauce, 2 cups	• ¾ cup tomato paste plus 1 cup water

alcohol substitutions

alcohol	substitution
Amaretto, 2 tablespoons	• ¼ to ½ teaspoon almond extract*
Bourbon or Sherry, 2 tablespoons	• 1 to 2 teaspoons vanilla extract*

**Brandy, fruit-flavored liqueur, port wine,
    rum, or sweet sherry:** ¼ cup or more
	• Equal amount of unsweetened orange or apple juice plus 1 teaspoon vanilla
	    extract or corresponding flavor

Brandy or rum, 2 tablespoons	• ½ to 1 teaspoon brandy or rum extract*

Grand Marnier or other orange liqueur,
    2 tablespoons
	• 2 tablespoons unsweetened orange juice concentrate or 2 tablespoons orange
	    juice and ½ teaspoon orange extract

Kahlúa or other coffee or chocolate liqueur,
    2 tablespoons
	• ½ to 1 teaspoon chocolate extract plus ½ to 1 teaspoon instant coffee dissolved
	    in 2 tablespoons water

Marsala, ¼ cup	• ¼ cup white grape juice or ¼ cup dry white wine plus 1 teaspoon brandy

Wine
    red, ¼ cup or more
    white, ¼ cup or more
	
	• Equal measure of red grape juice or cranberry juice
	• Equal measure of white grape juice or nonalcoholic white wine

Add water, white grape juice, or apple juice to get the specified amount of liquid (when the liquid amount is crucial).

equivalent measures

3 teaspoons	= 1 tablespoon		2 tablespoons (liquid)	= 1 ounce	⅛ cup	= 2 tablespoons
4 tablespoons	= ¼ cup		1 cup	= 8 fluid ounces	⅓ cup	= 5 tablespoons plus 1 teaspoon

5⅓ tablespoons	= ⅓ cup		2 cups	= 1 pint (16 fluid
				    ounces)
					⅔ cup	= 10 tablespoons
						    plus 2 teaspoons

8 tablespoons	= ½ cup		4 cups	= 1 quart		
16 tablespoons	= 1 cup		4 quarts	= 1 gallon	¾ cup	= 12 tablespoons

metric equivilants

The recipes that appear in this cookbook use the standard United States method for measuring liquid and dry or solid ingredients (teaspoons, tablespoons, and cups). The information on this chart is provided to help cooks outside the U.S. successfully use these recipes. All equivalents are approximate.

METRIC EQUIVALENTS FOR DIFFERENT TYPES OF INGREDIENTS

A standard cup measure of a dry or solid ingredient will vary in weight depending on the type of ingredient. A standard cup of liquid is the same volume for any type of liquid. Use the following chart when converting standard cup measures to grams (weight) or milliliters (volume).

Standard Cup	Fine Powder	Grain	Granular	Liquid Solids	Liquid
	(ex. flour)	(ex. rice)	(ex. sugar)	(ex. butter)	(ex. milk)
1	140 g	150 g	190 g	200 g	240 ml
¾	105 g	113 g	143 g	150 g	180 ml
⅔	93 g	100 g	125 g	133 g	160 ml
½	70 g	75 g	95 g	100 g	120 ml
⅓	47 g	50 g	63 g	67 g	80 ml
¼	35 g	38 g	48 g	50 g	60 ml
⅛	18 g	19 g	24 g	25 g	30 ml

USEFUL EQUIVALENTS FOR DRY INGREDIENTS BY WEIGHT

(To convert ounces to grams, multiply the number of ounces by 30.)

1 oz	=	¹⁄₁₆ lb	=		30 g
4 oz	=	¼ lb	=		120 g
8 oz	=	½ lb	=		240 g
12 oz	=	¾ lb	=		360 g
16 oz	=	1 lb	=		480 g

USEFUL EQUIVALENTS FOR LENGTH

(To convert inches to centimeters, multiply the number of inches by 2.5.)

1 in					=	2.5 cm		
6 in	=	½ ft	=		=	15 cm		
12 in	=	1 ft			=	30 cm		
36 in	=	3 ft	=	1 yd	=	90 cm		
40 in					=	100 cm	=	1 m

USEFUL EQUIVALENTS FOR LIQUID INGREDIENTS BY VOLUME

¼ tsp	=						1 ml	
½ tsp	=						2 ml	
1 tsp	=						5 ml	
3 tsp	=	1 tbls			=	½ fl oz	=	15 ml
	=	2 tbls	=	⅛ cup	=	1 fl oz	=	30 ml
	=	4 tbls	=	¼ cup	=	2 fl oz	=	60 ml
	=	5⅓ tbls	=	⅓ cup	=	3 fl oz	=	80 ml
	=	8 tbls	=	½ cup	=	4 fl oz	=	120 ml
	=	10⅔ tbls	=	⅔ cup	=	5 fl oz	=	160 ml
	=	12 tbls	=	¾ cup	=	6 fl oz	=	180 ml
	=	16 tbls	=	1 cup	=	8 fl oz	=	240 ml
	=	1 pt	=	2 cups	=	16 fl oz	=	480 ml
	=	1 qt	=	4 cups	=	32 fl oz	=	960 ml
						33 fl oz	=	1000 ml = 1 l

USEFUL EQUIVALENTS FOR COOKING/OVEN TEMPERATURES

	Fahrenheit	Celsius	Gas Mark
Freeze Water	32° F	0° C	
Room Temperature	68° F	20° C	
Boil Water	212° F	100° C	
Bake	325° F	160° C	3
	350° F	180° C	4
	375° F	190° C	5
	400° F	200° C	6
	425° F	220° C	7
	450° F	230° C	8
Broil			Grill

Menu Index

This index lists every menu by suggested occasion. Recipes in bold type are provided with the menu and accompaniments are in regular type.

Menus for Company

Backyard Picnic

SERVES 6
Apricot-Pecan Chicken Salad
(page 33)
Salad greens
Double Chocolate Candy Cookies
(page 215)

Appetizer Party

SERVES 10 TO 12
Herbed Goat Cheese Bites
(page 35)
Cheese-Jalapeño Jelly Thumbprints *(page 326)*
Easy Party Snack Mix *(page 57)*
Layered Lima Bean Dip *(page 37)*
Sweet- 'n'- Salty Honey Cheese Spread *(page 84)*
Assorted crackers and bread slices

Decadent Dessert Party

SERVES 10 TO 12
Triple Chocolate-Cookie Trifle Pie *(page 44)*
Free-form Strawberry Cheesecake (double recipe) *(page 87)*
Caramel-Pecan Bars *(page 251)*
Mississippi Mud Fondue *(page 257)*

Cozy Supper

SERVES 8
Baked Pork Loin Roast *(page 52)*
Crispy Eggplant With Tomatoes and Mozzarella *(page 130)*
Cornmeal Biscuits *(page 313)*
Hot Fudge Brownie Cake *(page 40)*

Casual Lunch

SERVES 12
(page 60)
Spicy Boiled Shrimp With Creamy Buttermilk-Avocado Sauce
Chicken Caesar Salad Bites
Blue Cheese-Walnut Finger Sandwiches
Corn-and-Lima Bean Salad (double recipe)
Mustard-Dill Tortellini Salad Skewers
Vanilla-Champagne Soaked Fruit

Weekend Brunch

SERVES 8 TO 10
(page 68)
Brown Sugar-Bourbon Baked Ham
Sweet-and-Spicy Mustard Sauce
Baked Grits and Greens
Pink-and-White Grapefruit Salad
Morning Glory Muffin Bread
Favorite biscuits

Guilt-Free Supper

Serves 6
(page 82)

Flank Steak With Radish
    Salsa
Balsamic Grilled Veggies
Italian-Herb Bread
Slightly Sweet Tea
Grilled Banana Splits With
    Chocolate Sauce

Light Bites

Serves 6
(page 102)

Orange-Basil Ice
Melon, Mozzarella, and Prosciutto
    Skewers
Fresh Herb Tomato Crostini
Mini Crab Cakes With Garlic-Chive
    Sauce

Spring Chesapeake Picnic

Serves 6 to 8
(page 98)

Jerk Chicken
Cornbread-and-Crab-Stuffed Fish
Jean's Potato Salad
Rice and Peas
Lemon Chess Pie
Seafarers' Cherries Jubilee

Seafood Supper

Serves 6
(page 142)

Fried Soft-Shell Crab With
    Florida Cocktail Sauce and
    Stone Crab Sauce
Crispy Hush Puppies
Heavenly Key Lime Pie
Wine and beer

Autumn Menu

Serves 6
(page 226)

Roasted Grape Chutney with
    cheese and crackers
Rosemary-Garlic Pork With
    Roasted Vegetables &
    Caramelized Apples
Hearts of Romaine Salad
Caramelized Onion Flatbread
Rich Chocolate Tart

Game-Day Gathering

Serves 6 to 8
(page 238)

Smoky "Pimiento" Cheese
    Sandwiches
Make-Ahead Muffuletta Party
    Sandwich
Bacon-Onion Dip
Simple Scotch Shortbread
Southern Sweet Tea

Easygoing Entertaining Menu

Serves 8
(page 254)

Cherry-Pecan Brie, Uptown Figs,
    or Bacon-Arugula-Apple Bites
Herbed Pork Roast
Roasted Fall Vegetables
Puffed Mashed Potatoes
Basil-and-Blue Cheese
    Salad
Brandy Alexander
    Cheesecake

Come by for Coffee

Serves 6 to 8
(page 268)

Caramel-Cream Macchiato
    Coffee
Cream Cheese-Olive Spread
Assorted bakery cookies and
    brownies

Holiday Cocktail Party

Serves 10 to 15
(page 292)

Red Pepper Jelly-Brie Bites
Cranberry-Orange Simple Syrup
    and Spiced Apple Simple Syrup
    with Champagne
Mocha Punch

Fiesta Night

Serves 4 to 6
(page 147)

Chicken-and-Green Chile
    Enchiladas
Avocado-Tomato Toss
Lemonade or Classic Margarita

Simple But Elegant Supper

Serves 4

Natalie's Cajun-Seasoned
    Pan-Fried Tilapia *(page 156)*
Spinach-Grape Chopped Salad
    (page 72)
Crusty bakery rolls
Caramel Pie *(page 314)*
Wine
Coffee

Menus for Family

Simple Supper

SERVES 4
(page 34)
Pecan-Crusted Tilapia
Herb Mashed Potatoes
Balsamic Green Beans
Quick Apple Bundles

Steak and Potatoes Supper

SERVES 4
(page 48)
Steak Balsamico With
    Mushrooms
Warm Roasted Red Potato
    Salad

Southern Comfort Food

SERVES 4
(page 48)
Turkey Scaloppine
Roasted Zucchini
Creamy Grits With Sweet Corn

Italian Inspired

SERVES 4
(page 49)
Pan-Fried Chicken-and-Ham
    Parmesan
Garlic-Herb Pasta
Sautéed Grape Tomatoes

New Orleans Supper

SERVES 4
(page 50)
Cajun Omelet
Green salad
French bread

Unbeatable Southern Supper

SERVES 6
(page 64)
Grilled Basil-and-Garlic
    Pork Chops
Basmati Rice and Peas
Okra-Tomato Sauce

Speedy Supper

SERVES 4
(page 105)
Mediterranean Turkey Cutlets
    and Pasta
Green vegetable or tossed salad
Blueberry-Pecan Cobbler
Iced tea or lemonade

Comfort Supper

SERVES 4
(page 120)
Onion-Topped Sausage 'n'
    Mashed Potato Casserole
Green Beans With Tangy
    Mustard Sauce
Raspberry-Lemonade Pie
Iced te

Rise and Shine Menu

SERVES 6 TO 10
(page 262)
One-Dish Blackberry French Toast
    or Ham-and-Cheese Croissant
    Casserole
Fresh fruit
Coffee
Orange juice

Texas Ranch Dinner

SERVES 8
Grilled Flat-Iron Steak *(page 296)*
Soufflé Potatoes *(page 310)*
Roasted Asparagus
Cornbread
Homemade Applesauce *(page 311)*

Meat and Potatoes Dinner

SERVES 6
Parmesan-and-Mushroom-Stuffed
    Meatloaf *(page 87)*
Oven-Roasted Smashed Potatoes
    (page 253)
Strawberry-Fruit Toss With
    Cornmeal Shortcakes *(page 85)*

Weekend Lunch

SERVES 4
Pressed Cuban Sandwiches
    (page 52)
Herbed Potato Salad *(page 133)*
Mini Mocha Ice-Cream Scoops
    (page 148)

Soup Supper

SERVES 6

Lemon-Chicken Soup *(page 290)*
Buttermilk biscuits
Ice-cream Crêpes *(page 149)*

Italian Supper

SERVES 4

Tomato Crostini *(page 306)*
Baked Ziti With Italian Sausage
    (page 157)
Caesar salad
Gelato

Southern Supper

SERVES 6

Mama's Fried Chicken *(page 309)*
**Classic Baked Macaroni and
    Cheese** *(page 235)*
Collard greens
Cobbler Custard Cups *(page 111)*

All-American Dinner

SERVES 8

Marian's Easy Roast Chicken
    (page 42)
**Green Beans With Mushrooms and
    Bacon** *(page 282)*
Mashed potatoes
So Good Brownies *(page 144)*

Mexican Breakfast

SERVES 4

**Huevos Rancheros on Cilantro
    Grits Cakes** *(page 194)*
Crispy Tex-Mex Potato Patties
    (page 284)
**Overnight Cinnamon-Pecan
    Coffeecake** *(page 285)*

Pork Chop Dinner

SERVES 8

Pan-Fried Pork Chops *(page 309)*
**Spinach-Apple Salad With Maple-
    Cider Vinaigrette** *(page 277)*
Basic Buttermilk Cornbread
    (page 312)

Simple Weeknight Dinner

SERVES 6

**Apple-Chicken Sausage With
    Apricot-Pepper Relish** *(page 295)*
Brown rice
Broccoli

Tex-Mex Soup Supper

SERVES 6

Creamy Chipotle-Black Bean Dip
    (page 306)
Southwestern Soup *(page 29)*
Tortilla chips

Down-Home Dinner

SERVES 4

**Pecan-Crusted Pork Burgers
    With Dried Apricot-Chipotle
    Mayonnaise** *(page 93)*
French fries
Espresso-Fudge Truffle Brownies
    (page 291)
Kentucky Lemonade *(page 199)*

Quick Chicken Dinner

SERVES 4

Pecan Chicken *(page 309)*
Steamed vegetables
**Hurry-Up Homemade Crescent
    Rolls** *(page 281)*
Iced tea

Breakfast for Dinner

SERVES 6

Creole Shrimp and Grits *(page 29)*
Caesar salad
Caramel-Nut Pull-Apart Bread
    (page 312)

Menus for Special Occasions

Easter Celebration

SERVES 8
(page 76)

Shrimp-and-Blue Cheese Spread
Pork Roast With Carolina Gravy
Asparagus-New Potato Hash
Watts Grocery Spoon Bread
Easter Cookies *(page 78)* or Lemon
    Curd-Filled Angel Food Cake
    (page 79)

Passover Menu

SERVES 8 TO 10
(page 88)

Mini Salmon Croquettes
Thin Potato Kugel
Flourless Peanut Butter-
    Chocolate Cookies
Chocolate-Pecan Meringues

Southern Cookout

SERVES 6
(page 124)

Herb-Marinated Flank Steak
Flank Steak Sandwiches With Blue
    Cheese
Double Grilled Cheese
    Sandwiches
Baked Bean Crostini
Peppery Grilled Okra With
    Lemon-Basil Dipping Sauce
Double Peanut Butter Candy Bites
    With Granola
Lemonade Iced Tea

Game-Day Menu

SERVES 4
(page 158)

Chopped Chicken Sandwich With
    Crunchy Pecan Slaw
Tex-Mex Butternut Bisque
Oatmeal-Pecan Snack Cookies
Spiked Arnold Palmer

Festive Fall Get-together

SERVES 12
(page 232)

The Great White Pumpkin
    Cheese Ball
Easy Barbecue Sliders
Blood Orange Martinis

Dressed-Up Holiday Dinner

SERVES 8 TO 10
(page 242)

Whiskey Sour
Crab Crostini
Roasted Dry-Rub Turkey With
    Gravy
Sautéed Green Beans
Smoky Cranberry-Apple Sauce
Cornbread Yeast Rolls
Peanut Butter-Banana Sandwich
    Bread Puddings With Dark
    Caramel Sauce

Hanukkah Celebration

SERVES 6 TO 8
(page 258)

Matzo Ball Soup
Carrot Kugel
Edible Chocolate Dreidels
Jelly Doughnuts (Sufganiyout)

Dashing Christmas Dinner

SERVES 8
(page 272)

Deviled Ham Terrine
Quick Winter Pickled Veggies
Fennel-Crusted Rib Roast
Warm Greens With Cornbread
    Croutons
Root Vegetable Gratin
Buttermilk Panna Cotta With
    Zinfandel Poached Figs
Kumquat Martini

Festive Breakfast

SERVES 6
(page 280)

Texas Toast Breakfast Bread
    Pudding
Spicy Cornmeal Bacon
Fresh fruit
Orange juice and coffee

Christmas Dinner

SERVES 8
(page 318)

Crab and Oyster Bisque
Coffee-Crusted Beef Wellingtons
Cast-Iron Herbed Potatoes Anna
Scalloped Greens
Cabbage and Apple Salad With
    Roasted Onions
Carrots With Country Bacon
Cardamom-Scented Sweet
    Potato Pie
Chocolate Tiramisù Charlotte
Wine
Coffee

Untraditional Feast

SERVES 4 TO 6
(page 264)

Baby Back Ribs With Jackie's
    Dry Rub
Butter Beans
Smoked Gouda Cheese Grits
Bakery rolls
White Chocolate Ice Cream With
    Raspberry Sauce

Indoor Barbecue

SERVES 6 TO 8

Slow-Cooker BBQ Pork *(page 308)*
Potato salad
Coleslaw
Slice-and-Bake Shortbread
    Cookies *(page 279)*

Recipe Title Index

This index alphabetically lists every recipe by exact title.

Month-By-Month Index

This index alphabetically lists every food article and accompanying recipes by month.

General Recipe Index

This index lists every recipe by food category and/or major ingredient.

Pies, Puffs and Pastries *(continued)*

Vegetable
Mushroom Puffs, Easy, 327
Tomato-Leek Pie, 134
Tomato Vegetable Pie, Southern, 135
PINEAPPLE
Bread, Morning Glory Muffin, 69
Ice, Pineapple-Basil, 102
Muffins, Morning Glory, 69
Ribs, Apricot-Pineapple Sweet, 113
Tacos Al Pastor, 119
Tacos, Spicy Chicken-Pineapple, 119
PISTACHIO
Pastry Twists, Pistachio, 332
PIZZA
Bread, Pizza, 326
Cheeseburger Pizza, Ultimate, 307
Cheese Pizza, Ultimate, 307
Hawaiian Pizza, 236
Steak and Gorgonzola Pizzas, Mini Grilled, 223
Strata, Pizza, 329
Veggie Pizza, Ultimate, 307
PLANTAINS
Caramelized Plantains With Honey-Peanut
Sauce, 214
POLENTA
Crust, Italian Beef Casserole With Polenta, 88
Crust, Tomato 'n' Beef Casserole With
Polenta, 88
PORK. *See also* **BACON, HAM, SAUSAGE.**
Burgers With Dried Apricot-Chipotle
Mayonnaise, Pecan-Crusted Pork, 93
Chops
Basil-and-Garlic Pork Chops, Grilled, 64
Caramelized Cajun Pork Chops, 139
Grillades Over Panko-Crusted Grits Patties,
Easy Pork, 193
Grilled Pork Chops With Balsamic
Syrup, 212
Pan-Fried Pork Chops, 309
Pan-Fried Pork Chops, Cajun-Seasoned, 156
Greens With Pork, Sautéed, 251
Quesadillas, Barbecued Pork, 296
Ribs
Apricot-Pineapple Sweet Ribs, 113
Baby Back Ribs With Jackie's Dry Rub, 264
Dry Rub, Rib, 113
Liquid Seasoning, Rib, 113
Roasts
Baked Pork Butt Roast, 52
Baked Pork Loin Roast, 52
BBQ Pork, Slow-Cooker, 308
Championship Pork Butt, 112
Dry Rub, Pork Butt, 113
Gravy, Pork Roast With Carolina, 77
Herbed Pork Roast, 255
Marinade, Pork Butt Injection, 113
Rosemary-Garlic Pork With Roasted
Vegetables & Caramelized Apples, 226
Shredded Pork With Carolina Gravy, 77
Slow-Cooker Pork Butt Roast, 52
Sweet 'n' Spicy Braised Pork, 212
Sandwiches, Barbecue, 53
Sandwiches, Italian-Style, 53
Sandwiches, Pressed Cuban, 52
Sliders, Easy Barbecue, 233
Tenderloin
Balsamico With Mushrooms, Pork, 48
Marinated Pork Tenderloin,
Bourbon-, 222
Salad, Island Jerk Pork Tenderloin, 212
Tacos Al Pastor, 119

POTATOES. *See also* **SWEET POTATOES.**
Chicken Thighs With Carrots and
Potatoes, 240
Chips and Ice Cream, Chocolate-Dipped
Potato, 220
French Fries, 310
Fries, Barbecue Oven, 198
Fries, Italian Oven, 198
Fries, Jerk Oven, 198
Fries, Salt-and-Pepper, 310
Fries, Salt-and-Pepper Oven, 198
Fries, Southwest Oven, 198
Hash, Asparagus-New Potato, 77
Herbed Potatoes Anna, Cast-Iron, 320
Kugel, Thin Potato, 89
Mashed
Buttermilk-Garlic Mashed
Potatoes, 310
Casserole, Onion-Topped Sausage 'n' Mashed
Potato, 121
Cheddar-Chive Mashed Potatoes, 284
Garlic-Parmesan Mashed Potatoes, 284
Gruyère-Thyme Mashed Potatoes, 284
Herb Mashed Potatoes, 34
Oven-Roasted Smashed Potatoes, 253
Perfect Mashed Potatoes, 283
Puffed Mashed Potatoes, 255
Tangy Mashed Potatoes, 284
New Potatoes, Garlic-Butter, 310
Pancakes, Chicken-and-Potato, 33
Patties, Breakfast Tex-Mex Potato, 284
Patties, Crispy Tex-Mex Potato, 284
Roasted Potato Wedges With Tarragon
Mayonnaise, 205
Salads
Dressing, Potato Salad, 115
Dry Rub, Potato Salad, 114
Grilled Fingerling Potato Salad, 138
Grilled Potato Salad, 114
Herbed Potato Salad, 133
Jean's Potato Salad, 99
Roasted Red Potato Salad, Warm, 48
Soufflé Potatoes, 310
Soup, Zucchini-Potato, 66
Twice-Baked Potatoes, 268
PRALINE
Bread, Praline-Apple, 196
Bread, Praline Pull-Apart, 284
PUDDINGS
Bread
Caramel-Pecan-Pumpkin Bread Pudding,
One-Dish, 229
Caramel-Pecan-Pumpkin Bread
Puddings, 228
Peanut Butter-Banana Sandwich Bread
Puddings With Dark Caramel Sauce, 244
Texas Toast Breakfast Bread
Pudding, 280
Vegetable Bread Pudding, Marian's
Savory, 157
Cake, Chocolate-Cherry Pudding, 40
Chocolate Pudding, 316
Coconut Pudding, Orange-and-Grapefruit
Brûlée With, 289
Corn Pudding, 311
PUMPKIN
Bread Pudding, One-Dish Caramel-Pecan-
Pumpkin, 229
Bread Puddings, Caramel-Pecan-
Pumpkin, 228
Cakes, Mini Pumpkin, 229
Cakes, Mini Pumpkin-Molasses, 230
Crisp, Pumpkin, 230
Pie Spectacular, Pumpkin, 249

Seeds, Roasted Pumpkin, 231
Soup, Kitchen Express Roasted Pumpkin-Acorn
Squash, 228
Soup, Pumpkin-Acorn Squash, 228
Vinaigrette, Harvest Wild Rice Salad With
Pumpkin, 195

QUESADILLAS
Pork Quesadillas, Barbecued, 296
Ratatouille Quesadillas, 232
Three-Cheese Blackberry Quesadillas With
Pepper-Peach Salsa, 111
Two-Cheese Blackberry Quesadillas, 111
QUICK & EASY RECIPES
Apple Bundles, Quick, 34
Green Beans, Balsamic, 34
Main Dishes
Meatloaves, Mini Apple-Cheddar Turkey, 73
Meatloaves, Mini Pesto-Turkey, 73
Tilapia, Pecan-Crusted, 34
Turkey Parmesan, 73
Turkey Tenderloins, Spice-Rubbed
Grilled, 73
Potatoes, Herb Mashed, 34
Sauce, Golden Rum-Butter, 34

RASPBERRIES
Frosting, Raspberry Buttercream, 63
Glaze, Raspberry, 44
Petits Fours, Chocolate-Raspberry, 331
Petits Fours, Raspberry-Red Velvet, 216
Pie, Raspberry-Lemonade, 121
Sauce, Raspberry, 265
RELISHES. *See also* **SALSAS, SAUCES,**
TOPPINGS.
Apricot-Pepper Relish, Apple-Chicken Sausage
With, 295
Cheese Relish, 294
RICE
Basmati Rice and Peas, 64
Basmati Rice and Pigeon Peas, 64
Brown Rice
Citrus-Asparagus Brown Rice, Savory, 206
Dirty Rice, Quick, 206
Feta, Pistachios, and Mint, Brown Rice With, 155
Salad, Herb-and-Pepper Brown Rice, 208
Cakes, Chicken-and-Rice, 33
Cakes With Lemon-Basil Sauce, Panko-Crusted
Rice, 207
Casserole, Chicken-and-Rice, 204
Chicken and Rice, Simple, 51
Chicken and Rice With Black Beans, Baked, 51
Citrus-Scented Rice With Fresh Basil, 155
Coconut-Lime Rice, 55
Coconut Rice With Fresh Ginger and Cilantro, 155
Fried Rice, Combination, 270
Fried Rice, Shrimp and Veggie, 207
Hoppin' John Salad, 127
Long-Grain Rice With Feta, Pistachios, and
Mint, 155
Peas, Rice and, 99
Pilaf, Rice, 311
Red Beans and Rice, Quick Skillet, 303
Red Beans and Rice, Slow-Cooker, 303
Red Beans and Rice, Vegetarian, 303
Salad, Sesame-Cilantro Chicken-and-
Rice, 206
Soup, Tex-Mex Chicken-and-Rice, 209

Favorite Recipes Journal

Jot down your family's and your favorite recipes for quick and handy reference. And don't forget to include the dishes that drew rave reviews when company came for dinner.

Recipe	Source/Page	Remarks